SELECTED READINGS FROM ECONOMETRICA

Joseph E. Stiglitz, General Editor

1. Selected Readings in Econometrics from *Econometrica* edited by John W. Hooper and Marc Nerlove

2. Selected Readings in Economic Theory from *Econometrica* edited by Kenneth J. Arrow

3. Selected Readings in Macroeconomics and Capital Theory from *Econometrica* edited by David Cass and Lionel W. McKenzie

Selected Readings in Macroeconomics and Capital Theory
from *Econometrica*

Selected Readings in

Macroeconomics and Capital Theory

from *Econometrica*

edited by

David Cass and Lionel W. McKenzie

The MIT Press

Cambridge, Massachusetts, and London, England

Library of Congress Cataloging in Publication Data

Cass, David, comp.
  Selected readings in macroeconomics and capital
theory from Econometrica.

  (Selected readings from Econometrica, 3)
  Includes 1 article in French.
  1. Macroeconomics — Mathematical models — Addresses,
essays, lectures. I. McKenzie, Lionel W., joint comp.
II. Econometrica. III. Title. IV. Title: Macroeconomics
and capital theory. V. Series.
HB141.C37   339   73-20096
ISBN 0-262-03051-9

CONTENTS

CONTENTS

PREFACE

This collection contains our choice of the best articles in the general area of macroeconomics and capital theory which appeared in *Econometrica* through 1966. The cutoff date was selected for the same reason expressed by the editors of earlier volumes in this series of reprints; roughly speaking, we feel that we lose perspective in trying to judge more recent articles. Except for the fact that the overall editor of the series, Joseph Stiglitz, suggested several articles he thought merited more consideration, appraised our choices, and thus partly implicates himself in the final decision, we accept full responsibility for the outcome.

There were a number of basic issues we faced in surveying the voluminous contributions *Econometrica* has made since its inception. Chief among these were: (1) What are the limits of the general area of macroeconomics? In particular, should we consider articles expressly microeconomic in original form but with obvious macroeconomic implications for later research? The inclusion of the pieces by Marschak, Muth, and Phelps clearly shows what we concluded on this question. (2) How comprehensive should we attempt to be? In this regard we did make some effort to include articles on a broad range of different topics within the general area of macroeconomics, basically to improve the usefulness of the volume. We did not, however, try to present some balance between theoretical and empirical work in the area, nor did we try to represent all authors who have made — in *Econometrica* and elsewhere — substantial contributions in the area. We believe these decisions, more than any other, shaped the final outcome on the margin. (3) Should we include articles readily available in other collections? Our answer here was unavoidably dictated by the recognition that the heart of our final selection (namely, almost half of the total in number, and more than that in quality) would have been excluded otherwise.

To end on a positive note: For the most part, scanning and reading back issues of *Econometrica* — and especially the articles included (or excluded on the margin) — was for us both very stimulating and very rewarding. We hope the resulting collection will be similarly appreciated by many others.

Econometrica, Vol. 3, No. 3 (July, 1935)

A MACRODYNAMIC THEORY OF BUSINESS CYCLES[1]

By M. Kalecki

Paper presented at the meeting of the Econometric Society, Leyden, October 1933.

I

In the following all our considerations concern an economic system *isolated and free of secular trend*. Moreover, we make with respect to that system the following assumptions.

1. We call real gross profit B the total real income of capitalists (business men and private capitalists), amortization included, per unit of time. That income consists of two parts, that consumed and that accumulated:

$$(1) \qquad\qquad B = C + A.$$

Thus, C is the total volume of consumers' goods consumed by capitalists, while A—*if we disregard savings of workpeople, and their "capitalistic" incomes*—covers goods of all kind serving the purpose of reproduction and expansion of fixed capital, as well as increment of stocks. We shall call A "gross accumulation."

The personal consumption of capitalists, C, is not very elastic. *We assume that C is composed of a constant part, C_1, and a variable part proportionate to the real gross profit λB:*

$$(2) \qquad\qquad C = C_1 + \lambda B$$

where λ is a small constant fraction.

From equations (1) and (2) we get:

$$B = C_1 + \lambda B + A$$

and

$$(3) \qquad\qquad B = \frac{C_1 + A}{1 - \lambda},$$

i. e., the real gross profit B is proportionate to the sum $C_1 + A$ of the constant part of the consumption of capitalists C_1 and of the gross accumulation A.

---

[1] The term "macrodynamic" was first applied by Professor Frisch in his work "Propagation problems and impulse problems in dynamics" (*Economic Essays in Honour of Gustav Cassel*, London, 1933), to determine processes connected with the functioning of the economic system as a whole, disregarding the details of disproportionate development of special parts of that system.

The gross accumulation A is equal to the sum of the production of capital goods and of the increment of stocks of all kinds.[2] *We assume that the total volume of stocks remains constant all through the cycle.* This is justified in so far as in existing economic systems totally or approximately isolated (the world, U.S.A.) the total volume of stocks does not show any distinct cyclical variations. Indeed, while business is falling off, stocks of finished goods decrease, but those of raw materials and semi-manufactures rise; during recovery there is a reversal of tendencies. From the above we may conclude that *in our economic system the gross accumulation A is equal to the production of capital goods.*

2. We assume further that *the "gestation period" of any investment is θ.* Of course, this by no means corresponds to the reality; θ is merely the average of various actual durations of "gestation periods," and our system in which θ is a constant value is to be considered as a simplified model of reality.

Whenever an investment is made, three stages can be discerned: (1) investment orders, i.e., all the orders for capital goods to serve the purpose of reproduction or expansion of industrial equipment; the total volume of such orders allocated per unit of time will be called I; (2) production of capital goods; the volume of that production per unit of time, equal, as said above, to the gross accumulation, is called A; (3) deliveries of finished industrial equipment; the volume of such deliveries per unit of time will be called L.[3]

The relation of L and I is simple. Deliveries L at the time t are equal to investment orders I at the time $t - \theta$:

$$(4) \qquad\qquad L(t) = I(t - \theta).$$

($I(t)$ and $L(t)$ are investment orders and deliveries of industrial equipment at the time t.)

The interrelationship of A and I is more complicated.

Let us call W the total volume of unfilled investment orders at the moment t. As each investment needs the time θ to be filled, $1/\theta$ of its volume must be executed in a unit of time. Thus, the production of capital goods must be equal to $1/\theta \cdot W$:

$$(5) \qquad\qquad A = \frac{W}{\theta}.$$

---

[2] Industrial equipment in course of construction is not included in "stocks of all kinds"; thus, change in the volume of the industrial equipment in course of construction is involved in the "production of capital goods."

[3] While A is the production of *all* capital goods, L is only that of *finished* capital goods. Thus, the difference $A - L$ represents the volume of industrial equipment in course of construction, per unit of time.

As regards W, it is equal to the total of orders allocated during the period $(t-\theta, t)$. Indeed, since the "gestation period" of any investment is θ, no order allocated during the period $(t-\theta, t)$ is yet finished at the time t, while all the orders allocated before that period are filled. We thus obtain the equation:

$$(6) \qquad W(t) = \int_{t-\theta}^{t} I(\tau)d\tau.$$

According to equations (4) and (5) we get:

$$(7) \qquad A(t) = \frac{1}{\theta} \int_{t-\theta}^{t} I(\tau)d\tau.$$

($A(t)$ is the production of capital goods at the time t.)

Thus A at the time t is equal to the average of investment orders $I(t)$ allocated during the period $(t-\theta, t)$.

3. Let us call K the volume of the existing industrial equipment. The increment of that volume within the given period is equal to the difference between the volume of deliveries of finished equipment and that of equipment coming out of use. If we denote by $K'(t)$ the derivative of K with respect to time, by $L(t)$ the volume of deliveries of industrial equipment per unit of time (as above), and by U the demand for restoration of equipment used up per unit of time, we get:

$$(8) \qquad K'(t) = L(t) - U.$$

We can assume that the demand for restoration of the industrial equipment—U—remains constant all through the cycle. The volume of the existing industrial equipment K shows, it is true, certain fluctuations,

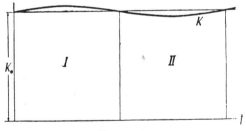

FIGURE 1

e.g., in the first part of the cycle K is above the average, and one might think that then the demand for restoration of equipment ought to be above the average too. Yet, it should be borne in mind that the new equipment is "young" and that its "rate of mortality" is very low, as the average "lifetime" of industrial equipment is much longer than the duration of a cycle (15–30 years as against 8–12 years). Thus, the fluctuations of the demand for restoration of equipment are of no importance, and may safely be disregarded.

4. The proportions of the investment activity at any time depend on the expected net yield. When the business man will invest a capital k in the construction of industrial equipment, he will first evaluate the probable gross profit b, while deducting (1) the amortization of the capital k, i.e., βk (β—the rate of amortization); (2) the interest on the capital k, i.e., pk (p—the interest rate); (3) the interest on the future working capital, the ratio of which to the invested capital k will be denoted by $\gamma - p\gamma k$. The probable yield of the investment will thus be:

$$\frac{b - \beta k - pk - p\gamma k}{k} = \frac{b}{k} - \beta - p(1 + \gamma).$$

The coefficients β and γ may be considered constant all through the cycle. p is the money rate at the given moment, b/k is the probable future yield evaluated after that of the existing enterprises. The volume of the existing industrial equipment is K, the total real gross profit is B. Thus, the average real gross profit per unit of the existing fixed capital is B/K (that quotient will be called further gross yield B/K).

We may conclude that $\frac{b}{k}$ is evaluated after B/K, and that investment activity is controlled by the gross yield B/K and the money rate p. As a matter of fact, the function of B/K and p is not the very volume of investment orders I, but the ratio of that volume to that of industrial equipment K, i.e., I/K. In fact, when B and K rise in the same proportion, B/K remains unchanged, while I rises (probably) as did B and K. Thus, we arrive at the equation:

$$(9) \qquad \frac{I}{K} = f\left(\frac{B}{K}, p\right)$$

where f is an increasing function of B/K and a decreasing function of p.

It is commonly known that, except for *financial panic* (the so-called crises of confidence), the market money rate rises and falls according to general business conditions. We make on that basis the following simplified assumption: *The money rate p is an increasing function of the gross yield B/K.*

From the assumption concerning the dependence of the money rate p on the gross yield B/K, and from (8), it follows *that I/K is a function of B/K.* As B is proportionate to $C_1 + A$, where C_1, is the constant part of the consumption of capitalists, and A the gross accumulation equal to the production of capital goods, we thus obtain:

$$\frac{I}{K} = \phi\left(\frac{C_1 + A}{K}\right)$$

(10)

ϕ being, of course, an increasing function. We further assume *that ϕ is a linear function*, i.e., that:

$$\frac{I}{K} = m\frac{C_1 + A}{K} - n$$

where the *constant m is positive*, ϕ being an increasing function. Multiplying both sides of the equation by K we get:

(11) $$I = m(C_1 + A) - nK.$$

* * *

We have seen that between I (investment orders), A (gross accumulation equal to the production of capital goods), L (deliveries of industrial equipment), K (volume of the existing industrial equipment), and the time t, there are interrelationships:

(4) $$L(t) = I(t - \theta)$$

(7) $$A(t) = \frac{1}{\theta}\int_{t-\theta}^{t} I(\tau)d\tau$$

(8) $$K'(t) = L(t) - U$$

resulting from technics of the capitalistic production, and the relation:

(11) $$I = m(C_1 + A) - nK$$

resulting from the interdependence between investments and yield of existing enterprises. From these equations the relation of I and t may be easily determined.

Let us differentiate (11) with respect to t:

(12) $$I'(t) = mA'(t) - nK'(t).$$

Differentiating the equation (7) with respect to t, we get:

(13) $$A'(t) = \frac{I(t) - I(t - \theta)}{\theta}$$

and from (4) and (8):

(14) $$K'(t) = I(t - \theta) - U.$$

Putting into (12) values of $A'(t)$ and $K'(t)$ from (13) and (14), we have:

(15) $I'(t) = \dfrac{m}{\theta} \left[I(t) - I(t - \theta) \right] - n\left[I(t - \theta) - U \right].$

Denoting the deviation of $I(t)$ from the constant demand for restoration of the industrial equipment U by $J(t)$:

(16) $J(t) = I(t) - U,$

we can transform (15) as follows:

$$J'(t) = \frac{m}{\theta} \left[J(t) - J(t - \theta) \right] - nJ(t - \theta)$$

or

(17) $(m + \theta n)J(t - \theta) = mJ(t) - \theta J'(t).$

The solution of that equation will enable us to express $J(t)$ as a function of t and to find out which, if any, are the endogenous cyclical fluctuations in our economic system.

II

It may be easily seen that the equation (17) is satisfied by the function $De^{\alpha t}$ where D is an arbitrary constant value and α a definite value which has to be determined. Replacing $J(t)$ by $De^{\alpha t}$, we get:

$$D(m + \theta n)e^{\alpha(t-\theta)} = Dme^{\alpha t} - D\alpha\theta e^{\alpha t}$$

and, dividing by $De^{\alpha t}$, we obtain an equation from which α can be determined:

(18) $(m + \theta n)e^{-\alpha\theta} = m - \alpha\theta.$

By simple transformations we get further:

$$e^{-m}(m + \theta n)e^{m-\alpha\theta} = m - \alpha\theta$$

and setting

(19) $m - \alpha\theta = z$

(20) $e^{-m}(m + \theta n) = l$

we have

(21) $le^z = z$

where z is to be considered as a complex number:

(22) $z = x + iy.$

Thus, (19) can be given the following form:

(23)
$$\alpha = \frac{m - x}{\theta} - i\frac{y}{\theta}$$

and (21) be transformed into:

(24)
$$x + iy = le^x(\cos y + i \sin y).$$

Adopting the method of Tinbergen,[4] we discern two cases: Case I— when $l > 1/e$, and Case II—when $l \leq 1/e$.

Case I. As Tinbergen has shown, in that case all the solutions will be complex numbers, and they will be infinite in number. Let us arrange them by increasing y_k:

$$\cdots x_k - iy_k, \cdots x_2 - iy_2, \ x_1 - iy_1, \ x_1 + iy_1, \ x_2 + iy_2 \cdots x_k + iy_k \cdots.$$

(It is easy to see that when $x_k + iy_k$ is a root of (24), that equation is satisfied as well by $x_k - iy_k$).

From the equation (23) we get values of α:

$$\alpha_k = \frac{m - x_k}{\theta} - i\frac{y_k}{\theta}$$

and

$$\alpha_{-k} = \frac{m - x_k}{\theta} + i\frac{y_k}{\theta}.$$

Functions:

$$D_k e^{\alpha_k t} = D_k e^{(m-x_k)t/\theta}\left(\cos y_k \frac{t}{\theta} - i \sin y_k \frac{t}{\theta}\right)$$

and

$$D_{-k} e^{\alpha_{-k} t} = D_{-k} e^{(m-x-k)t/\theta}\left(\cos y_k \frac{t}{\theta} + i \sin y_k \frac{t}{\theta}\right)$$

satisfy (17).

The general solution of (17), which is at the same time a differential and a functional equation, depends upon the form of the function $J(t)$ in the initial interval $(0, \theta)$; that form is quite arbitrary. Yet, we can develop (with sufficient approximation) the function $J(t)$ in the initial interval into the series $\sum D_k e^{\alpha_k t}$ where the constants D_k depend upon the form of the function $J(t)$ in the initial interval.[5] As functions $D_k e^{\alpha_k t}$ satisfy (17), the function $\sum D_k e^{\alpha_k t}$, which represents with sufficient approximation $J(t)$ in the initial interval, will be a general solu-

---

[4] "Ein Schiffbauzyklus?" *Weltwirtschaftliches Archiv*, B. 34, H.1.
[5] *Loc. cit.*, p. 158.

tion of (17).[6] That solution is, of course, a real one, thus D_k and D_{-k} must be complex conjugate numbers, and $J(t)$ can be represented as follows:

(25)
$$J(t) = e^{(m-x_1)t/\theta}\left(F_1 \sin y_1 \frac{t}{\theta} + G_1 \cos y_1 \frac{t}{\theta}\right)$$
$$+ e^{(m-x_2)t/\theta}\left(F_2 \sin y_2 \frac{t}{\theta} + G_2 \cos y_2 \frac{t}{\theta}\right) \cdots.$$

On the basis of that solution we cannot yet say anything definite about the character of fluctuations of $J(t)$, as the constants F_k and G_k depend upon the form—unknown to us—of the function $J(t)$ in the initial interval. But here we can take advantage of the following circumstance. It may be inferred from Tinbergen's argument when he solves the equation (24) that

(26)
$$x_1 < x_2,\ x_1 < x_3 \cdots.$$

Let us divide $J(t)$ by:
$$e^{(m-x_1)t/\theta}\left(F_1 \sin y_1 \frac{t}{\theta} + G_1 \cos y_1 \frac{t}{\theta}\right).$$

According to the inequality (26), for a sufficiently great t the sum of all the expressions other than the first one will be equal to an arbitrarily small value ω:

$$\frac{J(t)}{e^{(m-x_1)t/\theta}\left(F_1 \sin y_1 \dfrac{t}{\theta} + G_1 \cos y_1 \dfrac{t}{\theta}\right)} = 1 + \omega.$$

At a time sufficiently distant from the initial interval, the following equation will be true with an arbitrarily small relative error:

(27)
$$J(t) = e^{(m-x_1)t/\theta}\left(F_1 \sin y_1 \frac{t}{\theta} + G_1 \cos y_1 \frac{t}{\theta}\right).$$

That equation represents harmonic vibrations with an amplitude decreasing, constant, or increasing, according as $x_1 \gtreqless m$. Their period, and the degree of progression or degression they show, do not depend on the form of the function $J(t)$ in the initial interval. (It is worth mentioning that, as follows from Tinbergen's analysis, vibrations represented by (27) have a period longer than 2θ, while vibrations represented by the expressions on the right side of the equation [25] which we dropped, have a period shorter than θ).

---

[6] *Loc. cit.*, p. 157.

If now we fix the origin of the time axis so as to equate $J(t)$ from (27) to zero for $t = 0$, that equation will assume the form:

$$J(t) = F_1 e^{(m-z_1)t/\theta} \sin y_1 \frac{t}{\theta}$$

or, taking into consideration (16):

(28) $$I(t) - U = F_1 e^{(m-z_1)t/\theta} \sin y_1 \frac{t}{\theta}.$$

Case II. In that case (24) has two real roots z_1' and z_1'', among complex roots like $x_1 \pm iy$. As in the first case, we get here, for a time sufficiently distant from the initial interval:

$$J(t) = D_1' e^{(m-z_1')t/\theta} + D_1'' e^{(m-z_1'')t/\theta}.$$

It follows from that equation that there are no cyclical vibrations.

The results of the above analysis can be summarized as follows:

Cyclical variations occur in our economic system only when the following inequality is satisfied:

$$l > \frac{1}{e},$$

transformed, by putting the value of l from (20) into:

(29) $$m + \theta n > e^{m-1}.$$

As we know, m is positive (see p. 331). We can easily prove that a necessary, though insufficient, condition, at which (29) is satisfied, i.e., there are cyclical variations, is that n be positive too.

Fluctuations of I at a time sufficiently distant from the initial interval $(0, \theta)$ *will be represented by the equation:*

(28) $$I(t) - U = F_1 e^{(m-z_1)t/\theta} \sin y_1 \frac{t}{\theta}.$$

The amplitude of fluctuations is decreasing, remains constant, or rises, according as $x_1 \gtreqless m$.

The period is equal to

(30) $$T = \frac{2\pi}{y_1} \theta.$$

On the basis of equations

(7) $$A(t) = \frac{1}{\theta} \int_{t-\theta}^{t} I(\tau) d\tau$$

and

$$(4) \qquad\qquad L(t) = I(t - \theta)$$

we can show L and A as functions of t, and see that these values are fluctuating, like I, around the value U. K is obtained by integration of:

$$(8) \qquad\qquad K'(t) = L(t) - U.$$

It also fluctuates around a certain constant value, which we denote by K_0. The whole calculation will be given in the next chapter with respect to a particular case when the amplitude of fluctuations is constant.

III

If, while $x_1 = m$, the amplitude of fluctuations remains constant, (28) assumes the form:

$$(31) \qquad\qquad I(t) - U = a \sin y_1 \frac{t}{\theta}$$

where a is the constant amplitude.

That case is of a particular importance as it appears to be nearest to actual conditions. Indeed, in reality we do not observe any *regular* progression or degression in the intensity of cyclical fluctuations.

Putting the value of I from (31) into (7) and (4) we get

$$(32) \qquad \begin{aligned} A - U &= \frac{1}{\theta} \int_{t-\theta}^{t} \left(a \sin y_1 \frac{\tau}{\theta} + U \right) d\tau - U \\ &= a \, \frac{\sin \dfrac{y_1}{2}}{\dfrac{y_1}{2}} \sin y_1 \frac{t - \dfrac{\theta}{2}}{\theta} \end{aligned}$$

and

$$(33) \qquad\qquad L - U = a \sin y_1 \frac{t - \theta}{\theta}.$$

From (8) and (33)

$$K'(t) = a \sin y_1 \frac{t - \theta}{\theta}.$$

Integrating:

$$(34) \qquad K - K_0 = - a \frac{\theta}{y_1} \cos y_1 \frac{t - \theta}{\theta}$$

where K_0 is the constant around of which K is fluctuating, equal here to the average volume of the industrial equipment K during a cycle.

In a similar way, the average values of I, A, and L, during a cycle will be equal in our case of constant amplitude to the constant U around which I, A, and L, are fluctuating.

Taking into consideration the condition of a constant amplitude $x_1 = m$ we shall get now from (20) and (24):

$$(35) \qquad \cos y_1 = \frac{m}{m + \theta n}$$

and

$$(36) \qquad \frac{y_1}{tg y_1} = m.$$

These equations allow us to determine y_1; moreover, they define the interrelationship of m and n.

Between m and n there is still another dependency. They are both coefficients in the equation:

$$(11) \qquad I = m(C_1 + A) - nK$$

which must be true for one-cycle-averages of I and A equal to U, and for the average value of K equal to K_0:

$$U = m(C_1 + U) - nK_0.$$

Hence:

$$(37) \qquad n = (m - 1) \frac{U}{K_0} + m \frac{C_1}{K_0}.$$

Thus, if values of U/K_0 and C_1/K_0 were given, we could determine m and n from (35), (36), and (37). U/K_0 is nothing else but the rate of amortization, as U is equal to the demand for restoration of equipment, and K_0 is the average volume of that equipment. C_1 is the constant part of the consumption of capitalists. U/K_0 and C_1/K_0 may be roughly evaluated on the basis of statistical data. If we also knew the average gestation period of investments θ, we could determine y_1 and the duration of the cycle $T = 2\pi\theta/y$.

We evaluate the *gestation period of investments* θ on the basis of data of the German *Institut fuer Konjunkturforschung*. The lag between the curves of beginning and termination of building schemes (dwelling

houses, industrial and public buildings) can be fixed at 8 months; the
lag between orders and deliveries in the machinery-making industry
can be fixed at 6 months. We assume that the average duration of θ is
0.6 years.

The rate of amortization U/K_0 is evaluated on the basis of combined
German and American data. On that of the German data, the ratio of
amortization to the national income can be fixed at 0.08. With a certain approximation, the same is true for U.S.A. Further, according to
official estimates of the wealth of U.S.A. in 1922, we set the amount of
fixed capital in U.S.A. at \$120 milliards (land excepted). The national
income is evaluated at \$70 milliards for 5 years about 1922. The rate
of amoritization would thus be $0.08 \cdot 70/120$, i.e., *ca.* 0.05.

Most difficult is the *evaluation of* C_1/K_0. K_0 was fixed at \$120 mil-
liards, C_1 is, as we know, the constant part of the consumption of
capitalists. Let us evaluate first the average consumption of capitalists
in U.S.A. in the period 1909–1918. The total net profit in that period
averaged, according to King, \$16 milliards deflated to the purchasing
power of 1913. The average increment of total capital in that period is
estimated by King at \$5 milliards. That figure includes savings of work-
people, but, on the other hand, 16 milliards of profits cover also "capitalistic" incomes of workpeople (use of own houses, etc.). Thus, the
difference, $16 - 5 = 11$ millards of 1913-dollars, represents with a sufficient degree of accuracy the consumption of capitalists (farmers included). The average national income amounted in the period 1909–
1918 to \$36 milliards with the purchasing power of 1913 (King). The
ratio of the consumption of capitalists to the national income would
thus be 0.3. As, further, the average income during 5 years around 1922
amounted, as mentioned, to \$70 milliards of current purchasing power,
the consumption of capitalists in these years may be estimated at \$21
milliards. Now, we have to determine the constant part of that consumption. In order to do that, we assume that when the volume of
capitalists' gross profits deviates from the average by, say, ± 20 per
cent, the corresponding relative change in their consumption is but 5
per cent, i.e., 4 times smaller. That assumption is confirmed by statistical evidence. Accordingly, the constant part of the consumption of
capitalists, equal to $C_1 + \lambda B$ (see above, λ is a constant fraction,
B—the total gross profit), amounts to 3/4 of \$21 milliards, i.e., to \$16
milliards. The ratio C_1/K_0 would then be 16/120 or *ca.* 0.13.

Equations (35), (36) and (37), if we put:

$$\theta = 0.6; \qquad \frac{U}{K_0} = 0.05; \qquad \frac{C_1}{K_0} = 0.13;$$

give:

$$\cos y_1 = \frac{m}{m + 0.6n}$$

$$\frac{y_1}{tg y_1} = m$$

$$n = 0.05(m - 1) + 0.13m.$$

The solution of these equations gives:

$$m = 0.95; \quad n = 0.121; \quad y_1 = 0.378.$$

Thus, the duration of the cycle is:

$$T = \frac{2\pi}{y_1}\theta = \frac{2\pi}{0.378} \cdot 0.6 = 10.0.$$

The figure of 10 years thus obtained as the time of duration of a cycle is supported by statistical evidence: 8 to 12 years.[7] It may be objected that values θ_1 U/K_0, C_1/K_0, on which our calculation was based, were but roughly estimated, and that the conformity between facts and theory can be merely a coincidence. Let us calculate T for such values of θ_1 U/K_0, C_1/K_0 as would be quite different from those previously taken:

θ	$\dfrac{U_0}{K_0}$	$\dfrac{C_1}{K_0}$	T
0.6	0.05	0.13	10.0
0.6	0.03	0.13	10.0
0.6	0.07	0.13	10.0
0.6	0.05	0.07	13.2
0.6	0.05	0.19	8.5
0.3	0.05	0.13	7.1
0.9	0.05	0.13	12.5

We see that the value of U/K_0 plays no great rôle with respect to the result of our calculation. We see further that when values of C_1/K_0 and θ differ by almost 50 per cent from those adopted before (C_1/K_0 =0.13 and U/K_0=0.05) solutions for T move between 7 and 13 years. The actual duration of the cycle being, as already mentioned, 8 to 12

[7] Shorter cycles can be considered as "short-wave" fluctuations.

years, we can safely say that, irrespective of the degree of accuracy in estimating θ, U/K_0, C_1/K_0, there is no flagrant incongruity between the consequences of our theory and reality.

There is one more question to be dealt with. During the whole time we considered, as stated at the very beginning of the study, an economic system free of secular trend. But a case when the trend is uniform, and when gross accumulation, consumption of capitalists, and the volume of industrial equipment, show the same rate of development, can be easily reduced to a state "free of trend" simply by dividing all these values by the denominator of the trend. Interrelationships stated in our chapter I will remain true for these quotients, with the following changes: (1) The value U will be no longer equal to the demand for restoration of the used-up equipment, but it will cover as well the steady demand for the expansion of the existing equipment as a result of the uniform secular trend. Thus U/K_0 will be equal not to the rate of amortization 0.05, but, assuming the rate of net accumulation equal, say, to 3 per cent, to 0.08. (2) Also stocks of goods, previously considered constant, will increase in the same proportion under the influence of the trend. That steady increment of stocks per unit of time—let us call it C_2—will be a component of the gross profit B, now equal to $C+C_2+A$, where C is the personal consumption of capitalists, C_1 the steady increment of stocks, and A the production of capital goods. If we now consider that, according to equation (2), the consumption of capitalists C is equal to $C_1+\lambda B$, we see that B is proportionate to C_1+C_2+A. The constant C_1+C_2 will play in our considerations the same rôle as C_1 previously did. According to the official estimate of the national wealth of the U.S.A., the volume of stocks of goods amounts to 0.3 of the volume of the industrial equipment, i.e., to $0.3 \cdot K_0$. If the rate of net accumulation be 3 per cent, C_2 will be $0.03 \cdot 0.3 \cdot K_0$. Hence, instead of $C_1/K_0=0.13$ we must take $(C_1+C_2)/K_0=0.14$. From the above table we may easily see that both modifications—0.08 instead of 0.05 for U/K_0 and 0.14 instead of 0.13 for C_1/K_0,—will have but little effect on the result of the calculation of T.

We shall now determine, on the basis of (31), (32), (33), and (34), equations of curves I, A, L, and K, with $\theta=0.6$ and $T=10.0$:

$$I-U = a \sin 0.63t$$
$$A-U = 0.98a \sin 0.63 \, (t-0.3)$$
$$L-U = a \sin 0.63 \, (t-0.6)$$
$$K-K_0 = -1.59a \cos 0.63 \, (t-0.6).$$

Assuming, in conformity with the above estimate, $U/K_0=0.05$, we find the following formulae for the relative deviations from the state of equilibrium:

$$\text{(38)} \qquad \frac{I - U}{U} = \frac{a}{U} \sin 0.63t$$

$$\text{(39)} \qquad \frac{A - U}{U} = \frac{a}{U} \cdot 0.98 \cdot \sin 0.63(t - 0.3)$$

$$\text{(40)} \qquad \frac{L - U}{U} = \frac{a}{U} \sin 0.63(t - 0.6)$$

$$\text{(41)} \qquad \frac{K - K_0}{K_0} = -\frac{a}{U} \cdot 0.08 \cos 0.63(t - 0.6).$$

IV

Figure 2 represents the curves of investment orders I, of production of capital goods A, of deliveries of industrial equipment L, and of the volume of industrial equipment K, which correspond to the formulae (38), (39), (40), and (41).

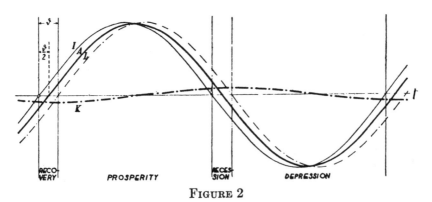

FIGURE 2

Let us recall the dependence (11), $I = m(C_1 + A) - nK$, wherefrom it follows, if m and n are positive (see p. 333), that the volume of investment orders is an increasing function of the gross accumulation equal to the production of capital goods, and a decreasing function of the volume of the existing industrial equipment. Having these in mind, we can, on the basis of the Figure 2, explain the mechanism of the business cycle.

Recovery is the phase of the cycle of a duration θ, when the volume of investment orders begins to exceed the volume of the demand for restoration of the industrial equipment. But the very volume of the existing industrial equipment is not yet increasing, as deliveries of new equipment still remain below the demand for restoration of equipment.

The output of capital goods A, equal to the gross accumulation, is on the increase. Meanwhile, the volume of the existing industrial equipment K is still on the decrease, and, as a result, investment orders rise at a rapid pace.

During *prosperity* also deliveries of equipment exceed the demand for restoration of the equipment, thus the volume of the existing equipment is increasing. The rise of K at first hampers the rise of investment orders, and at last causes their drop. The output of capital goods follows suit, and begins to fall off in the second part of prosperity.

During *recession* investment orders are below the level of the demand for restoration of the industrial equipment, but the volume of the existing industrial equipment K is still on the increase, since deliveries are still below the demand for restoration. As the volume of production of capital goods, equal to the gross accumulation A, continues to fall off, the volume of investment orders I is decreasing rapidly.

During *depression* deliveries of equipment are below the level of the demand for restoration of the equipment, and the volume of the existing equipment is falling off. The drop in K at first smoothes the downward tendency in investment orders, and then calls forth their rise. In the second part of depression the production of capital goods, too, begins to increase.

*   *   *

We have seen a plot of investment orders, gross accumulation, and existing industrial equipment. But the fluctuations in the volume of the gross accumulation, which appear as a result of the functioning of the business cycle mechanism, must necessarily affect the movement of prices and the total volume of production. Indeed, the real gross profit B is, on the one hand, an increasing function of the gross accumulation A (B being proportionate to $C_1 + A$, where C_1 is the constant part of the consumption of capitalists, see above) and, on the other hand, it can be represented as a product of the general volume of production and of the profit per unit of production. In that way, the general volume of production and prices (or rather the ratio of prices to wages determining the profit per unit) rises in the upward part of the cycle as the gross accumulation increases.

The interdependence of gross accumulation, equal to the production of capital goods, and of the general movement of production and prices, is realized in the following way. While the output of capital goods increases by a certain amount, in the general volume of production, beside that increment, there is another increment because of the increased demand for consumers' goods on the part of workers recently hired by industries making capital goods.[8] The consequent increase in employment in industries making consumers' goods results, in its turn, in an increase in the demand for consumers' goods on the part of workers. As simultaneously there is an advance of prices, the new demand is but partly met by the new production. The remaining part of that demand is satisfied at the expense of the "old" workers, whose real earnings suffer a reduction. The general level of production and prices must eventually rise, so as to provide for an increment of the real profit equal to the increment of the production of capital goods.

That description is incomplete in so far as it does not reckon with changes in the personal consumption of capitalists. That consumption—C—is dependent, to a certain extent, on the proportions of the total profit B, and increases in accordance with the gross accumulation A (from equations (2) and (3) it follows that $C = (C_1 + \lambda A)/(1 + \lambda)$, where λ is a constant fraction). The increase in the consumption of capitalists has the same effect as the increase in production of capital goods: there is an increase in the volume of production of consumers' goods for the use of capitalists; as a result, employment increases, hence an additional demand for consumers' goods for the use of workers, and, eventually, a further rise of production and prices.

The general level of production and prices must rise, eventually, so as to provide for an increment of the real profit equal to the increment of the production of capital goods and of the consumption of capitalists.

* \quad * \quad *

The question may arise wherefrom capitalists take the means to increase at the same time the production of capital goods and their own consumption. Disregarding the technical side of the money market such as, e.g., the variable demand for means of payment, we may say that these outlays are "financing themselves." Imagine, for instance, that some capitalists withdraw during a year a certain amount from their savings deposits, or borrow that amount at the Central Bank, in order to invest it in the construction of some additional equipment. In the course of the same year that amount will be received by other capitalists under the form of profits (since, according to our assumptions, workers do not save), and put again into a bank as a savings deposit or used to pay off a debt to the Central Bank. Thus, the circle will close itself.

Yet in reality, just because of the technical side of the money market, which, as a matter of fact, forms its very nature, a credit inflation becomes necessary for two reasons.

---

[8] We take for granted that there is a reserve army of unemployed.

The first is the fact of the curve I of investment orders not coinciding exactly with that of production of capital goods A, equal to the gross accumulation. When giving an investment order, the entrepreneur has to provide first some corresponding fund, out of which he will currently finance the filling cf that order. At any time the corresponding bank account will be increased (per unit of time) by the amount I equal to the volume of orders allocated, and simultaneously decrease by an amount A spent on the production of capital goods.[9]

In that way, at any time the investment activities require an amount I (per unit of time), notably: $I-A$ to form new investment reserves, and A to be spent on the production of capital goods. The actually spent amount A "finances itself," i.e., comes back to the bank under the form of realized profits, while the increment of investment reserves $I-A$ is to be created by means of a credit inflation.

Another reason for the inflation of credit is the circumstance that the increase in the production of capital goods or in the consumption of capitalists, i.e., increased profits, calls forth a rise of the general level of production and prices. This has the effect of increasing the demand for means of payment under the form of cash or current accounts, and to meet that increased demand a credit inflation becomes necessary.

M. KALECKI

Polish Institute for Economic Research
Warsaw, Poland

[9] The values concerned are not exactly the real values of I and A but corresponding amounts of money, calculated at current prices.

Econometrica, Vol. 5, No. 2 (April, 1937)

THE SUMMATION OF RANDOM CAUSES AS THE SOURCE OF CYCLIC PROCESSES*

By Eugen Slutzky

I. SCOPE OF THE INVESTIGATION

ALMOST ALL of the phenomena of economic life, like many other processes, social, meteorological, and others, occur in sequences of rising and falling movements, like waves. Just as waves following each other on the sea do not repeat each other perfectly, so economic cycles never repeat earlier ones exactly either in duration or in amplitude. Nevertheless, in both cases, it is almost always possible to detect, even in the multitude of individual peculiarities of the phenomena, marks of certain approximate uniformities and regularities. The eye of the observer instinctively discovers on waves of a certain order other smaller waves, so that the idea of harmonic analysis, viz., that of the possibility of expressing the irregularities of the form and the spacing of the waves by means of the summation of regular sinusoidal fluctuations, presents itself to the mind almost spontaneously. If the results of the analysis happen sometimes not to be completely satisfactory, the discrepancies usually will be interpreted as casual deviations superposed on the regular waves. If the analyses of the first and of the second halves of a series give considerably divergent results (such as, for example, were found by Schuster while analyzing sunspot periodicity),[1] it is, even then, possible to find the solution without giving up the basic concept. Such a discrepancy may be the result of the interference of certain factors checking the continuous movement of the process and substituting for the former regularity a new one which sometimes may

* Professor Eugen Slutzky's paper of 1927, "The Summation of Random Causes as the Source of Cyclic Processes," *Problems of Economic Conditions,* ed. by The Conjuncture Institute, Moskva (Moscow), Vol. 3, No. 1, 1927, has in a sense become classic in the field of time-series analysis. While it does not give a complete theory of the time shape that is to be expected when a given linear operator is applied to a random (auto-non-correlated) series, it has given us a number of penetrating and suggestive ideas on this question. It has been, and will no doubt continue to be, highly stimulating for further research on this vast and—not least for business-cycle analysis—most important problem. Unfortunately Professor Slutzky's paper so far has been available only in Russian (with a brief English summary). Some years ago Professor Henry Schultz had the original article translated into English by Mr. Eugene Prostov, and suggested that it be published in ECONOMETRICA. At the request of the Editor Professor Slutzky has prepared for our Journal a revised English version with which he has incorporated also a number of important results obtained after 1927.— EDITOR.

[1] Arthur Schuster, "On the Periodicities of Sunspots," *Phil. Trans.,* Series A, Vol. 206, 1906, p. 76.

even happen to be of the same type as the former one. Empirical series are, unfortunately, seldom long enough to enable one definitely to prove or to refute such an hypothesis. Without dwelling on the history of complicated disputes concerning the above-mentioned problem, I will mention only two circumstances as the starting points for the present investigation—one, so to speak, in the field of chance, the other in the field of strict regularity.

One usually takes the analysis of the periodogram of the series as the basis for the discovery of hidden periodicities. Having obtained from the periodogram the values of the squares of the amplitudes of the sinusoids, calculated by the method of least squares for waves of varying length, we ask whether there is a method of determining those waves which do not arise from chance. Schuster apparently has discovered a suitable method;[2] but we must give up his criterion when we remember that among his assumptions is that of independence of the successive observations. As a general rule we find that the terms of an empirical series are not independent but correlated and at times correlated very closely. This circumstance, as is known, may very perceptibly heighten the oscillation of the derived characteristics of the series, and it is quite conceivable that waves satisfying Schuster's criterion would in fact be casual—just simulating the presence of a strict regularity.[3] Thus we are led to our basic problem: is it possible that a definite structure of a connection between random fluctuations could form them into a system of more or less regular waves? Many laws of physics and biology are based on chance, among them such laws as the second law of thermodynamics and Mendel's laws. But heretofore we have known how regularities could be derived from a chaos of disconnected elements because of the very disconnectedness. In our case we wish to consider the rise of regularity from series of chaotically-random elements because of certain connections imposed upon them.

Suppose we are inclined to believe in the reality of the strict periodicity of a business cycle, such, for example, as the eight-year period postulated by Moore.[4] Then we should encounter another difficulty. Wherein lies the source of the regularity? What is the mechanism of

[2] A. Schuster, "On the Investigation of Hidden Periodicities, etc.," *Terrestrial Magnetism*, Vol. 3, 1898.

[3] The further development of Schuster's methods, which we find in his extremely valuable paper, "The Periodogram of the Magnetic Declination as Obtained from the Records of the Greenwich Observatory during the Years 1871–1895," *Trans. of the Cambridge Philos. Soc.*, Vol. 18, 1900, p. 107, seems to overcome this difficulty. Because it is rather unfinished in mathematical respects, however, the influence of this paper seems not to have been comparable to its importance.

[4] H. L. Moore, *Generating Economic Cycles*, New York, 1923.

causality 'which, decade after decade, reproduces the same sinusoidal wave which rises and falls on the surface of the social ocean with the regularity of day and night. It is natural that even now, as centuries ago, the eyes of the investigators are raised to the celestial luminaries searching in them for an explanation of human affairs. One can dauntlessly admit one's right to make bold hypotheses, but still should not one try to find out other ways?[5] What means of explanation, however, would be left to us if we decided to give up the hypothesis of the superposition of regular waves complicated only by purely random components? The presence of waves of definite orders, the long waves embracing decades, shorter cycles from approximately five to ten years in length, and finally the very short waves, will always remain a fact begging for explanation. The approximate regularity of the periods is sometimes so distinctly apparent that it, also, cannot be passed by without notice. Thus, in short, *the undulatory character of the processes and the approximate regularity of the waves* are the two facts for which we shall try to find a possible source in random causes combining themselves in their common effect.

The method of the work is a combination of induction and deduction. It was possible to investigate by the deductive method only a few aspects of the problem. Generally speaking, the theory of chance waves is almost entirely a matter of the future. For the sake of this future theory one cannot be too lavish with experiments: it is experiment that shows us totally unexpected facts, thus pointing out problems which otherwise would hardly fall within the field of the investigator.[6]

II. COHERENT SERIES OF CONSEQUENCES OF RANDOM
CAUSES AND THEIR MODELS

There are two kinds of chance series: (1) those in which the probability of the appearance, in a given place in the series, of a certain value of the variable, depends on previous or subsequent values of the variable, and (2) those in which it does not. In this way we distinguish

[5] A similar viewpoint is found in the remarkable work of G. U. Yule, "Why Do We Sometimes Get Nonsense-Correlations between Time Series?" *Journal of the Royal Statistical Society*, Vol. 89, 1926. This work approaches our theme rather closely.

[6] The following exposition is based on a large amount of calculation. The author expresses special gratitude to his long-time collaborator, E. N. Pomeranzeva-Ilyinskaya and also to O. V. Gordon, N. F. Rein, M. A. Smirnova and E. V. Luneyeva. The calculations were carefully checked, almost all work having been independently performed by two individuals. It is very unlikely that undetected errors are sufficiently significant to affect to any perceptible degree our final conclusions. A few errors, detected in the course of time in Tables I, III, and IX of the original paper, are noted at the end of this paper, and an error in Figure 7, B_4, has been corrected when it was re-drawn.

between *coherent*[7] and *incoherent* (or random) series. The terms of the series of this second kind are not correlated. In series in which there is correlation between terms, one of the most important characteristics is the value of the coefficient of correlation between terms, considered as a function of the distance between the terms correlated. We shall call it the *correlational function* of the corresponding series and shall limit our investigation to those cases in which the distribution of probabilities remains constant. The coefficient of correlation, then, is exclusively determined by the distance between the terms and not by their place in the series. The coefficient of correlation of each member with itself (r_0) will equal unity, and its coefficient of correlation (r_t) with the tth member following will necessarily equal its coefficient (r_{-t}) with the tth member preceding.

Any concrete instance of an experimentally obtained chance series we shall regard as a *model* of empirical processes which are structurally similar to it. As the basis of the present investigation we take three models of purely random series and call them the first, second, and third basic series. These series are based on the results obtained by the People's Commissariate of Finance in drawing the numbers of a government lottery loan. For the first basic series, we used the last digits of the numbers drawn; for the second basic series, we substituted 0 for each even digit and 1 for each odd digit; the third basic series was obtained in the same way as the second, but from another set of numbers drawn.[8]

Let us pass to the coherent series. Their origin may be extremely varied, but it seems probable that an especially prominent role is played in nature by the process of *moving summation* with weights of one kind or another; by this process coherent series are obtained from other coherent series or from incoherent series. For example, let causes $\cdots x_{i-2},\ x_{i-1},\ x_i,\ \cdots$ produce the consequences $\cdots y_{i-2},\ y_{i-1},\ y_i,$ $\cdots$, where the magnitude of each consequence is determined by the influence, not of one, but of a number of the preceding causes, as for instance, the size of a crop is determined, not by one day's rainfall, but by many. If the influence of causes in retrospective order is expressed by the weights $A_0, A_1, A_2, \cdots A_{n-1}$, then we shall have

$$(1) \quad \begin{cases} y_i = A_0 x_i + A_1 x_{i-1} + \cdots + A_{n-1} x_{i-(n-1)}, \\ y_{i-1} = \qquad\quad A_0 x_{i-1} + \cdots + A_{n-2} x_{i-(n-1)} + A_{n-1} x_{i-n}, \\ \cdots \cdots \cdots \cdots \cdots \cdots \cdots \cdots \cdots \cdots \cdots \cdots \cdots \cdots \end{cases}$$

---

[7] I venture to propose this name because it seems to me that it truly expresses what is intended, namely, the existence of some connection between the elements or parts of a thing (for example, of a series), but not a connection between this thing as a whole and another.

[8] The tables giving these series and seven others derived from them will be found in the original paper (*loc. cit.*, pp. 57–64) and are not repeated here.

Each of two adjacent consequences has one particular cause of its own, and $(n-1)$ causes in common with the other consequence. Because the consequences possess causes in common there appears between them a correlation even though the series of causes are incoherent. When all the weights are equal (*simple* moving summation) the coefficient of correlation expresses the share of the common causes in the total number of independent causes on which the consequences

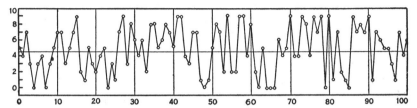

FIGURE 1.—The first 100 terms of the first basic series.

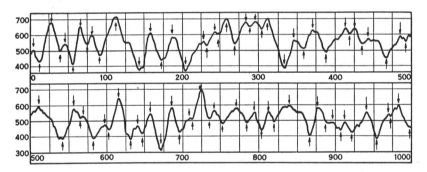

FIGURE 2.—The first 1000 terms of Model II.

depend (as has long been known from the theory of the experiment of Darbishire); then

$$r_0 = 1, r_1 = r_{-1} = \frac{n-1}{n}, r_2 = r_{-2} = \frac{n-2}{n}, \cdots, r_{n-1} = r_{-(n-1)} = \frac{1}{n},$$

further coefficients being equal to zero. By taking a ten-item moving summation of the first basic series, Model I was obtained.[9] A small section of Model I is plotted in Figure 3 with an index[10] of the English

[9] In addition, 5 was added to each sum. This does not change the properties of the series. Neither does it make any difference as to the method of numbering consequences in comparison with the scheme used in formula (1). At the outset of the work, it seemed to be technically more convenient to give the consequence the same number as the earliest cause and not the latest. Thus, for example, for Model I,
$$y_0 = x_0 + x_1 + x_2 + \cdots + x^9 + 5.$$

[10] Dr. Dorothy S. Thomas, "Quarterly Index of British Cycles," in W. L. Thorp, *Business Annals*, New York, 1926, p. 28.

business cycles for 1855–1877 in juxtaposition—an initial graphic demonstration of the possible effects of the summation of unconnected
causes.

In turn the consequences become causes. Taking a ten-item moving
summation of Model I, we obtained the 1000 numbers of Model II.
Performing a two-item moving summation twelve times in succession
on the third basic series,[11] we obtained the 1000 numbers of Model IVa.
First and second differences of Model IVa give Models IVb and IVc
respectively (See Figure 4). Furthermore, the application of scheme
(1) to the second basic series gives[12] Model III if the weights used are

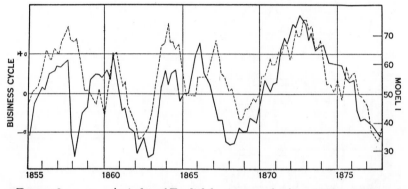

FIGURE 3.————An index of English business cycles from 1855 to 1877; scale
on the left side. ﹣﹣﹣﹣﹣﹣﹣Terms 20 to 145 of Model I; scale on the right side.

10^4 times the ordinates of the Gaussian curve taken at intervals of
0.1σ. Because this model was very smooth it appeared sufficient to
use only the 180 even members out of the 360 items (see Figure 11
under the numbers 0, 2, 4, $\cdots$ 358). Model IIIa—the last one—is 10^4

[11] It actually was computed by applying the scheme (1) to the third basic
series with the weights 1, 12, 66, 220, 495, 792, 924, 792, $\cdots$, 12, 1, because
s-fold simple summation of two items is equivalent, as can be shown easily, to
direct summation with the weights $C_0^s, C_1^s, C_2^s, \cdots, C_s^s$, (where C_k^s is the number of
combinations of s things taken k at a time.

[12] The exact values of Model III could be obtained by multiplying the corresponding items of the basic series by the exact values of the function $10^4 \exp$
$\{-\frac{1}{2}(0.1t)^2\}/\sqrt{2\pi}$, for integral values of t. This function was the basis of obtaining the 4th differences of Model III. Approximate values of Model III were
found by using a set of weights composed of 95 numbers corresponding to the
values of the above function for integral values of t from -47 to $+47$, with the
numbers less than 1 rounded off to the nearest tenth and numbers greater than 1
to whole units. The numbers of the basic series were written on a ribbon which
we slid along the column of weights. Inasmuch as the basic series consisted of
zeros and ones, all of the computations were plain additions. For Model IVa, a
ribbon with holes in the place of unities was constructed.

times the 4th differences of the numbers of Model III from the 7th to the 97th.[13]

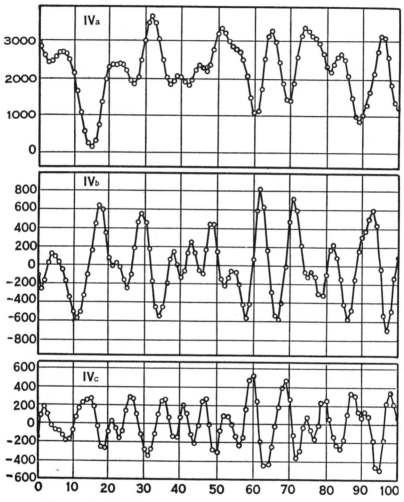

FIGURE 4.—The first 100 terms of Models IVa, IVb, and IVc.

We could not be satisfied by a smaller number of models because it was necessary to observe their various properties and to have illustra-

[13] For the calculation of these differences the accuracy with which we determined the items of Model III was not sufficient, so the following method was used: It is easy to see that the *n*th order differences of the items of the series obtained by scheme (1) are equivalent to those computed by the same scheme but applying weights equal to the differences of the original weights (keeping in mind that the series of original weights is extended at both ends with zeros).

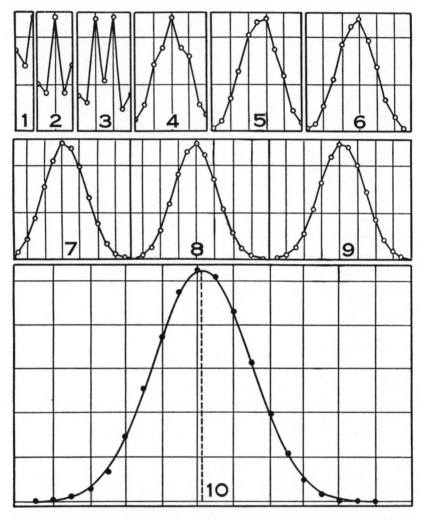

FIGURE 5.—An example of the crossing of random weights. The weights of the causes for each of 10 successive summations are shown, i.e., $A_k'^{(1)}$, $A_k'^{(2)}$, $\cdots$, $A_k'^{(10)}$. See Appendix, Section 1.

With the help of S. Pineto's *Tables de logarithmes vulgaires a dix decimales*, St. Petersburg, 1871, the values of the function
$$\exp\left\{-\tfrac{1}{2}(0.1t)^2\right\}/\sqrt{2\pi}$$
were obtained to ten decimal places for integral values of t from 0 to 44; this series was completed by using Sheppard's tables, and the differences of the entire series up to and including the 4th differences were taken. Multiplying the latter by 10^8 and expressing the result in integers, we obtained weights with the help of which—and by using scheme (1)—the values of $10^4\,\Delta^4 y_{III}$ were obtained from the second basic series.

tions for the elucidation of the different aspects of the problem. We could not aspire to imitate nature in forming a set of weights; still, in the course of the work, we have come across an exceptionally curious circumstance. First, each multifold simple summation of n items at a time gives a set of weights which approaches the Gaussian curve as a limit. In the Appendix, Section 1, there is given the instance of a tenfold summation of three items at a time with the weights chosen absolutely at random for each successive summation. The ten con-

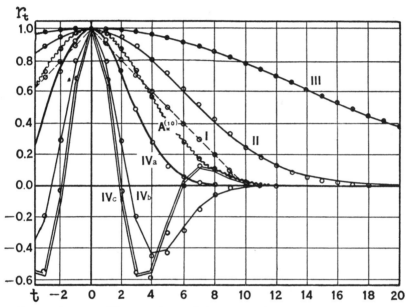

FIGURE 6.—oooo The correlational functions of Models I–IVc, and of the scheme of the crossing of the chance weights $(A_k'^{(10)})$.

〜〜〜〜 〉 Corresponding Gaussian curves and the reduced differences of the ══════ 〉 ordinates of the Gaussian curve.

secutive sets of weights are depicted in Figure 5. It is easily seen how they gradually become more and more like the Gaussian curve, and for the tenth summation the weights approach the Gaussian curve very closely.

This is far from being a chance result. From further considerations (Appendix, Section 1) we find that we have here actually encountered a law which, under certain conditions, must necessarily realize itself in the chaos of random entanglements and crossings of endless numbers of series of causes and consequences. The problem is specially important for the reason that the correlational function of a derived series is defined entirely by the respective weights-function. It is possible to prove (see Appendix, Sections 1, 2, and 3) that if the series of weights follows the Gaussian curve, the correlational function of the resulting consequence series is capable of being expressed by a similar curve with a greater or smaller degree of approximation. For the series of consequences proportionate to the increments of the cause—that is, the differences of order k of the series of causes—the correlational function can be represented by the series of the differences (of order $2k$) of the ordinates of the Gaussian curve. It could not be by chance that the correlational function of all of our models, with the exception of the most elementary one (Model I), belong to one of the two types mentioned (see Figure 6). No exception is found in the correlational

TABLE 1

Distance between terms	Correlation coefficients with random weights	Ordinates of Gaussian curve	Differences
t	r_t	R_t	$r_t - R_t$
0	1.000	1.000	0.000
1	0.965	0.965	0.000
2	0.868	0.866	+0.002
3	0.727	0.723	+0.004
4	0.567	0.562	+0.005
5	0.410	0.407	+0.003
6	0.275	0.274	+0.001
7	0.171	0.171	0.000
8	0.097	0.100	−0.003
9	0.051	0.054	−0.003
10	0.024	0.027	−0.003
11	0.011	0.013	−0.002
12	0.004	0.006	−0.002
13	0.001	0.002	−0.001
14	0.000	0.001	−0.001

function for the series of consequences of the 10th order obtained in the course of the crossing of the random weights in the example mentioned above. The values of these correlation coefficients (r_t), together with the ordinates of the corresponding Gaussian curve (R_t), are given in Table 1 (for the calculation see Appendix, Section 2).

III. THE UNDULATORY CHARACTER OF CHANCE SERIES; GRADUALITY AND FLUENCY AS TENDENCIES

Our models, representing several sets of experiments, give an inductive proof of our first thesis, namely, *that the summation of random causes may be the source of cyclic, or undulatory processes.*[14] It is, however

[14] The definition of the business cycle as being a process (not necessarily periodic) characterized by successive rises and falls, is given by W. C. *Mitchell* in Introduction to W. L. *Thorp, Business Annals*, New York, 1926, pp. 32–33.

not difficult to determine the reason why it must be so inevitably. We shall first observe a series of independent values of a random variable. If, for the sake of simplicity, we assume that the distribution of probabilities does not change, then, for the entire series, there will exist a certain horizontal level such that the probabilities of obtaining a value either above or below it would be equal. The probability that a value, which has just passed from the positive deviation region to the negative, will remain below at the subsequent trial is $\frac{1}{2}$; the probability that it will remain below two times in succession is $\frac{1}{4}$; three times $\frac{1}{8}$; and so on. Thus the probability that the values will remain for a long time above the level or below the level is quite negligible. It is, there-

TABLE 2

Length of half-wave	Actual frequency	Theoretical frequency
i	n'_i	n_i
1	261	256
2	137	128
3	65	64
4	29	32
5	14	16
6	4	8
7	1	4
8 and more	1	4
Total	512	512

fore, practically certain that, for a somewhat long series, the values will pass many times from the positive deviations to the negative and vice versa. Let us designate as a *half-wave* a portion of the series in which the deviation does not change sign. Thus, for 1000 numbers of the third basic series we find 540 half-waves (instead of the theoretically expected 500). Taking from this number the first 512 half-waves we find among them a number of half-waves of the length 1,2, etc. In Table 2 the actual (n_i') and theoretical[15] (n_i) frequencies for half-waves of various lengths are shown. That the observed series is consistent with the theoretical series can be found by the calculation of the χ^2 criterion of goodness of fit.[16]

If a variable can have more than two values and if, in a certain interval of a more or less considerable length, it happens to remain above

[15] L. von Bortkiewicz, *Die Iterationen*, 1917, Formel 75, p. 99.
[16] We find, indeed,

$$\chi^2 = \sum \frac{(n_i' - n_i)^2}{n_i} = 7.78,$$

the corresponding probability being $P = 0.35$; see *Tables for Statisticians and Biometricians*, ed. by K. Pearson, Part I, Table XII.

(or below) its general level, then in that interval it will have a temporary level about which it almost certainly will oscillate. Thus on the
waves of one order there appear superimposed waves of another order.

The unconnected random waves are usually called irregular zigzags.
A correlation between the items of a series deprives the waves of this
characteristic and introduces into their rising and falling movements
an element of *graduality*. In order to make the reasoning more concrete,
let us consider a series obtained from an incoherent series by means of
a ten-item moving summation. Our Model I will be used as the example. Any items of this model separated from each other by more than
9 intervals (as, for example, the values y_0, y_{10}, y_{20}, $\cdots$) are not correlated with each other and consequently form waves of the above con-
sidered type, i.e., irregular zigzags. But if we consider the entire series,
we shall certainly find gradual transitions from the maximum point of a
wave to its minimum and vice versa, since the correlation between
neighboring items of the series makes small differences between them
more probable than large ones. This we find to be true for all of our
models.

We must distinguish between the *graduality* of the transitions and
their *fluency*. We could speak about the absence of the latter property
if a state of things existed where there would be an equal probability
for either a rise or a fall after a rise as well as after a fall. If fluency were
missing we should obtain waves covered by zigzags such as we find in
Model I (see Figure 3).

For example, we have for Model I,

$$y_0 = 5 + x_0 + x_1 + x_2 + \cdots + x_9,$$
$$y_1 = 5 \qquad + x_1 + x_2 + \cdots + x_9 + x_{10},$$
$$y_2 = 5 \qquad\qquad + x_2 + \cdots + x_9 + x_{10} + x_{11},$$
$$\cdots\cdots\cdots\cdots\cdots\cdots\cdots\cdots\cdots$$

from which we obtain

$$\Delta y_0 = y_1 - y_0 = x_{10} - x_0,$$
$$\Delta y_1 = y_2 - y_1 = x_{11} - x_1,$$
$$\cdots\cdots\cdots\cdots\cdots\cdots$$

Thus we see that the adjacent first differences do not have any
causes in common, and hence are not correlated. The same applies to
differences which are further apart, with the exception of such as
$y_1 - y_0 = x_{10} - x_0$ and $y_{11} - y_{10} = x_{20} - x_{10}$. The series of differences is almost incoherent and hence the waves will be covered by chaotically
irregular zigzags such as we find in Model I.

Let us assume further that adjacent differences are positively correlated. Then, in all probability, after a rise another rise will occur,
after a fall a further fall; a steep rise will have the *tendency* to continue

with the same steepness, a moderate one with the same moderateness. So small sections of a wave will tend to be straight lines; and the greater the coefficient of correlation between adjacent differences the closer the sections approximate straight lines.[17]

Correlation between second differences plays an analogous role. The greater this correlation coefficient, the greater the tendency toward the preservation of the constancy of the second differences. Over more or less considerably long intervals a series with approximately constant second differences will tend to approximate a second-degree parabola as all "good" curves do. In Table 3 are given, for Models, I, II, and III, the values of the correlation coefficients between the adjacent items of the series (r_1), between the adjacent first differences $(r_1^{(1,1)})$, and between the adjacent second differences $(r_1^{(2,2)})$. The coefficients were calculated by the formulas of the Appendix, Section 1. As we go from the first basic series to Model I and then to Models II and III, we find progressive changes in their graphic appearance (see Figures, 3, 2, 8, and 11 respectively). These changes are produced at first by the introduction and then by the growth of graduality and of fluency in the movements of the respective chance waves. The growth of the degree of correlation between items (or between their differences) as we go from the first basic series to Model I, etc. (see Table 3) corresponds to the changes in the graphic appearance of our series.

TABLE 3

Model	Coefficient of correlation between:		
	Terms	First differences	Second differences
	r_1	$r_1^{(1,1)}$	$r_1^{(2,2)}$
I	0.9	0.0	−0.5
II	0.985	0.85	0.0
III	0.9975	0.9925	0.9876

IV. EMPIRICAL EVIDENCE OF THE APPROXIMATE REGULARITY OF CHANCE WAVES

Our first thesis, that is, the demonstration of the possibility of the appearance of undulatory processes of a more or less fluent character as the result of the summation of random causes, may be considered

[17] The term *tendency* is used here in a strict sense. To each equation of regression (giving the value of the conditional mathematical expectation of a variable as a function of some other variable) there corresponds an approximate equation between the variables themselves. The closer to unity the absolute value of the coefficient of correlation lies, the greater is the probability that this functional relationship will be maintained within the limits of the desired accuracy; i.e., the stronger will be the *tendency*.

as practically proved. However, our second thesis, that is, the demonstration of *the approximate regularity of the waves*, offers considerably greater difficulties. Again we shall begin with the inductive method.

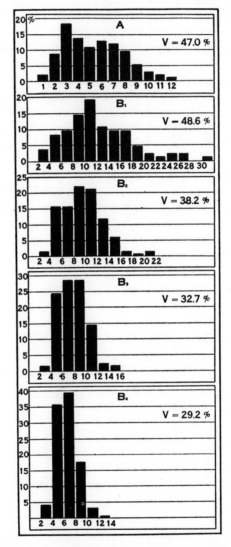

FIGURE 7.—The frequency distributions of the lengths of waves and half-waves: *A*, Business cycles of 12 countries, not including England (Mitchell); B_1 to B_4, Models II, IVa, IVb, and IVc respectively.

In Figure 2 are plotted 1000 points of Model II; a continuous line has been passed through them, which, because of the small scale, seems to be a comparatively fluent curve. One can distinguish on the curve waves of different orders—even down to insignificant zigzags, of which a number are not apparent on the graph because of their minuteness. The maxima and minima having been listed, together with the length of their half-waves and amplitudes, we have found that, since an empirically descriptive point of view, in its very nature, permits only approximate solutions,[18] it was legitimate to draw a boundary between waves and *ripples:* maxima and minima with amplitudes of ten units or less being discarded as ripples. The remaining maxima and minima are indicated by arrows in Figure 2. The distribution of the lengths of the 83 half-waves for Model II is given graphically in Figure 7 (B_1). Figure 7 includes the distribution (A) of the lengths of 93 cycles of economic life for 12 countries outside of England, as given by Mitchell.[19] The coefficient of variation for the latter is 47.0%[20] as compared to 48.6% for Model II. Thus we find variation of the same degree in the two distributions. The distributions for Models IVa, IVb, and IVc are also shown in Figure 7. The average lengths of waves are 9.23, 7.36 and 6.15, while the coefficients of variation are 38.2%, 32.7% and 29.2% respectively. In general appearance these last three distributions are similar to the first two, although the last three have less variation, in spite of the fact that for Models IV, a, b, and c, the data are taken without discarding the ripples. Our models being based on some a priori schemes, it appears quite likely that some day it will be possible to calculate the mathematical expectation and variability of the distances between maxima and minima. In this respect, therefore, the chance waves in coherent series must be subject to some kind of regularity, the regularity of this type being observed even in the chaotic zigzags of purely random series.[21]

We are interested, however, in a different aspect of the problem. The attempt of Mitchell to deny the periodicity of business cycles is a result of his tendency to stick to a purely descriptive point of view. The means of description which he uses and which we tried to imitate for our models are far too crude. If we try to apply the same method to a sum of two or three sinusoids the result would be approximately the same. Those investigators of economic life are right who believe in their acumen and instinct and subscribe to at least an approximate correctness in the concept of the periodicity of business cycles. Let us

[18] Cf. E. Husserl, *Ideen zu einer reinen Phänomenologie und phänomenologischen Philosophie*, Halle a.d.S., 1922, § 74: *Deskriptive und exakte Wissenschaften*, p. 138–139.

[19] W. L. Thorp, *Business Annals*, Introduction by W. C. Mitchell, p. 58.

[20] *Ibid.*

[21] Cf. L. von. Bortkiewicz, *Die Iterationen*, 1917.

again examine Model II (Figure 2). In many places there are, apparently, large waves with massive outlines as well as smaller waves lying, as it were, over them; sometimes these are detached from them, sometimes they are almost completely merged into them. For example, at the beginning of Figure 2, three waves of nearly equal length are apparent, that is, from the first to the third minimum, from the third to the fifth, and from the fifth to the sixth. Upon these waves smaller

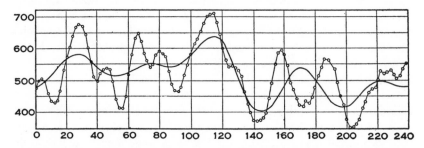

FIGURE 8.—o-o-o The first 120 even terms of Model II. ———Sum of the first five harmonics of Fourier series: $y = 518.14 - 20.98 \cos (2\pi t/240) + 50.02 \sin (2\pi t/240) + 17.30 \cos (2\pi t/120) - 3.16 \sin (2\pi t/120) - 10.93 \cos (2\pi t/80) + 35.66 \sin (2\pi t/80) + 17.18 \cos (2\pi t/60) - 21.92 \sin (2\pi t/60) - 38.53 \cos (2\pi t/48) - 3.65 \sin (2\pi t/48)$.

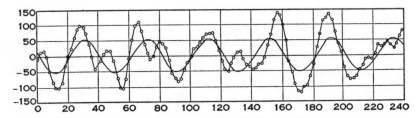

FIGURE 9.—o-o-o The deviations of Model II from the sum of the first five harmonics of Fourier series. ——— 6th sinusoid: $y = 12.98 \cos (2\pi t/40) - 51.50 \sin (2\pi t/40)$.

ones can be seen having also approximately equal dimensions. A careful examination of the graphs of our models will disclose to the reader a number of places where the approximate equality of the length of the waves is readily apparent. If we had a much shorter series, such as a series offered by the ordinary statistics of economic life with its small number of waves, we should be tempted to consider the sequence as strictly periodic, that is, as composed of a few regular harmonic fluctuations complicated by some insignificant casual fluctuations. For instance, let us consider two sections of Model II, lying one directly above the other in Figure 2, namely, the section from item 100 to item 250 and the one from 600 to 750. The similarity between the waves in these sections is apparent.

The accuracy of the above deduction is limited by the imperfection of a visual impression. To eliminate this shortcoming, let us analyze one or two sections of our models harmonically by means of Fourier's analysis. This has been done for a section of 240 points of Model II and the 360 points of Model III. Because of the great fluency of these series it was sufficient to use only the even-numbered ordinates (i.e., 0, 2, $\cdots$ 238, and 0, 2, $\cdots$ 358, respectively), thus saving some computation. The results for the 120 points of Model II are shown in Figures 8, 9 and 10, those for the 180 points of Model III in Figures 11 and 12.

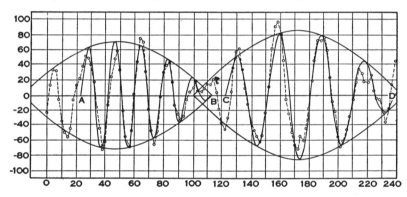

FIGURE 10.—o-o-o The deviations of Model II from the sum of six harmonics.

$$A\text{———}B: y_I = 71 \sin \frac{2\pi}{264}(t + 18) \sin \frac{2\pi}{18}(t - 24).$$

$$C\text{———}D: y_{II}\ 85 \sin \frac{2\pi}{288}(t - 100) \sin \frac{2\pi}{14\frac{2}{3}}(t - 122\frac{1}{3})$$

First let us consider Model II. In Figure 8 the sum of the first five sinusoids of the Fourier series are shown, while in Figure 9 the deviations from that sum are shown together with the sixth sinusoid. It is known, of course, that practically any given curve can be represented by a sum of a series of sinusoids provided a large enough number of terms is taken. It is not for every empirical series, however, that we can obtain such a significant correspondence and such a sharply expressed periodicity with a comparatively small number of harmonics. The approximately regular waves which were apparent even in the crude series are much more distinct now when they are isolated by deducting the sum of the first five harmonics. Of course, we cannot assert that the rest of Model II would follow the same periodicity, but, for our purposes, it is sufficient that successive waves should maintain an approximate equality of length for six periods. This hardly can be considered to be a chance occurrence; the explanation of such an effect must be found in the mechanism of the connection of the random values.

The deviations from the sum of six harmonics are plotted in Figure 10 together with the corresponding fluent curves. These curves are obtained as interference waves of two sinusoids with equal amplitudes and approximately equal periods. In other words, such a curve can be represented as the product of two sinusoids or as a sinusoid with an amplitude also changing along a sinusoid. These *bending sinusoids*

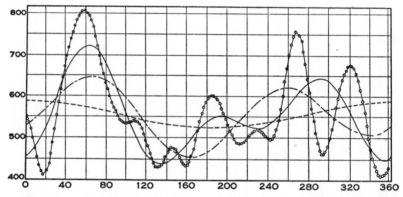

FIGURE 11.—o-o-o The first 180 even terms of Model III. ----$y_I = 554.8$ $+31.79 \cos (2\pi t/360) + 3.40 \sin (2\pi t/360)$. ------ $y_{II} = y_I - 58.82 \cos (2\pi t/180)$ $+46.63 \sin (2\pi t/180)$. ———$y_{III} = y_{II} - 75.36 \cos (2\pi t/120) + 0.61 \sin (2\pi t/120)$.

separate on the graph the regions which place our empirical series in a definite *regime*.[22] Over a large part of the first region the regime is maintained for three or four periods with a correspondence that is much greater than could reasonably be expected between an analytical curve and a random series. At the beginning and end of a region the regime is broken. The point where a bending sinusoid cuts the axis of abscissas is the *critical point*. After this point a regime is replaced by another regime of the same type, but having different parameters. Throughout the greater part of the second region, as in the first, the regime is quite well sustained.[23]

[22] The term *regime* has been borrowed for the purposes of theoretical statistics from hydrography by N. S. Tchetverikov. See his work: "Relation of the Price of Wheat to the Size of the Crop," *The Problems of Economic Conditions*, Vol. 1, Issue 1, Moscow, 1925, p. 83.

[23] The parameters of a regime,
$$y = A \sin [(360°/L)(x - a)] \sin [(360°/l)(x - b)]$$
are easy to determine by means of graphical construction after a few trials. It is also possible to make corrections, using the method of least squares, but in our case we did not think it necessary.

If a result like the foregoing is not due to chance, a much better proof could be expected from an analysis of Model III for which the correlation between the elements is greater than for Model II. In Figure 11 the even-numbered points from 0 to 358 of Model III are plotted together with the first harmonic of the Fourier series, the sum of the first two, and the sum of the first three sinusoids. Instead of the six sinusoids needed for Model II, only three are here necessary for our purposes. The deviations from these are shown in Figure 12. Three regions are apparent with a change of regimes at the critical

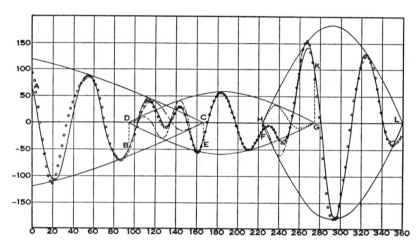

FIGURE 12.—oooo Deviations of Model III from the sum of the first three harmonics. A———B----C, Regime I: $y_I = 136 \sin\ [2\pi(t-167)/960]\ \sin\ [2\pi(t-39)/64]$. D—··—·-E, Regime II': $y_{II}' = 58 \sin\ [2\pi(t-94)/360]\ \sin\ [2\pi(t-98)/36]$. E———F····G, Regime II'': $y_{II}'' = 58 \sin\ [2\pi(t-94)/360]\ \sin\ [2\pi(t-170)/54.4]$. H—··—··-K———L, Regime III: $y_{III} = 182 \sin\ [2\pi(t-222)/276]\ \sin\ [2\pi(t-250.6)/59.6]$. B———E; $y = y_I + y_{II}'$. F———K: $y = y_{II}'' + y_{III}$.

points. In addition we find one more regularity: to the overlapping parts of the said regions corresponds every time the partial superposition of the regimes, i.e., the algebraical addition of the respective curves.

Let us try now to summarize our observations in the following tentative and hypothetical manner:

The summation of random causes generates a cyclical series which tends to imitate for a number of cycles a harmonic series of a relatively small number of sine curves. After a more or less considerable number of periods every regime becomes disarranged, the transition to another regime occurring sometimes rather gradually, sometimes more or less abruptly, around certain critical points.

V. THE TENDENCY TO SINUSOIDAL FORM

In addition to the tendencies towards graduality and fluency (that is towards linear and parabolic forms for small sections) we find a third tendency, namely, the tendency toward a sinusoidal form.

Let $y_i, y_{i+1}, y_{i+2}, \cdots$ be the ordinates of a sinusoid. Then it is always true that

$$(2) \qquad\qquad \Delta^2 y_i = -ay_{i+1},$$

where $\Delta^2 y_i = (y_{i+2} - y_{i+1}) - (y_{i+1} - y_i)$, that is, the ith second difference of the series.

Conversely, it can easily be proved that the function defined by an equation of the form (2) in case $0 < a < 4$ must be a sinusoid.[24] Now, if there is a high correlation between the second differences ($\Delta^2 y_i$) and the ordinates (y_{i+1}) of a series, then equation (2) will be approximately true and there will exist a tendency toward a sinusoidal form in the series. The closer the correlation coefficient between $\Delta^2 y_i$ and y_{i+1}, denoted by us by $r_1^{(2,0)}$, is to -1, the more pronounced (or strong) is the tendency to a sinusoidal form.

A tendency toward either linear or parabolic forms cannot appear in a very large section of a coherent series because it would disrupt its cyclic character. The accumulation of deviations necessarily destroys every linear or parabolic regime even though the respective correlations are very high. After a regime is disrupted the new section will have a new, let us say a parabolic, regime (i.e., a regime of parabolas with different parameters). This process continues throughout the entire series, so that each coherent series of the type considered here is patched together out of a number of parabolas with variable parameters whose variations generally cannot be foreseen.

A sinusoidal regime is also bound to disrupt gradually, this being a property which distinguishes every tendency from an exact law. But under favorable conditions the sinusoidal tendency can be maintained over a number of waves without contradicting the basic property of a coherent series. In order to obtain a result of this kind it is necessary that the respective correlations be sufficiently high. But, as a matter of fact, $r_1^{(2,0)}$ for Model II is approximately the same as for Model I (-0.315 and -0.316), while Model III with its great smoothness has an $r_1^{(2,0)}$ less than that of Model IVa (-0.578 as compared to -0.599). It seems, however, to be very probable that this criterion is insufficient just because we have to deal here not with one sinusoid but with a whole series of sinusoids having different periods. Equation (2), of

---

[24] The condition $0 < a < 4$ is always satisfied in our case since $a = 2 \ (1 - r_1)$ where r_1 is a correlation coefficient between the adjacent terms of the series (between y_i and y_{i+1}). See Appendix, Section 4.

course, is true only for a single sinusoid and cannot be applied to a sum of sinusoids.

To find an instance more apt to illustrate the tendency in question, let us consider the differences of various orders for Model III, the series best adapted for such purposes. If a curve is represented by a sum of sinusoids, then the differences of all orders are sums of sinusoids having waves of the same periods as the curve. The higher the order of the difference, the more pronounced are the shorter periods, since the differencing process weights the shorter periods as against the longer ones. Thus, by applying the formulas of the Appendix, Section 1, we find

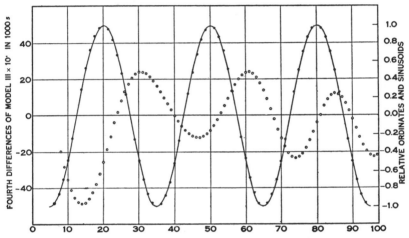

FIGURE 13.—oooo The fourth differences of Model III $\times 10^4$. —·—·— Their relative ordinates, together with the sinusoid.

that the coefficients of correlation, $r_1^{(2,0)}$, for Model III itself, and for its first, second, third, and fourth differences, are -0.5781, -0.7756, -0.8462, -0.8830, and -0.9057, respectively. The following considerations will show us to what extent the simple sinusoidal regime is maintained at least over small portions of the last series.

Let us determine the highest (or lowest) point of a typical wave (A or B, respectively, in Figure 14) as the apex of a second-degree parabola which passes through the three highest (or the three lowest) points of the wave. Then, let us draw a horizontal line bisecting the distance between the highest and lowest points of the wave. Further, let us denote the point where this horizontal line crosses the straight line joining the two points between which the horizontal line passes as C. This point divides AB into two quarter-waves, AC and BC. For each of these, let us make the following construction: Dividing the base line DC (D having the same abscissa as A) into six equal parts, we obtain seven points corresponding to 0°, 15°, 30°, 45°, 60°, 75°, and 90°. At the five central points construct perpendiculars and extend them to the parabola fitted to the three empirical points (interpolated according to Newton's formula). These perpendiculars are the ordinates of an empirical half-wave and, if we divide through by the maximum ordinate AD, we obtain the relative ordinates y_{15}, y_{30}, y_{45}, y_{60}, and y_{75}. If our wave is a sinusoid, these relative ordinates will equal the sines of 15°, 30°, 45°, 60°, and 75°, respectively. The empirical relative ordinates for the 12 quarter-waves of $\Delta^4{}_{VIII}$ are shown by black dots around the regular sinusoid of Figure 13, while the relative ordinates of the first, second, etc., quarters of every empirical wave are shown on the first,

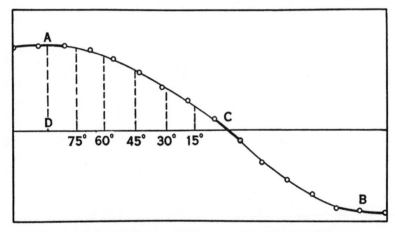

FIGURE 14.—A Scheme for Calculation of the Relative Ordinates.

second, etc., quarters of the sinusoid. The points can hardly be distinguished from the curve. Thus the tendency to a sinusoidal form is shown rather distinctly. If we compute the arithmetic averages of the relative ordinates having the same abscissa (e.g., $\bar{y}_{15} = 1/12(y_{15}{}^{(1)} + y_{15}{}^{(2)} + \cdots + y_{15}{}^{(12)})$ and compare them with the corresponding sines (e.g., sin 15°), we shall see that the deviations are less than $\frac{1}{2}$ in the second decimal place (see Table 4). The agreement is, therefore, close enough

TABLE 4

Phase-angle (α)	15°	30°	45°	60°	75°
$\bar{y}_\alpha$	0.258	0.496	0.703	0.863	0.964
Sin α	0.259	0.500	0.707	0.866	0.966
Deviations	−0.001	−0.004	−0.004	−0.003	−0.002

to be considered as the clear manifestation of the tendency toward a sinusoidal form, and thus displays once more the ability of chance waves to simulate regular harmonic oscillations.

VI. ON THE PSEUDO-PERIODIC CHARACTER OF THE EMPIRICAL CORRELATIONAL FUNCTION[25]

As a further illustration of the sinusoidal tendency, I shall consider here a chance series satisfying, to a rather high degree of approximation, the equation

$$(3) \qquad \Delta^4 z_i - p\Delta^2 z_{i+1} - q z_{i+2} = 0,$$

corresponding, if treated as a precise one, to the sum of two sinusoids.

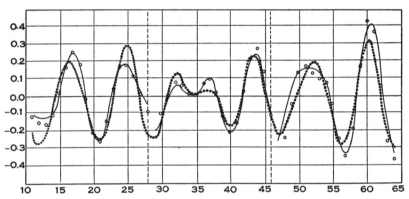

FIGURE 15.— o o o o The reduced empirical correlation function of Model IVc. ——— Sum of two sinusoids, separately for each of three intervals. ..... Sum of three sinusoids.

Let us denote the series in question by the symbols

$$\rho'_{11}, \ \rho'_{12}, \ \cdots, \ \rho'_{64},$$

the values of ρ'_t (see Figure 15) being given by the equation

$$(4) \qquad \rho'_t = \sqrt{\frac{128 - t}{128}} \, \rho_t,$$

where ρ_t is the empirical correlation coefficient between the terms (y_i, y_{i+t}) of the series made up by 128 items of Model IVc. As the values of ρ_t have been calculated from very different numbers of items varying from 117 (that is, $128 - 11$) to 64 (that is, $128 - 64$), the reduction

[25] Eugen Slutzky, "On the Standard Error of the Correlation Coefficient in the Case of Homogenous Coherent Chance Series" (in Russian, with English summary). Transactions of the Conjuncture Institute, Vol. 2, 1929, pp. 94–98, 154.

by (4) has been thought useful in order to bring the respective standard deviations to approximate equality.

Before going further, the following remarks will be made. Let y_0, y_1, $\cdots$ be a stationary chance series. This implies that the mathematical expectation, $E(y_i)$, is a constant, that the standard deviation, σ, is a constant, and that the correlation coefficient, r_t, between y_i and y_{i+t}, is a function of t only. Then, putting, without loss of generality, $E(y_i) = 0$, we shall have $\sigma^2 = E(y_i^2)$ and $r_t = E(y_i y_{i+t})/\sigma^2$. This being the *theoretical* correlation coefficient, let us suppose that $r_t = 0$ if $t > \omega$. Then the correlation coefficient, r'_u, between the empirical correlation coefficients, ρ_t and ρ_{t+u}, will be given by the equation

$$(5) \qquad r'_u = r(\rho_t, \rho_{t+u}) = \frac{\sum\limits_{-\omega}^{\omega} r_t r_{t+u}}{\sum\limits_{-\omega}^{\omega} r_t^2},$$

this formula being approximately correct if it be supposed (1) that ρ_t and ρ_{t+u} are calculated from the same number of values, n; (2) that n is sufficiently large; and (3) that $t > 2\omega$, $n - t > \omega$, and $u > 0$.[26]

Let us suppose now that the values of r'_u calculated from (5) may be held to be approximately true for the series of the reduced correlation coefficients $(\rho'_{11}, \rho'_{12}, \cdots \rho'_{64})$ defined above. Then we have to consider the following problem:

The series given (ρ'_t) being a chance series, there can exist no periodicity in the strict sense of the word. Its cyclical character being, however, obvious (see Figure 15), it may be asked whether the law of its composition from simple harmonics cannot be detected when its correlational function is known.

Let us try to solve this problem to the first approximation by supposing that our series can be duly approximated by the sum of two sinusoids with constant periods and varying amplitudes and phases. To this end, let us find the parameters of the regression equation which can be written in the form

$$(6) \qquad \Delta^4 \rho'_u = p\Delta^2 \rho'_{u+1} + q\rho'_{u+2} + \epsilon,$$

ϵ being the "error," and p and q being determined by the method of least squares. If we denote the correlation coefficients between the pairs of values

$$(\Delta^4\rho'_u, \Delta^2_r\rho'_{u+1}), \ (\Delta^4\rho'_u, \rho'_{u+2}), \ (\Delta^2\rho'_{u+1}, \rho'_{u+2}),$$

by r_{12}, r_{13}, r_{23} respectively, then, using the formulae (43)–(44) (Appendix, Section 1), we obtain

[26] Cf. Slutsky, *loc. cit.* in note 25, pp. 91–94.

(7) $r_{12} = \dfrac{\Delta^6 r'_{-3}}{\sqrt{\Delta^8 r'_{-4} \Delta^4 r'_{-2}}}$; $r_{13} = \dfrac{\Delta^4 r'_{-2}}{\sqrt{\Delta^8 r'_{-4}}}$; $r_{23} = \dfrac{\Delta^2 r'_{-1}}{\sqrt{\Delta^4 r'_{-2}}}$,

where $r'_{-u} \ (= r'_u)$ is the correlation coefficient defined by the equation (5). These values are

$$r'_{-4} = r'_4 = -0.761,874,30,$$
$$r'_{-3} = r'_3 = -0.618,465,96,$$
$$r'_{-2} = r'_2 = -0.013,793,10,$$
$$r'_{-1} = r'_1 = -0.689,655,17,$$

whence, using (7),

$$r_{12} = 0.945,847, \quad r_{13} = 0.760,844, \quad r_{23} = -0.919,999.$$

Then, by the well-known formula of linear regression, we obtain

$$p = -1.419,386, \quad q = -0.425,828,$$

the multiple correlation coefficient, between $\Delta^4 \rho_u$ on the one hand, and $\Delta^2 \rho_{u+1}$ and ρ_{u+2} on the other, being $r_{1.23} = 0.986$. The correlation is thus very high and so it is quite reasonable to omit ϵ in (6) and to treat the resulting approximate equation according to the rules of the calculus of finite differences. We find thus that the solution of this equation is the sum of two sinusoids with the periods

$$L_1 = 9.40, \quad L_2 = 6.04.$$

Let us, then, divide our series $(\rho'_{11}, \rho'_{12}, \cdots \rho'_{64})$ into three parts, of 18 items each, and let us find, for each part separately, two sinusoids with the periods $L_1 = 9, L_2 = 6$, these being the whole numbers nearest to the theoretical values just obtained. We find the results given in Table 5.

TABLE 5

	Part I		Part II		Part III	
	$L_1 = 9$	$L_2 = 6$	$L_1 = 9$	$L_2 = 6$	$L_1 = 9$	$L_2 = 6$
Amplitude	0.19790	0.07820	0.12614	0.12527	0.29123	0.13340
Phase	231°37′	52°39′	218°2′	295°2′	270°52′	2°33′

A glance at Fig. 15 shows that the theoretical curves fit the empirical points very satisfactorily and it seems fairly certain that, if we had included one or two sinusoids more, we could have obtained a quite satisfactory fit, even if treating our empirical series as a whole. This can be proved by the fact that the sum of three sinusoids

$$z = 0.1893 \sin \left[(360°/8.80)t - 47°3'\right]$$
$$+ 0.1000 \sin \left[(360°/7.14)t + 168°24'\right]$$
$$+ 0.0794 \sin \left[(360°/5.87)t - 76°3'\right],$$

though found by rather a rough graphical estimate, fits our empirical curve in a fairly satisfactory manner.[27]

VII. THE LAW OF THE SINUSOIDAL LIMIT

Many tendencies dealt with rather empirically in the preceding discussion will be more clearly understood, and their significance more fully appreciated, if we take into consideration the following propositions.[28]

THEOREM A: (*The Law of the Sinusoidal Limit*)

Let $y_1, y_2, \cdots$ *be a chance series fulfilling the conditions,*

$$E(y_i) = 0, \quad E(y_i{}^2) = \sigma^2 = f(n),$$

$$\frac{E(y_i y_{i+t})}{E(y_i{}^2)} = r_t = \phi(t, n),$$

where n is a parameter specifying the series as a whole, and $f(n)$ and $\phi(t, n)$ are independent of i. If, furthermore, the correlation coefficient, r_1, between y_i and y_{i+1}, satisfies the condition

$$\left| r_1 \right| \leqq c < 1, \qquad\qquad (n \to \infty),$$

and the correlation coefficient between $\Delta^2 y_i$ and y_{i+1}, that is, ρ_1, is such that

$$\lim \rho_1 = -1, \qquad\qquad (n \to \infty),$$

then (1) ϵ and η being taken arbitrarily small and s arbitrarily large, there will exist a number, n_0, such that for every $n > n_0$, the probability, that the absolute values of the deviations of $y_i, y_{i+1}, \cdots y_{i+s}$ from a certain sinusoid will not exceed $\epsilon\sigma$, will be $> 1 - \eta$; (2) the period of this sinusoid will be determined by the equation

$$\cos (2\pi/L) = r_1;$$

(3) the number of the periods in the interval $(i, i+s)$ will be arbitrarily large provided s and n be taken large enough.

This proposition (for its proof see Appendix, Section 4) would be of no interest could we not give at least a single instance of a chance series satisfying the conditions of Theorem A. This is done by

[27] The above illustration seems to throw some light on the difficulties connected with the idea of a correlation periodogram. Cf. Dinsmore Alter, "A Group or Correlation Periodogram," etc., *Monthly Weather Review*, Vol. 55, No. 6, June, 1927, pp. 263–266; Sir Gilbert Walker, "On Periodicity in Series of Related Terms," *Proc. Royal Soc.*, Ser. A, Vol. 131, No. A 818, 1931, pp. 518–532.

[28] E. Slutsky, "Sur un théorème limite relatif aux séries des quantités éventuelles," *Comptes Rendus*, Paris, t. 185, seance du 4 Juli, 1927, p. 169.

THEOREM B: Let $x_1, x_2, \cdots$ be a random series fulfilling the conditions

$$E(x_i) = 0, \ E(x_i^2) = \sigma_x^2 = \text{const.}, \ E(x_i x_j) = 0, \qquad (i \neq j).$$

Now, if we put

$$x_i^{(1)} = x_i + x_{i-1}, \ x_i^{(2)} = x_i^{(1)} + x_{i-1}^{(1)}, \cdots ,$$
$$x_i^{(n)} = x_i^{(n-1)} + x_{i-1}^{(n-1)},$$

and

$$y_i = \Delta^m x_i^{(n)},$$

then the series $y_1, y_2, \cdots$ will tend to obey the law of the sinusoidal limit, provided m and n be increasing indefinitely and m/n = constant (for the proof see Appendix, Section 4).

Both propositions can be generalized to the case of a chance series practically coinciding, not with one sinusoid, but with the sum of a certain number of sinusoids.[29] In every case, however, the practical coincidence (and it is a very essential character of the series under consideration) does not extend itself to the series as a whole, the respective sinusoids of closest fit being different for different partial series. This is plainly evident for the chance series of Theorem B, for, s being arbitrarily large and n and m being sufficiently large, the values y_i and y_{i+t} will be wholly independent of each other as soon as $t > m + n + 1$, whence it follows that the phases and the amplitudes of the sinusoids practically coincident with the partial series, $y_i, y_{i+1}, \cdots$ y_{i+s}, and $y_{i+t+s}, y_{i+t+s+1}, \cdots y_{i+t+2s}$, respectively, will also be independent of each other provided $t > m + n + 1$.

The following considerations will show us the same problem from a somewhat different standpoint. Let us suppose a certain mechanism is being subjected to damped vibrations of a periodic character and to casual disturbances accumulating energy just sufficient to counterbalance the damping.[30] Then the movement of the system could be regarded as consisting of the two parts: of the vibrations determined by the initial conditions at some given moment, and of the vibrations generated by the disturbances that have occurred since. As soon as the first part has been nearly extinguished by the damping process after due lapse of time, the actual vibrations will be reduced practically to the second part, that is, to the accumulated consequences of the chance

[29] V. Romanovsky, "Sur la loi sinusoidale limite," *Rend. d. Circ. mat. di Palermo*, Vol. 56, Fasc. 1, 1932, pp. 82–111; V. Romanovsky, "Sur une generalisation de la loi sinusoidal limite," *Rend d. Circ. mat. di Palermo*, Vol. 57, Fasc. 1, pp. 130–136; cf. Sir Gilbert Walker, *op. cit.*, in note 27.

[30] Cf. G. Udney Yule, "On a Method of Investigating Periodicities in Disturbed Series with Special Reference to Wolfer's Sunspot Numbers," *Phil. Trans. Roy. Soc. of London*, Ser. A. Vol. 226, 1927, pp. 267–298.

causes. The latter, after a due time, being again reduced to a value not different practically from zero, the vibrations will consist of the disturbances accumulated during the second interval of time and so on. It is evident that the vibrations ultimately will have the character of a chance function, the described process being a particular instance of the summation of random causes. Should the disturbances be small enough, there would exist an arbitrarily large, but finite, number, L_0, such that the resulting process would be practically coincident, in every interval of the length, $L \leqq L_0$, with a certain periodic (or nearly periodic) function, obeying thus the law of the sinusoidal limit.

Analogous considerations may be applied to the motion of planetary, or star systems, the innumerable cosmic influences being considered as casual disturbances. The paths of the planets, if regarded during billions of years, should be considered, therefore, as chance functions, but if we do not wish to go beyond thousands of years their approximate representation must be taken as not casual.

The chance functions of the type just considered appearing on the one end of the scale, and the random functions on the other, there evidently must exist all possible intermediate gradations between these extremes. The ability of the coherent chance series to simulate the periodic, or the nearly periodic, functions, seems thus to be definitely demonstrated.

It remains for us to try to clear up theoretically the remarkable property of some specimens of chance series, which do not belong to the extreme classes of their type, of being approximately representable by a small number of sinusoids, over a shorter or longer interval.

It is well known that every empirical series consisting of a finite number of terms ($N = 2n$ or $2n+1$) can be represented precisely by a finite Fourier series, that is by the sum of a finite number (n) of sinusoids. Further, it is plainly evident, the series under consideration being chance series and the coefficients of the Fourier expansion,

$$y_t = A_0 + \sum_1^n A_k \cos (2\pi kt/N) + \sum_1^n B_k \sin (2\pi kt/N),$$

that is, the values $A_0, A_1, \cdots A_n$, and $B_0, B_1, \cdots B_n$, being linear functions of $y_1, y_2, \cdots y_n$, that the variables A_k and B_k will also be chance variables. Their mathematical expectations, standard deviations, and the correlation coefficients between them can be easily obtained.[31] Denoting by R_k^2 the intensity of the kth harmonic, that is,

[31] E. Slutsky, "Alcuni applicazioni di coefficienti di Fourier al analizo di sequenze eventuali coherenti stazionarii," *Giorn. d. Istituto Italiano degli Attuari*, Vol. 5, No. 4, 1934; see also E. Slutsky, "Sur l'extension de la theorie de periodogrammes aux suites des quantités dependentes." *Compte Rendus*, t. 189, seance du 4 novembre, 1929, p. 722.

the square of its amplitude, we shall have

$$R_k^2 = A_k^2 + B_k^2,$$

and

(8)
$$E(R_k^2) = (4\sigma_y^2/N)\left[1 + 2\sum_1^{N-1} r_t \cos (2\pi kt/N)\right]$$
$$- (8\sigma_y^2/N^2) \sum_1^{N-1} tr_t \cos (2\pi kt/N),$$

whence, for the case of a random series, we obtain at once the formula of Schuster,

(9)
$$E(R_k^2) = 4\sigma_y^2/N,$$

the probability distribution being the same in both cases,

(10)
$$P(R_k^2 > Z^2) = \exp\left[-Z^2/E(R_k^2)\right].$$

Let us suppose the m intensities happening to have the largest values in some given case are those with the indices: $\alpha, \beta, \cdots \mu$ and let

$$\tfrac{1}{2}(R_\alpha^2 + R_\beta^2 + \cdots + R_\mu^2) = ps^2,$$

s^2 being the square of the empirical standard deviation and p the coefficient measuring the degree of approximation reached in the given case by means of m harmonics. By taking account of (8), (9), and (10), we see at once that, in the case of a random series, the indices $\alpha, \beta, \cdots \mu$ are able to assume any values with equal probability but that in the case of a coherent series those having the largest values of $E(R_k^2)$ will be the most probable. As half of the sum of the intensities is equal to the square of the empirical standard deviation (Parceval's theorem), it is but natural that the coherent chance series, in many cases at least, may be represented—the degree of approximation being the same—by a smaller number of harmonics than the random series.

It can be proved further (under suppositions of a not very restrictive character) that the correlation coefficients between the intensities belonging to the same interval, as well as between those belonging to the adjacent intervals, are quantities of the order $1/N^2$, and that the standard deviation of the intensity, σ_{R^2}, tends to be equal to its probable value, $E(R_k^2)$. Whence it is evident that the indices of the harmonics which happen to be the most suited for the representation of the series in a certain interval must also be practically independent of the indices of the "best" harmonics in adjacent intervals, the length of these intervals being sufficiently large. The larger the probable value of the intensity the larger also must be the extent of its casual variation. These are properties quite consistent with a considerable degree of regularity—as well as with the abrupt changes of the "regimes" determined by studying the empirical series dealt with in the foregoing pages.

APPENDIX

MATHEMATICAL NOTES OF THE THEORY OF RANDOM WAVES

1. Let $x_0, x_1, \cdots x_i, \cdots$ be a random series, that is, a series of chance values independent of each other. Let this be our basic series and let it be considered as a model of incoherent series of random causes. Denoting by the symbol E the mathematical expectation, let us suppose that

(1) $E(x_i) = 0, \ E(x_i{}^2) = \sigma_x{}^2 = \text{const.}; \ E(x_i x_j) = 0, \qquad (i \neq j).$

From the basic incoherent series of causes let us construct a coherent series of "consequences," $\cdots y_{i-2}, y_{i-1}, y_i, \cdots$, by the scheme

(2) $$y_i = \sum_{k=0}^{n-1} A_k x_{i-k},$$

where the quantities A_k are constants.[32] Then, by using (1) and (2), it can easily be shown that

(3) $$E(y_i) = 0,$$

(4) $$E(y_i{}^2) = \sigma_y{}^2 = \sigma_x{}^2 \sum_{k=0}^{n-1} A_k{}^2,$$

(5) $$E(y_i y_{i+t}) = \sigma_x{}^2 \sum_{k=0}^{(n-1)-t} A_k A_{k+t}.$$

Since equations (4) and (5) do not depend on i, the coefficient of correlation between y_i and y_{i-t}, that is, r_t, is also independent of i, and we have

(6) $$r_t = \frac{\sum_{k=0}^{(n-1)-t} A_k A_{k+t}}{\sum_{k=0}^{n-1} A_k{}^2},$$

from which it immediately follows that

(7) $$r_0 = 1; \ r_t = r_{-t}; \ r_t = 0, \ (t \geqq n).$$

The process of moving summation can be repeated. As before, let us take $\cdots x_{i-2}, x_{i-1}, x_i, \cdots$ as the basic series underlying the conditions

---

[32] Cf. Prof. Birger Meidell's valuable investigation of the analogous cumulative processes in his paper, "Über periodische und angenäherte Beharrungs-zustände," *Skandinavisk Aktuarietidskrift*, 1926, p. 172.

(1). Then on performing an s-fold moving summation we obtain the following successive consequence series:

(8)
$$x_i^{(1)} = \sum_{k=0}^{n-1} \alpha_k^{(1)} x_{i-k}; \quad x_i^{(2)} = \sum_{k=0}^{n-1} \alpha_k^{(2)} x_{i-k}^{(1)}; \cdots$$

$$x_i^{(s)} = \sum_{k=0}^{n-1} \alpha_k^{(s)} x_{i-k}^{(s-1)}.$$

After the s-fold summation we have an expression of type (2) with $y_i = x_i^{(s)}$. Hence, if we take $n=2$ and $\alpha_k^{(j)} = 1$, it can easily be shown that

(9)
$$y_i = x_i^{(s)} = \sum_{k=0}^{s} C_k^s x_{i-k}.$$

If we put

(10)
$$\phi(t) = \frac{1}{\sqrt{2\pi}} \exp\left(- \tfrac{1}{2}t^2\right),$$

we can, by the use of well-known transformations, obtain the approximate expression (which we write for an *even* s)

(11)
$$y_i = D \sum_{k=0}^{s} x_{i-k} \phi\left(\frac{k - s/2}{\sqrt{s/4}}\right),$$

D being a coefficient, the value of which need not concern us here.

It is very remarkable that a similar result will always be obtained for s sufficiently great, whatever be the weights used, provided it is supposed (1) that the weights are not negative, (2) that they remain constant at every given stage of the process, and (3) that the summation does not tend to degenerate into a mere repetition of the same values, which would be the case should all $\alpha_k^{(s)}$ but one tend to approach 0; (the sum of the weights is supposed, without loss of generality, to be constant).

To prove this, let us remark first that the result of the s-fold summation given by (8) can evidently be obtained by a similar s-fold summation with the weights

$$p_0^{(j)}, p_1^{(j)}, \cdots, p_{n-1}^{(j)}, \qquad (j = 1, 2, \cdots, s),$$

where

$$p_k^{(j)} = \frac{\alpha_k^{(j)}}{m_j}, \quad m_j = \sum_{k=0}^{n-1} \alpha_k^{(j)},$$

if we multiply the resulting weights by the proportionality factor $m_1 \cdot m_2 \cdots m_s$.

Now to prove our proposition we shall use the following analogy (kindly suggested to the author by Prof. A. Khinchin).

Let $z_1, z_2, \cdots z_s$ be a set of random variables whose possible values are $0, 1, 2, \cdots, n-1$, the respective probabilities being $p_0^{(i)}, p_1^{(i)}, \cdots p_{n-1}^{(i)}, (j=1, 2, \cdots s)$. Then it is easy to see that the probability of the equation

$$(12) \qquad k = z_1 + z_2 + \cdots + z_s$$

must be equal to the coefficient of x^k in the expansion of

$$(13) \qquad \prod_{j=1}^{s} (p_0^{(i)} + p_1^{(i)}x + p_2^{(i)}x^2 + \cdots + p_{n-1}^{(i)}x^{n-1}).$$

On the other hand, it can be proved that the same coefficient, multiplied by $m_1 \cdot m_2 \cdots m_s$, will be equal to the coefficient A_k in the equation (2) obtained by an s-fold summation according to the scheme (8) with the weights

$$m_j p_0^{(i)}, \; m_j p_1^{(i)}, \; \cdots, \; m_j p_{n-1}^{(i)}, \qquad\qquad (j = 1, 2, \cdots, s).$$

This is easily seen for $s=2$ and the result can be generalized by mathematical induction from s to $s+1$.

This analogy leads us to the following considerations. Let us put

$$(14) \qquad \begin{cases} a_j = E(z_j) = \displaystyle\sum_{k=0}^{n-1} k p_k^{(i)}, \\[2mm] b_j = E[(z_j - a_j)^2] = \displaystyle\sum_{k=0}^{n-1} (k - a_j)^2 p_k^{(i)}, \\[2mm] c_j = E[\,|z_j - a_j|^g\,] = \displaystyle\sum_{k=0}^{n-1} |\,k - a_j\,|^g p_k^{(i)}, \qquad (g > 2). \end{cases}$$

It is evident that $b_j = 0$ only if every $(k - a_j)^2 p_k^{(i)} = 0$ for $k = 0, 1, 2, \cdots (n-1)$, and that this is possible only when every $p_k^{(i)}$ but one is equal to zero, the exceptional p being 1, in which case the values $x_k^{(i)}$ are merely repetitions of the values $x_k^{(i-1)}$.

This case being excluded, we shall have, on the average at least,

$$(15) \qquad\qquad (1/s) \sum_1^s b_i > \epsilon > 0;$$

whence

$$(16) \qquad \frac{\left[\displaystyle\sum_1^s c_i\right]^2}{\left[\displaystyle\sum_1^s b_i\right]^g} < \frac{\left[(1/s) \displaystyle\sum_1^s c_i\right]^2}{s^{g-2}\epsilon^g} \to 0.$$

But this is the well known Liapounoff's condition, under which the probability distribution of the sum $z_1 + z_2 + \cdots + z_s$, that is, the distribution of the coefficients A_k, tends to the normal law.[33]

Let us put, for instance,

$$\alpha_0{}^{(i)} = \alpha_1{}^{(i)} = \cdots = \alpha_{n-1}{}^{(i)} = 1, \qquad (j = 1, 2, \cdots, s).$$

Then we obtain

$$m_j = \sum_{k=0}^{n-1} \alpha_k{}^{(i)} = n,$$

(17)
$$m_1 m_2 \cdots m_s = n^s,$$

$$p_k{}^{(i)} = 1/n,$$

for

and
$$j = 1, 2, \cdots, s, \quad \text{and} \quad k = 0, 1, \cdots, n - 1;$$

$$a_j = E(z_j) = \sum_{k=0}^{n-1} k p_k{}^{(i)} = (n - 1)/2,$$

(18)

$$b_j = E[(z_j - a_j)^2] = (1/n)\left\{ \sum_{k=0}^{n-1} k^2 - n a_j{}^2 \right\} = (n^2 - 1)/12.$$

Whence

(19)
$$k_0 = E(k) = E\left[\sum_{1}^{s} z_j \right] = s(n - 1)/2,$$

and

(20)
$$\sigma_k = \sqrt{s b_j} = \sqrt{s(n^2 - 1)/12}.$$

As s tends towards ∞, the value of A_k will thus approach a limit, which enables us to write, for s large but finite, the following approximate equations:[34]

[33] It is evident that, since Liapounoff's theorem is a proposition about the limit properties of certain integrals and not of the individual ordinates, the above demonstration must be interpreted also in the same sense. For many cases, however, for example, in the case of the illustration below, the additional conditions are satisfied under which the values of the variables A_k themselves are tending toward the ordinates of the Gaussian curve.

Cf. Liapounoff, "Nouvelle forme du théorème sur la limite de probabilité," *Memoires de l'Academie de science de St.-Petersbourg*, serie 8, Vol. 12, No. 5.

R. von Mises, *Vorlesungen aus dem Gebiete der Angewandten Mathematik*, Bd. I—*Wahrscheinlichkeitsrechnung und ihre Anwendungen*, 1931, p. 200–212.

R. von Mises, "Generalizzazione di un teorema sulla probabilità della somma di un numero illimitato di variabili casuali," *Giornale dell'Istituto Italiano degli Attuari*, Anno 5, N4, p. 483–495.

[34] This result coincides with that given in the first edition of this memoir in 1927; it was supplied to the author by the courtesy of Prof. A. Khinchin who derived it by the application of the well-known Cauchy theorem to the evaluation of the coefficient of x^k in the expansion of
$$(1 + x + x^2 + \cdots + x^{n-1})^s.$$
I am sorry that the calculations are too long to be reproduced here.

(21) $A_k \stackrel{a}{=} n^s \sqrt{6/\pi s(n^2-1)} \exp\left\{-6(k-k_0)^2/s(n^2-1)\right\}.$

For the general case, we shall give here the following illustration Let the weights for a set of successive summations be certain random numbers. For this purpose, let us choose consecutive groups of three numbers from the first basic series (Column 2, Table I, Appendix II). For the first moving summation the weights will be $\alpha_0^{(1)}=5$, $\alpha_1^{(1)}=4$, $\alpha_2^{(1)}=7$; for the second $\alpha_0^{(2)}=3$, $\alpha_1^{(2)}=0$, $\alpha_2^{(2)}=3$, etc. Performing the substitutions indicated by formula (8) we obtain the resulting weights corresponding to A_k of formula (2), $A_k^{(1)}=\alpha_k^{(1)}$, $A_k^{(2)}$, $A_k^{(3)}$, $\cdots A_k^{(10)}$. For each given s, we divide the weights by the largest $A_k^{(s)}$ to obtain the relative weights, $A'_k^{(s)}$ (see Table VIII, Appendix II, of the original paper, and Figure 5). The series of quantities $A'_k^{(10)}$ does not differ greatly from the Gaussian curve obtained by putting[35]

(22) $B'_k^{(10)} = 1004 \exp\left\{-\tfrac{1}{2}[(k-9.26)/2.67]^2\right\}.$

2. The coefficients of correlation between the terms of a coherent series are, in many cases, easy to obtain by using formula (6). For a simple moving summation of n equally weighted items at a time, we have $A_0=A_1=\cdots=A_{n-1}=1$. It is easy to see that

(23) $\begin{cases} r_t = (n-|t|)/n, & (|t| \leq n) \\ r_t = 0, & (|t| \geq n). \end{cases}$

From formulas (4), (5), (9) and the properties of $\overset{\bullet}{C}_k$, we find for the s-fold moving summation of two terms, that is, $(n=2)$, that

(24) $\sigma_y^2 = \sigma_x^2[1 + (\overset{\bullet}{C_1})^2 + (\overset{\bullet}{C_2})^2 + \cdots + (\overset{\bullet}{C_{s-1}})^2 + 1] = \sigma_x^2 \overset{\bullet}{C_s^{2s}},$

and

(25) $E(y_i y_{i+t}) = \sigma_x^2[\overset{\bullet}{C_0^s}\overset{\bullet}{C_t^s} + \overset{\bullet}{C_1^s}\overset{\bullet}{C_{t+1}^s} + \cdots + \overset{\bullet}{C_{s-t}^s}\overset{\bullet}{C_s^s}] = \sigma_x^2\overset{\bullet}{C_{s-t}^{2s}}.$

Hence

(26) $r_t = \overset{\bullet}{C_{s-t}^{2s}}/\overset{\bullet}{C_s^{2s}} = \dfrac{s(s-1)\cdots(s-t+1)}{(s+1)(s+2)\cdots(s+t)}.$

Consider another case. Let us form, from a basic series, a coherent series by the scheme:

[35] Let us pass a second degree parabola through $A_0'^{(10)}$, $A_1'^{(10)}$, $A_2'^{(10)}$; another through $A_2'^{(10)}$, $A_3'^{(10)}$, $A_4'^{(10)}$; etc. Denote the area of this figure by S, its maximum ordinate by y_0, and the abscissa bisecting the area by k_0. Then, in the Gaussian equation

$$B'_k^{(10)} = [S/\sigma\sqrt{2\pi}] \exp\left\{-\tfrac{1}{2}[(k-k_0)/\sigma]^2\right\},$$

all of the parameters are known, since

$$k_0 = 9.26, \quad y_0 = S/\sigma\sqrt{2\pi} = 1004,$$

and hence

$$\sigma = S/y_0\sqrt{2\pi} = 2.67.$$

$$(27) \qquad y_i = D \sum_{k=0}^{2k_0} x_{i-k} \phi[(k - k_0)/\sigma],$$

where $\phi(t)$ is given by formula (10), D is a constant, and k_0 is a number large enough so that $\phi(t)$ can be neglected for $|t| > k_0/\sigma$. Then, from (6), the coefficient of correlation is

$$(28) \qquad r_t = \frac{\displaystyle\sum_{k=0}^{2k_0-t} \phi[(k - k_0)/\sigma]\phi[(k - k_0 + t)/\sigma]}{\displaystyle\sum_{k=0}^{2k_0} \{\phi[(k - k_0)/\sigma]\}^2}.$$

If σ is sufficiently large we can substitute integrals for the summations in (28). Inserting $z = k - k_0$, we then obtain the approximation formula

$$(29) \qquad r_t = \frac{\displaystyle\int_{-\infty}^{+\infty} \exp\left[-\tfrac{1}{2}\frac{z^2 + (z + t)^2}{\sigma^2}\right]dz}{\displaystyle\int_{-\infty}^{+\infty} \exp\left[-\frac{z^2}{\sigma^2}\right]dz}$$

$$= \exp\left(-t^2/4\sigma^2\right) = \frac{\phi(t/\sigma\sqrt{2})}{\phi(0)}.$$

Inasmuch as Model III is formed by the scheme of formula (27), with $D = 10^4$, $k_0 = 48$, and $\sigma = 10$, we can calculate the correlation function by formula (29). The values for $[\phi(t/\sqrt{200})]/\phi(0)$, ($t = 0, 1, 2,$ $\cdots$), were calculated with the aid of Sheppard's tables.[36] The symbol $R_{t(III)}$, instead of $r_{t(III)}$, indicates that an approximate, and not an exact, formula was used in the calculation.

Model IVa was obtained by a 12-fold moving summation of two items; therefore, its correlation function, $r_{t(IVa)}$, is obtained by using formula (26), which, if we consider (11), gives $R_{t(IVa)} = \phi(t/\sqrt{6})/\phi(0)$. The discrepancies between the two results are rather small. The correspondence between $r_{t(IVb)}$ and $R_{t(IVb)}$ is somewhat less, as is also that between $r_{t(IVc)}$ and $R_{t(IVc)}$. Both sets were computed by formula (45) (see next paragraph), but for the calculation of $r_{t(IVb)}$ and $r_{t(IVc)}$ the actual values of $r_{t(IVa)}$ were used as the base, while for $R_{t(IVb)}$ and $R_{t(IVc)}$ the approximate values of $R_{t(IVa)}$, obtained by the Gaussian formula, were used. Even here the discrepancies are not very great when regarded from the same point of view (see Figure 6).

[36] *Tables for Statisticians and Biometricians*, ed. by K. Pearson, Cambridge, 1914, Table II.

Finally, for Model II, corresponding to the scheme

$$(30) \qquad y_i = x_i^{(2)} = \sum_{k=0}^{18} A_k^{(2)} x_{i+k} + 50,$$

$$(A_k^{(2)} = 1, 2, \cdots, 9, 10, 9, \cdots, 2, 1),$$

the coefficients of correlation can be obtained directly from formula (6). It is worth noting that, even in this case, a good approximation, $R_{t(II)}$, can be obtained by the use of the Gaussian curve, the equation being

$$(31) \qquad R_{t(II)} = \exp\left[-\tfrac{1}{2}(t/5.954)^2\right],$$

where $\sigma = 5.954$ was obtained by equating the areas of the Gaussian curve and of the empirical curve, and the computations were carried through with the help of Simpson's rule (see Figure 6).

A few more words may be said about the correlational function for the weights, $A'_k{}^{(10)}$, of our example of the crossing of random weights (see Section 2 of the text, Appendix, Section 1, and Figure 6). The exact values of the coefficients of correlation (r_t) were found by formula (6), while approximate values (R_t) were obtained from the equation

$$(32) \qquad R_t = \exp\left[-\tfrac{1}{2}(t/3.727)^2\right],$$

which was obtained in the same manner as was equation (31). Both the exact and approximate values are given in Table 1 (see also Figure 6). Also, let us note that, from the equation of the Gaussian curve which approximates the weights, $A'_k{}^{(10)}$ (see formula (22) above), it is possible to find an approximate expression for the coefficients of correlation by using formula (29). An expression analogous to (32) would be obtained, but instead of $\sigma = 3.727$, we would have $\sigma = 3.776$. The correlation coefficients are only slightly less accurate than those found from formula (32), the deviations are all of one sign, and none is greater than 0.009.

Let us make one more observation. If a chance variable $y_i = u_i + v_i$, where u_i is a coherent series and v_i is a random series, it is easy to show that

$$(33) \qquad E(y_i y_{i+t}) = E(u_i u_{i+t}),$$

$$(34) \qquad (E y_i^2) = \sigma_u^2 + \sigma_v^2,$$

$$(35) \qquad r_{v_i, v_{i+t}} = \frac{r_{u_i, u_{i+t}}}{1 + (\sigma_v^2/\sigma_u^2)},$$

where $E(u_i)$ and $E(v_i)$ are taken equal to zero.

If $r_{u_i, u_{i+t}}$ lies along the Gaussian curve, then $r_{v_i, v_{i+t}}$ will lie along a similar curve with ordinates proportionally reduced, except that r_0 will, as formerly, equal unity; the *chapeau de gendarme* has taken on the spike of the *budenovka* (a Soviet military cap). It is to be expected that this figure and the analogous figures for the correlation function of the differences (formula (45) of the following paragraph) will be encountered in the investigation of empirical series.[37]

3. Let us now investigate the differences of various orders of the series y_i, i.e., $\Delta^\alpha y_i$, $\Delta^\beta y_i$, and their coefficients of correlation.[38] As before, let

$$(36) \qquad E(y_i) = 0; \; E(y_i{}^2) = \sigma_y{}^2 = \text{constant}; \; E(y_i y_{i+t})/\sigma_y{}^2 = r_t,$$

where r_t is supposed to be independent of i. Let us introduce the notation

$$(37) \qquad r_t{}^{(\alpha,\beta)} = r_{\Delta^\alpha y_i, \Delta^\beta y_{i+t}}, \qquad\qquad (\alpha \geqq \beta);$$

and, in particular,

$$(38) \qquad r_t{}^{(\alpha,\alpha)} = r_{\Delta^\alpha y_i, \Delta^\alpha y_{i+t}} \qquad r_t{}^{(\alpha,0)} = r_{\Delta^\alpha y_i, y_{i+t}}.$$

By using the equality

$$(39) \qquad C_k^{2\alpha} = C_{\alpha-k}^\alpha C_0^\alpha + C_{\alpha-(k-1)}^\alpha C_1^\alpha + \cdots + C_{\alpha-1}^\alpha C_{k-1}^\alpha + C_\alpha^\alpha C_k^\alpha,$$

it can be shown that

$$\sigma_{\Delta^\alpha y_i}{}^2 = E[(\Delta^\alpha y_i)^2] = E[(C_\alpha^\alpha y_{i+\alpha} - C_{\alpha-1}^\alpha y_{i+\alpha-1} + C_{\alpha-2}^\alpha y_{i+\alpha-2}$$
$$(40) \qquad - \cdots + (-1)^\alpha C_0^\alpha y_i)^2] = (-1)^\alpha \Delta^{2\alpha} r_{-\alpha} \sigma_y{}^2.$$

From (40), by using the equality,

$$(41) \qquad C_k^{\alpha+\beta} = C_{\alpha-k}^\alpha C_0^\beta + C_{\alpha-k+1}^\alpha C_1^\beta + \cdots + C_{\alpha-1}^\alpha C_{k-1}^\beta + C_k^\beta,$$

we obtain

$$(42) \qquad E[\Delta^\alpha y_i \Delta^\beta y_{i+t}] = (-)^\alpha \Delta^{\alpha+\beta} r_{t-\alpha} \sigma_y{}^2, \qquad\qquad (\alpha \geqq \beta),$$

and from this we have

$$(43) \qquad r_t{}^{(\alpha,\beta)} = \frac{(-1)^\alpha \Delta^{\alpha+\beta} r_{t-\alpha}}{\sqrt{(-1)^{\alpha+\beta} \Delta^{2\alpha} r_{-\alpha} \Delta^{2\beta} r_{-\beta}}}.$$

In the same manner we obtain

$$(44) \qquad r_t{}^{(\alpha,0)} = \frac{(-1)^\alpha \Delta^\alpha r_{t-\alpha}}{\sqrt{(-1)^\alpha \Delta^{2\alpha} r_{-\alpha}}},$$

[37] Cf. Figure 19 of Yule, "Why Do We Sometimes Get Nonsense-Correlations $\cdots$," *loc. cit.*, p. 43.

[38] Cf. O. Anderson, "Über ein neues Verfahren bei Anwendung der 'Variate-Difference' Methode," *Biometrika*, Vol. 15, 1923, pp. 142 ff.

and, as a special case of formula (43), we have

$$(45) \qquad r_t^{(\alpha,\alpha)} = \frac{\Delta^{2\alpha} r_{t-\alpha}}{\Delta^{2\alpha} r_{-\alpha}}.$$

By this formula and by (26) the correlation coefficients for Models IVb and IVc have been computed.

4. Let us now prove Theorem A (see Section VII above). The regression coefficient of $\Delta^2 y_i$ on y_{i+1} being

$$E(\Delta^2 y_i \cdot y_{i+1})/\sigma_y^2 = -2(1 - r_1),$$

we obtain the approximate equation

$$\Delta^2 y_i \overset{a}{=} -2(1 - r_1)y_{i+1}.$$

Whence

$$(46) \qquad y_{i+2} \overset{a}{=} 2r_1 y_{i+1} - y_i,$$

the errors of both equations being evidently identical. If we denote this error by α_2 and put $\beta_2 = \alpha_2/\sigma_y$, we may apply the well-known formula of correlation theory and thus obtain

$$(47) \qquad E(\beta_2^2) \doteq E(\Delta^2 y_i)(1 - \rho_1^2)/\sigma_y^2 = (1 - \rho_1^2)(6 - 8r_1 + 2r_2).$$

Now, under the suppositions of Theorem A,

$$\lim_{n \to \infty} \beta_2^2 = 0;$$

whence, applying Tchebycheff's theorem, we see that β_2 has the stochastical limit $E(\beta_2) = 0$, $(n \to \infty)$; that is, ϵ and η being arbitrarily small, the probability

$$P\{|\beta_2| > \epsilon\} < \eta,$$

provided n is sufficiently large.

On the other hand, if we put

$$y_{i+2} = 2r_1 y_{i+1} - y_i + \alpha_2,$$
$$y_{i+3} = 2r_1 y_{i+2} - y_{i+1} + \alpha_3,$$
$$\cdot \ \cdot \ \cdot \ \cdot \ \cdot \ \cdot \ \cdot \ \cdot \ \cdot \ \cdot \ \cdot \ \cdot$$
$$y_{i+s} = 2r_1 y_{i+s-1} - y_{i+s-2} + \alpha_s;$$

and if we insert y_{i+2} in the second equation of this system, y_{i+3} in the third, and so on, we obtain, after reduction,

$$(48) \qquad y_{i+s} = C_1 y_{i+1} + C_2 y_i + \lambda_s \sigma_y,$$

where

(49) $$\lambda_s = a_0\beta_s + a_1\beta_{s-1} + \cdots + a_{s-2}\beta_2,$$

the values $a_0, a_1, \cdots a_{s+2}$, being determined by the conditions

(50) $$\begin{cases} a_0 = 1, \quad a_1 = 2r_1, \\ a_{k+2} = 2r_1 a_{k+1} - a_k. \end{cases}$$

This equation is identical with

(51) $$y_{i+2} = 2r_1 y_{i+1} - y_i,$$

that is, with (46) considered as a precise equation. The solution of (51) or (50) can be obtained easily. We find

(52) $$y_t = A \cos (2\pi t/L) + B \sin (2\pi t/L),$$

and

(53) $$a_k = C \cos (2\pi k/L) + D \sin (2\pi k/L),$$

where we have put

(54) $$\cos (2\pi/L) = r_1,$$

L being the period of the respective sinusoid. It is evident that, under the assumptions of Theorem A, $(|r_1| \leq \lambda < 1)$, we shall have

(55) $$L \leq 2\pi/\text{arc cos } \lambda = H = \text{constant}.$$

Two sinusoids must now be considered. The first, which will be denoted by S_1, is determined by (51), or (52), and the initial points y_i, y_{i+1}. It is evident that $C_1 y_{i+1} + C_2 y_i$ in (48) is the ordinate of S_1 which could be obtained in this form from (51) by successive substitutions. The deviation of the actual value of y_{i+s} from S_1 is $\lambda_s \sigma_y$ as given by (48) and (49), the coefficients a_k being the ordinates of the second sinusoid (S_2) determined by (50) or (53), and the initial values $a_0 = 1$, $a_1 = 2r_1$. But, if we put, in (53), $k = 0$, and then $k = 1$, we obtain

$$C = 1, \quad D = r_1/\sqrt{1 - r_1^2}.$$

Hence the amplitude of S_2 is

$$\sqrt{C^2 + D^2} = 1/\sqrt{1 - r_1^2} \leq 1/\sqrt{1 - \lambda^2} = K = \text{constant}.$$
$$C = 1, \quad D = r_1/\sqrt{1 - r_1^2}.$$

Thus, taking into account that every a_k in (49) has an upper limit $\leqq \sqrt{C^2+D^2}$, $(n\to\infty)$ and remembering the theorems of my *Metron* memoir[39] we conclude that λ_s has the stochastical limit $=0$ and that, ϵ and η being arbitrarily small and s arbitrarily large, the probability that the conditions

$$\lambda_2 < \epsilon, \, \lambda_3 < \epsilon, \, \cdots, \, \lambda_s < \epsilon,$$

are simultaneously satisfied will be $>1-\eta$ provided n is sufficiently large. The formulas (54) and (55) complete the proof.

To prove theorem B, we may proceed here as follows: It is seen by (43) and (45) that the correlation coefficient between y_i and y_{i+1} is

$$(56) \qquad r_1 = r_1{}^{(m,m)} = \frac{\Delta^{2m}r_{-m+1}}{\Delta^{2m}r_{-m}},$$

and the correlation coefficient between $\Delta^2 y_i$ and y_{i+1} is given by

$$(57) \qquad \rho_1 = r_1{}^{(m+2,m)} = \frac{(-1)^m \Delta^{2m+m}r_{-(m+1)}}{\sqrt{\Delta^{2(m+2)}r_{-(m+2)}\Delta^{2m}r_{-m}}},$$

where, using (26) we must put

$$r_t = \frac{C^{2n}_{n-t}}{C^{2n}_n}.$$

On the other hand, r_{-t} being equal to r_t, it can easily be seen that

$$(58) \qquad C^{2n}_n \Delta^{2m}r_{-m} = \sum_{k=0}^{2m}(-1)^k C^{2m}_k C^{2n}_{n-m+k} = A_{n+m},$$

where A_{n+m} is the coefficient of x^{n+m} in the expansion of $(1+x)^{2n}(1-x)^{2m}$. Applying Cauchy's theorem we have

$$A_{n+m} \quad \frac{1}{2\pi i}\int_{|1|}\frac{(1+x)^{2n}(1-x)^{2m}}{x^{n+m+1}}\,dx.$$

If we put $x=e^{i\phi}$, we obtain, after reduction,

$$A_{n+m} = \left[(-1)^m 2^{2(n+m)}/\pi\right]\int_0^\pi \cos^{2n}\phi \sin^{2m}\phi \, d\phi.$$

[39] E. Slutsky, "Über Stochastische Asymptoten und Grenzwerte," *Metron*, Vol. 5, N. 3, 1925, pp. 61–64.

Hence

$$(59) \quad A_{n+m} = \frac{(-1)^m 2^{n+m} 1 \cdot 3 \cdots (2n-1) \cdot 1 \cdot 3 \cdots (2m-1)}{1 \cdot 2 \cdot 3 \cdots (n+m)}.$$

Thus we obtain, by (58),

$$(60) \quad \Delta^{2m} r_{-m} = \frac{(-1)^m 2^m 1 \cdot 3 \cdots (2m-1)}{(n+1)(n+2) \cdots (n+m)}.$$

If we notice that

$$\Delta^{2m+2} r_{-(m+1)} = \Delta^{2m} r_{-(m+1)} - 2\Delta^{2m} r_{-m} + \Delta^{2m} r_{-(m-1)},$$

where, evidently,

$$\Delta^{2m} r_{-(m+1)} = \Delta^{2m} r_{-(m-1)},$$

we get

$$\Delta^{2m} r_{-m+1} = \tfrac{1}{2}\Delta^{2(m+1)} r_{-(m+1)} + \Delta^{2m} r_{-m}$$

$$(61) \qquad = \frac{(-1)^m 2^m 1 \cdot 3 \cdots (2m-1)(n-m)}{(n+1)(n+2) \cdots (n+m+1)},$$

so that, by (56), (57), (60), and (61), we obtain

$$(62) \qquad r_1 = (n-m)/(n+m+1)$$

and[40]

$$(63) \qquad \rho_1 = -\sqrt{\frac{(2m+1)(n+m+2)}{(2m+3)(n+m+1)}}.$$

Now, it is evident that, n/m being constant,

$$r_1 < \frac{n/m - 1}{n/m + 1} < 1$$

and

$$\rho_1 \to -1, \qquad\qquad (n \to \infty),$$

which proves Theorem B.

CORRECTIONS OF BASIC DATA

The tables of figures which contain the series used in the present investigation are to be found in the original paper (*loc. cit.*, pp. 57–64). As the preparation of them has involved a great deal of time and labor

---

[40] To apply this formula in the case of No. V, we should notice that Model III is approximately equivalent to the series (y_1) of Theorem B, with $n = 400$.

EUGEN SLUTZKY

and as it may be expected that someone will make use of them for the purpose of analogous studies, we give here correct readings for the *errata* found after the figures had been published. (Those relating to Table VI are immaterial and are omitted here.)

Table	Column					
	1	2	6	7	8	10
I	300				−453	
	418			−361		
	637				332	
	638			− 10	461	
	639		1367	451	295	
	807			255		
	819				211	
	820			496	−252	
	821		2290	244	−488	
	971				− 99	
	972			263	− 98	
	973		2134	165	−186	
III	23	− 4551				
	72	−20219				
IX	9		0.0007			
	11					0.0059
	13					0.0001
	14					0.0000

EUGEN SLUTZKY

*Mathematical Institute of the Moscow State University
Moscow, U.S.S.R.*

Econometrica, Vol. 5, No. 2 (April, 1937)

MR. KEYNES AND THE "CLASSICS";
A SUGGESTED INTERPRETATION[1]

By J. R. Hicks

I

IT WILL BE ADMITTED by the least charitable reader that the entertainment value of Mr. Keynes' *General Theory of Employment* is considerably enhanced by its satiric aspect. But it is also clear that many readers have been left very bewildered by this Dunciad. Even if they are convinced by Mr. Keynes' arguments and humbly acknowledge themselves to have been "classical economists" in the past, they find it hard to remember that they believed in their unregenerate days the things Mr. Keynes says they believed. And there are no doubt others who find their historic doubts a stumbling block, which prevents them from getting as much illumination from the positive theory as they might otherwise have got.

One of the main reasons for this situation is undoubtedly to be found in the fact that Mr. Keynes takes as typical of "Classical economics" the later writings of Professor Pigou, particularly *The Theory of Unemployment*. Now *The Theory of Unemployment* is a fairly new book, and an exceedingly difficult book; so that it is safe to say that it has not yet made much impression on the ordinary teaching of economics. To most people its doctrines seem quite as strange and novel as the doctrines of Mr. Keynes himself; so that to be told that he has believed these things himself leaves the ordinary economist quite bewildered.

For example, Professor Pigou's theory runs, to a quite amazing extent, in real terms. Not only is his theory a theory of real wages and unemployment; but numbers of problems which anyone else would have preferred to investigate in money terms are investigated by Professor Pigou in terms of "wage-goods." The ordinary classical economist has no part in this *tour de force*.

But if, on behalf of the ordinary classical economist, we declare that he would have preferred to investigate many of those problems in money terms, Mr. Keynes will reply that there is no classical theory of money wages and employment. It is quite true that such a theory cannot easily be found in the textbooks. But this is only because most of the textbooks were written at a time when general changes in money wages in a closed system did not present an important problem. There can be little doubt that most economists have thought that they had

[1] Based on a paper which was read at the Oxford meeting of the Econometric Society (September, 1936) and which called forth an interesting discussion. It has been modified subsequently, partly in the light of that discussion, and partly as a result of further discussion in Cambridge.

a pretty fair idea of what the relation between money wages and employment actually was.

In these circumstances, it seems worth while to try to construct a typical "classical" theory, built on an earlier and cruder model than Professor Pigou's. If we can construct such a theory, and show that it does give results which have in fact been commonly taken for granted, but which do not agree with Mr. Keynes' conclusions, then we shall at last have a satisfactory basis of comparison. We may hope to be able to isolate Mr. Keynes' innovations, and so to discover what are the real issues in dispute.

Since our purpose is comparison, I shall try to set out my typical classical theory in a form similar to that in which Mr. Keynes sets out his own theory; and I shall leave out of account all secondary complications which do not bear closely upon this special question in hand. Thus I assume that I am dealing with a short period in which the quantity of physical equipment of all kinds available can be taken as fixed. I assume homogeneous labour. I assume further that depreciation can be neglected, so that the output of investment goods corresponds to new investment. This is a dangerous simplification, but the important issues raised by Mr. Keynes in his chapter on user cost are irrelevant for our purposes.

Let us begin by assuming that w, the rate of money wages per head, can be taken as given.

Let x, y, be the outputs of investment goods and consumption goods respectively, and N_x, N_y, be the numbers of men employed in producing them. Since the amount of physical equipment specialised to each industry is given, $x = f_x(N_x)$ and $y = f_y(N_y)$, where f_x, f_y, are *given* functions.

Let M be the *given* quantity of money.

It is desired to determine N_x and N_y.

First, the price-level of investment goods = their marginal cost = $w(dN_x/dx)$. And the price-level of consumption goods = their marginal cost = $w(dN_y/dy)$.

Income earned in investment trades (value of investment, or simply Investment) = $wx(dN_x/dx)$. Call this I_x.

Income earned in consumption trades = $wy(dN_y/dy)$.

Total Income = $wx(dN_x/dx) + wy(dN_y/dy)$. Call this I.

I_x is therefore a given function of N_x, I of N_x and N_y. Once I and I_x are determined, N_x and N_y can be determined.

Now let us assume the "Cambridge Quantity equation"—that there is some definite relation between Income and the demand for money. Then, approximately, and apart from the fact that the demand for money may depend not only upon total Income, but also upon its distribution between people with relatively large and relatively small demands for balances, we can write

$$M = kI.$$

As soon as k is given, total Income is therefore determined.

In order to determine I_x, we need two equations. One tells us that the amount of investment (looked at as demand for capital) depends upon the rate of interest:

$$I_x = C(i).$$

This is what becomes the marginal-efficiency-of-capital schedule in Mr. Keynes' work.

Further, Investment = Saving. And saving depends upon the rate of interest and, if you like, Income. $\therefore I_x = S(i, I)$. (Since, however, Income is already determined, we do not need to bother about inserting Income here unless we choose.)

Taking them as a system, however, we have three fundamental equations,

$$M = kI, \quad I_x = C(i), \quad I_x = S(i, I),$$

to determine three unknowns, I, I_x, i. As we have found earlier, N_x and N_y can be determined from I and I_x. Total employment, $N_x + N_y$, is therefore determined.

Let us consider some properties of this system. It follows directly from the first equation that as soon as k and M are given, I is completely determined; that is to say, total income depends directly upon the quantity of money. Total employment, however, is not necessarily determined at once from income, since it will usually depend to some extent upon the proportion of income saved, and thus upon the way production is divided between investment and consumption-goods trades. (If it so happened that the elasticities of supply were the same in each of these trades, then a shifting of demand between them would produce compensating movements in N_x and N_y, and consequently no change in total employment.)

An increase in the inducement to invest (i.e., a rightward movement of the schedule of the marginal efficiency of capital, which we have written as $C(i)$) will tend to raise the rate of interest, and so to affect saving. If the amount of saving rises, the amount of investment will rise too; labour will be employed more in the investment trades, less in the consumption trades; this will increase total employment if the elasticity of supply in the investment trades is greater than that in the consumption-goods trades—diminish it if *vice versa*.

An increase in the supply of money will necessarily raise total income, for people will increase their spending and lending until incomes have risen sufficiently to restore k to its former level. The rise in income will tend to increase employment, both in making consumption goods and in making investment goods. The total effect on employment depends upon the ratio between the expansions of these industries; and that depends upon the proportion of their increased incomes which people desire to save, which also governs the rate of interest.

So far we have assumed the rate of money wages to be given; but so long as we assume that k is independent of the level of wages, there is no difficulty about this problem either. A rise in the rate of money wages will necessarily diminish employment and raise real wages. For an unchanged money income cannot continue to buy an unchanged quantity of goods at a higher price-level; and, unless the price-level rises, the prices of goods will not cover their marginal costs. There must therefore be a fall in employment; as employment falls, marginal costs in terms of labour will diminish and therefore real wages rise. (Since a change in money wages is always accompanied by a change in real wages in the same direction, if not in the same proportion, no harm will be done, and some advantage will perhaps be secured, if one prefers to work in terms of real wages. Naturally most "classical economists" have taken this line.)

I think it will be agreed that we have here a quite reasonably consistent theory, and a theory which is also consistent with the pronouncements of a recognizable group of economists. Admittedly it follows from this theory that you may be able to increase employment by direct inflation; but whether or not you decide to favour that policy still depends upon your judgment about the probable reaction on wages, and also—in a national area—upon your views about the international standard.

Historically, this theory descends from Ricardo, though it is not actually Ricardian; it is probably more or less the theory that was held by Marshall. But with Marshall it was already beginning to be qualified in important ways; his successors have qualified it still further. What Mr. Keynes has done is to lay enormous emphasis on the qualifications, so that they almost blot out the original theory. Let us follow out this process of development.

II

When a theory like the "classical" theory we have just described is applied to the analysis of industrial fluctuations, it gets into difficulties in several ways. It is evident that total money income experiences great variations in the course of a trade cycle, and the classical theory can only explain these by variations in M or in k, or, as a third and last alternative, by changes in distribution.

(1) Variation in M is simplest and most obvious, and has been relied

on to a large extent. But the variations in M that are traceable during a trade cycle are variations that take place through the banks—they are variations in bank loans; if we are to rely on them it is urgently necessary for us to explain the connection between the supply of bank money and the rate of interest. This can be done roughly by thinking of banks as persons who are strongly inclined to pass on money by lending rather than spending it. Their action therefore tends at first to lower interest rates, and only afterwards, when the money passes into the hands of spenders, to raise prices and incomes. "The new currency, or the increase of currency, goes, not to private persons, but to the banking centers; and therefore, it increases the willingness of lenders to lend in the first instance, and lowers the rate of discount. But it afterwards raises prices; and therefore it tends to increase discount."[2] This is superficially satisfactory; but if we endeavoured to give a more precise account of this process we should soon get into difficulties. What determines the amount of money needed to produce a given fall in the rate of interest? What determines the length of time for which the low rate will last? These are not easy questions to answer.

(2) In so far as we rely upon changes in k, we can also do well enough up to a point. Changes in k can be related to changes in confidence, and it is realistic to hold that the rising prices of a boom occur because optimism encourages a reduction in balances; the faling prices of a slump because pessimism and uncertainty dictate an increase. But as soon as we take this step it becomes natural to ask whether k has not abdicated its status as an independent variable, and has not become liable to be influenced by others among the variables in our fundamental equations.

(3) This last consideration is powerfully supported by another, of more purely theoretical character. On grounds of pure value theory, it is evident that the direct sacrifice made by a person who holds a stock of money is a sacrifice of interest; and it is hard to believe that the marginal principle does not operate at all in this field. As Lavington put it: "The quantity of resources which (an individual) holds in the form of money will be such that the unit of money which is just and only just worth while holding in this form yields him a return of convenience and security equal to the yield of satisfaction derived from the marginal unit spent on consumables, and equal also to the net rate of interest."[3] The demand for money depends upon the rate of interest! The stage is set for Mr. Keynes.

[2] Marshall, *Money, Credit, and Commerce*, p. 257.

[3] Lavington, *English Capital Market*, 1921, p. 30. See also Pigou, "The Exchange-value of Legal-tender Money," in *Essays in Applied Economics*, 1922, pp. 179–181.

As against the three equations of the classical theory,

$$M = kI, \quad I_x = C(i), \quad I_x = S(i, I),$$

Mr. Keynes begins with three equations,

$$M = L(i), \quad I_x = C(i), \quad I_x = S(I).$$

These differ from the classical equations in two ways. On the one hand, the demand for money is conceived as depending upon the rate of interest (Liquidity Preference). On the other hand, any possible influence of the rate of interest on the amount saved out of a given income is neglected. Although it means that the third equation becomes the multiplier equation, which performs such queer tricks, nevertheless this second amendment is a mere simplification, and ultimately insignificant.[4] It is the liquidity preference doctrine which is vital.

For it is now the rate of interest, not income, which is determined by the quantity of money. The rate of interest set against the schedule of the marginal efficiency of capital determines the value of investment; that determines income by the multiplier. Then the volume of employment (at given wage-rates) is determined by the value of investment and of income which is not saved but spent upon consumption goods.

It is this system of equations which yields the startling conclusion, that an increase in the inducement to invest, or in the propensity to consume, will not tend to raise the rate of interest, but only to increase employment. In spite of this, however, and in spite of the fact that quite a large part of the argument runs in terms of this system, and this system alone, *it is not the General Theory*. We may call it, if we like, Mr. Keynes' *special theory*. The General Theory is something appreciably more orthodox.

Like Lavington and Professor Pigou, Mr. Keynes does not in the end believe that the demand for money can be determined by one variable alone—not even the rate of interest. He lays more stress on it than they did, but neither for him nor for them can it be the only variable to be considered. The dependence of the demand for money on interest does not, in the end, do more than qualify the old de-

---

[4] This can be readily seen if we consider the equations

$$M = kI, \quad I_x = C(i), \quad I_x = S(I),$$

which embody Mr. Keynes' second amendment without his first. The third equation is already the multiplier equation, but the multiplier is shorn of his wings. For since I still depends only on M, I_x now depends only on M, and it is impossible to increase investment without increasing the willingness to save or the quantity of money. The system thus generated is therefore identical with that which, a few years ago, used to be called the "Treasury View." But Liquidity Preference transports us from the "Treasury View" to the "General Theory of Employment."

pendence on income. However much stress we lay upon the "speculative motive," the "transactions" motive must always come in as well.
Consequently we have for the General Theory

$$M = L(I, i), \quad I_x = C(i), \quad I_x = S(I).$$

With this revision, Mr. Keynes takes a big step back to Marshallian
orthodoxy, and his theory becomes hard to distinguish from the revised
and qualified Marshallian theories, which, as we have seen, are not
new. Is there really any difference between them, or is the whole thing
a sham fight? Let us have recourse to a diagram (Figure 1).

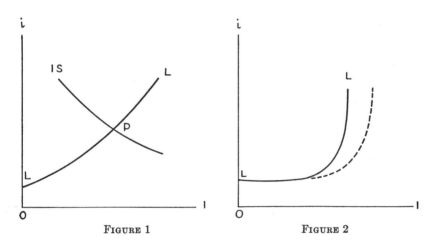

FIGURE 1   FIGURE 2

Against a given quantity of money, the first equation, $M = L(I, i)$,
gives us a relation between Income (I) and the rate of interest (i).
This can be drawn out as a curve (LL) which will slope upwards, since
an increase in income tends to raise the demand for money, and an
increase in the rate of interest tends to lower it. Further, the second
two equations taken together give us another relation between Income
and interest. (The marginal-efficiency-of-capital schedule determines
the value of investment at any given rate of interest, and the multiplier
tells us what level of income will be necessary to make savings equal
to that value of investment.) The curve IS can therefore be drawn
showing the relation between Income and interest which must be
maintained in order to make saving equal to investment.

Income and the rate of interest are now determined together at P,
the point of intersection of the curves LL and IS. They are determined
together; just as price and output are determined together in the
modern theory of demand and supply. Indeed, Mr. Keynes' innovation
is closely parallel, in this respect, to the innovation of the marginalists.

The quantity theory tries to determine income without interest, just as the labour theory of value tried to determine price without output; each has to give place to a theory recognising a higher degree of inter-dependence.

III

But if this is the real "General Theory," how does Mr. Keynes come to make his remarks about an increase in the inducement to invest not raising the rate of interest? It would appear from our diagram that a rise in the marginal-efficiency-of-capital schedule must raise the curve *IS*; and, therefore, although it will raise Income and employment, it will also raise the rate of interest.

This brings us to what, from many points of view, is the most important thing in Mr. Keynes' book. It is not only possible to show that a given supply of money determines a certain relation between Income and interest (which we have expressed by the curve *LL*); it is also possible to say something about the shape of the curve. It will probably tend to be nearly horizontal on the left, and nearly vertical on the right. This is because there is (1) some minimum below which the rate of interest is unlikely to go, and (though Mr. Keynes does not stress this) there is (2) a maximum to the level of income which can possibly be financed with a given amount of money. If we like we can think of the curve as approaching these limits asymptotically (Figure 2).

Therefore, if the curve *IS* lies well to the right (either because of a strong inducement to invest or a strong propensity to consume), *P* will lie upon that part of the curve which is decidedly upward sloping, and the classical theory will be a good approximation, needing no more than the qualification which it has in fact received at the hands of the later Marshallians. An increase in the inducement to invest will raise the rate of interest, as in the classical theory, but it will also have some subsidiary effect in raising income, and therefore employment as well. (Mr. Keynes in 1936 is not the first Cambridge economist to have a temperate faith in Public Works.) But if the point *P* lies to the left of the *LL* curve, then the *special* form of Mr. Keynes' theory becomes valid. A rise in the schedule of the marginal efficiency of capital only increases employment, and does not raise the rate of interest at all. We are completely out of touch with the classical world.

The demonstration of this minimum is thus of central importance. It is so important that I shall venture to paraphrase the proof, setting it out in a rather different way from that adopted by Mr. Keynes.[5]

If the costs of holding money can be neglected, it will always be

---

[5] Keynes, *General Theory*, pp. 201–202.

profitable to hold money rather than lend it out, if the rate of interest is not greater than zero. Consequently the rate of interest must always be positive. In an extreme case, the shortest short-term rate may perhaps be nearly zero. But if so, the long-term rate must lie above it, for the long rate has to allow for the risk that the short rate may rise during the currency of the loan, and it should be observed that the short rate can only rise, it cannot fall.[6] This does not only mean that the long rate must be a sort of average of the probable short rates over its duration, and that this average must lie above the current short rate. There is also the more important risk to be considered, that the lender on long term may desire to have cash before the agreed date of repayment, and then, if the short rate has risen meanwhile, he may be involved in a substantial capital loss. It is this last risk which provides Mr. Keynes' "speculative motive" and which ensures that the rate for loans of indefinite duration (which he always has in mind as *the* rate of interest) cannot fall very near zero.[7]

It should be observed that this minimum to the rate of interest applies not only to one curve *LL* (drawn to correspond to a particular quantity of money) but to any such curve. If the supply of money is increased, the curve *LL* moves to the right (as the dotted curve in Figure 2), but the horizontal parts of the curve are almost the same. Therefore, again, it is this doldrum to the left of the diagram which upsets the classical theory. If *IS* lies to the right, then we can indeed increase employment by increasing the quantity of money; but if *IS* lies to the left, we cannot do so; merely monetary means will not force down the rate of interest any further.

So the General Theory of Employment is the Economics of Depression.

[6] It is just conceivable that people might become so used to the idea of very low short rates that they would not be much impressed by this risk; but it is very unlikely. For the short rate may rise, either because trade improves, and income expands; or because trade gets worse, and the desire for liquidity increases. I doubt whether a monetary system so elastic as to rule out both of these possibilities is really thinkable.

[7] Nevertheless something more than the "speculative motive" is needed to account for the system of interest rates. The shortest of all short rates must equal the relative valuation, at the margin, of money and such a bill; and the bill stands at a discount mainly because of the "convenience and security" of holding money—the inconvenience which may possibly be caused by not having cash immediately available. It is the chance that you may want to discount the bill which matters, not the chance that you will then have to discount it on unfavourable terms. The "precautionary motive," not the "speculative motive," is here dominant. But the prospective terms of rediscounting are vital, when it comes to the *difference* between short and long rates.

IV

In order to elucidate the relation between Mr. Keynes and the "Classics," we have invented a little apparatus. It does not appear that we have exhausted the uses of that apparatus, so let us conclude by giving it a little run on its own.

With that apparatus at our disposal, we are no longer obliged to make certain simplifications which Mr. Keynes makes in his exposition. We can reinsert the missing i in the third equation, and allow for any possible effect of the rate of interest upon saving; and, what is much more important, we can call in question the sole dependence of investment upon the rate of interest, which looks rather suspicious in the second equation. Mathematical elegance would suggest that we ought to have I and i in all three equations, if the theory is to be really General. Why not have them there like this:

$$M = L(I, i), \quad I_x = C(I, i), \quad I_x = S(I, i)?$$

Once we raise the question of Income in the second equation, it is clear that it has a very good claim to be inserted. Mr. Keynes is in fact only enabled to leave it out at all plausibly by his device of measuring everything in "wage-units," which means that he allows for changes in the marginal-efficiency-of-capital schedule when there is a change in the level of money wages, but that other changes in Income are deemed not to affect the curve, or at least not in the same immediate manner. But why draw this distinction? Surely there is every reason to suppose that an increase in the demand for consumers' goods, arising from an increase in employment, will often directly stimulate an increase in investment, at least as soon as an expectation develops that the increased demand will continue. If this is so, we ought to include I in the second equation, though it must be confessed that the effect of I on the marginal efficiency of capital will be fitful and irregular.

The Generalized General Theory can then be set out in this way. Assume first of all a given total money Income. Draw a curve CC showing the marginal efficiency of capital (in money terms) at that given Income; a curve SS showing the supply curve of saving at that *given* Income (Figure 3). Their intersection will determine the rate of interest which makes savings equal to investment at that level of income. This we may call the "investment rate."

If Income rises, the curve SS will move to the right; probably CC will move to the right too. If SS moves more than CC, the investment rate of interest will fall; if CC more than SS, it will rise. (How much it rises and falls, however, depends upon the elasticities of the CC and SS curves.)

The IS curve (drawn on a separate diagram) now shows the relation between Income and the corresponding investment rate of interest. It has to be confronted (as in our earlier constructions) with an *LL* curve showing the relation between Income and the "money" rate of interest; only we can now generalise our *LL* curve a little. Instead of assuming, as before, that the supply of money is given, we can assume that there is a given monetary system—that up to a point, but only up to a point, monetary authorities will prefer to create new money rather than allow interest rates to rise. Such a generalised *LL* curve will then slope upwards only gradually—the elasticity of the curve depending on the elasticity of the monetary system (in the ordinary monetary sense).

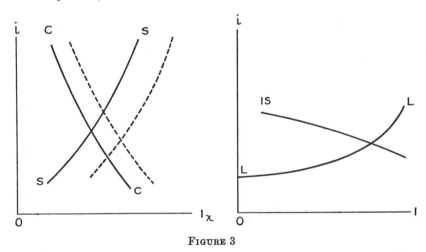

FIGURE 3

As before, Income and interest are determined where the *IS* and *LL* curves intersect—where the investment rate of interest equals the money rate. Any change in the inducement to invest or the propensity to consume will shift the *IS* curve; any change in liquidity preference or monetary policy will shift the *LL* curve. If, as the result of such a change, the investment rate is raised above the money rate, Income will tend to rise; in the opposite case, Income will tend to fall; the extent to which Income rises or falls depends on the elasticities of the curves.[8]

---

[8] Since $C(I, i) = S(I, i)$, $\quad \dfrac{dI}{di} = -\dfrac{\partial S/\partial i - \partial C/\partial i}{\partial S/\partial I - \partial C/\partial I}.$

The savings investment market will not be stable unless $\partial S/\partial i + (-\partial C/\partial i)$ is positive. I think we may assume that this condition is fulfilled.

If $\partial S/\partial i$ is positive, $\partial C/\partial i$ negative, $\partial S/\partial I$ and $\partial C/\partial I$ positive (the most probable state of affairs), we can say that the *IS* curve will be more elastic, the

　　　　　J. R. HICKS

When generalised in this way, Mr. Keynes' theory begins to look very like Wicksell's; this is of course hardly surprising.[9] There is indeed one special case where it fits Wicksell's construction absolutely. If there is "full employment" in the sense that any rise in Income immediately calls forth a rise in money wage rates; then it is *possible* that the CC and SS curves may be moved to the right to exactly the same extent, so that IS is horizontal. (I say possible, because it is not unlikely, in fact, that the rise in the wage level may create a presumption that wages will rise again later on; if so, CC will probably be shifted more than SS, so that IS will be upward sloping.) However that may be, if IS is horizontal, we do have a perfectly Wicksellian construction;[10] the investment rate becomes Wicksell's *natural rate*, for in this case it may be thought of as determined by real causes; if there is a perfectly elastic monetary system, and the money rate is fixed below the natural rate, there is cumulative inflation; cumulative deflation if it is fixed above.

This, however, is now seen to be only one special case; we can use our construction to harbour much wider possibilities. If there is a great deal of unemployment, it is very likely that $\partial C/\partial I$ will be quite small; in that case IS can be relied upon to slope downwards. This is the sort of Slump Economics with which Mr. Keynes is largely concerned. But one cannot escape the impression that there may be other conditions when expectations are tinder, when a slight inflationary tendency lights them up very easily. Then $\partial C/\partial I$ may be large and an increase in Income tend to *raise* the investment rate of interest. In these circumstances, the situation is unstable at *any* given money rate; it is only an imperfectly elastic monetary system—a rising LL curve— that can prevent the situation getting out of hand altogether.

These, then, are a few of the things we can get out of our skeleton apparatus. But even if it may claim to be a slight extension of Mr. Keynes' similar skeleton, it remains a terribly rough and ready sort of affair. In particular, the concept of "Income" is worked monstrously hard; most of our curves are not really determinate unless something is said about the distribution of Income as well as its magnitude. Indeed, what they express is something like a relation between the price-system and the system of interest rates; and you cannot get that into a curve. Further, all sorts of questions about depreciation have been neglected; and all sorts of questions about the timing of the processes under consideration.

---

greater the elasticities of the CC and SS curves, and the larger is $\partial C/\partial I$ relatively to $\partial S/\partial I$. When $\partial C/\partial I > \partial S/\partial I$, the IS curve is upward sloping.

[9] Cf. Keynes, *General Theory*, p. 242.

[10] Cf. Myrdal, "Gleichgewichtsbegriff," in *Beiträge zur Geldtheorie*, ed. Hayek.

The *General Theory of Employment* is a useful book; but it is neither the beginning nor the end of Dynamic Economics.

J. R. HICKS

Gonville and Caius College
Cambridge

Econometrica, Vol. 6, No. 4 (October, 1938)

MONEY AND THE THEORY OF ASSETS

By J. Marschak

1. THE SCOPE

There has been until recently little connection between what is usually taught as Monetary Theory and the General Theory of Prices (or Value). Furthermore, there is little connection between the two compartments of Monetary Theory: the Theory of the "Equation of Exchange" with its underlying concepts, Price Level, Velocity of Circulation, Real Income, etc., on the one hand and, on the other, the Theory of Credit and Banking. The Babylonian lack of common language between the two compartments of Monetary Theory is well illustrated by the fact that, while "Exchange Value of Money" (Wicksell, Robertson) is defined as the reciprocal of the Price Level, the term Price of Money is often used to designate interest rates on short loans—although usually economists agree to use Exchange Value of a thing and Price, of a thing as equivalent terms. In neither of the two compartments of Monetary Theory is much use made of the fundamentals of economic theory. The Price Level is treated as if it had nothing to do with prices. The velocity of circulation has been, thanks to the Cambridge School, associated with cash holdings instead of being left in the air; but the next step, to treat cash holdings on the same lines on which holdings of any other Stocks are treated in the General Theory of Prices, has been made by few economists only, of whom Dr. Hicks is the most outstanding.[1] Similarly, the Interest Rate of the treatises on Banking and Trade Cycle seems to be ashamed of any connection with its less adventurous and "dynamic" but more scholarly relation, the Interest Rate of the marginal productivity theory: the parentage is casually mentioned, if at all, in a few hurried phrases only.

F. Divisia has suggested[2] to add the Equation of Exchange to the Paretian system of equations. This makes it possible to determine the absolute and not only the relative price of goods if the velocity of circulation is given. But we may refuse to regard the velocity of circulation as given because we want to find the factors determining it, or determining Walras' *encaisse désirée,* just as we look for the factors determining the desired quantity of houses, stocks of materials in the factory or in a housewife's larder, securities, bills, or any other balance-sheet items. We do not want the Velocity of Circulation to save the situation like a *deus ex machina.* Yet there is the difficulty that money

---

[1] *Economica,* 1935. See also the interesting article by P. Rosenstein-Rodan, *Economica,* 1936.

[2] *Économie Rationelle.*

is neither a production good nor a consumers' good, and the technique used to explain the causation of quantities and prices of such goods may not apply to money unless we find some way of generalizing the concepts used.

Recently, the rigid (i.e., given) velocity of circulation has been discarded, and the cash holdings expressed as a function of the interest rate, a kind of demand function. Mr. Keynes' "liquidity preference" is a great step forward, provided it is not taken to be simply another word for the old and mysterious "love of money"; provided that it yields itself to a further rational analysis.

The desire to treat monetary problems and indeed, more generally, problems of investment with the tools of a properly generalized Economic Theory is not merely one of aesthetics or disciplinarianism—although the example of the gradual unification of the various forms of Energy in Nineteenth Century Physics might in itself encourage the search for unity. The unsatisfactory state of Monetary Theory as compared with general Economics is due to the fact that the principle of determinateness so well established by Walras and Pareto for the world of perishable consumption goods and labour services has never been applied with much consistency to durable goods and, still less, to claims (securities, loans, cash). To do this requires, first, an extension of the concept of human *tastes:* by taking into account not only men's aversion for waiting but also their desire for safety, and other traits of behaviour not present in the world of perfect certainty as postulated in the classical static economics. Second, the *production conditions,* assumed hereto to be objectively given, become, more realistically, mere subjective expectations of the investors—and *all* individuals are investors (in any but a timeless economy) just as all market transactions are investments. The problem is: to explain the objective quantities of goods and claims held at any point of time, and the objective market prices at which they are exchanged, given the subjective tastes and expectations of the individuals at this point of time.

2. PROCEDURE[3]

Our procedure is as follows: we recapitulate the theory of economic determinateness[4] properly generalised so as to include the case of joint demand and supply (which will be found to be important later). We

[3] Cp. Makower and Marschak, *Economica,* 1938.

[4] We prefer this term to "economic equilibrium" as the stability of a given system of quantities *in time* is not implied. For brevity only, we shall occasionally use expressions like "the *equilibrium amount a* of an asset" to mean "the amount which satisfies the set of determining equations"; taking the point of view of the individual concerned we may also use, instead, the expression "the *best accessible amount* of an asset."

treat perfect competition as a special, imperfect competition as a general case. We then gradually extend the meaning of the symbols so as to take account of uncertainty and ignorance. At no stage do we assume a "timeless" economy—an assumption which has always made the economics of production extremely vague.

For each of the r individuals in the market there are two sets of unknowns: (1) his best accessible balance sheet, or best accessible collection of m present *assets* a, b, $\cdots$; and (2) his best accessible consumption plan, or best combination of n future consumption items x, y, $\cdots$ which we shall call for brevity "*yields*," because unfortunately "consumptions" would be ungrammatical. A further set of unknowns are (3) the m market *prices* of assets: p (of a), q (of b), etc.

The yields, or amounts consumed, $x, y, \cdots$, differ either in quality or with respect to the time interval in which the consumption takes place. Thus, x may be first year's milk consumption, y second year's milk consumption, z first year's meat consumption, etc. Yields cannot be stocked or exchanged. Assets are stocks of either goods or claims. Assets are thus a wider concept than "producers' goods" or indeed than any goods in stock. Yields, on the other hand, are not stocks of consumers' goods, but flows of amounts consumed. Assets are items (positive or negative) in a balance sheet; yields are items in a family budget. By buying and selling assets in the market the individual arranges his present balance sheet in the time point 1 so as to be able to enjoy the best accessible consumption plan, i.e., the most satisfactory series of family budgets for the time intervals 1–2, 2–3, etc. The yields $x, y, \cdots$ refer thus to the future. The assets $a, b, \cdots$ as well as their prices $p, q, \cdots$ refer to the present. It is not necessary to introduce here the concept of "future assets." Exchanges in the market of "futures" can be regarded as exchanges of present claims.

It is seen that the assets are "jointly demanded"; the significance of an asset to the investor depends on what other items he has on his balance sheet. And a given balance sheet enables him to receive not one yield but a whole set of mutually dependent yields; yields are "jointly supplied."

3. THE CRUSOE CASE

Certain rudimentary features of the system can be studied already in the case of an isolated producer-consumer. There are here n unknowns only: the yields $x, y, \cdots$. The assets $a, b, \cdots$ are fixed since there is no exchange, but the individual can choose between various consumption plans. His *tastes* are given by the utility function

$$U(x, y, \cdots)$$

(or any monotonically increasing function of U), which has to be maximized, subject to the restricting *transformation condition*

(3.1) $$T(x, y, \cdots ; a, b, \cdots) = 0,$$

which describes what consumption plans the individual expects to be accessible with the given asset collection. Equating to zero the complete differential of U, and comparing it to the complete differential of T, we obtain $n-1$ equations of the type

(3.2) $\qquad U_x/U_y = T_x/T_y$, (yield-substitution equation),

which together with (3.1) give a determinate system.[5] The left-hand side of (3.2) may be called rate of preference between x and y (e.g., rate of time preference if x and y are amounts of milk to be consumed in two periods); it depends on tastes. The right-hand side may be called transformation rate between x and y, i.e., the rate at which x and y can be substituted for one another if assets and all other yields are kept constant: it depends on transformation (in Crusoe case, production) conditions. The two rates are equal "in equilibrium."

It will be noticed that the transformation condition, $T(x, y, \cdots ; a, b, \cdots) = 0$, describes the case of joint supply *and* joint demand. Each combination of m assets ($=$each balance sheet) can produce an n-dimensional set of yield combinations ($=$consumption plans). To select from this set the best consumption plan is, for the individual, "a matter of taste" as shown by the condition $U=\max$. If there is only one consumption good (and only one time period), the function T degenerates into the "production function" treated in the theory of distribution, wages, etc.: the case of joint supply only. If $a, b, \cdots$ (as in the Crusoe case) are fixed, T is identical with Irving Fisher's "opportunity function."[5a]

4. A MAN IN THE MARKET

Next, let us consider the case of a producer exchanging assets at give prices $p, q, \cdots$. The unknowns are: m asset quantities $a, b, \cdots$ and n yields $x, y, \cdots$.

The transformation condition $T(x, y, \cdots ; a, b, \cdots) = 0$ describes again all the consumption plans which are accessible to a present possessor of the amounts $a, b, \cdots$ of the assets, according to his judgement. The individual can realize these plans not only by future production (as in the Crusoe case) but also by future buying and selling of

---

[5] We shall not give the well-known discussion of second derivatives and the conditions under which a maximum, and not a minimum, is obtained.

[5a] R. G. D. Allen calls this rudimentary T a "transformation function" (*Mathematical Analysis for Economists*, pp. 121–124). He also treats the usual "production function" but he does not give a general function involving several production and several consumers' goods. Pareto (*Manuel*, App. 78) introduces a set of equations (in our notation): $a = F(x, y \cdots)$, $b = G(x, y \cdots)$; but these may become incompatible if there *are* more production goods than consumption goods.

assets. The transformation condition thus depends, not only on the expected technical conditions (including future inventions, weather, etc.) but also on the expected future market prices. We are thus concerned not only with "productive" but also with "speculative" stocks of goods and claims, i.e., those to be sold later.

Writing $a_0, b_0, \cdots$ for the initial quantities of assets (now to be distinguished from the unknown best amounts $a, b, \cdots$), we have

(4.1) $T(x, y, \cdots; a, b, \cdots) = 0$, (transformation equation),

(4.2) $p(a - a_0) + q(b - b_0) + \cdots = 0$, (balance equation),

and the requirement that $U(x, y, \cdots)$ should be a maximum. Differentiating,

$$U_x dx + U_y dy + \cdots = 0$$
$$T_x dx + T_y dy + \cdots + T_a da + T_a db = 0$$
$$p da + q db + \cdots = 0.$$

Keeping the assets constant and letting only two yields vary at a time we get, as before, $n-1$ equations of the type

(4.3) $U_x/U_y = T_x/T_y$, (yield-substitution equations).

Keeping, on the other hand, yields constant and varying two assets at a time, we get $m-1$ equations of the type

(4.4) $p/q = T_a/T_b$, (asset-substitution equations).

We have thus $m+n$ equations for the same number of unknowns. The equation (4.4) shows that "in equilibrium" the price ratio between two assets is equal to their rate of transformation. It is more usual to state that "prices of production goods are proportionate to their marginal productivities" but the latter have seldom been defined so as to cover the case of joint demand and joint supply. Consider the derivative dT/da which is obtained from (4.1) if all yields but only one asset are regarded as variable:

$$\frac{dT}{da} = T_a + T_x \frac{dx}{da} + T_y \frac{dy}{da} + \cdots = 0;$$

similarly

$$\frac{dT}{db} = T_b + T_x \frac{dx}{db} + T_y \frac{dy}{db} + \cdots = 0.$$

Therefore, and in consequence of (4.3),

$$\frac{T_a}{T_b} = \frac{U_x \dfrac{dx}{da} + U_y \dfrac{dy}{da} + \cdots}{U_x \dfrac{dx}{db} + U_y \dfrac{dy}{db} + \cdots},$$

so that we can write, instead of (4.4), the following "marginal productivity theorem":

$$(4.4') \quad \frac{p}{q} = \frac{U_x \dfrac{dx}{da} + U_y \dfrac{dy}{da} + \cdots}{U_x \dfrac{dx}{db} + U_y \dfrac{dy}{db} + \cdots}, \quad \text{(marginal productivity equations)}.$$

The numerator in the right-hand part of the last equation may be called for brevity the "marginal productivity" of the asset a; although a more precise name would be "the utility of the best accessible combination of marginal yields of the asset a"; or "the asset's largest possible contribution to the total utility of the consumption plan."[6]

Let x and y be the amounts of some definite item in the family budgets of two successive years; and suppose that the asset a contributes to nothing but the consumption of this item in the first year, while the asset b contributes the same amount to the consumption of the second year only. (These are, in fact, the assumptions tacitly made in the usual explanation of the interest rate as the "price of waiting.") We have then $dx/da = dy/db$; $dx/db = dy/da = 0$; while terms involving dz, etc., vanish. It follows from (4.4') that $p/q = U_x/U_y$, i.e., the price ratio is equal to the time-preference rate. The expression $(U_x/U_y - 1)$ is occasionally called the subjective rate of interest (for the two years concerned), and it must be equal, in equilibrium, to the market rate of interest $(p/q - 1)$. The assumptions made do not, however, apply in reality, except in the case of the lending of a consumption good, to be repaid *in one single lump*. In general there is no simple relationship between the market price of assets and the preference rates between yields (of which the preference, for a given kind of yield, between two given years is a special case). There is, therefore, strictly, no single "market rate of interest."

The usual assumptions are unrealistic also for the further reason that loans are seldom made in the form of consumption goods. The thing borrowed and lent is *cash*. Let, then, our asset a be "present cash," and our asset b be "a claim on next year's cash." The ratio p/q between the present prices of these two assets depends not only (as in the preceding paragraph) on the preference rates such as U_y/U_x but also on the comparative size of the marginal yields dx/da, dy/db; in the preceding paragraph these were assumed equal; but in the present meaning of a and b they depend on the money prices of consumption goods in the two years. This influence of the expected price tendency

---

[6] It is easily seen that Marshall's "Mathematical Appendix XIV" treats quite a different question.

of goods upon the present price of loans (or, loosely, upon the "market rate of interest") has been discussed in detail by Irving Fisher[7] and others.

Let a still be present cash; but let b be, not a present claim on future cash, but some present commodity stock. The numerator in (4.4′) is again the smaller, the higher the expected money prices of consumption goods: the well-known "flight from money into things" in times of expected inflation.[8]

The equation (4.4′) shows that the system may become incompatible (and therefore, in the economists' language, no equilibrium possible) if the preference rates U_x/U_y, etc., as well as the ratios $(dx/da)/(dx/db)$, etc., are constant. Preference rates are variable if there is some "law of changing (e.g., diminishing), marginal utilities"; while the ratios $(dx/da)/(dx/db)$, etc. are variable if there is some "law of changing (e.g., diminishing) returns." The latter must be generalized so as to include—in accordance with the definition of the transformation function—not only yields from production but also from speculation. The condition that $(dx/da)/(dx/db)$ should depend on a, b implies in this case that the investor must not assume the future market to be perfect; while the constancy of p/q assumed in this section implies a perfect present market. A speculator with a constant time-preference ("patience") rate would pile up "infinite" commodity stocks if he could buy spot and sell forward in perfect markets and was sure that future commodity prices will exceed present ones. In reality this limiting case is precluded not only by the imperfection of markets, both future and present, but also by uncertainty: limitations which we shall study later.

In the Crusoe case no utility was, of course, provided by holding cash. Under the assumptions of the present section cash holding receives some explanation in so far as cash may be held, even in conditions of certainty, to benefit from an expected *fall* of commodity prices. It has been shown how this affects the price of cash both in terms of commodities and of loans. This speculative aspect of cash holding is, however, obviously insufficient to explain it in general.

5. PRICE FORMATION IN A PERFECT MARKET

In the preceding section the asset prices p, q, $\cdots$ of the assets a, b, $\cdots$ were regarded as data given to the individual. Their formation can now be explained by the tastes, transformation conditions, and initial assets of all (say r) individuals in the market. The unknowns are:

---

[7] In the concluding part of his *Theory of Interest*.

[8] The "self-acceleration" of inflation follows from the above only if an additional, dynamic assumption holds true: that the expected price change has the same sign as the preceding one.

mr assets, nr yields, m prices; total, $mr+nr+m$. There are $(m+n)r$ equations of the types discussed in Section 4: r transformation equations (4.1), r balance equations (4.2), $r(n-1)$ yield-substitution equations (4.3), and either $r(m-1)$ asset-substitution equations (4.4) or $r(m-1)$ marginal-productivity equations (4.4′). In addition, there are m equations of the type

$$(5.1) \qquad \sum(a - a_0) = 0, \text{ etc., (clearing-of-the-market equations)},$$

the summation being performed over the r individuals. One of the equations of the type (5.1) is redundant because multiplying each by the corresponding price and adding we get the sum of all balance equations of the type (4.2). On the other hand, assuming a to be the numéraire, the equation

$$(5.2) \qquad\qquad p = 1$$

makes the necessary total, $mr+nr+m$ equations.

The contents of this section are well known but had to be briefly restated, as a link with the further discussion.

6. IMPERFECT PRESENT MARKET

The preceding sections did not exclude the imperfection (in the investor's eyes) of the *future* market: it was, indeed, indicated that it is more realistic to assume it, which simply meant that the transformation function $T(x, y, \cdots ; a, b, \cdots)$ was nonlinear everywhere: imperfection of the future market (prices decreasing as sales increase) was treated as a case of "decreasing returns." If we had introduced the concept of "future assets" we could have distinguished formally between future exchange and future production; but this advantage would only have been gained at the expense of a much more complicated notation which I prefer to avoid at present. It suffices to remember always that the transformation function has been generalised so as to include under yields $x, y, \cdots$ all possible future consumption, whether made possible by future physical transformation or by future exchange.

The preceding sections did, however, assume the *present* market to be perfect. The rates of exchange between assets are, in a perfect market, independent of amounts exchanged. The linear "balance equation" (cf. 4.2)

$$(6.1) \quad pa + qb + \cdots - (pa_0 + qb_0 + \cdots) = 0, \text{ (balance equation)},$$

expresses the fact that each individual's receipts equal his expenditure in terms of any one asset chosen as a numéraire. In conditions of perfect competition, (6.1) can, however, also be interpreted as a "market equation": the partial derivatives of its left-hand side taken at any point $(a, b, \cdots)$ with respect to a or b, etc., are proportionate to the respective prices. In conditions of imperfect competition, (6.1) remains valid as a balance equation; $p, q, \cdots$ being interpreted as the market prices actually paid for the total amounts bought—"average revenues." But it ceases to be valid as a "market equation" because the prices become dependent on the amounts $a, b, \cdots$; they become proportionate to functions, say, $p^*(a, b, c, \cdots)$, $q^*(a, b, c, \cdots)$ instead of $p, q, \cdots$. The market plane becomes a more general market surface. The individual has to choose not one out of the family of all "market planes" (6.1) through the initial point, but one of the family of "market surfaces" through the initial point, say

$$(6.2) \quad M(\mu, a, b, c, \cdots) - M(\mu, a_0, b_0, c_0, \cdots) = 0, \text{ (market equation)},$$

where $M = \int(p^*da + q^*db + \cdots)$, (assuming the right-hand side integrable). The r parameters μ (one for each individual) are new unknowns of the system which remains determined because r new equations (6.2) have been added. Thus, if the forms of the M-functions are given, the μ's (and, therefore, the relevant market surfaces for each individual) are determined by the tastes, initial assets, and transformation conditions of all individuals. The form of each M-function is determined by other data than those enumerated and is loosely described as the individual's "bargaining power," his "strategic position," etc. (In a perfect market, M degenerates into a linear form.) Substituting partial derivatives ("marginal revenues") $M_a, M_b, \cdots$ for $p, q, \cdots$ in the equations (4.4) or (4.4') we get now

$$(6.3) \qquad M_a/M_b = T_a/T_b, \text{ (asset-substitution equations)},$$

or

$$(6.3') \quad \frac{M_a}{M_b} = \frac{U_x \dfrac{dx}{da} + U_y \dfrac{dy}{da} + \cdots}{U_x \dfrac{dx}{db} + U_y \dfrac{dy}{db} + \cdots}, \quad \begin{array}{l}\text{(marginal-productivity} \\ \text{equations).}\end{array}$$

The equations (6.1) to (6.3) or (6.3'), together with (4.1), (5.1), and (5.2), constitute a determinate system.

For the problem of asset holdings, and in particular cash holdings, the imperfection of the present market is mainly relevant in connection with "decreasing selling costs": selling costs are expenses to improve the bargaining power (i.e., to straighten a market function); if they decrease, per unit of amount sold, with increasing sales, small sales will be avoided and stocks accumulated: e.g., stocks of cash waiting for investment. Stocks (of cash or, say, wheat) due to the different timing of receipts and outgoings are cases of the same type.

7. UNCERTAINTY*

Since, in the actual uncertain world, the future production situation (technique, weather, etc.) and future prices are not known, the transformation equation $T(a, b, \cdots ; x, y, \cdots) = 0$ is not strictly valid so long as it means that, in the mind of the producer, to each combination of assets there corresponds one and only one n-dimensional set of yield combinations. It is more correct to assume (although this assumption will also be revised later) that to each combination of assets there corresponds, in his mind, an n-dimensional joint-probability distribution of the yields. Thus, instead of assuming an individual who thinks he knows the future events we assume an individual who thinks he knows the probabilities of future events. We may call this situation the situation of a game of chance, and consider it as a better although still incomplete approximation to reality, and to relevant monetary problems, than the usual assumption that people believe themselves to be prophets.

We may, then, use the previous formal set-up if we reinterpret the notation: $x, y, \cdots$ shall mean, not future yields, but parameters (e.g., moments and joint moments) of the joint-probability distribution of future yields. Thus, x may be interpreted as the mathematical expectation of first year's meat consumption, y may be its standard deviation, z may be the correlation coefficient between meat and salt consumption in a given year, t may be the third moment of milk consumption in second year, etc. We know of the economic relevance of certain of these parameters: e.g., in our illustration, x, z, and, in many cases, t are positive utilities, while y is a disutility: people usually like to eat more, rather than less, meat; they dislike (with the exception of passionate gamblers) situations in which the amounts of meat can be anything within a wide range; they like meat consumption to be accompanied by salt consumption; and (witness football pools) they like "long odds," i.e., high positive skewness of yields. It is sufficiently realistic, however, to confine ourselves, for each yield, to two parameters only: the mathematical expectation ("lucrativity") and the coefficient of variation ("risk"); while it would be definitely unrealistic (as pointed out in Keynes' *Treatise on Probability* as well as by Irving Fisher, A. C. Pigou, S. Florence, and J. R. Hicks), to confine ourselves to the mathematical expectation only.

The system of our Sections 3–6 holds good with this new interpretation. The unknowns are: the present quantities and prices of assets,

---

* For the author's later views on the subject matter of Sections 7–9, see "Role of Liquidity under Complete and Incomplete Information," *American Economic Review*, vol. 39, 1949, pp. 182–195; and "Decision-Making: Economic Aspects," in *International Encyclopedia of the Social Sciences*, New York, 1968, especially Sections 5–6.

and the parameters of yield distributions. The data are: initial balance sheets, tastes of men (in terms of lucrativities and risks of various yields), and transformation conditions (expressed in terms of assets, and of the lucrativities and risks of various yields). As before, the rate of preference (or aversion) between x and y (say between risk and lucrativity of meat) equals, in equilibrium, their rate of transformation; and the price of each asset is proportionate to its marginal productivity, the latter being redefined as the utility of the best set of its marginal contributions to various parameters (e.g., to risk or lucrativity of meat, salt, etc.).

This application of the methods of the general price theory to the conditions of uncertainty is obviously relevant to monetary theory because of the relatively low risk which is usually attached to money. Cash always produces constant (namely zero) dividends; and, if it is disposed of, the consumption made thus possible depends on commodity prices only. Bonds also produce constant dividends; but the consumption made possible by selling a bond depends not only on commodity prices (in terms of cash) but also on loan prices (in terms of cash). Finally, with shares both prices and dividends vary. The marginal contribution of cash to the variability of future yields (i.e., consumption amounts) is therefore smaller than that of shares (and also plants, etc.) or even bonds (or houses, landed property, etc.).[9] A change in tastes in the sense of increasing risk aversion leads to decreasing prices of relatively risky assets, or to hoarding, or to both. The same result can be due to changes of transformation conditions in the sense of an increasing expected variability of yields (for given amounts of assets), i.e., to increased "insecurity feeling."

8. PLASTICITY, SALEABILITY, LIQUIDITY

Suppose the individual has fixed his present assets, as determined by the conditions described in the previous section. It can be shown that the range of variations of the *best* yields compatible with the assets thus fixed is the larger (1) the larger the dispersion of the probability distribution of *possible* yields, (2) the greater the difficulty of substitution between the various yields, as measured by the curvature of the transformation function, (3) the larger the curvature of the indifference lines. We shall confine ourselves to a simple case of two kinds of yields only, say x and y.

[9] This is sometimes expressed by using the concept of a market rate of interest: the price of a share or bond is said to vary "owing" to fluctuations in the interest rate; (the price of a share varying also on account of fluctuations in dividends). Since the "market rate of interest" is only another word for relative asset prices (see Section 4), this is a tautology rather than an explanation.

Let the assets a, b, $\cdots$ assume their best present values. For yields, use the notation of the sections previous to 7. Express the random character of the transformation relationship between the yields x and y (a, b, $\cdots$ being fixed) not by using means and coefficients of variation, but by using a *random term* h, thus

$$(8.1) \qquad\qquad y = f(x + h).$$

As h assumes various values with given probabilities, the best values of x and y, as required by the taste condition $U(x, y) = \max$, also change. They must satisfy the condition—cp. (3.2)—

$$(8.2) \qquad\qquad \frac{d}{dx} f(x + h) = - \frac{U_x}{U_y} \cdot$$

Writing for brevity $- U_x/U_y = v(x, y)$, we have from (8.1) and (8.2)

$$v[x, f(x + h)] = f'(x + h).$$

Differentiating completely and separating the terms in dx and dh

$$(8.3) \qquad dx = dh \left[-1 + \frac{\dfrac{\partial v}{\partial x}}{\dfrac{\partial v}{\partial x} + \dfrac{\partial v}{\partial f} f'(x + h) - f''(x + h)} \right].$$

The fraction on the right-hand side has a positive numerator because $|v|$, the numerical value of the exchange ratio of x in terms of y, usually decreases as x increases. Since, on the other hand, $|v|$ increases with increasing y, and because of the law of diminishing returns, the denominator appears to be a sum of positive terms

$$\left(\frac{\partial v}{\partial x} + \frac{\partial v}{\partial f} \cdot v \right) \qquad \text{and} \qquad [- f''(x + h)],$$

and is larger than the numerator. Hence dx/dh lies between -1 and 0, approaching -1 as the numerical value of $f''(x+h)$, i.e., the curvature of the transformation line, increases, or the sum of the two other terms of the denominator, i.e., the curvature of the indifference line, increases, or both.

If, therefore, the addition of a unit of some asset in forming a present balance sheet makes the curvature $f''(x)$ larger than the addition of a unit of some other asset, the risk contributed by the former is larger, and its marginal productivity (in the sense of Section 7), accordingly, smaller.

With a given dispersion of the transformation function (i.e., given degree of "insecurity feeling")—measured, e.g., by the mean square root of the values of the random shifts (such as h), the price of the asset a is affected by the magnitude $(d/da)[f''(x)]$. Its reciprocal may be called "plasticity" of an asset: the easiness of manœuvring into and out of various yields after the asset has been acquired. When plasticity is due to the fact that the future market of this asset is perfect, we may call it "saleability": the more imperfect the future market of an asset the more difficult it is to sell it in order to adapt the yields consequent upon its acquisition to the transformation conditions as they take actual shape in the course of time.

The future market of cash is probably less imperfect than that of most assets. Cash is "universally acceptable" or has at least a very wide market. Cash is therefore held partly for the special purpose of future manœuvring. Holdings of cash and its price in terms of other assets must therefore be larger th larger the dispersion of the estimates of future transformation conditions.

Money's saleability, or plasticity, is probably meant when people use the word "liquid"—as opposed to "frozen." Yet the other property of cash already mentioned in Section 7—the low variability of its price, due to the low variability of its contribution to yields—is also important, and it may be useful to indicate the two properties by the single word "liquidity," admitting, however, that it denotes a bundle of two measurable properties and is therefore itself not measurable.

Future adjustment of yields can be performed by physical transformation of assets, as well as by selling and buying assets: saleability is not the only form of plasticity. Stocks of raw materials are more plastic than those of finished goods because they are more easily put into various physical shapes according to needs.[10]

9. DEGREE OF KNOWLEDGE

In the preceding two sections, the individual was assumed to know the relevant probabilities: the parameters of the transformation function as defined were assumed to be known. But this knowledge of probabilities—a situation approached in the games of chance—is a limiting case only. In reality the man does not regard himself as enabled by his experience to assign definite probabilities to each yield combination. Let the form of the transformation function (8.1) depend on a set of parameters S. For each set of values, say, S_1 assigned to these parameters there can be stated a probability $P(E|S_1)$ that the actual observed facts E (e.g., the crops and outputs, prices, etc., of

---

[10] To distinguish formally between the two kinds of plasticity would imply the treatment of "future assets" as variables of the system. We have found it unnecessary to use that more complicated approach.

the past, or any other information available) would have happened if S_1 was true. We obtain thus a likelihood function $L(S)$ of the variable set S, viz.,

$$L(S) = P(E \mid S).$$

If knowledge is small, the function does not show any conspicuous peaks: a set of parameters, S_1, may be nearly as much in agreement with the facts E as some other set, say, S_2 in its neighbourhood, i.e. $P(E \mid S_1)$ may be nearly equal to $P(E \mid S_2)$. Greater knowledge means a concentration of the most likely rival hypotheses within a narrow region. Characteristic parameters can be used to measure this: e.g., the steepness of $L(S)$ near its maximum, or some measure analogous to measures of dispersion, or Dr. Neyman's "confidence limits," etc.

This may be the *rationale* of Professor Knight's important distinction between "risk" and "uncertainty": the former is a known parameter of a probability distribution, the latter, the lack of knowledge of this (or any other) parameter.[11]

The importance of this from the point of view of economic theory lies in the distinction between gambler and entrepreneur. Some assets may produce higher known risks than others, and gamblers may develop a higher preference for them than other people. On the other hand, some assets may contribute to the yields—their mean values as well as their variabilities—in a less-known way than others; and "entrepreneurs" have a higher preference for them than other people. Cash is usually regarded as an asset, the future productivity of which is definitely zero, and the future price of which (in terms of consumption goods) is assumed to remain known. Cash holdings grow whenever the prevailing preferences are nonentrepreneurial.

10. STATIC REWARDS AND DYNAMIC LOSSES

The above discussion has not included any statement as to whether the transformation functions expected by each individual have proved right or wrong in the next point of time after his "present" best collection of assets has been formed. Usually the forecasts will have proved more or less wrong; the total utility of each individual will have proved smaller than it would have been if he had known the future: these will be *dynamic losses*—(or malinvestment losses)—the larger, the less the man's skill (or luck) in forecasting. In what way dynamic losses influence the man's further revision of his expectations and thus

---

[11] We prefer to use "lack of knowledge" for Prof. Knight's "uncertainty" and to reserve the latter term for its ordinary use, viz., for expressing the fact that not all probabilities—even if known—equal 1 (and therefore not all dispersions equal 0).

affect the equilibrium of the day after tomorrow (as perhaps suggested by Mr. Keynes' phrase of "profits and losses being the mainspring of action"), is a problem in Economic Dynamics where the causation of changes of data (tastes, expectations, present market conditions) is to be studied.

Dynamic losses resulting from the change in data have clearly little to do with "static rewards" accruing to any individual whose tastes or expectations are different from those of the mass of other men. If meat abstinence is scarce, vegetarians profit by low prices of vegetables; a man who has a small time preference, or a small risk aversion, or optimistic ideas about future transformation, or an entrepreneurial taste for "dark horses" in times when these attitudes are scarce gets higher total utility than in times when they are common: the assets for which he is relatively more keen than others are cheaper, in terms of other assets, than in times when everyone develops those characteristics.

It follows from the preceding discussion that hoarding of cash is "rewarded" in those times. On the other hand, risk aversion, pessimistic transformation functions, and lack of either knowledge or entrepreneurial spirit, although analytically distinguishable, usually go, in fact, together, and all make for "cheap money."

All Souls College
  Oxford, England

Econometrica, Vol. 10, No. 1 (January, 1942)

PROCESS ANALYSIS AND EQUILIBRIUM ANALYSIS*

By A. Smithies

I

The primary purpose of this paper is to attempt to bridge the gulf between the equilibrium and the process approach to economic problems. Such a gulf does exist: the equilibrium theorists, in their enthusiasm for existence theorems, have too frequently ignored the equally important problem of whether a possible equilibrium will in fact be approached by an economy starting from an arbitrary disequilibrium position. The process theorists on the other hand have been too prone to overlook the possibility that the process which they analyze may eventually result in equilibrium. This is true of the exposition of Robertson and Lundberg.[1] Indeed, the arithmetical method of these writers exhausts the physical endurance of the investigator long before equilibrium is in sight. Many of the mathematical theorists also have been interested in proving that cycles exist to the exclusion of the possibility of equilibrium being attained. In fact, Kalecki[2] has gone so far as to *assume* that the cycles be obtained are undamped. The assumption has met with considerable criticism, e.g., by Frisch and Holme[3] whose paper stresses the importance of the damping factor. Frisch, in his own paper on propagation problems in dynamic economics[4] arrives at the conclusion that the cycles in his hypothetical model will eventually converge to equilibrium unless new shocks occur to propagate further cyclical movements. It is with this point of view that I am in sympathy and this paper will be largely concerned with determining under what conditions the process resulting from theoretical model will converge to an equilibrium position.

The secondary purpose of the paper is to throw some light on the modern controversy on interest theory. The equilibrium resulting from the process I shall set up will differ from Keynes'[5] equilibrium theory

* Paper presented at the New Orleans meeting of the Econometric Society, December 30, 1940.

[1] D. H. Robertson, "Saving and Hoarding," *Economic Journal*, September, 1933, p. 399; Erik Lundberg, *Studies in the Theory of Economic Expansion*, London, 1937.

[2] M. Kalecki, "A Macrodynamic Theory of Business Cycles," Econometrica, Vol. 3, 1935, p. 327.

[3] Ragnar Frisch and Harald Holme, "Solution of a Mixed Difference and Differential Equation," Econometrica, Vol. 3, 1935. p. 225.

[4] "Propagation Problems and Impulse Problems in Dynamic Economics," *Economic Essays in Honor of Gustav Cassel*, 1933, p. 171.

[5] J. M. Keynes, *General Theory of Employment, Interest and Money*, New York, 1936.

only to the extent of my disagreement with that theory (which is confined to one point), while the consideration of the process analysis itself will, I hope, throw some light on the suggestive but unrigorously defined *ex ante* concepts.[6]

The essential feature of process analysis, whether arithmetical or mathematical is that the behavior of the economic system can be determined by considering that solution of a difference equation[7] in a single variable, which fits arbitrary values of the variable over two initial intervals. The arithmetical method consists in solving this equation empirically while the mathematical method consists in finding its analytic solutions. Since this latter method offers greater theoretical possibilities for present purposes, it is the method I shall adopt.

II

The economic system proposed for examination will be subject to the following simplifying assumptions:

(1) The gross rate of investment I at time t will depend on plans made and finance at $t-1$. This assumption obviously fails to do justice to the fact that a longer planning period is required, say, for the construction of fixed equipment than for the accumulation of inventories. However, I do not think the assumption of a single lag period affects the theoretical validity of the results. I am fortified in this view by the work of James and Belz.[8]

(2) All investment is financed by borrowing at a uniform rate of interest, and all borrowing is for new investment. An entrepreneur reinvesting profits or an individual buying equities is considered to be borrowing from himself.

(3) I follow Keynes in assuming that the potential total quantity of money M is determinate and constant. By this quantity I mean the total cash and deposits in the hands of others than the banks in conditions where the credit system is expanded to its maximum extent. I assume, moreover, that banks and individuals holding idle balances are prepared to make loans on the same terms.

(4) M is assumed to consist of deposits—active deposits M_1, and idle deposits M_2. Deposits are active when they are held either for use in

---

[6] Bertil Ohlin, "The Stockholm Theory of Savings and Investment," *Economic Journal*, 1937, pp. 53 and 221.

[7] Of course if the arithmetic method is eschewed, the investigator has greater freedom and may prefer models yielding differential or mixed difference and differential equations in cases where he believes that his theory demands consideration of rates of change of the principal variables at a point of time rather than the average rate of change over a finite period.

[8] R. W. James and M. H. Belz, "The Influence of Distributed Lags on Kalecki's Theory of the Trade Cycle," ECONOMETRICA, Vol. 6, 1938, p. 159.

current transactions or when they have been earmarked for investment —according to assumption 1. All other deposits are idle. It is assumed as an approximation that M_1 is proportional to national income.

(5) All relevant economic quantities will be expressed in constant prices.

(6) We are dealing with a closed economic system.

The essential feature of our model economy is that its production activities at time t are independent of its money-market activities. The latter determine the rate of investment and income at $t+1$, but are themselves dependent on the general economic situation at t and $t-1$, or, perhaps more significantly, on the situation at time t and the extent to which that situation has changed over the preceding unit of time.

We shall make use of the following symbols for the variables of the system:

Y = national income,

S = saving,

I = investment,

D = demand for investment funds on the money market (assumption 2),

F = supply of funds on the money market,

r = rate of interest (assumption 2).

All these variables are functions of time; and the subscripts -1 and -2 will denote lags of one and two units of time respectively.

We can now formulate the fundamental relationships.

(1) The demand for funds for investment is assumed to depend linearly on the present level of national income and on its increase over the last unit period, and inversely on the rate of interest. The relation is as follows:

(1) $$D = cY + d(Y - Y_{-1}) - gr - m,$$

where c, d, g, and m are positive, and m enters negatively to give effect to the fact that investment becomes zero for a positive value of income. Y and r obviously enter positively and negatively respectively. The term involving $Y - Y_{-1}$ is intended to take account of expectations; it is assumed that a recent increase of income will give rise to expectation of a further increase, so that $Y - Y_{-1}$ will enter positively into (1).

(2) Our next relation concerns the supply of funds on the money market. This supply can come either from holdings of idle deposits or from holdings of active deposits. The way in which funds are re-

leased from the latter source is by saving. Thus the total supply of funds at time t will depend on the rate at which people are prepared to release their idle deposits and on the extent to which they are prepared to lend their savings. It should be recalled that the rate of saving at t, which is equal to the rate of investment at that time, is independent of the behavior of the money market at t, having been determined by investment plans made at $t-1$. The willingness of the economy to lend will depend firstly on the volume of idle deposits (which we shall denote by $M - lY$, lY being active deposits according to assumption 4) and the rate of saving and secondly on the inducement that is offered by way of interest to exchange nonliquid assets for liquid assets. The supply of funds is assumed to depend linearly on each of these factors. Thus

$$(2) \qquad F = h(M - lY) + pS + kr - n,$$

where h, p, k, and n are positive, h and p are less than unity, and n is introduced negatively in order to do justice to the fact that lending and saving can both be zero, with the volume of idle deposits $M - lY$ and r both positive—a common phenomenon of the depths of a severe depression.

(3) Next, the demand for funds on the money market is equated to the supply, i.e.,

$$(3) \qquad\qquad\qquad D = F.$$

As we have said, the money-market situation at $t-1$, will determine investment at t. Hence from (1) we can write

$$(4) \qquad I = cY_{-1} + d(Y_{-1} - Y_{-2}) - gr_{-1} - m,$$

where r denotes the equilibrium rate of interest established at $t-1$.

We must now introduce saving into our scheme. I adopt the Keynesian common-sense definition of saving as being the difference between national income and consumers' outlay, and accept, without prejudice the Keynesian "law" that saving can be expressed as a unique function of present income such that the proportion of income saved increases as income increases. Since the limitations of our methods require savings to depend linearly on income we must then have

$$(5) \qquad\qquad\qquad S = aY - b,$$

where a and b are positive.

Next current savings is equal to current investment.

$$(6) \qquad\qquad\qquad I = S.$$

In this formulation it is to be noted that I have ignored a phenomenon which has been noted by Keynes and stressed by Robertson[10] and which is important for an understanding of the relation of saving to investment, but not important, I think, for present purposes. (5) and (6) give, for the multiplier relationship, $\Delta Y = \Delta I/a$. It has been pointed out, however, by Keynes and Robertson that the impact of an increased flow of investment on income will first be partially absorbed by an increase in a but as the economy adapts itself to the new situation, a assumes its normal level.[11]

If we solve (1) and (2) and (3) for r, and lag all the variables by one unit of time, we obtain

$$(7) \quad r_{-1} = \frac{1}{g + k} \left[(c + d + hl - pa)Y_{-1} - dY_{-2} - hM + pb - m + n) \right].$$

Equations (4), (5), (6), and (7) are the relations which determine our process. By combining them we obtain our required second-order difference equation in Y, namely

$$(8) \quad Y = AY_{-1} + B(Y_{-1} - Y_{-2}) + C,$$

where

$$A = [kc + g(pa - hl)] \div a(g + k),$$
$$B = kd \div a(g + k),$$
$$C = [g(b + hM - pb - n) + k(b - m)] \div a(g + k).$$

Having constructed our theoretical apparatus, we shall now use it, firstly, to consider the equilibrium system to which it corresponds, especially in relation to contemporary discussion on the subject of "monetary equilibrium"; and secondly, to determine the conditions under which our process actually converges to that equilibrium position.

---

[10] *General Theory*, p. 123; D. H. Robertson, "Notes on Mr. Keynes' General Theory of Employment," *Quarterly Journal of Economics*, 1937, p. 168.

[11] To illustrate this point, the well-known device of demonstrating the multiplier as the limit of the sum of an infinite series may be used. Let $k = 1 - a$ be the normal value of the marginal propensity to consume, then we have

$$\Delta Y = (1 + k + k^2 + \cdots)\Delta I$$
$$= \Delta I \sum_{r=0}^{\infty} k^r = \frac{1}{1 - k} \Delta i.$$

If we assume each "round" to occur during unit time intervals, 1, 2, $\cdots$, then the value of the marginal propensity to save after the nth will be $1/\sum_{r=0}^{n} k^r$, that is, the marginal propensity to save will have the value unity for $t = 1$, and as $t \to \infty$, it will approach a.

III

If equilibrium is assumed to exist, that implies that Y, I, s, and r will become unchanging functions of t, and we can obtain the equilibrium relationships merely by dropping the subscripts in relations (4) to (7) inclusive. These will then take the following general form.

(9) $$S = f(Y),$$

(10) $$I = \phi(Y, r),$$

(11) $$I = S,$$

(12) $$M = \psi(Y, r).$$

It will be readily seen that these relations correspond formally to the Keynesian system of equilibrium as set forth in the *General Theory*. Although Keynes never reduces his system formally to one of mutual determination, it is obvious that this is what he has in mind. In fact the above relations (9) to (12) are set out in Mr. W. B. Reddaway's review of the *General Theory*[12]—a review of more than ordinary significance since at the time of writing it, Mr. Reddaway was Keynes' envoy extraordinary to Australia.

Although the formal correspondence exists, there is an interesting difference between my equation (7) and Keynes'[13] relation:

(13) $$M = L_1(Y) + L_2(r),$$

where L_1 and L_2 are active and idle deposits respectively, thus implying that the volume of idle deposits is a unique function of the rate of interest. It is on this point that my formulation differs from Keynes'. The difference can be demonstrated best by introducing S explicitly as a variable. In equilibrium we shall have $D = F = I = S$. Hence from (2), we have:

$$S = h(M - lY) + pS + kr - n,$$

(14)
$$M - lY = \frac{1 - p}{h} S + \frac{n - kr}{h}.$$

Now lY is active deposits, hence we have a functional relation between idle deposits, the rate of saving, and the rate of interest. Relation (14) will only reduce to (13) if $p = 1$, and I see no reason for assuming this to be so.[14]

---

[12] *Economic Record*, 1936, p. 28.

[13] Keynes, *op. cit.*, p. 199.

[14] This, however, seems to be what Mr. A. P. Lerner has done in his article "Alternative Formulations of the Theory of Interest," *Economic Journal*, 1938, p. 211.

Relation (14) can best be explained by regarding r as the dependent variable. Thus we have

(15) $$r = \frac{S(1 - p)}{k} - \frac{h(M - lY)}{k} + \frac{n}{k}.$$

The inverse relation of r to the volume of idle deposits $M - lY$ is the Keynesian relation, and requires no explanation. What we have to explain is why r depends directly on S. The reason is as follows. Our assumption that p is less than unity means that there exists a propensity to hoard savings (language which, *pace* Mr. Keynes, we are permitted to use in our process analysis); and in order to evoke a given supply of funds the interest rate must be higher than if there were no such propensity to hoard savings. The form which I have given to relation (2) implies that the greater the volume of savings, the greater the rate of interest required to avoid hoarding. Hence, given the parameters of relation (2), the rate of interest depends directly on the rate of saving. If we do not resort to the process formulation, we can state the position in Keynesian language as follows: In equilibrium the rate of interest must be such that the volume of idle deposits (M_2) is constant. According to the hypotheses of the present paper, the propensity of the economy to increase its holdings of idle deposits depends directly, *ceteris paribus*, on the rate of saving. Hence it follows by Keynes' own arguments, that the greater the rate of saving the greater the rate of interest required to keep the volume of idle deposits constant—a proposition to which relation (15) does justice but to which Keynes' relation (13) does not.

The above proposition is not to be confused with the Keynes-Robertson proposition[15] that an increase of thriftiness, that is, an increase in the *propensity to save* which results in a contraction of income, will *tend* to lower the rate of interest through its effect in increasing the volume of idle deposits. Our proposition implies that an increased propensity to save will be associated with an increased propensity to hoard, and in order to overcome the latter, and avoid a decrease of income, there must be an increased demand for funds at a higher rate of interest.

The difference between relations (15) and (13) is the extent of my disagreement with Mr. Keynes' equilibrium theory. And this is the difference, I think, between a theory of interest based on the demand and supply of loanable funds and Mr. Keynes' version of the holding-of-money approach. Although our model is a very simple structure, I cannot see that its simplicity destroys the validity of the relation we have found between the rate of interest and the rate of saving.

[15] D. H. Robertson, "Mr. Keynes and Finance," *Economic Journal*, 1938, p. 555.

We can also use our model to throw some light on Ohlin's *ex ante* theory of interest.[16] If our model is correct, there is no place in the theory of interest for *ex ante* savings. It is the current flow of savings that is relevant, and expected future savings are only relevant in so far as they influence the current rate of savings. We could take account of this phenomenon, subject to the limitations of our method, by making the rate of saving depend not only on present income, but on the rate of change of income over the last unit period—assuming that this affords an adequate index of expectations as to the future behavior of income. On the other side, our model gives a precise meaning to *ex ante* investment; *ex ante* investment at t is the rate of investment planned for t to take effect at $t+1$. Thus in our formulation *ex ante* investment at t is equal to *ex post* investment at $t+1$. This equality in our scheme indicates, I think, a greater generality in Ohlin's scheme; for, if I understand him correctly, these two rates could differ by the rate at which undesigned changes in inventories occur at $t+1$. This phenomenon has been excluded from our model by assumption 1. This paragraph is to a large extent supererogatory in view of Keynes' own criticisms of Ohlin's theory,[17] so will not be carried further.

Finally, our model can be interpreted on Wicksellian lines, in terms of the natural and market rates of interest.[18] Since in equilibrium S and I are constant, at any time t the rate at which funds allocated for investment at time $t+1$ must be equal to the rate of savings at t. If we define the natural rate of interest as the rate which brings about this equality, we can say that the equilibrium position of our system is characterized by equality between the market rate and the natural rate. Further, for an expansion of income it is necessary that investment at $t+1$ should be greater than savings at t. Since by (1) the demand for investment is a decreasing function of the interest rate, it follows that in this case the market rate must be less than the natural rate.

Our next problem is to determine the equilibrium level of income. This is obtained by dropping the subscripts from (8) and solving for the equilibrium value of Y which we shall denote by Y_E. Thus we have

$$(16) \qquad Y_E = \frac{C}{1 - A},$$

and, substituting for C and A their values,

$$(17) \qquad Y_E = \frac{g(b + hM - pb - n) + k(b - m)}{g(a + hl - pa) + k(a - c)}.$$

[16] *Op. cit.*

[17] J. M. Keynes, "The '*ex ante*' Theory of the Rate of Interest," *Economic Journal*, 1937, p. 663.

[18] Cf. Haberler, *Prosperity and Depression*, League of Nations, 1939, p. 35.

We shall now discuss the dependence of this equilibrium level of income on the values of the parameters of our system.

We are entitled to assume that Y_E is positive, which means that both the numerator and the denominator of (17) are of the same sign. Suppose them to be negative, then it follows, from (17) that the greater m, or n, or both, the greater Y_E. But it follows from (1), (2), and (3) that an increase in m, or n, or both, will decrease the rate of investment, which from (5) and (6) will decrease income. Hence we conclude that both the numerator and the denominator of (17) are positive. Applying this conclusion to (16), we have

(18) $$A < 1, \qquad C > 0.$$

This result will be useful later.

It is also evident from (1), (2), and (3) that the smaller g and the greater k, the greater will be the value of investment, and consequently of income, by (5) and (6). That is, Y_E depends directly on the responsiveness of lenders to a rise and on the responsiveness of investors to a fall in the rate of interest.

By inspection of (17) we can now conclude that Y_E depends:

(a) inversely on a, and directly on b; that is, inversely on the propensity to save;

(b) directly on M, the quantity of money;

(c) directly on c, the parameter relating investment to income;

(d) inversely on $hl-pa$. This quantity is the rate at which the supply of loanable funds decreased as a result of a change in income. Its value depends on the relative rates at which funds become available for lending through saving and become unavailable through the increased requirements of active deposits respectively. This can be seen by differentiating (2) and (5) partially with respect to Y. We have

(19) $$\frac{\partial F}{\partial Y} = -hl + p\frac{dS}{dY} = -(hl - pa).$$

This rate can safely be assumed to be negative, for, by assumption (4), active deposits include funds earmarked for investment, and for an increase in income the rate at which funds are being earmarked must be greater than the rate of savings. Thus, *a fortiori*, funds are absorbed at a greater rate than that at which they are released by saving.

Our conclusion as to the determinants of the equilibrium level of income correspond closely to Keynes' theory, except for (d). Keynes' system recognizes the propensity to save only as a factor limiting the expansion of income. Our analysis also emphasizes the importance of this factor [see (a) above], but states, in addition, that the propensity to save and the propensity not to hoard savings p are positive factors in determining the supply of loanable funds.

IV

We now have to inquire whether the equilibrium level of income Y_E is in part attained if our system is initially in a nonequilibrium position. We shall be interested not only in answering this question in the affirmative or negative, but also in determining whether the path followed, whether towards equilibrium or not, is cyclical or exponential.

Our problem involves finding the complete solution of (8). This can be done by finding the general solution of the homogeneous equation

$$(20) \qquad Y = (A + B)Y_{-1} - BY_{-2}$$

and adding to it the constant solution of (8), namely Y_E.

Let $Y(t) = y^t$; then by substituting in (20), we obtain for y the equation:

$$(21) \qquad y^2 - (A + B)y + B = 0.$$

Solving for y we get:

$$(22) \qquad y = \frac{A + B \pm \sqrt{(A + B)^2 - 4B}}{2}.$$

Let these two roots be denoted by y_1 and y_2 respectively. The complete solution of (8) then will be

$$(23) \qquad Y = \alpha y_1^t + \beta y_2^t + Y_E,$$

where α and β are periodic functions of time of period 1, such that the solution will fit arbitrary values of Y over two initial unit periods.

From (23) it is clear that, if y_1 and y_2 are imaginary, the solution will be expocyclic, fluctuating about the equilibrium value Y_E, while, if y_1 and y_2 are real and positive, the solutions will be noncyclical. Further, if the absolute values of y_1 and y_2 are less than unity, the equilibrium level of income Y_E will be approached as $t \to \infty$. We have now to give economic content to these results.

Whether y_1 and y_2 are real and positive, or imaginary, will depend on whether the discriminant of (22) is positive or zero, or negative. We thus obtain as necessary and sufficient conditions for

(a) y_1 and y_2 real: $A \geqq \sqrt{B}(2 - \sqrt{B})$;

(b) y_1 and y_2 imaginary: $A < \sqrt{B}(2 - \sqrt{B})$.

We repeat here for the sake of convenience, the values of A and B, namely

$$A = [kc + g(pa - hl)] \div a(g + k),$$
$$B = kd \div a(g + k).$$

Consider now the function $f(B) = \sqrt{B}(2-\sqrt{B})$. Differentiating $f(B)$ with respect to B, we have $f'(B) = 1/\sqrt{B} - 1$. Now $B > 0$, and as B increases from zero to unity, for given A, condition (a) becomes less likely to be fulfilled, while as B increases further, this condition is more likely to be fulfilled. And if $B \geq 4$, condition (a) is necessarily fulfilled, since A may be assumed to be positive. We conclude therefore that the existence of a noncyclical solution depends on *either A or B* being sufficiently great relative to the other for its effect always to dominate the solution.

Now the magnitude of A relative to B depends on the influence of the present level of income and on the rate at which there is a net release of money through the process of saving and absorbing cash for transactions purposes. The magnitude of B, on the other hand, depends on the influence exercised by the increase in income in the immediate past on present investment plans, or, better from the economic point of view, B depends on the expectations of future income derived from the experience of immediate past. Considering the formulas for A and B, it appears that there is little empirical likelihood of noncyclical solutions where $B > A$. On the other hand, condition (b) indicates that cyclical solutions can occur with $A > B$.

We turn next to the question of the magnitude of the roots, in order to answer the question whether our solution will converge to its equilibrium value Y_E. For convergence to occur it is necessary and sufficient that both y_1 and y_2 are less than unity in absolute value.

Let us consider first the case where these roots are real. It will be sufficient if we consider the root

$$(24) \qquad y_1 = \tfrac{1}{2}\left[A + B + \sqrt{(A + B)^2 - 4B}\,\right]$$

since this is obviously the greater root.

Differentiating with respect to B, we get:

$$(25) \qquad \frac{dy_1}{dB} = \frac{1}{2}\left(1 + \frac{A + B - 2}{\sqrt{(A + B)^2 - 4B}}\right).$$

The fraction on the right is clearly greater than unity in absolute value. Hence, since $A < 1$, for $0 \leq B \leq 1$, $dy_1/dB < 0$. Also for $B = 0$, its lowest possible value, we have, from (24), $y_1 = A$, i.e., y_1 is less than unity. Thus for all values of B less than unity, the real roots are less than unity, and the system will converge to equilibrium. We have seen above, however, that the roots may be real for $B > 1$. Since for real roots we must have, by condition (a), $A + B > 2\sqrt{B}$, we have from (24) $y_1 > \sqrt{B} > 1$. Thus in this case the system will diverge from equilibrium. However, as we have pointed out above, this case seems empirically unlikely, hence we conclude that, it is probable that if the solution of our problem is noncyclical it will converge to equilibrium.

The magnitude of the imaginary roots will be $\sqrt{B}$ for each root. The factors making for a large value of B depend on the role expectations play in determining the level of income, i.e., the magnitude of d and the willingness of lenders to lend in response to the rate of interest: i.e., on k. The damping factors are the marginal propensity to save a, and the coefficient g, which depends on the influence of the rate of interest as a deterrent to investment. There seems no a priori reason why our solution should be damped.

Our last problem is to determine the period of the cycles. From (22), if y_1 and y_2 are complex conjugates, their argument ϕ will be given by

$$\phi = \tan^{-1} \frac{\sqrt{4B - (A + B)^2}}{A + B},$$

and, since $A + B > 0$, we conclude that $\tan \phi > 0$, so that $\phi < \pi/2$ and $y_1{}^t$ and $y_2{}^t$ are of period greater than 4. The cyclical component of the complete solution may then also be said to be of period greater than 4 units of time.

V

To put forward yet another elementary "macrodynamic" model at the present time requires a final word, if not of apology, at least of justification. On the one hand we have Professor Schumpeter's obvious lack of sympathy, summarized in his statement that "no attempt at technical improvement . . . can do away with the fact that a picture of business behavior is being drawn, not from reality, but from the needs of the theorist."[19] On the other hand, our model looks exceedingly rudimentary when compared with the picture of the economy revealed by Professor Tinbergen's microscope.[20]

I think Tinbergen himself has provided an answer to Schumpeter. Although both writers agree that a model constructed with unchanging parameters can afford no more than a partial explanation of the business cycle, Tinbergen has, at the very least, made a strong *prima facie* case for believing that economic events from 1919–1932 in the United States can be explained by a system with substantially unchanging parameters, which is far more than I think Schumpeter would have conceded. As to Tinbergen himself, I find it extremely difficult to comprehend his picture of the whole economy in all its complexity, and so find it necessary, as an aid to understanding, to reduce his system to a model, of about the

[19] J. A. Schumpeter, *Business Cycles*, New York, 1939, p. 192.

[20] J. Tinbergen, *Business Cycles in the United States of America*, League of Nations, 1939.

same degree of complexity as that presented in this paper. I therefore believe that the simple aggregative models still have their place—even though it be a subordinate one—in economic theory.

As to the usefulness of the particular model we have been studying, it confirms the general conclusion of business-cycle theory that equilibrium is not necessarily the "natural state" of any given economy; and even if it is, the economy, starting from an initial position of disequilibrium, may only reach equilibrium after a considerable period of time. From the point of view of public policy designed to achieve stability, it is therefore unlikely that, even in the absence of outside disturbances, it will be sufficient merely to fix the value of one of the variables, say the interest rate, or one of the parameters, say the marginal propensity to save, at a value that, *ceteris paribus*, is consistent with a high equilibrium level of income.

University of Michigan

Econometrica, Vol. 12, No. 1 (January, 1944). Postscript from
Henry Hazlitt, ed., *The Critics of Keynesian Economics* (Princeton,
New Jersey: D. Van Nostrand Company, Inc., 1960), pp. 183–184.

LIQUIDITY PREFERENCE AND THE THEORY OF INTEREST AND MONEY

By Franco Modigliani

PART I

1. INTRODUCTION

THE AIM OF this paper is to reconsider critically some of the most important old and recent theories of the rate of interest and money and to formulate, eventually, a more general theory that will take into account the vital contributions of each analysis as well as the part played by different basic hypotheses.

The analysis will proceed according to the following plan:

I. We start out by briefly re-examining the Keynesian theory. In so doing our principal aim is to determine what is the part played in the Keynesian system by the "liquidity preference," on the one hand, and by the very special assumptions about the supply of labor, on the other. This will permit us to distinguish those results that are due to a real improvement of analysis from conclusions that depend on the difference of basic assumptions.

II. We then proceed to consider the properties of systems in which one or both Keynesian hypotheses are abandoned. We thus check our previous results and test the logical consistency of the "classical" theory of money and the dichotomy of real and monetary economics.

III. From this analysis will gradually emerge our general theory of the rate of interest and money; and we can proceed to use this theory to test critically some recent "Keynesian" theories and more especially those formulated by J. R. Hicks in *Value and Capital*[1] and by A. P. Lerner in several articles.

IV. Finally, to make clear the conclusions that follow from our theory, we take issue in the controversial question as to whether the rate of interest is determined by "real" or by monetary factors.

In order to simplify the task, our analysis proceeds in general, under "static" assumptions; this does not mean that we neglect time but only that we assume the Hicksian (total) "elasticity of expectation" to be always unity. In Hicks's own words this means that "a change in current prices will change expected prices in the same direction and in the same proportion."[2] As shown by Oscar Lange, this implies that we assume the "expectation functions," connecting expected with present prices, to be homogeneous of the first degree.[3]

[1] J. R. Hicks, *Value and Capital*, Oxford University Press, 1939, 331 pp.
[2] *Ibid.*, p. 205.
[3] Cf. O. Lange, "Say's Law: a Restatement and Criticism" in *Studies in Mathematical Economics and Econometrics*, edited by Lange, McIntyre, and Yntema, The University of Chicago Press, 1942, pp. 67–68.

Since all the theories we examine or formulate in this paper are concerned with the determinants of equilibrium and not with the explanation of business cycles, this simplification, although it is serious in some respects, does not seem unwarranted.

2. THREE ALTERNATIVE MACROSTATIC SYSTEMS

As a first step in the analysis, we must set up a system of equations describing the relation between the variables to be analyzed. In doing this we are at once confronted with a difficult choice between rigor and convenience; the only rigorous procedure is to set up a complete "Walrasian" system and to determine the equilibrium prices and quantities of each good: but this system is cumbersome and not well suited to an essentially literary exposition such as we intend to develop here. The alternative is to work with a reduced system: we must then be satisfied with the rather vague notions of "physical output," "investment," "price level," etc. In what follows we have chosen, in principle, the second alternative, but we shall check our conclusions with a more general system whenever necessary.

The equations of our system are:

$$(1) \qquad M = L(r, Y),$$
$$(2) \qquad I = I(r, Y),$$
$$(3) \qquad S = S(r, Y),$$
$$(4) \qquad S = I,$$
$$(5) \qquad Y \equiv PX,$$
$$(6) \qquad X = X(N),$$
$$(7) \qquad W = X'(N)P.$$

The symbols have the following meaning: Y, money income; M, quantity of money in the system (regarded as given); r, rate of interest; S and I, saving and investment respectively, all measured in money; P, price level; N, aggregate employment; W, money wage rate; X, an index of physical output.[4] We may also define C, consumption measured in money, by the following identity:

$$(8) \qquad C \equiv Y - I.$$

Identity (5) can be regarded as defining money income. There are

---

[4] This system is partly taken from earlier writings on the subject. See especially O. Lange, "The Rate of Interest and the Optimum Propensity to Consume," *Economica*, Vol. 5 (N. S.), February, 1938, pp. 12–32, and J. R. Hicks, "Mr. Keynes and the 'Classics'; A Suggested Interpretation," ECONOMETRICA, Vol. 5, April, 1937, pp. 147–159.

so far 8 unknowns and only 7 equations; we lack the equation relating the wage rate and the supply of labor. This equation takes a substantially different form in the "Keynesian" system as compared with the "classical" systems.

In the classical systems the suppliers of labor (as well as the suppliers of all other commodities) are supposed to behave "rationally." In the same way as the supply of any commodity depends on the relative price of the commodity so the supply of labor is taken to depend not on the money wage rate, but on the real wage rate. Under the classical hypothesis, therefore, the last equation of the system takes the form:

$$(9a) \quad N = F\left(\frac{W}{P}\right); \text{ or, in the inverse form: } W = F^{-1}(N)P.$$

The function F is a continuous function, although not necessarily monotonically increasing.

The Keynesian assumptions concerning the supply-of-labor schedule are quite different. In the Keynesian system, within certain limits to be specified presently, the supply of labor is assumed to be perfectly elastic at the historically ruling wage rate, say w_0. The limits mentioned above are given by equation (9a). For every value of W and P the corresponding value of N from (9a) gives the maximum amount of labor obtainable in the market. As long as the demand is less than this, the wage rate remains fixed as w_0. But as soon as all those who wanted to be employed at the ruling real wage rate w_0/P have found employment, wages become flexible upward. The supply of labor will not increase unless the money wage rate rises relative to the price level.

In order to write the last equation of the "Keynesian" form of our system, we must express this rather complicated hypothesis in functional form. Taking (9a) as a starting point, we may write:

$$(9) \quad\quad\quad\quad W = \alpha w_0 + \beta F^{-1}(N)P,$$

where α and β are functions of N, W, P, characterized by the following properties:

$$(10) \quad \begin{aligned} \alpha &= 1, \quad \beta = 0, \quad \text{for} \quad N \leqq N_0, \\ \alpha &= 0, \quad \beta = 1, \quad \text{for} \quad N > N_0, \end{aligned}$$

where N_0 is said to be "full employment." Equations and inequalities (10) thus state that, unless there is "full employment" ($N = N_0$), the wage rate is not really a variable of the system but a datum, a result of "history" or of "economic policy" or of both. Equation (9) then reduces to $W = w_0$. But after "full employment" has been reached at wage rate w_0, the supply of labor ceases to be perfectly elastic: W becomes a variable to be determined by the system and (9) becomes a "genuine" equation. We should add that, even in the "Keynesian" system, it is admitted that the wage rate will begin to be flexible downward before employment has reached the zero level: but in order not to complicate equation (9) still further we can, without serious harm, leave the hypothesis in its most stringent form.

For generality we may also use equation (9) as it now stands, as the "supply of labor" function of the "classical" theory. But instead of conditions (10) we have the identities (for all values of N)

$$(11) \qquad\qquad \alpha \equiv 0, \qquad \beta \equiv 1.$$

Some remarks are also necessary concerning the "demand for money" equation. According to the "quantity theory of money," the demand for money does not depend on the rate of interest but varies directly with money income. Under this hypothesis equation (1) reduces to

$$(1a) \qquad\qquad M = kY.$$

By properly combining the equations and conditions written above, we obtain three different systems which we will analyze in turn.

I. A "Keynesian" system consisting of equations (1) to (7) and (9) and conditions (10).

II. A "crude classical" system consisting of equations (1a), (2) to (7), and (9), and identities (11).

III. A "generalized classical" system consisting of the equations listed under II but with (1a) replaced by (1).

3. A RECONSIDERATION OF THE KEYNESIAN THEORY

In reconsidering the Keynesian system we shall essentially follow the lines suggested by J. R. Hicks in his fundamental paper, "Mr. Keynes and the 'Classics.'"[5] Our main task will be to clarify and develop his arguments, taking into account later theoretical developments.

Close consideration of the Keynesian system of equations [equations (1) to (7) and (9) to (10)] reveals that the first 4 equations contain only 4 unknowns and form a determinate system: the system of monetary equilibrium. We therefore begin by discussing its equations and its solution.

4. THE TRANSACTION DEMAND FOR MONEY

In a free capitalistic economy, money serves two purposes: (a) it is a medium of exchange, (b) it is a form of holding assets. There are accordingly two sources of demand for money: the transaction demand for money and the demand for money as an asset. This is the fundamental proposition on which the theory of the rate of interest and

[5] ECONOMETRICA, Vol. 5, April, 1937, pp. 147–159.

money rests; it is therefore necessary to analyze closely each source of demand and the factors that determine it.

The transaction demand for money is closely connected with the concept of the income period. We may define the income period as the (typical) time interval elapsing between the dates at which members of the community are paid for services rendered. We shall assume for the moment that this income period is approximately the same for every individual and that it coincides with the expenditure period.[6]

Each individual begins the income period with a certain income arising out of direct services rendered or out of property and with assets (physical and nonphysical) having a certain market value. In his endeavor to reach the highest level of satisfaction he is confronted with two sets of decisions: (a) he must decide what part of his income he will spend on consumption and what part he will save, (b) he must determine how to dispose of his assets.

The first set of decisions presents no special difficulty of analysis. On the basis of his tastes, his income, and market prices he will make a certain plan of expenditure to be carried out in the course of the income period. The amount of money that is necessary for individuals to carry out their expenditure plans is the *transaction demand for money by consumers*, as of the beginning of the period. The average transaction demand, on the other hand, depends on the rate at which expenditure takes place within the period.[7]

The difference between the individual's money income and the amount he decides to spend in the fashion discussed above is the money value of his savings (dissavings) for the income period. It represents the net increment in the value of his assets.

5. THE DEMAND FOR MONEY AS AN ASSET

Having made his consumption-saving plan, the individual has to make decisions concerning the assets he owns. These assets, let us note, consist of property carried over from the preceding income period *plus current savings*.

There are essentially three forms in which people can keep their assets: (a) money, (b) securities,[8] and (c) physical assets.

---

[6] This means, for instance, that people are required by custom or contract to pay within the income period for what they have consumed in the period (rent, grocery bill, etc.) or else must rely on "consumers' credit."

[7] Thus if expenditure should proceed at an approximately even rate, it would be one-half the initial demand.

[8] Under the name of securities we include both fixed-income-bearing certificates and common stocks or equities. From the strictly economic point of view, common stocks should perhaps be considered as a form of holding physical assets. For institutional reasons, however, equities have very special properties which make them in many respects more similar to bonds than to physical assets.

We shall for the moment eliminate the third alternative by distinguishing between entrepreneurial and nonentrepreneurial decisions. We consider as entrepreneurs individuals who hold assets in physical form; decisions concerning the acquisition or disposal of physical assets will accordingly be treated as entrepreneurial decisions and will be analyzed in connection with the schedule of the propensity to invest [equation (3)]. An individual's decision to acquire directly physical assets (say a house) or to reinvest profits in his enterprise can be split into two separate decisions, a decision to lend (to himself) and a decision to increase his entrepreneurial risk by borrowing (from himself).

We are therefore concerned here exclusively with decisions concerning nonphysical assets and with those factors that influence the choice between the first two alternatives. Our problem is to determine whether there is any reason for individuals to wish to hold some or all of their assets in the form of money and thus to demand money over and above the quantity they need for transactions.

In this respect there is little to add to the exhaustive treatment that this subject has received in recent literature.[9]

There are two properties that all assets, whether physical or not, share in different degrees: liquidity and risk. Following a criterion particularly stressed by Jacob Marschak, we shall define liquidity of an asset in terms of the perfection of the market in which it is traded. An asset is liquid if this market is perfect, i.e., an individual's decision to buy or sell does not affect the price finitely; it is illiquid in the opposite case. It is riskless if the price at which it sells is constant or practically so; it is risky if the price fluctuates widely.

Securities clearly share with money the property of being highly liquid assets. Where there is an organized market, securities will not be significantly inferior to money in this respect. They have, however, two clear drawbacks in comparison with cash:

(a) They are not a medium of exchange. Assets generally accrue in the form of money through savings, and a separate transaction is necessary to transform them into securities. This transaction involves both subjective and objective costs.

(b) They are more risky than money since their market price is not constant. Even the "safest" type of securities, on which the risk of default can be neglected, fluctuates in price as the rate of interest moves. There are, it is true, some types of loans for which this last risk can be neglected, namely very-short-term loans. Let us assume, for the sake

---

[9] See, for instance, J. R. Hicks, *Value and Capital*, Chapters XIII and XIV and *passim;* J. M. Keynes, *The General Theory of Employment, Interest and Money*, New York, Harcourt, Brace and Company, 1936, 403 pp.; Mabel Timlin, *Keynesian Economics*, University of Toronto Press, 1942, Chapters V and VI; etc.

of precision, that the money market is open only on the first day of the income period; then the shortest type of loans will be those that mature at the end of said period. These types of assets will not be subject to the risk mentioned under (b) since, by assumption, the rate of interest cannot change while they are outstanding.[10]

It is just for this type of assets, however, that the disadvantage mentioned under (a), namely the cost of investment, weighs more heavily: for the yield they promise for the very short duration of the loan can only be small, so that even a moderate cost is sufficient to wipe it out. If, as is likely, the cost of investment does not rise in proportion to the amount invested, then short loans may be an interesting investment for large sums, but not so for small investors. Thus, if this were the only possible form of investment, we should expect that any fall in the rate of interest, not accompanied by a corresponding fall in the cost of investing, would induce a growing number of potential investors to keep their assets in the form of money, rather than securities; that is to say, we should expect a fall in the rate of interest to increase the demand for money as an asset.

In this respect, securities of longer maturity would appear to be superior, since the yield to be gathered by holding them until maturity is larger, while the cost of acquiring them need not be different. But as the importance of the cost element decreases, the importance of the risk element grows. As is well known, a given change in the rate of interest will affect most the present value of those bonds whose maturity is furthest away. If the only reason for owning assets were to earn the income they produce, these price fluctuations would not be so important. For, as long as the owner is in a position to hold the asset until maturity, there would be only a potential loss, a loss of better opportunities. There can be little doubt, however, that for a large part of the community the main reason for holding assets is as a reserve against contingencies. A form of assets whose value is not certain must be, *ceteris paribus*, inferior to one whose value is certain, namely money.

This very fact, besides, gives an additional reason why bonds of longer maturity should be a less safe form of holding assets. For there is much less certainty about faraway income periods than there is about the near future and the possibility that one will have to realize the assets before their maturity, if any, increases accordingly; while, on the other hand, it becomes increasingly difficult to make reliable forecasts about the level of the rate of interest and the future market value of the assets.

[10] Even if this assumption were relaxed, the possible fluctuations in the rate of interest would be negligible and the extent to which they would affect the present value of the securities mentioned above could be disregarded.

Securities, on the other hand, are clearly superior to money in that they yield an income. The ruling rate of interest measures the remuneration to be obtained by accepting the drawbacks and assuming the risks that are characteristic of securities as compared with money. Or, to look at it from another point of view, it measures the cost of holding money instead of securities in terms of forgone income. Thus a fall in the rate of interest has, in any event, the effect of making cash cheaper and hence more attractive as a form of holding assets.

In addition, several other reasons can be mentioned that cause a low rate of interest to discourage the holding of securities. In the first place, the risk element involved in holding securities becomes more pronounced when the rate of interest is low, for a smaller fall in the capital value of the asset is sufficient to wipe out the income already earned by holding the asset. Thus, for instance, the smaller the rate of interest, the smaller is the *percentage change* in the rate itself necessary to absorb the yield obtained by holding the asset a given length of time. Again, it has been pointed out by some authors that, as the rate of interest becomes lower, there is some ground to expect that possible movements will be predominantly in the direction of an increase and therefore unfavorable to the holders of securities.

In conclusion then, the lower the rate of interest, the larger will be the number of owners of assets who will prefer to hold these assets in the form of money for the income period; the demand for money to hold (as distinguished from money to spend, previously considered) or demand for money as an asset is a decreasing function of the rate of interest. Denoting this demand by D_a, we can write

$$D_a = D_a(r)$$

for the schedule of demand for money to hold.

What can we say about the characteristics of this function? It must clearly be a monotonically decreasing function of the rate of interest; in addition, however, it must have, in the author's opinion, two important properties:

In the first place, there must be some value of r, say r', such that $D_a(r) = 0$ for $r \geq r'$. For there must be, for every individual, some minimum net yield per income period that will induce him to part entirely with money as an asset. Hence, if he can find some type of securities such that by holding them for a given number of income periods he expects to obtain a net yield equal to or larger than the minimum, his demand for money to hold will fall to zero.[11]

---

[11] Let i_0 denote the minimum yield (per income period) at which an individual is ready to hold no assets in the form of money during the period. We may also assume, without being unrealistic, that this minimum yield is the same for each

Since this is true for every individual, there must also be some system of interest rates which is sufficient to reduce the aggregate demand to zero.

The second characteristic is more peculiar. Since securities are an "inferior" way of holding assets, it is generally recognized that there must be some minimum rate of interest, say r'', at which nobody will be willing to hold nonphysical assets except in the form of money. When this level is reached, the demand for money to hold becomes "absolute" and the rate of interest cannot fall any lower. Hence, $D_a'(r) = \infty$ for $r \gtreqless r''$.

6. THE DEMAND FOR MONEY: CONCLUSION

We have so far discussed the demand for money as an asset and the transaction demand for money by individuals; to complete the analysis we must consider the transaction demand by firms. In principle, the same considerations apply here as were stated in connection with individuals' transaction demand. Firms, as well as individuals, have an institutional expenditure-receipt pattern and, given this pattern, the average demand depends on the volume of transactions. We must however recognize that, in the case of firms, generalizations are less meaningful since their expenditure and receipt flows are generally less certain and uniform than for individuals.

Then, too, we must admit that we may have oversimplified the consumers' transaction demand by assuming that individuals have a rigorously defined plan of expenditure at the beginning of the income period. It may very well be that under more realistic conditions they will de-

---

income period. Suppose that the securities which, in his opinion, present the best opportunity are expected by him to produce a net yield (including capital appreciation) $i_0', i_1', \cdots, i_n'$ in periods $1, 2, \cdots, n$. He will be induced to invest provided there is some value of n for which

$$(1 + i_0')(1 + i_1') \cdots (1 + i_n') \geq (1 + i_0)^n.$$

From M. Timlin's treatment of this subject (*Keynesian Economics*, Chapter III) it would appear that marginal holders should expect any security to yield the same net income, at least during the current period. This however is correct only if the expectations of all dealers about the future short rates of interest agree with the market expectation as shown by the forward rates established in the market. [The forward rate for the nth income period ahead can always be found by comparing the price of riskless securities maturing n periods ahead with those maturing $(n+1)$ periods ahead.] But if an individual believes this forward rate to be too high he may acquire the security at once even though he may expect that it will yield in the current period less than some other security. For, assuming that he is right, he will be able to realize his capital gain as soon as the market recognizes its error and there is no telling when this will occur. If he should wait until the next income period and hold for the current one the asset that promises to pay a higher yield, he may lose his chance of making the expected capital gain.

sire to carry some cash above the amount they plan to spend as a reserve and to avoid ending the period with a zero cash balance. This however does not substantially affect our argument. All we are interested in establishing is that, within an institutional framework, there must be for any given volume (value) of transactions a certain amount of money that is necessary to carry them out. This amount clearly depends on such institutional factors as the length of the income period and the prevailing customs as to the settlement of current purchases by firms and must therefore be substantially independent of the level of the rate of interest. The level of the rate of interest influences decisions concerning the disposition of assets, and *money needed to carry out transactions planned for the coming income period is not an asset*. In particular, there must be some level of the rate of interest that is sufficient to reduce to zero the demand for money to hold, and hence the total demand to its minimum institutional level which depends on the volume of transactions. As the rate of interest rises above this level, the demand for money will be substantially unaffected and will depend exclusively on the level of money income.

On the basis of these considerations we may, in a first approximation, split the total demand for money into two parts: the demand for money to hold, $D_a(r)$, and the demand for money to spend or for transactions, $D_T(Y)$; and write

(12) $$L(r, Y) = D_a(r) + D_T(Y) = M.$$

This is not really necessary for our argument, but is very useful since it will constantly remind us of the two sources of demand for money and it will permit us to analyze more conveniently the part played by each variable.

With this in mind we shall find it useful to consider the functioning of the money market in which decisions concerning the disposition of nonphysical assets are carried out.

7. THE MONEY MARKET AND THE SHORT-RUN EQUILIBRIUM OF THE RATE OF INTEREST

There are two ways of looking at this market: (a) in terms of flows (savings and net borrowing) and (b) in terms of stocks. It is from this latter point of view that we shall consider it at this moment.

The supply in this market consists of the stock that is not needed for transactions. On the basis of our first approximation (12), this supply, denoted by S_a, will be

$$S_a = M - D_T(Y),$$

and is determined for any value of the money income and the fixed supply of money.

A position of equilibrium in the money market is reached when a system of interest rates is established at which dealers are willing to hold for the income period all the available supply. Or, from a different angle, the system of interest rates is determined by the price (in terms of forgone income) that dealers are willing to pay to hold assets in the form of money for the coming income period.

This can easily be translated into the usual Marshallian supply and demand apparatus, provided we replace the system of interest rates by a single rate r, as shown in Figure 1.

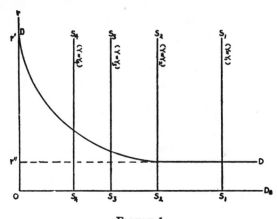

DD is the demand curve for money to hold, sloping downward and to the right (when the price, the rate of interest, rises, the demand falls, as in the case of ordinary commodities). The vertical lines are various supply curves corresponding to different values of Y and the fixed value of M. As the income increases, the supply falls: hence

$$Y_4 > Y_3 > Y_2 > \cdots .$$

Since a fall in supply causes a rise in price, the graph shows clearly that equation (1) gives r as an increasing function of Y.

The characteristics of the D_a function described above are shown in in the graph. We noted that, for $r \geq r'$ the demand falls to zero; hence the graph of DD joins the vertical axis and coincides with it.

On the other hand, when the rate of interest falls to the level r'', the demand for money to hold becomes infinitely elastic. Any increase in the supply of money to hold now fails to affect the rate of interest, for the owners of the extra supply will either desire to hold this in the form of cash; or else they will find some owners of securities, who, being just indifferent as to holding cash or securities, will be willing to sell without any necessity for bidding up the price of securities (lowering the rate of interest). Thus, in Figure 1, when the interest rate r'' is reached, the graph of DD becomes parallel to the D_a axis; the income corresponding to r'' cannot be more than Y_2; but if income should fall below Y_2 it would not change the interest rate.[12] This situation that plays such an important role in Keynes's *General Theory* will be referred to as the "Keynesian case."

In the diagram we have assumed that there is a single rate of interest r, instead of a whole system of rates for loans of different duration. While it may be assumed that in principle all the rates tend to move in the same direction, we must bear in mind that the extent to which a change in the supply of money changes the rates on loans of different maturities depends on the character of interest expectations.

A change in the supply will necessarily affect the short rates (unless the short rate has already reached its minimum). But the extent to which it will affect longer rates depends on the relation between the current spot rate and expected future rates.

To denote the relationship between current and expected rates we may again use the Hicksian elasticity of expectation. If this elasticity is unity, expected short rates move in the same direction and in the same proportion as the spot rate; if it is less than unity, a given percentage change in short rates leads to a smaller percentage change in expected rates; and vice versa for elasticity larger than one.

If the expectations about future short rates are based predominantly on the current shorter rates, then the elasticity of expectation tends toward one and the whole system of rates moves in close conformity. But if dealers have rigid expectations based on different elements, the elasticity of expectation will be low and a change in short rates will affect longer rates only to the extent that some of the discount rates, which determine the present value of the assets, are changed.

In practice we may expect that this elasticity will be larger than zero and smaller than one and that it will be larger for the rates expected in the near future.[13]

To the extent that this is true there will be two reasons why rates on loans of shorter maturity should move in closer agreement with the very short rate: (a) because they are more affected by a change in the current short rate, (b) because the other future short rates (of which they are an average) are more influenced by such a change.

---

[12] From equation (1) we obtain $dr/dY = -L_Y/L_r$, where the subscripts denote partial derivatives. Hence $dr/dY = 0$ if $|L_r| = \infty$.

[13] Denoting by $r_1, r_2, \cdots, r_n$ the short rate of interest anticipated for periods $1, 2, \cdots, n$, we may expect that

$$\frac{\partial r_1}{\partial r_0} > \frac{\partial r_2}{\partial r_0} > \cdots > \frac{\partial r_n}{\partial r_0}.$$

These necessary qualifications do not alter our previous conclusions concerning the determination of equilibrium in the money market. The equilibrium system of interest rates is determined in each period by the condition that the supply of money to hold, which (given M) depends on the transaction demand for money and hence on income, be equal to the demand for money to hold. We may therefore proceed to draw the graph of equation (1), $M = L(r, Y)$. This is the LL curve of Figure 3. Any point on this curve shows the equilibrium value of r corresponding to a value of Y and the fixed value of M: it shows therefore positions of possible equilibrium in the money market. We must prove next that only one point on this curve is consistent with the long-run equilibrium of the system.

8. SAVING, INVESTMENT, AND THE *IS* FUNCTION

The first part of our system yields a second relationship between interest and income. Making use of equations (2) and (3) and the equilibrium condition (4) we obtain: $I(r, Y) = S(r, Y)$. In order to gain some idea of the shape of this curve we may again make use of a graphical method illustrated in Figure 2.

Figure 2-B is the graph of equation (3). Since $\partial S/\partial r$ is usually considered small and of unknown sign we have simplified the drawing by eliminating r. This curve describes the relationship between money income and the proportion of it that people choose not to consume. Its position depends on the value of the fixed money wage rate w_0: given the wage rate, to any level of money income there corresponds a certain real income and price level and, therefore, a certain level of money saving. In this diagram Y_2 denotes the highest money income that can be reached with the money wage rate w_0, and A is the full employment relationship between saving and income.

The straight line beginning at A gives the relationship between money income and money saving once full employment has been reached and the second part of condition (10) replaces the first.[14] We have then what is usually called inflation: real income cannot change but money income can rise to any level. As all prices rise simultaneously the amount of real income saved is unchanged while its money value rises in the same proportion as the price level and money income.[15] The dotted curved line, on the other hand, gives a potential

---

[14] This line is the continuation of the radius vector from the origin to A.

[15] This is strictly correct only if inflation does not provoke any permanent redistribution of income; or if the redistribution does not affect the aggregate propensity to save. Since wages rise with prices we can exclude redistributions from working class to nonworking class. But we cannot exclude redistribution from fixed-income receivers (especially owners of securities) to profits. It is difficult to say whether this will change sensibly the aggregate propensity to save; it is probably a good approximation to assume that the effect will be negligible.

relation between S and I if it were possible to raise the real income above the full employment level.

Figure 2-A is the graph of equation (2). Each curve in this graph shows the amount of investment that would be undertaken at different levels of the rate of interest and for a fixed value of the income. To larger values of Y correspond investment curves higher and to the right.

Since the vertical scale is the same in both Figure 2-A and Figure 2-B, we may use the following method to find the shape of $S(Y) = I(r, Y)$: For any value of Y, say Y_1, the corresponding amount of saving, S_1, can be read from the SS curve. But in equilibrium $S = I$, hence we can draw a line parallel to the Y axis at height S_1 and prolong it until it inter-

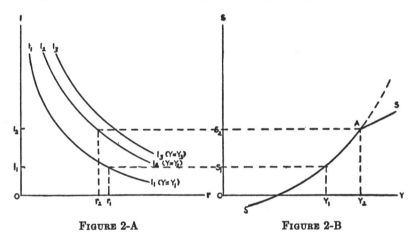

FIGURE 2-A   FIGURE 2-B

sects the investment curve of Figure 2-A corresponding to the income Y_1. We may thus find the rate of interest r_1 that corresponds to the given income Y_1.

The character of the relationship between r and Y that emerges from this diagram cannot be established a priori as in the case of the LL curve discussed before. For, as Y increases, S in Figure 2-B increases too, but the corresponding value of r in Figure 2-A may increase or decrease. It all depends on the way the change in income affects the position of the investment curves. If the increase in income tends to raise the desire to save more than the desire to invest, the rate of interest will fall; in the opposite case it will rise.[16] This last possibility is, in our opinion, unlikely to occur, but it may materialize when entrepreneurs are highly optimistic and the existing equipment is already working at capacity.

[16] From $S(r, Y) = I(r, Y)$ we obtain $dr/dY = (S_Y - I_Y)/(I_r - S_r)$, where the subscripts denote partial derivatives. Since $I_r - S_r$ may be expected to be negative, we have $dr/dY \lessgtr 0$ as $S_Y \lessgtr I_Y$.

The relationship between r and Y emerging from equations (2) and (3) and the equilibrium condition (4) is shown as the IS curve of Figure 3. In the normal case it will slope downward and to the right as in this diagram, but it is conceivable that, at least in a certain range, it may slope upward to the right. In this case $S_Y < I_Y$ and it is usually assumed that the equilibrium of the system will be unstable (and neutral if $S_Y = I_Y$). We shall see, however, that, with inelastic money supply, the negative slope of the IS curve is a sufficient but not necessary condition for stability.

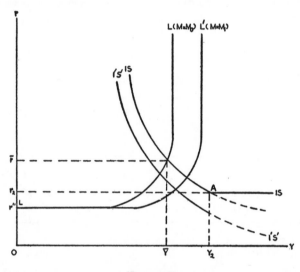

FIGURE 3

The IS curve must also have another important property. In Figure 3, A denotes the equilibrium relationship between full-employment income (Y_2) and rate of interest (r_2). Money income cannot rise above the full-employment level denoted by Y_2 except through inflation, i.e., if wages and prices rise in the same proportion as income. As the stage of inflationary prices and wage increases is reached, the "real" value of investment that it pays to undertake at any interest rate is unchanged since yields and costs change in the same proportion.[17] The

---

[17] Following the example of Mr. Keynes we may define the marginal efficiency of an asset as the discount rate that makes the sum of the expected marginal discounted yields equal to the marginal cost of the asset. The expected yields need not all be equal since they depend on the expected net physical yield as well as on expected future prices; and neither is necessarily constant in time. But the expected physical yield does not depend on prices; and, owing to our "static assumption" of unit elasticity of expectation, expected prices change in the same proportion as present prices. Therefore the summation of the yields changes in

money value of profitable investments, on the other hand, rises proportionally to prices and money income. As we have seen above, the same will be true of money savings. It follows that inflationary increases in income raise saving and investment in the same proportion and must therefore leave the equilibrium value of the rate of interest unchanged at the full-employment level r_2. It is for this reason that in Figure 3, to the right of A, the IS curve becomes parallel to the income axis. The dotted curved line beyond A is again the hypothetical relationship between r and Y if it were possible to raise real income above the full-employment level (and if the wage rate should remain unchanged at the level w_0).

9. THE MONEY MARKET AND THE DETERMINANTS OF MONETARY EQUILIBRIUM

We may now finally proceed to consider the process by which the equilibrium of the system is established. For this purpose we must once more revert to the money market which we must, this time, consider in terms of flows rather than in terms of stocks.

In Section 5 we have seen that the rate of interest is established in the money market by the condition that supply of and demand for the stock of money to hold must be equal. This condition is sufficient to determine a position of short-run equilibrium, i.e., a position of equilibrium for the income period. We must now consider under what conditions this level of the rate of interest will also represent a position of long-run equilibrium. As in the textbook analysis of demand and supply, a position of long-run equilibrium is characterized by the fact that neither price nor quantity (demanded and supplied) tend to change any further. In the present case a position of long-run equilibrium will be reached only when the rate of interest does not tend to change from one income period to the other and this in turn is possible only if the stock of money to hold remains constant in time.

Now in each income period people increase their assets by current savings; the money thus saved, since it is not needed for transactions, constitutes an increase in the supply of money to hold. Borrowing, on the other hand, automatically decreases the supply of money to hold by taking cash out of the money market and putting it into active circulation again, through expenditure on investments. If net saving exceeds net borrowing then, on balance, the supply of money to hold

---

the same proportion as marginal cost and so does the aggregate value of investments having marginal efficiency equal to or larger than r_2. Under unit elasticity of expectation a given change in all present prices does not modify entrepreneurs' production plans.

will increase above the level of the previous period, say $D_{a \cdot 0}$. But at the old rate of interest (r_0) people will not want to hold the extra supply; they will therefore try to purchase securities and thus will lower the rate of interest. If, on the other hand, at the interest rate r_0 borrowers desire to borrow in the period more than the current amount of money savings, they must induce dealers in the money market to reduce the demand for money as an asset below the previous level $D_{a \cdot 0}$; and this is possible only if the rate of interest rises. There are then three possibilities. (The subscripts 0 and 1 denote quantities in periods zero and one, respectively.)

(1) $S_1 > I_1$: then $D_{a \cdot 1} > D_{a \cdot 0}$ and the rate of interest falls.

(2) $S_1 = I_1$: here $D_{a \cdot 1} = D_{a \cdot 0}$ and the rate of interest is unchanged.

(3) $S_1 < I_1$: then $D_{a \cdot 1} < D_{a \cdot 0}$ and the rate of interest rises.

Recalling our definition of long-run equilibrium, we see at once that only situation (2) satisfies it. In equilibrium then, both demand for and supply of the stock of money to hold and demand for and supply of the flow of saving must be equal.[17a] In addition, however, it is necessary that the flows of saving and of borrowing be themselves constant in time. This is possible only if two conditions hold: (a) The borrowing that occurs must be equal to the amount of investment that entrepreneurs wish to undertake at the given rate of interest and income level. The relationship between I_1, r_1, and Y_1 must be described by a point on the corresponding curve of Figure 2-A. (b) The income (and the rate of interest) must be as large as is required to induce people to go on saving an amount S_1. The relationship between Y_1, S_1, and r_1 must be described by a point lying on the curve of Figure 2-B. But if conditions (a) and (b) are satisfied the relationship between Y and r will be described by a point lying on the IS curve of Figure 3. Thus a position of full equilibrium must be represented by a point lying at the same time on the LL curve (denoting equilibrium between demand for and supply of the stock of money to hold) and on the IS curve (denoting equality and constancy in time of the inflow and outflow of cash in the money market); hence it must be given by the intersection of these two curves.

This is shown in Figure 3 where the equilibrium values of r and Y, thus determined, are denoted by $\bar{r}$ and $\bar{Y}$. Analytically this corresponds to the simultaneous solution of the two relationships between the income and the rate of interest obtained from equations (1), (2), (3), and (4): $M = L(r, Y)$ and $S(r, Y) = I(r, Y)$.

[17a] The classical example of the level of water in a reservoir fits this case perfectly. The rate of interest, like the level of the water, can be constant only if inflow and outflow are equal.

10. A DYNAMIC MODEL OF THE KEYNESIAN THEORY AND
THE STABILITY OF EQUILIBRIUM

So far our analysis has apparently been "timeless"[18] since it was based on the system of equations of Section 2, in which time does not appear explicitly. A close examination of the last sections, and especially Sections 7 and 9, will reveal, however, that dynamic elements have gradually slipped into our analysis, thanks to the device of "long- and short-run equilibrium," the oldest and simplest device of developing a dynamic theory with a static apparatus. Actually the criterion that distinguishes short- from long-run equilibrium is essentially a dynamic one: namely, the length of time that is required for certain decisions to be carried out, or, more generally, for certain causes to show their effects.

In our case, the equilibrium of the "money market" is a condition of short-run equilibrium (that determines the rate of interest for each period) because it is the result of decisions that can be carried into effect immediately. The condition saving = investment, on the other hand, is a condition of long-run equilibrium because the equality of *ex ante* saving and investment cannot be brought about instantaneously. This is a different way of stating the familiar proposition that the multiplier takes time to work out its full effect. This well-known fact is in turn explained essentially by the existence of a fundamental time lag: the lag between the time when income is earned and the time when it becomes available for expenditure. In the economic systems in which we live, people are usually paid for services already rendered. The income earned (or produced) in a period is the value of services rendered which will be paid for at the end of the normal income period; while the income available for expenditure represents payment for services rendered in the previous period. Decisions as to spending and saving can refer only to the disposable income, and are essentially motivated by it, even though income earned may have some influence.

This explains why the graph of the *IS* curve, unlike the *LL* curve, describes not instantaneous relationships but only possible positions of long-run equilibrium. When the two curves intersect we have a position of full equilibrium since both short- and long-run conditions are satisfied.

It will therefore be useful at this point to give explicit recognition to the dynamic elements that form the basis of our approach. This is the purpose of the following system of difference equations which may be considered as the simplest dynamic model of our theory.

---

[18] The word "timeless" has been used here to avoid confusion since the word "static" has already been used to denote the assumption of homogeneity of the first degree of the "expectations functions."

$$(2.1) \qquad M = L(r_t, Y_{d \cdot t}),$$

$$(2.2) \qquad I_t = I(r_t, Y_{d \cdot t}),$$

$$(2.3) \qquad S_t = S(r_t, Y_{d \cdot t}),$$

$$(2.4) \qquad Y_{d \cdot t} = C_t + S_t,$$

$$(2.5) \qquad Y_t = C_t + I_t,$$

$$(2.6) \qquad Y_{d \cdot t} = Y_{t-1}.$$

In this system Y denotes income earned and Y_d income disposable. This is a new variable to which corresponds the new equation (2.6). The remaining equations of the system are unchanged.

By repeated substitution the system reduces to the two equations

$$Y_t = Y_{t-1} - S_t + I_t = Y_{t-1} - S(Y_{t-1}, r_t) + I(Y_{t-1}, r_t),$$
$$M = L(r_t, Y_{t-1}).$$

Solving the second equation for r_t and substituting in the first, we obtain a single equation of the form: $Y_t = f(Y_{t-1})$ which determines the time path of the income. By similar procedure we obtain the time sequence of the other variables.

If the system is stable, each variable approaches some definite value which it will maintain in time until there occurs some change in the form of the functional relationship or in some parameter (M or w_0). Equation (2.1) is again the "equation of the money market" that determines the value of r for any period; but we have a position of long-run equilibrium only when $r_t = r_{t-1}$. And this implies $Y_t = Y_{d \cdot t} = Y_{t-1}$ and therefore $S_t = I_t$.

The importance of this system is not limited to the fact that it defines rigorously concepts that were loosely used in our previous analysis. It serves also another important purpose: namely it permits us to determine the conditions of stability for the system.

Following the usual method, we proceed to expand equations (2.1) to (2.3) by Taylor series around the equilibrium values neglecting all terms of degree higher than one. We then obtain:

$$0 = L_r \dot{r}_t + L_Y \dot{Y}_{t-1} + \cdots ,$$
$$I_t = I(\bar{r}, \bar{Y}) + I_r \dot{r}_t + I_Y \dot{Y}_{t-1} + \cdots ,$$
$$S_t = S(\bar{r}, \bar{Y}) + S_r \dot{r}_t + I_Y \dot{Y}_{t-1}.$$

Subscripts denote partial derivatives taken around the equilibrium values ($\bar{r}$, $\bar{Y}$) and $\dot{r}_t = \dot{r}_t - \bar{r}$, $\dot{Y}_t = Y_t - \bar{Y}$. By making use of (4) and (5) and by repeated substitution we obtain the following linear difference equation with constant coefficients:

$$\dot{Y}_t = \dot{Y}_{t-1} \left[1 + \frac{L_Y}{L_r} (S_r - I_r) + I_Y - S_Y \right].$$

The solution of this equation takes the form: $\dot{Y} = \kappa\lambda^t$ or $Y = (Y_0 - \overline{Y})\lambda^t$, since $\dot{Y}_0 = Y_0 - \overline{Y} = \kappa$. Y_0 is determined by the initial conditions and

$$\lambda = 1 + \frac{L_Y}{L_r}(S_r - I_r) + I_Y - S_Y.$$

The stability condition is $|\lambda| < 1$; in the present case this reduces to

(2.7) $\qquad -\dfrac{L_Y}{L_r} - \dfrac{r}{S_r - I_r} < \dfrac{I_Y - S_Y}{S_r - I_r} < -\dfrac{L_Y}{L_r}.$

Since the middle term is the slope of the IS curve and the right-hand term is the slope of the LL curve, the right-hand condition has a very clear graphical meaning. Stability requires that the slope of the IS curve be algebraically smaller than the slope of the LL curve. The slope of the LL curve cannot be negative ($L_Y > 0$, $L_r \geqq 0$). Also general economic considerations suggest that $S_r - I_r > 0$. Hence this condition is necessarily satisfied if $I_Y - S_Y < 0$, i.e., when the IS curve falls from left to right. But this is not necessary. Stability is also possible when the IS curve rises in the neighborhood of the equilibrium point as long as it cuts the LL curve from its concave toward its convex side.[19]

If the stability conditions are satisfied, the variables approach their equilibrium values, which are the same as those obtained by solving the static system of Section 2. In the opposite case they diverge more and more from these values in a process of cumulative contraction or expansion. In the same way, a change in some of the data will lead to a new stable equilibrium if the new functions satisfy the conditions written above.

It is interesting to note that, as long as the money supply is inelastic, the system must always have at least one stable solution since eventually the LL curve becomes perpendicular to the horizontal axis and hence its slope must become larger then the slope of the IS curve.

11. THE DETERMINANTS OF REAL EQUILIBRIUM

It is now time to consider the role of the second part of the system in the determination of equilibrium. Equations (5), (6), and (7) *explain* the forces that determine the real variables of the system: physical output, employment, real wage rate.[20]

---

[19] It is only as $L_r \to \infty$ (demand for money to hold infinitely elastic, LL curve parallel to the horizontal axis) that the condition $I_Y - S_Y < 0$ becomes necessary for equilibrium. This holds equally if the supply of money is infinitely elastic for this has the same effect as $L_r = \infty$.

[20] The price level is also necessary to determine the real wage rate, given the money wage rate W.

The most important of these equations is (7), which states the conditions of equilibrium in the production of goods whether for consumption or for investment.[21] Production will be extended up to the point at which the given and fixed money wage rate w_0 is equal to the marginal net product of labor, or, if we prefer, up to the point at which price equals marginal labor cost.[22] This assumes that the only variable factor is labor and the quantity of equipment is fixed; a condition that is approximately satisfied in the case we are considering. Eliminating equation (5) by substitution into (7) we can reduce this part of the system to two equations in the two unknowns X and N, where X' is used for dX/dN:

$$W_0 = X'(N)\, \frac{Y}{X}, \qquad X = X(N).$$

Since the money income is determined exclusively by the *monetary* part of the system, the price level depends only on the amount of output. If, at any given price level, the fixed wage is less than the marginal product of labor, the forces of competition lead to an expansion of employment and output which forces prices down. This lowers the marginal product of labor until it becomes equal to the wage rate. If the wage rate exceeded the marginal product of labor, output and employment would contract, which would force prices up. We see clearly from Figure 3 that the amount of employment thus determined will, in general, not be "full employment"; that is, unless the LL curve intersects the IS curve at (Y_2, r_2) or to the right of it.

12. UNDEREMPLOYMENT EQUILIBRIUM AND LIQUIDITY PREFERENCE

This last result deserves closer consideration. It is usually considered as one of the most important achievements of the Keynesian theory that it explains the consistency of economic equilibrium with the presence of involuntary unemployment. It is, however, not sufficiently recognized that, except in a limiting case to be considered later, this result is due entirely to the assumption of "rigid wages"[23] and not to the Keynesian liquidity preference. Systems with rigid wages share the common property that the equilibrium value of the "real" variables is determined essentially by monetary conditions rather than by "real" factors (e.g., quantity and efficiency of existing equipment, relative

[21] The equilibrium price of each type of physical asset is found by capitalizing a series of expected marginal yields at the current rate of interest. The expected yields of the marginal unit need not be equal in each period.

[22] This is a sufficient condition under assumption of perfect competition; the modifications necessary in the case of monopolies cannot be considered here.

[23] The expression "rigid wages" refers to the infinite elasticity of the supply curve of labor when the level of employment is below "full."

preference for earning and leisure, etc.). The monetary conditions are sufficient to determine money income and, under fixed wages and given technical conditions, to each money income there corresponds a definite equilibrium level of employment. This equilibrium level does not tend to coincide with full employment except by mere chance, since there is no economic mechanism that insures this coincidence. There may be unemployment in the sense that more people would be willing to work at the current real wage rate than are actually employed; but in a free capitalistic economy production is guided by prices and not by desires and since the money wage rate is rigid, this desire fails to be translated into an economic stimulus.

In order to show more clearly that wage rigidities and not liquidity preference explain underemployment equilibrium we may consider the results to be obtained by giving up the liquidity-preference theory and assuming instead the crudest quantity-of-money theory while keeping the assumption of rigid wages. This can be done by merely replacing equation (1) of our system by the equation

(1a) $$M = kY.$$

Since M and k are constant this equation is sufficient to determine money income. Equations (5), (6), and (7) determine directly physical output and employment as we saw in Section 10. Once more there is no reason to expect that the level of employment thus determined will be "full employment"; and yet the system will be in equilibrium since there will be no tendency for income, employment, and output to change.

It is very interesting to see what part is played under these conditions by equations (2) and (3), the saving and investment equations that have been so much stressed by all the Keynesians. Since the income is determined by equation (1a), equation (2) reduces to an "orthodox" supply-of-saving schedule, giving saving as a function of the rate of interest. For the same reason, equation (3) reduces to a demand-for-saving schedule. Both schedules can be represented in a Marshallian supply and demand diagram as is done in Figure 4. The intersection of these curves, i.e., the equilibrium condition, demand = supply, determines the level of the rate of interest.

Finally let us notice that, in this system also, the rate of interest depends on the quantity of money, or more exactly on the ratio M/W. A change in M (W constant) raises real income and shifts both the SS and II curves to the right. The net result will be a fall in the rate of interest, if the increase in income raises the desire to save more than the desire to invest (normal case); a rise, in the opposite case.

In spite of these significant similarities between the present system and the Keynesian system, in which we recognize the existence of liquidity demand for money, there remains one very important difference; this difference is to be found in the role played by the rate of interest in the determination of equilibrium. In both cases the level of employment depends on the quantity of "active" money. But in the Keynesian system this depends on the rate of interest and consequently also on the propensities to save and invest. In the present case the quantity of active money is fixed and independent of the rate of interest. Hence the propensities to save and invest are not a part of the mechanism determining employment; they merely determine the amount of resources devoted to the improvement of the means of production.

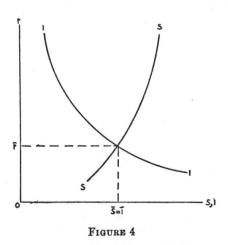

FIGURE 4

We now proceed to consider the determinants of equilibrium in a system in which we do away not only with the liquidity-preference theory but also with the assumption of rigid wages.

13. THE LOGICAL CONSISTENCY OF THE QUANTITY THEORY OF MONEY AND THE DICHOTOMY OF MONETARY AND REAL ECONOMICS

In order to discuss the quantity theory of money we substitute equation (1a) for (1) and replace conditions (10) by the identities (11).

It was shown in Section 8 that a given change in prices will change income, investment, and saving in the same proportion. Consequently, after Y in equations (2) and (3) is replaced by the expression given in (5), the saving and investment equations may be written in the form

$$(3.2) \qquad \frac{I}{W} = I\left(r, \frac{P}{W}X\right),$$

$$(3.3) \qquad \frac{S}{W} = S\left(r, \frac{P}{W}X\right).$$

Next we divide both members of equations (4) and (5) by W obtaining

(3.4)
$$\frac{S}{W} = \frac{I}{W},$$

(3.5)
$$\frac{Y}{W} \equiv \frac{P}{W} X,$$

(3.6)
$$X = X(N),$$

(3.7)
$$\frac{W}{P} = X'(N),$$

(3.9)
$$N = F\left(\frac{W}{P}\right),$$

$$\left[(3.8) \qquad \frac{Y}{W} \equiv \frac{I}{W} + \frac{C}{W} \right].$$

Equations (3.2) to (3.7) and (3.9) form a system of 7 equations in the 7 unknowns I/W, S/W, P/W, Y/W, r, X, N. These unknowns are therefore determined. Next we can write equation (1a) in the form $M = kPX = Wk(P/W)X$. But since P/W and X have already been determined, this equation determines the money wage rate and hence the price level, money income, etc. This is essentially the "classical" procedure, and we can only repeat the classical conclusions to the effect that the real part of the system, namely, employment, *interest rate*, output, or real income, do not depend on the quantity of money. The quantity of money has no other function than to determine the price level.

This result does not, of course, depend on any special feature of our system. It will always follow, provided all the supply and demand functions for commodities[24] and labor are homogeneous of the zero degree; and since we are proceeding under "static" assumptions, all the supply and demand functions must be homogeneous of zero degree, if people behave rationally.[25]

This conclusion, which is very old indeed, has some interest since it has been recently challenged by Oscar Lange. Of all the recent attacks against the traditional dichotomy of monetary and real economics, Lange's criticism is by far the most serious because it maintains that "the traditional procedure of the theory of money involves a

[24] "Commodities" are, in this context, all goods except money.

[25] For a proof of this statement see O. Lange, "Say's Law: A Restatement and Criticism," *op. cit.*, pp. 67 and 68. Professor Lange shows that the homogeneity of first degree of all expectation functions is a sufficient condition for all demand and supply equations for "commodities" to be homogeneous of zero degree.

[logical] contradiction."[26] We propose to show, however, that, while Lange's criticism of Say's law cannot be questioned, it does not invalidate the logical consistency of the procedure of the quantity theory of money.

According to Lange, Say's law implies that the amount of cash people desire to hold is always identically equal to the quantity in existence: denoting by D_n and S_n the demand and supply of money respectively, we can write this as $S_n \equiv D_n$. Lange then states that "a proportional change of all prices does not induce a substitution between different commodities"[27] and concludes that "the demand and supply functions of commodities are, *when Say's law holds*, homogeneous of zero degree."[28] But the homogeneity of the supply and demand functions for commodities does not depend on Say's law: it depends on the assumption of rationality and the homogeneity of the expectation functions. Since a proportional change in all prices does not change the price ratios it also does not change the marginal rate of substitution, and therefore does not induce a substitution between different commodities.

Let us now consider a system in which there are n goods ($n-1$ commodities and money). As is well known, there are only $n-1$ prices to be determined, the price of money being unity, and $n-1$ independent supply and demand equations, for one follows from the rest. Since the supply and demand functions for commodities are homogeneous of zero degree, the quantities demanded of the $n-1$ commodities are functions of the $n-2$ price ratios p_i/p_{n-1} ($i=1, 2, \cdots, n-2$), where p_{n-1} is chosen arbitrarily.[29] At the same time the demand and supply function to be eliminated is also arbitrary; we may, if we choose, eliminate one of the $n-1$ referring to commodities; we are then left with $n-2$ equations for commodities to determine the $n-2$ price ratios. Hence the price ratios are determined. To determine the actual prices we use the demand and supply equation for money as was done above. In Lange's system this is written:

$$k \sum_{i=1}^{n} p_i S_i = M, \quad \text{or also} \quad k p_{n-1} \sum_{i=1}^{n} \frac{p_i}{p_{n-1}} S_i = M,$$

where S_i denotes the equilibrium quantity supplied and demanded of the ith commodity. Since k is a constant this equation determines p_{n-1} and consequently all other prices.

As long as Say's law is not assumed, this procedure is perfectly legitimate; and we cannot escape the classical conclusion that money

---

[26] *Ibid.*, p. 65.

[27] *Ibid.*, p. 63.

[28] *Ibid.*, p. 63. Italics ours.

[29] In our own system p_{n-1} was arbitrarily chosen as the wage rate.

is "neutral," just a "veil." If, however, Say's law holds, the demand and supply of money are identically equal. The nth equation is therefore not a genuine equation. Thus we have only $n-2$ independent equations to determine $n-1$ prices: the system is not determinate. In Lange's own formulation, the nth equation degenerates into the identity

$$kp_{n-1} \sum_{i=1}^{n} \frac{p_i}{p_{n-1}} S_i \equiv M,$$

which is satisfied by any value of p_{n-1} whatever; the price level is thus indeterminate.[30]

Hence one of Lange's conclusions, namely that "Say's law precludes any monetary theory,"[31] is perfectly justified. But Lange goes on to draw a conclusion which does not follow, namely that "the traditional procedure of the theory of money involves a contradiction. Either Say's law is assumed and money prices are indeterminate, or money prices are made determinate—but then *Say's law and hence the neutrality of money* must be abandoned."[32] But the traditional theory of money is not based on Say's law. The necessary condition for money to be neutral is that the $n-1$ "real" demand and supply equations be homogeneous of order zero and this homogeneity does not "disappear when Say's law is abandoned."[33] Under "static" assumptions money is neutral even without assuming Say's law, if only people are assumed to behave "rationally"; this is all that the classical theory assumes and needs to assume.[34]

The most serious charge against the classical dichotomy can thus be dismissed, as long as we maintain our "static" assumptions.

14. LIQUIDITY PREFERENCE AND THE DETERMINANTS OF THE RATE OF INTEREST UNDER THE ASSUMPTION OF FLEXIBLE WAGES[35]

With this in mind we may now proceed to analyze our third system consisting of equations (1) to (7), (9), and identities (11). In this system we recognize that there are two sources of demand for money,

[30] Then k changes in inverse proportion to p_{n-1} instead of being a constant.

[31] O. Lange, *op. cit.*, p. 66.

[32] *Ibid.*, p. 65. Italics ours.

[33] *Ibid.*, p. 66.

[34] Lange's result seems due to a failure to distinguish between necessary and sufficient conditions. Say's law is a sufficient condition for the neutrality of money but not a necessary one. Lange asks me to inform the reader that he agrees with my conclusion. This conclusion, however, does not invalidate his result that under Say's law the money prices are indeterminate.

[35] The expression "flexible wages" is used here and in the following pages for brevity in place of the more exact expression "homogeneity of zero degree of the supply-of-labor function."

the transaction demand and the liquidity demand. But, as in the case just analyzed, we make no restrictive assumptions as to the supply-of-labor equation. The suppliers of labor as well as the suppliers of all other commodities are supposed to behave "rationally." It follows that the only difference between the present case and the case just considered is in equation (1). As in the previous case, the last 7 equations form a determinate system which is sufficient to determine the 7 unknowns it contains, namely *the "real" variables of the system and the rate of interest.*

By use of equation (5) or (3.5) equation (1) takes the form

$$(3.1) \qquad\qquad M = L\left(r,\, W\frac{P}{W}X\right).$$

Since r and P/W are already determined, this equation determines the 8th unknown of the system, the wage rate: and therefore also the price level, money, income, etc.[36]

We thus reach the conclusion that under "static" assumptions and "flexible" wages, *the rate of interest and the level of employment do not depend on the quantity of money.*

Two questions arise at once: (a) what determines the rate of interest and (b) what part do the rate of interest and liquidity demand for money play in the determination of equilibrium.

Strictly speaking, the rate of interest is determined by all the equations of a Walrasian system *except the supply-of-and-demand-for-money equation.* But it is clear that in the first approximation of partial-equilibrium analysis, the determination of the rate of interest must be associated with equations (3.2) and (3.3), the saving and investment schedules. To explain the level of the rate of interest we could use once more Figure 4, changing the variables measured on the horizontal axis from S or I into S/W or I/W. We must add at once, however, that these two schedules should in no way be confused with the schedules of supply of and demand for savings (or supply of and demand for securities) used in the textbook explanation of the determination of the rate of interest.

Equation (3.3) only tells us what part of their real income people wish to devote to increasing their assets rather than to consumption, at different levels of the rate of interest.

In a similar fashion equation (3.2) shows that by devoting output worth I/W to the improvement of the means of production, it is possible to increase real income by an amount $(I/W)(1+r)$ per unit of time. The value of r depends on the given technical conditions, on the

---

[36] Except in the Keynesian case considered later (Section 16).

quantity I/W and $(P/W)X$ according to the relation expressed by equation (3.2). This shows clearly the fundamental factors that determine the rate of interest. The given technical conditions, expressed by the production function [equation (3.6)], together with *tastes* of people for earning and leisure, expressed by the supply-of-labor function [equation (3.9)], give the level of real income that can be reached.[37] The saving schedule, equation (3.3), tells us what part of this income the community desires to save. The technical conditions (inventions, quantity of capital already in existence, etc.) expressed by the marginal-efficiency-of-investment function (3.2), determine the marginal efficiency of the amount of investment that the giving up of consumption permits undertaking: this is the equilibrium rate of interest.

Let us now examine what part is played by liquidity preference in the present system. On the basis of the given rate of interest determined in the fashion discussed above, people decide what quantity of money they want to hold as an asset. Hence, provided the liquidity demand is finite, the rate of interest, together with the supply of money, determines the quantity of active money and therefore the price level. Thus under "flexible" wages, *the desire to hold assets in liquid form does not determine the rate of interest, but determines the price level.* It follows that any factor that influences the demand for money as an asset, either directly or through the rate of interest, will have a repercussion on the price level, unless it is counteracted by an appropriate change in the quantity of money. This will in particular be the case with changes in the propensities to save and to invest.

15. LIQUIDITY PREFERENCE UNDER RIGID AND FLEXIBLE WAGES—AN EXAMPLE

In order to see clearly the different implications of the liquidity-preference theory under different hypotheses as to the supply of labor we may briefly consider the effects of a shift in the investment schedule [equation (2) or (3.2)].

Suppose that the system is in equilibrium at money income Y_0: the flow of investments is I_0, and its marginal efficiency, r_0, is the equilibrium rate of interest. Now let us assume that for some reason the rate of investment that seems profitable at any level of the rate of interest falls. In particular the marginal efficiency of the rate of investment I_0 falls to the level $r_1 < r_0$. In order for the system to reach a new position of equilibrium, it is necessary that the rate of interest fall to this level. Except under special circumstances, to be considered later, as

---

[37] Under flexible wages there is, of course, always full employment under the conditions mentioned in Section 16.

the rate of interest falls, the demand for money as an asset rises, and a certain amount of current money savings remains in the *money market* to satisfy the increased demand. If the supply of money is not properly increased, this, in turn, implies a fall in money income.

Under the conditions of our last model (flexible wages) the fall is brought about by an all-around reduction in wages and prices. The price level reaches its new equilibrium position when the supply has been increased sufficiently to satisfy the liquidity demand for money associated with the interest rate r_1.[38] The net effect of the shift is then to depress the interest rate, the money income, and money wages without affecting the real variables of the system, employment, output, real wage rate.[39]

But if money wages are rigid downward, the reduction in money income, made necessary by the fall in the rate of interest, becomes a reduction in real income and employment as well. The effect of the shift in the investment schedule is now to start a typical process of contraction so frequently described in Keynesian literature. As producers of investment goods make losses, they have no other choice than to dismiss workers, even though their physical productivity is unchanged. This, in turn, reduces the demand for consumption goods and causes unemployment to spread to this sector. Real income falls along with money income (the price level is likely to fall to a smaller extent). The fall in money income increases the supply of money to hold; the fall in real income decreases saving and raises its marginal efficiency above the level r_1.[40] This double set of reactions leads finally to a new equilibrium, with a smaller money and real income, less employment, higher real wages (since the price level falls) and a rate of interest somewhere below r_0 and above the new "full employment interest" r_1.[41] In terms of our graphic apparatus, a decreased marginal efficiency of capital (or increased propensity to save), shifts the IS curve to the left, as shown by the curve $I'S'$, and lowers interest rate and income, money as well as real income.

[38] The rate of interest must necessarily fall to the level r_1, for the real income and therefore the amount of real savings will be unchanged, and the marginal efficiency of this amount of real savings is r_1, by hypothesis.

[39] The real wage rate clearly cannot fall. If the real wage rate had fallen, entrepreneurs would try to expand employment while the supply of labor would, if anything, contract. If it had risen, the opposite situation would occur, and neither of these situations is compatible with equilibrium.

[40] Except if the IS curve is not monotonic decreasing, in which case the process of contraction will be more pronounced.

[41] If there was no full employment in the initial situation, then r_1 is simply the rate of interest that would maintain the old level of employment. This conclusion is also subject to the qualification mentioned in footnote 40.

16. TWO LIMITING CASES: (A) THE KEYNESIAN CASE

There is one case in which the Keynesian theory of liquidity preference is sufficient by itself to explain the existence of underemployment equilibrium without starting out with the assumption of rigid wages. We have seen (Section 5) that, since securities are inferior to money as a form of holding assets, there must be some positive level of the rate of interest (previously denoted by r'') at which the demand for money becomes infinitely elastic or practically so. We have the Keynesian case when the "full-employment equilibrium rate of interest" is less than r''. Whenever this situation materializes, the very mechanism that tends to bring about full-employment equilibrium in a system with "flexible" wages breaks down, since there is no possible level of the money wage rate and price level that can establish full-employment equilibrium.

From the analytical point of view the situation is characterized by the fact that we must add to our system a new equation, namely $r = r''$. The system is therefore overdetermined since we have 9 equations to determine only 8 unknowns.

Equations (3.2) and (3.3) are sufficient to determine the value of the real income (since r is already determined). But this value will in general not be consistent with the value of the real income determined by the last four equations. More workers would be willing to work at the ruling real wage rate than are employed, but efforts at reducing real wages and increasing employment are bound to fail. For any fall in wages and prices increases the supply of money to hold but cannot lower the rate of interest below the level r'' since the demand for money as an asset is infinitely elastic. As Keynes would say, labor as a whole will not be able to fix its own real wage rate.

It appears clearly that, in this case, equilibrium is determined by those very factors that are stressed in the typical Keynesian analysis. In particular, real income and employment is determined by the position and shape of the saving and investment function, and changes in the propensity to invest or to save change real income without affecting the interest rate.

The price level on the other hand is in neutral equilibrium (at least for a certain range of values). It will tend to fall indefinitely as long as workers attempt to lower money wages in an effort to increase employment; and it can only find a resting place if and when money wages become rigid.

In this case the Keynesian analysis clearly departs from the classical lines and it leads to conclusions that could scarcely have been reached by following the traditional line of approach.

Whether the situation we have characterized as the "Keynesian case" is typical of some or all modern economic systems is a factual question which we cannot attempt to answer here. It is beyond doubt however that its interest is not purely theoretical.[42]

(B) THE CLASSICAL CASE

We have the classical case when the equilibrium rate of interest is sufficiently high to make the demand for money to hold zero or negligible. Graphically, the IS curve of Figure 3 intersects the LL curve in the range in which LL is perpendicular to the income axis. Under these conditions changes in the rate of interest (except possibly if they are of considerable size) tend to leave the demand for money unchanged or practically so; $L_r = 0$ or negligible and $M = L(Y)$. The properties of a system satisfying this condition have already been sufficiently analyzed in Sections 11 and 12.[43]

17. PRELIMINARY CONCLUSIONS

This brings to an end the first part of our analysis which aimed principally at distinguishing, as far as possible, to what extent the results of the Keynesian analysis are due to a more refined theoretical approach (liquidity preference) and to what extent to the assumption of rigid wages. We may summarize the results of our inquiry in the following propositions:

I. The liquidity-preference theory is not necessary to explain under-

---

[42] In the *General Theory* Keynes explicitly recognizes that the situation described as the "Keynesian case" does not seem, so far, normally to prevail in any economic system. This situation, on the other hand, certainly plays an important part in some phases of the business cycle, when a great feeling of uncertainty and the anticipation of price reductions increase the attractiveness of liquidity and, at the same time, decreases the propensity to invest. Besides, it may also soon become a normal feature of some economies if there should come to prevail a real scarcity of investment outlets that are profitable at rates of interest higher than the institutional minimum. Modifying a well-known statement of Hicks we can say that the Keynesian case is either the Economics of Depression or the Economics of Abundance. (Hicks's original statement: "The General Theory of Employment is the Economics of Depression" is found in "Mr. Keynes and the 'Classics,'" *op. cit.*, p. 155.)

[43] To what extent the "classical case" is met in practice is again a factual question. In our opinion a moderately high rate of interest is sufficient to make it unattractive to hold assets in the form of cash and therefore to induce members of the community to limit their holdings to the amount necessary for transactions (which is determined by the institutional set-up). It is perhaps not unreasonable to expect that under normal conditions a "pure" rate of interest (i.e., net of default risk) in the neighborhood of 5 per cent might be sufficient to reduce the demand for money to hold to negligible proportions.

employment equilibrium; it is sufficient only in a limiting case: the "Keynesian case." In the general case it is neither necessary nor sufficient; it can explain this phenomenon only with the additional assumption of rigid wages.

II. The liquidity-preference theory is neither necessary nor sufficient to explain the dependence of the rate of interest on the quantity of money. This dependence is explained only by the assumption of rigid wages.

III. The result of the liquidity-preference theory is that the quantity of active money depends not only on the total quantity of money but also on the rate of interest and therefore also on the form and position of the propensities to save and to invest. Hence in a system with flexible wages the rate of interest and the propensities to save and to invest are part of the mechanism that determines the price level. And in a system with rigid wages they are part of the mechanism that determines the level of employment and real income.

We proceed now to make use of our results for two purposes: (a) To examine critically some of the theories that have their logical foundation in the Keynesian analysis. (b) To state some general conclusions about the determinants of the rate of interest.

PART II

18. GENERAL REMARKS ABOUT THE ASSUMPTION OF WAGE RIGIDITY IN THE KEYNESIAN THEORIES

In the *General Theory* Keynes does of course recognize the fundamental importance of the relation between money wages and the quantity of money as is shown by his device of the wage units. This very fact, on the other hand, has had the effect of obscuring the part played by wage rigidities in the determination of economic equilibrium. This can be clearly seen in a large body of literature based on the Keynesian analysis, and will be illustrated with a few examples.

(A) Let us first consider the role of investment.

The statement that unemployment is caused by lack of investment, or that a fall in the propensity to invest or an increase in the propensity to save will decrease employment, has become today almost a commonplace.

As we have seen, however, lack of investment is sufficient to explain underemployment equilibrium only in the "Keynesian case," a situation that is the exception and not the rule.

It is true that a reduced level of employment and a reduced level of investment go together, but this is not, in general, the result of causal relationship. It is true instead that the low level of investment and employment are both the effect of the same cause, namely a basic maladjustment between the quantity of money and the wage rate. It is the fact that money wages are too high relative to the quantity of money that explains why it is unprofitable to expand employment to the "full employment" level. Now to each level of employment and income corresponds a certain distribution of the employment between the production of consumption and investment goods determined by the saving pattern of the community. Hence, when the over-all level of employment is low there will be a reduced level of investment as well as a reduced level of consumption. And the level of investment is low because employment is low and not the other way around.

What is required to improve the situation is an increase in the quantity of money (and not necessarily in the propensity to invest); then employment will increase in every field of production including investment. Again, it is true that, in general, a fall in the propensity to invest (the propensity to save being constant) tends to decrease employment (and that an increase in the same propensity has the opposite effect), but this occurs only because it decreases (or increases) the quantity of money available for transactions relative to the money wage rate and therefore makes it profitable to expand employment. Exactly the same result could be obtained by deflating (or inflating) the quantity of money directly. That a change in the marginal efficiency of investment has no direct influence on aggregate employment can be clearly seen in the "classical case" when the demand for money to hold is zero or negligible. In this case the change mentioned above does not affect employment, but only the rate of interest and therefore, at most, the distribution of the unchanged amount of employment between consumption and investment.

In conclusion, then, the statement that unemployment is caused by lack of investment assumes implicitly that every possible economic system works under the special conditions of the "Keynesian case"; and this is clearly unwarranted. In general the reduced level of employment is not a cause, but just a symptom of unemployment, which in turn is due to essentially monetary disturbances.

This formulation is not only more correct but carries also important implications about the concrete form of economic policies necessary to relieve unemployment.

(B) Another typical result of understressing the assumption of rigid wages is to be found in connection with the concepts of a "natural rate of interest" and of "cumulative inflation" and "deflation" of Wicksellian analysis.[44]

[44] See J. Marschak, "Wicksell's Two Interest Rates," *Social Research*, Vol. 8, November, 1941, pp. 469–478.

This "natural rate" is the equilibrium (and therefore full-employment) interest rate of a system with flexible wages and not of a Keynesian system with rigid wages. Under "flexible" wages, as we know, the equilibrium rate of interest does not depend on the quantity of money. But, because of the time required for a new position of equilibrium to be reached when some of the conditions change, it will depend on the rate of change of M. Thus the money authority will be able to keep r below (or above) its equilibrium value by increasing (or decreasing) the quantity of money without limit; we thus get a process of cumulative inflation or deflation. Under Keynesian assumptions this ceases to be true; but only because wages are assumed rigid and in this condition, as we have seen, it is in general possible to change the rate of interest with a finite change in the quantity of money.[45]

(C) As a last example, we may quote Lange's "optimum propensity to consume."[46] This concept, outside of its theoretical interest, is only of practical importance if for some reason, money wages and money supply are absolutely inelastic. In general all that is required to increase employment is to expand the quantity of money (or at worst reduce wages) without any necessity for interfering with the propensity to consume.[47]

19. LERNER'S THEORY OF THE RATE OF INTEREST

We proceed now to consider the typically "Keynesian" theory of the rate of interest and money due to A. P. Lerner. We choose Lerner's theory, because its extremism and its clear-cut formulation permit of a useful criticism.

[45] The case is more complicated if the relation between Y and r described by the IS curve is not monotonic decreasing in the relevant range. It might then appear that an attempt of the money authority at reducing the interest rate will result in a fall in income and employment. This is the result reached by Marschak. Actually as the money authority expands the quantity of money by open-market policy it finds that the rate of interest eventually rises along with income and employment instead of falling. If the money authority insists on keeping the interest rate at the planned level it will have to go on expanding the quantity of money. This will either push the system to some new equilibrium if the planned rate is equal to or larger than the full-employment rate, or it will cause inflation if the planned rate is below this level. But in no event will an initial attempt at lowering r by open-market policy lead to a contraction of income.

[46] Oscar Lange, "The Rate of Interest and the Optimum Propensity to Consume," *Economica*, Vol. 5 (N. S.), February, 1938, pp. 12–32.

[47] If the demand for money is infinitely elastic the propensity to consume plays an important role in the determination of employment. In this case the optimum level of consumption C' would clearly be $C' = Y' - I(r'', Y')$, where Y' is full-employment income and r'' the critical level of the rate of interest for which $L_r = \infty$.

The substance of Lerner's argument, as far as we can make out, is this: The "classical theory" that saving and investment determine the rate of interest must be rejected: saving and investment, being identically equal, cannot determine interest. This is instead determined by the quantity of money according to a demand-for-money function, say $M = f(r)$.[48]

The first argument is clearly unimportant since it is based on definitions. If one accepts the Keynesian definitions then, of course, actual (or *ex post*) saving and investment are identical; and clearly the *ex post* identity, saving $\equiv$ investment, cannot determine either the rate of interest or income. This however does not prove that the propensities to save and to invest are irrelevant to the determination of interest.

We know on the contrary, that, under assumption of flexible wages, neither of Lerner's arguments holds. In this case the rate of interest is independent of the quantity of money and, except in limiting cases, is determined only by the propensities to save and to invest [equations (3.2) and (3.3)].

Let us stress, in order to avoid misunderstandings, that we perfectly agree with Lerner and with all the Keynesians that saving and lending are the result of two independent decisions; our equation (3.3) is a saving schedule and not a schedule of supply of loanable funds. However we cannot agree with Lerner that to treat saving as a "demand-for-securities schedule" is, without qualifications, a serious blunder, or that the classical analysis as to the effect of shifts in the desire to invest or to save is right by pure chance. We must remember that saving and lending coincide when the demand for money to hold is zero or constant. The quantity theory of money starts out with the assumption that the demand for money to hold is identically zero: $D_a'(r) \equiv 0$ or $M = L(Y)$. Now this assumption is unsatisfactory for a general theory, but may be fully justified under certain conditions.

We know that, when the equilibrium rate of interest is sufficiently high, the demand for money to hold does become zero, even if it is not assumed to be identically zero. And, under historically realized conditions, the equilibrium rate of interest may be sufficiently high to make the demand for money to hold so negligible and so scarcely affected by observed changes in the interest rate that this demand can, safely, be neglected. Interest becomes a factor of secondary importance and can

[48] See especially, "Alternative Formulations of the Theory of Interest," *Economic Journal*, Vol. 48, June, 1938, pp. 211–230; and "Interest Theory—Supply and Demand for Loans or Supply and Demand for Cash?" This latter paper has been recently made available to me by Mr. Lerner in manuscript form; it is to be published in the *Review of Economic Statistics*. The present criticism is also the result of a long personal discussion and correspondence.

be dropped along with many others which certainly do influence the demand for money but are not sufficiently relevant to warrant separate consideration. Under these conditions, the assumption $M = L(Y)$ will give a satisfactory approximation to economic reality.[49] Under changed historical conditions this assumption is no longer justified and it becomes necessary to take into account new factors to avoid oversimplifications.[50]

When we recognize that the demand for money to hold need not be zero (and as long as it is finite), saving and lending coincide only when the demand for money to hold is constant, that is to say, in equilibrium. The equality of money savings and lending becomes an equilibrium condition which, under flexible wages, *determines the price level, not the rate of interest*. And this in turn may explain the traditional lack of attention to the demand for money to hold in connection with the theory of interest.

Thus Lerner's theory cannot explain the rate of interest in a system with "flexible" wages. Let us then see whether it holds within the limits of his (tacit) assumption of rigid wages. We will agree at once that under this assumption the rate of interest depends on the quantity of money, but this is true only in a very special sense. If we look at our "Keynesian" model we find that we have 7 equations in 7 unknowns and two arbitrary quantities or "parameters," M and W_0. The solution of the system gives each of the 7 variables as functions of these arbitrary parameters: $\bar{r} = r(M, W)$, $\bar{Y} = Y(M, W)$, $\bar{N} = N(M, W)$, etc. On the basis of previous considerations these can be written:

$$(5.1) \qquad \bar{r} = r\left(\frac{M}{W}\right), \qquad (5.2) \qquad \bar{Y} = Y\left(\frac{M}{W}\right), \text{ etc.}$$

If this is the sense in which Lerner states that r is a function of M, his statement is formally correct. But in the first place it is not very helpful for understanding the determinants of the rate of interest. In a system with rigid wages practically every economic variable depends on the quantity of money (and the money wage). The rate of interest depends on M as much as the price of shoes or employment in ice-

---

[49] The fact that hoarding and unemployment have always developed in certain phases of the business cycle is not an objection to that. For these are features for a theory of business cycles to explain. Here we are only comparing static theories.

[50] Thus for example, the outcome of a certain physical experiment may be influenced, to a slight extent, by changes in humidity. Then, if the experiment is carried out in a place in which the observed variations in humidity are not sufficient to affect the outcome sensibly, it is perfectly justifiable to neglect it. If the same experiment were conducted somewhere else, where humidity is known to be highly unstable, precautions should be taken in interpreting the results.

cream manufacturing. In the second place it has nothing to do with Keynes's liquidity preference: r depends on M even if we neglect the liquidity demand for money (see Section 11). Hence if Lerner's equation, $M = f(r)$, corresponds to our equation (5.1), then it is not a demand-for-money schedule, but an empirical relationship obtained by previous solution of a system of equations of which the demand for money itself is one. And his approach certainly throws no light on the determinants of the rate of interest.

The only alternative is to consider Lerner's equation as a true demand for money corresponding to our equation (1): $M = L(r, Y)$. But why has the second variable been omitted? The answer is clear; by concentrating attention on the liquidity preference and the demand for money to hold, sight has been lost of the demand for money to spend. Thus we go from one extreme to the other; instead of neglecting the influence of the rate of interest as in the "quantity theory," we neglect the part played by income in determining the demand for money. The results of this unjustified omission are serious in many respects. The most serious is that it leads to the conclusion (reached by Lerner) that saving and investment play no part in the determination of the rate of interest.[51] Figure 3 shows on the contrary that equations (2) and (3) play as vital a role as the demand-for-money equation. It is clear also that changes in the propensity to save or to invest or in the wage rate, lead directly to changes in the interest rate.

To defend his point Lerner is forced to say that changes in these propensities affect the rate of interest *because* they change the demand for money, i.e., because they shift the graph of $M = f(r)$.[52] But this is true and by definition only if Lerner identifies $M = f(r)$ with our equation (5.1). Since this equation is obtained by previously solving the whole system, it contains the relevant parameters of the functions which determine the rate of interest. A change in any of these parameters changes or shifts the function $r = r(M/W)$ accordingly. But, as we

[51] In "Alternative Formulations of the Theory of Interest," Lerner writes: "For the first, easy step [from the classical to the modern theory of interest] is the insinuation of Liquidity Preference as a junior partner in the old established one-man firm in the business of interest-determination, and the second . . . step is to put Saving-Investment, the senior partner, to sleep, as a preliminary to kicking him out" (*op. cit.*, p. 221).

[52] That this is Lerner's point of view may be seen for instance in the following passage from a letter written to me in June, 1943. Discussing the effects of an increase in the propensity to invest in the "classical case" (demand for money to hold equal zero) he writes: "Even in that case there must be a fall in income which decreases the need for cash which lowers the rate of interest so that the investors have a signal that they should increase investment, but an infinitesimal decrease in employment is sufficient to bring about any necessary fall in the rate of interest. . . ."

have already seen, equation (5.1) cannot possibly help us in under-standing the determinants of the rate of interest.[53]

Another consequence of Lerner's formulation is that it leads to the conclusion that the interest rate can always be lowered by increasing the quantity of money, at least to the point where the demand becomes infinitely elastic; while the truth is that no finite change in the quantity of money can hold the interest rate below the full-employment level.[54]

Let us finally note that Lerner's theory is not fully satisfactory even in the "Keynesian case." It is true that in this case saving and invest-ment do not determine the rate of interest, but it is equally clear that the rate of interest does not depend on the quantity of money.

In conclusion, to say that the rate of interest is determined by the schedule $M = f(r)$ is useless and confusing if this schedule is arrived at by previous solution of the entire system; it is an unwarranted simplifi-cation, full of serious consequences, if this function is treated as an ordinary demand function. And the statement that the propensity to save and invest plays no part in determining the rate of interest is true only in a limiting case: the Keynesian case.

20. HICKS'S THEORY—THE RATE OF INTEREST AND THE COST OF INVESTING IN SECURITIES

In *Value and Capital* Hicks has developed what is probably the most daring attempt at reducing the rate of interest to a purely monetary phenomenon.

In Hicks's own words the rate of interest is explained by the "imper-fect moneyness" of securities. "The imperfect moneyness of those bills which are not money is due to their lack of general acceptability: it is this lack of general acceptability which causes the trouble of investing in them"[55] and it is this trouble, namely "the trouble of making trans-actions [i.e., of purchasing securities] which explains the short rate of interest."[56] And these same factors also explain the long rate since the long rate is some average of the short rates plus a premium to cover the risk of (unanticipated) movements in the future short rates.[57]

Thus the rate of interest is explained by the fact that securities are not a medium of exchange and is determined essentially by the cost of

---

[53] To give another example, we can solve the system to obtain, say, the equi-librium output of shoes (Q) as a function of the quantity of money: $Q = f(M, W)$ or $M = F(Q, W)$. But to say that a change in tastes changes the output *because* it shifts this function is formally correct but perfectly useless as a tool of analysis.

[54] Proper qualifications must be made for the case in which the *IS* curve is not monotonic decreasing.

[55] *Value and Capital*, p. 166.

[56] *Ibid.*, p. 165.

[57] *Ibid.*, Chapter XI.

making loan transactions. This is certainly an unusual theory of interest and an astonishing one, to say the least; it appears irreconcilable with the theory we have developed throughout this paper.

Hicks's theory finds its origin in an attempt to answer a question posed by the Keynesian analysis. The reason that induces people to hold assets in the form of cash rather than securities is that the value of even the safest type of securities is not certain: it is subject to changes due to movements in the rate of interest. Now, as we have seen, this risk decreases as the duration of the loan transaction becomes shorter: and it disappears entirely on loans that last only one "Hicksian week" (or one income period in our model) since by hypothesis the rate of interest cannot change. There must then be some other reason to stop people from holding all of their assets in the form of securities and thus reducing their demand for "money to hold" to zero; this reason can only be the cost of investing in this riskless type of loans. This is Hicks's starting point: and so far there seems to be no difference from our own approach as developed in Section 5. But from these correct premises Hicks draws the wrong conclusion: namely *that it is the cost of investing that explains the rate of interest.* To say that the cost of investing is necessary to explain *why* the demand for money to hold is not always zero and to say that it *explains* the rate of interest are quite different statements. There is a logical gap between the two. Thus, for example, from the correct premise that the cost of automobiles in New York cannot fall to zero because they have to be transported from Detroit, there does not logically follow the conclusion that the cost of cars in New York is explained or determined by the cost of transporting them.

There is a different way of explaining the rate of interest, which is not less satisfactory for the fact of being obvious: namely that for certain categories of people (entrepreneurs as well as spendthrifts) it is worth while to pay a premium to obtain spot cash against a promise to pay cash in the future. This is the course we have followed: and it is clearly all that is necessary to explain the existence of the rate of interest. The cost of investing continues to play an important part in our theory: (a) it explains why the demand for money to hold is not identically zero; (b) it explains why the rate of interest can never fall below a certain level in a free capitalistic economy; and hence it explains the pecularities of the Keynesian case. But it is clear that it is not necessary to explain the rate of interest.

Our next task is to show that the cost of investing is also not sufficient to explain the nature of interest. To this end we must disprove Hicks's statement that if people were to be "paid in the form of bills . . . there would be no cost of investment and therefore . . . no reason for the bills to fall to a discount,"[58] i.e., no rate of interest. It is easy to show that, even if "bills" were to be used as medium of exchange, there would be no reason for the rate of interest to fall to zero.

Let us consider first the case of a "stationary state." It is well known that the stationary state is characterized by the fact that the rate of change of the quantity of capital is zero; the marginal efficiency of the existing quantity of capital is equal to the rate of interest, say r_0, that makes net saving equal to zero.[59] Now it is theoretically conceivable that, in this state, securities might replace money as a medium of exchange;[60] their purchasing power would be objectively determined by their discounted value since, by hypothesis, the future rate of interest is known and constant. Their aggregate value would also be constant but, since individual savings need not be zero, there would be a net flow from dissavers to savers. Under these conditions it is clear that securities would continue to yield the rate of interest r_0, even though they would be performing the function of a medium of exchange. Thus, as far as the stationary state goes, Hicks's conclusion does not follow: the interest rate would be zero only in the special case $r_0 = 0$.

Next let us consider an expanding economy, in which the net level of saving and investment is not zero, and let us assume again that it is technically possible for securities to be accepted as a medium of exchange.[61]

In this economy, if there is to be no inflation, it is necessary that the rate of money investment be not larger than the rate of (ex ante) saving. Now there are two possibilities:

(a) There exists some mechanism by which the net increase in outstanding securities cannot exceed net savings. Then the competition of borrowers to obtain loans will automatically determine the level of the rate of interest.

(b) There is no limitation as to the issuance of new securities per unit of time. Then, of course, the rate of interest would be zero, since there would be no necessity for borrowers to compete. But the result would clearly be a situation of unending and progressive inflation. In the first case the stability of the quantity of active money and therefore of the price level is assured by the fact that savers would increase their "hoards" of securities-money, at a rate equal to the net increase in the value of outstanding securities. But in the second case there is nothing

---

[58] *Ibid.*, p. 165.

[59] For a more detailed description of the conditions that give rise to a stationary state see, for instance, M. Timlin, *Keynesian Economics*, Chapter IV.

[60] See, for instance, *ibid.*, p. 53.

[61] This would require that all people agree at all times on the present value of every security.

to stop the price level from rising indefinitely, except if it so happens that the "full employment" rate of interest is zero or negative.[62]

We may therefore safely conclude that the rate of interest is not explained by the fact that securities are not money. Once we recognize this, the complicated and confusing Hicksian theory about the imperfect moneyness of securities becomes unnecessary and should, in our opinion, be abandoned.

To say that different assets share in different degrees the quality of "moneyness" either has no meaning or it is based on a confusion between liquidity and the properties of a medium of exchange. It is true that different assets have different degrees of liquidity, since the liquidity depends on the perfection of the market in which a good is traded. And it is also true that money is probably, under normal conditions, the most liquid of all assets. But the property of money is that it is accepted (freely or by force of law) as a medium of exchange: and liquidity does not make money out of something that is not money. Whatever one's definition of liquidity, to say that a government bond, a speculative share, a house, are money in different degrees, can at best generate unnecessary confusion. It is true that money and securities are close substitutes, but this connection is to be found elsewhere than in degrees of moneyness; it depends on the fact that both money and securities are alternative forms of holding assets in nonphysical form. Securities are thus close substitutes for money, but not for money as a medium of exchange, only for money as an asset.

Having shown that the cost of investment neither explains nor determines the rate of interest, we will agree with Hicks that "the level of that [short] rate of interest measures the trouble involved in investing funds . . . to the marginal lender."[63] One cannot disagree with this statement any more than with the statement that the price of butter measures the marginal utility of butter to each member of the community.[64] Both statements are either tautologies or definitions of rational behavior. They are tautologies if they mean that all those who found it convenient to perform a certain transaction have done so. They are definitions of rational economic behavior if they state the conditions under which economic agents will maximize their satisfac-

---

[62] We are well aware of the fact that the excess of money investment over (ex ante) saving does not lead to inflation, unless there is full employment to begin with, or until full employment is reached. It remains true however that, except in the case mentioned in the text, a zero rate of interest must eventually lead to inflation.

[63] *Op. cit.*, p. 165.

[64] More exactly: the ratio of the price of butter to that of any other commodity measures the ratio of their respective marginal utilities.

tion.[65] But it is clear that whether these statements are tautologies or definitions they are not sufficient to explain either the price of butter or the level of the rate of interest.

To conclude then we agree with Hicks that the rate of interest is at least equal to the cost of investing to the marginal lender, but this statement is not very helpful for understanding the rate of interest. But the Hicksian theory that the rate of interest is determined or simply explained by the imperfect moneyness of securities must be discarded as faulty.

21. SAVING AND INVESTMENT OR SUPPLY OF AND DEMAND FOR CASH?—CONCLUSIONS

It will now be useful, in concluding this paper, to restate in brief form the general theory of interest and money that emerges from our analysis.

We believe that the best way of achieving this aim is to show how, by means of our theory, we can answer the controversial question that has caused so much discussion in recent economic literature.

Is the rate of interest determined by the demand for and supply of cash? Or is it determined by those "real factors," psychological and technological, that can be subsumed under the concepts of propensity to save and marginal efficiency of investment?

We consider it to be a distinct advantage of our theory that we can answer both questions affirmatively. We do not have to choose between these two alternatives any more than between the following two: Is the price of fish determined by the daily demand and the daily supply; or is it determined by the average yearly demand and the cost of fishing?

Since we have maintained throughout this paper that, in general, saving and lending are independent decisions, we must clearly agree that the "daily" rate of interest is determined by the demand for and supply of money to hold (or, for that matter, by demand for and supply of loanable funds).[66] It is this very principle that has formed the base of our analysis of the money market (Section 7). But we cannot stop at this recognition and think that this is sufficient for a general theory of the rate of interest.

To come back to our example, it is certainly true that the daily price

[65] If anything, Hicks's statement is less illuminating, since there is, at least theoretically, the possibility that the rate of interest may exceed the cost of lending idle funds to the marginal lender: it is this very possibility that gives rise to the "classical case."

[66] In this respect we have nothing to add to the arguments developed by Hicks in Chapter XII of *Value and Capital*. There are enough equations to determine all the prices on each Monday and it makes no difference which equation is eliminated.

of fish is entirely explained by the daily catch of fish. But if we want to understand why the daily price fluctuates around a certain level and not around a level ten times as high, we must look for something more fundamental than the good or bad luck of the fishermen on a particular day. We shall then discover that the number of fishermen and the amount of equipment used does not change daily but is determined by the condition that the average returns, through good and bad days, must be sufficiently high to make the occupation of fishing (and investment in fishing equipment) as attractive as alternative ones.

What is obviously true for the price of fish must also hold for the price of loans. The statement that the "daily" rate is determined by the "daily" demand for and supply of money (or, more exactly, of money to hold) does not greatly advance us in the understanding of the true determinants of the rate of interest. This theory by itself is insufficient to explain, for instance, why in countries well-equipped and of great saving capacity, like England or the United States, the system of rates of interest fluctuates around low levels (2 or 3 per cent for the pure long rate and much less for short rates); while it fluctuates around much higher levels (5 or 6 per cent or more for the long rate) in countries poor in savings or rich but scarcely developed. Is that because in the last-mentioned countries the supply of cash is insufficient? Clearly not. The explanation for this difference can only run in terms of those more fundamental factors, technological and psychological, that are included in the propensity to save and the marginal efficiency of investment.

As we have shown in our model the equality of demand and supply of loanable funds is the equilibrium condition for the week (or for our income period) and determines the equilibrium rate of interest (or system of rates) for the week. It corresponds to the short-run equilibrium condition of the Marshallian demand and supply analysis: price equals marginal cost. But the stock of money to hold (the supply) tends itself to change and thus push the "daily" rate toward the level at which the flow of money saving equals the flow of money investment. The condition, (ex ante) saving = (ex ante) investment, corresponds to the long-run Marshallian condition (under perfect competition): price = average cost including rent.

The first condition is satisfied even in the short period since it is the result of decisions that can be carried out instantaneously (see Section 5). The second is a long-run condition and therefore may actually never be satisfied: but it is necessary to explain the level toward which the weekly rate tends (even though this level may never be reached since the long-run equilibrium rate of interest itself changes).

Thus, to complete our theory, we must be able to explain what determines the level of long-run equilibrium. At this point we find that our answer is not unique since it depends on the assumptions concerning the form of the supply-of-labor schedule.

I. As long as wages are flexible, the long-run equilibrium rate of interest is determined exclusively by real factors, that is to say, essentially by the propensity to save and the marginal efficiency of investment. The condition, money saving = money investment, determines the price level and not the rate of interest.

II. If wages are rigid it is still true that the long-run equilibrium rate of interest is determined by the propensities to save and to invest but the situation is now more complicated; for these propensities depend also on money income and therefore on the quantity of active money which in turn depends itself on the level of the rate of interest. Thus, unless wages are perfectly flexible or the supply of money is always so adjusted as to assure the maintenance of full employment, the long-run equilibrium rate of interest depends also on the quantity of money and it is determined, together with money income, by equations (1), (2), and (3) of our model. We want however to stress again that the dependence of the rate of interest on the quantity of money does not depend on liquidity preference. In a system with rigid wages not only interest but also almost every economic variable depends on the quantity of money.

III. Finally our theory of the rate of interest becomes even less uniform when we take into account the "Keynesian case." In this case clearly the long-run equilibrium rate of interest is the rate which makes the demand for money to hold infinitely elastic. The economic theorist here is forced to recognize that under certain conditions the rate of interest is determined exclusively by institutional factors.

Bard College of Columbia University

Postscript

I want to take the opportunity offered by this reprinting to warn the reader that the latter part of section 13, beginning with the second paragraph on page 125, contains several errors which vitiate the argument — though the main conclusion can be salvaged. These errors and their implications were first pointed out by D. Patinkin, in "Relative prices, Say's Law and the Demand for Money," *Econometrica*, April 1948, and elaborated in *Money Interest and Prices*, Row, Peterson, 1956, appendix to Chapter 8. While it is not possible in this postscript to provide a rigorous restatement, we offer a brief sketch of the correct formulation.

In the first place, in line with the model used throughout the rest of the paper, one must add to the $n - 1$ commodities and money mentioned on page 126, an $n + 1$ good, namely bonds, a good whose quantity may be positive (credits) or negative (debts). Also, when credits and debts are taken into account, the homogeneity of zero degree in prices of the *individual* demand functions for commodities no longer logically follows from rational behavior. Nor can homogeneity be introduced as a plausible, ad hoc, behavior assumption.

On the other hand it can be verified that, provided (a) the given money supply consists entirely of bank money which is offset by the debt of the private sector to the banking system, and (b) all existing bonds represent claims on, or liabilities to, the private sector (including banks), then *aggregate* private real wealth will be invariant under a proportional change of all prices (no Pigou effect exists). Under these conditions it is both permissible and justifiable to postulate that (c) the *market* demand for each commodity is homogeneous of zero degree and the *market* demand for money is homogeneous of first degree, in all commodity prices. Indeed (c) is then equivalent to assuming that the aggregate demand for each commodity and for money is unaffected by a mere redistribution of wealth. Such an assumption does not seem unreasonable, at least as a convenient first approximation. (It follows of course from assumptions (a) to (c) that the net demand for bonds by household and banks combined is not homogeneous in prices, as can be verified from the budget equation of individuals plus banks).

Under assumptions (a) to (c) the argument in the rest of the paper remains valid. That the bond market is, at times, not given explicit treatment, is accounted for by the fact that, through the so-called Walras Law, one of the markets is necessarily cleared when the remaining ones are cleared, and hence need not be explicitly exhibited.

January 1960.

Econometrica, Vol. 13, No. 4 (October, 1945)

MULTIPLIER EFFECTS OF A BALANCED BUDGET*†

By Trygve Haavelmo

1. INTRODUCTION

It has commonly been argued that public spending, to be a remedy against unemployment, must be *deficit* spending and not spending balanced by an equal amount of taxes, since, in the latter case, the government would only be taking back with one hand what it gives with the other. One necessary qualification of this statement is, of course, well known, namely, that taxes corresponding to an equal amount of public spending may lead to a redistribution of incomes which, in turn, may lead to a higher level of national consumption at a given level of private investment. The effect of such redistribution, however, depends essentially on whether or not there is any substantial difference in the marginal propensities to consume, as between the various income groups. If, for example, the propensity-to-consume function of the individual is a linear function of personal income the marginal propensity to consume will be constant for all levels of income, and there could be no redistribution effect (unless the redistribution had an effect on private investment).

In this latter case it might then be thought that public spending balanced by an equal amount of taxes would have no effect upon total income and employment in the society (apart from a possible effect, indirectly, on the propensity to invest). This commonly made conjecture is, however, false, as has already been pointed out by several writers on the subject.[1] In a situation with unemployment and idle resources there is a definite employment-creating effect of public outlays even when they are fully covered by tax revenues. And this is true quite

* Cowles Commission Papers, New Series, No. 12.

† I wish to express my sincere thanks to Professor J. Marschak for many helpful suggestions.

[1] See, e.g., P. A. Samuelson, "Full Employment After the War" in *Postwar Economic Problems*, edited by S. E. Harris, New York, 1943, p. 44.

A. H. Hansen and H. S. Perloff, *State and Local Finance in the National Economy*, New York, 1944, pp. 245–246.

N. Kaldor, "The Quantitative Aspects of the Full Employment Problem in Britain," Appendix C in William H. Beveridge, *Full Employment in a Free Society*, New York, 1945, pp. 346–347.

Henry C. Wallich, "Income-generating Effects of a Balanced Budget," *Quarterly Journal of Economics*, Vol. 59, November, 1944, pp. 78–91. (My attention has been drawn to this important article which I had not heard of at the time when my manuscript was submitted for publication. Mr. Wallich's paper, I am sure, deserves more extensive comments than those I had occasion to add to the present article).

apart from whatever other effects the taxes and the expenditures might have on the distribution of income or on the behavior of consumers and investors.

Although this idea is not a new one, there still seems to be much need for a rigorous theoretical analysis of the whole subject. The existing literature is not altogether clear on the matter. Mr. Kaldor, for example, in discussing the possibility of full employment under a balanced budget, explains the matter as follows:

> Full employment could be secured, however, by means of increased public outlay, even if the State expenditure is fully covered by taxation—for the reason that an increase in taxation is not likely to reduce private outlay by the full amount of the taxes paid. It may be assumed that all taxes have some influence on the savings of the individuals on whom they fall; taxes which fall on the poor have a relatively large effect on consumption and a relatively small effect on savings; with taxes paid by the rich it is probably the other way round. Hence an increase in public expenditure will cause a net addition to the total outlay of the community even if it is covered by taxation; . . . .[2]

This statement would seem to convey the idea that taxes equal to public expenditure can create employment only to the extent that they cut down on people's savings. This is not correct. We shall show below that public expenditures covered by taxes have an employment-generating effect which is *independent* of the numerical value of the propensity to consume.

Hansen and Perloff, in their comments on the same subject, write as follows:

> . . . Moreover, an increase in useful governmental expenditures (the initial expenditure being financed by borrowing) will tend to raise the national income even though subsequently financed from consumption taxes. Thus, when additional government expenditures are paid out to the public, the income receipts of individuals are increased. If, now, subsequently a consumption tax is imposed equivalent to the enlarged income, it follows that private expenditures after taxes remain as before. The Gross National Product is increased by the amount of the new government spending while private expenditures remain the same. Thus in this case the total Gross National Product (governmental expenditures plus private expenditures) is enlarged roughly by the amount of the new expenditure but not by a magnified amount.[3]

Here the final conclusion, namely that expenditures covered by taxes will raise income (and employment) by the amount of the tax, is correct. The assumption of the initial expenditure's being financed by borrowing is, however, unnecessary. Indeed, if this assumption were necessary, the conclusion would not hold in the second year, the third year, etc., since then current expenditure would equal current taxes.

---

[2] Kaldor, *op. cit.*, p. 346.
[3] Hansen and Perloff, *op. cit.*, p. 245.

Mr. Wallich, in his recent article dealing directly with the subject discussed here, has reached the same conclusion as Hansen and Perloff. He has a clear illustration in terms of a numerical example. His more general discussion of the "reason why," however, might perhaps give rise to misunderstandings. He writes, in part:

> The reason why national income can increase in this instance, without an increase in investment and without a redistribution of income from the higher to the lower income groups, is that the additional income financed by the Government does not give rise to new net saving. It is true that the previously unemployed will save part of their new income, but an equal volume of savings of the initially employed is absorbed by the additional tax. Since the two groups are assumed to be similar, the savings of one are offset by the reduction in the savings of the other. [Footnote omitted] By absorbing part of originally existing income and respending it in its entirety, the Government prevents some fraction of this amount from being saved, as it otherwise would be. . . .[4]

If investment is assumed to remain constant it seems unnecessary to prove that saving remains constant. What is needed is a rigorous proof that under these circumstances total income will actually rise as a result of the taxation and spending. For this purpose the argument that the government spends income that otherwise would have been partly saved is dangerous as it might lead to the false belief that the higher the propensity to save for the public the larger the effect of the fiscal policy discussed. As already mentioned we shall see that this is not the case.

The whole matter may in fact be stated much more simply as follows: Let us use the words "net income" to designate the sum of incomes at the individuals' disposal after they had paid the taxes. The words "gross income" will mean the sum of individuals' incomes before taxes. Gross income is thus the sum of earnings made by individuals in producing goods and services: it is equal to the money value of goods and services produced, either for private or for public needs. Thus while the demand of private people for goods and services depends on net income, their employment depends on gross income. Extra public expenditure covered, simultaneously, by taxes can obviously be added to the existing gross income in such a way that it will leave the people with exactly the same amount of net income, and hence will leave the private demand at exactly the same level as before the tax was imposed (provided the tax policy does not lead to a change in the distribution of net incomes and, thereby, to a change in the marginal propensity to consume of the society as a whole). But, while the government collects the tax money without any direct compensation to the individual taxpayer, the government requires goods and services from

[4] Wallich, *op. cit.*, p. 80.

the public in return for money expenditures. Now, if there were already
full employment before the tax was imposed, the result would be that
the public as a whole would have to work partly for the government
instead of working for their own direct benefit. Then they could not pay
the taxes by working more. If, however, there is a sufficient amount of
idle manpower and resources the amount of employment and productive services required by the government will come forth in *addition* to
what is wanted by the private sector of the economy. The gross income,
i.e., the money value of all goods and services produced (for private as
well as public needs) will have increased, although the net income has
remained unchanged. In fact, from an employment point of view, the
result for the society as a whole will be exactly the same as if the government had ordered idle manpower and resources to work without any
direct compensation.

In the following we propose to give a more accurate demonstration
of this simple conclusion.

2. THE SIMPLEST CASE: A LINEAR CONSUMPTION FUNCTION

The assumption of a linear consumption function is of particular interest here, since, in that case, as already mentioned, no multiplier
effect can result from a redistribution of incomes. This simplifying assumption, therefore, allows us to isolate whatever "pure" multiplier
effects might be generated by public spending balanced by taxes.

We shall use the symbol r to denote gross individual money income,
while $\bar{r}$ will denote gross average individual money income, and R gross
total national money income. (Throughout this study we shall assume
that there are sufficient unused manpower and resources available to
justify the assumption of a constant level of prices. We shall further
assume that we are dealing with a "closed economy.") Since we shall be
interested in comparing incomes before and after imposing a certain
income tax we shall indicate by r_0, $\bar{r}_0$, and R_0 the individual, average,
and total income, respectively, *before* any tax is imposed, while r, $\bar{r}$,
and R will be used to denote the same income concepts (gross, i.e.,
including taxes paid) after a certain income tax is imposed. The total
number of individuals, N, is assumed to remain constant.

We assume that the private consumption expenditure, $u(r_0)$, of an
individual having the net income r_0 is given by

$$(2.1) \qquad u(r_0) = ar_0 + b,$$

where a and b are positive constants $(0 < a < 1)$. Then, whatever be the
income distribution, the average consumer expenditure $\bar{u}$ is given by

$$(2.2) \qquad \bar{u} = u(\bar{r}_0) = a\bar{r}_0 + b$$

and the total consumer expenditure of all the individuals, $U(R_0)$, is given by

$$(2.3) \qquad U(R_0) = aR_0 + Nb.$$

Let V denote total private investment. In all that follows we shall assume V to remain constant. The average investment V/N, then also a constant, we shall denote by v. Total national income R_0 (=total consumer and investment expenditures) is then defined implicitly by

$$(2.4) \qquad R_0 = aR_0 + Nb + V,$$

which gives

$$(2.5) \qquad R_0 = \frac{Nb + V}{1 - a}.$$

If now a tax totalling T dollars is imposed on incomes, and the tax money is fully spent by the government, the resulting total gross national income, earned in the production of goods and services for both private and government use (=consumer expenditure+private investment+government spending) is defined implicitly by

$$(2.6) \qquad R = a(R - T) + Nb + V + T,$$

which gives

$$(2.7) \qquad R = \frac{Nb + V}{1 - a} + T.$$

Comparing (2.5) and (2.7) we have the following

THEOREM I: *If the consumption function is linear, and total private investment is a constant, a tax, T, that is fully spent will raise total gross national income by an amount T and leave total private net income and consumption unchanged. And this holds regardless of the numerical value of the marginal propensity to consume, a.*

The result obtained may also be expressed as follows: If the government spends T dollars and at the same time covers this expenditure by taxes, the multiplier effect, per dollar spent, will be equal to 1.

This, of course, does not mean that the net income and consumption of every single individual necessarily remain the same after the tax has been imposed. For the tax is a certain loss of net income to every individual while the gain from the government expenditure is only an average gain. The individual gains might differ widely.

From (2.7) it follows that by making T sufficiently large one can reach a full-employment level of R. It is interesting to consider the *rate* of taxation that such a full-employment policy might require. Let λ be the tax rate imposed on R. [The distribution of the taxes as between the various individual incomes is here irrelevant, owing to the assumption (2.1).] Then we have

$$(2.8) \qquad R = aR(1 - \lambda) + Nb + V + \lambda R$$

or

$$(2.9) \qquad R = \frac{Nb + V}{(1 - a)(1 - \lambda)} = \frac{R_0}{(1 - \lambda)} .$$

In other words, a tax rate of, say, 50 per cent will double the total gross income that existed before the tax was imposed.

In the preceding analysis it has of course been assumed that the various services and benefits which the government is able to provide through the spending of the tax money are not counted by the individuals as a part of their consumption or their savings. This assumption is necessary in order to consider a and b as independent of the tax. The government might no doubt provide such services and benefits in return for the taxes that, in particular, the demand for private savings would be reduced. The government might, on the other hand, provide goods and services that would cover a certain part of regular consumer needs. If, as a result of the tax and spending policy, the propensity to consume were changed from a to, say, $a(\lambda)$ then, instead of (2.9), we would have

$$(2.10) \qquad R_1 = \frac{R_0(1 - a)}{(1 - \lambda)[1 - a(\lambda)]} .$$

If $a(\lambda) > a$, $R_1 > R$; if $a(\lambda) < a$, $R_1 < R$.

It would no doubt take a considerable amount of research to obtain actual information on the influence on consumers' behavior of the various types of services and benefits provided directly or indirectly by the government. But such a study might be well worth while.

3. MORE GENERAL CASE: NONLINEAR CONSUMPTION FUNCTION

We shall first study the effect of a proportional income tax imposed on all individual incomes, the total tax revenue being spent by the government. Since we assume that the consumption function might be nonlinear we shall have to make some additional assumptions about the behavior of the income distribution through this process of taxation and public spending. The usual simplifying assumption is that "the income distribution remains unchanged." Taken literally, this assumption makes little sense, since a "constant income distribution" would mean that the total (or average) income as well as all other parameters of the distribution would have to remain constant at one level. Usually, what is meant is that, if the average income varies, the income distribution will be subject only to a proportional stretch or squeeze.

Let $\Phi(x)$ denote a certain relative frequency distribution where the average of x is equal to 1, and let us assume that the ratio $r/\bar{r}$ is distributed as x, for all values of $\bar{r}$. The distribution of r will then be

$$(3.1) \qquad \Phi\left(\frac{r}{\bar{r}}\right)\frac{1}{\bar{r}},$$

i.e., the distribution will belong to a parametric class defined by the form Φ, and the parameter $\bar{r}$. We shall assume here that the structure of the economy is such that the income distribution always must belong to this class.

Let r_0 denote individual incomes before the tax is imposed, and let us assume as before that the average investment per individual, v, is a given constant. Further, let the consumption function be $u(r_0)$. Then the average income, $\bar{r}_0$, is given by

$$(3.2) \qquad \bar{r}_0 = \int_0^\infty u(r_0)\,\Phi\left(\frac{r_0}{\bar{r}_0}\right)\frac{1}{\bar{r}_0}\,dr_0 + v.$$

If now a proportional tax rate λ is imposed, the resulting gross average income, $\bar{r}$, is defined by

$$(3.3) \qquad \bar{r} = \int_0^\infty u[r(1-\lambda)]\,\Phi\left(\frac{r}{\bar{r}}\right)\frac{1}{\bar{r}}\,dr + \lambda\bar{r} + v.$$

If we denote the net income, namely $(1-\lambda)r$, by r_t, and the average of r_t by $\bar{r}_t$, this relation may be written as

$$(3.4) \qquad \bar{r}_t = \int_0^\infty u(r_t)\,\Phi\left(\frac{r_t}{\bar{r}_t}\right)\frac{1}{\bar{r}_t}\,dr_t + v.$$

Comparing (3.2) and (3.4) we see that the implicit definition of $\bar{r}_0$ by (3.2) is identical with the implicit definition of $\bar{r}_t$ by (3.4). Hence, if this definition is unique, we have

$$(3.5) \qquad \bar{r}_t = \bar{r}_0, \qquad \bar{r} = \frac{\bar{r}_0}{1-\lambda}.$$

We therefore have

THEOREM II: *If the income distribution has the property of always remaining within the class defined by (3.1) the effect of a proportional tax, fully spent, will be exactly the same as if the propensity-to-consume function had been linear, i.e., private net income and consumption remain unchanged while gross national income rises by the total amount of the tax, and this result is independent of the form of u.*

We have studied the particular case of a proportional tax rate because this seemed the most reasonable assumption in connection with the assumption that the income distribution always must belong to the one-parameter class (3.1). But the particular assumption about a proportional tax rate is not essential. If the assumption is made that also the distribution of net income, r_t, always must belong to the same parametric family of the type (3.1) then our results will follow without making any separate restrictions upon the manner in which the taxes are collected and spent. For we can then write down the equation (3.4) directly. This equation defines $\bar{r}_t$ as a function of v independently of the size and the distribution of the tax. We must, therefore, have $\bar{r}_t = \bar{r}_0$, and $\bar{r} = \bar{r}_0 +$ the average amount of tax. This gives us:

THEOREM III: *If the structure of the economy is such that it maintains a constant "relative" distribution of net incomes whatever the tax is, then the average net income will be the same as before the tax was imposed, while total gross income will increase by the total amount of the tax.*

It might perhaps be worth while in this connection to point out that the assumption we have made about the income distribution is *not* exactly equivalent to saying that "all incomes change in the same proportion." For let $\Phi(r_0/\bar{r}_0)/\bar{r}_0$ and $\Phi(r_t/\bar{r}_t)/\bar{r}_t$ be the income distribution before and after imposing the tax, respectively. Then these two distributions are only the *marginal* distributions of the two variables r_0 and r_t. The knowledge of these two distributions does not uniquely determine the *joint* distribution of r_0 and r_t. If, for example—and only as an illustration—the two distributions were normal distributions, the correlation coefficient would still be free to take any value from -1 to $+1$. The practical meaning of this remark is that a study of the income distribution before and after the introduction of a tax will not fully reveal the eventual "reshuffling" that the individual income receivers might have been subject to as a result of the tax and spending policy of the government.

* * *

It would of course be interesting to study the effects of more general forms of tax rates and more general forms of respending the tax money. Such an analysis, however, would take us into a general discussion of the effects of a redistribution of incomes, and that was not our objective. We only wanted to demonstrate that a "balanced budget" has a direct multplier effect, with a multiplier equal to 1, in *addition* to whatever (positive or negative) effects there might be from a redistribution of income.

Washington, D. C.

Reprinted from Evsey D. Domar, *Essays in the Theory of
Economic Growth* (New York: Oxford University Press, 1957),
pp. 70–82

Capital Expansion, Rate of Growth, and Employment*[1]

I

Introduction

This paper deals with a problem that is both old and new—the relation between capital accumulation and employment. In economic
literature it has been discussed a number of times, the most notable
contribution belonging to Marx. More recently, it was brought forth
by Keynes and his followers.

A thorough analysis of the economic aspects of capital accumulation is a tremendous job. The only way in which the problem can be
examined at all in a short paper like this is by isolating it from the
general economic structure and introducing a number of simplifying
assumptions. Some of them are not entirely necessary and, as the
argument progresses, the reader will see how they can be modified
or removed.

The following assumptions and definitions should be noted at the
start: (a) there is a constant general price level; (b) no lags are
present; (c) savings and investment refer to the income of the same

* [Reprinted by permission from *Econometrica*, Vol. 14 (Apr., 1946), pp.
137–47. Essay IV presents much of the discussion of this paper in a less technical language, but lacks its mathematical derivations.

As indicated in the Foreword of my work *Essays in the Theory of Economic
Growth*, I am not quite happy with the concepts used here. A concurrent reading of
the relevant part of the Foreword (pp. 6–8) is recommended.]

[1] This is a summary of a paper presented before a joint session of the Econometric Society and the American Statistical Association in Cleveland on Jan.
24, 1946. Many thanks for help and criticism go to my fellow members of the
'Little Seminar': Paul Baran, Svend Laursen, Lloyd A. Metzler, Richard A.
Musgrave, Mary S. Painter, Melvin W. Reder, Tibor Scitovsky, Alfred Sher-
rard, Mary Wise Smelker, Merlin Smelker, and most of all to James S.
Duesenberry.

period; (d) both are net of depreciation; (e) depreciation is not measured by historical costs, but by the cost of replacing the depreciated asset by another one of the same productive capacity;[2] (f) productive capacity of an asset or of the whole economy is a measurable concept.

The last assumption, on which (e) also depends, is not at all safe. Productive capacity, whether of a certain piece of capital equipment or of the whole economy, depends not only on physical and technical factors, but also on the whole complex of economic and institutional conditions, such as distribution of income, consumers' preferences, relative wage rates, relative prices, and the structure of industry, many of which are in turn affected by the behavior of the variables analyzed here. We shall nevertheless assume all these conditions to be given, and shall mean by the productive capacity of an economy its total output when its labor force is fully employed in some conventional sense.[3]

The economy will be said to be in equilibrium when its productive capacity P equals its national income Y. Our first task is to discover the conditions under which this equilibrium can be maintained, or more precisely, the rate of growth at which the economy must expand in order to remain in a continuous state of full employment.

II

The Problem of Growth

The idea that the preservation of full employment in a capitalist economy requires a growing income goes back (in one form or another) at least to Marx. It has been fully recognized in numerous

---

[2] If the original machine worth $1,000 and producing 100 units is replaced by another one worth also $1,000, but producing 120 units, only $833.33 will be regarded as replacement, and the remaining $166.67 as new investment. A similar correction is made when the new machine costs more or less than the original one. The treatment of depreciation, particularly when accompanied by sharp technological and price changes, presents an extremely difficult problem. It is quite possible that our approach, while convenient for present purposes, may give rise to serious difficulties in the future. [No distinction is made in this paper between replacement and depreciation. This distinction is developed in Essay VII.]

[3] It is undoubtedly possible to work out a more precise definition of productive capacity, but I prefer to leave the matter open, because a more precise definition is not entirely necessary in this paper and can be worked out as and when

studies (recently made in Washington and elsewhere) of the magnitude of gross national product needed to maintain full employment.
But though the various authors come to different numerical results,
they all approach their problem from the point of view of the size
of the labor force. The labor force (manhours worked) and its productivity are supposed to increase according to one formula or
another, and if full employment is to be maintained, national income
must grow at the combined rate. For practical relatively short-run
purposes this is a good method, but its analytical merits are not
high, because it presents a theoretically incomplete system: since
an increase in labor force or in its productivity only raises productive
capacity and does not by itself generate income (similar to that
produced by investment), the demand side of the equation is missing.
Nor is the difficulty disposed of by Mr. Kalecki's method according
to which capital should increase proportionally to the increase in
labor force and its productivity.[4] As Mrs. Robinson well remarked,
'The rate of increase in productivity of labor is not something given
by Nature.'[5] Labor productivity is not a function of technological
progress in the abstract, but technological progress embodied in
capital goods, and the amount of capital goods in general. Even
without technological progress, capital accumulation increases labor
productivity, at least to a certain point, both because more capital
is used per workman in each industry and because there is a shift
of labor to industries that use more capital and can afford to pay a
higher wage. So if labor productivity is affected by capital accumulation, the formula that the latter should proceed at the same rate as
the former (and as the increase in labor force) is not as helpful as it
appears.

The standard Keynesian system does not provide the tools for
deriving the equilibrium rate of growth. Growth is entirely absent

needed. [In the original version of the paper, productive capacity of an economy
was defined as 'its total output when all productive factors are fully employed.'
I have changed the definition because it contradicted the meaning in which the
concept of productive capacity was used throughout the paper. This important
correction was suggested by Edith T. Penrose.]

[4] See his essay, 'Three Ways to Full Employment' in *The Economics of Full
Employment* (Oxford, 1944), p. 47, and also his 'Full Employment by Stimulating Private Investment?' in *Oxford Economic Papers*, No. 7 (Mar., 1945), pp.
83–92.

[5] See her review of *The Economics of Full Employment*, *The Economic Journal*,
Vol. 55 (Apr., 1945), p. 79.

from it because it is not concerned with changes in productive capacity. This approach permits the assumption that employment is a function of national income (and the wage unit), an assumption which can be justified for short periods of time, but which will result in serious errors over a period of a few years. Clearly, a full employment level of income of five years ago would create considerable unemployment today. *We shall assume instead that employment is a function of the ratio of national income to productive capacity.* While this approach seems to me to be superior to that of Keynes, it should be looked upon as a second approximation rather than a final solution: it does not allow us to separate unused capacity into idle machines and idle men; depending upon the circumstances, the same ratio of income to capacity may yield different fractions of the labor force employed.

Because investment in the Keynesian system is merely an instrument for generating income, the system does not take into account the extremely essential, elementary, and well-known fact that investment also increases productive capacity.[6] This *dual* character of the investment process makes the approach to the equilibrium rate of growth from the investment (capital) point of view more promising: if investment both increases productive capacity and generates income, it provides us with *both* sides of the equation the solution of which may yield the required rate of growth.

Let investment proceed at the rate I per year, and let s be the ratio of the productive capacity net of depreciation (net value added) of the new projects to capital invested in them (I).[7] The net annual potential output of these projects will then be equal to Is. But the productive capacity of the whole economy may increase by a smaller amount, because the operations of these new projects may involve a transfer of labor (and other factors) from other plants, whose productive capacity is therefore reduced.[8] We shall define σ, the

[6] Whether every dollar invested increases productive capacity is essentially a matter of definition. It can safely be said that investment taken as a whole certainly does. To make this statement hold in regard to residential housing, imputed rent should be included in the national income. See also note 19.

[7] The use of the word 'project' does not imply that investment is done by the government, or that it is always made in new undertakings. I am using 'project' (in the absence of a better term) because investment can mean the act of investing and the result of the act.

[8] I am disregarding the external economies and diseconomies of the older plants due to the operation of the new projects.

potential social average investment productivity, as

$$(1) \qquad \sigma = \frac{\dfrac{dP}{dt}}{I}.$$

The following characteristics of σ should be noted:

1. It does not imply that factors of production other than capital and technology remain constant. On the contrary, its magnitude depends to a very great extent on technological progress. It would be more correct to say that σ refers to an increase in capacity accompanying rather than caused by investment.

2. σ refers to the increase in *potential* capacity. Whether or not this potential increase results in a larger income depends on the behavior of expenditures.

3. σ is concerned with the increase in productive capacity of the whole society, and not with the rate of return derived or expected from investment. Therefore σ is not affected directly by changes in distribution of income.

4. s is the maximum that σ can attain. The difference between them will depend on the magnitude of the rate of investment on the one hand, and on the growth of other factors, such as labor and natural resources, and on technological progress on the other. A misdirection of investment will also produce a difference between s and σ.

We shall make the heroic assumption that s and σ are constant. From (1) it follows that

$$(2) \qquad \frac{dP}{dt} = I\sigma.$$

It is important to note that, with a given σ, dP/dt is a function of I, and not of dI/dt. Whether dI/dt is positive or negative, dP/dt is always positive so long as σ and I are positive.

Expression (2) showing the increase in productive capacity is essentially the supply side of our system. On the demand side we have the multiplier theory, too familiar to need any comment, except for an emphasis on the obvious but often forgotten fact that with any given marginal propensity to save, *dY/dt is a function not of I, but of dI/dt*. Indicating the marginal propensity to save by α, and assuming it to be constant,[9] we have the simple relationship that

$$(3) \qquad \frac{dY}{dt} = \frac{dI}{dt} \frac{1}{\alpha}.$$

Let the economy be in an equilibrium position so that[10]

$$(4) \qquad P_0 = Y_0.$$

To retain the equilibrium position, we must have

$$(5) \qquad \frac{dP}{dt} = \frac{dY}{dt}.$$

Substituting (2) and (3) into (5) we obtain our fundamental equation

$$(6) \qquad I\sigma = \frac{dI}{dt} \frac{1}{\alpha},$$

the solution of which gives

$$(7) \qquad I = I_0 e^{\alpha\sigma t}.$$

$\alpha\sigma$ is the equilibrium rate of growth. So long as it remains constant, *the maintenance of full employment requires investment to grow at a constant relative or compound interest rate.*

If, as a crude estimate, α is taken at 12 per cent and σ at some 30 per cent, the equilibrium rate of growth will be some 3.6 per cent per year.[10a]

[9] Over the period 1879–1941 the average propensity to save (ratio of net capital formation to national income) was fairly constant and approximately equal to some 12 per cent. See Simon Kuznets, *National Product Since 1869*, National Bureau of Economic Research (mimeographed, 1945), p. II-89 [since published under the same title (New York, 1946), p. 119] and the *Survey of Current Business*, Vol. 22 (May, 1942), and Vol. 24 (Apr., 1944). In a cyclical problem the assumption of a constant propensity to save would be very bad. Since we are interested here in a secular problem of maintaining continuous full employment, this assumption is not too dangerous.

[10] The problem can be also worked out for the case when $P_0 > Y_0$.

[10a] After this paper was sent to the printer, I found a very interesting article by E. H. Stern, 'Capital Requirements in Progressive Economies,' *Economica*, n.s., Vol. 12 (Aug., 1945), pp. 163–71, in which the relation between capital and output in the U.S. during 1879–1929 is expressed (in billions of dollars) as *capital* = 3.274 *income* − 3.55. My estimates gave roughly similar results. This would place *s* around 30 per cent, though this figure should be raised to account for the underutilization of capital during a part of that period. It is also not clear how the junking process (see below) was reflected in these figures.

The average rate of growth of real national income over the period 1879–1941 was some 3.3 per cent. See Table V and Appendix B of Essay II.

The reader will now see that the assumption of constant α and σ is not entirely necessary, and that the whole problem can be worked out with variable α and σ.

III

The Effects of Growth

Our next problem is to explore what happens when investment does grow at some constant percentage rate r, which, however, is not necessarily equal to the equilibrium rate $\alpha\sigma$. It will be necessary to introduce two additional concepts: average propensity to save I/Y and the average ratio of productive capacity to capital P/K. To simplify the problem, we shall assume that

1. $I/Y = \alpha$, so that the average propensity to save is equal to the marginal.

2. $P/K = s$, i.e. the ratio of productive capacity to capital for the whole economy is equal to that of the new investment projects.

We shall consider first the special simple case $\sigma = s$, and then the more general case when $\sigma < s$.[11]

Case 1: $\sigma = s$. Since $I = I_0 e^{rt}$, capital, being the sum of all net investments, equals

$$(8) \qquad K = K_0 + I_0 \int_0^t e^{rt} dt = K_0 + \frac{I_0}{r}(e^{rt} - 1).$$

As t becomes large, K will approach the expression

$$(9) \qquad \frac{I_0}{r} e^{rt},$$

so that capital will also grow at a rate approaching r.

As $Y = (1/\alpha) I_0 e^{rt}$, the ratio of income to capital is

$$(10) \qquad \frac{Y}{K} = \frac{\dfrac{1}{\alpha} I_0 e^{rt}}{K_0 + \dfrac{I_0}{r}(e^{rt} - 1)},$$

[11] It is also possible that, owing to capital-saving inventions in existing plants, $\sigma > s$. Formally this case can be excluded by falling back on the definition of depreciation given in note 2. This, however, is not a very happy solution, but the approach used in this paper will hardly offer a better one. I think, however, that α in our society is sufficiently high to make $\sigma > s$ in a continuous state of full employment more an exception than a rule.

and

(11) $$\lim_{t \to \infty} \frac{Y}{K} = \frac{r}{\alpha}.$$

Thus so long as r and α remain constant (or change in the same proportion) no 'deepening' of capital takes place. This, roughly speaking, was the situation in the United States over the last seventy years or so prior to World War II.

Substituting $K = P/s$ into (11) we obtain

(12) $$\lim_{t \to \infty} \frac{Y}{P} = \frac{r}{\alpha s}.$$

Since in the present case $\sigma = s$,

(13) $$\lim_{t \to \infty} \frac{Y}{P} = \frac{r}{\alpha \sigma}.$$

The expression

(14) $$\theta = \frac{r}{\alpha \sigma}$$

may be called the *coefficient of utilization*. When the economy grows at the equilibrium rate, so that $r = \alpha\sigma$, $\theta = 100$ per cent and productive capacity is fully utilized. But as r falls below $\alpha\sigma$, a fraction of capacity $(1 - \theta)$ is gradually left unused.[12] *Thus the failure of the economy to grow at the required rate creates unused capacity and unemployment.*

Case 2: $\sigma < s$. As investment proceeds at the rate I, new projects with a productive capacity of Is are built. Since the productive capacity of the whole economy increases only by $I\sigma$, it follows that somewhere in the economy (not excluding the new projects) productive capacity is reduced by $I(s - \sigma)$. Therefore every year an amount of capital equal to $I(s - \sigma)/s$ becomes useless.

The problem can now be approached from two points of view. The amounts $I(s - \sigma)/s$ can be looked upon as capital losses, which are not taken into account in calculating income and investment.[13] In this case, I still indicates the rate of net investment, and all other

[12] It should be noted that if r, α, and σ are constant, θ is also a constant. Even though the economy fails to grow at the required rate, the relative disparity between its capacity and income does not become wider, because its capital also grows not at the $\alpha\sigma$ but at the r rate.

[13] These losses are not necessarily losses in the accounting sense. See note 14.

symbols retain their old meaning, except that capital has to be redefined as the integral of investment *minus* capital losses: every year chunks of capital (over and above depreciation) are written off and junked. The annual addition to capital will then be

(15) $$\frac{dK}{dt} = I - \frac{I(s - \sigma)}{s} = I\frac{\sigma}{s},$$

and

(16) $$K = K_0 + I_0 \frac{\sigma}{s} \int_0^t e^{rt} dt = K_0 + I_0 \frac{\sigma}{sr}(e^{rt} - 1).$$

Also,

(17) $$\lim_{t \to \infty} \frac{Y}{K} = \frac{r}{\alpha} \cdot \frac{s}{\sigma},$$

and

(18) $$\lim_{t \to \infty} \frac{Y}{P} = \frac{r}{\alpha\sigma},$$

which is exactly the same result we had in (13).

The second approach consists in treating the amounts $I(s - \sigma)/s$ not as capital losses but as a special allowance for obsolescence. Net investment would then have to be defined not as I, but as $I\sigma/s$. Other symbols would have to be redefined accordingly, and the whole problem could then be reworked in the same way as on pp. 76–7.

In a sense the choice between these two methods is a matter of bookkeeping; depending upon the character of the problem in hand, one or the other can be used, though I suspect that the second method can easily become misleading. The nature of the process will be the same whichever method is used. The fact is that, owing to a difference between s and σ, the construction of new investment projects makes certain assets (not excluding the new projects themselves) useless, because under the new conditions brought about by changes in demand, or a rise in the wage rates, or both, the products of these assets cannot be sold.[14] As stated on p. 73 the difference

[14] To be strictly true, the statement in the text would require considerable divisibility of capital assets. In the absence of such divisibility, the expression 'junking' should not be taken too literally.

The fact that these assets may still be operated to some extent or that their products are sold at lower prices or that both these conditions exist does not invalidate our argument, because σ, being expressed in real terms, will be higher than it would be if the assets were left completely unused.

between s and σ is created either by misdirection of investment or by the lack of balance between the propensity to save on the one hand, and the growth of labor, discovery of natural resources, and technological progress on the other. So long as mistakes are made or this lack of balance exists, the junking process is inevitable.

From a social point of view, the junking process is not necessarily undesirable. In this country, where saving involves little hardship, it may be perfectly justified. But it may present a serious obstacle to the achievement of full employment, because the owners of capital assets headed for the junk pile will try to avoid the losses. So long as they confine themselves to changes in their accounting practices, no special consequences will follow. But it is more likely that they will try to accumulate larger reserves either by reducing their own consumption or by charging higher prices (or paying lower wages). As a result, the total propensity to save may rise. This will be exactly the opposite measure from what is needed to avoid the junking process, and will of course lead to greater trouble, though I am not prepared to say to what extent capital owners will succeed in passing on these losses.

In so far as they are able to control new investment, they will try to avoid losses by postponing it. Consequently, the rate of growth may well be depressed below the required $\alpha\sigma$, and unused capacity will develop. Our present model does not allow us to separate unused capacity into idle capital and idle men, though most likely both will be present.[15] For humanitarian reasons we are more concerned with unemployed men. But *unemployed capital is extremely important, because its presence inhibits new investment.*[16] It presents a grave danger to a full employment equilibrium in a capitalist society.

IV

Guaranteed Growth of Income

In the preceding sections it was shown that a state of full employment can be maintained if investment and income grow at an annual

[15] The presence of unemployed men may be obscured by inefficient utilization of labor, as in agriculture.

[16] It is true that a given capital owner may often have a hard time distinguishing between capital idle because of $\sigma < s$, and capital idle because of $r < \alpha\sigma$. The first kind of idleness, however, is relatively permanent, and cannot be corrected by greater expenditures, while the second is temporary (it is hoped) and is due to poor fiscal and monetary policies.

rate $\alpha\sigma$. The question now arises as to what extent the argument can be reversed: suppose income is guaranteed to grow at the $\alpha\sigma$ rate; will that call forth sufficient investment to generate the needed income?

We are concerned here with a situation where spontaneous investment (i.e. investment made in response to changes in technique, shifts in consumers' preferences, discovery of new resources, etc.) is not sufficient, and therefore a certain amount of induced investment (made in response to a rise in income) is also required.[17] To simplify the argument, let us assume that spontaneous investment is absent altogether. It should also be made clear that the problem is treated from a theoretical point of view, without considering the numerous practical questions that the income guarantee would raise.

If an economy starts from an equilibrium position, an expected rise in income of $Y\alpha\sigma$ will require an investment equal to $Y\alpha\sigma/s$. As before, two cases have to be considered.

1. If σ is equal or reasonably close to s, the resulting amount of investment of $Y\alpha$ will equal the volume of savings that will be made at that level of income, and equilibrium will be maintained.[18] *Thus a mere guarantee of a rise in income* (if taken seriously by the investors) *will actually generate enough investment and income to make the guarantee good without necessarily resorting to a government deficit.*

2. If σ is appreciably below s, investment will probably fall short of savings and equilibrium will be destroyed. The difficulty arises because a full employment rate of investment in the face of a $\sigma < s$ makes the junking process (discussed above) inevitable, while a mere guarantee of a rise in income, as a general rule, lacks the instrument to force the capital owners to discard their equipment. They will simply invest $Y\alpha\sigma/s$ instead of $Y\alpha$. Only if in the economy as a whole there is a considerable number of products the demand for which is highly elastic with respect to income, and a good number of others the demand for which is negatively elastic with respect to income, will a larger amount than $Y\alpha\sigma/s$ be invested and a corresponding amount of capital junked. Of course, if the rise in income is accompanied by shifts in consumers' preferences, the appearance

---

[17] Cf. Alvin H. Hansen, *Fiscal Policy and Business Cycles* (New York, 1944), Part Three, and particularly p. 297.

[18] There is a slight error in the magnitudes in the text because of the use of discontinuous functions.

of new products, aggressive competition, and other changes, the junking process will be speeded up, but if these changes do take place they may give rise to spontaneous investment of their own and the guaranteed *rise* in income will not be important. Still, the assurance of a high and rising income is undoubtedly one of the best methods for encouraging investment.

As explained before, a substantial difference between s and σ simply indicates that with the available labor force and the current progress of technology, the maintenance of full employment under a given α requires the accumulation of capital at a faster rate than it can be used. As a general rule, this applies equally well to both private and public investment, though there may be special cases when, owing to the development of particular consumers' preferences (e.g. for vacations), or to technological reasons (e.g. need for power), or to institutional conditions (as in urban redevelopment), considerable need for public investment still exists.[19]

I am not prepared to say whether we already are or shall soon be faced with a serious difference between s and σ, though I doubt that it was an important problem in the past, except perhaps for the short boom years. My own guess is that we shall be more concerned with the disparity between $\alpha\sigma$ and r, that is, with the failure of income to grow at the required rate.

If, however, the difference between σ and s becomes serious and inhibits investment, or if the junking process proceeds at a faster rate than is deemed socially desirable, the society will have at its disposal two not mutually exclusive methods: (1) the reduction of the propensity to save, or (2) the speeding up of technological progress. I hope that the main emphasis will be placed on the latter.

*   *   *   *

This paper attempted to analyze the relation between investment, rate of growth, and employment. The analysis was carried out on a

[19] As soon as the government enters the picture we find ourselves in a maze of definitional problems. From the point of view of this paper, saving and investment should be understood in reference to the whole economy, including the government, and not to its private sector only. But which government expenditures should be regarded as investment? The difficulty is present in the private sector as well, except that there we can take refuge in formal definitions, which cannot be well applied to government. I leave the question open. Certainly, investment need not be limited to inventories, steel, and concrete.

very abstract and simplified level—a procedure which may be justified at the beginning of an investigation, but which must be corrected later on. In general, there is no such a thing as an absolutely
good or bad assumption: what may be safe in one kind of a problem
can become fatal in another. Of the several assumptions made here,
that regarding depreciation is likely to cause the greatest difficulties,
but it is by no means the only one. I hope to develop the whole
subject further at a later date.

The central theme of the paper was *the rate of growth*, a concept
which has been little used in economic theory, and in which I put
much faith as an extremely useful instrument of economic analysis.
One does not have to be a Keynesian to believe that employment is
somehow dependent on national income, and that national income
has something to do with investment. But as soon as investment
comes in, growth cannot be left out, because for an individual firm
investment may mean *more* capital and *less* labor, but for the economy as a whole (as a general case) investment means *more* capital
and *not less* labor. If both are to be profitably employed, a *growth*
of income must take place.

Econometrica, Vol. 14, No. 2 (April, 1946)

MACROECONOMICS AND THE THEORY OF RATIONAL BEHAVIOR[1]

By Lawrence R. Klein

I. THE PROBLEM

Many of the newly constructed mathematical models of economic systems, especially the business-cycle theories, are very loosely related to the behavior of individual households or firms which must form the basis of all theories of economic behavior. In these mathematical models, the demand equations for factors of production in the economy as a whole are derived from the assumption that entrepreneurs collectively attempt to maximize some aggregate profit; whereas the usually accepted assumption is that the individual firm attempts to maximize its own profit. For example Evans,[2] Keynes,[3] Hicks,[4] and Pigou[5] all have in their systems marginal-productivity (i.e., profit-maximizing) equations for the total economy or for some very large subsections such as the consumer-goods or producer-goods industries. These marginal-productivity equations are written, without justification, for the economy as a whole, in exactly the same form as the marginal-productivity equations for a single firm producing a single commodity. These aggregative theories have often been criticized on the grounds that they mislead us by taking attention away from basic individual behavior. The problem of bridging the gap between the traditional theories based on individual behavior and the theories based on community or class behavior is, to a large extent, a problem of proper measurement. This paper attempts to make a very modest contribution towards the formulation and solution of the problem.

We have a body of theory which develops the economic behavior of

[1] Cowles Commission Papers, New Series, No. 14. Part of the work on this paper was done under a fellowship of the Social Science Research Council. The author is indebted to other members of the Cowles Commission staff for constructive criticism.

[2] "Maximum Production Studied in a Simplified Economic System," Econometrica, Vol. 2, January, 1934, pp. 37–50.

[3] *The General Theory of Employment, Interest and Money*, New York, Harcourt Brace, 1936.

[4] "Mr. Keynes and the 'Classics': A Suggested Interpretation," Econometrica, Vol. 5, April, 1937, pp. 147–159.

[5] *Employment and Equilibrium*, London, Macmillan, 1941.

individual households and firms. We also have many index numbers compiled according to definite formulas from individual observations. If we consider the index numbers as transformations of the variables that appear in the behavior equations of microeconomics, there possibly exists a definite set of relations among the index numbers which we may call our model of macroeconomics. But for most of the common index numbers, it is very difficult to determine whether a well-defined macrosystem follows from our theories of microeconomics. Consequently we may be forced to attempt to solve our problem in another way. Instead of assuming the theory of microeconomics and the index numbers, let us assume the theory of micro- and of macroeconomics, and then construct aggregates (usually in the form of index numbers) which are consistent with the two theories.

All too often, index-number theorists have devised arbitrary and even mutually inconsistent criteria which are imposed upon the construction of index numbers. We can well begin by setting down objective criteria of properly constructed economic aggregates which are consistent with the practices and aims of business-cycle theory. The general economic system is composed of equations relating to the behavior of households, firms, and interactions in the market between households and firms. We shall give detailed consideration in this paper only to those equations relating to the behavior of firms. Many of the propositions can be easily carried over to the equations of household behavior.

II. TWO CRITERIA FOR AGGREGATES

Our first criterion that an aggregate must satisfy is that *if there exist functional relations that connect output and input (production functions) for the individual firm, there should also exist functional relations that connect aggregate output and aggregate input for the economy as a whole or an appropriate subsection.* For example, we have for the firm, in microeconomics,

$$(1) \qquad F_\alpha(x_{1\alpha}, \cdots, x_{m\alpha}; n_{1\alpha}, \cdots, n_{r\alpha}; z_{1\alpha}, \cdots, z_{s\alpha}) = 0,$$

$$\alpha = 1, 2, \cdots, A.$$

This relation states that the αth firm produces the m commodities $\{x_{i\alpha}\}$ through the input of the services of r kinds of labor $\{n_{i\alpha}\}$ and of s kinds of capital $\{z_{i\alpha}\}$. We demand now that there exist a function, in macroeconomics,

$$(2) \qquad\qquad F(X, N, Z) = 0$$

which states that the entire community of firms produces the aggregate output X through the input of the services of labor N and of capital Z.

A second criterion that we shall impose upon our aggregates is the following: *If profits are maximized by the individual firms so that the marginal-productivity equations,*

(3)
$$\frac{\partial x_{i\alpha}}{\partial n_{j\alpha}} = \frac{w_j}{p_i},$$

$$i = 1, 2, \cdots, m,$$
$$j = 1, 2, \cdots, r,$$
$$\alpha = 1, 2, \cdots, A,$$

$$\frac{\partial x_{i\alpha}}{\partial z_{j\alpha}} = \frac{q_j}{p_i},$$

$$i = 1, 2, \cdots, m,$$
$$j = 1, 2, \cdots, s,$$
$$\alpha = 1, 2, \cdots, A,$$

hold under perfect competition, then the aggregative marginal-productivity equations,

(4)
$$\frac{\partial X}{\partial N} = \frac{W}{P},$$

$$\frac{\partial X}{\partial Z} = \frac{Q}{P},$$

must also hold, where w_j = the wage of the jth type of labor, p_i = the price of the ith commodity, q_j = the price of the jth type of capital service, W = the wage aggregate, P = the output-price aggregate and Q = the capital-service-price aggregate.

Obviously the second criterion cannot be satisfied without the first.

These criteria imply that we derive our macrosystem of N commodities and M factors as though we were writing down the equations for a hypothetical microsystem of N commodities and M factors. Particular interest is attached to the case where $N = 1$ and $M = 2$.

A theory based on the second criterion alone has been studied extensively by Dresch[6] and has also been treated by Hicks[7] and Lange.[8] Hicks has shown that the "fundamental equation of value theory" (Slutsky equation) remains formally invariant if we lump together (treat as one good) any group of goods whose prices change all in the same proportion. This is clearly a sufficient condition for the solution of the aggregation problem, but it may not be the most satisfactory condition to impose because most prices do not change in the same proportion.

[6] "Index Numbers and the General Economic Equilibrium," *Bulletin of the American Mathematical Society*, Vol. 44, February, 1938, pp. 134–141.

[7] *Value and Capital*, Oxford, Clarendon Press, 1939, p. 312.

[8] *Price Flexibility and Employment*, Cowles Commission Monograph No. 8, Bloomington, Indiana, Principia Press, 1944, pp. 103–106.

III. THE ATTEMPT OF FRANCIS DRESCH

Dresch,[9] in a suggestive article, has attempted to show that all the necessary conditions for maximum profits in the case of firm behavior hold in analogy for the economy as a whole if the macrovariables are properly defined in terms of the microvariables. Dresch's properly defined variables are Divisia[10] index numbers in every case. We shall show below that Dresch's aggregates do not satisfy our criteria.

We can best discuss the Dresch theory in a simple case of competitive firms making one product each. Let the production function for the αth good produced by the αth firm be

$$(5) \qquad x_\alpha = f_\alpha(n_{1\alpha}, \cdots, n_{r\alpha}; z_{1\alpha}, \cdots, z_{s\alpha}), \qquad \alpha = 1, 2, \cdots, A.$$

Profit maximization under perfect competition leads to the necessary conditions

$$(6) \qquad \frac{\partial x_\alpha}{\partial n_{i\alpha}} = \frac{w_i}{p_\alpha}, \qquad \begin{matrix} i = 1, 2, \cdots, r, \\ \alpha = 1, 2, \cdots, A, \end{matrix}$$

$$(7) \qquad \frac{\partial x_\alpha}{\partial z_{i\alpha}} = \frac{q_i}{p_\alpha}, \qquad \begin{matrix} i = 1, 2, \cdots, s, \\ \alpha = 1, 2, \cdots, A, \end{matrix}$$

where w_i is the wage rate paid to the ith type of labor, p_x is the price of the αth good and q_i is the cost of the services of the ith type of capital.

The Divisia index of total output, X, is defined by the differential equation

$$(8) \qquad dX = \frac{X}{V_x} \sum_{\alpha=1}^{A} p_\alpha dx_\alpha; \qquad V_x \equiv \sum_{\alpha=1}^{A} p_\alpha x_\alpha.$$

But from the production function (5) we obtain

$$(9) \qquad dx_\alpha = \sum_{i=1}^{r} \frac{\partial f_\alpha}{\partial n_{i\alpha}} dn_{i\alpha},$$

if all $dz_{i\alpha} = 0$, i.e., if we consider variations in output when labor alone varies and capital services of all types are held constant. Hence on substitution of (9) into (8) we get

$$(10) \qquad (dX)_N = \frac{X}{V_x} \sum_{\alpha=1}^{A} \sum_{i=1}^{r} p_\alpha \frac{\partial f_\alpha}{\partial n_{i\alpha}} dn_{i\alpha},$$

where $(dX)_N$ is defined as the change in total output when labor alone varies. Similarly the Divisia definition of the labor index is obtained from the differential equation

---

[9] F. W. Dresch, *op. cit.*

[10] F. Divisia, *Économique Rationnelle*, Paris, Doin, 1928, pp. 265–280.

(11) $$dN = \frac{N}{V_N} \sum_{\alpha=1}^{A} \sum_{i=1}^{r} w_i dn_{i\alpha}; \qquad V_N \equiv \sum_{\alpha=1}^{A} \sum_{i=1}^{r} w_i n_{i\alpha}.$$

The definition of marginal productivity is now taken to be the ratio $(dX)_N/dN$ or

(12) $$\frac{(dX)_N}{dN} = \frac{\dfrac{X}{V_X} \sum_{\alpha=1}^{A} \sum_{i=1}^{r} p_\alpha \dfrac{\partial f_\alpha}{\partial n_{i\alpha}} dn_{i\alpha}}{\dfrac{N}{V_N} \sum_{\alpha=1}^{A} \sum_{i=1}^{r} w_i dn_{i\alpha}}.$$

But if we substitute the equilibrium conditions for profit maximization (6) we obtain

(13) $$\frac{(dX)_N}{dN} = \frac{\dfrac{X}{V_X} \sum_{\alpha=1}^{A} \sum_{i=1}^{r} p_\alpha \dfrac{w_i}{p_\alpha} dn_{i\alpha}}{\dfrac{N}{V_N} \sum_{\alpha=1}^{A} \sum_{i=1}^{r} w_i dn_{i\alpha}} = \frac{\dfrac{V_N}{N}}{\dfrac{V_X}{X}}.$$

The ratio V_N/N represents the wage bill deflated by an employment index and can be called the average wage rate, an aggregate. Also V_X/X represents the value of output deflated by an output index, and can be called the price aggregate. Thus the proposition that the marginal productivity of labor equals the real wage rate in equilibrium holds in analogy for the macrosystem if the corresponding proposition holds for the microsystem. By a parallel procedure it follows that

(14) $$\frac{(dX)_Z}{dZ} = \frac{\dfrac{V_Z}{Z}}{\dfrac{V_X}{X}}.$$

It is also true that this technique can be extended to the theory of consumer behavior except for the fact that the aggregations can only be taken over groups of commodities and not over individuals because of the difficulties of interpersonal comparisons of utility.

What is the meaning of the ratio $(dX)_N/dN$? Can this ratio properly be defined as marginal productivity, $\partial X/\partial N$? If such a partial derivative is to have meaning, then there must exist a differentiable aggregate production function, from which we can derive the marginal productivity for the economy as a whole or for some subsection of the economy.

This means that our first criterion must be satisfied. Formally, if there exists a set of production functions referring to the individual firms,

(5) $\qquad x_\alpha = f_\alpha(n_{1\alpha}, \cdots, n_{r\alpha}; z_{1\alpha}, \cdots, z_{s\alpha}) \qquad\qquad \alpha = 1, 2, \cdots, A,$

with well-defined partial derivatives

$$\frac{\partial f_\alpha}{\partial n_{i\alpha}}, \qquad\qquad \begin{matrix} i = 1, 2, \cdots, r, \\ \alpha = 1, 2, \cdots, A, \end{matrix}$$

$$\frac{\partial f_\alpha}{\partial z_{i\alpha}}, \qquad\qquad \begin{matrix} i = 1, 2, \cdots, s, \\ \alpha = 1, 2, \cdots, A, \end{matrix}$$

then the criterion requires that there must also exist a function

(15) $\qquad\qquad\qquad X = f^*(N, Z)$

with well-defined partial derivatives

$$\frac{\partial f^*}{\partial N}, \qquad \frac{\partial f^*}{\partial Z}.$$

It is by no means evident that an acceptable production function measured in terms of Divisia indexes exists; furthermore it is not evident that, if such a production function does exist, it has a partial derivative equal to $(dX)_N/dN$ as calculated above.

A precise statement of the conditions under which an aggregate production function exists can be made with the help of some propositions from the theory of functional dependence.[11] Let us write individual production functions, for the most general case, as

(1) $\qquad F_\alpha(x_{1\alpha}, \cdots, x_{m\alpha}; n_{1\alpha}, \cdots, n_{r\alpha}; z_{1\alpha}, \cdots, z_{s\alpha}) = 0,$

$$\alpha = 1, 2, \cdots, A.$$

If these production functions are sufficiently well-behaved, as is generally assumed, we can rewrite them as

(16) $\qquad x_{1\alpha} = f_\alpha(x_{2\alpha}, \cdots, x_{m\alpha}; n_{1\alpha}, \cdots, n_{r\alpha}; z_{1\alpha}, \cdots, z_{s\alpha}),$

$$\alpha = 1, 2, \cdots, A.$$

We shall now define our aggregates as

(17) $\qquad\qquad X = G(x_{11}, \cdots, x_{m1}, \cdots, x_{1A}, \cdots, x_{mA}),$

(18) $\qquad\qquad N = H(n_{11}, \cdots, n_{r1}, \cdots, n_{1A}, \cdots, n_{rA}),$

(19) $\qquad\qquad Z = I(z_{11}, \cdots, z_{s1}, \cdots, z_{1A}, \cdots, z_{sA}).$

The definitions of the output, labor, and capital aggregates define three transformation functions sending the variables $\{x_{i\alpha}\}$, $\{n_{i\alpha}\}$, and $\{z_{i\alpha}\}$ into X, N, Z, subject to the restraints of the production functions.

[11] Leonid Hurwicz was very helpful in formulating the proposition to follow.

It is well known that the transformed variables are functionally related, uniquely, by a relation

(20) $\Phi(X, N, Z) = 0,$

if the following rectangular matrix is of rank 2:

$$\begin{Vmatrix} \left[\dfrac{\partial G}{\partial x_{1\alpha}} \dfrac{\partial x_{1\alpha}}{\partial x_{i\alpha}} + \dfrac{\partial G}{\partial x_{i\alpha}} \right] & 0 & 0 \\[3ex] \left[\dfrac{\partial G}{\partial x_{1\alpha}} \dfrac{\partial x_{1\alpha}}{\partial n_{i\alpha}} \right] & \left[\dfrac{\partial H}{\partial n_{i\alpha}} \right] & 0 \\[3ex] \left[\dfrac{\partial G}{\partial x_{1\alpha}} \dfrac{\partial x_{1\alpha}}{\partial z_{i\alpha}} \right] & 0 & \left[\dfrac{\partial I}{\partial z_{i\alpha}} \right] \end{Vmatrix}.$$

Each of the elements of this matrix are column vectors, the vectors of the first row having $(m-1)A$ elements $(i = 2, 3, \cdots, m; \alpha = 1, 2, \cdots, A)$, the vectors of the second row having rA elements $(i = 1, 2, \cdots, r; \alpha = 1, 2, \cdots, A)$, and the vectors of the third row having sA elements $(i = 1, 2, \cdots, s; \alpha = 1, 2, \cdots, A)$.

The conditions that all third-order determinants vanish, *identically*, where $\partial H / \partial n_{i\alpha}$ and $\partial I / \partial z_{i\alpha}$ are not all zero, are

(21) $$\frac{\partial x_{1\alpha}}{\partial x_{i\alpha}} \equiv - \frac{\dfrac{\partial G}{\partial x_{i\alpha}}}{\dfrac{\partial G}{\partial x_{1\alpha}}}, \qquad \begin{aligned} & i = 2, \cdots, m, \\ & \alpha = 1, 2, \cdots, A, \end{aligned}$$

(22) $$\frac{\dfrac{\partial x_{1\alpha}}{\partial n_{i\alpha}}}{\dfrac{\partial x_{1\beta}}{\partial n_{j\beta}}} \equiv \frac{\dfrac{\partial H}{\partial n_{i\alpha}}}{\dfrac{\partial H}{\partial n_{j\beta}}} \cdot \frac{\dfrac{\partial G}{\partial x_{1\beta}}}{\dfrac{\partial G}{\partial x_{1\alpha}}}, \qquad \begin{aligned} & i = 1, 2, \cdots, r, \\ & j = 1, 2, \cdots, r, \\ & \alpha = 1, 2, \cdots, A, \\ & \beta = 1, 2, \cdots, A, \end{aligned}$$

(23) $$\frac{\dfrac{\partial x_{1\alpha}}{\partial z_{i\alpha}}}{\dfrac{\partial x_{1\beta}}{\partial z_{j\beta}}} \equiv \frac{\dfrac{\partial I}{\partial z_{i\alpha}}}{\dfrac{\partial I}{\partial z_{j\beta}}} \cdot \frac{\dfrac{\partial G}{\partial x_{1\beta}}}{\dfrac{\partial G}{\partial x_{1\alpha}}}, \qquad \begin{aligned} & i = 1, 2, \cdots, s, \\ & j = 1, 2, \cdots, s, \\ & \alpha = 1, 2, \cdots, A, \\ & \beta = 1, 2, \cdots, A. \end{aligned}$$

The choice of the aggregative functions, G, H, and I must be such as to satisfy these identical relationships. The relationships state in a loose sense that marginal rates of substitution among variables of the aggregative functions must be the same as the marginal rates of substitution among the variables of the production function. It seems clear from these conditions that there must be some similarities in form between the basic production functions and the aggregative functions. It will be necessary to have some specifications, in any case, on the individual functions in order to know how to construct the aggregates so as to satisfy the theorem on functional dependence.

The conditions (21), (22), (23) give us an exact judgment as to the desirability of any particular type of aggregation. For example, there may be considered the special case in which the different types of output and of factors are of the same dimensionality. Then we may be led to believe that simple summation is the natural type of aggregation. We would have

$$(17a) \qquad X = \sum_{\alpha=1}^{A} \sum_{i=1}^{m} x_{i\alpha},$$

$$(18a) \qquad N = \sum_{\alpha=1}^{A} \sum_{i=1}^{r} n_{i\alpha},$$

$$(19a) \qquad Z = \sum_{\alpha=1}^{A} \sum_{i=1}^{s} z_{i\alpha},$$

and (21), (22), (23) would become

$$\frac{\partial x_{1\alpha}}{\partial x_{i\alpha}} \equiv -1, \qquad \begin{aligned} & i = 1, 2, \cdots, m, \\ & \alpha = 1, 2, \cdots, A, \end{aligned}$$

$$\frac{\partial x_{1\alpha}}{\partial n_{i\alpha}} \equiv \frac{\partial x_{1\beta}}{\partial n_{j\beta}}, \qquad \begin{aligned} & i = 1, 2, \cdots, r, \\ & j = 1, 2, \cdots, r, \\ & \alpha = 1, 2, \cdots, A, \\ & \beta = 1, 2, \cdots, A, \end{aligned}$$

$$\frac{\partial x_{1\alpha}}{\partial z_{i\alpha}} \equiv \frac{\partial x_{1\beta}}{\partial z_{j\beta}}, \qquad \begin{aligned} & i = 1, 2, \cdots, s, \\ & j = 1, 2, \cdots, s, \\ & \alpha = 1, 2, \cdots, A, \\ & \beta = 1, 2, \cdots, A. \end{aligned}$$

This seemingly obvious type of aggregation would thus be suitable only if the marginal productivity of any type of labor (capital) in any firm were *identically* the same as the marginal productivity of any other type of labor (capital) in any firm. The restriction can be somewhat reshaped if the sums in (17a), (18a), and (19a) are changed to linear combinations. Then the marginal productivities need not be equal, but merely proportional.

It should be remarked that the functions G, H, I were made to depend only upon the physical quanties $\{x_{i\alpha}\}$, $\{n_{i\alpha}\}$, $\{z_{i\alpha}\}$. Most index numbers are constructed so that quantity indexes depend upon prices as weights, as well as upon quantities. We might construct our transformations as follows:

$$(17b) \qquad X = \frac{\dfrac{\sum\limits_{\alpha=1}^{A} \sum\limits_{i=1}^{m} p_i x_{i\alpha}}{\sum\limits_{\alpha=1}^{A} \sum\limits_{i=1}^{m} p_i x_{i\alpha}{}^0}}{\sum\limits_{\alpha=1}^{A} \sum\limits_{i=1}^{m} p_i{}^0 x_{i\alpha}{}^0},$$

$$(18b) \qquad N = \frac{\dfrac{\sum\limits_{\alpha=1}^{A} \sum\limits_{i=1}^{r} w_i n_{i\alpha}}{\sum\limits_{\alpha=1}^{A} \sum\limits_{i=1}^{r} w_i n_{i\alpha}{}^0}}{\sum\limits_{\alpha=1}^{A} \sum\limits_{i=1}^{r} w_i{}^0 n_{i\alpha}{}^0},$$

$$(19b) \qquad Z = \frac{\dfrac{\sum\limits_{\alpha=1}^{A} \sum\limits_{i=1}^{s} q_i z_{i\alpha}}{\sum\limits_{\alpha=1}^{A} \sum\limits_{i=1}^{s} q_i z_{i\alpha}{}^0}}{\sum\limits_{\alpha=1}^{A} \sum\limits_{i=1}^{s} q_i{}^0 z_{i\alpha}{}^0}.$$

The aggregates (17b), (18b), (19b) are all value aggregates deflated by fixed-base price indexes.

By differentiating (17b), we find

$$(24) \qquad -\frac{\dfrac{\partial X}{\partial x_{i\alpha}}}{\dfrac{\partial X}{\partial x_{1\alpha}}} \equiv -p_i/p_1.$$

This relation holds identically because of the definition of the aggregative function. It is also true that

$$(25) \qquad \frac{\partial x_{1\alpha}}{\partial x_{i\alpha}} = -\frac{p_i}{p_1},$$

but this relation does *not* hold identically; it holds only for the equilibrium conditions under profit maximization. It is not a relation that depends solely upon technological possibilities of substitution via the production function. Hence condition (21) is not *identically* satisfied for a very common type of index number. The same is true of (22) and (23).

It needs to be further pointed out that the inclusion of prices and wages as variables in the aggregation functions, G, H, and I complicates the functional matrix by the addition of more rows provided it is desired to find a relation

$$(20) \qquad \Phi(X, N, Z) = 0$$

that does not depend explicitly on the individual prices and wages. The simple addition of more rows, however, will have no influence on the previously stated conditions (21), (22), (23) that the matrix be of rank 2. These conditions become necessary but not sufficient in this case.

It can be seen from this discussion that the use of some very common types of index numbers is not justified on the basis of the criteria which have been stated at the outset.

The Divisia-type indexes which Dresch has employed are not covered by the functions G, H, and I above because these functions are ordinary point functions, while it is well known that the Divisia indexes are line integrals, i.e., functionals They depend upon the entire paths of prices and quantities rather than merely upon point values An investigation of the conditions under which a functional relation exists among X, N, Z when they are defined by functionals as opposed to point functions is more complicated. But it happens in that case also, that the appropriate determinants do not vanish identically. Dresch's theory has intuitive significance, but fails to satisfy both of the criteria put forth at the beginning of this paper.

IV. A SUGGESTION

An alternative approach that retains the same goals can now be shown in an example. This approach is not general or unique but holds for a class of production functions that are very significant. By specifying, more closely, the shape of the production functions, we can derive a satisfactory explanation of the meaning of an aggregative production function.

Let

$$(26) \qquad x_\alpha = B_\alpha f_\alpha(n_{1\alpha}, \cdots, n_{r\alpha}) g_\alpha(z_{1\alpha}, \cdots, z_{s\alpha}), \qquad \alpha = 1, 2, \cdots, A,$$

be the production function for the αth firm. A special case of this function is the logical extension of the Cobb-Douglas type function

$$(26a) \qquad x_\alpha = C_\alpha \prod_{i=1}^{r} n_{i\alpha}{}^{a_i} \cdot \prod_{i=1}^{s} z_{i\alpha}{}^{b_i}.$$

Our requirement is that the production function partition into a product of a labor function and a capital function. We also attribute a single output variable to each firm, but this is done for simplicity; it is not essential.

The transformations[12] will be defined according to

$$(27) \qquad X = \left[\prod_{\alpha=1}^{A} x_\alpha \right]^{1/A},$$

$$(28) \qquad N^a = \left[\prod_{\alpha=1}^{A} f_\alpha(n_{1\alpha}, \cdots, n_{r\alpha}) \right]^{1/A},$$

$$(29) \qquad Z^b = \left[\prod_{\alpha=1}^{A} g_\alpha(z_{1\alpha}, \cdots, z_{s\alpha}) \right]^{1/A},$$

$$(30) \qquad X = D N^a Z^b.$$

The first criterion is satisfied because the aggregate production (30) does exist in explicit form. In order to apply the second criterion, we distinguish between two cases.

Case I: *a and b, the elasticities of output, are constants.* If p_α is the price of the αth good, w_i is the wage rate paid to the ith type of labor, and q_i is the cost of the ith type of capital services, then we define

$$(31) \qquad P = \frac{\sum\limits_{\alpha=1}^{A} p_\alpha x_\alpha}{A \cdot X},$$

$$(32) \qquad W = \frac{\sum\limits_{\alpha=1}^{A} \sum\limits_{i=1}^{r} w_i n_{i\alpha}}{A \cdot N},$$

$$(33) \qquad Q = \frac{\sum\limits_{\alpha=1}^{A} \sum\limits_{i=1}^{s} q_i z_{i\alpha}}{A \cdot Z},$$

as the corresponding aggregates for average price of output, average

[12] In this discussion, the macrovariables are averages, but the entire analysis also follows if the averages are changed to aggregates. We use averages in order that the macrovariable be made less sensitive to variations in the output or input of a single firm.

It should also be pointed out that firms with zero output are excluded; otherwise the entire aggregate would vanish if a single term vanished.

wage, and average price of capital. These definitions lead by simple division to

$$(34) \qquad \frac{W}{P} = \frac{X}{N} \frac{\sum\limits_{\alpha=1}^{A} \sum\limits_{i=1}^{r} w_i n_{i\alpha}}{\sum\limits_{\alpha=1}^{A} p_\alpha x_\alpha},$$

$$(35) \qquad \frac{Q}{P} = \frac{X}{Z} \frac{\sum\limits_{\alpha=1}^{A} \sum\limits_{i=1}^{s} q_i z_{i\alpha}}{\sum\limits_{\alpha=1}^{A} p_\alpha x_\alpha}.$$

Also by differentiation of the aggregate production functions, we get

$$(36) \qquad \frac{\partial X}{\partial N} = a \frac{X}{N},$$

$$(37) \qquad \frac{\partial X}{\partial Z} = b \frac{X}{Z}.$$

Combining (34), (35), (36), (37), we have

$$(38) \qquad \frac{\partial X}{\partial N} = \frac{W}{P} \left\{ a \frac{\sum\limits_{\alpha=1}^{A} p_\alpha x_\alpha}{\sum\limits_{\alpha=1}^{A} \sum\limits_{i=1}^{r} w_i n_{i\alpha}} \right\},$$

$$(39) \qquad \frac{\partial X}{\partial Z} = \frac{Q}{P} \left\{ b \frac{\sum\limits_{\alpha=1}^{A} p_\alpha x_\alpha}{\sum\limits_{\alpha=1}^{A} \sum\limits_{i=1}^{s} q_i z_{i\alpha}} \right\}.$$

The aggregative marginal productivities are not in general equal to W/P or Q/P, but they will be when

$$(40) \qquad a = \frac{\sum\limits_{\alpha=1}^{A} \sum\limits_{i=1}^{r} w_i n_{i\alpha}}{\sum\limits_{\alpha=1}^{A} p_\alpha x_\alpha},$$

$$(41) \qquad b = \frac{\sum\limits_{\alpha=1}^{A} \sum\limits_{i=1}^{s} q_i z_{i\alpha}}{\sum\limits_{\alpha=1}^{A} p_\alpha x_\alpha} .$$

Equations (40) and (41) are to be considered as equilibrium conditions for the macrosystem. The constant elasticities, a and b, are to be chosen as the average values over the time path of the *observed* ratios

$$\frac{\sum\limits_{\alpha=1}^{A} \sum\limits_{i=1}^{r} w_i n_{i\alpha}}{\sum\limits_{\alpha=1}^{A} p_\alpha x_\alpha}$$

and

$$\frac{\sum\limits_{\alpha=1}^{A} \sum\limits_{i=1}^{s} q_i z_{i\alpha}}{\sum\limits_{\alpha=1}^{A} p_\alpha x_\alpha}$$

respectively. The observed values of labor's share and capital's share will fluctuate about the average or equilibrium values and, therefore, cause $\partial X/\partial N$ and $\partial X/\partial Z$ in (38) and (39) to deviate from their equilibrium values W/P and Q/P. The macroequations for the firm will assume their equilibrium forms only when labor's share and capital's are at their equilibrium values.

Our equilibrium system, in abbreviated form, is then

$$(30) \qquad X = DN^a Z^b,$$

$$(42) \qquad \frac{\partial X}{\partial N} = \frac{W}{P},$$

$$(43) \qquad \frac{\partial X}{\partial Z} = \frac{Q}{P}.$$

This is a complete analogue of the equilibrium system of microeconomics.

Case II: *a and b, the output elasticities, are not constant.*
Define

$$a_{i\alpha} = \frac{n_{i\alpha}}{x_\alpha} \frac{\partial x_\alpha}{\partial n_{i\alpha}}, \qquad \begin{aligned} i &= 1, 2, \cdots, r, \\ \alpha &= 1, 2, \cdots, A, \end{aligned}$$

$$b_{i\alpha} = \frac{z_{i\alpha}}{x_\alpha} \frac{\partial x_\alpha}{\partial z_{i\alpha}}, \qquad \begin{aligned} i &= 1, 2, \cdots, s, \\ \alpha &= 1, 2, \cdots, A. \end{aligned}$$

In addition to the transformation equations (27), (28), (29), we also have

$$(44) \qquad a = \frac{\sum\limits_{\alpha=1}^{A} \sum\limits_{i=1}^{r} a_{i\alpha} p_\alpha x_\alpha}{\sum\limits_{\alpha=1}^{A} p_\alpha x_\alpha},$$

$$(45) \qquad b = \frac{\sum\limits_{\alpha=1}^{A} \sum\limits_{i=1}^{s} b_{i\alpha} p_\alpha x_\alpha}{\sum\limits_{\alpha=1}^{A} p_\alpha x_\alpha}.$$

According to (44) and (45), the elasticities of output for the aggregative system are weighted averages of the elasticities of the individual firms. We retain the same definitions of P, W, Q given in (31), (32), (33); consequently (38) and (39) still hold. We now propose to show that the equilibrium conditions (40) and (41) are true profit-maximizing conditions which hold whenever profits are at a maximum for each individual firm. In the microsystem, we have for equilibrium,

$$(6) \qquad \frac{\partial x_\alpha}{\partial n_{i\alpha}} = \frac{w_i}{p_\alpha}, \qquad \begin{aligned} i &= 1, 2, \cdots, r, \\ \alpha &= 1, 2, \cdots, A, \end{aligned}$$

$$(7) \qquad \frac{\partial x_\alpha}{\partial z_{i\alpha}} = \frac{q_i}{p_\alpha}, \qquad \begin{aligned} i &= 1, 2, \cdots, s, \\ \alpha &= 1, 2, \cdots, A. \end{aligned}$$

Then, on substituting the definitions of $a_{i\alpha}$ and $b_{i\alpha}$ into (6) and (7), we get

$$(46) \qquad a_{i\alpha} = \frac{w_i n_{i\alpha}}{p_\alpha x_\alpha},$$

$$(47) \qquad b_{i\alpha} = \frac{q_i z_{i\alpha}}{p_\alpha x_\alpha}.$$

Summing over the i subscript in each case and then over the α subscript, we get

$$(48) \qquad \sum_{\alpha=1}^{A} \sum_{i=1}^{r} a_{i\alpha} p_\alpha x_\alpha = \sum_{\alpha=1}^{A} \sum_{i=1}^{r} w_i n_{i\alpha},$$

$$(49) \qquad \sum_{\alpha=1}^{A} \sum_{i=1}^{s} b_{i\alpha} p_{\alpha} x_{\alpha} = \sum_{\alpha=1}^{A} \sum_{i=1}^{s} q_i z_{i\alpha}.$$

Divide both sides of (48) and (49) by $\sum_{\alpha=1}^{A} p_{\alpha} x_{\alpha}$ to get our previously stated equilibrium conditions,

$$(40) \qquad a = \frac{\displaystyle\sum_{\alpha=1}^{A} \sum_{i=1}^{r} a_{i\alpha} p_{\alpha} x_{\alpha}}{\displaystyle\sum_{\alpha=1}^{A} p_{\alpha} x_{\alpha}} = \frac{\displaystyle\sum_{\alpha=1}^{A} \sum_{i=1}^{r} w_i n_{i\alpha}}{\displaystyle\sum_{\alpha=1}^{A} p_{\alpha} x_{\alpha}},$$

$$(41) \qquad b = \frac{\displaystyle\sum_{\alpha=1}^{A} \sum_{i=1}^{r} b_{i\alpha} p_{\alpha} x_{\alpha}}{\displaystyle\sum_{\alpha=1}^{A} p_{\alpha} x_{\alpha}} = \frac{\displaystyle\sum_{\alpha=1}^{A} \sum_{i=1}^{s} q_i z_{i\alpha}}{\displaystyle\sum_{\alpha=1}^{A} p_{\alpha} x_{\alpha}}.$$

The abbreviated equilibrium system, (30), (42), (43), holds as before in Case I.

In the formulations above, a and b are like elasticities in that they are invariant under a change of units. But the quantity aggregates, X, N, Z, like any physical variable of economics, depend upon the choice of units.

If the functions f_{α} and g_{α} are known explicitly, then it is possible to show the precise manner in which the aggregates should be calculated. For example if

$$(28a) \qquad N^a = \left(\prod_{\alpha=1}^{A} f_{\alpha} \right)^{1/A} = \left(\prod_{\alpha=1}^{A} \prod_{i=1}^{r} n_{i\alpha}{}^{a_i} \right)^{1/A},$$

$$(29a) \qquad Z^b = \left(\prod_{\alpha=1}^{A} g_{\alpha} \right)^{1/A} = \left(\prod_{\alpha=1}^{A} \prod_{i=1}^{s} z_{i\alpha}{}^{b_i} \right)^{1/A},$$

then the logarithm of N is a linear combination of the logarithms of the various types of labor employed by the various firms, and similarly for capital.

As a practical method of procedure, we should calculate functions of the type (26a) for a large sample of cases. From the sample, calculate weighted geometric means of output, labor, and capital and weighted arithmetic means of the elasticities of output of labor and of capital. Knowing these averages and the numbers of firms, products, and factors, we can get good approximations of the proper aggregates. The problem of calculating the aggregates is mainly one of sampling.

The above demonstration has to be somewhat modified for the case of imperfect competition, but in any event the idea is clear for an important case. If we want to simplify mathematical models of general equilibrium into a small number of equations, it is useful to know that operationally significant concepts exist which justify such simplifications. It is only in models of macroeconomics that we can see through all the complex interrelationships of the economy in order to form intelligent judgments about such important magnitudes as aggregate employment, output, consumption, investment.

Cowles Commission for Research in Economics
  The University of Chicago

Econometrica, Vol. 16, No. 3 (July, 1948)

SUR LA POSSIBILITÉ DE CONSTRUCTION DE CERTAINS MACROMODÈLES

Par André Nataf

RÉSUMÉ

Le système des équations T de l'équilibre comprend un nombre énorme d'équations, chaque entité économique (producteur, ou consommateur) faisant l'objet d'un groupe d'équations.

Le problème de l'aggrégation en économie, pour autant qu'il est avancé, peut se proposer:

1. Sans resoudre explicitement ou implicitement, selon la méthode envisagée, le système T, d'essayer de le séparer en sous-systèmes indépendants les uns des autres, T', la résolution de chaque T' étant à priori plus simple que celle de T.

2. Toujours sans résolution explicite ou implicite, de rechercher s'il n'est pas possible de combiner certaines équations de T en une équation unique, ce qui facilite le rassemblement des éléments statistiques globaux et permet éventuellement une vérification des théories au moyen de sondages statistiques, même si cette méthode ne permet pas de déterminer tous les paramètres économiques individuellement.

3. De fabriquer un modèle V, réduit de T, en correspondance connue avec T et dégageant bien la structure de T, tout en étant plus simple à embrasser.

Il importe évidemment de rechercher si ces intentions sont réalisables, ce qui n'est nullement prouvé a priori.

Lawrence R. Klein a posé entre autres, le problème suivant (Econometrica, Vol. 14, Avril, 1946, pp. 93–108):

Etant données A entreprises ayant chacune une fonction de production technique,

F_α (production, maind'oeuvre, capital) $= 0$,

est-il possible de déduire de ces A équations une seule équation de production globale

Φ (indice de production, indice de main d'oeuvre, indice de capital) $= 0$?

Nous répondons à ce problème bien délimité de la façon suivante:

Ceci n'est possible que si l'on peut réduire la forme des équations de production à une fonction linéaire de 3 termes indépendants mathématiquement: la production, la main d'oeuvre, le capital.

Dans ces conditions la fonction Φ se réduit purement et simplement à la somme des fonctions F_α et les 3 indices sont chacun en ce qui le concerne, la somme des termes relatifs à la production, la main d'oeuvre, le capital.

Il s'ensuit qu'a priori il y a très peu de chances que cette façon d'aborder le problème de l'aggrégation soit efficace, sauf lorsqu'on considère de faibles variations autour d'une position donnée.

* * *

Cet article contient la solution à une question posée par M. Lawrence R. Klein dans Econometrica (Vol. 14, avril, 1946). L'article porte le titre suivant: "Macroeconomics and the Theory of Rational Behavior." Le problème que se pose l'auteur peut ainsi se résumer: Admettons que la production de chaque entreprise individuelle puisse se calculer en supposant que chaque firme considérée essaye de réaliser le profit le plus grand possible compatible avec une équation de production

(1) $F_\alpha(x_{1\alpha}, \cdots, x_{m\alpha}; n_{1\alpha}, \cdots, n_{r\alpha}; z_{1\alpha}, \cdots, z_{s\alpha}) = 0, \alpha = 1, 2, \cdots, A$

(les m $x_{i\alpha}$ désignant les produits de fabrication, les r $n_{j\alpha}$ désignant les paramètres relatifs au travail et les s $z_{k\alpha}$ les paramètres relatifs aux capitaux investis). D'une façon générale, nous admettrons que la connaissance de l'equation $F(\alpha) = 0$ et des prix des produits, du travail, et des capitaux permet de déterminer tous les paramètres x_α, n_α, et z_α à l'équilibre.

Beaucoup d'auteurs essayent de déterminer l'allure du marché en se bornant à calculer certaines fonctions: X de tous les x_α et des x_α seuls, N des n_α, et Z des z_α. Toutes ces économies essayent du reste, pour faire ces calculs, d'étendre pour les fonctions X, N, Z les calculs faits pour les x_α, n_α, z_α. Dans ces conditions, l'on est amené (toujours en supposant que l'on se trouve dans une économie caractérisée par la recherche d'un profit maximum) à postuler l'existence d'une relation entre X, N, Z que Klein note sous la forme

(2) $$F(X, N, Z) = 0.$$

Klein pose alors la question suivante: Désignant (et nous garderons toujours ses notations, sauf pour les expressions nouvelles que nous serons amenés à considérer) par

(17) $X = G(x_{11}, \cdots, x_{m1}; \cdots; x_{1A}, \cdots, x_{mA})$,

(18) $N = H(n_{11}, \cdots, n_{r1}; \cdots; n_{1A}, \cdots, n_{rA})$,

(19) $Z = I(z_{11}, \cdots, z_{s1}; \cdots; z_{1A}, \cdots, z_{sA})$,

les fonctions X, N, Z (qui sont de véritables indices respectivement de la production, du marché du travail, du marché des capitaux), Klein recherche quelles conditions nécessaires et suffisantes (K) doivent rem-

plir les A fonctions (1) et les 3 fonctions G, H, I pour que ces derni-
ères puissent être liées par une relation

(20) $$\Phi(X, N, Z) = 0.$$

Klein met en évidence un système de *variables indépendantes* qui sont:
toutes les variables $x_{i\alpha}$ sauf les variables $x_{1\alpha}$ ($\alpha = 1, \cdots, A; i = 2, \cdots,$
m) et toutes les variables $n_{1\alpha}$ et $z_{i\alpha}$ sans exception. A cet effet il écrit
(ce qui est toujours possible, par un choix convenable de notations le
cas échéant) les équations (1) sous la forme

(16) $$x_{1\alpha} = f_\alpha(x_{2\alpha}, \cdots, x_{m\alpha}; n_{1\alpha}, \cdots, n_{r\alpha}; z_{1\alpha}, \cdots, z_{s\alpha}).$$

Les conditions (K) s'écrivent alors, en supposant (ce qui semble évi-
dent de par la nature économique de la question) que les dérivées
$\partial H/\partial n_{i\alpha}$ et $\partial I/\partial z_{j\beta}$ ne sont pas toutes nulles:

(21) $$\frac{\partial x_{1\alpha}}{\partial x_{i\alpha}} \equiv -\frac{\dfrac{\partial G}{\partial x_{i\alpha}}}{\dfrac{\partial G}{\partial x_{1\alpha}}}, \qquad \begin{array}{l} i = 2, 3, \cdots, m, \\ \alpha = 1, 2, \cdots, A, \end{array}$$

(22) $$\frac{\dfrac{\partial x_{1\alpha}}{\partial n_{i\alpha}}}{\dfrac{\partial x_{1\beta}}{\partial n_{j\beta}}} \equiv \frac{\dfrac{\partial H}{\partial n_{i\alpha}}}{\dfrac{\partial H}{\partial n_{j\beta}}} \cdot \frac{\dfrac{\partial G}{\partial x_{1\beta}}}{\dfrac{\partial G}{\partial x_{1\alpha}}}, \qquad \begin{array}{l} i = 1, 2, \cdots, r, \\ j = 1, 2, \cdots, r, \\ \alpha = 1, 2, \cdots, A, \\ \beta = 1, 2, \cdots, A, \end{array}$$

(23) $$\frac{\dfrac{\partial x_{1\alpha}}{\partial z_{i\alpha}}}{\dfrac{\partial x_{1\beta}}{\partial z_{j\beta}}} \equiv \frac{\dfrac{\partial I}{\partial z_{i\alpha}}}{\dfrac{\partial I}{\partial z_{j\beta}}} \cdot \frac{\dfrac{\partial G}{\partial x_{1\beta}}}{\dfrac{\partial G}{\partial x_{1\alpha}}}, \qquad \begin{array}{l} i = 1, 2, \cdots, s, \\ j = 1, 2, \cdots, s, \\ \alpha = 1, 2, \cdots, A, \\ \beta = 1, 2, \cdots, A. \end{array}$$

Klein applique ces conditions (K) à l'étude de cas particuliers. Dans
le cas général, il pressent qu'il doit exister quelques similitudes de
formes entre les fonctions G, H, I et les fonctions (1) $F(\alpha) = 0$. C'est
ce que nous allons voir en intégrant dans le cas général le système des
équations (21), (22), et (23) que nous appellerons encore système (K).

M. Divisia, à qui nous avons soumis nos résultats, a remarqué
que même sans intégrer (K) on pouvait utiliser les conditions (21), (22),
et (23) pour éprouver les modèles macroéconomiques déjà existants ou
bien à venir.

Intégration du système (K)

1° Faisons d'abord quelques remarques générales mais qui nous seront utiles dans l'étude de (K)

R.1°—Les couples de variables et fonctions n et H d'une part, z et I d'autre part jouent des rôles manifestement symétriques dans tout le problème. A tout résultat établi à n'importe quel moment de l'étude pour l'un des couples correspondra un résultat symétrique pour l'autre.

R. *2°*—Au lieu de calculer les $x_{i\alpha}$ dans les équations (1) $F(\alpha)=0$ nous aurions pu, sans rien changer à la forme définitive des fonctions G, H, I calculer les $n_{i\alpha}$ ou les $z_{i\alpha}$. Dans ces conditions, nous pouvons compléter notre première remarque générale en disant que tout résultat établi pour l'un des couples n, H et z, I pourra se transcrire à la fin des calculs sur les couples x, G; n, H; g, I par une permutation convenable.

2° Intégration des équations (22) [et par suite (23)]

Les équations (22) doivent être vérifiées lorsqu'on y fait $\alpha=\beta$, i et j prenant par ailleurs toutes les valeurs possibles.

Ces équations deviennent alors:

$$(\overline{22\alpha}) \qquad \dfrac{\dfrac{\partial x_{1\alpha}}{\partial n_{i\alpha}}}{\dfrac{\partial x_{1\alpha}}{\partial n_{j\alpha}}} \equiv \dfrac{\dfrac{\partial H}{\partial n_{i\alpha}}}{\dfrac{\partial H}{\partial n_{j\alpha}}}, \qquad \begin{aligned} i &= 1, 2, \cdots, r, \\ j &= 1, 2, \cdots, r, \end{aligned}$$

qui peuvent s'écrire plus symétriquement

$$\dfrac{\dfrac{\partial x_{1\alpha}}{\partial n_{1\alpha}}}{\dfrac{\partial H}{\partial n_{1\alpha}}} \equiv \dfrac{\dfrac{\partial x_{1\alpha}}{\partial n_{2\alpha}}}{\dfrac{\partial H}{\partial n_{2\alpha}}} \equiv \dfrac{\dfrac{\partial x_{1\alpha}}{\partial n_{3\alpha}}}{\dfrac{\partial H}{\partial n_{3\alpha}}} \equiv \cdots \equiv \dfrac{\dfrac{\partial x_{1\alpha}}{\partial n_{r\alpha}}}{\dfrac{\partial H}{\partial n_{r\alpha}}},$$

ce qui montre qu'il y a $(r-1)$ équations (22) indépendantes, celles que l'on obtient en fixant j égal à 1 et en faisant varier i de 2, 3, $\cdots$, à r. Ceci donne les équations

$$(22\alpha) \qquad \dfrac{\dfrac{\partial x_{1\alpha}}{\partial n_{i\alpha}}}{\dfrac{\partial x_{1\alpha}}{\partial n_{1\alpha}}} \equiv \dfrac{\dfrac{\partial H}{\partial n_{i\alpha}}}{\dfrac{\partial H}{\partial n_{1\alpha}}} \equiv u_{i\alpha}, \qquad i = 2, 3, \cdots, r,$$

$u_{i\alpha}$ désignant la valeur commune des rapports.

D'après

$$\frac{\dfrac{\partial x_{1\alpha}}{\partial n_{i\alpha}}}{\dfrac{\partial x_{1\alpha}}{\partial n_{1\alpha}}} \equiv u_{i\alpha},$$

$u_{i\alpha}$ ne dépend que des variables *indépendantes*:

$$x_{2\alpha}, \; x_{3\alpha}, \; \cdots \; , \; x_{m\alpha},$$
$$n_{1\alpha}, \; n_{2\alpha}, \; n_{3\alpha}, \; \cdots \; , \; n_{r\alpha},$$
$$z_{1\alpha}, \; z_{2\alpha}, \; z_{3\alpha}, \; \cdots \; , \; z_{s\alpha}.$$

Donnons à $n_{1\alpha}, n_{2\alpha}, \cdots, n_{r\alpha}$ des valeurs fixes ainsi qu'aux variables $n_{1\beta}$, $n_{2\beta}, \cdots, n_{r\beta}$, β arbitraire, $\neq \alpha$. Faisons par contre varier arbitrairement $x_{2\alpha}, x_{3\alpha}, \cdots, x_{n\alpha}$ et $z_{1\alpha}, z_{2\alpha}, \cdots, z_{s\alpha}$. D'après

$$u_{i\alpha} \equiv \frac{\dfrac{\partial H}{\partial n_{i\alpha}}}{\dfrac{\partial H}{\partial n_{1\alpha}}}$$

où H ne dépend que des variables n on voit que $u_{i\alpha}$ ne change pas de valeur. C'est donc que $u_{i\alpha}$ n'est pas fonction de $x_{2\alpha}, x_{3\alpha}, \cdots, x_{m\alpha}$, ni de $z_{1\alpha}, z_{2\alpha}, \cdots, z_{s\alpha}$ mais des seules variables indépendantes restantes dans son expression sous la forme

$$\frac{\dfrac{\partial x_{1\alpha}}{\partial n_{i\alpha}}}{\dfrac{\partial x_{1\alpha}}{\partial n_{1\alpha}}}$$

soient: $n_{1\alpha}, n_{2\alpha}, \cdots, n_{r\alpha}$. On peut donc écrire $u_{i\alpha} \equiv u_{i\alpha}(n_{1\alpha}, n_{2\alpha}, \cdots, n_{r\alpha})$. Les équations (22α) montrent que $x_{1\alpha}$ et H sont des fonctions de $n_{1\alpha}, n_{2\alpha}, \cdots, n_{r\alpha}$ et d'autres variables (que nous n'avons pas besoin d'expliciter pour $x_{1\alpha}$ et H mais que nous appellerons génériquement v_k) qui sont solutions d'un système $[P]$ d'équations aux dérivées partielles (où nous désignerons par P l'inconnue)

$$[P] \quad \begin{cases} \dfrac{\partial P}{\partial n_{2\alpha}} \equiv u_{2\alpha} \dfrac{\partial P}{\partial n_{1\alpha}} & [P]_2, \\[2.5ex] \dfrac{\partial P}{\partial n_{3\alpha}} \equiv u_{3\alpha} \dfrac{\partial P}{\partial n_{1\alpha}} & [P]_3, \\[2ex] \quad \cdot \quad \cdot \quad \cdot \quad \cdot \quad \cdot \quad \cdot \\[1ex] \dfrac{\partial P}{\partial n_{r\alpha}} \equiv u_{r\alpha} \dfrac{\partial P}{\partial n_{1\alpha}} & [P]_r. \end{cases}$$

Pour intégrer $[P]$ supposons que nous ayons trouvé une solution $\mathcal{P}$ fonction des seules variables $n_{1\alpha}$, $n_{2\alpha}$, $\cdots$, $n_{r\alpha}$, P, fonction des $n_{i\alpha}$ et des v_k vérifiera alors le système de relations

$$[P'] \qquad \frac{\dfrac{\partial P}{\partial n_{1\alpha}}}{\dfrac{\partial \mathcal{P}}{\partial n_{1\alpha}}} \equiv \frac{\dfrac{\partial P}{\partial n_{2\alpha}}}{\dfrac{\partial \mathcal{P}}{\partial n_{2\alpha}}} \equiv \cdots \equiv \frac{\dfrac{\partial P}{\partial n_{r\alpha}}}{\dfrac{\partial \mathcal{P}}{\partial n_{r\alpha}}} \qquad \text{équivalent à } [P].$$

Pour chaque système de valeurs des v_k ces équations expriment que P est fonction de la seule combinaison $\mathcal{P}(n_{1\alpha}, n_{2\alpha}, \cdots, n_{r\alpha})$ cette fonction dépendant évidemment des v_k considérés comme des paramètres. En définitive on voit que P est une fonction de $\mathcal{P}(n_{1\alpha}, n_{2\alpha}, \cdots, n_{r\alpha})$; et de $v_1, \cdots, v_k, \cdots$:

$$P = P[\,\mathcal{P}(n_{1\alpha}, n_{2\alpha}, \cdots, n_{r\alpha}); v_1, \cdots, v_k, \cdots\,].$$

Remarque—Nous n'avons pas, à vrai dire, intégré $[P]$. Mais le résultat obtenu suffira pour ce qui suit. Notons 1°—que d'après sa forme analytique, ce système peut se ramener à l'intégration de systèmes d'équations différentielles; 2°—que les

$$u_{i\alpha} \equiv \frac{\dfrac{\partial \mathcal{P}}{\partial n_{i\alpha}}}{\dfrac{\partial \mathcal{P}}{\partial n_{1\alpha}}}$$

ne doivent pas être quelconques pour que le système admette des solutions différentes de la solution banale $P = P$ (des seules variables v) constante par rapport aux $n_{i\alpha}$. En fait, les $u_{i\alpha}$ sont surtout des intermédiaires de calcul.

Forme des fonctions H, I, f_α, G

Appliquons ces résultats à H et aux $x_{1\alpha}$ en donnant à α toutes les valeurs possibles. On voit que *nécessairement* H est seulement fonction de A fonctions $\mathcal{H}_\alpha(n_{1\alpha}, n_{2\alpha}, \cdots, n_{r\alpha})$ $(\alpha = 1, 2, \cdots, A)$ (qui jouent alternativement les rôles de $\mathcal{P}$ et des v_k) ce que nous noterons plus brièvement $\mathcal{H}_\alpha$.

Donc $N = H(\mathcal{H}_1, \mathcal{H}_2, \cdots, \mathcal{H}_A)$.

D'après R. 1°, de même $Z = I(\mathcal{I}_1, \mathcal{I}_2, \cdots, \mathcal{I}_A)$ avec $\mathcal{I}_\alpha = \mathcal{I}_\alpha$ $(z_{1\alpha}, \cdots, z_{s\alpha})$.

Par suite $x_{1\alpha} = f_\alpha(x_{2\alpha}, \cdots, x_{m\alpha}; \mathcal{H}_\alpha; \mathcal{I}_\alpha)$, les fonctions $\mathcal{H}_\alpha$ et $\mathcal{I}_\alpha$ intervenant dans N, Z, et $x_{1\alpha}$ ayant exactement la même signification, d'après l'étude du système $[P]$. Remontons aux fonctions $F(\alpha)$. On voit que

(50-I) $F(\alpha) \equiv F_\alpha(x_{1\alpha}, x_{2\alpha}, \cdots, x_{m\alpha}; \mathcal{K}_\alpha; \mathcal{I}_\alpha) = 0.$

Mais enfin d'après R. 2°, X est une fonction G de A fonctions: $\theta_\alpha(x_{1\alpha}, \cdots, x_{m\alpha})$, que nous noterons

$$X = G(\theta_1, \theta_2, \cdots, \theta_A),$$

et de même

(50-II) $F(\alpha) = \overline{F}_\alpha(\theta_\alpha; n_{1\alpha}, n_{2\alpha}, \cdots, n_{r\alpha}; \mathcal{I}_\alpha) = 0.$

Dans ces conditions établissons que F_α est une fonction des seules combinaisons θ_α, $\mathcal{K}_\alpha$, et $\mathcal{I}_\alpha$.

Pour cela il nous suffira d'établir que si un système D de valeurs numériques des $x_{i\alpha}$, $n_{j\alpha}$, $z_{l\alpha}$ vérifie (50-I) [et par suite (50-II)] tout autre système D' de valeurs numériques donnant les mêmes valeurs à θ_α, $\mathcal{K}_\alpha$, $\mathcal{I}_\alpha$ vérifiera aussi bien (50-I) par example. Or de par la forme de (50-I) nous pouvons donner aux n et z les mêmes valeurs que dans D, les x gardant les valeurs attribuées dans D'. Appelons $\overline{D}$ ce $3^{\text{ème}}$ système de valeurs; $\mathcal{K}_\alpha$ et $\mathcal{I}_\alpha$ auront les mêmes valeurs. Mais (50-II) s'annulle chaque fois que (50-I) s'annulle et vice-versa. (50-II) s'annullera pour $\overline{D}$ étant donné que $\overline{D}$ et D attribuent les mêmes valeurs aux familles de variables n, z entrant dans l'expression de (50-II) et la même valeur à θ_α. Mais par suite (50-I) également s'annulle pour $\overline{D}$. Mais $\overline{D}$ et D' annulent en même temps (50-I). Donc D' et D annullent en même temps (50-I).

On voit donc, que F_α s'annulle pour des valeurs convenablement associées des seules combinaisons θ_α, $\mathcal{K}_\alpha$, $\mathcal{I}_\alpha$.

Par conséquent, nous pouvons exprimer θ_α sous une forme commode remplaçant la $1^{\text{ère}}$ expression de la fonction de production soit:

(50) $\theta_\alpha = \chi_\alpha(\mathcal{K}_\alpha, \mathcal{I}_\alpha)$

χ_α désignant une forme de fonction des 2 variables, $\mathcal{K}_\alpha$ et $\mathcal{I}_\alpha$.

3° Poursuite de l'intégration de (K)

Reprenons les équations (22) et (23). Nous n'avons intégré que celles pour lesquelles $\alpha = \beta$. Nous allons maintenant revenir sur les équations où $\alpha \neq \beta$. Tout d'abord étant donné ce que nous savons maintenant (22) et (23) s'écrivent:

$$\overline{(22')} \qquad \dfrac{\dfrac{\partial x_{1\alpha}}{\partial \mathcal{K}_\alpha} \dfrac{\partial \mathcal{K}_\alpha}{\partial n_{i\alpha}}}{\dfrac{\partial x_{1\beta}}{\partial \mathcal{K}_\beta} \dfrac{\partial \mathcal{K}_\beta}{\partial n_{j\beta}}} \equiv \dfrac{\dfrac{\partial H}{\partial \mathcal{K}_\alpha} \dfrac{\partial \mathcal{K}_\alpha}{\partial n_{i\alpha}} \dfrac{\partial G}{\partial x_{1\beta}}}{\dfrac{\partial H}{\partial \mathcal{K}_\beta} \dfrac{\partial \mathcal{K}_\beta}{\partial n_{j\beta}} \dfrac{\partial G}{\partial x_{1\alpha}}}$$

ou plus simplement:

$$(\overline{22}) \qquad \frac{\dfrac{\partial x_{1\alpha}}{\partial \mathcal{H}_\alpha}}{\dfrac{\partial x_{1\beta}}{\partial \mathcal{H}_\beta}} \equiv \frac{\dfrac{\partial H}{\partial \mathcal{H}_\alpha}}{\dfrac{\partial H}{\partial \mathcal{H}_\beta}} \cdot \frac{\dfrac{\partial G}{\partial x_{1\beta}}}{\dfrac{\partial G}{\partial x_{1\alpha}}}, \qquad \begin{array}{l} \alpha = 1, 2, \cdots, A, \\ \beta = 1, 2, \cdots, A, \end{array}$$

et de même

$$(\overline{23}) \qquad \frac{\dfrac{\partial x_{1\alpha}}{\partial \mathcal{I}_\alpha}}{\dfrac{\partial x_{1\beta}}{\partial \mathcal{I}_\beta}} \equiv \frac{\dfrac{\partial I}{\partial \mathcal{I}_\alpha}}{\dfrac{\partial I}{\partial \mathcal{I}_\beta}} \cdot \frac{\dfrac{\partial G}{\partial x_{1\beta}}}{\dfrac{\partial G}{\partial x_{1\alpha}}}, \qquad \begin{array}{l} \alpha = 1, 2, \cdots, A, \\ \beta = 1, 2, \cdots, A. \end{array}$$

Eliminant entre ces équations le rapport

$$\frac{\dfrac{\partial G}{\partial x_{1\beta}}}{\dfrac{\partial G}{\partial x_{1\alpha}}}$$

il vient

$$(51) \qquad \frac{\dfrac{\partial x_{1\alpha}}{\partial \mathcal{H}_\alpha} \cdot \dfrac{\partial I}{\partial \mathcal{I}_\alpha}}{\dfrac{\partial x_{1\alpha}}{\partial \mathcal{H}_\beta} \cdot \dfrac{\partial I}{\partial \mathcal{I}_\beta}} \equiv \frac{\dfrac{\partial x_{1\alpha}}{\partial \mathcal{I}_\alpha} \cdot \dfrac{\partial H}{\partial \mathcal{H}_\alpha}}{\dfrac{\partial x_{1\beta}}{\partial \mathcal{I}_\beta} \cdot \dfrac{\partial H}{\partial \mathcal{H}_\beta}} .$$

(51) montre que le 1er membre fonction des seules variables $x_{i\alpha}$ $(i=2, \cdots, m)$, $\mathcal{H}_\alpha$, $\mathcal{I}_\alpha$; $x_{j\beta}$ $(j=2, \cdots, m)$, $\mathcal{H}_\beta$, $\mathcal{I}_\beta$; $\mathcal{I}_1$, $\mathcal{I}_2$, $\cdots$, $\mathcal{I}_A$ est identique au $2^{\text{ème}}$ membre fonction des seules variables $x_{i\alpha}$ $(i=2, \cdots, m)$, $\mathcal{H}_\alpha$, $\mathcal{I}_\alpha$; $x_{j\beta}$ $(j=2, \cdots, m)$, $\mathcal{H}_\beta$, $\mathcal{I}_\beta$; $\mathcal{H}_1$, $\mathcal{H}_2$, $\cdots$, $\mathcal{H}_A$. Toutes ces variables étant indépendantes, il s'ensuit que celles figurant dans un seul membre n'interviennent pas en réalité. Mais ces variables provenaient respectivement seulement de

$$\frac{\dfrac{\partial I}{\partial \mathcal{I}_\alpha}}{\dfrac{\partial I}{\partial \mathcal{I}_\beta}} \qquad \text{pour } \mathcal{I}_1, \mathcal{I}_2, \cdots, \mathcal{I}_A,$$

et de

$$\frac{\dfrac{\partial H}{\partial \mathcal{H}_\alpha}}{\dfrac{\partial H}{\partial \mathcal{H}_\beta}} \qquad \text{pour } \mathcal{H}_1,\ \mathcal{H}_2,\ \cdots,\ \mathcal{H}_A.$$

On voit donc que

$$\frac{\dfrac{\partial H}{\partial \mathcal{H}_\alpha}}{\dfrac{\partial H}{\partial \mathcal{H}_\beta}}$$

par exemple n'est fonction que de $\mathcal{H}_\alpha$, et $\mathcal{H}_\beta$ et non des autres $\mathcal{H}_i$. Désignons par $h_{\alpha\beta}(\alpha, \beta)$ cette fonction:

$$(52) \qquad \frac{\dfrac{\partial H}{\partial \mathcal{H}_\alpha}}{\dfrac{\partial H}{\partial \mathcal{H}_\beta}} \equiv h_{\alpha\beta}.$$

Nous allons voir que $h_{\alpha\beta}$ est de la forme $h_\alpha(\alpha)/h_\beta(\beta)$. Nous pouvons en effet écrire avec un $3^{\text{ème}}$ groupe de variables

$$(53) \qquad \frac{\dfrac{\partial H}{\partial \mathcal{H}_\beta}}{\dfrac{\partial H}{\partial \mathcal{H}_\gamma}} \equiv h_{\beta\gamma}(\beta, \gamma) \quad \text{et} \quad \frac{\dfrac{\partial H}{\partial \mathcal{H}_\alpha}}{\dfrac{\partial H}{\partial \mathcal{H}_\gamma}} \equiv h_{\alpha\gamma}$$

en combinant (52) et (53) à $h_{\alpha\beta}/h_{\gamma\beta}$

$$(54) \qquad h_{\alpha\gamma} \equiv \frac{h_{\alpha\beta}}{h_{\gamma\beta}}.$$

Nous pouvons dans (54) donner à β une valeur fixe puisque $h_{\alpha\gamma}$ ne dépend pas de $\mathcal{H}_\beta$. $h_{\alpha\beta}$ et $h_{\gamma\beta}$ seront des fonctions de $\mathcal{H}_\alpha$ et $\mathcal{H}_\gamma$ seuls. D'où

$$(55) \qquad h_{\alpha\gamma} \equiv \frac{h_\alpha(\mathcal{H}_\alpha)}{h_\gamma(\mathcal{H}_\gamma)}.$$

Dans (55) jusqu'ici γ peut prendre toute valeur 1, 2, $\cdots$, A sauf peut-être la valeur β. Les équations (55) nous permettent en tous cas d'écrire

(56)
$$\frac{\dfrac{\partial H}{\partial \mathcal{K}_1}}{h_1} \equiv \frac{\dfrac{\partial H}{\partial \mathcal{K}_2}}{h_2} \equiv \cdots \equiv \frac{\dfrac{\partial H}{\partial \mathcal{K}_\alpha}}{h_\alpha} \equiv \frac{\dfrac{\partial H}{\partial \mathcal{K}_\gamma}}{h_\gamma} \equiv \cdots \equiv \frac{\dfrac{\partial H}{\partial \mathcal{K}_A}}{h_A}$$

Mais en intervertissant le rôle des variables α et β par exemple nous pouvons écrire k_i désignant une fonction de le seule variable $\mathcal{K}_i$.

(57)
$$\frac{\dfrac{\partial H}{\partial \mathcal{K}_1}}{k_1} \equiv \frac{\dfrac{\partial H}{\partial \mathcal{K}_2}}{k_2} \equiv \cdots \equiv \frac{\dfrac{\partial H}{\partial \mathcal{K}_\beta}}{k_\beta} \equiv \frac{\dfrac{\partial H}{\partial \mathcal{K}_\gamma}}{k_\gamma} \equiv \cdots \equiv \frac{\dfrac{\partial H}{\partial \mathcal{K}_A}}{k_A} .$$

Mais la comparaison de (56) et (57) montre immédiatement que les fonctions h et k de même indice sont proportionnelles, le coefficient de proportionnalité étant constant. On peut donc dans (57) remplacer les k par les h de même indice: k_β sera remplacée par une fonction proportionnelle et (56) se complètera par un A-ième rapport égal $(\partial H/\partial \mathcal{K}_\beta)/h_\beta$.

Désignons maintenant par H_i une fonction de $\mathcal{K}_i$ seule, primitive de h_i. On a donc

(58)
$$\frac{dH_i}{d\mathcal{K}_i} \equiv h_i$$

i variant de 1 à A.

Posons

(59)
$$\overline{H} \equiv H_1 + H_2 + \cdots + H_A.$$

D'où

$$\frac{\partial \overline{H}}{\partial \mathcal{K}_i} \equiv \frac{dH_i}{d\mathcal{K}_i} \equiv h_i.$$

(56) complété s'écrit donc sous la forme équivalente:

(56')
$$\frac{\dfrac{\partial H}{\partial \mathcal{K}_1}}{\dfrac{\partial \overline{H}}{\partial \mathcal{K}_1}} \equiv \frac{\dfrac{\partial H}{\partial \mathcal{K}_2}}{\dfrac{\partial \overline{H}}{\partial \mathcal{K}_2}} \equiv \cdots \equiv \frac{\dfrac{\partial H}{\partial \mathcal{K}_A}}{\dfrac{\partial \overline{H}}{\partial \mathcal{K}_A}} .$$

Nous voyons encore que H est une fonction arbitraire de $\overline{H}$ seul. De même I sera une fonction arbitraire d'une fonction $\overline{I}$ de la forme

(60)
$$\overline{I} \equiv I_1(\mathfrak{I}_1) + I_2(\mathfrak{I}_2) + \cdots + I_A(\mathfrak{I}_A)$$

et G une fonction arbitraire de $\overline{G}$

(61)
$$\overline{G} \equiv G_1(\theta_1) + G_2(\theta_2) + \cdots + G_A(\theta_A).$$

Formes associées des fonctions $\chi_i(\mathcal{K}_i, \mathcal{I}_i)$, *H, I, G*

Il n'est pas moins général (et il sera plus simple pour les calculs) de prendre pour *H, I, G*, des fonctions de la forme $\overline{H}, \overline{I}, \overline{G}$.

Il est clair par ailleurs que les variables essentielles sont les $\mathcal{K}$, les $\mathcal{I}$, et les θ. Pour exprimer que $\overline{H}, \overline{I}, \overline{G}$, sont liées par une relation Φ il va nous être commode d'écrire que pour chaque système de valeur des variables indépendantes $\mathcal{K}_j$, $\mathcal{I}_j$ les differentielles $d\overline{H}$, $d\overline{G}$, $d\overline{I}$ sont liées par une relation linéaire et homogène, le coefficient de dG n'étant pas nul (la production n'est en effet pas indépendante du travail et des capitaux)

$$(62) \qquad\qquad d\overline{G} \equiv ad\overline{H} + bd\overline{I}.$$

L'identité (62) entraîne pour les variables $\mathcal{K}_j$, $\mathcal{I}_j$ quelque soit j:

$$\frac{\partial \overline{G}}{\partial \chi_j} \frac{\partial \chi_j}{\partial \mathcal{K}_j} \equiv a \frac{dH_j}{d\,\mathcal{K}_j}, \qquad j = 1, 2, \cdots, A.$$

D'où

$$a \equiv \frac{\dfrac{\partial \overline{G}}{\partial \chi_j} \dfrac{\partial \chi_j}{\partial \mathcal{K}_j}}{\dfrac{dH_j}{d\,\mathcal{K}_j}} \quad \text{quelque soit } j.$$

Donc a est une même fonction des groupes de variables indépendantes d'indice arbitraire j: c'est dire que a est une constante absolue, de même que b par conséquent.

Mais alors (62) s'intègre et donne

$$(63) \qquad\qquad \overline{G} \equiv a\overline{H} + b\overline{I} + c,$$

a, b, c, étant des constantes.

Nous pouvons supposer c nul en le faisant rentrer par exemple dans une des fonctions H_j ou I_k. Rapprochant (61) et (63) on voit que l'on doit avoir identiquement

$$(64) \qquad G_j(\theta_j) \equiv aH_j + bI_j \text{ (à une } c^{te} \text{ additive près sans intérêt).}$$

Désignons par G_j^{-1} le fonction inverse de $G_j(\theta_j)$, il vient

$$(65) \qquad\qquad \theta_j \equiv G_j^{-1}(aH_j + bI_j)$$

qui donne la forme nécessaire des θ_j.

Expressions des formes H, I, G, à partir des θ_j

N'oublions pas que dans notre problème les relations (1) $F_\alpha = 0$ nous sont données. Nous pouvons alors interpréter ainsi l'équation (65) (en gardant nos notations sur la signification desquelles nous insisterens légèrement):

Pour que l'on puisse trouver une relation (20) $\Phi(X, N, Z)$ il faut que tous les $F(\alpha)$ puissent se ramener à la forme suivante $\theta_\alpha(x_{1\alpha}, x_{2\alpha}, \cdots, x_{m\alpha})$ $=\chi_\alpha[H_\alpha(n_{1\alpha}, n_{2\alpha}, \cdots, n_{r\alpha})+I_\alpha(z_{1\alpha}, \cdots, z_{s\alpha})]$ (en désignant maintenant par H_j la fonction aH_j et par I_j la fonction bI_j, ce qui ne change absolument rien à la généralité des résultats), ce qui s'énonce encore: Les fonctions de productions individuelles doivent pouvoir se ramener à la forme suivante:

$\theta_\alpha=$fonction χ_α de la somme de 2 fonctions des n_α seuls et des z_α seuls.

Dans ces conditions, on pourra toujours prendre (et cette restriction n'a rien de limitatif puisque G, H, I ne sont évidemment définis qu'à une fonction d'eux-mêmes près)

$$H \equiv H_1 + H_2 + \cdots + H_\alpha + \cdots + H_A,$$

$$I \equiv I_1 + I_2 + \cdots + I_\alpha + \cdots + I_A,$$

$$G \equiv \chi_1^{-1}(\theta_1) + \cdots + \chi_\alpha^{-1}(\theta_\alpha) + \cdots + \chi_A^{-1}(\theta_A),$$

et, dans ces conditions (20) s'écrira

$$G \equiv I + H$$

ou

$$X \equiv N + Z.$$

Autres formes simples

M. L. R. Klein a considéré (p. 102 de son article) des fonctions de production explicitées sous la forme

$$(26) \quad x_\alpha = B_\alpha f_\alpha(n_{1\alpha}, \cdots, n_{r\alpha}) g_\alpha(z_{1\alpha}, \cdots, z_{s\alpha}), \quad \alpha = 1, 2, \cdots, A.$$

Au fait près qu'il ne considère qu'une seule variable x_α que, pour plus de généralités, nous devons remplacer par $\theta_\alpha(x_{1\alpha}, \cdots, x_{m\alpha})$ nous pouvons voir maintenant qu'il a considéré la forme la plus générale possible des fonctions de production pour lesquelles le problème posé admet une solution (il suffit en effet de remplacer H, I, G par u^H, v^I, w^G, u, v, w étant des constantes).

Dans ces conditions il n'est pas étonnant que nous puissions étendre au cas général les remarques faites par Kenneth May[1] sur les résultats de Klein.

K. May met en relief (p. 61) le fait que les indices X, N, Z dépendent essentiellement des fonctions de production. Nous pouvons maintenant littéralement dire que ces indices sont des sommes de parties des fonctions de production.

---

[1] Kenneth May, "Technological Change and Aggregation," ECONOMETRICA, Vol. 15, January, 1947, pp. 51–63, esp. pp. 61, 62.

Mais nous devons aller plus loin et insister sur le fait que les fonctions de production trouvées ont une forme analytique invraisemblable dans un domaine moyen de variations des facteurs de production: la forme trouvée ne s'applique en pratique que pour de petits déplacements de ces facteurs autour d'une position donnée.

D'autre part, l'utilisation des variables indépendantes pose en fait le problème du domaine de variation de ces variables. Il y a une difficulté double sous ce rapport:

1°—Il est certain qu'il y a des relations techniques entre les facteurs de production (il ne viendra jamais à l'idee de décupler le nombre d'ouvriers en laissant intact l'état des machines par exemple).

2°—D'autre part, il serait illusoire d'utiliser toutes ces relations techniques pour éliminer certaines variables et ne garder que des variables indépendantes.

N'insistons pas sur les autres difficultés que pose la notion de fonction de production. K. May y a excellement insisté (p. 63). Portons notre attention sur le point suivant, qui n'a rien de nouveau mais qui ressort bien de la question étudiée: *Que peut-on prendre comme variables indépendantes?*

En fait, de fil en aiguille on serait probablement amené à n'utiliser que le temps comme variable indépendante.

Ceci nous amène à comparer le problème économique à un problème de mécanique où l'on utilise bien, pour des commodités de calcul, les paramètres de liberté du système mais où l'on détermine ces paramètres en fonction du temps.

Et sans doute si l'on pouvait essayer des modèles économiques dynamiques et non statiques, bien des contradictions s'évanouiraient-elles et l'efficacité de ces modèles comme guides pratiques serait-elle bien plus grande.

Centre National de la Recherche Scientifique
Paris

Econometrica, Vol. 17, Nos. 3–4 (October, 1949)

NOTE: SOME CONDITIONS OF MACROECONOMIC STABILITY

By David Hawkins and Herbert A. Simon

In a recent paper by one of us[1] there is an error in the statement of a supposed sufficient condition that a system of linear homogeneous equations should have solutions all of the same sign. The present note is intended to correct that error, to state and prove an apparently new, necessary and sufficient condition that the stated consequence should hold, and finally to interpret the significance of this condition in economic terms.

Two preliminary remarks are in order. First, the error in the theorem originally stated does not affect the substance of the paper to which reference is being made. That paper sets forth theorems on the stability of systems which *do* have stationary solutions with all variables positive. The lemma under consideration here gives necessary and sufficient conditions that a system *will* have stationary solutions with all variables positive. That is, it gives a criterion to test whether the theorems in the body of the paper are applicable to any particular system of equation.

Second, the conditions under which the variables satisfying a system of linear equations will be all positive are of economic interest in their own right. They are, in fact, the conditions determining whether a system of linear production functions is capable, given a sufficient supply of the "fixed" factors of production, of producing any desired schedule of consumption goods.

The system of equations[2] is the following:[3]

$$(1) \qquad \sum_{j=1}^{n} b_{ij} x_j = 0, \qquad (i = 1, \cdots, n)$$

with $\Delta = 0$ and of rank $n - 1$; $b_{ij} > 0$ for all $i \neq j$; $b_{ii} < 0$ for all i.

Instead of dealing directly with the system (1), it will be more convenient to consider the associated nonhomogeneous system:

$$(2) \qquad \sum_{j=1}^{m} a_{ij} x_j - k_i = 0, \qquad (i = 1, \cdots, m)$$

---

[1] David Hawkins, "Some Conditions of Macroeconomic Stability," Econometrica, Vol. 16, October, 1948, pp. 309–322. The theorem under discussion is on page 312.

[2] The system (1) is essentially that introduced by W. W. Leontief in *The Structure of American Economy*, 1919–1929, Cambridge: Harvard University Press, 1941. p. 48.

[3] In Hawkin's original system we require only that $b_{ij} \geq 0$ for $i \neq j$. The stronger condition $b_{ij} > 0$ employed here simplifies the statement of the theorem and its proof and, because of the continuity of solutions of these equations with respect to variations of these coefficients, does not involve any essential loss of generality.

with

$$m = n - 1; k_i = b_{in}; a_{ij} = -b_{ij}, \quad (i, j = 1, \cdots, m); |A| = |a_{ij}| \neq 0.$$

It is clear that, for $x_n = 1$, the solution of (1) is identical with that of (2), and the $[x_i]$ satisfying (1) will all be of the same sign if and only if the $[x_i]$ satisfying (2) are all positive. Further, without loss of generality, we can take $a_{ii} = -b_{ii} = 1$.

In equations (2), x_i is the total quantity of the ith commodity produced; k_i is the quantity of the ith commodity consumed; $-a_{ij}x_j$ is the quantity of the ith commodity used in producing the jth commodity. The nth equation in system (1), which is linearly dependent upon the first m equations, may be interpreted as a consumption function. Alternatively, the vector $[k_i]$ in (2), which gives the relative quantities of the various commodities consumed, may be considered the schedule of consumption goods.

The production system (2) is economically meaningful only if the $[x_i]$ satisfying it are all positive. Conceivably, the signs of the $[x_i]$ may depend upon the magnitude of the $[k_i]$—that is, upon the schedule of consumption goods. Hence we will be interested in knowing under what conditions the $[x_i]$ will be positive for some given set $[k_i]$, and under what conditions the $[x_i]$ will be positive for *any* set $[k_i \geqslant 0]$.

The defective theorem is the following: LEMMA: *The system of equations* (1) *is satisfied only for x_i all of the same sign.*

This theorem is true only for $n \leqslant 3$, as shown by the following counter-example:

$$-2x_1 + 4x_2 + x_3 + x_4 = 0$$

$$4x_1 - 2x_2 + x_3 + x_4 = 0$$

$$x_1 + x_2 - 2x_3 + 4x_4 = 0$$

$$x_1 + x_2 + 4x_3 - 2x_4 = 0$$

We verify immediately that $\Delta = 0$, and is of rank $n - 1$, and that $b_{ij} > 0$ for all $i \neq j$, while $b_{ii} < 0$ for all i. But the general solution of this system is: $x_1 = K; x_2 = K; x_3 = -K; x_4 = -K$; where K is an arbitrary constant.

The fallacy in the proof offered for the lemma lies in paragraph III of Hawkins' paper. Specifically, it is not correct that: if all members of a set of hyperplanes intersect in a common line through the origin, and if each member of the set has points lying in the first quadrant, then the common line of intersection must lie in the first quadrant.

We now proceed to a valid, necessary and sufficient condition that the equations (2) be satisfied only for $[x_i]$ all positive. THEOREM: *A necessary and sufficient condition that the x_i satisfying (2) be all positive is that all principal minors of the matrix $||a_{ij}||$ be positive.*

To prove this theorem we first consider the augmented $m \cdot n$ matrix $||a_{ij} - k_i||$ and proceed to reduce this matrix, row by row, to triangular form. That is, by adding to each row an appropriate linear combination of the preceding rows, we obtain a matrix in which all elements to the left of the main diagonal are zero. This procedure can always be carried out step by step until a row (say the jth) is reached with a nonpositive diagonal term. It does not alter the solution of the system and does not alter the values of the principal minors consisting of the first i rows and columns ($i = 1, \cdots, m$).

Because of the arrangement of signs in our particular matrix, all elements in the first column except the first can be made zero by adding to each row an appropriate *positive* multiple of the first row. The signs of all other elements off the main diagonal will remain negative. The sign of a_{22} may remain positive or become negative. In the former case, the third and all following elements in the second column can be made zero by adding to the corresponding rows an appropriate *positive* multiple of the second row. In general, if the first i elements on the main diagonal remain positive after the first $i-1$ steps in the triangularization, then the ith step in triangularization can be carried out by adding to the remaining rows a *positive* multiple of the ith row; otherwise by adding a *negative* multiple of the ith row. We carry out the triangularization until we reach a row with a nonpositive diagonal term.

For the matrix finally obtained, we distinguish two cases: (A) all the diagonal terms in the triangular matrix are positive, (B) at least one term on the main diagonal is nonpositive (and the jth term, say, is the first nonpositive one). We now prove that in case (A) all the principal minors are positive and all the x_i are positive; while in case (B) at least one principal minor is nonpositive and at least one of the x_i is negative—a statement equivalent to our theorem.

A. In case (A) we solve the corresponding system of equations successively for $x_m, x_{m-1}, \cdots, x_1$ in terms of the k_i. Since $k_m > 0$, we must have $x_m > 0$. Since $k_{m-j} > 0$, it follows that if all $x_{m-i} > 0$ $(i < j)$, then $x_{m-j} > 0$. Hence by induction, all the x_i must be positive. But, since a triangular determinant equals the product of the elements on its main diagonal, all principal minors consisting of the first k rows and columns of the triangular matrix are positive ($k = 1, \cdots, m$). But these minors are equal to the corresponding minors of the original matrix $||a_{ij}||$.

B. In case (B), all elements to the right of the main diagonal in the jth row of the diagonalized matrix are negative, and the diagonal term is nonpositive. Suppose now that all x_i for $i > j$ are positive.

Then, since k_j is positive, x_j must be negative.[4] But the principal minor of the first j rows and columns of the triangularized matrix will be negative or zero, since the jth element in the principal diagonal is nonpositive, the others positive. Hence the corresponding minor in $|\,|\,a_{ij}\,|\,|$ will be nonpositive.

Since the signs of the x_i obviously do not depend on the order in which the equations are arranged before triangularization, in case (A) *all* the principal minors of $|\,|\,a_{ij}\,|\,|$ must be positive.

This completes the proof of the theorem. Moreover, our proof gives a direct method of testing whether the x_i satisfying a given matrix are all positive.

COROLLARY: *A necessary and sufficient condition that the x_i satisfying* (2) *be all positive for any set* $[k_i > 0]$ *is that all principal minors of the matrix* $|\,|\,a_{ij}\,|\,|$ *are positive.* This corollary follows immediately from the theorem, and from the consideration that the elements of the matrix $|\,|\,a_{ij}\,|\,|$ are independent of the $[k_i]$.

Economic Interpretations. From the corollary, we see that if the production equations are internally consistent in permitting the production of some fixed schedule of consumption goods, then these consumption goods can be obtained in any desired proportion from this production system. Hence the system will be consistent with *any* schedule of consumption goods.

The condition that all principal minors must be positive means, in economic terms, that the group of industries corresponding to each minor must be capable of supplying more than its own needs for the group of products produced by this group of industries. If this is true, and if the condition $\Delta = 0$ for equations (1) is satisfied, then we can say that each group of industries must be just capable of supplying its own demands upon itself *and* the demands of the other industries in the economy. For example, if the principal minor involving the ith and jth commodities is negative, this means that the quantity of the ith commodity required to produce one unit of the jth commodity is greater than the quantity of the ith commodity that can be produced with an input of one unit of the jth commodity. Under these circumstances, the production of these two commodities could not be continued, for they would exhaust each other in their joint production.

University of Colorado and
Illinois Institute of Technology

---

[4] Or, if the diagonal term is zero, we have a contradiction—i.e., all x for $i > j$ cannot be positive.

Econometrica, Vol. 18, No. 4 (October, 1950)

A MULTIPLE-REGION THEORY OF INCOME AND TRADE[1]

By Lloyd A. Metzler

This paper deals with the effects of investment in one region or country upon income in all regions of an n-region system, and with the relations between these income movements and the pattern of trade among the various regions or countries. It includes both a static system of n equations based upon the usual definition of income and a corresponding dynamic system based upon the assumption that the output of a given region or country tends to rise when demand exceeds supply and to contract when supply exceeds demand. Under the assumed conditions, it is shown that stability of the system may be described in terms of Hicks's "conditions of perfect stability." The Hicks conditions, in turn, are dependent upon the marginal propensities to spend of the various regions. Throughout the discussion of the static problems, the system is assumed to be dynamically stable.

I. INTRODUCTION

THE THEORY of employment and income that was developed during the decade of the thirties was concerned primarily with the economic forces governing the level of output in a closed economic system. From the outset, however, it was apparent that the new ideas had important applications to interregional and international problems. In particular, the theory of employment added considerably to our understanding of the mechanism by which an expansion or contraction of income in one region or country is transmitted to other regions or countries. But much of the early discussion of such problems was devoted to a highly simplified model in which the world was divided into two regions or countries; in this model an expansion or contraction of income was assumed to originate in one of the two regions or countries, and the repercussions upon income in the other region or country, and upon the balance of payments between the two, were then examined in some detail.[2] The purpose of the

---

[1] This paper was written in 1945 but was not submitted for publication because there seemed to be no widespread interest in the subject. In recent months, however, it has become apparent that the general principles of regional income movements are applicable to many other fields besides international trade. Most of the propositions developed in this paper, for example, are applicable to the theory of linear programming and to input-output studies within a single country. See, for instance: David Hawkins and Herbert A. Simon, "Note: Some Conditions of Macroeconomic Stability," ECONOMETRICA, Vol. 17, July–October, 1949, pp. 245–248; R. M. Goodwin, "The Multiplier as Matrix," *Economic Journal*, Vol. 59, December, 1949, pp. 537–555; and John S. Chipman, "The Multi-Sector Multiplier," appearing in this issue, pp. 355–374. In addition to these published papers, I have recently read an unpublished manuscript by H. A. John Green dealing with some aspects of the problem discussed in the present paper. In view of the renewed interest in the subject, it seems to me appropriate to present the results of my own investigation.

[2] See, for example, my own papers, "Underemployment Equilibrium in Inter-

present paper is to generalize the earlier discussion by considering a model of an economic system composed of n regions or countries, where n may be either large or small. Although I shall speak hereafter of "n countries," I assume it is clear that the conclusions apply without modification to the regions within a single country or, indeed, to any regional classification of the world economy, such as the economy composed of Eastern Europe, Western Europe, Latin America, and similar regions.

The procedure followed in this paper is essentially the same as that employed in the earlier discussions of the two-country model. The level of output in each of the n countries is assumed, initially, to be in a state of balance in the sense that the country's rate of output of goods and services is equal to the demand for such goods and services. A disturbance of the economic forces governing income is then assumed to take place in one of the countries, and the effects of this disturbance are traced throughout the n-country system. Both movements of real income or employment and movements of the international balance of trade are taken into account. In order to isolate the effects of employment and real income, the assumption is made that all prices, costs, and exchange rates remain unaltered. In other words, commodities and services are assumed to be produced and sold at constant supply prices. Exchange rates are assumed to be kept at fixed levels, either by central bank activity or by the normal operations of the gold standard. A free market for foreign exchange is postulated for each of the n countries, and imports are thus supposed to be limited by a country's income or purchasing power, and not by the size of its foreign-exchange reserves.

In the present world of unbalanced trade, dollar shortages, exchange controls, and "hard" or "soft" currencies, this last assumption will doubtless strike the reader as highly unrealistic. I should therefore add that the model of international trade discussed below is not intended as a description of the abnormal conditions prevailing today. Whether the model will or will not be a reasonable description of world trade and employment in the future is a question that can hardly be answered at the present time; the answer obviously depends upon numerous and unpredictable political influences as well as upon more narrow economic

national Trade," ECONOMETRICA, Vol. 10, April, 1942, pp. 97–112, and "The Transfer Problem Reconsidered," *Journal of Political Economy*, Vol. 50, June, 1942, pp. 397–414. See also F. Machlup, *International Trade and the National Income Multiplier*, Philadelphia: The Blakiston Co., 1943, 237 pp. Machlup presents an economic model involving three countries and has also described models involving a larger number. In his more complex models, however, a considerable amount of symmetry is assumed with respect to propensities to spend and to import, and for this reason his results cannot be regarded as completely general.

considerations, such as the fate of exchange controls, import quotas, and other governmental measures for controlling world trade. But whatever the future development of international trade may be, there are two reasons, it seems to me, why economic models such as the one given in this paper are useful. In the first place, there are almost certain to be large areas of the world, even in an economic system having extensive trade controls, in which payments between one region and another are made more or less freely. It is unlikely, for example, that any limitations other than the limitation of purchasing power will ever be placed upon transactions between Kansas and Nebraska or upon payments between the North Central States and the New England States in the United States. Likewise, payments between members of the sterling area of the British Commonwealth now occur quite freely despite the limitations upon payments outside the area.[3] Thus whatever happens to inter*national* trade, the model discussed below remains useful as a description of inter*regional* trade. The second and less important reason for regarding the model as useful is the fact that it can be helpful in interpreting economic events of the past. There have been long periods of time—the period under the gold standard before the first world war is an example—when international payments were made without restriction throughout the world. There is no doubt that during these periods limited income was the principal constraint upon imports, and the assumption made above regarding foreign exchange markets is accordingly appropriate for describing such periods.

The international theory of income to be presented below is, in at least two respects, a short-run theory. It is short-run, in the first place, in the same sense that Keynes's *General Theory* is a short-run theory: it takes the rate of current investment in each country either as a given amount or as a given function of income in that country, and makes no allowances either for the effects of continuous investment upon a country's capacity to produce or for the repercussions of a change in such capacity upon the demand for new investment. The theory, in brief, is a *static* theory of income and not a theory of growth; and for this reason it is obviously inapplicable over an extended period of economic development. The theory given below is short-run, in the second place, in its treatment of each country's balance of payments. The procedure followed in this regard is simply to investigate the effects of a given disturbance upon each country's balance of payments on current account, and not to

[3] This second example is perhaps slightly misleading, inasmuch as all of the countries concerned have far-reaching import controls which to a considerable extent take the place of exchange controls. It does not seem overly optimistic, however, to conjecture that the import controls within the area, if not those pertaining to imports from countries outside the area, will be gradually relaxed.

inquire about how a given deficit or surplus in this balance is offset. Nothing is said, in other words, about the role of capital movements in establishing and maintaining equilibrium in the flow of international payments and receipts. Thus, quite apart from the problems of growth, the position of equilibrium described below must be regarded as temporary. For, unless capital movements occur more or less automatically in response to discrepancies in a country's balance of payments on current account, a country with a deficit in its current account will sooner or later have to take measures such as cost deflation or currency depreciation to eliminate the deficit; and these measures, in turn, will affect the equilibrium of income. In other words, the equilibrium of income to be discussed in this paper can exist over a considerable period of time only if international monetary reserves are large or if capital movements are of the equilibrating type.

In demonstrating how an economic disturbance in one country affects income and employment throughout the world, any one of a considerable number of economic events could be selected as the disturbing force. We might, for example, investigate the repercussions of an increase in domestic investment in one of the n countries or of an increase in the consumption of domestic goods; or we might consider the effects of technological changes or changes in tastes which tend to shift the demand for goods and services in some particular country from domestic goods to imports; or we might, following more traditional lines, examine the economic consequences of reparations payments or some other form of income transfer between countries. The international repercussions of all such disturbances, however, have many common features, and it would, accordingly, be needlessly repetitious to consider each of them separately. Indeed, it seems to me that the important elements of an interregional or international theory of employment can, for the most part, be demonstrated by considering only one type of disturbance, namely, a change in domestic investment in one of the n countries. The effects of other, more complex, types of disturbances can then be determined by regarding these complex disturbances as combinations of movements of investment in one or more countries. Thus, for the purpose of income analysis, a reparations payment may be regarded as a combination of investment in the receiving country and disinvestment of the same amount in the paying country. In view of this possibility of transforming other disturbing forces into combinations of movements in investment, the international theory of employment presented below is developed entirely by considering the adjustment of the world economy to a change in investment in one country. The conclusions reached for this particular disturbance may readily be applied to other disturbances as well.

II. A SYSTEM OF INCOME EQUATIONS

Neglecting income transfers between countries, the current net income of a particular country is simply the market value of that country's net output of goods and services. The word "net" as used in this connection implies that two deductions are made from the total value of goods and services produced. First, the usual allowance is made for the depreciation of capital. Second, and more important for present purposes, the value of all imported goods and services employed in production is deducted from the market value of such production. This second deduction is necessary because a country's output incorporates not only the services of domestic factors of production, but also many materials and services purchased abroad; and the latter do not constitute income produced within the given country. The concept of income in an open economy is thus a sort of value-added-by-manufacture concept, except that the unit of account is a country or region rather than an industry.

Consider, now, a sum of values consisting of the following items: (1) all expenditures by the residents of a particular country upon consumers' goods and services, including imported as well as domestic goods and services; (2) net investment in plant, equipment, inventories, etc., including investment in equipment produced abroad as well as investment in things domestically produced; (3) exports of goods and services. In what respects does this sum differ from net income as defined in the preceding paragraph? The sum includes, in the first place, the value of imported materials and services employed in domestic production, and these obviously must be deducted in computing the net income produced within the given country. The sum also includes, in the second place, imported finished goods which may have been used either for consumption, for net investment, or for re-export; and since these imported finished goods obviously do not constitute a part of the particular country's current production, their value must likewise be deducted from the total in computing national income. Thus, we find that the total of domestic expenditures for consumption and investment plus receipts from exports exceeds national income by the value of imports, including both imports of finished goods and services and imports of intermediate goods and services. In terms of the final uses of goods and services, national income may accordingly be written as follows:

national income *equals* expenditures on consumers' goods and services
plus net investment *plus* exports of goods and services
less imports of goods and services.

Three of the items in this summation—consumption, net investment, and imports—are dependent upon the level of income and employment at home, while the remaining item, exports, depends upon income in all of the countries to which the given country is selling goods and services.[4] This immediately suggests that for the world economy it might be convenient to set up a tabular presentation of income similar to the input-output tables developed by Leontief in the study of inter-industry relations.[5] Such a table would show how each country's income is *earned* —in sales at home and sales to other countries—and how income is *spent*—in purchases at home and purchases from other countries. Individual countries or regions, in other words, would replace the individual industries in the Leontief tables; and imports and exports would replace inputs and outputs.

Let $m_i(y_i)$ be the function which shows how *total* imports of the ith country from all other countries in the table are related to national income, y_i, of the importing country. This total import function will be composed of a number of subfunctions showing how imports from each of the other countries are related to income in the ith country. Thus, if $m_{ji}(y_i)$ represents the imports of the ith country from the jth country, stated as a function of income in the ith country, we will have $m_i(y_i) \equiv m_{1i}(y_i) + m_{2i}(y_i) + \cdots$, where the summation is extended over all countries from which the ith country imports goods or services. Since one country's imports are another country's exports, the entire pattern of world trade may be described in terms of the import functions, $m_{ji}(y_i)$. The tabular presentation of world income may then be completed by inserting functional relations for each country's expenditures on *all* goods and services. In setting up such total expenditure functions, there is no necessity to distinguish between consumers' goods and net investment, since the one affects income in the same way as the other. Suppose that both consumers' goods expenditures and net investment are dependent to some extent upon income at home, and let $u_i(y_i)$ represent such an expenditure function; $u_i(y_i)$, in other words, shows how expenditure in the ith country on *both* consumers' goods and net investment is related to the ith country's income. Hereafter, the function $u_i(y_i)$ will be called simply an "expenditure function"; it plays the same role in the present theory of employment that is usually attributed to the consumption

[4] If the import content of a country's exports differs from the import content of the goods and services produced for home use, total imports will depend not only upon income but also on the composition of income; i.e., upon the way output is divided between exports and goods or services produced for domestic use. Since the demand for the given country's exports is governed in part by income in other countries, and since imports in this instance depend partly upon exports, it follows that imports should really be expressed as a function of income in all countries. But this is a refinement which cannot be incorporated in the present model without complicating it unduly.

[5] W. W. Leontief, *The Structure of American Economy, 1919–1929*, Cambridge, Mass.: Harvard University Press, 1941, *passim*.

function. The quantity $u_i(y_i)$ represents *all* expenditures of the ith country on consumers' goods and net investment, irrespective of the source of goods and services purchased. It includes imported finished goods as well as the import-content of domestic production. In order to show how expenditure by a given country affects that country's net income, total imports, $m_i(y_i)$, must therefore be subtracted from the expenditure function, $u_i(y_i)$.

The foregoing relations are summarized in the accompanying table, which presents a hypothetical case of a world economy consisting of three countries. The items in a given *row* of this table provide a classification of the components of a country's national income according to the *sources* from which it was earned, while the items in the corresponding *column*

	Expenditures by Country 1 (1)	Expenditures by Country 2 (2)	Expenditures by Country 3 (3)	National Income (1) + (2) + (3)
Receipts from Sales by Country 1 (1)	$u_1(y_1) - m_1(y_1)$	$m_{12}(y_2)$	$m_{13}(y_3)$	y_1
Receipts from Sales by Country 2 (2)	$m_{21}(y_1)$	$u_2(y_2) - m_2(y_2)$	$m_{23}(y_3)$	y_2
Receipts from Sales by Country 3 (3)	$m_{31}(y_1)$	$m_{32}(y_2)$	$u_3(y_3) - m_3(y_3)$	y_3
Total Expenditures of Each Country (1) + (2) + (3)	$u_1(y_1)$	$u_2(y_2)$	$u_3(y_3)$	

indicate the *uses* of national income. The sum of the items in row 1 thus represents national income of Country 1, while the sum of the items in column 1 shows the total expenditures of Country 1 on all goods and services. In summing column 1, the positive items of imports, $m_{21}(y_1)$ and $m_{31}(y_1)$, will exactly cancel against total imports, which enter negatively in row 1, column 1, leaving only the total expenditure, $u_1(y_1)$.

Consider, now, a more general economic system consisting of n countries. Using the same notation as in the table, we can set up n equations which express the fact that, in equilibrium, each country's output is equal to the demand for this output. Thus we have

$$y_1 = [u_1(y_1) - m_1(y_1)] + m_{12}(y_2) \qquad\qquad + \cdots + m_{1n}(y_n),$$
$$y_2 = m_{21}(y_1) \qquad\qquad + [u_2(y_2) - m_2(y_2)] + \cdots + m_{2n}(y_n),$$

(1) . . . .

$$y_n = m_{n1}(y_1) \qquad\qquad + m_{n2}(y_2) \qquad\qquad + \cdots$$
$$\qquad\qquad\qquad\qquad\qquad\qquad\qquad + [u_n(y_n) - m_n(y_n)].$$

Since there are n countries in all, these n equations are sufficient, with given prices and exchange rates, to determine the level of income in each country.

III. STABILITY OF THE SYSTEM

Equations (1) are *static* equations; they indicate the levels of income which the system would achieve if consuming and investing habits remained unchanged over a sufficient period of time. They are accordingly useful in solving economic problems such as the ones mentioned earlier. Suppose, for example, that the propensity to consume or to invest in domestic goods were to increase in Country 1; the demand for goods and services would then rise throughout the world economy, and if the system were stable a new equilibrium, corresponding to the higher level of demand in Country 1, would eventually be established in all countries. Equations (1) enable us to show how the new position of equilibrium in each of the n countries compares with the old. This problem is nothing more than a generalization of the familiar investment multiplier.

Before discussing the static theory of income, however, there is a closely related dynamic problem that it will be useful to discuss first. As we shall see, solution of the dynamic problem provides a considerable amount of information about the static theory. If income in one or more of the n countries is not in a state of equilibrium, so that the current level of output differs from the current demand, then the current levels of income, y_1, y_2, $\cdots$, y_n, will not satisfy equations (1). In some instances, the level of output or income, y_i, may fall short of demand, while in other instances output will probably be in excess of current demand. Under these circumstances there will be a tendency for the level of output in each country to change, as producers try to bring their production plans in line with current requirements. The changes in output, in turn, will alter the level of income in each country, thereby bringing about shifts of demand and creating further discrepancies between supply and demand. The dynamic problem I wish to discuss is whether such a system has a natural tendency to approach a balanced state or whether discrepancies between demand and supply tend to produce still larger discrepancies. In short, is the system of income equations stable or unstable?

In order to answer this question, some assumptions must be made as to what happens in each country when output differs from current demand.

Although no simple model can possibly do justice to such a complex problem, it seems to me reasonable to suppose that producers as a group will react to a discrepancy between output and demand by altering the rate of output. I shall therefore assume that output, and hence income, increases whenever demand exceeds current output and falls when demand is less than current output. Moreover, I shall also assume that the speed with which output plans are altered is directly proportional to the size of the discrepancy between demand and supply; a big discrepancy, in other words, leads to a more rapid response than a small one. Although this second assumption is not absolutely essential, it is an assumption which will simplify our problem somewhat without altering the results in any important respects. Throughout the period of time when income is out of equilibrium, discrepancies between demand and supply are assumed to be met by appropriate adjustments of business inventories.

For any given country, say Country 1, the rate of current net output or national income is y_1 , while the net demand for this output is $u_1(y_1) - m_1(y_1) + m_{12}(y_2) + \cdots + m_{1n}(y_n)$. The preceding assumptions concerning the behavior of producers may therefore be embodied, as a first approximation, in the following system of dynamic equations:

$$\frac{dy_1}{dt} = k_1[u_1(y_1) - m_1(y_1) + m_{12}(y_2) + \cdots + m_{1n}(y_n) - y_1],$$

(2) $$\frac{dy_2}{dt} = k_2[u_2(y_2) - m_2(y_2) + m_{21}(y_1) + \cdots + m_{2n}(y_n) - y_2],$$

$$\cdots \cdots \cdots \cdots \cdots \cdots \cdots \cdots \cdots \cdots \cdots \cdots \cdots \cdots \cdots$$

$$\frac{dy_n}{dt} = k_n[u_n(y_n) - m_n(y_n) + m_{n1}(y_1) + \cdots$$
$$+ m_{n,n-1}(y_{n-1}) - y_n].$$

The constants, k_i , in these equations are positive numbers which represent the speeds of adjustment of output in the various countries.

Equations (2) cannot be solved without knowing the explicit form of the expenditure functions and import functions. Since we are primarily interested in the stability of the system and not in its explicit solution, however, we may consider only a linear approximation to (2). Stability of the linear approximation is obviously a necessary condition, although not always a sufficient condition, for stability of equations (2). Expanding the right-hand side of (2) in a Taylor expansion about the equilibrium values y_1^0 , y_2^0 , $\cdots$, y_n^0 , and dropping all except linear terms, we have

$$\frac{dy_1}{dt} = k_1(u_1' - m_1' - 1)(y_1 - y_1^0)$$
$$+ k_1 m_{12}'(y_2 - y_2^0) + \cdots + k_1 m_{1n}'(y_n - y_n^0),$$

[Equations (3) continued on p. 338]

(3) $\dfrac{dy_2}{dt} = k_2\, m'_{21}(y_1 - y_1^0)$

$\qquad\qquad + k_2(u'_2 - m'_2 - 1)(y_2 - y_2^0) + \cdots + k_2\, m'_{2n}(y_n - y_n^0),$

. . . .

$\qquad \dfrac{dy_n}{dt} = k_n\, m'_{n1}(y_1 - y_1^0)$

$\qquad\qquad + k_n\, m'_{n2}(y_2 - y_2^0) + \cdots + k_n(u'_n - m'_n - 1)(y_n - y_n^0),$

where $u'_i \equiv (du_i/dy_i)_{v_i^0}$, $m'_{ji} \equiv (dm_{ji}/dy_i)_{v_i^0}$, etc. Equations (3), being linear with constant coefficients, can be solved for any given initial conditions so as to express each of the incomes, y_i , as a function of time, as follows:

(4) $\qquad y_i(t) = y_i^0 + A_{i1}e^{\lambda_1 t} + A_{i2}e^{\lambda_2 t} + \cdots + A_{in}e^{\lambda_n t},$

where the A_{ij} are constants dependent upon the initial value of income at time $t = 0$, and where the λ_j are roots of the following equation:

(5) $\begin{vmatrix} k_1(1 + m'_1 - u'_1) + \lambda & -k_1 m'_{12} & -k_1 m'_{1n} \\ -k_2 m' {}_{\,t} & k_2(1 + m'_2 - u'_2) + \lambda \cdots & -k_2 m'_{2n} \\ \cdots\cdots\cdots\cdots\cdots\cdots & \cdots\cdots\cdots\cdots\cdots & \\ -k_n m'_{n1} & -k_n m'_{n2} & \cdots k_n(1 + m'_n - u'_n) + \lambda \end{vmatrix} = 0.$

In order for $y_i(t)$ to approach its equilibrium value, y_i^0 , as t increases, it is apparent from (4) that the real parts of $\lambda_1, \lambda_2, \cdots, \lambda_n$ must all be negative. The necessary and sufficient conditions for this to be true may conveniently be expressed in terms of the following nth-order determinant:

(6) $\qquad M \equiv \begin{vmatrix} 1 + m'_1 - u'_1 & -m'_{12} & \cdots & -m'_{1n} \\ -m'_{21} & 1 + m'_2 - u'_2 & \cdots & -m'_{2n} \\ \cdots\cdots\cdots\cdots\cdots & \cdots\cdots\cdots\cdots & & \cdots\cdots\cdots \\ -m'_{n1} & -m'_{n2} & \cdots & 1 + m'_n - u'_n \end{vmatrix}$

The coefficient m'_{ij} of the determinant (6) represents, of course, the marginal propensity of the jth country to import from the ith country; i.e., it shows how the demand in Country j for imports from Country i is affected by a small increase in the former country's income. Similarly, the coefficient m'_j represents the marginal propensity of the jth country to import from all other countries together, so that $m'_j \equiv m'_{1j} + m'_{2j} + \cdots + m'_{nj}$. Throughout this paper, coefficients such as m'_{ij} are assumed to be positive or zero, which means that all of the off-diagonal elements of M are negative or zero.[6] The coefficient, u'_j , represents the marginal

---

[6] If one country's imports from another consisted predominantly of inferior commodities, the former's propensity to import from the latter might conceivably

propensity of the jth country to spend, including the marginal propensity to invest, if any, as well as the marginal propensity to consume, and including expenditure on imported finished goods as well as upon domestic goods. Normally u'_j will be less than unity, but, if the propensity to invest is large, this need not be true.

I have demonstrated in an earlier paper that, for dynamic systems such as (3) in which all off-diagonal coefficients of the y_i are positive or zero, the necessary and sufficient conditions of stability are identical with the so-called Hicksian conditions of perfect stability.[7] This means that the determinant, M, and any set of its principal minors such as

$$1 + m'_i - u'_i, \quad \begin{vmatrix} 1 + m'_i - u'_i & -m'_{ij} \\ -m'_{ji} & 1 + m'_j - u'_j \end{vmatrix},$$

$$\begin{vmatrix} 1 + m'_i - u'_i & -m'_{ij} & -m'_{ik} \\ -m'_{ji} & 1 + m'_j - u'_j & -m'_{jk} \\ -m'_{ki} & -m'_{kj} & 1 + m'_k - u'_k \end{vmatrix},$$

etc., must be positive. Hereafter, any determinant satisfying these conditions will be called a "Hicksian determinant."[8]

Since the speeds of adaptation, k_j, do not appear in the Hicks conditions, it follows that stability of (3) is independent of such speeds. A system which is stable for one set of speeds of adaptation will therefore be stable for all other possible sets. The fact that producers in one country change their production plans more rapidly than producers in another country has no effect upon the stability of the system.

Having established a general set of conditions which must be fulfilled in order that the income equations shall be stable, it is possible to go a step further and show that these Hicksian conditions depend, in a unique

---

be negative. In this event many of the theorems of the present paper would be invalid. The presence of negative propensities to import makes the conditions of stability considerably more complicated. Compare, for example, my conclusions concerning stability with those of John S. Chipman in the paper which follows this one.

[7] L. A. Metzler, "Stability of Multiple Markets: The Hicks Conditions," ECONOMETRICA, Vol. 13, October, 1945, pp. 277–292.

[8] In my earlier paper the conditions of stability were expressed in terms of a determinant whose elements all had signs opposite to the signs of the corresponding elements of M. As a result, the formal appearance of the stability conditions was not the same as in the present paper. In the terminology of my earlier paper, stability of the system required that the principal minors, when arranged as above, should be alternately negative and positive, and that the basic determinant itself should have the sign of $(-1)^n$. By changing the sign of each of the elements of M, the reader can easily verify that these earlier stability conditions are identical with the ones given in the present paper.

way, upon the propensities to spend in all countries. In particular, two propositions will be demonstrated. First, if the marginal propensity to spend, including expenditure on investment goods as well as on consumers' goods, is less than unity in every country, the system is necessarily Hicksian and therefore stable. Second, if the marginal propensity to spend is *greater* than unity in every country, the system cannot be Hicksian and must therefore be unstable.

To prove these propositions, it is convenient to use a theorem developed by Mosak.[9] Mosak's theorem, in slightly modified form, is as follows: If an nth-order determinant is Hicksian, and if the off-diagonal elements $-m'_{ij}$ are all negative, then the cofactor, M_{ij}, of the element $-m'_{ij}$ is positive for all i and j. The proof of this theorem is a simple proof by induction. Expanding M_{ij} about the row containing the elements $-m'_{j1}$, $-m'_{j2}$, $\cdots$, $-m'_{jn}$, we may write

$$(7) \qquad\qquad M_{ij} \equiv \sum_k - m'_{jk} M_{ij,jk},$$

where $M_{ij,jk}$ is the cofactor of the element $-m'_{jk}$ in the determinant, M_{ij}, and where the summation extends over all values of k from 1 to n except $k = j$. Since $M_{ij,jk} \equiv -M_{jj,ik}$, (7) may be written as follows:

$$(8) \qquad\qquad M_{ij} \equiv \sum_k m'_{jk} M_{jj,ik}.$$

Now M_{jj} is a Hicksian determinant of order $n - 1$. Suppose that Mosak's theorem is true for such an $(n - 1)$th-order determinant. Then $M_{jj,ik}$ is positive, and it follows, from (8), that M_{ij} must likewise be positive. Thus, if the theorem is true for the cofactors of an $(n - 1)$th-order determinant obtained by deleting the jth row and jth column of M, it is also true for the cofactors of the nth-order determinant, M. A similar argument applies, of course, to the cofactors of any lower-order Hicksian determinants obtained from M by deleting like rows and columns. To complete the proof we must show that the theorem is true for a low-order principal minor of M, such as a second-order minor. A typical second-order minor of M is

$$\begin{vmatrix} 1 + m'_i - u'_i & -m'_{ij} \\ -m'_{ji} & 1 + m'_j - u'_j \end{vmatrix}.$$

The cofactors of the off-diagonal elements of this minor are m'_{ij} and m'_{ji}, respectively, and these are both positive. Thus, Mosak's theorem is proved; i.e., we have shown that if the nth-order determinant is Hicksian, the cofactors of its off-diagonal elements are all positive.

    [9] Jacob L. Mosak, *General-Equilibrium Theory in International Trade*, Cowles Commission Monograph No. 7, Bloomington, Ind.: The Principia Press, 1944, pp. 49–51.

With the aid of this theorem, the two propositions stated above concerning the relations between marginal propensities to spend and the determinant, M, may easily be proved. Consider, first, the case in which the marginal propensity to spend is *less* than unity in each country. According to our first proposition, the determinant M is necessarily Hicksian and the dynamic system (3) is therefore stable under these conditions. The proposition will be proved by induction. Since $m_i' \equiv m_{1i}' + m_{2i}' + \cdots + m_{ni}'$, it is clear that the sum of the elements of the ith column of M is equal to $1 - u_i'$, where u_i' is the marginal propensity to spend of the ith country. Thus, if all u_i' are less than unity, the sum of the elements of each column of M will be positive. Adding all other rows of M to the first row, we may write:

$$
(9) \qquad M \equiv
\begin{vmatrix}
1 - u_1' & 1 - u_2' & 1 - u_3' & \cdots & 1 - u_n' \\
-m_{21}' & & & & \\
-m_{31}' & & & M_{11} & \\
\cdots & & & & \\
-m_{n1}' & & & &
\end{vmatrix},
$$

where M_{11} denotes the cofactor of M obtained by deleting the first row and first column. Now it is evident that under our assumed conditions M_{11} is an $(n-1)$th-order determinant having the same essential characteristics as M itself; i.e., the sum of the elements of each column of M_{11} is positive. The first column of M_{11}, for example, contains all of the elements of the corresponding column of M except the negative quantity, $-m_{12}'$, and similarly for all other columns. It follows that if the sum of the elements of a given column of M is positive, the same will be true a fortiori of the sum of the elements in the corresponding column of M_{11}. Any theorems concerning M which are based upon this characteristic will therefore be equally applicable to M_{11}. And a similar argument applies to lower-order principal minors of M, such as $M_{11,22}$, $M_{11,22,33}$, etc.

Suppose, now, that our theorem is true for the $(n-1)$th-order determinant, M_{11}; i.e., suppose that M_{11} is Hicksian. It can then be shown that the nth-order determinant, M, is also Hicksian. Expanding (9) on the first row and first column, in a Cauchy expansion, we find:[10]

$$
(10) \qquad M \equiv (1 - u_1')M_{11} + \sum_k \sum_j m_{j1}'(1 - u_k')M_{11,jk}.
$$

If M_{11} is a Hicksian determinant it must be positive, and $M_{11,jj}$, $M_{11,kk}$, etc., must likewise be positive. Moreover, by Mosak's theorem, $M_{11,jk}$ is positive. Since the m_{j1}' are positive or zero, and since $1 - u_1'$ and $1 - u_k'$

[10] See A. C. Aitken, *Determinants and Matrices*, New York: Interscience Publishers, Inc., 1944, pp. 74-75.

are positive by hypothesis, it follows immediately from (10) that, if M_{11} is a Hicksian determinant, M is positive and is therefore Hicksian.

It has now been demonstrated that if all u_k' are less than unity, and if M_{11} is Hicksian, then M is likewise Hicksian. By a similar argument it can be shown that, if $M_{11,22}$ is Hicksian and if the u_k' are less than unity, M_{11} is necessarily Hicksian. To complete the proof that M is always a Hicksian determinant when the marginal propensity to spend, u_k', is less than unity in every country, it is sufficient to show that the theorem is true for any low-order principal minor of M. Consider, for example, the following second-order minor:

$$\begin{vmatrix} 1 + m_i' - u_i' & -m_{ij}' \\ -m_{ji}' & 1 + m_j' - u_j' \end{vmatrix}.$$

Since $m_i' \geqslant m_{ji}'$ and $m_j' \geqslant m_{ij}'$, it is easy to show by expanding the above determinant that it is necessarily positive whenever u_i' and u_j' are both less than unity. Moreover, it may be seen by inspection that, under the prescribed conditions, the principal minors are positive. The second-order minor of M is therefore Hicksian, and our proof that M is a Hicksian determinant is complete.

If M is a Hicksian determinant, it follows from the results of my earlier paper that the dynamic system represented by equations (3) is a stable system. This conclusion will perhaps not surprise anyone, since it is simply a generalization of the theory of income stability of a single, closed economic system. It is well known that the multiplier in such a one-country system cannot have a finite value unless the country's marginal propensity to spend is less than unity. I have now established an analogous condition—sufficient but not necessary—for the case of an n-country economy.

Consider, now, an extreme case in which the marginal propensity to spend is *greater* than unity in every country. I have suggested above that in this event the determinant M cannot be Hicksian and the dynamic system (3) must therefore be unstable. The proof of this proposition consists of showing that if all u_k' exceed unity the assumption that M is Hicksian involves a contradiction. If M is Hicksian, the principal minor M_{11} is, of course, also Hicksian, which means that $M_{11,jk}$ and M_{11} are both positive. But if the marginal propensity to spend is greater than unity in all countries, $1 - u_k'$ is negative for all values of k. From (10) it follows that M must be negative. This contradicts the assumption that M is a Hicksian determinant and proves, in fact, that M cannot be Hicksian. It shows, in other words, that if the determinant is Hicksian so far as its principal minors are concerned, and if all marginal propensities to spend exceed unity, the determinant itself is negative and is therefore non-Hicksian. Employing again the results of my previous paper, it is clear that under such conditions the dynamic system (3) must necessarily be unstable.

I have now examined the stability of income for two different situations. The first, which might be called the normal situation, is the case in which the marginal propensity to spend is less than unity in every country. The second, which goes to the opposite extreme, is the case in which every country has a marginal propensity to spend exceeding unity. In the first situation the system was found to be Hicksian, and therefore stable, while in the second it was found to be non-Hicksian and therefore unstable. Between these two extremes may be found a large number of intermediate situations in which the propensity to spend is less than unity in some countries and greater than unity in others. The basic determinant, M, of these intermediate systems may or may not be Hicksian, which means that the systems may or may not be dynamically stable. Broadly speaking, we may say that M will be Hicksian and the system will be stable if the countries with low propensities to spend dominate, while in the converse case M will be non-Hicksian and the system unstable. In any event, the discussion that follows in Sections IV and V below concerning the international repercussions of added investment in one of the n countries is based upon the explicit assumption that the income equations form a dynamically stable system. In other words, the assumption is made that an increase of investment in one of the countries leads ultimately to a new equilibrium of income in all countries, and does not set off a continuous process of expansion culminating in a runaway inflation. This means that, while the propensity to spend may exceed unity in some countries, it cannot do so in all countries; at least one of the countries must have a propensity to spend of less than unity, and the low-propensity countries must be sufficiently important so that the basic determinant, M, is a Hicksian determinant.

IV. INVESTMENT AND INCOME

Having examined the conditions of stability of our income equations, we are now in a position to investigate some problems of comparative statics. Suppose that national income is initially in equilibrium in all countries and that this equilibrium is disturbed by an increase of investment in one of the countries, say in Country 1. If the increase of investment is sustained over a sufficient period of time, and if the income equations are dynamically stable, a new equilibrium corresponding to the higher rate of investment will eventually be established throughout the system. The income of every country will probably be affected to some extent by the expansion of investment in Country 1; and, as national incomes are altered, each country's exports and imports, or its balance of payments on current account, will likewise be changed. The present section is concerned with the changes in income brought about by the higher level of investment in Country 1.

Let α_1 represent autonomous or noninduced investment in Country 1. The first equation of the static system (1), including the additional investment, then becomes:

(11) $\qquad y_1 = u_1(y_1) - m_1(y_1) + m_{12}(y_2) + \cdots + m_{1n}(y_n) + \alpha_1$.

Assuming no change in autonomous investment in the other countries, the remaining $n - 1$ equations of (1) are unaltered. Equation (11) and the last $n - 1$ equations of (1) thus form a closed system of n equations in which the income of each country may be regarded as a function of α_1 . In order to see how the increase of investment in Country 1 affects each country, we may differentiate (11) and the last $n - 1$ equations of (1) with respect to α_1 , and solve the resulting linear equations for $dy_1/d\alpha_1$ and $dy_k/d\alpha_1$. It will then be found that

(12) $\qquad \dfrac{dy_1}{d\alpha_1} = \dfrac{M_{11}}{M} , \qquad \dfrac{dy_k}{d\alpha_1} = \dfrac{M_{1k}}{M} ,$

where, as before, M is the determinant of marginal propensities given by (6). Now, we know from the conditions of stability and from Mosak's theorem that M_{11} , M_{1k} , and M must all be positive. Both $dy_1/d\alpha_1$ and $dy_k/d\alpha_1$ must therefore be positive, which shows that an increase in investment in one of the n countries increases the level of income in every country in the system. There is, of course, nothing startling or profound about this conclusion; indeed, it is a conclusion which could have been reached intuitively without any mathematics at all.[11] It is therefore important only insofar as it leads to less obvious relations.

The expression, M_{11}/M, which shows how income in the first country is affected by an increase of investment in that country, is a generalized form of investment multiplier. I wish to show, now, how this generalized multiplier is related to two simpler multipliers that one encounters frequently in the theory of employment. The first of these simple multipliers is the ordinary investment multiplier of a closed economic system, i.e., the multiplier which ignores foreign-trade leakages; the second is the

[11] Any economist who gives the matter any thought will probably feel that to develop the rather complicated theorems of Section III concerning Hicksian determinants and conditions of stability simply in order to prove that an increase in investment in one country causes income to rise in all countries is like using a bulldozer to move an ant hill. His intuitive feeling may be so strong, in fact, that he will prefer to reverse the procedure of the present paper and use what he "knows" about the economic system to prove the theorems concerning determinants in Section III! While the mathematician will doubtless object to this procedure as completely lacking in rigor, I must confess that I have considerable confidence in it, particularly since it was substantially such a trend of thought which first led me to suspect the truth of the mathematical propositions of Section III above.

so-called foreign trade multiplier, which makes allowance for foreign-trade leakages but does not take into account the effects of income movements in other countries upon the demand for a given country's exports. If, as before, u_1' denotes the marginal propensity to spend of the first country, and m_1' denotes that country's marginal propensity to import, the ordinary investment multiplier, which assumes that all demand is for home goods, is simply $1/(1 - u_1')$. The foreign trade multiplier, on the other hand, is $1/(1 - u_1' + m_1')$. What is the relation of these two simple multipliers to the generalized multiplier given by (12)? Using the stability conditions and Mosak's theorem, it may be shown that, in the normal case in which the marginal propensity to spend is less than unity in every country, the value of the generalized multiplier lies between the ordinary multiplier and the foreign trade multiplier. To prove this proposition, notice first that by adding all other rows to the first row of M, expanding on the elements of this new row, and dividing both numerator and denominator by M_{11}, we may write:

$$(13) \quad \frac{dy_1}{d\alpha_1} \equiv \frac{M_{11}}{M}$$

$$\equiv \frac{1}{(1 - u_1') + [(1 - u_2')M_{12}/M_{11}] + \cdots + [(1 - u_n')M_{1n}/M_{11}]}.$$

Since M_{1k}/M_{11} is positive for any value of k, and since all of the u_k' are assumed to be less than unity, it is clear that the expression in (13) is less than the ordinary investment multiplier, which in this instance has a value of $1/(1 - u_1')$.

The second limit to $dy_1/d\alpha_1$ may be found by expanding M on its first *column* and again dividing both numerator and denominator of the resulting expression for $dy_1/d\alpha_1$ by M_{11}. It will then be found that

$$(14) \quad \frac{dy_1}{d\alpha_1} = \frac{1}{1 - u_1' + m_1' - [m_{21}'M_{21}/M_{11}] - \cdots - [m_{n1}'M_{n1}/M_{11}]}.$$

Again, since M_{k1}/M_{11} is positive, the value of $dy_1/d\alpha_1$ given by (14) is clearly *greater* than the foreign trade multiplier, $1/(1 - u_1' + m_1')$. Thus, I have shown that in the normal case in which all marginal propensities to spend are less than unity, the generalized investment multiplier has the following limits:

$$(15) \quad \frac{1}{1 - u_1' + m_1'} < \frac{dy_1}{d\alpha_1} < \frac{1}{1 - u_1'}.$$

These limits derive their importance from the fact that they represent two forms of the multiplier which have played prominent roles in the historical development of the theory of employment.

If one or more of the other countries—i.e., Countries 2, 3, $\cdots$, n—has a marginal propensity to spend greater than unity, one of the limits given by (15) *may* not hold. In particular, while the generalized multiplier is always greater than the foreign trade multiplier, as (14) shows, it may in special cases also be greater than the ordinary investment multiplier. Consider, for example, the following system:

$$(16) \qquad y_1 = 0.4y_1 + 0.5y_2 + \alpha_1, \qquad y_2 = 0.2y_1 + 0.7y_2.$$

For this system, $dy_1/d\alpha_1 = 3.75$, while $1/(1 - u_1') = 2.5$. Thus, when the marginal propensity to spend of one or more of the "other" countries exceeds unity, the true investment multiplier for a given country may be larger than the ordinary investment multiplier. In most cases, however, it seems probable that the true multiplier will lie between the two simple multipliers, as indicated in (15).

It may be useful at this point to give a brief intuitive explanation of the relations between the three multipliers. The foreign trade multiplier is the smallest of the three because it assumes that a country's exports are given and independent of its imports. In a period of rising domestic income, in other words, the foreign trade multiplier tacitly assumes that increased expenditures on imports represent net leakages from the country's circular flow of income; no allowance is made for the fact that as imports rise the level of income in other countries also rises, and the demand for the particular country's exports therefore rises, to some extent, along with its imports. The generalized multiplier takes account of this secondary rise in the country's exports, and it is therefore larger than the foreign trade multiplier. The ordinary investment multiplier, on the other hand, makes no allowance either for the leakages from the circular flow of income arising from increased imports or for the return of some of these leakages in the form of increased exports; it assumes, instead, that every increase in expenditure represents an equivalent increase in domestic income. Now, since the secondary rise in exports is normally smaller than the increase in imports with which it is associated, it follows that foreign trade usually exerts a retarding effect upon a rise in income originating in domestic investment. In short, the effect of foreign trade is to spread the stimulating effects of investment in one country over the entire economic system, thereby diluting to some extent the stimulus to income in the country originating the expansion. And, because it ignores this diluting effect, the ordinary investment multiplier overstates the rise in income at home to be expected from a given increase in domestic investment.

V. INVESTMENT AND THE PATTERN OF TRADE

So much for the effects of investment upon income and employment. I turn now to the related problem of the pattern of trade. As income expands throughout the system, each country's exports and imports will rise, and it is almost inevitable under such conditions that the balance of trade of most if not all of the countries will be affected. In the new position of equilibrium, some countries will have more favorable balances while others will have less favorable balances than in the old. What can be said, in a general way, about the new network of trade compared with the old?

With respect to bilateral balances between individual pairs of countries, there is very little that a general theory such as the one outlined in this paper can predict. The outcome depends entirely upon the particular values of the propensities to spend and to import, and may show wide variation from one economic system to another. With respect to each country's balance of trade as a whole, on the other hand, certain broad generalizations are possible. In particular, we can specify the conditions under which a general expansion originating in Country 1 is likely to lead to an improvement or to a deterioration in a given country's balance of trade with the rest of the world. Since there is no difficulty in forecasting how a given expansion will *initially* affect the balance of international payments, the problem before us is essentially a problem of comparing the initial, or primary, effects with the secondary repercussions. We want to know, in particular, whether the secondary repercussions are likely to reinforce or to offset the primary effects. Consider, for example, the balance of payments of some country other than Country 1, say Country k. As investment and income expand in Country 1, the initial effect will probably be an increase in exports from Country k to the expanding country, thereby giving the latter a temporary surplus in its balance of payments. A similar initial effect may be anticipated, of course, in all of the other countries dealing with Country 1. But, as the other countries' exports to Country 1 rise, their incomes will also rise, and the increase in incomes, in turn, will increase the demand for imports in these countries. The secondary income movements thus tend to offset the initial changes in balances of payments of the other countries.[12] There is no obvious reason, however, why the offsetting movement in each country's balance of payments should always be exactly equal to the initial disturbance. In the new equilibrium some countries will probably have more favorable balances of payments while others will have less favorable ones. What are the circumstances that distinguish the "surplus" countries from the "deficit" countries?

[12] It was no doubt this offsetting tendency that Nurske had in mind when he said that the theory of employment provides both an explanation of the adjusting process of the balance of payments and a theory of the transmission of business cycles from one country to another. (Ragner Nurske, "Domestic and International Equilibrium," in *The New Economics*, S. E. Harris, ed., New York: Alfred A. Knopf, Inc., 1947, p. 264.)

The question may be answered by considering the interrelations between balances of payments and incomes. Although the balance of trade of a given country depends upon the incomes of all countries in the system, there is a convenient way of relating each country's balance of trade to the *income of that country alone*. Thus, from the definition of national income given in (1) above, it follows that the excess of a country's exports over its imports is equal to the excess of its national income over its total expenditure on both consumers' goods and net investment. This is no more than a technical way of stating the common-sense proposition that a country with an export surplus is producing more than it uses itself, while a country with an import surplus is using more than it produces. But it is a technique, as we shall see, which saves a good deal of tedious algebra. Consider, for example, the balance of payments of Country k. If b_k denotes this balance, then it is clear from (1) that

(17) $$b_k = y_k - u_k(y_k),$$

whence

(18) $$\frac{db_k}{d\alpha_1} = (1 - u_k') \frac{dy_k}{d\alpha_1}.$$

Since $dy_k/d\alpha_1$ is positive, (18) shows that the direction of change of Country k's balance of payments depends upon that country's marginal propensity to spend. If its propensity to spend is less than unity, as will normally be the case, the balance of payments of Country k will be improved by the expansion in Country 1 even after allowing for the secondary rise of imports. But if the country's propensity to spend is *greater* than unity, (18) shows that its balance of payments on current account will be worsened by the expansion in Country 1. In this instance, the secondary rise of Country k's imports will be *more* than sufficient to offset the initial rise of its exports.

Now suppose that the marginal propensity to spend of each of the countries 2, 3, $\cdots$, n is less than unity. Under such conditions, the expansion of income in Country 1 improves the trade balances of all other countries in the system; and from this it follows that the trade balance of the country initiating the expansion must be less favorable than before the expansion began. In short, an expansion of income originating in one country normally moves the balance of trade *against* that country and *in favor* of all other countries in the system; as long as marginal propensities to spend are all less than unity, this proposition holds true regardless of the relative sizes of the marginal propensities to import. For this reason we cannot say that, if the other countries' propensities to import from Country 1 are high, the induced expansion of their imports is likely to over-balance the initial rise of their exports, leaving them with less favorable trade balances than before the expansion began. The outcome depends not upon the relative magnitudes of import propensities, but upon the absolute size of each of the propensities to spend. If the marginal propensities to spend are less than unity, the result will be an improvement in the balances of payments of all countries except Country 1, irrespective of the size of import propensities.

If marginal propensities to spend in some of the countries exceed unity, on the other hand, it is possible that some or all of the conclusions of the preceding paragraph will have to be reversed. Consider first an extreme case. Suppose that the propensities to spend exceed unity in *all* of the countries 2, 3, $\cdots$, n. Under these circumstances it is clear from (18) that the balance of trade of each of these countries would become less favorable as a result of expansion in Country 1; the secondary rise of imports in each of the countries would overbalance the primary increase in exports. But if Countries 2, 3, $\cdots$, n all have less favorable balances of payments, Country 1 must necessarily have a *more* favorable balance. After allowing for all repercussions, in other words, expansion of income in Country 1 increases that country's exports more than its imports are increased. Public works, encouragement of private investment, and other measures to expand the employment of resources in Country 1 would not, under the circumstances, create a balance-of-payments problem for the expanding country. Each time Country 1 increased its imports it could count upon an even larger secondary increase in its exports.

It is conceivable that this conclusion would be valid even under less extreme circumstances. Suppose, for example, that some of the countries 2, 3, $\cdots$, n had propensities to spend greater than unity while others had spending propensities less than unity. From (18) it is clear that some of these countries would then suffer a worsening of their balances of payments when Country 1 started an expansion, while others would find their balances of payments improved. And if the sum of all the adverse and favorable changes together were adverse, then Country 1 would obviously have a more favorable balance of payments than in the initial equilibrium. On the other hand, if the sum of changes in the balances of payments of Countries 2, 3, $\cdots$, n were favorable, then the movement of Country 1's balance would necessarily be adverse. Thus, when some of the spending propensities of Countries 2, 3, $\cdots$, n exceed unity, while others are less than unity, it is impossible without additional information to predict the effect of expansion on the balance of payments of the country initiating the expansion. The outcome depends upon a balancing of forces, i.e., upon a balancing of the influence of the stable countries against the influence of the unstable ones.

Thus far we have regarded the balance of payments of Country 1 as a sort of residual; we have described its movement only after seeing what happened to the balances of payments of the other countries in the system. Although this procedure is satisfactory for some purposes, it does not allow us to say much about the *magnitude* of the movement in Country 1's balance of payments. It is therefore useful to examine this balance directly . From (11) and (1) the balance of payments of Country 1 may be written as follows:

$$(19) \qquad\qquad b_1 = y_1 - u_1(y_1) - \alpha_1 .$$

In words, this says that Country 1's balance of payments on current account is the difference between its income and its total expenditure on goods and services, *including in the latter autonomous expenditures*, α_1 , as well as $u_1(y_1)$. Differentiating b_1 with respect to α_1 , we find:

$$(20) \qquad\qquad \frac{db_1}{d\alpha_1} = (1 - u_1') \frac{dy_1}{d\alpha_1} - 1.$$

In evaluating (20) we may begin with what I have called the normal case, namely, the case in which all marginal propensities to spend are less than unity. In this case we know from Section IV above that $dy_1/d\alpha_1$ is less than the ordinary investment multiplier; i.e., it is less than $1/(1 - u_1')$. From this fact we can derive the following limits for the movement of the balance of payments on current account of Country 1:

$$(21) \qquad\qquad -1 < \frac{db_1}{d\alpha_1} < 0.$$

The limits given by (21) show that in the normal case an increase of investment in Country 1 moves the balance of payments on current account *against* the expanding country; and the amount of the unfavorable movement is normally less than the increase of investment. A one billion dollar public works program consisting exclusively of expenditure on domestic goods and services, for example, could not under normal circumstances create a foreign-trade deficit in the expanding country greater than the amount of public works.

If the marginal propensity to spend in the expanding country were *greater* than unity, however, the limits given by (21) would no longer apply. It is apparent from (20) that under such a condition $db_1/d\alpha_1$ would be less, algebraically, than -1. The unfavorable movement of Country 1's balance of payment on current account would thus be *greater* than the amount of autonomous investment. An economy characterized by such a high propensity to spend would, of course, be highly unstable, and its instability, in turn, would lead to frequent and severe balance-of-payments problems vis-a-vis the rest of the world.

If the instability is in the rest of the world rather than in Country 1, there may be no balance-of-payments problem at all in the country initiating the expansion. In other words, if a larger number of the "other countries" have marginal propensities to spend greater than unity, while Country 1 has a propensity to spend *less* than unity, (20) shows that the change in the balance of payments of Country 1 may be favorable rather than unfavorable. This would be true whenever $dy_1/d\alpha_1$ were greater than $1/(1 - u_1')$. In such a situation the secondary rise in exports of the expanding country would exceed the rise in imports; the secondary effects, in other words, would more than offset the primary effects. But such an outcome could be expected only under the rather unusual circumstances of high propensities to spend in a considerable number of the other countries.

VI. TWO-COUNTRY AND MULTIPLE-COUNTRY MODELS COMPARED

The classical theory of international trade, including the theory of comparative advantage as well as the closely-related theory of the international price mechanism, was developed almost entirely in terms of two countries. Most of the important problems in international economics during the nineteenth century were discussed as though the world economy were divided into two regions, one region being the home country—usually England—and the other region being the "rest of the world." During the interwar period of the present century, this classical procedure came under heavy attack, particularly by the late Professor Graham, who argued with considerable cogency and force that the classical procedure involved a persistent bias.[13] Graham insisted that the traditional, two-country theory greatly exaggerated the role of international demand and neglected the role of shifts in output in determining the terms of international exchange. He argued, specifically, that if one considers a complex world economy in which a large number of countries are trading in a considerable number of commodities, the process of adjustment to a disturbing event in international trade is fundamentally similar to the process of adjustment within a single country. In Graham's view, then, the fact that resources, particularly labor, are more or less immobile between countries does not require, as the classical economists had supposed, a theory of *international* prices, separate and distinct from the theory of prices within a single country.

In concluding the present paper, which has dealt with an international theory of income rather than a theory of prices, there is no need to

[13] F. D. Graham, "The Theory of International Values Re-examined," *Quarterly Journal of Economics*, Vol. 38, November, 1923, pp. 54–86, and "The Theory of International Values," *ibid.*, Vol. 46, August, 1932, pp. 581–616. The ideas contained in these two articles were considerably elaborated in book form. (See F. D. Graham, *The Theory of International Values*, Princeton: Princeton University Press, 1948, 349 pp.)

discuss at length the controversy between Graham and the classical economists. My purpose in raising the issue is not to try to settle it but to raise a similar issue with respect to the international theory of income. If it is true, as Graham argues, that the traditional two-country model of international *price* theory involves a persistent and significant bias, is it also true that an analogous two-country model of international *income* theory involves a similar bias? To put the question another way, is a theory of international income that is founded upon the simplifying assumption that the world economy consists of two regions likely to involve any fundamental errors? The two-country income model, as I indicated earlier, has been discussed by a number of economists, and it should be possible to answer the question raised above by comparing the results of the two-country analysis with those of the generalized theory presented here. Since I am most familiar with my own version of the two-country model, I shall employ it to make the comparison.[14]

On the whole, the comparison does not reveal any basic flaws in the two-country model.[15] There are no processes of income adjustment in the *n*-country model which are not also revealed by the simple two-country model, and in the main the conclusions reached by employing the latter are the same as those reached by employing the former. In my earlier paper, using a terminology slightly different from that used here, I considered altogether three different cases of the two-country model. The first, or "normal," case was one in which the marginal propensity to spend was less than unity in both countries. The analogue of this case for the *n*-country model is the situation in which the propensity to spend is less than unity in each of the *n* countries. Under these circumstances both models reveal that an autonomous increase of investment in one country creates a deficit in that country's balance of payments on current account and that the amount of the deficit is less than the autonomous investment. This conclusion of the two-country model, in other words, is in no way vitiated by the complex interactions of trade among a large number of countries. The second case, in the two-country model, was one in which the propensity to spend of the country initiating the expansion, say Country 1, was less than unity, while the propensity to spend of the second country was greater than unity. The analogous situation, in the *n*-country model, is that in which the propensity to spend is less than unity in Country 1 but greater than unity in all other countries. Again, both the two-country and the *n*-country models lead to the same conclusion: autonomous investment in Country 1 actually *improves* the balance of trade of that country; the induced rise of Country 1's exports exceeds the rise of its imports. The third and final case, in the two-country model,

---

[14] Metzler, "Underemployment Equilibrium in International Trade," *op. cit.*
[15] Cf. Machlup, *op. cit.*, p. 197.

was a situation in which the propensity to spend in Country 1 was greater than unity, while the propensity to spend in Country 2 was less than unity; and the analogue of this situation, in the n-country model, is the situation in which Country 1 has a propensity to spend greater than unity, while all other countries have propensities less than unity. In this case also, as in the two preceding ones, the results of the two-country model are consistent with those of the n-country model. Either model supports the conclusion that, under the assumed conditions with respect to the propensities to spend, an increase in autonomous investment in Country 1 leads to an unfavorable movement in that country's balance of trade, the amount of the unfavorable movement being greater than the amount of autonomous investment.

Considering the large measure of agreement between the two-country and the n-country models, the reader may wonder what purpose is served by studying the generalized theory at all. If the simple theory and the general one both lead to the same results, why bother with the latter? To this question a number of answers may be given. The first and most obvious one is that hindsight is better than foresight. While we might have felt intuitively that the two-country model is satisfactory for most purposes, I doubt whether we could have been sure of this without a careful study of the more general system. A second reason for studying the general theory is that there are certain situations in the n-country model for which no analogue exists in the two-country model. This is true, for example, if the marginal propensity to spend is less than unity in Country 1 and in some but not all of the remaining countries. In situations such as this the effects of expansion can be described only by the general, n-country model. A third reason for preferring the n-country model to the two-country model is that the former provides a good deal more information than the latter about the dynamic stability of our income equations. Although I have used the stability conditions developed above primarily in studying the characteristics of the static equations, these stability conditions are also interesting and useful in other connections as well. It is useful, for example, to know that, if the propensity to spend is less than unity in all regions or subregions of the system, the stability of the income equations does not depend in any way upon how the world economy happens to be divided into national units. As a second example, it could easily be shown from Section III above and from my earlier paper on the stability of multiple markets that any cyclical solutions of the dynamic system are likely to be overshadowed by noncyclical solutions. This means, I believe, that the answer to the riddle of the business cycle is not to be found in horizontal transactions between one region and another, such as those depicted in our n-country system.

Perhaps the most important reason of all for studying the n-country model is that such a model will probably prove to be the most satisfactory theoretical foundation for an empirical study of the international aspects of income and employment. Although our study of the n-country model has not taken us very far, it has, I fear, taken us about as far as we can expect to go without introducing actual numbers in place of our hypothetical propensities to import and to spend. Unfortunately, the limits that we can expect to place upon the movements of our variables from a study of the theory alone are far too broad to be of much practical assistance in the formulation of economic policy. To a country considering the feasibility of a public works program, for example, it is little comfort to know that the unfavorable movement in its balance of trade engendered by such a program will normally be less than the amount of the public works. The country needs to know, in addition, what the approximate magnitude of its trade deficit will be and what the repercussions will be on incomes and trade balances in other countries. In order to answer questions such as these, it is obvious that the theory described above must be transformed into an empirical system; and for this purpose the n-country system is clearly the appropriate one. Eventually, then, an import-export matrix, similar in many respects to Leontief's input-output matrix for a single country, must be developed for the world economy. Many of the facts needed for such a table are already at hand. Reasonably accurate figures are available, for example, regarding the network of world trade. If these trade figures are to be transformed into propensities to import and to spend, however, they must be supplemented by statistics of national income for each of the countries. Lack of such income statistics has been responsible, more than anything else, for our inability to provide the empirical counterpart of the international theory of income set out above. With the improvement in statistics throughout the world since the end of the war, it is to be hoped that this gap in our knowledge will soon be filled.

The University of Chicago

Econometrica, Vol. 19, No. 1 (January, 1951)

THE NONLINEAR ACCELERATOR AND THE PERSISTENCE OF BUSINESS CYCLES[1]

By R. M. Goodwin

By taking account of obvious and inescapable limitations on the functioning of the accelerator, we explain some of the chief characteristics of the cycle, notably its failure to die away, along with the fact that capital stock is usually either in excess or in short supply. By a succession of increasingly complex models, the nature and methods of analyzing nonlinear cycle models is developed. The roles of lags and of secular evolution are illustrated. In each case the system's equilibrium position is unstable, but there exists a stable limit cycle toward which all motions tend.

INTRODUCTION

ALMOST without exception economists have entertained the hypothesis of linear structural relations as a basis for cycle theory. As such it is an oversimplified special case and, for this reason, is the easiest to handle, the most readily available. Yet it is not well adapted for directing attention to the basic elements in oscillations—for these we must turn to nonlinear types. With them we are enabled to analyze a much wider range of phenomena, and in a manner at once more advanced and more elementary.

By dropping the highly restrictive assumptions of linearity we neatly escape the rather embarrassing special conclusions which follow. Thus, whether we are dealing with difference or differential equations, so long as they are linear, they either explode or die away with the consequent disappearance of the cycle or the society.[2] One may hope to avoid this unpleasant dilemma by choosing that case (as with the frictionless pendulum) just in between. Such a way out is helpful in the classroom, but it is nothing more than a mathematical abstraction. Therefore,

---

[1] This paper, with the exception of a few modifications in the last section, was presented at the 1948 meeting of the Econometric Society in Cleveland, and it was summarized in ECONOMETRICA for April, 1949 (Vol. 17, pp. 184–185). In its various metamorphoses it was followed with great interest and many helpful comments by the late J. A. Schumpeter. His influence on the whole of it is so pervasive, and I hope so evident, that particular acknowledgment would be inadequate.

[2] Cf. any good book on mechanics, e.g., A. A. Andronow and C. E. Chaikin, *Theory of Oscillations* (English translation by S. Lefschetz), Princeton: Princeton University Press, 1949, Chapter I.

economists will be led, as natural scientists have been led, to seek in
nonlinearities an explanation of the maintenance of oscillation. Advice to
this effect, given by Professor Le Corbeiller in one of the earliest issues
of this journal, has gone largely unheeded.[3]

Mention should also be made of the fact that there exists an alternative way out of the dilemma—that of an impulse-excited mechanism.
There are two basically different classes of such mechanisms to be distinguished. (a) There are the synchronized systems of which the most
familiar is the ordinary pendulum clock. Here the pendulum executes
damped motion, but its own motion is used to time regular shocks so
that it settles down to a steady routine in which the energy which is
dissipated in friction during each cycle is exactly replaced. The wider
system, including the feedback mechanism (the escapement) for de-
livering the shocks, is a particular type of nonlinear oscillator since it
is autonomous and maintains a uniform cycle independently of initial
conditions. (b) Significantly different is a system subject to random
shocks. Here the mechanism itself is damped, but an outside, unexplained
source keeps it going, and in this sense it is not a complete theory, for
the source of maintenance lies outside the theory. Also, since the shocks
are not synchronized with the cycle, they work both with and against

---

[3] Ph. Le Corbeiller, "Les systèmes autoentretenus et les oscillations de relaxation," ECONOMETRICA, Vol. 1, July, 1933, pp. 328–332. "If statistical data lead us
to believe that a given magnitude varies periodically, and if we look for the cause
of these oscillations, we may suppose that that magnitude executes either (a)
forced oscillations, or (b) maintained oscillations, which may be either (bα) sine-
like, or (bβ) relaxation type." My debt to Professor Le Corbeiller is very great,
not only for the original stimulation to search for the essential nonlinearities,
but also for his patient insistence, in the face of the many difficulties which turned
up, that this type of analysis *must* somehow be worked out.

Since the statement in the text was written, I have discovered that there has
been an increasing amount of work on nonlinear theories, culminating in Professor
Hicks's admirable book, *A Contribution to the Theory of the Trade Cycle* (Oxford:
Clarendon Press, 1950, 199 pp.), which appeared while I was making final revi-
sions on this paper. Professor Tinbergen has also attacked the subject in his
article, "Ligevægtstyper Og Konjunkturbevægelse" (*Nordisk Tidsskrift for
Teknisk Økonomie*, Vol. 32, Nos. 2–4, 1943, pp. 45–63). This development cor-
roborates the position of Professor Le Corbeiller and promises much good for
economics. In Hicks's book the reader will find reference to other investigations
as well as a much more complete statement of why nonlinear cycle theory is
necessary. I find most impressive the extent to which he and I have hit on the
same problems and, substantially, the same answers, although his techniques
appear, on the surface, to be quite different since he deals with difference equations and since he does not approach the subject in terms of formal, nonlinear
theory. The similarities are not purely accidental, partly because we have both
started from the unsatisfactory, but profoundly stimulating, dynamical closure
of the Keynesian system put forth by Mr. Harrod in his book, *The Trade Cycle*
(Oxford: Clarendon Press, 1936, 234 pp.).

it so that their effects largely cancel out. That they do not entirely cancel out can be seen by the fact that, if the system were to come to rest, the next shock would excite it and the motion would be cyclical, so that there will always be a small tendency to cyclical motion. The shocks, however, would have to be large to produce much of a continuing cycle, which would make it desirable to analyze the individual causes and consequences of each shock rather than to treat them as a random element collectively. It also raises the question of whether or not the cycle would be more swamped in the random motions than is actually the case. Somewhere in between these two types lies the theory which might be called the Schumpeter clock (although it would be a chronometrically bad clock). The steady evolution of ideas leads to intermittent, irregular, but not random, bursts of expenditure. If these large and variable outlays impinge on a damped cycle, they may seriously alter its character and keep it from dying away. Professor Frisch has provided the basic analysis of this range of problems, and I shall attempt to indicate its relevance to nonlinear theories below.[4] The difficult question remains as to what extent the explanation lies entirely with the innovation, giving forced oscillations, and to what extent there is mutual conditioning, leading to an erratic clockwork (and hence nonlinear) theory.

Along with explaining the maintenance of oscillation, nonlinear theory does away with the necessity for "initial conditions." No matter how the mechanism is started, it tends to a certain type of cycle. Otherwise we are involved in believing that the magnitude and turning points, for example, of a cycle now are completely determined by events which took place many years ago. The absurdity of such an assumption is obvious.

Another advantage lies in the possible treatment of the acceleration principle. Because statistical studies (e.g., Tinbergen's "Statistical Evidence on the Acceleration Principle")[5] have shown that it does not correspond to the facts, many economists favor dropping it entirely. Yet this would surely be mistaken since it is merely the statement of a simple consequence of the one omnipresent, incontestable dynamic fact in economics—the necessity to have both stocks and flows of goods. In any case, it is worth while to try assumptions which take account of this fact but do not require any rigid proportionality. In doing this we

[4] Cf. Frisch, "Propagation Problems and Impulse Problems in Dynamic Economics," in *Economic Essays in Honour of Gustav Cassel*, London: George Allen and Unwin Ltd., 1933, pp. 171–205, and also my own "Innovations and the Irregularity of Economic Cycles," *Review of Economic Statistics*, Vol. 28, May, 1946, pp. 95–104.
[5] *Economica*, Vol. 5 (New Series), May, 1938, pp. 164–176.

may avoid another shortcoming of linear theory—the requirement that the upswing be essentially the same type of thing as the downswing. With nonlinear theory we may make the depression as different from the boom as we wish; in fact this is one way of assessing the degree of nonlinearity.

I shall proceed in order of increasing difficulty, taking up a series of models which are all variants of the simple multiplier and accelerator principles. The first is a threshold oscillator in which the economy once started up continues until it removes the capital deficiency which started it, and then it goes down until it removes the excess capacity with which it started downward. The second model introduces a simple linear trend (which is more important to nonlinear systems than to linear) which makes it unnecessary to await the wearing out of all the capital from the preceding boom before beginning the coming one. A third model consists of a combination of a dynamical accelerator and a less crude form of the nonlinear accelerator. This gives a more complicated evolution, but it still contains sudden shifts from declining to rising income and the reverse. This unreality is eliminated in the final model by taking account of the lag between investment decisions and the resulting outlays.

THE SIMPLEST MODEL

The central difficulty with the acceleration principle is that it assumes that actual, realized capital stock is maintained at the desired relation with output. We know in reality that it is seldom so, there being now too much and now too little capital stock. For this there are two good reasons. The rate of investment is limited by the capacity of the investment goods industry. Furthermore, entrepreneurial expectations are such that, even if it were possible to expand plant in the boom, there would be a great resistance to it. At the other extreme there is an even more inescapable and effective limit. Machines, once made, cannot be unmade, so that negative investment is limited to attrition from wear, from time, and from innovations. Therefore, capital stock cannot be increased fast enough in the upswing, nor decreased fast enough in the downswing, so that at one time we have shortages and rationing of orders and at the other excess capacity with idle plants and machines.

Call k capital stock, ξ the desired capital stock (proportional to income or output), c consumption, y income, and α, β, and κ constants. Then, with a linear consumption function,

(1) $\xi = \kappa y,$

(2) $c = \alpha y + \beta,$

(3) $y = c + k,$

where $\dot{k}$ is dk/dt, the rate of change in capital stock and, hence, net investment. I shall assume that the economy seeks the perfect adjustment of capital to output and that it does so in either of two extreme ways, capacity output of investment goods or zero gross investment. If actual capital equals desired capital, no adjustment is necessary and capital is simply maintained with zero net investment. When the stock of capital, k, is insufficient, the rate of investment, $\dot{k}$, proceeds at capac-

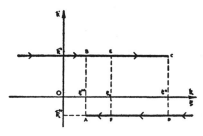

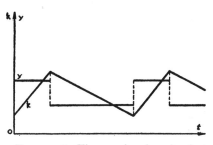

FIGURE 1—Simplest limit cycle in phase space.

FIGURE 2—Time series for simplest model.

ity, $\dot{k}^*$, and when it is in excess, it is retired by scrapping at a rate, $\dot{k}^{**}$, so that

(4)
$$\dot{k} = \begin{cases} \dot{k}^*, & \xi > k, \\ 0, & \xi = k, \\ \dot{k}^{**}, & \xi < k. \end{cases}$$

Combining (1), (2), (3), and (4) we have

$$\xi = \frac{\kappa}{1-\alpha}\dot{k} + \frac{\kappa\beta}{1-\alpha},$$

which gives ξ^*, ξ_0, ξ^{**} upon substitution of the corresponding values for $\dot{k}$. ξ has therefore only three possible values because it is linearly related to $\dot{k}$, which has only three by hypothesis.

If we plot this system in phase space we get the picture given in Figure 1. By contrast, a linear system would be a single straight line sloping upward to the right. The arrows indicate the direction of movement. The point ξ_0 is an equilibrium point ($k = \xi$ and consequently $\dot{k} = 0$) and satisfies the relationships defining the system. It is, however, an unstable equilibrium, since a small displacement in the phase plane leads to a large displacement from which it never returns. For example, if to ξ_0 we add $\Delta\xi$, then $\dot{k}$ changes from zero to $\dot{k}^*$ and ξ becomes ξ^*, and hence we are transferred to a point near E in the phase diagram. From there we travel continuously to C, at which point the system exhibits discontinuous change in k. At C, $k = \xi$, which means k drops to zero, but that makes $\xi = \xi_0 < k$; hence $k = 0$ is not a possible value and k^{**} is required. Thus the representative point in the phase plane jumps discontinuously from C to D and then travels continuously at a much slower pace, to A, where it jumps, for the opposite reasons, to B and thence to C, and so on indefinitely. Therefore we arrive at the limit cycle $ABCD$, and it is always the same cycle no matter where we start. The time series of k and y corresponding to the limit cycle are shown in Figure 2. For any initial stock of capital we get a determinate path for all subsequent time. To the left of B we travel on the top line, to the right of D on the bottom one. Between these two limits we have to specify not only the stock of capital but also whether it is increasing or decreasing since, as in any oscillation, the same quantity position must be traversed twice, once going up and once coming down. It is to be noted that very rapid changes are possible in investment but are quite impossible in the stock of capital. Hence, whenever the system reaches an impasse of any sort, the necessary discontinuity (which may be taken as an idealization of a very rapid change) must occur in k, not in k.

It would be difficult to imagine a cruder or more oversimplified model of the business cycle, but it does serve to illustrate clearly the general characteristics of nonlinear oscillators:

A. The final result is independent of the initial conditions.

B. The oscillation maintains itself without the need of any outside "factors" to help in the explanation. In this sense it is a complete, self-contained theory.

C. The equilibrium is unstable and therefore the mechanism starts itself given even the smallest disturbance. Yet in spite of this instability it is a usable theory because the mechanism does not explode or break down but is kept within limits by the nonlinea : .y.

D. No questionable lags are introduced. The mechanism operates by its own structure.

While such a crude model cannot claim to be a representation of actual cycles, it does have many of the basic characteristics (as opposed to the refinements) of the picture of cycles that economists have agreed on. In particular, its nature is such that when there is heavy investment, businessmen desire more capital than they have and when there is no investment, they have too much capital. Yet neither of these apparently circular and hence self-sustaining conditions can persist indefinitely because of an *inherent* dynamical contradiction. The boom generates its own ruin by fulfilling its purpose, and the depression brings about its own cure by removing the source of its being. One striking shortcoming of the mechanism is its tendency to spend much more of its time in depression than in boom, since capital can be built much more rapidly than it is worn out. Our mechanism gets rid, during depression, of all the capital created during the boom. Clearly, any account of growth will change this and remove the shortcoming.

TECHNOLOGICAL PROGRESS

To make a crude allowance for technological progress, we may assume a steady growth in the desired amount of capital. Altering (1) accordingly, we get

(1a) $$\xi = at + \kappa y; \quad \dot{\xi} = a,$$

where t is time and a the constant growth rate in the capital requirements. Keeping the other relations (2), (3), (4), we find that, as might be expected, no equilibrium exists, since $\dot{k} = 0$ means that k is constant

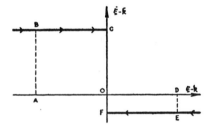

FIGURE 3—Phase diagram with steady growth.   FIGURE 4—The nonlinear accelerator-multiplier.

and hence that ξ would become greater than k and hence that $\dot{k}$ would cease to be zero.

Desired capital, ξ, depends on time and on the level of income, and hence

$$\xi = \begin{cases} at + \xi^* , & \xi - k > 0; \\ at + \xi^{**}, & \xi - k < 0. \end{cases}$$

It is more convenient to plot $\dot{\xi} - \dot{k}$ against $\xi - k$, as is done in Figure 3. $\dot{\xi}$ is always equal to a except at the points of discontinuity, whereas $\dot{k}$ has two values, $\dot{k}^*$ and $\dot{k}^{**}$. If a is greater than $\dot{k}^*$, the economy can never catch up with its capital needs. Excluding this unrealistic case, we find that in boom the economy proceeds slowly along the path EF, gradually catching up with its requirements (desired capital, ξ, is greater than actual capital stock, k). When enough capital has been accumulated $(\xi = k)$, investment ceases, but this means a great fall in income and hence capital requirements, so that decumulation begins. Hence we *add* to $\dot{\xi} = a$ the *negative* net investment $\dot{k}^{**}$, and hence (with $k > \xi$)

we proceed rapidly along the line BC—rapidly because excess capacity is being eliminated both through failure to replace and the steady occurrence of capital-using innovations. The distance AO is equal to OD since in each case the distance from the origin represents the jump in the value of ξ consequent upon a shift from k^* to k^{**} or vice versa. But while ξ shifts by the difference between ξ^* and ξ^{**}, k does not alter at the time of shift. Given any initial value of $\xi - k$, the path of the system is uniquely determined. If the mechanism was not already oscillating, it will, in the course of one motion, commence to vibrate on the closed cycle $BCEFBC$, and so on indefinitely in the absence of a change from "outside."

In addition to the characteristics of the first example, this one has certain other important aspects:

A. So long as there is technological progress, it has no equilibrium point; it can never settle down, even for a moment. It strains to get to its equilibrium point, but once there it relaxes, and that relaxation means that so much capital is no longer needed. Then it strains to slough off the excess capital, which, once eliminated, changes the situation again.

B. The depression is almost certain to be shorter than the boom and in any case is not symmetrical with it. The relative length of the two phases depends entirely on the rate of secular progress.

C. There is secular progress with capital accumulation.

D. The mode of action of this progress has considerable affinity with the Schumpeterian theory of innovations. New ideas requiring investment occur regularly, but nonetheless investment goes by spurts. Thus one of the most fundamental aspects of nonlinear oscillators is demonstrated: they are frequency converters. A steady change (zero frequency) is converted into a fluctuating motion with a positive frequency, or period.

E. In the simplest possible way, autonomous and induced investments are combined.

By virtue of its simplicity, this model has great flexibility. We may consider any variable rate of progress that we wish by taking short periods of constant rates of progress but allowing the rate to be different in each short space of time. In this manner we may easily introduce an historical element, prolonging or shortening the boom or depression according to the actually realized rate of progress.

THE DYNAMICAL MULTIPLIER AND THE NONLINEAR ACCELERATOR

There are two directions in which we may soften the crudities of the theory. The first is by considering the dynamical operation of the multiplier and the second by doing the same for investment decisions and outlays (to be taken up only in the next section). The use of the instantaneous multiplier introduces a quite unreal and unnecessary awkwardness, while clarifying and simplifying the problem. It is certain that the process of multiplication takes time, and in any dynamical situation it is important to take this into account. I propose to do this by replacing equations (2) and (3) by

(5) $$y = \alpha y + \beta + \dot{k} - \epsilon \dot{y}.$$

This is a multiplier, with a lag introduced by $\epsilon \dot{y}$, where ϵ is analogous to the lag in the usual time period analysis.[6] If we rewrite (5) in the form,

$$y = \frac{1}{1-\alpha} (\beta + \dot{k} - \epsilon \dot{y}),$$

we see that it states that income is the multiplier value of investment plus consumer injections less a kind of saving or disinvestment (it can be interpreted as either) resulting from a changing level of income.

The investment, $\dot{k}$, consists of an autonomous part, $l(t)$, and an induced part, φ. About induced investment we may make the less crude (than the previous one) assumption that the acceleration principle ($\xi = \kappa y$) holds over some middle range but passes to complete inflexibility at either extreme, as is shown in Figure 4. The upper limit is the k^* of the previous models and the lower limit the k^{**}. $d\varphi(\dot{y})/d\dot{y}$ is equal to the acceleration coefficient, κ, in its middle range and zero (or some quite small value) at either extremity. If we let

(6) $$\psi(\dot{y}) = \varphi(\dot{y}) - \epsilon \dot{y},$$

it will have the shape shown in Figure 5 when it is merely "multiplied" by $1/(1 - \alpha)$. It is assumed that $d\varphi(0)/d\dot{y}$ is greater than ϵ. If, for the moment, we measure y in deviations from its (dis-) equilibrium value, we may ignore β and l. Thus we get the result shown in Figure 5 which represents the equation

(5a) $$y = \frac{1}{1-\alpha} \psi(\dot{y}).$$

Thus for every value of y we can find whether it is increasing or decreasing and by how much. Therefore, once we specify an initial income, its whole subsequent evolution is determined.

We find that there is an equilibrium point, E, at the origin, but that it is unstable, as indicated by the arrows. Therefore, a small change in outside conditions leads, for example, to explosive growth to A, where

[6] Cf. my paper, "Secular and Cyclical Aspects of the Multiplier and the Accelerator," in *Employment, Income, and Public Policy*, Essays in Honor of Alvin H. Hansen, New York: W. W. Norton and Co., 1948, pp. 108–132.

the development becomes untenable with a discontinuous change in $\dot{y}$ to point B. And thence to C to D to A, and so forth, so that we have a closed path constituting a self-sustaining cycle.

The points A and C are critical points and there one of the variables suffers a discontinuous jump. Which variable can only be decided in terms of knowledge about the variables involved. In our case it is clearly $\dot{y}$ and not y, which is analogous to the jump from k^* to k^{**}. The discontinuity should be considered as an approximation to a rapid change. That there must be a jump can be deduced from the two facts that (a) the point, representative of the economy, must be on the curve, and (b) it must follow the direction of the arrows.

The model abstracts from secular progress, and by taking account of it we escape the peculiarity that the model spends more of its time in

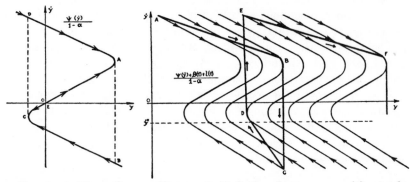

FIGURE 5—Phase dia-   FIGURE 6—Path in phase space with steady
gram for accelerator-   growth.
multiplier.

depression than in boom. As our system stands, income always returns to its previous low, but if we introduce a shifting of the curve to the right, then it is intuitively evident that the upswing will be lengthened and the downswing shortened. In order to include autonomous as well as induced investment we must rewrite (5a) as

$$(5b) \qquad y = \frac{\psi(\dot{y})}{1-\alpha} + \frac{\beta(t)}{1-\alpha} + \frac{l(t)}{1-\alpha},$$

where $l(t)$ is the historically given investment outlay, which does not depend on output and which may be roughly associated with innovations and governmental injections of purchasing power. As an interesting, though not essential, refinement, we may say that $l(t)$ is identically zero whenever $\dot{y}$ is below some negative threshold value, indicated as $\dot{y}^*$ in Figure 6. $\beta(t)$ is the historically given upward drift of the consumption function. This may be associated with rising population (because a given level of output means ever greater numbers of unemployed, all of whom consume without income) and with the accumulation of capital leading to greater *fixed*, short-run outlays of business. It is also possible to regard the long-run consumption function (with β as zero) as basic and the short-run one as a deviation from it depending on the previous high income.[7] The graphical technique is somewhat more complicated (the ψ curve is elongated in the upper phases of the boom) but the results are otherwise much the same. For simplicity of exposition only, I shall take the simple case of a steady increase in $\beta(t)$ and an $l(t)$ irregularly positive in boom and zero in deep depression. The effect of any increase in β and l is to translate the $\psi(\dot{y})$ curve to the right by the multiplier value of the current rates of outlay which they represent.

The resulting trajectory is no longer a closed curve, which merely expresses the fact that it is an evolutionary and not a stationary economy. It goes from A to B to C to D to E to F, and so on. The most important formal result is that the boom is lengthened and the depression shortened, thus avoiding the unrealistic behavior that the depression would otherwise have to last long enough to wear out all the capital constructed in the boom. It is possible to construct a good approximation to the trajectory in this phase space for any arbitrary $l(t)$. Thus every cycle may be (and certainly will be) different in shape and duration. Large innovational outlays lengthen the boom and carry it further. On the other hand, if there is only induced investment the upswing will not last so long. If innovational outlays commence early in the depression they will shorten it but not (unless very large) stop it. But, coming late in the depression, they may well reverse the downward motion of income; it is this case which is shown in Figure 6. Should no innovational outlays occur, the depression may drag out for a long time.

By graphical integration from Figure 6, we may determine the behavior of national income over time. The rate of growth of income is greatest at the beginning of the boom and then declines somewhat but not to zero. It changes at the peak to a decline, first great and then ever milder. The kind of behavior implied is shown roughly in Figure 7

EXPANDED MODEL WITH INVESTMENT LAG

The second lag that must be considered in order to come closer to reality is the lag between decisions to invest and the corresponding outlays. We may say that outlays will tend to lag behind decisions by

[7] Cf. James S. Duesenberry, *Income, Saving, and the Theory of Consumer Behavior*, Cambridge, Mass.: Harvard University Press, 1949, 128 pp.; and Franco Modigliani, "Fluctuations in the Savings-Income Ratio: A Problem in Economic Forecasting," in *Studies of Income and Wealth*, Vol. XI, New York: National Bureau of Economic Research, 1949, pp. 371–438.

approximately one half the length of time required for fabrication, which is longer than the time required for consumption goods. Therefore we may say

$$O_I(t + \theta) \approx O_D(t) = \varphi[\dot{y}(t)],$$

where O_I equals investment outlays, O_D investment decisions, and θ is one half the construction time of new equipment. Hence equation (5) is more correctly written as

(5c) $\epsilon \dot{y}(t + \theta) + (1 - \alpha)y(t + \theta) = O_A(t + \theta) + \varphi[\dot{y}(t)],$

where O_A stands for the sum of the autonomous outlays β and l. Expanding the two leading terms in a Taylor series and dropping all but the fist two terms in each, we get

(5d) $\epsilon \dot{y} + \epsilon \theta \ddot{y} + (1 - \alpha)y + (1 - \alpha)\theta \dot{y} - \varphi(\dot{y}) = O_A(t + \theta),$

where $\dot{y} = dy/dt$ and $\ddot{y} = d^2y/dt^2$. Or, shifting our autonomous injections by θ time units and calling it O^*, we get

(5e) $\epsilon \theta \ddot{y} + [\epsilon + (1 - \alpha)\theta]\dot{y} - \varphi(\dot{y}) + (1 - \alpha)y = O^*(t).$

For the moment we may take $O^*(t)$ to be a constant, O^*. Then we may study deviations from the equilibrium income $O^*/(1 - \alpha)$ by substituting

$$z = y - O^*/(1 - \alpha),$$

which gives us

(5f) $\epsilon \theta \ddot{z} + [\epsilon + (1 - \alpha)\theta]\dot{z} - \varphi(\dot{z}) + (1 - \alpha)z = 0.$

If $d\varphi(0)/d\dot{z} < \epsilon + (1 - \alpha)\theta$, we get damped oscillations, and if it is considerably less, we get nonoscillatory stable motion. In these cases we may write a linear approximation by taking $d\varphi(0)/d\dot{z}$ as a constant, and thus we will get a valid representation for small motions around the equilibrium point. But if $d\varphi(0)/d\dot{z} > \epsilon + (1 - \alpha)\theta$, which there is good reason to suppose to be the case, the system explodes beyond the limited region of valid linear approximation. Then we must resort to the Poincaré-Liénard method of graphical integration.[8] First, however, (5f) must be reduced to a dimensionless form. Let

$$\psi(\dot{z}) = [\epsilon + (1 - \alpha)\theta]\dot{z} - \varphi(\dot{z}),$$

[8] A particularly lucid and illuminating account of the entire subject, as well as of the Liénard construction, may be found in Ph. Le Corbeiller, "The Non-Linear Theory of the Maintenance of Oscillations," *Journal of the Institution of Electrical Engineers*, London, Vol. 79, September, 1936, pp. 361–378. A good account of the general methods employed in this, as well as of a much wider range of topics, will be found in the English translation, already referred to, of the important work of the two Russian scientists, Andronow and Chaikin.

$$x = \sqrt{(1 - \alpha)/\epsilon\theta}\; z/\dot{z}_0,$$

$$\dot{x} = dx/dt_1 = \dot{z}/\dot{z}_0,$$

$$\ddot{x} = d^2x/dt_1^2,$$

$$t_1 = \sqrt{(1 - \alpha)/\epsilon\theta}\; t.$$

$\dot{z}_0$ is any convenient unit in which to measure velocity. Noting that

$$\ddot{z} = \dot{z}_0 \frac{d^2x}{dt_1\,dt} = \dot{z}_0 \sqrt{\frac{1 - \alpha}{\epsilon\theta}} \frac{d^2x}{dt_1^2},$$

we may substitute these new variables in (5f), which becomes, after simplification,

(7) $$\ddot{x} + \frac{\psi(\dot{z}_0\dot{x})}{\dot{z}_0\sqrt{\epsilon\theta(1 - \alpha)}} + x = 0.$$

Letting

(7a) $$X(\dot{x}) = \frac{\psi(\dot{z}_0\dot{x})}{\dot{z}_0\sqrt{\epsilon\theta(1 - \alpha)}},$$

we get

(7b) $$\ddot{x} + X(\dot{x}) + x = 0.$$

An illuminating way to regard this is to write it as

(7c) $$\ddot{x} + [X(\dot{x})/\dot{x}]\dot{x} + x = 0,$$

where the expression in square brackets may be regarded as a variable damping coefficient. As is well known, a positive coefficient leads to an attenuating cycle and a negative one to an exploding cycle. $X(\dot{x})$ differs only in scale from $\psi(\dot{y})$, and therefore $X(\dot{x})/\dot{x}$ has the general form shown in Figure 8. Consequently the system oscillates with increasing violence in the central region, but as it expands into the outer regions, it enters more and more into an area of positive damping with a growing tendency to attenuation. It is intuitively clear that it will settle down to such a motion as will just balance the two tendencies, although proof requires the rigorous methods developed by Poincaré. It is interesting to note that this is how the problem of the maintenance of oscillation was originally conceived by Lord Rayleigh and that our equation is of the Rayleigh, rather than the van der Pol, type. The result is that we get, instead of a stable equilibrium, a stable motion. This concept is the more general one, for a stable equilibrium point may be considered as a stable motion so small that it degenerates into a point. Perfectly general conditions for the stability of motion are complicated and diffi-cult to formulate, but what we can say is that any curve of the general shape of $X(\dot{x})$ [or $\psi(\dot{y})$] will give rise to a *single, stable* limit cycle. Of another equation mathematically equivalent to ours, Andronow and Chaikin say: "Thus while there is no convenient method for solving van der Pol's equation, it is known that: (a) there is a unique periodic solution and it is stable; (b) every solution tends asymptotically to the periodic solution. These two properties manifestly provide most valuable practical information."[9] Therefore, making only assumptions acceptable to most business cycle theorists, along with two simple approximations, we have been able to arrive at a stable, cyclical motion which is self-generating and self-perpetuating.

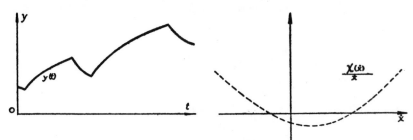

FIGURE 7—Time series with steady   FIGURE 8—The variable damping
growth.   coefficient.

For performing the graphical integration it is convenient, letting $v = \dot{x}$, to rewrite (7b) as

(7d) $$v\frac{dv}{dx} + X(v) + x = 0.$$

Thus we have an extremely simple, nonlinear, first order, differential equation, which may easily (the Liénard method makes it truly easy) be integrated graphically, provided we have an empirically given $X(v)$ curve. $X(v)$ need not be expressible in any simple mathematical form, although some approximation, say by a cubic expression, does facilitate qualitative discussion of the type of system. In our case we have only a very rough idea of the X function, which we may derive from the structural parameters, ϵ, θ, α, and the acceleration coefficient operative when there is no excess capacity. Regarding these parameters we have but a crude idea of their order of magnitude, nothing more. In estimating the fabrication period (twice the time lag) of consumption goods we must remember that it includes not only the time required to make any one article but also the raw materials that go to make it, and those that go to make the raw materials, and so on. If we replace all this by a single hypothetical firm producing consumption goods, we

[9] Andronow and Chaikin, *op. cit.*, pp. 4 and 302 ff.

must make the assumption of a fairly long fabrication time, say one-half to one and one-half years. Taking the mean of this range, we might put the time at one and hence ϵ at 0.5. Professor Frisch estimated the fabrication time for capital goods on the average at three years, and I shall take it to be two, which makes θ equal to 1.0. There is good evidence that in the course of the cycle α is around 0.6.[10] The acceleration coefficient is the ratio of national capital to national income, which was around 4.0 for Britain in the 1930's and was undoubtedly of this

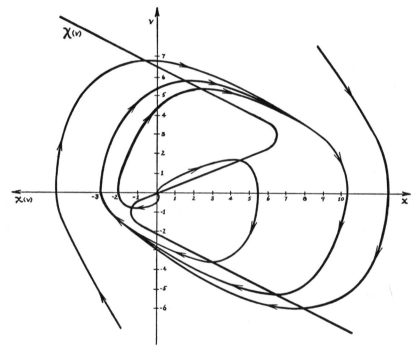

FIGURE 9—Phase portrait of the accelerator-multiplier with investment lag.

order of magnitude for the United States, although accurate statistics are still lacking. There is no doubt, however, that the marginal coefficient operative in a boom is much smaller. I shall assume that the slope of $\varphi(\dot{y})$ (the acceleration coefficient, κ) is 2.0 in the middle range and zero at either end. There remains only to determine the possible

[10] For simplicity I choose to ignore the thesis of Professors Duesenberry and Modigliani that the marginal propensity to consume has different values according to the recent past levels of income. But it is interesting to note that such hereditary effects (level dependent on path) have few terrors here since analytic solutions are impossible and graphical or arithmetical methods are used in any case.

limits of net annual investment. From Kuznets' data for the great boom and depression, these might be placed at −3.0 and +9.0 billions of dollars per year.

In Figure 9 is given the Poincaré limit cycle for the foregoing values of parameters. Also represented are four possible phase trajectories, starting from arbitrary initial conditions and approaching asymptotically the unique limit cycle. All points in the phase plane represent pairs of initial conditions, the vertical axis giving the initial velocities and the horizontal axis the initial levels of income (in deviations from some steady level). Through every point in the phase plane passes a single trajectory, which leads ultimately to the one limiting motion. In Figure 9 we have velocity as a function of income, and hence, by a second graphical integration, we can get income as a function of time for the undisturbed or limiting cyclical form. The range of fluctuation

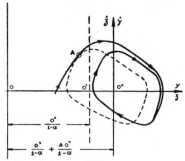

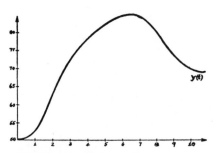

FIGURE 10—Effect of a single shift on phase path.

FIGURE 11—Time series of a non-sinusoidal cycle with growth.

is from −5.0 in the trough to +19.0 billions of dollars per year at the peak, and the period is slightly over nine years. The ease with which such models explain long cycles is a notable feature, and it does not depend in any great degree on the lags but rather on the amount of time it takes to produce the desired amount of capital goods.[11] Figure 9 also gives an idea of the extent of departure from simple harmonic motion as represented by a sine curve. The closed phase diagram for a sine curve is a circle, whereas this phase diagram is very uncircular. The upswing gets under way more quickly and the high level of activity is held longer than with a sine curve. The upper turning point is followed by a rapid decline and a tendency to remain longer at a depressed

[11] This can be seen perhaps more clearly in the model without time lags which I have presented in Chapter XXI of *Business Cycles and National Income* (New York: W. W. Norton and Co., 1950) by Alvin H. Hansen. There I have also indicated how we may take general full employment rather than full employment in the investment goods trades as our upward limiting factor.

level. In spite of the obvious asymmetry of $X(v)$, the two phases have approximately the same duration, a little more than four years being spent in the region of increasing income and a little more than four and one-half years with decreasing income. Our model is, however, of an unprogressive economy in which income and capital always return to their previous lows. In a progressive society the limit cycle would shift irregularly to the right and the representative point would pursue it in a complicated spiral to the right. We can see this by considering a single shift to the right brought about by an increase in O^* to $O^* + \Delta O^*$, as shown in Figure 10. The origin for y is O and the origin for z is O'; the previous steady regime is given by the broken contour and the new one by the solid one. The representative point will be at some point, say A, on the broken contour at the moment of the shift. This then specifies the initial conditions (level and rate of change) for a transient motion towards the new regime. We may consider a continual, regular or irregular, shifting to the right so long as it is not too rapid as compared with the undisturbed motion (i.e., adiabatic change).

Plotted roughly in Figure 11 is the resulting time series of income from a steady shifting (about 3% per year) to the right of the limit cycle. We see that the upswing is prolonged to 6.5 years and the downswing shortened to 4.2 years. The whole cycle is moderately lengthened to 10.7 years. Income rises from 50 to 85 billions of dollars and falls back to 69. The introduction of historically given innovational outlays would make each cycle different.

Finally, it should be noted that, while I have assumed a particular shape for $\varphi(\dot{y})$, the power of the Liénard construction is shown by the fact that an equation containing any given curve may be easily integrated. Therefore, whatever sort of investment function is found actually to hold, that type may be completely analyzed in its cyclical functioning. If we look closely into this problem, we find that what is really necessary is to take individual account of many different industries because, while one industry may still have excess capacity, another may be short of fixed capital. Therefore, the combined operation may depend as much on the points at which different industries fire into investment activity as on the actual shape of the X function for each industry or any conceivable aggregation of all of them. Thus we will have a kind of propagation of an impulse through an industry space with the (possibly quite slow) staggered responses of the various industries, with a resultant sluggishly cumulative boom.

Harvard University

Econometrica, Vol. 19, No. 2 (April, 1951)

THE RATE OF INTEREST

By Joan Robinson

This article sets out an analysis of interest rates in a simplified model market with only four, sharply distinguished, types of asset. There are shown to be three layers to the analysis: the basic pattern of demand and supply of assets of different types, the demand and supply of money, and the state of expectations. The analysis follows the lines opened up by Keynes and elaborates upon them at some points. It does not fit into static equilibrium theory, but is intended to link up with the analysis of an economy undergoing continuous change and development.

The problem to be discussed is the determination of the rate of interest in a closed economy, working under *laisser faire* in the sense that the authorities use no means to influence conditions except monetary policy.

The question is to some extent imaginary because, in the days when *laisser faire* ruled, an important influence on the rate of interest in any one country was the state of its balance of payments, and the objective of monetary policy was control of the foreign exchanges. Now the break-up of the world capital market, and exchange control, have largely insulated interest rates in each country. But there is no longer *laisser faire* in other respects. However, our problem is sufficiently complicated to justify drastic simplification.

INTRODUCTION

The most important influences upon interest rates—which account for, say, the difference between 30% in a Chinese village and 3% in London—are social, legal, and institutional. Side by side with the industrial revolution went great technical progress in the provision of credit and the reduction of lender's risk and great changes in social habits favourable to lending; and in the broad sweep of history these considerations are more significant than any others. But we are here concerned with an economy in which the most up-to-date credit facilities may be taken for granted and a capitalist system is fully developed.

First let us consider the influence upon interest rates of the "fundamental phenomena of Productivity and Thrift."[1] It is generally agreed that a fall in interest rates tends to stimulate investment and that a low rate of interest is more likely to discourage than to encourage saving. In any given situation, then, we may say that there is some value of the rate of interest so low as to lead to full employment (but at times this rate may be negative). The full-employment rate is strongly influenced by the "real force" of thrift and, if not by the "real force" of productivity, at least by beliefs about the future profitability of capital, which

---

[1] Robertson, *Essays in Monetary Theory* [**12**, p. 25].

is related to it. In a *laisser faire* competitive economy, with free wage-bargaining, if the full-employment rate were ever above the actual rate, inflation would set in through a rise of money-wage rates and the rate of interest would be driven up.[2] The full-employment value of the rate of interest may therefore be regarded as, in a certain sense, a lower limit to the possible value of the rate of interest. If this limit always lies far below any value of the actual rate of interest ever experienced, it has little influence on the actual rate. But if from time to time the "real forces" sweep the full-employment rate above the actual rate, and force the actual rate up (whether by causing inflation or by inducing the monetary authorities to raise the actual rate in order to avoid inflation), then clearly they do play a part in determining the course of the actual rate.[3]

Moreover, an important influence upon the actual rate, at any moment, are expectations of the future course of interest rates, and expectations are strongly influenced by the historical experience of interest rates which the community has lived through. If the real forces play some part in shaping that historical experience, they have some influence upon the position of the rate of interest even when the full-employment rate, at the moment, is far below it. Thus the real forces have a roundabout influence on the actual rate of interest, as well as upon the full-employment rate. There is then, after all, a Cheshire cat to grin at Professor Robertson,[4] but it often happens that the grin, cheerful or sour, remains after the circumstances which gave rise to it in the past have completely vanished from the present scene.

THE STRUCTURE OF THE MARKET

Let us turn to the monetary forces acting on the rate of interest. Keynes' theory treated the rate of interest as determined by the demand

[2] Cf. my *Essays in the Theory of Employment* [13, p. 17 et seq.].

[3] The theory (put forward by Professor Pigou, in "Real and Money Wage Rates in Relation to Unemployment" [11], after the appearance of the *General Theory* [7], and elaborated, for example, by Klein in *The Keynesian Revolution* [9] and by Modigliani in "Liquidity Preference and the Theory of Interest and Money" [10]) that when there is unemployment money-wage rates fall and reduce the demand for money, so that if the quantity of money is constant the rate of interest falls, and that this process goes on until ultimately the rate of interest reaches its full-employment value, means that the actual rate in a very long run is brought into equality with the full-employment rate (the run must be long enough for the economy to digest the consequences of a rising value of money; the first effect of a fall in money wages and prices is likely to be to reduce the full-employment rate more than it reduces the actual rate). Even when this theory can be made to seem plausible on its own ground, it has no application here, for it belongs to long-period static theory, while the purpose of this paper is to sketch a theory of interest which might be useful in historical analysis.

[4] [12, *loc. cit.*]

and supply of money. This was a useful simplification in the pioneering days of the theory, but it was always obvious that there is no such thing as *the* rate of interest and that the demand and supply of every type of asset has just as much right to be considered as the demand and supply of money.

To develop a more refined theory the notion of liquidity preference, measured by the reward required to induce owners of wealth to hold assets other than money, must be broken up into a number of aspects. Among the disadvantages of various kinds of assets compared to money we may distinguish:

1. Illiquidity in the narrow sense. Liquidity partly consists in the capacity of an asset to be realised in money. A limited and imperfect market, the cost and trouble of making a sale, and the time required to effect it, reduce the liquidity of an asset quite apart from variability in its price. Liquidity in the narrow sense depends upon the power to realise its value in cash, whatever the value may be at the moment. To avoid confusion with Keynes' language we will call this quality "convenience" instead of "liquidity."

2. Uncertainty of future capital value, or capital-uncertainty for short, due not to any fear of failure by the borrower but to the possibility of changes in capital values owing to changes in the ruling rate of interest. (This is the main ingredient in Keynes' conception of liquidity preference. He regards the rate of interest primarily as a premium against the possible loss of capital if an asset has to be realised before its redemption date.)

3. Lender's risk, that is, the fear of partial or total failure of the borrower.

Further, when comparing long-term bonds with other paper assets we have to add one more factor:

4. Uncertainty as to the income that a sum of money now committed to the asset will yield in the future, or income-uncertainty for short.

These qualities make up the character, or, so to say, natural colour, of various types of assets. (The relationship of present to expected prices is a separate element in the complex of influences governing the demand for the various assets at any moment.)

A modern capital market represents a bewildering variety of assets, with these qualities in all sorts of combinations. To make our inquiry manageable we must draw a simplified and stylised picture of the market, selecting only a few sharply defined types of asset, say three months' bills, irredeemable bonds, and ordinary shares.[5] We will further

---

[5] That is, common stocks. The distinction between shares and loans raises some legal and philosophical problems. At one point in the *General Theory* [7, Chapter XII] Keynes creates confusion by calling ordinary shares "real assets," and describing a purchase of shares on the Stock Exchange as an act of investment.

simplify by assuming that owners of wealth hold only money or paper assets, while real assets are owned by entrepreneurs who hold them against borrowed funds;[6] that money consists only of bank deposits, without distinction between demand and time accounts; and that the quantity of money is rigidly determined by the basis of credit which the Central Bank chooses to provide, as in the ideal text-book picture of the British banking system.[7]

Bills we will assume to be perfectly "good" in the sense that they are free of lender's risk, and they are so short-dated that capital-uncertainty is very small.[8] Bills then differ from money in little except their inferior "convenience." Our bonds, we may suppose, also are perfectly good, and no less "convenient" than bills, in the sense that they can be readily marketed at any time (or pledged against a loan).

The difference between them arises from uncertainty. In a world where past experience has been that interest rates vary from time to time there is uncertainty about future interest rates, in the sense that, whatever an individual may believe about the most probable future course of interest rates, he does not hold his belief with perfect conviction. An owner of wealth who buys a bill to-day knows what his capital will be in three months' time, but he is uncertain what interest he will then be able to get by re-investing it.[9] If he buys a bond, he knows his

It seems both simpler and less unrealistic to go to the opposite extreme, treating shares as a type of paper asset like the rest and regarding their yield as one of the rates of interest. This is, in essence, the way that those in charge of real investment decisions probably most often look at the matter. To the managing director of a joint-stock company there is a great deal in common between a share-holder and a creditor. The conception of yield also presents some complications. It may be calculated on the basis of earnings or of dividends, and on the basis of expected future returns or past realised returns. We shall not enter into these difficulties in the present discussion, but in general we are concerned with prospective yield.

[6] An entrepreneur operating real capital which he owns is regarded as *pro tanto* an owner of wealth lending to himself. Cf. Modigliani [10, p. 30]. Where a citizen lives in his own house, we may regard him as an owner of wealth lending to himself as an entrepreneur who sells to himself as a consumer.

When there is doubt about the future purchasing power of money, owners of wealth become entrepreneurs; that is to say, there is "flight into real values." The whole question of liquidity then takes on quite a different aspect, and money ceases to be the asset to which liquidity preference attaches. We shall not concern ourselves with this problem, but assume that we are discussing a community which has confidence in the future purchasing power of its money.

[7] The argument can easily be modified to fit the case where the supply of money has some elasticity and responds to changes in the rate of interest which the banks can earn.

[8] But see below, p. 100.

[9] It is uncertainty about the whole complex of interest rates that is relevant, not expectations about the bill rate only. Mr. Kalecki [5, p. 37] takes as typical the case of a person comparing the result of "holding one or the other type of

income for as long as he likes to hold the bond, but he is uncertain about what his capital will be worth at any date in the future. Perfectly good bills thus offer negligible capital-uncertainty, but relatively high income-uncertainty, while perfectly good bonds offer perfect certainty of income, but relatively high capital-uncertainty.

Shares are subject to income-uncertainty of a special kind because of uncertainty about the future profits to be earned by the real assets to which they correspond. They are therefore subject to a double dose of capital-uncertainty, for their prices vary both with changes in profit-expectations and with changes in the rates of interest. Moreover, they are subject to lender's risk, in varying degrees, according to the standing and reputation of the firms which they represent.

These qualities of the various types of asset are differently evaluated by different individuals. Some (widows and orphans) set great store on income-certainty, and do not bother much about capital-uncertainty, as they do not intend to realise in any case. Financial institutions set great store on their balance sheets, and value capital-certainty very highly. Owners of wealth with a taste for speculation, or those who have such a large fortune that they can spread their risks widely, have a smaller aversion than either to uncertainty about any particular asset. The general pattern of interest rates depends upon the distribution of wealth between owners with different tastes, relative to the supplies of the various kinds of assets.

Each type of asset is a potential alternative to every other; each has, so to speak, a common frontier with every other, and with money. Equilibrium in the market is attained when the interest rates are such that no wealth is moving across any frontier. Prices are then such that the market is content to hold just that quantity of each type of asset which is available at the moment.

The complex of demands and supplies is not static, but is moving slowly through time. Over any period there is an increment to total wealth from saving equal to the borrowing for investment (and budget deficits) that has taken place during the period. The total of wealth, representing a demand for paper assets, increases with the supply. But the supply of any particular type may alter relatively to the demand for it. For instance, a budget deficit, financed by selling bonds, will generate savings which the owners wish to put partly into money or shares. The supply of bonds is then increasing relatively to demand. A borrower

---

security over a few years"—that is, choosing between buying a bond now and deciding now not to buy a bond for a few years, holding bills during that time. But usually an owner of wealth feels himself free to switch his capital from one asset to another at any time in the future if it seems good to him. Mr. Kaldor [4, p. 13] uses a similar argument, which is subject to the same objection.

who is free to choose the kind of paper assets he creates will try to offer those which require the lowest interest, and this sets up a certain tendency for supply gradually to be adjusted to demand (though changes in business methods—the growth of self-financing, the decay of the trade bill—may alter supply in a way quite unrelated to changes in demand).

There is also a much more immediate way in which supply is adjusted to demand. Where there is a difference between interest rates there is a possible source of profit. If the short rate were found on the average to rule above the long, because of the dominance in the market of widows and orphans with a strong preference for bonds, and if this situation were expected to continue, financial houses could issue bonds, which would be taken up by the widows and orphans, and use the funds thus obtained to carry bills. They would undergo a risk, for if there were an unforeseen change, and the short rate fell permanently, they could only get out of the now unprofitable business by redeeming their bonds, which might meanwhile have risen in price. Thus the long rate would still have to remain normally lower than the short rate.

In the reverse case (which is the usual one, at least in recent times) where preference for capital-certainty predominates in the market, so that the bond rate exceeds the bill rate, there is an income to be made by borrowing short and lending long. This is commonly done by taking a bank advance. Assuming the basis of credit to remain constant, the banks must sell other assets when they increase advances, and their assets are short-dated (in our simplified world they could only hold bills) so that the effect is the same as though dealers in credit issued bills in order to hold bonds. The risk involved in this operation is that there may be an unforeseen rise in the bill rate, so that the dealers have either to renew their loans at a higher cost or to sell out bonds whose price may have fallen. Thus, these operations require a margin between long and short term rates and, since there is not an unlimited amount of credit available to dealers, the margin they require will be larger the greater the amount of bonds that they are holding.

Investment trusts issue what are intended to be less speculative securities in order to carry more speculative ones.

Operations such as these to some extent smooth out the differences in demand for securities of different types and bring the various interest rates closer together.

CHANGES IN THE QUANTITY OF MONEY AND IN EXPECTATIONS

Preferences for various types of asset, relative to the supplies of them, determine the general pattern of interest rates, and it is against this sort of background that day-to-day changes in interest rates occur. The pattern most commonly found in actual markets is such that normally the bill rate is lower than the bond rate, and the yields of shares higher.

Given the general background, there are two quite distinct types of influence which play upon the equilibrium pattern of rates. One is the state of expectations and the other is the supply of money. To discuss them separately we require that one be assumed constant when the other varies. It is difficult to frame the assumption that expectations are given without sawing off the bough we are sitting on. It is easiest to discuss expectations if they are quite definite. Everything can then be reduced to arithmetic. But if we assume that owners of wealth have clear and unanimous expectations about the exact future course of the prices of assets, in which they believe with perfect confidence, then we have ruled out uncertainty and stepped into a world quite unlike the one we want to discuss. Moreover, we have landed ourselves in a logical impasse, for either the expectations will turn out to be correct, in which case there is no more to be said, or they will turn out mistaken, in which case perfect confidence cannot persist.

The whole subject of expectations bristles with psychological and philosophical difficulties,[10] and I can offer only a sketchy and superficial treatment of it. For the moment let us be content to assume that the bond rate is expected to move around the average level that has been experienced in the recent past, so that when it falls below that level it is expected to rise, some time or other, and when it rises above, to fall, but that everyone's view is hazy as to how long it will take to return to the average value and how far it will go meanwhile, so that there is great uncertainty about what its value will be at any particular date in the future. For simplicity of exposition we will suppose that we are examining the market at a moment when to-day's bond rate is equal to the average value. Further, we will assume that profits are expected to continue at the same level as in the recent past, so that the prices of shares are not expected to move except in response to changes in the rate of interest. Finally, we will neglect speculators operating on day-to-day changes in the price of assets.

Having thus tethered expectations, let us examine the effect upon the market of a change in the quantity of money. A change in the amount of bank deposits is a special case of the kind of change in the stock of assets relative to the total of wealth which we have already discussed.[11]

---

[10] Cf. Shackle, *Expectation in Economics* [15, especially Chapter VII], and Fellner, *Monetary Policies and Full Employment* [1, p. 152 *et seq.*].

[11] When a change in the quantity of money comes about as the result of a Government deficit financed by printing notes, or through an inflow of gold due to an excess of exports over imports, the analysis is complicated by factors which are not relevant here. See my *Introduction to the Theory of Employment* [14, Chapter X].

The essence of the matter is that when the Central Bank, say, increases the basis of credit the member banks buy assets from the market to an amount which restores the normal ratio of their cash reserves to other assets. They thus reduce the amount of assets to be held by the market and so raise their prices. To maintain our simplifying assumptions we will assume that the banks buy only bills. The immediate consequence is a fall in the rate of interest on bills. What effect does this have upon the bond rate?

The bond rate is bound to be affected, for even if all owners of wealth have strong preferences, and are settled far from the frontier between bonds and bills, so that it would need a very large change in values to shift them, yet dealers in credit will react to small changes and so provide a continuously sensitive frontier between bills and bonds. The profit to be made by selling a bill and buying a bond is the difference in the interest on them for three months *minus* the fall (or *plus* the rise) in the price of the bond over three months. Dealing at to-day's prices, the difference in interest which will be enjoyed is known, but the change in price of the bond is unknown. A fall in the short rate increases the difference in interest rates, and so raises the demand for bonds, but the consequent rise in the price of bonds enhances the likelihood of a fall in their price in the future. If expectations are clear and definite, only a very small fall in the long-term rate of interest can occur. It needs a fall of only $\frac{1}{4}\%$ in the price of bonds over three months to wipe out the effect of a fall of 1% in the bill rate per annum, and a rise in to-day's price of bonds by $\frac{1}{4}\%$ means a fall in the bond rate of interest in the ratio $400:401$.[12] Suppose, for example, that there is a clear expectation that the bond rate will be back to its average in three months' time; then to-day's rate cannot fall by more than this ratio in response to each 1% fall in the bill rate.[13] But if expectations of what the bond rate will be in three months' time are vague and dubious, the power of a rise in to-day's price of bonds to wipe out the attraction of holding them is so much the weaker. Thus, the effect of a fall in the short rate upon the long is greater, the greater the uncertainty in which the market dwells.

In the *Treatise on Money*, Keynes, so to speak, dramatised uncertainty as the existence of "two views" leading to a "bull-bear position"—that is, a dispersion of opinions, each confidently held.[14] The degree of un-

---

[12] Cf. *General Theory* [**7**, p. 168].

[13] This relationship is quite sufficient to account for the observed sluggishness in the movement of the long-term rate of interest in response to changes in the short rate. It is unnecessary as well as unplausible to maintain that the long rate responds only to changes in the *expected future* short rate. Cf. above, footnote 9.

[14] In the *Treatise* [**8**, Chapter XV] the two views refer to future share prices, but Keynes applies the same idea to views about the rate of interest (*General Theory* [**7**, pp. 169 and 173]).

certainty in the market as a whole then depends on the variety of opinion within it. The same effects follow where everyone is alike, but no-one feels confident that his own best guess of what the future holds will turn out to be right. In any situation where there is inadequate evidence on which to base predictions, both elements will be present. Thus a rise in to-day's price of bonds will induce some holders of bonds to sell before others, and will cause many holders to sell out to some extent. The greater the dispersion of opinion and the less confidently are opinions held, the greater the movement of bond prices in response to a given change in the quantity of money.

We have assumed that expectations of profit are constant. With lower interest rates the frontiers between bills and shares and bonds and shares are no longer in equilibrium at the old rate, and there is a sympathetic movement in the price of shares, governed by similar considerations to those which influence the movement of bond prices. Thus an increase in the quantity of money lowers the whole complex of interest rates.

We may now look at the same situation the other way up and inquire what has happened to the increment of money which has been created. At any moment some money is in course of travelling round the active circulation—from income earner to shopkeeper, from shopkeeper to producer, from producer to income earner, and so back again. Some is in the financial circuit, passing between buyers and sellers of paper assets. Some is lodged in what we may call a "short hoard" either because its owner, who has recently made some savings is shortly going to spend it in buying securities, or because its owner (who may be an entrepreneur) has some large-scale purchase of goods shortly to make. These short hoards may reasonably be classed as part of the active circulation. Some money is lodged, at any moment, in "long hoards" because it has come into the hands of owners who choose to hold a part of their wealth in the form of money. Some is in "bear hoards" whose owners are waiting for a fall in bond and share prices to go back into the market.

Some bears, and some owners of wealth with a high preference for capital-certainty, hold bills rather than money. But it is natural to assume that, in the main, money is preferred to bills for long hoards because dealing in bills is a specialized business, for which many owners of long hoards have no inclination, and because it is not practicable in small sums. The advantage of money over bills for bear hoards is that it makes it possible to switch back into securities in less than three months, if that seems desirable, without the cost and the capital risk of switching into and out of bills.

Short hoards, long hoards, and bear hoards correspond to convenience, precaution, and speculation, mentioned by Keynes as motives for holding money.[15]

Now, the fall in interest rates which has occurred may slow down the active circulation somewhat. Money may idle a little longer in short hoards—the motive for economising balances is less[16]—but this effect will be slight, for the velocity of active circulation is fixed by fairly rigid habits. Thus, when there is an increase in money relative to national income, most of the new money cannot find a lodgement unless long or bear hoards are increased.[17]

The yields of all paper assets have fallen, and this in itself may lead some owners of wealth to prefer money. But the main effect is that the rise in the price of bonds and shares has enhanced the fear of a fall in their value in the future, and so set a bearish movement on foot. Money, we have supposed, is usually preferred to bills for bear hoarding; if, however, some of the bears prefer bills, the bill rate is reduced all the more, and there is a further movement over the bill frontier into money.

Thus the result of increasing the quantity of money is to lower the short rate and to pull the long rate below its expected value to the point where the combined effect of these two movements increases hoards by the amount of the increase in the quantity of money.[18] (If the fall in interest rates induces an increase in national income, of course, part of the new money is required for active circulation, and the interest rates will not fall so far.)

A fall in national income relative to the stock of money (abstracting from a consequent change in expectations) has effects similar to the above. A reduction in the quantity of money or rise in national income has the converse effects.

To summarise: given the state of expectations, the long and short rates of interest both fall as the quantity of money increases relatively

[15] *General Theory* [7, pp. 195–196]. It is, of course, impossible to draw a hard and fast line between them. Convenience shades into precaution, and precaution would not give rise to a demand for money unless there was an element of speculation present. Cf. Fellner [1, p. 147].

[16] Mr. Kalecki [5] suggests that it is only the short rate which is relevant here. But surely this is a mistake. If an individual (or a firm) decides to economise balances in order to enjoy interest he is just as likely to put the money into bonds as bills. See also Kaldor [4, *loc. cit.*].

[17] Mr. Kaldor seems to deny that hoarding ever occurs [4, p. 13, footnote], but on closer examination his argument appears to be purely verbal, as he calls deposits money only if they are in active circulation.

[18] If the above is correct, it is misleading to say that the short rate is determined by demand and supply of money while the long rate is determined by the expected future short rate, for one of the main determinants of the demand for money is expectations about the course of the long rate itself.

to national income. The fall in the short rate is steeper than the fall in the long,[19] so that the gap between the two increases with the quantity of money. The less the uncertainty (the more confident and unanimous the market that a departure of the rate of interest from its average value will quickly be reversed), the smaller is the response of the rates of interest to changes in the quantity of money, and the smaller is the gap between the two rates. In the limit, if the market confidently believes that it knows that from to-morrow the rate of interest will be at its past average value, the long and the short rate will be equal to that value today. (In this case liquidity preference in Keynes' sense is absolute.)

So far we have been discussing the situation at a moment of time, with given expectations, but time marches on. We have supposed that expectations of the future interest rates depend upon past experience. When the bond rate is below its past average, expectations tend to be revised as time goes by, and the demand for money tends gradually to fall, but this is a slow process, and before it has had time to produce any effect all sorts of changes occur. Thus uncertainty is kept alive by the chances of history.

It has been objected against this theory that it leaves the rate of interest hanging by its own boot straps.[20] But there is no escape from

[19] Unless uncertainty is so great that expectations about the future price of bonds have no influence at all upon the long rate.

[20] Both Mr. Hicks (*Value and Capital* [3, p. 164]) and Mr. Kaldor [4, p. 12] display a lively horror of boot straps, but it is not clear how they propose to escape from them. The view that the long rate can be determined solely from expectations about the short rate is untenable.

It is true, in a world in which expectations are definite and unanimous, that when we know to-day's bond rate and to-day's bill rate, we can reckon what change in the price of bonds is expected over the life of the bills. Then, looking into a further future, we can assume that the bill rate then expected to rule is known, and that by then the expected price of bonds is expected to obtain. Then we can reckon the expected change in bond prices over the further future, and so on to Kingdom Come. Then the whole pattern of expectations could be described in terms of the expected short rates alone. But all this means is that rational expectations must be self-consistent. It certainly does not detach the rate of interest from dependence on its boot straps for, in such a world, the only reason for a difference between short and long rates is the expectation of a change in the long rate. Indeed, one might say that there the short rate is simply an expression of expectations about bond prices. Moreover, the conception of expectations without uncertainty plunges us into philosophical difficulties (see above).

In real life it would be perfectly rational for a man to expect (on the basis of experience) that, for example, over the next year or two the bill rate will continue to be held steady at a low value while the bond rate fluctuates round, say, 3%. But it would not be rational for him to think that he knows exactly what the rates of interest will be every day from to-day till Kingdom Come.

Professor Robertson [12, *loc. cit.*] appears to hold (though he states positively the fact that the price to-day of any long-lived object with low carrying costs is strongly influenced by expectations about what its price will be in the future. If the rate of interest is hanging by its boot straps, so is the price of Picasso's paintings.

We have very little knowledge of the influences shaping expectations. Past experience is no doubt the major element in expectations, but experience, as far as one can judge, is compounded in the market with a variety of theories and superstitions and the whole almagam is played upon from day to day by the influences (including the last Bank Chairman's speech) which make up what Keynes called "the state of the news." Any theory that is widely believed tends to verify itself, so that there is a large element of "thinking makes it so" in the determination of interest rates.[21] This is all the more true when short-term speculation is prevalent.

A speculator has not the same attitude as an owner of wealth to liquidity, income-uncertainty, or capital-uncertainty. He is concerned with making money by forestalling changes in prices from day to day by "anticipating what average opinion expects the average opinion to be."[22] So long as the great bulk of transactions is made by owners of wealth and dealers in credit, the speculator has to guess how they will behave. The effect of speculation is then to speed up the movement of to-day's prices towards expected future prices. But, as soon as speculators become an important influence in the market, their business is to speculate on each other's behaviour. The market then becomes unstable, and falls into the condition described by Keynes under that misleading chapter heading, "The State of Long-Term Expectations."[23] The operations of the speculators cast a thick fog over future prospects

only what he does *not* hold) that the long rate is determined partly by the "real forces" and partly by beliefs about how the real forces are going to behave in the future. But, if so, with these beliefs he has admitted a Trojan horse full of expectations and liquidity preference into the citadel of the real forces.

In Mr. Kalecki's system expectations about the long rate, based on past experience, are a separate determinant of to-day's rate, and the system here set out is broadly the same as his (except for the point made above, footnote 9) and owes a great deal to it.

My chief debt is to some pregnant hints to be found in Mr. Harrod's *Dynamic Economics* [2, see especially p. 62].

[21] This gives the "real forces" one more card of entry (cf. above, p. 92). If it is widely believed that, for example, an increase in the rate of investment raises the rate of interest, then the appearance of any symptom which is taken to indicate that investment is going to increase will have a tendency to raise interest rates.

[22] *General Theory* [7, p. 156]. In reality, of course, there can be no quite clear-cut demarcation between speculators and owners of wealth who take a view about future prices, and the two classes shade into each other at the edges.

[23] *General Theory* [7, Chapter XII].

for the owners of wealth, increase uncertainty all round, and so raise the general level of interest rates.

They also create a fog for the economist describing the capital market, which very much reduces the cogency of the above type of analysis, and totally deprives it of utility as a source of tips.

AN INCREASE IN THE RATE OF INVESTMENT

Abstracting from speculation (for if we do not, there is little to be said) we will now examine the effects of an increase in the rate of investment (say, induced by an improvement in prospective profits) which increases national income but does not go far enough to hit full employment and create inflationary conditions. If the banking system follows the policy of meeting the needs of trade, interest rates are held constant. To make the story interesting we will assume that the quantity of money is not altered.

Investment plans must be made before any actual outlay takes place. If entrepreneurs proceed by issuing shares before they begin to place orders for new capital goods and hold money in short hoards for the time being, there is an increase in demand for money relative to the supply and an increase in supply of shares relative to demand, and the interest rates rise before the actual investment begins. (This is the famous problem of "finance.")[24] It is more natural to suppose, however, that entrepreneurs take bank advances as required and retire them by the issue of shares after the investment has been under way for some time.

Possible cases offer an endless variety of patterns. To simplify, we will assume that investment remains steady at the new higher rate during the period that we are discussing, that all investment is financed in the same way, and that the way it is financed is by taking over-drafts which are repaid by issuing securities at a certain interval after they have been drawn upon. With these assumptions, while the investment continues there is a certain volume of bank advances outstanding at any moment, and the supply of securities keeps pace with the addition to wealth due to saving, after an initial wobble, which may go either way according as the issue of securities begins before or after the pattern of saving has become adjusted to the new rate of investment.

We will abstract from the gradual effect of a rise in the proportions of shares to total wealth, and consider only the immediate influences upon interest rates coming from the change in the rate of investment.

Let us compare a date in Period II, when the multiplier has run its course and national income has settled at the level appropriate to the

---

[24] Keynes, "Alternative Theories of the Rate of Interest" [6].

new higher rate of investment, with a date in Period I, when investment was being carried out at the old rate.

There is now a larger national income, and a larger demand for money
in active circulation, including a swollen demand for short hoards,
corresponding to the higher level at which saving is running.[25] Entrepreneurs have taken bank advances, and the banks sold out bills, so
that the short rate has risen. Bond rates, as usual, have risen in sympathy.

The rise in interest rates puts a brake on the rise in demand for money
by increasing the velocity of active circulation; at the same time it
has drawn money out of bear and long hoards. The rates of interest
have risen to the point where equilibrium is restored at the frontiers
around money.

What has happened to shares? The same cause which induces the
increase in investment—a rise in prospective profits—gives rise to
better and more confident expectations of future dividends. For the
time being, at least, the optimism which started investment off appears
justified, for profits are in fact ruling higher while investment goes on.
The price of shares has therefore risen at least sufficiently to keep yields
at the level corresponding to the rate on bonds. (If we allow speculators
out of the cage where we are keeping them assumed away, the price
of shares may rise to any extent, and the normal relationship between
bond and share yields may be reversed.) If this were all, share yields
would move sympathetically with the bond rate—that is to say, they
would be raised slightly by the increase in demand for money. But there
is a further effect. With greater confidence in future profits, credit is
improved and the risk attached to shares is felt to be reduced. Different
shares will be differently affected. On the very "good" ones, for which
the risk premium is in any case small, the yield will have risen in sympathy with bonds; on others, particularly those whose firms are taking
the biggest part in the industrial boom, it will have fallen. Lumping all
shares together, their yield, on balance, is most likely to be reduced.

Our interest rates now stand thus, at a date in Period II compared
to Period I: The short rate is higher. Bond rates are higher than in
Period I (but not by much) and share rates are likely to be lower.

The yield on existing paper assets has a strong influence on the cost
of new borrowing. Concerns which borrow at near the gilt-edged rate
will find borrowing a little dearer and may be inclined to defer investment plans (though it is more likely that, in the general atmosphere of
optimism, they will take the rise in their stride). Industrialists in the

[25] Mr. Fellner [1, p. 149] suggests that hoards held by entrepreneurs fall as
general confidence increases. If this effect were to predominate, the rates of interest would normally fall as investment increases.

main find borrowing cheaper. The improved prospect of profit counts twice over—once in promoting investment at a given cost of borrowing and once in lowering the cost of borrowing.[26]

Keynes himself makes this point,[27] but the habit of thinking in terms of *the* rate of interest led him to overlook the fact that the most relevant interest rate is likely to be falling when investment is increasing, and to make the quite unnecessary concession to classical ideas that the movement in interest rates which accompanies a boom sets a drag upon the increase in investment.

AN INCREASE IN THRIFTINESS

We may now consider the much debated question of the effect of thriftiness on the rate of interest.[28] Our discussion of the real forces implied that, in a very broad sense and in a very long run, a high state of thriftiness relative to investment opportunities helps to keep interest rates low. In so far as it does so, accumulation of real capital may be greater than it would have been if interest rates had been higher, though not necessarily greater than it would have been if thriftiness had been less. In what follows we are not concerned with such long-run considerations, but with examining the impact of an increase in thriftiness upon interest rates in a very short and in a medium run.

Let us suppose that the thriftiness of our community has increased, which shows itself in the first instance in a reduction in the rate of outlay for consumption goods by some section of the public. We will first consider how the situation would develop *if* planned investment were unaffected, and then re-examine the influence of what has happened upon investment plans. It simplifies exposition if we postulate that the rate of planned investment is zero, but this means only that sentences such as "the stock of capital is unchanged" are substituted for "the stock of capital is the same as it would have been if this had not happened," and so forth. We must divide time up into periods, not necessarily of the same length. Period I is the time before the change occurred. In Period II consumption is lower than in Period I, by the amount of the designed increase of saving, but nothing else has had time to alter. Stocks have piled up in the shops. If we value the stocks at full retail prices, including the retailers' profit, we may say that national income is unchanged. At the end of Period II *ex-post* saving

---

[26] This argument has not much force in the case of a large established firm, for which there need not be any close connection between the timing of borrowing and of investment, but there is much investment which cannot be undertaken until finance for it has been secured.

[27] *General Theory* [7, p. 158].

[28] Cf. Robertson [12, p. 18 *et seq.*].

has occurred equal to the undesigned rise in stocks. In Period III (which is likely to be longer than II) retailers reduce purchases, the fall in national income works its way through the system, and there will be a secondary decline in consumption on top of the first. Stocks have to be reduced to the level appropriate to the new rate of consumption, so that there will be an extra fall in income and fall in employment while the redundant stocks of Period I and the undesigned accumulation of Period II are worked off. In Period IV disinvestment in stocks has come to an end, there is a recovery of employment relative to Period III, and we settle down to a new position of short-period equilibrium with a lower level of consumption appropriate to the new higher thriftiness and the unchanged rate of investment.

How have the rates of interest been behaving? Let us place ourselves at the point of time where Period II ends. We find members of the public with an increment of wealth compared to their position in Period I. There are a great many possible consequences in the financial sphere. Let us pick out two simple cases:

1) The savers are holding short hoards, equal to their increment of wealth, which they have not yet placed in securities.

2) They have already purchased bonds.

Retailers have acquired real assets to the value of the undesigned increase in stocks. Part of this value is represented by profits which they have failed to realise. According to the convention we have adopted, of considering the national income constant, the missing profits must be regarded as savings which the retailers have, willy-nilly, invested in stocks. The rest of the value of stocks represents outgoings which they would normally have paid out of receipts, and for which they now require finance. This division of the value of the stocks into two parts complicates the argument. At first we will abstract from it by assuming that the retailers finance the whole value of the stocks in the same way. Methods of finance vary greatly according to the way business is conducted. Again we may pick out a few simple cases from amongst all the possibilities:

a) The retailers have run down cash balances.

b) They have taken bank advances.

c) They have sold bonds which they were formerly holding.

Combining (1) with (a), cash released from retailers' balances matches the increase in cash held by savers, and nothing alters. Combining (2) with (c), the retailers sell bonds equivalent to those that the savers buy, and again nothing alters. Combining (1) with (c), the savers hoard money and the retailers sell bonds. The demand for money has increased, which raises interest rates in the converse of the manner described above. Besides this, the demand for bonds has fallen, which tends to

increase the gap between long and short rates. Combining (2) with
(a), the savers have bought bonds and the retailers have parted with
money. The rates of interest fall, and the gap between them tends to
narrow.

In case (b) the banks have made advances and, since the quantity
of money is assumed constant, they have sold out bills. This raises
the short rate of interest, and the long rate tends to rise in sympathy.
If we combine this with case (1) (savers holding money), the increase
in demand for money reinforces the rise in interest rates. If we combine it with (2) (savers holding bonds), the increase in demand for
bonds tends to counteract it.

In so far as the various types of case occur together they tend to
offset each others' effects upon the interest rates.

Slight differences are introduced if we take account of the retailers'
missing profits. Suppose that their savings in Period I exceeded the
missing profits, and that their personal expenditure is the same in
Period II as in Period I; then, in the case which combines (1) and (a),
the absorption of cash by savers is equal to the full value of the undesigned accumulation of stocks, while the release of cash by retailers
which finances them is short of the full value by the amount of the
missing profits. There is thus a net increase in demand for money, and
the interest rates rise. And so on.

But the argument has grown tedious. Its upshot is that in Period II
the effect upon interest rates is not likely to be large, and, in so far as
there is an effect, it may go either way.

Let us now jump over the turbid eddies of Period III and place ourselves at a point of time some way along in Period IV, when things have
settled down.

Still assuming, provisionally, that planned investment is unchanged
at zero, we have a national income lower than that in Period I by the
reduced consumption of the first group of savers *plus* the reduction
brought about by the secondary decline in incomes and employment
in accordance with the multiplier. A smaller amount of money is required in active circulation than in Period I. Bank advances have been
paid off and (assuming a constant quantity of money) the short rate
of interest is lower than in Period I. No net investment has taken
place; therefore there has been zero *ex-post* saving over the period as
a whole (neglecting the effect of disinvestment in stocks and working
capital owing to the fall in the level of output), so that the total of
outstanding assets and the total of privately owned wealth are unchanged. Abstracting from any change in expectations about the long
rate of interest owing to the experiences of the transition period, there
has been a fall in the bond rate, in sympathy with the short rate. The

consumption trades are doing badly compared to Period I, and shares are likely to be adversely affected. On the very "good" ones the yield may move in sympathy with the fall in bond and short rates, but many will suffer from a rise in riskiness, owing to poor prospects of profit in the consumption trades. Thus our picture is: a lower short rate in Period IV compared to I, a slightly lower bond and best share rate, and a higher yield of shares in general. This pattern of interest rates does not look very encouraging to investment, and it seems that our provisional assumption of a constant rate of investment ought rather to be revised in the downward direction because of the surplus capacity and low profits in the consumption trades and the high cost of industrial borrowing. If investment falls, the interest rates are likely to fall all the farther.

A CHEAP MONEY POLICY

The last case we will examine is a cheap money policy. A campaign by the monetary authorities to lower interest rates to counter unemployment, if successful, will stimulate activity. Undertaken in a situation which is already inflationary, it will necessitate stronger anti-inflation measures (such as a larger budget surplus). We are not here concerned with discussing its effectiveness in the first case, or its advisability in the second, but merely to study the mechanics of its operation. This story necessarily depends very much upon its institutional and political setting. The following reflects the English scene as far as our stylised picture of the capital market permits.

The first move in the campaign is for the Central Bank to dose the banks with cash, by open market purchases. The amount of advances the banks can make is limited by the demand from good borrowers. The demand is very inelastic (though it shifts violently up and down with the state of trade), so the banks, between whom competition is highly imperfect, see no advantage in cheapening their price. The redundant cash reserve must go into bills. Any rate of return is better than none. The banks with redundant cash find themselves in much the same position as a group of firms with surplus capacity and zero prime costs. If perfect competition prevailed, the bill rate would go to next to nothing and the banks could not cover their costs. They therefore fix up a gentleman's agreement which keeps the bill rate steady at a low level. The bill rate is maintained at this low level by the Central Bank's giving another dose of cash whenever it threatens to rise.

If the Central Bank is operating in the old orthodox manner, its power ends here, and the authorities must rely on the dealers in credit to bring the long rates down. Nowadays the authorities reinforce the action of the banking system by going into the bond market directly. If necessary, they issue bills in order to buy bonds, the quantity of money being adjusted to whatever level is required to keep the bill rate at its bottom stop. The low interest rates may slow down the velocity of active circulation so that money, as the saying is, stagnates in pools. Long hoards are swollen by the fall in the current rates and bear hoards by the fact that expected future rates are not yet revised.

As time goes by, experience of a long rate that is persistently somewhat lower than the expected rate lowers the expected rate and so lowers the actual rate further. The yield on shares falls in sympathy with the bond rates. Thus the whole complex of rates gradually falls through time. If the authorities take it gently and do not try to push the rate down too fast, and if they stick consistently to the policy, once begun, so that the market never has the experience of to-day's rate being higher than yesterday's, it is hard to discern any limit to the possible fall in interest rates (except the mere technical costs of dealing) so long as the full-employment interest rate is below the actual level of rates or is held below it by a budget surplus or other means.

All goes smoothly so long as the authorities are working with the grain of market opinion. But if they embark on the policy and begin to buy bonds at a time when the long rate is generally expected to rise, they come sharply into conflict with market opinion. So long as the expected rate remains high, they have to go on holding bonds and supplying money for bear hoards. If they persist resolutely, a moment will come when the bears are convinced that the new low rate has come to stay. Money then moves out of bear hoards into bonds, and the authorities can gradually sell off to ex-bears the bonds they have been holding, retire bills, and reduce the quantity of money to the level which will just hold the bill rate at its bottom stop.

But if the authorities' nerves are shaken by the ferocious growls with which the bears have been deafening them all this time, and once allow bond prices to relapse, the growling of the bears turns to joyous yelps of "I told you so" and the expected future bond rate is so much the higher for ever after.

University of Cambridge

REFERENCES

[1] FELLNER, WILLIAM J., *Monetary Policies and Full Employment*, Berkeley and Los Angeles: University of California Press, 1946, 268 pp.

[2] HARROD, R. F., *Towards a Dynamic Economics*, London: Macmillan & Co., 1948, 169 pp.

[3] HICKS, J. R., *Value and Capital*, Oxford: The Clarendon Press, 1946, 340 pp.

[4] KALDOR, N., "Speculation and Economic Stability," *Review of Economic Studies*, Vol. 7, October, 1939, pp. 1–27.

[5] KALECKI, M., "The Short-Term and the Long-Term Rate of Interest," in *Studies in Economic Dynamics*, London: George Allen & Unwin, 1943, 92 pp.

[6] KEYNES, J. M., "Alternative Theories of the Rate of Interest," *Economic Journal*, Vol. 47, June, 1937, pp. 241–252.

[7] ———, *The General Theory of Employment, Interest, and Money*, New York: Harcourt, Brace & Co., 1936, 403 pp.

[8] ———, *A Treatise on Money*, New York: Harcourt, Brace & Co., 1930, 2 vols.

[9] KLEIN, L. R., *The Keynesian Revolution*, New York: The Macmillan Co., 1947, 218 pp.

[10] MODIGLIANI, F., "Liquidity Preference and the Theory of Interest and Money," ECONOMETRICA, Vol. 12, January, 1944, pp. 45–88.

[11] PIGOU, A. C., "Real and Money Wage Rates in Relation to Unemployment," *Economic Journal*, Vol. 47, September, 1937, pp. 405–422.

[12] ROBERTSON, D. H., *Essays in Monetary Theory*, London: P. S. King & Son, 1940, 234 pp.

[13] ROBINSON, JOAN, *Essays in the Theory of Employment*, New York: The Macmillan Co., 1937, 254 pp.

[14] ———, *Introduction to the Theory of Employment*, New York: The Macmillan Co., 1937, 127 pp.

[15] SHACKLE, G. L. S., *Expectation in Economics*, Cambridge: Cambridge University Press, 1949, 146 pp.

Reprinted from Kenneth J. Arrow and Tibor Scitovsky, eds.,
Readings in Welfare Economics (Homewood, Illinois:
Richard D. Irwin, Inc., 1969), pp. 645–681

Capital accumulation and efficient allocation of resources*†

EDMOND MALINVAUD

1. *Introduction.* Among the many questions concerning the accumulation of capital the following has been said to be the most important [31]. According to which rules should choices between direct and indirect processes of production be determined; that is, when can we say that it is efficient to save today in order to increase future consumption? The present paper is devoted to this problem, which is clearly relevant for both the theory of capital and for welfare economics. The results given below are not essentially new. The author thinks, however, that his approach is likely to show in a more vivid light a few facts which, although obscurely felt, are not yet generally accepted in economic science.

The reader acquainted with welfare economics and the theory of efficient allocation of resources knows how some appropriate price system is associated with an efficient state. Loosely speaking, such a state would be an equilibrium position for a competitive economy using the given set of prices. The model introduced to prove this result does not allow explicitly for investment and capital accumulation. Thus one may wonder whether it can be extended to the case of capitalistci production. Admittedly, this is very likely. The introduction of time does not seem to imply any new principle. Choices between commodities available at different times raise essentially the same problem as choices between different commodities available at the same time. How can

---

* *Econometrica*, 21(1953): pp. 233–68. The proof of Theorem 1 was then incorrect, as was pointed out to the author by several readers, notably H. Uzawa. A corrigendum was published in *Econometrica*, 30(1962), pp. 570–73. The necessary changes are inserted in the present text. Reprinted by courtesy of the author and *Econometrica*.

† Based on Cowles Commission Discussion Paper, Economics, No. 2026 (hectographed), and a paper presented at the Minneapolis meeting of the Econometric Society in September, 1951. Acknowledgment is due staff members and guests of the Cowles Commission and those attending econometrics seminars in Paris. Their interest in the subject greatly helped me to bring the study to its present formulation. I am particularly indebted to M. Allais, T. C. Koopmans, and G. Debreu. Anyone acquainted with their work will discern their influence in this paper. But the reader might not know how much I owe to their personal encouragement and friendly criticism. I am also indebted to Mrs. Jane Novick who read my manuscript carefully and made many stylistic improvements.

consumers' needs best be satisfied when the production of goods involves strong relations of interdependence?

However, one thing may not be clear: in a competitive economy there is a rate of interest that is used to discount future values both on the loan market and in business accounting. Is this rate a part of the price system associated with an efficient economic process? In particular, should prices of the same commodity available at different times stand in some definite ratio depending only on the time lag and not on the specific commodity considered?

In order to deal with this and related questions this paper is divided into four parts. In the first, the process of capitalistic production is analyzed. A general model is defined that may be given two equivalent presentations. An "extensive form" generalizes current capital-theory models, while a "reduced form" makes it possible to apply the usual welfare reasoning.

The second part is purely mathematical, the main result of the paper being proved there. It provides a somewhat straightforward generalization of what was already known for the timeless case, the only difficulty arising when the future is assumed not bounded by some given horizon. The economic meaning and implications of the main theorem are examined in Part III. As most of the previous work on the theory of capital was based on statonary economies, it is worth studying them carefully. This is attempted in Part IV.

Because this study is mainly concerned with formal results, heuristic comments are reduced as much as the subject permits. It is supposed that the reader is well acquainted with welfare economics.

2. *Notation.* The mathematical tools used here are primarily vectors and sets in finite-dimensional Euclidean spaces. A vector in m-dimensional Euclidean space is denoted by a Latin letter (x_t, for instance), with an index specifying the time considered. The components of x_t are denoted by x_{it}, the distinction between vectors and their components being shown by the placement of the index t.

The symbol $\{x_t\}$ represents a sequence of vectors $x_1, x_2, \ldots, x_t, \ldots,$ where t takes all positive integral values. This sequence is also written more simply as $\mathbf{x}$, where the index is removed and the symbol is printed in boldface type.

The inequality $x_i \leqq y_t$ (as well as $\mathbf{x} \leqq \mathbf{y}$) applied to vectors x_t and y_t (or to sequences $\mathbf{x}$ and $\mathbf{y}$) means that no component x_{it} of x_t (or x_{it} of $\mathbf{x}$) is greater than the corresponding components of y_t (or of $\mathbf{y}$). The inequality $x_t \leq y_t$ (as well as $\mathbf{x} \leq \mathbf{y}$) means $x_t \leqq y_t$ and $x_t \neq y_t$ (or $\mathbf{x} \leqq \mathbf{y}$ and $\mathbf{x} \neq \mathbf{y}$).

A vector x_t (as well as a sequence $\mathbf{x}$) is said to be nonnegative if $x_t \geqq 0$ (or if $\mathbf{x} \geqq 0$).

Sets are denoted by bold faced capitals. The addition of sets is defined as follows:

$\mathbf{V} = \mathbf{U}_1 + \mathbf{U}_2$ means: v is an element of $\mathbf{V}$ if and only if it can be written as $v = u_1 + u_2$, where u_1 and u_2 are elements of $\mathbf{U}_1$ and $\mathbf{U}_2$ respectively; that is, $u_1 \in \mathbf{U}_1, u_2 \in \mathbf{U}_2$. u_0 is said to be a minimal element of $\mathbf{U}$ if there is no $u \in \mathbf{U}$ with $u \leq u_0$.

I. GENERAL MODEL OF CAPITALISTIC PRODUCTION

3. *Time, commodities, and capital goods.* Although time is usually considered as some continuous variable taking any value from minus infinity to plus infinity, it is given here as a succession of periods beginning at the present and going to infinity in the future. Indeed, since the past cannot be changed by any present economic decision, we may disregard it; moreover, there is little harm in assuming a decomposition in periods since their length may be made as short as one wishes.

Formally time appears as an index t that can take any positive integral value; $t = 1$ refers to the present moment, which is the beginning of the coming period, called period 1; $t + 1$ refers to the end of period t, or to the beginning of period $t + 1$.

The description of all economic activity proceeds in terms of commodities. Commodities, therefore, must be understood in a very general sense, and so as to cover in particular all services. The total number of commodities is supposed to be finite and equal to m.[1]

Formally, a set of given quantities of commodities is represented by a vector x_t in the m-dimensional Euclidean space. The component x_{it} of x_t defines which quantity of commodity i is included in x_t.

The concept of capital does not appear explicitly in our treatment and it is not needed. But for the interpretation of the following parts it may be better to define at least capital goods. Capital goods at time t include everything that has been made in preceding periods and is transferred to period t for further use in production. This definition is the old "produced means of production."[2] It stems from the essential character of capital. Indeed, it is made in order to make possible the use in future periods of goods or services that do not exist as natural resources or are not available in sufficient quantity.

4. *"Chronics"—extensive form.* We shall mean by a "chronic"[3] a quantitative description of the economic activity occurring during all future periods. It is one of all possible courses of events. A chronic is completely determined when the quantities produced, traded, and consumed are known, i.e., it does not require the definition of any standard of value. Two different chronics, C^1 and C^2, are distinguished by their upper indexes; any vector written with an upper index 1, x_t^1 for instance, represents the value taken by the corresponding vector, x_t, in the chronic C^1.

---

[1] This assumption is not strictly necessary. All that follows remains true as long as there is only a finite number of commodities inside each period.

[2] This might be thought of as too inclusive. Indeed, there is little in our modern world that is not the result of previous economic activity. But the origin of existing wealth does not concern us here. The distinction between natural resources and produced means of production is not important as far as past activity is concerned. The only condition we need to keep in mind is the following: the available natural resources during all future periods must be independent of any present or future economic decision.

[3] This neologism was introduced by G. Th. Guilbaud in his study on time series [11] (Added for the 1967 reprint: The word "chronic" was not used in later writings but replaced by "program," which is now the appropriate technical term.)

More precisely, a chronic C provides the following picture. At the present time certain commodities are available and are represented by a vector $\bar{b}_1$. Parts of them are devoted to consumption during period 1, the rest being kept for further consumption or used in production. Let us call x_1^+ and c_1 these two parts:

$$\bar{b}_1 = x_1^+ + c_1.$$

For production during the first period c_1 is used, together with natural resources z_1 and services x_1^- obtained from consumer (labor). If a_1 represents the aggregate vector of productive factors, then

$$a_1 = x_1^- + z_1 + c_1,$$

which is reminiscent of the familiar trilogy: labor, land, and capital.[4]

Productive activity transforms a_1 into some other vector, b_2', available at time 2.

The description of the second period will be similar to that of the first, with vectors b_2, x_2^+, c_2, x_2^-, z_2, a_2, b_3, and so on, for all periods. This defines the "extensive form" of chronics C.

The following equations hold:

$$b_t = x_t^+ + c_t \qquad \text{(for all } t\text{)},\tag{1}$$

and

$$a_t = x_t^- + z_t + c_t \qquad \text{(for all } t\text{)}.\tag{2}$$

If we define

$$x_t = x_t^+ - x_t^-,\tag{3}$$

then, we also have

$$a_t = b_t - x_t + z_t.\tag{4}$$

C may be represented as in Figure 1.

Such a chronic is possible if and only if the transformation from a_t to b_{t+1} is technically possible and if the resources used, z_t, never exceed the resources available, given by a vector $\bar{z}_t$. The second condition is formally expressed as

$$z_t \leqq \bar{z}_t.\tag{5}$$

The condition that the transformation from a_t to b_{t+1} be technically possible may be translated into formal language by saying that the pair (a_t, b_{t+1}) must be in some set $\mathbf{T}_t$, given a priori from the state of technological knowledge at time t, or

$$(a_t, b_{t+1}) \in \mathbf{T}_t.\tag{6}$$

---

[4] The question of whether there are two or three primary factors of production has been much debated. However, the answer seems to be fairly clear. Considering any one period there are indeed three factors. But if economic development as a whole, past, present, and future, is considered, capital cannot be considered a primary factor.

Figure 1

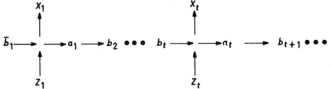

From this definition, T_t is clearly a set in the $2m$-dimensional Euclidean space.

5. *Assumptions concerning the sets of technological possibilities.* The theoretical results of the following sections make extensive use of some assumptions concerning the sets T_t of technological possibilities. The first assumption can hardly be objected to if one remembers that the limitation of resources is independently represented in the model.

ASSUMPTION 1 (additivity): *If from a_t^1 it is possible to obtain b_{t+1}^1 in period t, and from a_t^2 to obtain b_{t+1}^2 in the same period, then from $a_t^1 + a_t^2$ it is possible to obtain $b_{t+1}^1 + b_{t+1}^2$.*
Or, formally, if $(a_t^1, b_{t+1}^1) \in T_t$ and $(a_t^2, b_{t+1}^2) \in T_t$, then

$$(a_t^1 + a_t^2, b_{t+1}^1 + b_{t+1}^2) \in T_t.$$

The second assumption is not so immediate and could be challenged by many readers. But it is taken as a crude first approximation to reality. Moreover, it is necessary in the proofs of the following sections. So it is justified in some way by its usefulness.

ASSUMPTION 2 (divisibility): *If from a_t it is possible to obtain b_{t+1}, then from αa_t it is possible to obtain αb_{t+1}, where α is any positive number less than 1.*
Or, formally, if $(a_t, b_{t+1}) \in T_t$ and $0 < \alpha < 1$, then

$$(\alpha a_t, \alpha b_{t+1}) \in T_t.$$

When Assumptions 1 and 2 are made, T_t, considered as a set in the $2m$-dimensional Euclidean space, is a convex cone with vertex at the origin.

In most of the demonstrations given below, only convexity of T_t plays an essential role. For the sake of clarity, it is better to assume convexity alone, although in practice such an assumption is probably as restrictive as Assumptions 1 and 2 together.

ASSUMPTION 3 (convexity): *If from a_t^1 it is possible to obtain b_{t+1}^1 and from a_t^2 to obtain b_{t+1}^2, then from any combination $\alpha a_t^1 + \beta a_t^2$ it is possible to obtain the corresponding $\alpha b_{t+1}^1 + \beta b_{t+1}^2$, where α is any positive number less than 1 and $\beta = 1 - \alpha$.*

Or, formally, if $(a_t^1, b_{t+1}^1) \in T_t$ and $(a_t^2, b_{t+1}^2) \in T_t$, with $0 < \alpha < 1$ and $\alpha + \beta = 1$, then

$$(\alpha a_t^1 + \beta a_t^2, \alpha b_{t+1}^1 + \beta b_{t+1}^2) \in T_t.$$

The next and last assumption is trivial; it amounts to saying that production is not restricted if more of each good is available.

ASSUMPTION 4 (free disposal): *If from a_t^1 it is possible to obtain b_{t+1}^1, then it is also possible to obtain it from any vector a_t such that $a_t \geq a_t^1$.*

Or, formally, if $(a_t^1, b_{t+1}^1) \in T_t$ and $a_t \geq a_t^1$, then

$$(a_t, b_{t+1}^1) \in T_t.$$

6. *Decentralization of production.* In an actual economy production is not planned by a central bureau but is accomplished by many different firms, each having its own technology. The activity of the kth production unit during period t consists in a transformation of the vector a_{tk} into the vector $b_{t+1,k}$.[5] This transformation can be performed if and only if $(a_{tk}, b_{t+1,k})$ is an element of some set of technological possibilities, T_{tk}, or if

$$(a_{tk}, b_{t+1,k}) \in T_{tk}. \tag{7}$$

For the economy as a whole the simultaneous operation of all production units, n in number,[6] results in a transformation of a_t into b_{t+1}, with

$$a_t = \sum_{k=1}^{n} a_{tk}, \qquad b_t = \sum_{k=1}^{n} b_{tk}. \tag{8}$$

Since (a_t, b_{t+1}) is in T_t, it is clear that in all cases

$$\sum_{k=1}^{n} T_{tk} \subset T_t,$$

which only means that, if some transformation is possible within the framework of given production units, it is also possible a priori for society as a whole. However, the decomposition into production units could be inefficient, in the sense that it would make impossible some transformations that we know to be

---

[5] The vectors a_{tk} and b_{tk} may be decomposed as follows:

$$a_{tk} = c_{tk} + q_{tk}, \qquad b_{tk} + g_{tk} = s_{tk} + c_{tk},$$

with c_{tk} representing capital equipment of firm k at time t; q_{tk}, current purchases of firm k at time t; g_{tk}, Purchases of equipment of firm k at time t; and s_{tk}, sales of firm k at time t. The following relations hold:

$$c_t = \sum_{k=1}^{n} c_{tk}, \qquad z_t + \sum_{k=1}^{n} s_{tk} = x_t + \sum_{k=1}^{n} q_{tk} + \sum_{k=1}^{n} g_{tk}.$$

[6] The reader might object that the decomposition into production units need not remain unchanged as time goes on. This is quite true. We do not want, however, to make the model too involved. From the treatment given below for consumption units the reader will see that our results hold true with little change as long as there is only a finite number of firms during each period.

possible a priori. In the following pages it is supposed that some decentralization of production has been found that is efficient, or, in other words, that

$$\sum_{k=1}^{n} \mathbf{T}_{tk} = \mathbf{T}_{t}. \tag{9}$$

The technological possibilities for the kth firm are given by a sequence of sets, $\{\mathbf{T}_{tk}\}$. The assumptions on each $\mathbf{T}_{tk}$ are the same as those made on $\mathbf{T}_{t}$.

The decomposition of $\mathbf{T}_{t}$ may also be used to overcome the following difficulty. The inequality $z_t \leqq \bar{z}_t$ would introduce in the following Part II some complications that can be avoided by supposing the equality sign to hold, i.e., the utilized resources to be always equal to the available resources. This can easily be done by assuming the existence of some $(n + 1)$th activity which uses $\bar{z}_t - z_t$ but does not produce anything.

Formally, there is an activity characterized by the vectors

$$\left. \begin{aligned} a_{t,n+1} &= \bar{z}_t - z_t \\ b_{t,n+1} &= 0 \end{aligned} \right\}. \tag{10}$$

The set associated with this activity is defined by

$$(a_{t,n+1}, b_{t+1,n+1}) \in \mathbf{T}_{t,n+1} \quad \text{if} \quad a_{t,n+1} \geqq 0, \quad b_{t+1,\,n+1} = 0. \tag{11}$$

From Assumption 4, the following is obvious:

$$\mathbf{T}_t + \mathbf{T}_{t,n+1} = \mathbf{T}_t. \tag{12}$$

Throughout the following pages we shall write

$$z_t = \bar{z}_t \quad \text{(for all } t\text{)}. \tag{13}$$

The fictitious activity will be removed from the picture only when the final result is reached.

7. *Chronics—reduced form.* Let us now define the "input vector" y_t for time t as

$$y_t = a_t - b_t. \tag{14}$$

From equalities (4) and (13), it follows that

$$x_t + y_t = \bar{z}_t. \tag{15}$$

The "reduced form" of the chronic C is defined when the two sequences $\mathbf{x}$ and $\mathbf{y}$ are given, with the following necessary condition:

$$\mathbf{x} + \mathbf{y} = \bar{\mathbf{z}}. \tag{16}$$

From the limitation on technological knowledge, $\mathbf{y}$ is a possible sequence of input vectors if and only if

$$\mathbf{y} \in \mathbf{Y}, \tag{17}$$

where $\mathbf{Y}$ may be defined from $\{\mathbf{T}_t\}$ in the following way:

$\mathbf{y} \in \mathbf{Y}$ *if and only if there are two sequences* $\mathbf{a}$ *and* $\mathbf{b}$ *such that*[7]

$$\left. \begin{array}{l} b_1 = \bar{b}_1 \\ y_t = a_t - b_t \\ (a_t, b_{t+1}) \in \mathbf{T}_t \end{array} \right\} \quad \text{(for all } t\text{).} \qquad (18)$$

From the convexity of $\mathbf{T}_t$, $\mathbf{Y}$ is convex. If $\mathbf{y}^1$ and $\mathbf{y}^2$ are in $\mathbf{Y}$, then there are $\mathbf{a}^1$, $\mathbf{b}^1$ and $\mathbf{a}^2$, $\mathbf{b}^2$ satisfying (18). Now, if $0 < \alpha < 1$ and $\alpha + \beta = 1$, then $\{\alpha a_t^1 + \beta a_t^2\}$, $\{\alpha b_t^1 + \beta b_t^2\}$ satisfies (18). Hence, $\alpha \mathbf{y}^1 + \beta \mathbf{y}^2$ is in $\mathbf{Y}$.

To the decomposition of $\mathbf{T}_t$ into convex sets $\mathbf{T}_{tk}$ corresponds a decomposition of $\mathbf{Y}$ into convex sets $\mathbf{Y}_k$. Each $\mathbf{y}$ in $\mathbf{Y}$ can be written as[8]

$$\mathbf{y} = \sum_{k=1}^{n+1} \mathbf{y}_k$$

with $\mathbf{y}_k \in \mathbf{Y}_k$ and $y_{tk} = a_{tk} - b_{tk}$.

8. *Social choice among chronics.* According to principles first made clear by Pareto, it is sometimes possible to say that a chronic C^2 is "better" than some other chronic C^1. The exact definition of this preference may vary, but in all cases comparison is made only on the consumption vectors x_t. Indeed, economic organization aims at satisfying consumers' needs; hence, the technical process by which this is done is irrelevant to social choice.

The simplest possible criterion is undoubtedly the following: C^2 is said to be better than C^1 if the consumption sequences $\mathbf{x}^2$ and $\mathbf{x}^1$ fulfill the condition $\mathbf{x}^2 \geq \mathbf{x}^1$.

Loosely speaking, this means that there is at least as much of everything to consume in C^2 as in C^1 and that no more labor is required. This leads us to the concept of efficiency:[9]

DEFINITION 1: *A chronic* C^1 *is efficient if there is no possible chronic* C *leading to a consumption sequence* $\mathbf{x}$ *such that* $\mathbf{x} \geq \mathbf{x}^1$.

More generally, if there are any social preferences, then, attached to any given chronic C^1, there exists a set $\mathbf{X}$ of all $\mathbf{x}$ corresponding to chronics C that are preferred to C^1. The following assumption on $\mathbf{X}$ will be made:

ASSUMPTION 5: $\mathbf{X}$ *is convex and, if it contains* $\mathbf{x}^2$, *it also contains any* $\mathbf{x}$ *such that* $\mathbf{x} \geq \mathbf{x}^2$.

---

[7] The reader might find that the constraint $b_1 = \bar{b}_1$ does not pertain to technology and should not enter the definition of $\mathbf{Y}$. Nothing is changed in the following mathematical treatment and little in the economic interpretation if $\bar{z}_1$ is defined so as to include the services of natural resources *and* all existing commodities at time 1. As was pointed out in footnote 2, the exact content of initial capital has no real significance here; thus we are free to assume $\bar{b}_1 = 0$. If this is done, the first formula in (18) must be changed accordingly and the reasoning may proceed without any alteration.

[8] Using the definitions introduced in footnote 5, we may write $y_{tk} = q_{tk} + g_{tk} - s_{tk}$, so that the input vector for firm k at time t is the difference between purchases and sales.

[9] Because of its simplicity, this definition is not fully satisfactory. In particular, it does not provide for the existence of commodities that are not wanted for consumption. However, since we shall also deal with the most general criterion for social preferences, it is advisable to choose here the simplest possible definition of efficiency so as to make the treatment of this case easily understandable.

C^1 may be said to be optimal if there is no possible C with $\mathbf{x} \in \mathbf{X}$. In the following pages we shall, however, restrict the meaning of optimality and deal only with the usual welfare criterion. According to this criterion social choices are determined from individual preferences in the following way:

There are present and future consumers,[10] each of whom is characterized by an index j (a positive number). His activity is represented by a consumption sequence $\mathbf{x}_j$, which may also be written $\mathbf{x}_j = \mathbf{x}_j^+ - \mathbf{x}_j^-$.

Since the life of any consumer j is limited,[11] then necessarily $x_{tj} = 0$, except for a finite number of values of t. More precisely, let us suppose that the indexes j are so chosen that, for a given t, $x_{tj} = 0$, except for $j_t^0 \leq j \leq j_t^1$. (There is only a finite number of consumers living at any time.) For a given j we also have $x_{tj} = 0$, except for $t_j^0 \leq t \leq t_j^1$ and, for any j, $t_j^1 - t_j^0 \leq 0$.

With these assumptions we may write

$$\mathbf{x} = \sum_j \mathbf{x}_j. \tag{19}$$

Now, for each consumer j, there is a set X_j of all sequences $\mathbf{x}_j$ that are at least equivalent to $\mathbf{x}_j^1$, and a set $\mathbf{X}_j$ of all sequences $\mathbf{x}_j$ that are preferred to $\mathbf{x}_j^1$. According to the Pareto principle[12] we say that $\mathbf{x}$ is preferred to $\mathbf{x}^1$ (or $\mathbf{x} \in \mathbf{X}$) if it may be written as a sum of sequences $\mathbf{x}_j$ with

$$\mathbf{x}_j \in X_j \qquad \text{for all } j, \text{ and}$$

$$\mathbf{x}_j \in \mathbf{X}_j \qquad \text{for at least one } j.$$

In the following we shall suppose that X_j and $\mathbf{X}_j$ fulfill Assumption 5. We may now give the following definition.

DEFINITION 2: *A chronic C^1 is "optimal" if there is no possible chronic C such that $\mathbf{x} \in \mathbf{X}$, where $\mathbf{X}$ is defined according to the Pareto principle.*

It is not necessary to insist here on the meaning of such concepts as efficiency and optimality for practical economic policy. This has been done elsewhere.

---

[10] It might seem strange to introduce those consumers who do not yet exist. But if we consider all the consequences of our present economic decisions, however distant they might be, we have to take account of future generations, at least in a crude fashion. If they are not taken into consideration, production of certain very durable equipment would never be profitable.

[11] It would also be possible to introduce consumption units with infinite life, such as a national army. This would not create much difficulty.

[12] One might think the Pareto principle is still too restrictive as soon as choices involving time are concerned. Old people often say they would have planned their lives differently "if they had known." Clearly, only present individual preferences are considered in this paper. Each consumer is supposed fully to appreciate the relative urgency of his present and future needs. However, should this hypothesis be rejected, it would still be possible to introduce a weaker principle for social choices. One may say C is better than C^1 if it is preferred by all consumers now, and will still be preferred by them given all their future preference patterns. The latter concept has been used extensively by M. Allais [3, Chapter VI].

II. PROPERTIES OF EFFICIENT AND OPTIMAL CHRONICS

In this part, general properties of efficient and optimal chronics are studied. Nothing is assumed regarding the rhythm of expansion in the economy. In particular, some chronics may be efficient although they include periods with low levels of consumption and high investment followed by periods of disinvestment and high consumption. As usual in welfare economics and the theory of efficient allocation of resources, the final theorem introduces a price vector and rules of decentralization very similar to those which would hold in a competitive economy.

In order to make the main proof easier to understand, it is given in full detail for efficient chronics. The generalization to optimal chronics is merely sketched in the last paragraph. The reader will probably better understand the process of deduction if we first consider the case in which there is an economic horizon.

9. *Case of a finite horizon.* A chronic C^1 is efficient if there is no chronic C fulfilling[13]

$$\left.\begin{array}{l} \mathbf{x} \geq \mathbf{x}^1, \\ \mathbf{x} + \mathbf{y} = \bar{\mathbf{z}} \text{ and} \\ \mathbf{y} \in Y \end{array}\right\}. \tag{20}$$

Suppose now that there is some finite economic horizon h; in other words suppose that the result of economic activity is no longer an infinite sequence of consumption vectors but that there are only consumption vectors x_t for the $h - 1$ coming periods and the final stock of commodities b_h for the last period. Thus, the economic output is given by the finite set

$$\mathbf{x} = \{x_1, x_2, \ldots, x_t, \ldots, x_{h-1}, b_h\}.$$

$\mathbf{x}$ is a vector in the mh-dimensional Euclidean space. In the same way,

$$\mathbf{y} = \{y_1, y_2, \ldots, y_t, \ldots, y_{h-1}, \bar{z}_h - b_h\},$$

and Y becomes a convex set in the mh-dimensional Euclidean space.

In this form the problem is mathematically the same as in the static case. From previous works it is known that an efficient state is associated with some price vector,

$$\mathbf{p} = \{p_1, p_2, \ldots, p_t, \ldots, p_h\}.$$

The reader will find, for instance, a complete treatment of this finite case in Debreu's paper [8]. The price vector $\mathbf{p}$ is introduced, and its meaning when several periods are considered is indicated. See, in particular [8, p. 282, lines 10 to 14].

---

[13] Hence, we look for minimal elements in $\mathbf{Y}$. From a mathematical viewpoint, Theorem 1 provides a characterization of a minimal element in a convex set embedded in the linear space obtained by the Cartesian product of an infinite sequence of m-dimensional Euclidean spaces.

The existence of a price sequence will also be the essential result of the next section. But, as it stands now, it is somewhat unsatisfactory because nothing implies that the final stock of commodities is economically efficient in any sense.

In order to remove this limitation the efficiency of a chronic C^1 will be determined by successive steps. First C^1 will be compared to all C that are analogous to if after some given period h. Then h will be moved farther and farther into the future. If in this process there is never found any C better than C^1, then C^1 is efficient. This is indeed, the only way in which the problem can be handled in practice; hence, one may expect that it is also the only way in which economically meaningful results can be reached.

10. *Existence of a price vector.* To justify this procedure we need, however, to establish the following lemma:

LEMMA 1: *Under Assumption 4, C^1 is efficient if and only if, for all h, there is no possible C with*

$$\begin{cases} \mathbf{x} \ge \mathbf{x}^1, \\ x_t = x_t^1 \qquad \text{(for } t > h\text{).} \end{cases} \tag{21}$$

PROOF: If C^1 is efficient, there is clearly no C fulfilling (21). Conversely, suppose there is some possible C fulfilling $\mathbf{x} \ge \mathbf{x}^1$. Then, for at least one h, $x_h \ge x_h^1$. Given such an h, consider $\mathbf{x}^2$ defined by

$$x_t^2 = x_t \qquad \text{(for all } t \le h\text{), and}$$
$$x_t^2 = x_t^1 \qquad \text{(for all } t > h\text{).}$$

Clearly $\mathbf{x}^2 \le \mathbf{x}$, so that, by Assumption 4, there is associated with $\mathbf{x}^2$ some possible chronic C^2. C^2 satisfies (21), which completes the proof.

Given a chronic C^1, suppose we now restrict our attention to the possible chronic C fulfilling

$$\left.\begin{array}{l} \mathbf{y} \in T \\ x_t = x_t^1 \end{array}\right\} \qquad \text{(for } t > h\text{).} \tag{22}$$

This leads to the following lemma:

LEMMA 2: *Under Assumptions 3 and 4, if C^1 is efficient among all C satisfying (22), then there are h nonnegative vectors p_t, not all zero, such that*

$$\sum_{t-1}^{h} p_t y_t$$

is minimum for C^1 among all C satisfying (22).

PROOF: For all possible C satisfying (22) the following holds:

$$\begin{cases} \mathbf{y} \in T \\ y_t = \bar{z}_t - x_t^1 \qquad \text{(for all } t > h\text{).} \end{cases} \tag{23}$$

Thus, if C^1 is efficient among all C satisfying (22), $\mathbf{y}^1$ is minimal among all $\mathbf{y}$ satisfying (23).

Now, consider the following vector in the mh-dimensional Euclidean space: $\mathbf{y}_h = \{y_1, \ldots, y_t, \ldots, y_h\}$. $\mathbf{y}$ fulfills (23) only if the vector $\mathbf{y}_h$ obtained from it is in some set $\mathbf{Y}_h$ depending on C^1 and h. From the convexity of $\mathbf{Y}$ it follows that $\mathbf{Y}_h$ is convex. Thus, $\mathbf{y}_h^1$ has to be a minimal element in the convex set $\mathbf{Y}_h$. This implies the existence in $\mathbf{y}_h^1$ of a support plane to $\mathbf{Y}_h$ whose normal vector $\mathbf{p}_h$ is nonnegative;[14] or the existence of a nonnegative linear form

$$\sum_{t=1}^{h} p_t y_t$$

which is minimal for $\mathbf{y}_h^1$. Lemma 2 follows from this.

More precisely, if there are several support planes, the normal vectors generate a convex closed cone in the mh-dimensional Euclidean space.[15]

Going back to the extensive form of the chronics, we may write

$$\sum_{t=1}^{h} p_t y_t = -p_1 \bar{b}_1 + \sum_{t=1}^{h-1}(p_t a_t - p_{t+1}b_{t+1}) + p_h a_h. \tag{24}$$

Since the sets $\mathbf{T}_t$ are defined independently of the values taken by the y_t,

$$\sum_{t=1}^{h} p_t y_t$$

is minimal for C^1 among all C satisfying (22) if and only if:

---

[14] The following mathematical theorem is applicable here:

THEOREM: *In finite-dimensional Euclidean space, given a convex set* A *with a nonempty interior and a point x not interior to* A, *there is a plane* P *containing x and such that* A *is entirely contained in one of the closed half-spaces limited by* P.

For proof of this one may, for instance, transpose a proof by Banach [4, p. 28]. The reader may notice that A need not be closed.

y_h^1, being minimal, is necessarily a boundary point of $\mathbf{Y}_h$. So there is a nonzero vector p_h fulfilling the conditions of Lemma 2. The fact that $p_h \geqq 0$ follows directly from Assumption 4.

[15] If

$$\sum_{t=1}^{h} p_t(y_t - y_t^1) \geqq 0 \qquad \text{and} \qquad \sum_{t=1}^{h} p_t'(y_t - y_t^1) \geqq 0,$$

then, clearly

$$\sum_{t=1}^{h} (\alpha p_t + \beta p_t')(y_t - y_t^1) \geqq 0$$

for any $\alpha \geqq 0$ and $\beta \geqq 0$.

Also, if p_h^n is a sequence of vectors converging to p_h, and if

$$\sum_{t=1}^{h} p_t^n(y_t - y_t^1) \geqq 0 \qquad \text{for all } n,$$

then

$$\sum_{t=1}^{h} p_t(y_t - y_t^1) \geqq 0.$$

Figure 2

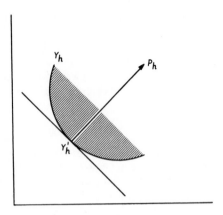

i) For all $t < h, p_t a_t - p_{t+1} b_{t+1}$ is minimal at (a_t^1, b_{t+1}^1) among all $(a_t, b_{t+1}) \in \mathbf{T}_t$;

ii) $p_h a_h$ is minimal at a_h^1 among all a_h that make possible $y_t = \bar{z}_t - x_t^1$ for all $t > h$.

If p_t is interpreted as a vector of discounted prices, $p_{t+1} b_{t+1} - p_t a_t$ will be the discounted profit from production during period t (see sections 14 and 15 below). Property (i) asserts that this profit should be maximized over the set of feasible productions. Property (ii) states that the value of capital at time h should be minimal over the set of chronics that permit the same consumption after time h as C^1 does.

We should now prove the existence of an infinite sequence $\mathbf{p}$ such that, for all h,

$$\sum_t p_t y_t$$

is minimal for C^1 among all C satisfying (22). But, in order to do so, we shall make a new assumption, which will be economically acceptable if we distinguish those commodities that cannot be produced or stored, essentially the various services of labor. Let us suppose they are the last n_2 commodities, and partition the vectors of inputs, outputs, and prices as follows:

$$a_t = \begin{bmatrix} d_t \\ e_t \end{bmatrix}, \qquad b_t = \begin{bmatrix} f_t \\ 0 \end{bmatrix}, \qquad p_t = \begin{bmatrix} q_t \\ s_t \end{bmatrix}, \tag{25}$$

where d_t, f_t, and q_t will be vectors of $n_1 = n - n_2$ components; e_t and s_t vectors of n_2 components, and 0 a vector of n_2 zeros.

Let us now make the following hypothesis about the optimum program C^1 and the technological sets $\mathbf{T}_t$.

ASSUMPTION 6. In any period t, it would be technically possible to produce outputs f_{t+1} larger than f_{t+1}^1 by using inputs of labor services e_t smaller than e_t^1 and some conveniently chosen inputs d_t of the other commodities.[16]

Formally, for any t, there is some $(a_t, b_{t+1}) \in T_t$ such that $f_{t+1} > f_{t+1}^1$ and $e_t < e_t^1$.

Since no restriction is placed on d_t, this assumption seems to be quite acceptable. A sufficiently large increase of the inputs of nonlabor commodities should permit reducing the inputs of labor services while increasing outputs. The assumption would, however, fail to hold if no input of some particular kind of labor service appeared in the optimum program, or if technology would imply strict proportionality between total labor inputs and total outputs.

We are now able to prove the following natural generalization of the efficiency theorem:

THEOREM 1: *Under Assumptions 3, 4, and 6, associated with an efficient chronic C^1, there is a nonnegative nonnull sequence* $\mathbf{p}$ *such that, for all h,*

$$\sum_{t=1}^{h} p_t y_t$$

is minimal for C^1 among all C satisfying (22).

PROOF: Let us define the following norm on the nonnegative prices:

$$|q_t| = \sum_{i=1}^{n_1} q_{it}, \qquad |s_t| = \sum_{i=n_1+1}^{n_2} s_{it}. \tag{26}$$

Assumption 6 implies the existence of numbers α_t such that, in any nh-dimensional nonnegative and nonzero vector $(p_1, p_2, \ldots, p_h)$ fulfilling conditions (i) and (ii):

$$q_1 \geq 0, \qquad |q_{t+1}| \leq \alpha_t |q_t|, \qquad |s_t| \leq \alpha_t |q_t|, \qquad \text{for all } t < h. \tag{27}$$

Indeed, write condition (i) for the input-output combination whose existence is asserted by Assumption 6:

$$q_{t+1}(f_{t+1} - f_{t+1}^1) - q_t(d_t - d_t^1) - s_t(e_t - e_t^1) \leq 0 \tag{28}$$

with

$$\begin{aligned} &q_{t+1} \geq 0; \qquad q_t \geq 0; \qquad s_t \geq 0; \\ &f_{t+1} - f_{t+1}^1 > 0; \qquad e_t - e_t^1 < 0. \end{aligned} \tag{29}$$

---

[16] Assumption 6 is now known in the technical literature as the "non tightness assumption". The proof also holds if all commodities can be produced ($ne = 0$). The condition on e_t may then obviously be deleted.

Suppose now $q_t = 0$; then (28) and (29) imply $q_{t+1} = 0$ and $s_t = 0$. Since $(p_1, p_2, \ldots, p_h)$ is nonzero, q_1 must then necessarily be nonzero and the first inequality in (27) is established. [17]

Let now φ_t and δ_t be any positive numbers such that

$$
\begin{aligned}
f_{i,t+1} - f_{i,t+1}^1 &\geq \varphi_t && \text{for all } i = 1, 2, \ldots, n_1, \\
e_{i,t} - e_{i,t}^1 &\leq -\varphi_t && \text{for all } i = n_1 + 1, \ldots, n_2, \\
d_{it} - d_{it}^1 &\leq \delta_t && \text{for all } i = 1, 2, \ldots, n_1.
\end{aligned}
$$

Then the left-hand side of (28) is not smaller than $|q_{t+1}|\varphi_t - |q_t|\delta_t + |s_t|\varphi_t$ which must therefore be nonpositive. Taking $\alpha_t = \delta_t/\varphi_t$, the last two inequalities in (27) follow directly.

After these preliminaries, it is possible to show how an infinite sequence of prices can be obtained. Suppose one nh-dimensional vector fulfilling condition (i) and (ii) has been found for each h ($h = 1, 2, \ldots$ ad infinitum). Let this vector be $(p_1^h, p_2^h, \ldots, p_t^h, \ldots, p_h^h)$. The first inequality in (27) shows that $q_1^h \geq 0$. We may therefore assume that the nh-dimensional vector has been normalized in such a way that $|q_1^h| = 1$. It then follows from the second and third inequalities in (27) that, for any t, p_t^h is bounded, uniformly in h.

The sequence $\{p_1^h\}$, for $h = 1, 2, \ldots$ ad infinitum, being bounded has a converging subsequence. Let $h_{\tau_1}^1$, with $\tau_1 = 1, 2, \ldots$ ad infinitum, be the indices of this subsequence and p_1 its limit point. Since q_1^h has been normalized p_1 is non-null.

The sequence $\{p_2^h\}$, for $h = h_{\tau_1}^1$ with $\tau_1 = 1, 2, \ldots$ ad infinitum, is bounded and has a converging subsequence. Let $h_{\tau_2}^2$, with $\tau_2 = 1, 2, \ldots$ ad infinitum, be the indices of this subsequence and p_2 its limit point.

By induction, we can find for any t a converging subsequence $\{p_t^h\}$ with $h = h_{\tau_t}^t$ and $\tau_t = 1, 2, \ldots$ ad infinitum. We may designate by p_t the limit point of this subsequence.

The $p_1, p_2, \ldots, p_t, \ldots$ so defined provide us with the sequence whose existence is asserted by Theorem 1. Indeed, for all h and in particular for $h = h_{\tau_t}^t$, $(a_{t-1}, b_t) \in T_{t-1}$ implies:

$$p_{t-1}^h(a_{t-1} - a_{t-1}^1) - p_t^h(b_t - b_t^1) \geq 0; \tag{30}$$

hence also, taking the limit for increasing τ_t,

$$p_{t-1}(a_{t-1} - a_{t-1}^1) - p_t(b_t - b_t^1) \geq 0. \tag{31}$$

Similarly, as soon as a_h makes possible $y_t = \bar{z}_t - x_t^1$ for all $t > h$:

$$p_h^{h'}(a_h - a_h^1) \geq 0 \tag{32}$$

---

[17] The reader might object that this argument does not exclude the case $p_t = 0$ for all $t < h$; $q_h = 0$, but $s_h \geq 0$. In fact, with the partitioning of the commodities into two groups, the n_2 last components should not appear in the last period. Instead of considering the nh-dimensional vector $(p_1, p_2, \ldots, p_h)$, we should consider the $(nh - n_2)$-dimensional vector $(p_1, p_2, \ldots, p_{h-1}, q_h)$ in Lemma 2 and in all the subsequent argument. For simplicity, I preferred not to introduce this complication here.

for all h' and in particular for $h' = h^h_{\tau_h}$; hence also, creasing τ_h,

$$p_h(a_h - a^1_h) \geqq 0. \tag{33}$$

Therefore, the sequence $p_1, p_2, \ldots, p_t, \ldots$, in which p_1 is nonnull, fulfills the two conditions (i) and (ii), and therefore

$$\sum_t p_t y_t$$

is minimal for C^1 among all C satisfying (22), as was to be proved.

The following lemma will give the converse of Theorem 1:

LEMMA 3: *Under Assumption 4, a sufficient condition for the efficiency of a chronic C^1 is the existence of a positive* [18] *sequence* **p** *such that, for all h,*

$$\sum_{t=1}^{h} p_t y_t$$

is minimum for C^1 among all C satisfying (22).

PROOF: Suppose C^1 is not efficient. Then, by Lemma 1, there exists an h and a C satisfying (22) such that $\mathbf{x} \geq \mathbf{x}^1$; hence $\mathbf{y} \leq \mathbf{y}^1$. Since $p_t > 0$, then

$$\sum_{t=1}^{h} p_t(y_t - y^1_t) < 0,$$

contradicting the hypothesis.

11. *Decentralization rule.* The preceding section provides a generalization of the first part of the efficiency theorem which was obtained in the static case. The second part of the same theorem specifies a rule of decentralization; more explicitly, it says that **py** is minimal for the society as a whole if and only if $\mathbf{py}_k$ is minimal for each firm. This will be the subject of Lemmas 4 and 5.

LEMMA 4: *Under Assumptions 3, 4 and 6, if C^1 is efficient there is a nonnegative sequence* **p** *such that, for all h and k,*

$$\sum_{t=1}^{h} p_t y_{tk}$$

is minimal at C^1 among all C satisfying

$$\left.\begin{array}{l} \mathbf{y}_k \in \mathbf{Y}_k, \text{ and} \\ y_{tk} = y^1_{tk} \end{array}\right\} \quad \text{(for } t > h\text{)}. \tag{34}$$

---

[18] The reader may notice we have $\mathbf{p} \geq 0$ in Theorem 1 and $\mathbf{p} > 0$ in Lemma 3, so that the lemma is not exactly the converse of the theorem. However, it does not seem to be worth extending our investigations here in order to reduce the gap. This would lead us into a rather long study. It was done for the static case in Koopmans' work. Moreover, in dealing with optimality we shall presently give a more satisfactory treatment of the difficulty.

PROOF: This follows directly from Theorem 1 because, if there were any C satisfying (34) such that

$$\sum_{t=1}^{h} p_t(y_{tk} - y_{tk}^1) < 0$$

for some k, then we could find a chronic C^2 identical with C^1 except for the input vectors of firm k. For the latter we would choose $y_{kt}^2 = y_{tk}$. Hence, C^2 would satisfy (22) and

$$\sum_{t=1}^{h} p_t(y_t^2 - y_t^1) < 0,$$

contradicting Theorem 1.

Let us first note as a consequence of Lemma 4 that C^1 is not efficient unless there is complete use of those resources which have a nonzero price. Indeed, for the $(n + 1)$th production unit we should have

$$\sum_{t=1}^{h} p_t(\bar{z}_t - z_t)$$

at a minimum. Since p_t and $\bar{z}_t - z_t$ are nonnegative, the minimum is reached when $p_t(\bar{z}_t - z_t) = 0$ for all t.

Even if $\mathbf{p} > 0$, the converse of Lemma 4 does not necessarily hold.[19] The difficulty lies in the possibility of having some C^2 such that

$$\begin{cases} y_t^2 = y_t^1 & \text{(for } t > h\text{), but not necessarily } y_{tk}^2 = y_{tk}^1, \\ \sum_{t=1}^{h} p_t(y_t^2 - y_t^1) < 0 \end{cases}$$

---

[19] The following counterexample illustrates the point. Suppose there are two commodities and two firms with the same technological set:

$$(a_{tk}, b_{t+1,k}) \in T_{tk} \text{ if } \begin{cases} a_{1tk} \geq 0, b_{1,t+1,k} \geq 0; \text{ and} \\ a_{1tk} + a_{2tk} - b_{1,t+1,k} - b_{2,t+1,k} \geq 0. \end{cases}$$

Consider C^1 defined by

$$C^1 \begin{cases} a_{1t} = 1, & a_{2t} = 2, & b_{1t} = 2, & b_{2t} = 1, & y_{1t} = -1, & y_{2t} = 1, \\ a_{1t1} = 0, & a_{2t1} = 2, & b_{1t1} = 2, & b_{2t1} = 0, & y_{1t1} = -2, & y_{2t1} = 2, \\ a_{1t2} = 1, & a_{2t2} = 0, & b_{1t2} = 0, & b_{2t2} = 1, & y_{1t2} = 1, & y_{2t2} = -1. \end{cases}$$

C^1 fulfills the condition of Lemma 4, with the price vector $p_t = (1, 1)$, but it is not efficient, as can be seen by comparison with the following

$$C \begin{cases} a_{1t} = a_{1t1} = 0, & a_{2t} = a_{2t1} = 1, & a_{1t2} = b_{1t2} = 0 & \text{(for all } t), \\ b_{2t} = b_{2t1} = 0, & b_{1t} = b_{1t1} = 1, & & \text{(for all } t > 1), \\ y_{t2} = 0, & y_{1t1} = -1, y_{2t1} = 1 & & \text{(for all } t > 1). \end{cases}$$

Indeed, C provides us with the same net output for all periods after the first one: $x_t = x_t^1 = \bar{z}_t + (1, -1)$ for $t > 1$. And it makes possible an increase in the first consumption vector $x_1 = \bar{z}_1 + (2, 0)$, $x_1^1 = \bar{z}_1 + (1, -1)$.

although there is no C such that

$$\begin{cases} y_{tk} = y_{tk}^1 \\ \sum_{t=1}^{h} p_t(y_t - y_t^1) < 0 \quad \text{(for } t > h \text{, and all } k \text{).} \end{cases}$$

Such a case corresponds to an inadequate distribution of capital among firms, which cannot be detected when comparisons are limited to any finite horizon.

However, the possibility of this can be ruled out if $p_h a_h$ tends to zero when h tends to infinity, i.e., if the present value of capital for period h decreases to zero when h tends to infinity. This is the meaning of the following lemma.

LEMMA 5: *Under Assumption 4, a sufficient condition for the efficiency of* C^1 *is that there is a positive sequence* **p** *such that*:
 i) *for all h and k,*

$$\sum_{t=1}^{h} p_t y_{tk}$$

is minimal at C^1 *among all* C *satisfying* (34);
 ii) $p_t a_t^1$ *tends to zero when t tends to infinity.*

PROOF: Suppose C^1 is not efficient. There is some h and some C^2 such that

$$\sum_{t=1}^{h} p_t(y_t^2 + y_t^1) < 0, \tag{35}$$

$$y_t^2 = y_t^1 \quad \text{or} \quad a_t^2 - b_t^2 = a_t^1 - b_t^1 \quad \text{(for all } t > h \text{).} \tag{36}$$

From Condition (i) it follows that $p_t a_{tk} - p_{t+1} b_{t+1,k}$ is minimal at $(a_{tk}^1, b_{t+1,k}^1)$ for all t and all $(a_{tk}, b_{t+1,k}) \in \mathbf{T}_{tk}$. Hence, for all t,

$$p_t(a_t^2 - a_t^1) \geqq p_{t+1}(b_{t+1}^2 - b_{t+1}^1). \tag{37}$$

(35) and (37) imply

$$p_h(a_h^2 - a_h^1) < 0. \tag{38}$$

Now, (36), (37), and (38) imply that the following is a nonincreasing sequence of negative vectors:

$$0 > p_h(a_h^2 - a_h^1) \geqq p_{h+1}(b_{h+1}^2 - b_{h+1}^1) = p_{h+1}(a_{h+1}^2 - a_{h+1}^1) \geqq \cdots .$$

But such a sequence cannot exist because $p_t a_t^2$ is nonnegative and, from condition (ii), $p_t a_t^1$ can be made smaller than any positive number, so that $p_h(a_h^2 - a_h^1)$ would have to be greater than any negative number.

12. *Properties of optimal chronics.* In dealing with optimal chronics the mathematical technique will be essentially the same as in the two preceding sections. Detailed demonstrations will therefore be omitted and only the main steps given.

Let us recall Definition 2: C^1 is optimal if there is no possible chronic C such that $\mathbf{x} \in \mathbf{X}$; i.e., if there is no $\mathbf{x} \in \mathbf{X}$ and $\mathbf{y} \in \mathbf{Y}$ such that $\bar{\mathbf{z}} = \mathbf{x} + \mathbf{y}$.

Let us define the set $\mathbf{Z} = \mathbf{X} + \mathbf{Y}$.

C^1 is optimal if and only if $\bar{\mathbf{z}}$ is not in $\mathbf{Z}$. From Assumptions 3, 4, and 5, $\mathbf{Z}$ is convex, and if it contains $\mathbf{z}^2$ it also contains any $\mathbf{z} \geq \mathbf{z}^2$. Hence, the following may be proved:[20]

THEOREM 1′: *Under Assumptions 3, 4, 5, and 6, if C^1 is optimal, there is a nonnegative sequence* $\mathbf{p}$ *such that*

$$\sum_{t=1}^{h} p_t(z_t - \bar{z}_t) \geq 0$$

for all h and all $\mathbf{z}$ *satisfying*

$$\left.\begin{array}{l} \mathbf{z} \in \mathbf{Z}, \\ z_t = \bar{z}_t \end{array}\right\} \quad (\text{for } t > h). \tag{39}$$

The following trivial lemma goes in the opposite direction:

LEMMA 3′: *Under the Assumptions 4 and 5, a sufficient condition for optimality of C^1 is the existence of a nonnegative sequence* $\mathbf{p}$ *such that*

$$\sum_{t=1}^{h} p_t(z_t - \bar{z}_t) > 0$$

for all h and $\mathbf{z}$ *fulfilling* (39).

Theorem 1′ and Lemma 3′ may be summed up into a single theorem if the following weak assumption on $\mathbf{X}$ is made:

ASSUMPTION 7: *If $\mathbf{x} \in \mathbf{X}$, then there is $\epsilon > 0$ such that if $|x_{it}^2 - x_{it}| < \epsilon$ for all i and t, it is implied that $\mathbf{x}^2 \in \mathbf{X}$.*

This says that, if $\mathbf{x}$ is preferred to $\mathbf{x}^1$, then any sequence $\mathbf{x}^2$ sufficiently close to $\mathbf{x}$ is also preferred to $\mathbf{x}^1$.[21]

We may now formulate

THEOREM 2. *Under Assumptions 3, 4, 5, 6, and 7, C^1 is optimal if and only if there is a nonnegative sequence* $\mathbf{p}$ *such that*

$$\sum_{t=1}^{h} p_t(z_t - \bar{z}_t) > 0$$

for all h and all $\mathbf{z}$ *satisfying* (39).

---

[20] As in Section 10, one would define finite sequences z_h and the sets $\mathbf{Z}_h$ of all z_h such that $\mathbf{z}^2 \in \mathbf{Z}$ if $z_t^2 = z_t$ for $t \leq h$, and $z_t^2 = \bar{z}_t$ for $t > h$. C^1 is optimal if and only if $\bar{z}_h \notin \mathbf{Z}_h$ for all h. Hence, the existence of finite nonnegative sequences $\mathbf{p}_h$ such that $z_h \in \mathbf{Z}_h$ implies

$$\sum_{t=1}^{h} p_t(z_t - \bar{z}_t) \geq 0$$

(cf. footnote 14), and hence, finally, the existence of an infinite nonnegative sequence $\mathbf{p}$.

[21] Although it is not satisfied by the efficiency concept, this assumption does not seem to be restrictive. It is clearly fulfilled if the individual preferences may be represented by continuous utility functions.

Along with the existence of a price vector, a scheme of decentralization may be introduced. This is included in Lemmas 4' and 5'.

LEMMA 4': *Under Assumptions 3, 4, 5, and 6, if C^1 is optimal, there is a nonnegative $\mathbf{p}$ such that, for all h, k, and j,*

i) $\sum_{t=1}^{h} p_t y_{tk}$ *is minimal at C^1 among all C satisfying (34)*;

ii) $\sum_{t} p_t(x_{tj} - x_{tj}^1) \geqq 0$ *for all $\mathbf{x}_j \in \mathbf{X}_j$.*

Since the vectors of the sequence $\mathbf{x}_j$ are null except for a finite number, the sum in Condition (ii) does make sense. Also, Condition (ii) may be written with the strict sign if Assumption 7 holds for the individual preference sets $\mathbf{X}_j$.

For the converse of Lemma 4' one more assumption is needed:

ASSUMPTION 8: *For all t and j, there exist vectors $\bar{u}_{tj}$ such that $\mathbf{x}_j \in \mathbf{X}_j$ implies $\mathbf{x}_{tj} \geqq \bar{u}_{tj}$.*

Since $x_{tj}^+ \geqq 0$, Assumption 8 means essentially that there is some upper limit to the amount of labor x_{tj}^- that can be required from consumer j. For society as a whole we shall write

$$\bar{u}_t = \sum_j \bar{u}_{tj}.$$

Hence we have the following lemma:

LEMMA 5': *Under Assumptions 3, 4, 5, 7, and 8, a sufficient condition for the optimality of C^1 is the existence of a nonnegative sequence $\mathbf{p}$ such that, for all h, j, and k,*

i) $\sum_{t=1}^{h} p_t y_{tk}$ *is minimal for C^1 among all C satisfying (34)*;

ii) $\sum_{t} p_t(x_{tj} - x_{tj}^1) \geqq 0$ *for all $\mathbf{x}_j \in \mathbf{X}_j$;*

iii) $p_t a_t^1$ *and $p_t(x_t^1 - \bar{u}_t)$ tend to zero when t tends to infinity.*

As in the efficiency case, Condition (iii) means that the present values of future capital and future consumption tend to zero when we consider periods that are farther and farther away in the future. Conditions (ii) in Lemmas 3' and 4' are not exactly the same. But they are equivalent if X_j is contained in the closure of $\mathbf{X}_j$, or if, for any $\mathbf{x}_j^2 \in X_j$ and any positive sequence $\mathbf{u}$, there is some $\mathbf{x}_j \in \mathbf{X}_j$ such that $\mathbf{x}_j - \mathbf{x}_j^2 \leqq \mathbf{u}$. This amounts to saying that there does not exist any complete saturation of all consumers' needs. By increasing the quantity of some conveniently chosen commodity, the consumer may be made better off, however small the increase might be.

III. EFFICIENCY AND THE RATE OF INTEREST

13. *Efficiency in actual societies.* The results of the last part were concerned mainly with the general properties of efficient and optimal chronics. They merely extended what was already known about the static case. It is, however, of paramount interest to study the extent to which these requirements are fulfilled in a real society. This is the purpose of the present part, in which we shall try to move closer to reality, introducing some institutional rules together with the general scheme of production and consumption. This inquiry aims at showing which restrictions are necessary in order to interpret the preceding formal lemmas as a justification of a competitive economic system.

We shall first rule out uncertainty in its two-fold aspect. Any firm will be supposed to know exactly which technical transformations are, and will be, possible; that is, firm k knows perfectly the sets $\mathbf{T}_{tk}$ for all values of t. In addition every economic unit, whether firm or consumer, also knows the present and future conditions of the market, i.e., prices and interest rates.

A second hypothesis concerns money. We shall suppose that firms and consumers do not hold money, either because they are not allowed to or because they do not want to. Once uncertainty is removed, this amounts to supposing that interest rates are positive and services of the banking system free (by which we mean only the fixed costs for any transfer from one account to another—not the normal interest discounts, which are, indeed, retained in the model). Thus, money will be a value unit only.

With these hypotheses we shall proceed to show, first, how interest rates do appear in the price system and, second, how the usual profit-maximizing principles coincide with the preceding decentralization rules. Then we shall be able to exhibit very simply some relations between private and national accounting. Finally, we shall deal with the question of why interest rates should be positive.

14. *Interest rates in actual economies.* As in Sections 11 and 12, the price system $\mathbf{p}$ apparently does not include a rate of interest. This may seem strange since, in society as we know it, interest rates are used on the loan market and in business accounting for discounting future values. The point may be made clearer by the following remark.

In the static case the efficiency theorem leads to a set of prices that are determined up to some common multiplicative scalar. Thus only a set of relative prices is given. Absolute prices may be fixed at any level in accordance with monetary conditions. Our result in the dynamic case is formally similar but entails a different interpretation: The whole set of present and future prices is still determined up to a multiplicative scalar; this, however, determines not only the relative prices for each period but also all future prices, given the present ones. If, as is usually the case, the institutional structure is such that that the absolute prices must satisfy some normalization condition within each period, then our lemmas must be modified.

A normalization rule states which multiple of p_t should be taken as the absolute price vector for period t. To avoid confusion, let us denote by p'_t the normalized price vector associated with p_t:

$$p_t = \beta_t\, p'_t, \tag{41}$$

where β_t is some convenient positive scalar.[22] Let us call it the discount coefficient for period t. Since the sequence $\mathbf{p}$ is determined up to a multiplicative constant, we shall suppose $\beta_1 = 1$.

In the following, the sequence $\mathbf{p}$ will be replaced by two sequences, one of nonnegative normalized price vectors $\mathbf{p}'$ and the other of the positive discount coefficients β_t. However, it should be clear that neither, taken alone, has any intrinsic meaning.

Let us define

$$1 + \rho_t = \beta_t/\beta_{t+1}. \tag{42}$$

ρ_t will appear as a rate of interest in the next section and later on in the treatment of stationary cases.

15. *Rules of behavior for consumers and firms.* As we have seen, the firm k should maximize in each period $p_{t+1}b_{t+1,k} - p_t a_{tk}$ subject to $(a_{tk}, b_{t+1,k}) \in \mathbf{T}_{tk}$. This is equivalent to maximizing

$$B_{tk} = p'_{t+1}(b_{t+1,k} - a_{tk}) + (p'_{t+1} - p'_t)a_{tk} - \rho_t p'_t a_{tk}. \tag{43}$$

B_{tk} is the usual net profit concept[23] for period t. It is computed as the sum of

$$+ \text{ value of net production,} \quad p'_{t+1}(b_{t+1,k} - a_{tk})$$

$$+ \text{ capital gains,} \quad (p'_{t+1} - p'_t)a_{tk}$$

$$- \text{ interest costs,} \quad \rho_t p'_t a_{tk}.$$

One may also note that if $a^1_{tk} = b^1_{tk} = 0$ after some horizon h, maximizing

$$\sum_{t=1}^{h} p_t\, y_{tk}$$

is equivalent to maximizing

$$F_{1k} - p'_1 c_{1k} = \sum_t \beta_{t+1} B_{tk}. \tag{45}$$

F_{1k}, so defined, may be interpreted as being the present value of the firm.

Formulas (42), (43), and (45) show that the theory of allocation of resources justifies the usual accounting procedures. The interest rates here introduced play the same role as they do in business accounting.

Let us also remark that, if additivity of the technical processes holds, together with divisibility, then necessarily

$$B_{tk} = 0 \quad \text{and} \quad F_{1k} = p'_1 c_{1k}. \tag{46}$$

---

[22] For the sake of simplicity, it is supposed that $p_t \neq 0$.

[23] It has not always been clear in economic literature which quantity the entrepreneur ought to maximize. (See, for instance, Boulding [7], Samuelson [28], Lutz [21], Rottier [27].) In any case, maximization of B_{tk} is a necessary but not a sufficient condition.

Indeed, if Assumptions 1 and 2 hold for firm k (i.e. if $\mathbf{T}_{tk}$ are convex cones), then Lemma 4 implies

$$-\beta_{t+1} B_{tk} = p_t a_{tk}^1 - p_{t+1} b_{t+1,k}^1 = 0.$$

Suppose for instance this quantity to be negative. Then, with

$$a_{tk} = \alpha a_{tk}^1 \quad \text{and} \quad b_{t+1,k} = \alpha b_{t+1,k}^1,$$

we would have

$$p_t a_{tk} - p_{t+1} b_{t+1,k} < p_t a_{tk}^1 - p_{t+1} b_{t+1,k}^1$$

for any α greater than 1, which would contradict the fact that $(a_{tk}^1, b_{t+1,k}^1)$ maximizes $(a_{tk}, b_{t+1,k})$ in $\mathbf{T}_{tk}$.

In interpreting the rule of behavior for consumers, suppose that they can receive or make loans. An account of their assets and liabilities is kept at some bank, and the net assets at the beginning of period t for consumer j is equal to A_{tj}. The consumer will be paid interest on it equal to

$$K_{tj} = \rho_{t-1} A_{t-1,j}. \tag{47}$$

K_{tj} may be called the consumer's capitalist income. During period t he will save

$$S_{tj} = A_{tj} - A_{t-1,j}.$$

If we write

$$C_{tj} = p_t' x_{tj}^+ \quad \text{and} \quad W_{tj} = p_t' x_{tj}^-,$$

the budget equation for j will be

$$C_{tj} + S_{tj} = Y_{tj} = W_{tj} + K_{tj}, \tag{48}$$

which may be read as *consumption + saving = income*. Formally it may be written

$$p_t x_{tj} = \beta_{t-1} A_{t-1,j} - \beta_t A_{tj}. \tag{49}$$

Minimizing

$$\sum_t p_t x_{tj}$$

subject to $\mathbf{x}_j \in \mathbf{X}_j$ amounts to maximizing the final assets $A_{tj,j}^1$ under the constraints $\mathbf{x}_j \in \mathbf{X}_j$, and $p_t x_{tj} = \beta_{t-1} A_{t-1,j} - \beta_t A_{tj}$.

Thus, roughly speaking, the rule advises us to choose C^1 if, among all chronics that are at least as good, it is associated with the greatest final assets.[24]

---

[24] This is clearly only one among many possible rules which would bring about a minimum of

$$\sum_t p_t x_{tj}$$

subject to $\mathbf{x}_j \in \mathbf{X}_j$.

The budget equation, together with this last rule, shows how the interest rates we have introduced play the usual role on the loan market.[25]

In fact, we shall introduce a somewhat different definition, which is a little more involved but makes the following section simpler. We shall suppose wages to be paid at the end of the period and to include conveniently the interest earned thereon. Thus the budget equation becomes

$$Y_{tj} = K_{tj} + (1 + \rho_{t-1})W_{t-1, j} = C_{tj} + S_{tj}. \tag{50}$$

Accordingly, formula (49) becomes

$$p_t x_{tj} = \beta_{t-1}(A_{t-1, j} + W_{t-1, j}) - \beta_t(A_{tj} + W_{tj}). \tag{51}$$

Since consumer j disposes of initial assets $A_{tj,j}^0$ but does not get any wage before the end of period t_j^0, the intuitive meaning of the behavior rule is still to maximize the final assets while enjoying a given level of utility.

16. *Real capital and assets; private and national accounting.* As was shown by Fetter [9], there are essentially two concepts of capital given in the economic literature. According to the first, capital includes all " owned sources of income "; thus, it may be defined as the totality of assets:

$$A_t = \sum_j A_{tj}.$$

According to the other definition it is a " stock of physical goods used as means of production." The latter concept is sometimes called " real capital " and could be written $p_t' c_t$.

But assets and real capital are not independent of each other. Indeed, if any net assets exist, they represent some " real " values. If, to simplify, we deal directly with aggregates and write

$$B_t = \sum_k B_{tk},$$

we may define:

$$A_t = L_t + F_t, \tag{52}$$

where L_t and F_t are the values of natural resources (land) and of firms, respectively.

$$L_t = \frac{1}{\beta_t} \sum_{\theta=t}^{\infty} \beta_\theta p_\theta' z_\theta, \tag{53}$$

$$F_t = p_t' c_t + \frac{1}{\beta_t} \sum_{\theta=t}^{\infty} \beta_{\theta+1} B_\theta, \tag{54}$$

supposing that the infinite sums are meaningful.

---

[25] Thus here, as in classical economics, interest rates appear in their two-fold aspect—as a marginal rate of return and as a price for loans.

From these definitions it is possible to give an expression for capitalist income:

$$K_{t+1} = \rho_t A_t = B_t + \rho_t p_t' c_t + (1 + \rho_t) p_t' z_t + G_t', \qquad (55)$$

where $G_t' = G_t - (p_{t+1}' - p_t') c_t$, $G_t = (L_{t+1} - L_t) + (F_{t+1} - F_t)$. Formula (55) shows that capitalist income is the sum of

+ *profits of firms* B_t

+ *interest from real capital,* $\rho_t p_t' c_t$

+ *rents from land,* $(1 + \rho_t) p_t' z_t$

+ *capital gains,* $G_t'.$

The capital gains on real capital, which are not included in G_t', are part of profits.[26]

It is now possible to show very simply how national production is related to national income. Let us define the latter by

$$Y_t = \sum_j Y_{tj}, \qquad (56)$$

and net national production by

$$P_t = p_{t+1}'(b_{t+1} - c_t). \qquad (57)$$

Let us also define net national investment as

$$I_t = p_{t+1}'(c_{t+1} - c_t). \qquad (58)$$

The reader may check that the following relations hold:

$$P_t = C_{t+1} + I_t, \qquad (59)$$

$$Y_t = C_t + S_t, \qquad (60)$$

$$S_{t+1} = I_t + G_t, \qquad Y_{t+1} = P_t + G_t. \qquad (61)$$

These relations bear a strong resemblance to the usual national accounting equations. However, the matter of capital gains seems to introduce some

---

[26] We considered firms and consumers as different units and found some behavior rules for them separately. But actually many consumers do perform productive activities; there is no such sharp distinction in reality between production and consumption units. It is therefore important to notice here that the two behavior rules are consistent. Nobody is faced with the difficult problem of choosing between a maximum of B_t and a maximum of A_t.

difficulty.[27] Needless to say, our relations are not directly transposable to actual societies because money and international trade have been deliberately excluded.

17. *Why should interest rates be nonnegative?* Interest theory, if not capital theory, has often been thought of as dealing only with one question: Why does competition not bring the rate of interest down to zero? The emphasis on this point seems to have been a little misplaced. Once it is understood that two equal quantities of the same thing available at two different moments are not economically equivalent, there is no a priori reason for the interest rate to be zero. However, we do observe in fact that interest rates have always been positive; thus, we may wonder why this is so. The following remarks are intended to reformulate a few reasons that seem to be important in this respect.

First, in a monetary economy, consumers may always hold money, so that there would not be any loans unless the interest rate were positive. This reason, however important as it is, does not provide a complete answer. It has been argued that not only monetary but also real interest rates[28] are always positive. We also want to see if positive interest rates in a nonmonetary economy can be explained.

Note that in such an economy interest rates alone do not have any intrinsic meaning, so that the question does not make sense unless one specifies the normalization rule on the price vector p'_t. This must be kept in mind to understand the following remarks.

1. Suppose first that the prices p'_t are such that

$$p'_t \bar{z}_t = p'_{t+1} \bar{z}_{t+1} \qquad \text{(for all } t\text{)}$$

---

[27] Of course, this difficulty could be avoided by changing our definitions. But there are good reasons for our choice. If income did not include capital gains, the behavior rules could no longer be interpreted in the frame of a competitive economy. If capital gains were included in national production and investment, these aggregates would no longer be evaluated from real physical net output and investment by using a unique set of prices. Concepts like the investment schedule would also be much more difficult to define.

The above equations should not, however, lead the reader to think that the whole of the present national accounting analysis is not well founded. If one considers what would happen in times of inflation, he will find that net national production is the very concept people have in mind when they speak of national income. As we have defined the latter it would include large capital gains which should be saved and invested on the loan market if capitalists wanted to keep constant the *real* value of their assets. Thus, both income and savings might seem to be largely overrated by our definitions.

One should also notice that the equation $S = I + G$ is not an equilibrium relation on any market but rather a necessary identity as soon as net assets are supposed to equate the value of firms and natural resources.

[28] Real interest rates are defined once the effect of changes in the general level of prices is removed. Here, the real interest rate associated with chronic C^1 appears if the normalization rule is such as to make invariant the value of some representative bundle of goods. Usually this concept is defined as follows: Let r be the monetary interest rate and P the general level of prices. The real interest rate is then given by the formula: $\rho = r - (1/P) \cdot (dP/dt)$.

so that ρ_t may be computed by

$$1 + \rho_t = \frac{p_t \bar{z}_t}{p_{t+1} \bar{z}_{t+1}}.$$

If the natural resources are privately owned, they must have some value. Formula (53) defining L_t must have meaning. This implies that

$$\lim_{h \to \infty} \sum_{\theta=t+1}^{h} \beta_\theta$$

exists for all t. This cannot be so unless

$$\lim_{t \to \infty} (\beta_t / \beta_{t+1}) \geqq 1,$$

or, equivalently, unless $\lim_{t \to \infty} \rho_t \geqq 0$. Such was the idea behind Turgot's theory of fructification.

2. Suppose now that the price of some commodity i_θ is kept constant: $p'_{i_0 t} = p'_{i_0 \cdot t+1}$ for all t, so that ρ_t may be computed by

$$1 + \rho_t = \frac{p_{i_0 t}}{p_{i_0, t+1}}.$$

If commodity i_0 may be stored without any cost, we may write $(a_t^2, b_{t+1}^2) \in \mathbf{T}_t$ with $a_{it}^2 = a_{it}^1, b_{i,t+1}^2 = b_{i,t+1}^1$, for $i \neq i_0$; $a_{i_0 t}^2 = a_{i_0 t}^1 + \alpha_t$ and $b_{i_0, t+1}^2 = b_{i_0, t+1}^1 + \alpha_t$, with $\alpha_t > 0$. If $p_t a_t - p_{t+1} b_{t+1}$ is minimum for C^1, then necessarily $(p_{i_0 t} - p_{i_0, t+1}) \alpha_t \geqq 0$; hence $\rho_t \geqq 0$.

3. With the same normalization rule as in 2, we may suppose $\mathbf{x}^2 \in \mathbf{X}$ when $\mathbf{x}^2$ is defined by $x_t^2 = x_t^1$ for $t > 2$; $x_1^2 = x_1^1 + a$; and $x_2^2 = x_2^1 - \beta a$, with $a_i = 0$ for $i \neq i_0$ and with $a_{i_0} > 0$ and $\beta > 1$. Thus, $\mathbf{x}^2$ is analogous to $\mathbf{x}^1$ except that it allows for a greater consumption of i_0 in the first period and a smaller consumption of i_0 in the second period, the total quantity of i_0 for both periods being smaller than in $\mathbf{x}^1$. And it is supposed that C^2 is preferred to C^1.

If C^1 is optimal, then $p_1(x_1^2 - x_1^1) + p_2(x_2^2 - x_2^1) \geqq 0$. Hence

$$\rho_1 \geqq \beta - 1 > 0.$$

This is the usual theory of preference for present commodities.

4. It is sometimes said that the rate of interest is, or should be, equal to the rate of expansion of the economy. More precisely, suppose that the rate of interest is computed from nonnormalized prices by

$$1 + \rho_t = \frac{p_t c_t}{p_{t+1} c_t},$$

or, equivalently, that the normalization rule specifies $p'_{t+1} c_t = p'_t c_t$. Let us define the rate of capital accumulation δ_t as

$$1 + \delta_t = \frac{p'_{t+1} c_{t+1}}{p'_{t+1} c_t}.$$

Then $\rho_t - \delta_t$ is of the same sign as $-p'_{t+1}(c_{t+1} - c_t) + \rho_t p'_t c_t$. In particular, if the $\mathbf{T}_t$ are cones, this is also the sign of

$$p'_{t+1}x^+_{t+1} - (1 + \rho_t)p'_t(x^-_t + z_t).$$

There does not seem to be, in general, any definite sign for this expression. However, if we suppose $x^+_{t+1} = x^-_t = z_t = 0$, then, clearly, $\rho_t = \delta_t$. Such was the case in von Neumann's model of 1937 [24].

IV. STATIONARY ECONOMICS

Usually in capital theory "production is defined in relation to economic equilibrium ... in the form of a stationary economy."[29] Indeed, if such an assumption is made, the interest rate appears quite naturally in the requirements for efficiency, along with the "marginal productivity of capital." In this part we shall deal first with the properties of efficient stationary chronics,[30] second with the marginal productivity of capital, and third with the concept of the optimum amount of capital. A last section will be devoted to some historical comments.

18. *Properties of efficient stationary chronics.* We shall now assume the set of technological possibilities and the available resource vector to be identical to a set $\mathbf{T}$ and to a vector $\bar{z}$ independent of time. The chronic C^1 is said to be stationary if the vectors characterizing the economic activity remain unchanged from one period to another. Thus, C^1 is fully described by the four m-dimensional vectors, a, b, z, and x, with the conditions

$$\left.\begin{array}{l} a = b + z - x, \\ (a, b) \in \mathbf{T}, \\ z \leqq \bar{z} \end{array}\right\}. \tag{62}$$

According to Theorem 1, if the stationary chronic C^1 is efficient, there is some nonnegative sequence $\mathbf{p}$ such that, for all t,

i) $p_t a - p_{t+1}b$ is minimal at (a^1, b^1) among all $(a, b) \in \mathbf{T}$;

ii) $p_t a$ is minimal at (a^1, b^1) among all $(a, b) \in \mathbf{T}$ such that $a - b = a^1 - b^1$.

Conversely, if there is a positive sequence $\mathbf{p}$ such that C^1 fulfills conditions (i) and (ii), then C^1 is efficient. More precisely, we state

LEMMA 7: *Under Assumptions 3, 4, and 6, if a stationary chronic C^1 is efficient, there exists a nonnegative vector p and a scalar $\rho > -1$ such that*

i) *$p(b - a) - \rho p a$ is maximal at (a^1, b^1) among all $(a, b) \in \mathbf{T}$;*

ii) *pa is minimal at (a^1, b^1) among all $(a, b) \in \mathbf{T}$ such that $a - b = a^1 - b^1$.*

Conversely, if there is a positive vector p and a scalar $\rho > -1$ such that the stationary chronic C^1 fulfills conditions (i) and (ii), then C^1 is efficient.

---

[29] Knight [15].
[30] Throughout this part we shall study efficiency alone. The introduction of consumers' preferences would make the whole treatment unnecessarily involved.

PROOF: The second statement of the lemma follows directly from Lemma 3 if we define the sequence **p** by $p_t = p/(1 + \rho)^{t-1}$.

Conversely, if C^1 is efficient, there is, by Theorem 1, a nonnegative sequence **p** such that $(p_t, -p_{t+1})$ is in the closed convex cone of normals to **T** at (a^1, b^1). This implies that this cone contains some vector of the form $(p, -\beta p)$ with $\beta > 0$.[31] Lemma 7 follows, with $1 + \rho = 1/\beta$.

Thus, associated with any efficient stationary chronic, there is some set of relative prices and some rate of interest. This seems to contradict the preceding result, according to which interest rates appear only when some monetary rule is given. But this last condition is in fact implicitly included in Lemma 7.

---

[31] This is obvious if the cone of normals is just a half line. In general, the proof is somewhat more difficult. It is given here for completeness. We want to prove

LEMMA: *Given a sequence* **p** *of vectors in the m-dimensional Euclidean space, with* $p_t \geq 0$ *and the convex closed cone* $\mathbf{\Gamma}$ *generated by* $(p_t, -p_{t+1})$ *in the 2m-dimensional space, there is some vector* $p \geq 0$ *and some positive* β *such that* $(p, -\beta p) \in \mathbf{\Gamma}$.

PROOF: Define

$$p_t^{(1)} = p_t, \quad p_t^{(h)} = p_t^{(h-1)} + p_{t+1}^{(h-1)} \qquad \text{(for } h > 1).$$

Let $\mathbf{C}^{(h)}$ be the convex closed cone generated by the $p_t^{(h)}$ in m-dimensional space $(t = 1, 2, \ldots, \textit{ad infinitum})$.

$$\mathbf{C}^{(h)} \subset \mathbf{C}^{(h-1)}.$$

Define

$$\mathbf{C}^\infty = \bigcap_{h=1}^{\infty} \mathbf{C}^{(h)}.$$

$\mathbf{C}^\infty$ is a nonempty closed convex cone.

By definition of $\mathbf{C}^{(h)}$, for any $u \in \mathbf{C}^{(h)}$ there is a sequence $\{u_n\}$ of vectors fulfilling the following:

$$\lim_{n \to \infty} u_n = u, \qquad (a)$$

$$u_n = \sum_t \alpha_{tn} p_t^{(h)}, \qquad (b)$$

with scalars $\alpha_{tn} \geq 0$, all zero except for a finite number.

Define

$$v_n = \sum_t \alpha_{tn} p_t^{(h-1)}, \qquad w_n = \sum_t \alpha_{tn} p_{t+1}^{(h-1)}.$$

Clearly, $u_n = v_n + w_n$. $\{v_n\}$ and $\{w_n\}$ are two bounded nondecreasing sequences of vectors in $\mathbf{C}^{(h-1)}$. They have limits v and w in $\mathbf{C}^{(h-1)}$, with $u = v + w$. It is trivial to note that $(v, -w) \in \mathbf{\Gamma}$.

Hence, for any $u \in \mathbf{C}^{(h)}$, there are two v and $w \in \mathbf{C}^{(h-1)}$, with

$$u = v + w, \qquad (a)$$

$$(v, -w) \in \mathbf{\Gamma}. \qquad (b)$$

It follows that, for any $u \in \mathbf{C}^\infty$, there are two v and $w \in \mathbf{C}^\infty$ such that (a) and (b) above are satisfied. [Indeed, for all h, $u \in \mathbf{C}^{(h+1)}$. Hence, there are $v^{(h)}$ and $w^{(h)}$ in $\mathbf{C}^{(h)}$ with $u = v^{(h)} + w^{(h)}$ and $(v^{(h)}, -w^{(h)}), \in \mathbf{\Gamma}$. $\{v^{(h)}\}$ is a sequence of positive bounded vectors; it has a limit point v which is in all $\mathbf{C}^{(h)}$. $w = u - v$ is a limit point of $\{w^{(h)}\}$; it is in all $\mathbf{C}^{(h)}$; and $(v, -w) \in \mathbf{\Gamma}$.]

Now, there is in $\mathbf{C}^\infty$ an extreme element, i.e., an element u such that $u = v + w$ with v and w in $\mathbf{C}^\infty$ implies $w = \alpha u = \beta v$ with positive scalars α and β.

Hence, for this element u, $(v, -w) = (v, -\beta v) \in \mathbf{\Gamma}$, which completes the proof.

Indeed, when prices are used in the computation of $p(b - a) - \rho pa$, it is supposed that absolute prices remain the same in all periods; or, in other words, that the normalization rule does not change.[32]

19. *Marginal productivity of capital.* It is a much debated question to know whether the interest rate is, or ought to be, equal to the marginal productivity of capital. As we shall see, the whole controversy boils down to the definition given to marginal productivity. Following Knight [15], we shall adopt here the most usual concept.

Given the efficient stationary chronic C^1, let us consider the class $\mathscr{C}$ of all possible stationary chronics for which the inputs x^- and z take the same values as in C^1. These chronics differ by their capital vector c and their consumption vector x^+. Let p^1 be an efficient price vector associated with C^1. The marginal productivity of capital for C^1 is defined as

$$\mu = \operatorname*{Sup}_{C \in \mathscr{C}} \frac{p^1(x - x^1)}{p^1(c - c^1)}. \tag{63}$$

This formula relates the gain in consumption, $p^1(x - x^1)$, to the corresponding increase of social capital, $p^1(c - c^1)$, both being evaluated from the set of prices p^1; μ is the maximum value taken by this ratio.

Now, from Lemma 7 it directly follows that

$$\rho^1 \geqq \mu, \tag{64}$$

where ρ^1 is the efficient interest rate associated with C^1. One might, moreover see that the equality holds if $\mathbf{T}$ is bounded by a differentiable surface.

On the other hand, a long line of economists[33] define marginal productivity of capital as the ratio between the increase in value of consumption, $px - p^1x^1$, to the increase in value of real capital, $pc - p^1c^1$. Or, in our present terminology,

$$\mu' = \operatorname*{Sup}_{C \in \mathscr{C}} \frac{px - p^1x^1}{pc - p^1c^1}. \tag{65}$$

Clearly, μ' is not related by any definite formula to ρ^1. Thus there is no reason why they should be equal.

There remains the question which of the two definitions should be adopted in economic theory. There seem to be at least three resaons for choosing

---

[32] Similar results may be obtained by an approach more in accordance with the usual technique in capital theory. One can say that a stationary chronic is not efficient if it is possible, without any present loss, to pass to some other stationary chronic allowing for a higher consumption.

Or, formally, C^1 is not efficient if there is some possible C such that:

i) $x \geq x^1$; and

ii) there are some b^2 and z^2 such that $(a^1, b^2) \in \mathbf{T}$, $z^2 \leqq \bar{z}$, $a = b^2 - x^1 + z^2$.

Condition (ii) says that it is possible to go from C^1 to C in one period with a consumption vector equal to x^1.

[33] Cf., for instance, Wicksell [33]. For more detailed references the reader may consult Metzler [23].

formula (63). First, it makes the marginal productivity of capital just equal to the interest rate. Second, it is the right measure for the ratio between the permanent future increase in national consumption and the necessary present savings, as one might easily see from our model. From this viewpoint, it provides welfare economics with a concept that has a much more profound meaning than the alternative, μ'. Finally, the definition of μ coincides with the general definition of marginal productivity, while formula (65) does not. Indeed, marginal productivity is always computed with a single set of prices. This may be made clearer if we suppose that $C - C^1$ is null except for its first component γ_1, a given quantity of commodity 1, while the corresponding increase in the consumption vector $x - x^1$ is null except for commodity 2, the component then being ξ_2. Formula (63) gives $\mu p_1^1/p_2^1 \geqq \xi_2/\gamma_1$, so that the ratio on the left-hand side is directly related to physical conditions of production, like any other substitution ratio in an efficient position. A similar result does not hold with formula (65).

μ is also equal to the marginal productivity of capital such as it is sometimes defined by considering a lengthening of a production or investment period. Indeed, let us compare C^1 with a stationary chronic C absolutely similar except for a one-unit increase of the investment period of commodity 1. If the invested quantity of commodity 1 in C^1 equal to γ, $c - c^1$ is null except for its first component, which is equal to γ, then $\mu \geqq p^1(x - x^1)/p_1^1 \gamma$. Thus, μ is also at least equal to the ratio between the increase in the product from a one-unit lengthening of the investment period of some commodity to the value of the quantity annually invested of the same commodity, or equivalently, to the value which is to be saved on consumption during the present period in order to realize the given lengthening of the investment period. Such was the essential idea behind the Jevonian analysis.

20. *Optimum amount of capital.* The concept of an optimum amount of capital is given in a few places in economic literature.[34] It appears in such situations as the following. The government thinks some sacrifice should be made in order to accumulate enough capital to raise consumption above its present level. The rate of accumulation is not required to be in accordance with present consumers' preferences; these could be neglected if necessary in order to ensure a better future for the community. Is it always profitable for this purpose to increase the quantity of capital? Or is there any optimum beyond which one should rather disinvest than invest?

Indeed, as long as some increase in a_t leads to some increase in b_{t+1}, consumption may be made larger during the next period if it is reduced during the present one. However, it would not be reasonable to impose any given decrease in x_t if the corresponding increase in b_{t+1} becomes too small. This may be better formulated for stationary chronics. For these an increase of the capital vector will be said to be advantageous if it results in a permanent

---

[34] Cf., for instance, Wicksell [33, p. 209], Ramsey [25], Meade [22], Knight [16, p. 402], Allais [3].

improvement in the future or, in other words, if the stationary chronic associated with the new capital vector is preferable to that associated with the former one. It may seem likely a priori that the greater the capital vector, the higher the consumption level. This is not necessarily true because in stationary chronics provision must be made for capital replacement. The latter may become so heavy as to exceed the increase in production.

We shall adopt the following formal definition:

DEFINITION: *The efficient stationary chronic* C^1 *is associated with an optimal capital vector if there is no possible stationary chronic C such that* $x \geqq x^1$, *whatever the value taken by the capital vector.*[35]

We shall show that if some optimal capital vector exists, it is associated with a zero interest rate. By comparison with Lemma 7 this is the result of the following:

LEMMA 8: *Under Assumptions* 3 *and* 4, *if* C^1 *is an efficient stationary chronic associated with an optimal capital vector, then there is a nonnegative price vector p such that* $p(b - a)$ *is maximum at* (a^1, b^1) *among all* $(a, b) \in T$.

PROOF: If C^1 is an efficient stationary chronic associated with an optimal capital vector, there is no $(a, b) \in T$ with $b - a \geqq b^1 - a^1$. Indeed, suppose there is such an (a, b); there would exist a possible stationary chronic C such that

$$x = b - a + \bar{z} \geqq b^1 - a^1 + z^1 = x^1.$$

Consider now the set **U** of all $u = b - a$ where $(a, b) \in T$. **U** is convex and has u^1 as a maximal element; hence, there is a nonnegative vector **p** such that *pu* is maximum at u^1 among all $u \in$ **U**.

As we noticed earlier, the rate of interest in a stationary chronic provides a measure of the marginal productivity of capital. It is therefore not surprising to find that it is equal to zero when the capital vector is optimal.

Finally, we must insist on the very restricted meaning of the concept of the optimal amount of capital and, hence, on the restricted applicability of Lemma 8.

---

[35] The objection that an optimal capital vector could not conceivably exist has frequently been raised against this concept, i.e., that a complete saturation of all capital needs can never occur, even under ideal conditions. Cf., for instance, Knight [16]. In the author's view this is not correct. It is indeed true that we shall probably never reach a state of complete saturation of all capital needs, but the reason is psychological or institutional and not technological.

The question of the existence of a stationary chronic C^1 associated with an optimal capital vector would be worth studying. Our present formulation, however, is not suitable for dealing with existence problems in a sufficiently precise way. The reader might find it interesting to consider the following example:

Suppose an economy with three commodities, the available resources vector $\bar{z} = (\bar{z}_1, \bar{z}_2, 0)$, and the technological set defined by $(a, b) \in T$ if $b_1 = 0$, $(b_2)^2 + (b_3)^2 \leqq 8a_1a_2$. The following stationary chronic is associated with an optimal capital vector:

$$a = (\bar{z}_1, 2\bar{z}_1 + \bar{z}_2, 0) \qquad b = (0, 4\bar{z}_1, \sqrt{8\bar{z}_1\bar{z}_2}), \qquad x = (0, 2\bar{z}_1, \sqrt{8\bar{z}_1\bar{z}_2}).$$

Indeed, as we have seen, optimal capital vectors cannot be defined except for stationary chronics whose practical significance could be disputed.

21. *Historical note on the theory of capital.*[36] Throughout the preceding pages the traditional theory of capital has been related to welfare economics. But this attempt is now new. In economic literature, any sound approach to the analysis of capital formation stemmed from the theory of value whose connection with welfare economics is obvious. Thus, it may be worthwhile to compare the main expositions of the theory of capital and interest with the model presented here.

For this purpose we need not consider whether the authors were concerned with problems of equilibrium or with welfare, nor whether they took account consumers' preferences. Moreover, we need not consider production or distribution theories that take capital as given; indeed, from our viewpoint they miss the essential problem, which is how choices are, or should be, made between direct and indirect processes of production.

We shall examine the principal theories of capital according to two criteria: first, the descriptive scheme of the productive process and, second, the author's solution.

Broadly speaking, the models describing capitalistic production may be classified under four main headings:

First, some theories start from a law, given a priori, of substitution between present and future commodities. This is made quite clear, for instance, in Irving Fisher's theory of interest [10]. In this approach the real nature of the substitution is not explored except for some heuristic comments. Thus, the theory is bound either to consider only a particular aspect of production (as, for instance, the growing of trees) or to assume the prices for each period to be independently determined. In this way, the substitution law must be interpreted as relating present to future income. This procedure, used extensively by Fisher, will be examined below.

Second, most theories of capital describe production as the result of the simultaneous operation of numerous elementary processes,[37] each of them specialized in the production of a particular commodity from labor and natural resources. Most often, roundabout methods are introduced so that the final product may be obtained after a very long time. But, in any case, labor and natural resources are considered as the only inputs in the process. Capital goods do not exist as such; they are expressed in terms of the original services invested in them at the time of their production. These services are said to "mature" when the final product is delivered for consumption. Such is the scheme underlying the theories of John Rae [26], Jevons [14], Böhm-Bawerk [5, 6], Wicksell [33], Åkerman [1], Lindahl [19], and

---

[36] We shall not consider the theories dealing with welfare economics or efficient allocation of resources. For a short analysis of these subjects and references, see Debreu [8].

[37] Usually the models were not as general as they could have been. Many unnecessary restrictions, which were intended to simplify the theoretical exposition, in fact often resulted in making the subject more abstruse.

Hayek [12, 13]. Sometimes it is also supposed that present and future prices are determined independently, so that somewhat less care is required in setting the problem.

To these theories is often attached the concept of the production or investment period. But, although it might be very helpful from an expository viewpoint, it is not at all necessary and could be deleted altogether. Furthermore, as has been shown repeatedly, the definition of these periods raises innumerable difficulties.

In fact, the fundamental shortcoming of this approach follows from the assumption that it is possible to impute the service of capital goods to the original factors, land and labor. This is surely not the case except in some particular instances. Thus, the whole theoretical construction is dangerously weakened.

As a third alternative one may consider the services used in production as originating either from original sources or from existing equipment. Accordingly, the commodities produced include new durable equipment as well as consumption goods. This approach was used first by Walras [22] and more recently by Allais [2]. In order to arrive at manageable equations, both supposed that any capital good, once produced, provides a series of services that cannot be altered by more or less intensive utilization. Even so, this third approach seems to provide a good approximation to the conditions of the real world, as was rightly pointed out by Lindahl [19] in his penetrating essay.

It is apparent that the theory we have built throughout this paper proceeded from an attempt to give to Walras' model a more general content and to explain how a substitution law may be obtained from it.

Finally, it is also possible to give a simple and completely general description of production if the economy is assumed to be stationary. In this case there is a law relating capital equipment to the permanent consumption which it makes possible. This is the idea underlying most of Knight's writings [16]. One may wonder, however, whether his analysis can provide an answer to the question: Why should the study of stationary, and therefore artificial, economies enable us to understand the conditions of production in our changing world? Moreover, as we have seen, the efficiency of any stationary chronic cannot be determined except by comparison with other chronics that are not stationary.

It may be noted also that a stationary economy has often been assumed in theories classified under the second heading (such as those of Jevons and Wicksell), but it does not play there the essential part it does in Knight's treatment.

What sort of answers do the theories give? Here again we may group them under three headings.[38]

---

[38] To do full justice to earlier theories, we should mention that they also wanted at times to study the effects of capital increments on wages, or similar questions related to distribution theory. But this does not concern us here.

First, a few of them try to determine which relations must hold for a firm in a competitive economy. They more or less implicitly assume that these also hold for the whole economy. This is particularly clear in papers by Åkerman [1], Leontief [20], Schneider [30], and Boulding [7]. The approach is, indeed, quite successful because it provides a simple answer to a difficult problem. However, a doubt may remain as to the generality of the results. Clearly, also, it is not suitable for dealing with efficiency or welfare.

Second, most theories aim at determining the interest rates, assuming the prices for all periods given a priori.[39] Although this method may bring sound results, there are strong objections to it. In the first place, prices are determined at the same time as interest rates; it is just in the philosophy of capitalistic production that no simple dichotomy exists between the markets for present and future goods. One may wonder, moreover, whether it has always been realized that interest rates to be associated with chronics do not exist independently of the monetary conditions ruling the economy. If any misunderstanding arose on that point, it should surely be attributed to those writers who studied interest formation independently of price formation.

Finally, a few writers did show how prices and interest rates were simultaneously determined. They made quite clear the connection between interest and the general theory of value. To the author's knowledge, Böhm-Bawerk [5], Wicksell [33], Landry [18], Lindahl [19], and Allais [2] provided us with valuable theories of capital. Unfortunately, their writings were largely misunderstood, if not unknown. The diffusion of their main ideas was greatly hampered by endless discussions on details in their exposition. It was the purpose of the present paper to make the analysis more general, and it is hoped in this way to help avoid in the future such lengthy debates as have occurred on the theory of capital in the past.

REFERENCES[40]

1. ÅKERMAN, GUSTAV. *Realkapital und Kapitalzins*, Stockholm, Centraltrycheriet, 1923.

2. ALLAIS, MAURICE. *A la recherche d'une discipline économique*, Tome I, Paris: Ateliers Industria, 1943; reprinted as *Traité d'économie pure*, Paris 1953.

3. ALLAIS, MAURICE. *Economie et intérêt*, Paris, Imprimerie Nationale, 1947.

4. *BANACH, STEFAN. *Théorie des opérations linéaires*, Warsaw: Subwencju Funduszu kultury narodowej, 1932, and New York: Hafner Publishing Co., 1949.

5. BÖHM-BAWERK, EUGEN VON. *Geschichte und Kritik der Kapitalzins Theorien*, 1884.

---

[39] Here again, simplicity of exposition was often thought necessary but such misplaced simplifications were needed because all deductions had to be made on two-dimensional diagrams.

[40] This bibliography contains writings on capital theory only, except for references marked with an asterisk, which do not deal with this theory but were specifically mentioned in this paper. For references on welfare economics, see Debreu [8].

6. BÖHM-BAWERK, EUGEN VON. *Positive Theorie des Kapitales*, first published 1888, dritte Auflage, Innsbrück: Wagner'schen Universitäts-Buchhandlung, 1912.

7. BOULDING, KENNETH. "The Theory of a Single Investment," *Quarterly Journal of Economics*, Vol. 49, May, 1935, pp. 475-94.

8. *DEBREU, GÉRARD. "The Coefficient of Resource Utilization," *Econometrica*, Vol. 19, July, 1951, pp. 273-92.

9. FETTER, FRANK A. "Capital," in Seligman and Johnson, eds., *Encyclopedia of the Social Sciences*, New York: Macmillan Co., 1932, pp. 187-90.

10. FISHER, IRVING. *The Theory of Interest*, New York: Macmillan Co., 1930

11. *GUILBAUD, GEORGES TH. "L'étude statistique des oscillations économiques," *Cahiers du Séminaire d'Econométrie*, N° 1, Paris: Librairie de Médicis, 1951, pp. 5-41.

12. HAYEK, F. A. VON. "The Mythology of Capital," *Quarterly Journal of Economics*, Vol. 50, February, 1936, and *Readings in the Theory of Income Distribution*, London: Allen and Unwin, 1950, pp. 355-83.

13. HAYEK, F. A. VON. *The Pure Theory of Capital*, London: Macmillan and Co., 1941.

14. JEVONS, WILLIAM STANLEY. *The Theory of Political Economy*, London, 1871.

15. KNIGHT, FRANK H. "The Theory of Investment Once More: Mr. Boulding and the Austrians," *Quarterly Journal of Economics*, Vol. 50, November, 1935, pp. 36-67.

16. KNIGHT, FRANK H. "Capital and Interest," *Encyclopedia Brittanica*, Chicago: University of Chicago Press, 1946, pp. 799-800, and *Readings in the Theory of Income Distribution*, London: Allen and Unwin, 1950, pp. 384-417.

17. *KOOPMANS, TJALLING C., ed. *Activity Analysis of Production and Allocation*, Cowles Commission Monograph 13, New York: Wiley and Sons, 1951.

18. LANDRY, ADOLPHE. *L'intérêt du capital*, Paris: V. Giard et E. Brière, 1904.

19. LINDAHL, ERIK ROBERT. *The Place of Capital in the Theory of Prices*, 1929, reprinted in *Studies in the Theory of Money and Capital*, London: G. Allen and Unwin, 1939.

20. LEONTIEF, WASSILY. "Interest on Capital and Distribution: A Problem in the Theory of Marginal Productivity," *Quarterly Journal of Economics*, Vol. 49, November, 1934, pp. 147-61.

21. LUTZ, FRIEDRICH A. "Théorie du capital et théorie de la production," *Economie appliquée*, Janvier, 1948.

22. MEADE, JAMES EDWARD. *An Introduction to Economic Analysis and Policy*, 2d ed., London, Oxford University Press, 1937.

23. METZLER, LLOYD A. "The Rate of Interest and the Marginal Product of Capital," *Journal of Political Economy*, Vol. 58, August, 1950, pp. 289-306, and "The Rate of Interest and the Marginal Product of Capital: A Correction," *Journal of Political Economy*, Vol. 59, February, 1951, pp. 67-68.

24. NEUMANN, JOHN VON. **"A Model of General Economic Equilibrium," *Review of Economic Studies*, Vol. 13, No. 1, 1945-46.

25. RAMSEY, FRANK P. **"A Mathematical Theory of Savings," *Economic Journal*, Vol. 38, December, 1928, pp. 543-59.

26. RAE, JOHN. *Statement of Some New Principles on the Subject of Political Economy*, Boston: Hilliard, Gray and Co., 1834.

27. ROTTIER, GEORGES. "Notes sur la maximation du profit," *Economie Appliquée*, Janvier-Mars, 1951, pp. 67–84.

28. SAMUELSON, PAUL A. "Some Aspects of the Pure Theory of Capital," *Quarterly Journal of Economics*, Vol. 51, May, 1937, pp. 469–96.

29. SAMUELSON, PAUL A. "The Rate of Interest under Ideal Conditions," *Quarterly Journal of Economics*, Vol. 53. February, 1939, pp. 286–97.

30. SCHNEIDER, ERICH. "Das Zeitmoment in der Theorie der Produktion," *Jahrbücher für Nationalökonomie und Statistik*, January, 1936, pp. 45–67.

31. SCHNEIDER, ERICH. "Bemerkung zum Hauptproblem der Kapitaltheorie," *Jahrbücher für Nationalökonomie Statistik*, February, 1938, pp. 183–88.

32. WALRAS, LÉON. *Eléments d'économie pure*, Lausanne, 1877.

33. WICKSELL, KNUTT. *Lectures on Political Economy*, London: Routledge and Kegan Paul, 1934.

Econometrica, Vol. 21, No. 3 (July, 1953)

BALANCED GROWTH UNDER CONSTANT RETURNS TO SCALE[1]

By Robert M. Solow and Paul A. Samuelson

The recent literature of long-run economic dynamics pays particular attention to the existence and stability of moving equilibrium paths characterized by steady compound-interest growth. In both aggregative and many-sector models the assumption is usually made that inputs are combined in fixed proportions. The present paper lifts this restriction and studies the steady-growth potentialities of a more general many-industry system which is closed in the sense that all of each period's output is plowed back as input in the next period.

1. INTRODUCTION

SYSTEMS of linear fixed-proportion production functions, or input-output models, were proposed by Walras and Wieser, revived by Leontief, and have recently been studied intensively. The capacity of such idealized economic systems for steady balanced growth was first explored in the well-known paper of von Neumann [12] and more recently by Samuelson [10] and Georgescu-Roegen [4, Chapter 4]. By balanced growth (or decay) we mean a state of affairs in which the output of each commodity increases (or decreases) by a constant percentage per unit of time, the mutual proportions in which commodities are produced remaining constant. The economy changes only in scale, but not in composition.

The object of this paper is to consider balanced growth properties in a way which will be more or less familiar to economists who are used to the formulation of dynamic models in terms of difference equations. In so doing, we replace the hypothesis of fixed proportions by the more general one that production functions are homogeneous of first degree. Thus we retain constant returns to scale, but permit continuous substitution of inputs. Our difference equations become nonlinear, but remain fairly simple.

On the other hand, we suppose all optimization and allocation problems to have been solved in one way or another. We do not question what happens inside the economic sausage grinder; we simply observe that inputs flow into the economy and outputs appear. Since the economy is assumed to be closed (with labor "produced" by consumption), all outputs become the inputs of the next period. Thus, it is as if we had a single joint production process with continuously variable proportions.

2. JOINT PRODUCTION WITH VARIABLE PROPORTIONS

In our formulation, a production process corresponds to the possibility of transforming present amounts a_1, a_2, $\cdots$, a_n of n perfectly defined

[1] An earlier version of Sections 1–8 of this paper was read by R. M. Solow at the Santa Monica meeting of the Econometric Society, August 1951.

commodities into definite and nonsubstitutive amounts b_1, b_2, $\cdots$, b_n. If the nth commodity is a nondepreciating capital good, then we simply enter $a_n = b_n$. It is assumed that amounts λa_1, λa_2, $\cdots$, λa_n of inputs will produce λb_1, λb_2, $\cdots$, λb_n of outputs, i.e., there are constant returns to scale. In linear programming the ratios $a_1 : a_2 : \cdots : a_n$ are fixed for each process, and optimization consists of determining which processes will be operated and with what intensities. We bypass this last question, drop the fixed-proportion assumption, and simply require that $b_1 = H^1(a_1, \cdots, a_n)$, $b_2 = H^2(a_1, \cdots, a_n)$, $\cdots$, $b_n = H^n(a_1, \cdots, a_n)$; where any proportions of inputs are permitted, and the functions H^i are all homogeneous of the first degree.

In a completely closed economy, outputs become inputs one unit of time later and this fact gives us the causal system of nonlinear difference equations

$$(1) \qquad X_i(t + 1) = H^i[X_1(t), X_2(t), \cdots, X_n(t)] \qquad (i = 1, \cdots, n),$$

where $X_i(t)$ is the output of the ith commodity in period t.

One other stipulated property of the H^i will be used later. As production functions, we suppose them to be continuous and monotonic nondecreasing functions of each argument; as one or more inputs are increased, other things being equal, no output can fall. For simplicity we rule out saturation cases and assume the functions to be strictly increasing; this implies among other things that so long as some inputs are positive, some of every output will be produced.[2] If the production functions are smooth enough to have marginal productivities, these latter are positive.

3. BALANCED GROWTH

This is not the only interpretation which can be given to the fundamental difference equations (1). Another possibility is to think of

---

[2] This restriction is somewhat stronger than it might at first seem. It implies, for instance, that if we start with a positive amount of one input, say bananas, then all other inputs and commodities would be produced from it in nonzero amounts. This could probably be weakened to require only that from bananas alone we could produce, say, bananas and labor in the next period; that from bananas and labor alone we could produce in one period bananas, labor, and something else; and so on until after at most n periods all commodities could be made available. This weaker property is analogous to indecomposability in linear systems [11]. The purpose of assumptions like this is to assure that there exists an equilibrium state with positive output of all commodities. Otherwise further considerations might apply only to one or more subsets of commodities. A concrete example of a system (1) satisfying these assumptions might be:

$$X_1(t + 1) = a_{11}X_1(t) + a_{12}X_2(t) + p_1 X_1(t)^{q_1} X_2(t)^{1-q_1},$$

$$X_2(t + 1) = a_{21}X_1(t) + a_{22}X_2(t) + p_2 X_1(t)^{q_2} X_2(t)^{1-q_2},$$

where a_{ij}, p_i, q_i, $1 - q_i$ are all positive. The linear part is needed to provide positive partial derivatives everywhere.

$X_i(t)$ as the size of a population in the ith age (or other) group. The increasing functions H^i would then represent combined fertility-mortality schedules.[3] We also remark that (1) generalizes systems of linear difference equations, all of whose coefficients are positive as studied by Chipman, Goodwin, Metzler, and others [11].

Balanced growth has been defined to mean $X_i(t + 1) = \lambda X_i(t)$ for each i and for some positive constant λ. This in turn implies, if we consider only integral values of t, that

$$(2) \qquad\qquad X_i(t) = x V_i \lambda^t \qquad\qquad (i = 1, \cdots, n);$$

and since the $X_i(t)$ are essentially positive, we must be able to choose the x, $V_1, \cdots, V_n$ all positive. Inserting (2) in (1) and using the homogeneity of H^i gives

$$(3) \qquad\qquad \lambda V_i = H^i(V_1, \cdots, V_n) \qquad\qquad (i = 1, \cdots, n).$$

The constant x can be adjusted to insure that $\sum_{j=1}^{n} V_j = 1$, and we suppose this done.

Thus, finding a balanced growth solution (2) to the difference equations is reduced to solving the nonlinear eigenvector problem (3) with positive λ, $V_1, \cdots, V_n$. This will determine the proportions $V_1 : V_2 : \cdots : V_n$ in which output may grow or decay steadily.

4. EXISTENCE OF A BALANCED GROWTH PATH

The existence of a solution to (3), and thus the possibility of balanced growth in (1), is not immediately apparent, but can be proved as follows. The vectors $V = (V_1, \cdots, V_n)$ with, let us recall, $V_i \geqslant 0$, $\sum V_j = 1$, define a closed simplex in Euclidean n-space. Consider the points $y = (y_1, \cdots, y_n)$ determined by

$$y_i = \frac{H^i(V_1, \cdots, V_n)}{\sum\limits_{j=1}^{n} H^j(V_1, \cdots, V_n)} \qquad\qquad (i = 1, \cdots, n).$$

Clearly $y_i \geqslant 0$, $\sum y_j = 1$, so that we have here a continuous mapping of the closed simplex into itself. According to the fixed-point theorem

[3] $X_i(t)$ may refer to age groups of each sex, with the H's involving nuptiality behavior. In some such cases, however, the monotonicity assumption may become unrealistic.

There is an extensive literature on the growth of animal and human populations, to which the interested reader may refer. Rather than give a complete bibliography here we refer to the following few papers, each of which contains numerous further references: (see [7], [8], [1], and [3]). The theory of random processes also runs somewhat parallel to our development (see [2]). Most of the works referred to here deal with linear problems.

of Brouwer [**6,** p. 117], such a mapping has a fixed-point. That is, there is at least one vector V^* carried into itself by this transformation of coordinates. For this vector V^* we can write

$$V_i^* \sum H^j(V_1^*, \cdots, V_n^*) = H^i(V_1^*, \cdots, V_n^*) \qquad (i = 1, \cdots, n).$$

Thus V^* is a solution to our problem, with $\lambda = \sum H^j(V_1^*, \cdots, V_n^*)$. For proper initial conditions, a steady geometric growth or decay is always possible for systems of homogeneous production functions. Should output once find itself in the proportion $V_1^* : V_2^* : \cdots : V_n^*$ it will remain in these proportions, and be multiplied by the factor λ each new unit of time. It follows from the stipulated properties of the H^i functions that every component of the equilibrium vector V^* is strictly positive.

5. PROOF OF UNIQUENESS OF GROWTH RATE

So far we have been concerned only with the existence of a steady-growth solution and its accompanying magnification factor λ. May there be more than one such solution? Not if the functions H^i are monotonic.

This is especially easy to see when $n = 2$. Let us suppose the contrary, that there exist two growth rates λ and μ with eigenvectors (V_1, V_2) and (U_1, U_2) respectively. This means we have

$$\lambda V_i = H^i(V_1, V_2) \qquad (i = 1, 2),$$

$$\mu U_i = H^i(U_1, U_2) \qquad (i = 1, 2);$$

and using the homogeneity property,

$$\lambda = H^1\left(1, \frac{V_2}{V_1}\right) = H^2\left(\frac{V_1}{V_2}, 1\right),$$

$$\mu = H^1\left(1, \frac{U_2}{U_1}\right) = H^2\left(\frac{U_1}{U_2}, 1\right).$$

Then $\lambda > \mu$ would imply, since we are assuming the H^i to be monotonically increasing functions, that $V_2/V_1 > U_2/U_1$ and also $V_1/V_2 > U_1/U_2$. This contradiction shows that λ cannot be greater than μ. By symmetry it cannot be less. Hence λ is unique.

For general n, a different line of proof is easier. We recall that $A_i \geqslant B_i$ for all i implies that $H^i(A_1, \cdots, A_n) \geqslant H^i(B_1, \cdots, B_n)$ for all i. Now suppose there exist vectors of positive components, U and V, such that

$$\lambda V_i = H^i(V_1, \cdots, V_n),$$

$$\mu U_i = H^i(u_1, \cdots, U_n), \qquad (i = 1, \cdots, n).$$

$$\sum U_j = \sum V_j = 1,$$

It is clear from the homogeneity of the H^i that U and V are not proportional if $\lambda \neq \mu$. There obviously exists a positive constant M so large that $V_i/M \leqslant U_i$ for each i. Then by the monotonicity assumption

$$\frac{\lambda V_i}{M} = H^i\left(\frac{V_1}{M}, \cdots, \frac{V_n}{M}\right) \leqslant H^i(U_1, \cdots, U_n) = \mu U_i;$$

and again

$$\frac{\lambda^2 V_i}{M} = H^i\left(\frac{\lambda V_1}{M}, \cdots, \frac{\lambda V_n}{M}\right) \leqslant H^i(\mu U_1, \cdots, \mu U_n) = \mu^2 U_i;$$

and by induction $\lambda^N(V_i/M) \leqslant \mu^N U_i$ for every i and every N. Since the larger exponential must ultimately dominate, this implies that $\lambda \leqslant \mu$. By an exactly symmetrical argument $\lambda \geqslant \mu$, and hence $\lambda = \mu$. Thus, there is only one possible rate of balanced growth.

6. PROOF OF UNIQUENESS OF PROPORTIONS

There is still one more uniqueness question to be answered. Is it possible that a rate of steady growth λ should be compatible with more than one set of proportions $V_1:V_2:\cdots:V_n$? Is there more than one composition of outputs capable of steady growth? Here again the answer is no. For if there were, we would have

$$\lambda V_i = H^i(V_1, \cdots, V_n),$$

$$\lambda U_i = H^i(U_1, \cdots, U_n),$$

and thus

$$H^1(1, V_2/V_1, \cdots, V_n/V_1) = H^1(1, U_2/U_1, \cdots, U_n/U_1),$$

$$H^2(V_1/V_2, 1, \cdots, V_n/V_2) = H^2(U_1/U_2, 1, \cdots, U_n/U_2),$$

$$\cdots\cdots\cdots\cdots\cdots\cdots\cdots\cdots\cdots\cdots\cdots\cdots\cdots\cdots\cdots\cdots$$

$$H^n(V_1/V_n, V_2/V_n, \cdots, 1) = H^n(U_1/U_n, U_2/U_n, \cdots, 1).$$

If U and V are not simply proportional, the assumed monotonicity tells us that in each of the above equations there must be at least one $V_i/V_j < U_i/U_j$ and at least one $V_k/V_j > U_k/U_j$. Suppose $V_2/V_1 < U_2/U_1$. Then in the second equation $V_1/V_2 > U_1/U_2$, and so, say, $V_3/V_2 < U_3/U_2$. Now this implies $V_3/V_2 \cdot V_2/V_1 = V_3/V_1 < U_3/U_2 \cdot U_2/U_1 = U_3/U_1$. Thus $V_1/V_3 > U_1/U_3$, $V_2/V_3 > U_2/U_3$, and in the third equation we must have, say, $V_4/V_3 < U_4/U_3$. This is enough to guarantee that $V_k/V_4 > U_k/U_4$ for $k = 1, 2, 3$. Proceeding in this way we will find $V_1/V_n > U_1/U_n$, $V_2/V_n > U_2/U_n$, $\cdots$, $V_{n-1}/V_n > U_{n-1}/U_n$ and this contradicts the last equation above. Thus U and V are proportional.

7. BOUNDS ON THE GROWTH RATE

Our result so far is that under the assumption of strict monotonicity of the functions H^i, there is only one possible rate of geometric growth or decay, and only one composition of output capable of growth or decay at this constant geometric rate. This uniqueness of the magnification factor λ means, disregarding the razor's edge of a stationary system, that a system is capable either of balanced growth or of balanced decay but never of both. Which will it be? When can we say whether λ will be greater or less than unity? Certainly without detailed knowledge of the functions H^i only very crude statements can be made, for λ is a characteristic of the entire structure of the system.

We are not entirely at a loss, however. One simple estimate is available. Under our assumptions, which are in accord with economic meaning, the transformation (1) maps the nonnegative hyperoctant into itself: outputs are always positive or zero. Suppose, in addition, the functions H^i are such that there exists a vector $(V_1, \cdots, V_n)$ with the property that for each i and for some positive constant c, $H^i(V_1, \cdots, V_n) \geqslant cV_i$. This means that there is a certain composition of output which, in one time period, is transformed into a new output in which the contribution of each commodity is multiplied by a factor *at least* equal to c. We can then conclude that the steady growth rate λ is *at least* equal to c. In intuitive terms this theorem[4] says that if the economy can increase output by, say, at least five per cent for each commodity and maybe more for some, then it can certainly increase all outputs in proportion at a rate not less than five per cent a year. As a corollary, if a simple system of the kind studied can increase every component of output in one year, then it is not capable of balanced decay but only of balanced growth. A similar upper-bound on the rate of growth can be found.

Another byproduct of this theorem is a characterization of the unique rate of steady growth λ. It is the largest positive number c with the property that there exists a positive vector V such that $H^i(V) \geqslant cV_i$ for every i. An alternative characterization can be found by using Euler's

---

[4] The statement in the text is a specialization of the following theorem of Krein and Rutman [5, p. 115]: A homogeneous, completely continuous operator c-monotone with respect to K, has in K a characteristic vector which corresponds to a positive characteristic number not less than c.

This theorem is proved for operators in a Banach space, which we specialize to Euclidean n-space. An operator A is defined to be homogeneous if $A(\lambda x) = \lambda A(x)$ for all $\lambda \geqslant 0$, completely continuous if it maps closed sets into compact sets, c-monotone with respect to a cone K if $x \leqslant y$ (vector inequality) implies $A(x) \leqslant A(y)$ and if there exists a vector u in K such that $A(u) \geqslant cu$. The nonnegative hyperoctant plays the role of the cone K. Actually, for the simple special case that we need, a quite elementary proof can be given.

theorem[5] in (3) to obtain

$$\lambda V_i = \sum_{j=1}^{n} H_j^i(V_1^*, \cdots, V_n^*) V_j^*,$$

so that λ is the unique real positive characteristic root of the Jacobian $J = [H_j^i(V^*)]$ to which corresponds a positive eigenvector. For this and other properties of Frobenius matrices like J with positive elements see [11] and the literature referred to there.

8. STABILITY OF PROPORTIONS

A second important circle of questions concerns the stability of the balanced growth solution. We know that if outputs should ever find themselves in the proportions $V_1^*:V_2^*:\cdots:V_n^*$, they will remain so. But if the system is *slightly* disturbed from this special path, will forces be set in action that tend to restore the original motion? This is the question of stability in the small of the solutions (2) of (1). Or more strongly: If the system (1) is started from *arbitrary* positive initial conditions, will a balanced growth time path (2) tend eventually to be established? This is stability in the large, and includes stability in the small.

Fairly straightforward calculations show that a sufficient condition for stability in the small of the solution (2) is that all the characteristic roots of $J'J$ be less than one, provided the H^i functions have bounded second derivatives. This type of sufficient condition is known in the linear case [9].

But this is not much of an advance. Smallness of the characteristic roots of $J'J$ will tend to be associated with smallness of the roots of J, and therefore (see end of preceding section) with balanced decay. Hence the case of balanced growth cannot be fruitfully handled by the above condition. This is, after all, only natural. In the case where the system is expanding geometrically, one unit of output lost in the distant past could have been the progenitor of an ever-growing quantity of output lost since that time. This is especially clear if, as suggested earlier, we think of $X_i(t)$ as being the size of a population in the ith age group. Now suppose one mother had been subtracted from the population many generations ago. If the population is expanding geometrically in the Malthusian manner, the number of potential descendants would also be increasing approximately geometrically. The loss in potential population attributable to the past disturbance would be increasing, not de-

---

[5] To do this requires that the H^i be differentiable, something which we have not assumed and do not need except for certain minor side results in Section 10 below. Where derivatives are not defined, the slopes of supporting hyperplanes of the H^i surfaces can be used to state a generalized Euler's theorem.

creasing. The steady-growth solution cannot be stable in the absolute sense that changes in initial conditions have effects ultimately damping to zero.

What we might expect, however, is that the equilibrium *relative* age distribution might tend to reestablish itself; that the population might tend to resume its geometrical expansion at the rate λ. In our notation, we might expect that the proportions $V_1^* : V_2^* : \cdots : V_n^*$ will be asymptotically regained and the system will asymptotically again expand at the rate λ, as a result of some initial conditions other than the original ones. This is in fact the case, and in the next section we will show that the system (1) is stable in this relative sense, and, moreover, stable *in the large*. In other words, from any arbitrary positive initial conditions, the equations (1) eventually generate steady growth in the unique proportions V^* and rate λ.

9. PROOF OF RELATIVE STABILITY IN THE LARGE

Let $X_i(t)$ be generated by the system (1) from positive initial conditions. In mathematical terms our object is to show that

$$(4) \qquad \lim_{t \to \infty} \frac{X_i(t)}{V_i^* \lambda^t} = \text{constant} = x \qquad (i = 1, \cdots, n)$$

where V_i^* and λ have their usual meanings and x is a constant depending on the initial conditions or last arbitrary displacement, but independent of i [see (2)].

Define

$$x_i(t) = \frac{X_i(t)}{V_i^* \lambda^t},$$

and substitute into (1) to obtain

$$V_i^* \lambda^{t+1} x_i(t+1) = H^i[V_1^* \lambda^t x_1(t), \cdots, V_n^* \lambda^t x_n(t)].$$

By use of the homogeneity property this becomes

$$(5) \quad \begin{aligned} x_i(t+1) &= H^i \left[\frac{V_1^*}{V_i^* \lambda} x_1(t), \cdots, \frac{V_n^*}{V_i^* \lambda} x_n(t) \right] \\ &= G^i[x_1(t), \cdots, x_n(t)] \end{aligned} \qquad (i = 1, \cdots, n)$$

where the G^i functions are *means* with the easily verifiable properties:

$$(6) \quad \begin{aligned} & G^i(1, \cdots, 1) = 1, \\ & G^i(mx_1, \cdots, mx_n) = mG^i(x_1, \cdots, x_n), && m \geqslant 0, \\ & G^i(x, \cdots, x) = x, && (i = 1, \cdots, n) \\ & G^i \text{ is strictly increasing, like } H^i, \end{aligned}$$

$\min (x_1, \cdots, x_n) \leqslant G^i(x_1, \cdots, x_n) \leqslant \max (x_1, \cdots, x_n)$, with the equality signs holding if, and only if, all the x's are equal.

In the trivial case where $x_1(0) = x_2(0) = \cdots = x_n(0) = x$, the balanced growth proportions are already established and we have automatically $x_i(t) = x$, confirming (4).

Now define the two sequences $\{m(t)\} = \{\min [x_1(t), \cdots, x_n(t)]\}$ and $\{M(t)\} = \{\max [x_1(t), \cdots, x_n(t)]\}$. From (5) and (6) we have, $m(t + 1) = \min \{G^1[x_1(t), \cdots, x_n(t)], \cdots, G^n[x_1(t), \cdots, x_n(t)]\} \geqslant m(t)$, the equality sign holding only in the trivial case that $x_1(t) = \cdots = x_n(t)$.

By an identical argument, we prove that $M(t)$ is a never-increasing sequence, and is, in fact, strictly decreasing except in the trivial case of equal initial conditions. Thus the two limits exist:

$$\lim_{t \to \infty} m(t) = m^* \leqslant M(0),$$

$$\lim_{t \to \infty} M(t) = M^* \geqslant m(0).$$

Clearly $M^* \geqslant m^*$, and it only remains to show that $M^* = m^*$. Suppose the contrary, that $M^* - m^* = \Delta > 0$. Given any small positive number ϵ, we can find a $T = T(\epsilon)$ so large that for $t \geqslant T$, $m(t) \geqslant m^* - \epsilon$. Now let $m_1 = m_1(\epsilon)$ be the smallest of the n^2 numbers $G^i(M^*, m^* - \epsilon, \cdots, m^* - \epsilon), G^i(m^* - \epsilon, M^*, m^* - \epsilon, \cdots, m^* - \epsilon), \cdots, G^i(m^* - \epsilon, \cdots, m^* - \epsilon, M^*), (i = 1, 2, \cdots, n)$. If, as has been assumed, $M^* > m^*$, we will have $m_1(0) > m^*$, by (6). Consider $m(T + 1)$. This quantity will surely be larger than $m_1(\epsilon)$, since $M^* < M(T)$ and M^* appear in place of the $x_k(T) = M(T)$ in at least one of the above G^i functions, while also $m^* - \epsilon \leqslant x_j(T)$, $j = 1, \cdots, n$, so that for each i at least one of the above G^i has each of its arguments less than the corresponding component of the vector $[X_1(T), \cdots, X_n(T)]$. Hence $m(T + 1) \geqslant m_1(\epsilon)$ and if we let ϵ tend to zero (and hence T tend to infinity), we get finally,

$$m^* = \lim m(T + 1) \geqslant \lim m_1(\epsilon) = m_1(0) > m^*,$$

a contradiction. Hence $M^* = m^*$.

We have

$$m(t) \leqslant x_i(t) \leqslant M(t) \qquad (i = 1, \cdots, n),$$

and

$$\lim_{t \to \infty} m(t) = \lim_{t \to \infty} M(t) = m^* = M^* = x.$$

Hence

$$\lim_{t \to \infty} x_i(t) = x \qquad (i = 1, \cdots, n),$$

and from the definition

$$\lim_{t \to \infty} \frac{X_i(t)}{V_i^* \lambda^t} = x \qquad\qquad (i = 1, \cdots, n);$$

i.e., for any initial conditions, the X's eventually grow like $xV_i^*\lambda^t$, which completes the proof.

10. SUFFICIENT CONDITIONS FOR RELATIVE STABILITY IN THE SMALL

Stability in the large, which we have just verified, implies the stability in the small of the balanced growth proportions. There is thus no further independent interest in the latter. But a necessary condition for stability in the small is that the characteristic roots of certain linearized difference equations should not exceed unity in absolute value. Thus the proof of the preceding section gives us gratis certain theorems on matrices, which we record for completeness.

The intensive variables or proportions $V_i(t)$ are defined by

$$V_i(t) = \frac{X_i(t)}{\sum X_j(t)} \qquad\qquad (i = 1, \cdots, n).$$

Substituting in (1) and using once more the homogeneity of the H^i we find that the $V_i(t)$ satisfy the difference equations

$$(7) \quad V_i(t + 1) = \frac{H^i[V_1(t), \cdots, V_n(t)]}{\sum H^j[V_1(t), \cdots, V_n(t)]} = Q^i[V_1(t), \cdots, V_n(t)],$$

where the Q^i are now homogeneous of zero degree. The now familiar balanced-growth proportions are obtained by putting $V_i(t + 1) = V_i(t) = V_i^*$ in (7), and the existence and uniqueness of V^* is assured. Our stability proof tells us that from any initial conditions $V_1(0), \cdots,$ $V_n(0)$, all positive and such that $\sum V_j(0) = 1$, the equations (7) generate sequences $V_i(t)$ such that $\lim_{t \to \infty} V_i(t) = V_i^*$, $i = 1, \cdots, n$. Hence (7) is stable under small disturbances. This implies that if we consider the linear approximations to (7), $V(t + 1) = QV(t)$, the matrix Q has all its characteristic roots less than or equal to unity in absolute value.

Now Q is simply[6] the Jacobian $[\partial Q^i / \partial V_j]$ evaluated at the equilibrium point V^*. Simple calculation and use of the fixed-point equation show that

$$Q_j^i = \frac{\partial Q^i}{\partial V_j} = \frac{H_j^i}{\sum H^k} - \frac{H^i \sum_k H_j^k}{(\sum H^k)^2} = \frac{H_j^i - V_i^* \sum_k H_j^k}{\sum H^k},$$

---

[6] We are now assuming the H^i to be continuously differentiable.

all evaluated at V^*. Incidentally, it is easily seen that $\sum_{i=1}^{n} Q_j^i = 0$, so that Q will not be a matrix of nonnegative elements. If $\bar{V}$ represents the matrix with V_1, V_2, $\cdots$, V_n down the main diagonal and zeros elsewhere and if 1 is the matrix with unity in every place, $Q = (1/\sum H^k)\{J - \bar{V}1J\} = (1/\sum H^k)\{I - \bar{V}1\}J$. J is the Jacobian (H_j^i) introduced in Section 7.

As a result of our stability proof we have the proposition:[7] if H^1, $\cdots$, H^n are homogeneous functions of first degree with positive partial derivatives and V^* is the solution of (3), then all the characteristic roots of $(1/\sum H^k)\{I - \bar{V}1\}J$ are less than or equal to one in modulus. Another way of saying this is that $\{I - \bar{V}1\}J$ has all its roots less than or equal to $\sum H^k(V^*)$ in modulus. Note that $\sum H^k(V^*)$ is the unique λ satisfying (3).

Since the characteristic equation is unaltered if we change the order of a product, $\{I - \bar{V}1\}J$ has the same roots as $J\{I - \bar{V}1\}$, the (i, j) element of which is simply $H_j^i(V^*) - H^i(V^*)$. Hence, none of the roots of this matrix exceed $\sum H^k(V^*) = \lambda$ in absolute value.

It is interesting that in these stability equations the Hessian matrices (H_{ij}^k) play no role; only first partial derivatives count. Thus, in this model, stability is entirely independent of the presence or absence of diminishing marginal returns.

11. DIFFERENTIAL-EQUATIONS ANALOGUES

Essentially the same methods and results carry over to differential equations

$$(8) \qquad \dot{Y}_i = F^i[Y_1(t), \cdots, Y_n(t)] \qquad (i = 1, \cdots, n),$$

where the functions F^i are homogeneous of first degree with positive partial derivatives. Substitution of $Y_i(t) = c u_i e^{\lambda t}$ leads to the eigenvalue problem

$$(9) \qquad \lambda u_i = F^i(u_1, \cdots, u_n),$$

where we can choose $\sum u_i = 1$. Our earlier results yield the existence and uniqueness of the positive constants $(\lambda, u_1, \cdots, u_n)$.[8]

To prove the relative stability in the large of the balanced growth solution $Y_i = c u_i e^{\lambda t}$, we define as before

[7] We could have dealt similarly with any positively-weighted sum of the V's, or, what is the same thing, made a dimensional transformation of the original variables.

[8] Note that since λ is positive, cases of balanced decay require different arguments. The true analogue in differential equations would be systems like $\dot{Y}_i = F^i(Y) - Y_i$, where F_j is positive so that the matrix $(F_j^i - \delta_{ij})$ has positive elements everywhere, or else has the Minkowski-like property of having all its off-diagonal elements positive.

$$y_i(t) = \frac{Y_i(t)}{u_i\, e^{\lambda t}}, \qquad \dot{Y}_i = u_i\, e^{\lambda t}(\lambda y_i + \dot{y}_i)$$

and find

(10) $$\dot{y}_i = F^i\left(\frac{u_1}{u_i}\, y_1, \cdots, \frac{u_n}{u_i}\, y_n\right) - \lambda y_i.$$

Let $m(t) = \min_i[y_i(t)]$. If at time t, $m(t) = y_k(t)$, we have

$$\dot{y}_k = F^k\left(\frac{u_1}{u_k}\, y_1, \cdots, \frac{u_n}{u_k}\, y_n\right) - \lambda y_k$$

$$= \frac{y_k}{u_k}\, F^k\left(u_1\, \frac{y_1}{y_k}, \cdots, u_n\, \frac{y_n}{y_k}\right) - \lambda y_k$$

$$> \frac{y_k}{u_k}\, \lambda u_k - \lambda y_k = 0$$

by the monotonicity of F^k and the fact that $y_i/y_k \geqq 1$ with inequality holding at least once. Thus $m(t)$ is bounded above [by $M(0)$] and increasing, and approaches a limit m^*. An analogous argument shows that $M(t) = \max_i[y_i(t)]$ has a limit M^*. It is not hard to show, by an argument much like that used in Section 9, that $M^* = m^*$, so that $y_i(t) \to y$ for every i. Thus the balanced growth solution is stable in the large.

As before we can define the intensive variables $Z_i = Y_i/\sum Y_j$ which satisfy the normalized equations $\dot{Z}_i = F^i(Z_1, \cdots, Z_n) - Z_i\sum F^k(Z_1, \cdots, Z_n)$. Relative equilibrium (i.e., a stable set of proportions Z_i) requires $\dot{Z}_i = 0$, or $Z_i^*\sum F^k(Z^*) = F^i(Z^*)$. Such an equilibrium exists and is unique and stable in the large. The matrix of the approximating linear equations in Z is

$$J_1 = \left(F_j^i - Z_i^* \sum_k F_j^k - \delta_{ij} \sum_k F^k\right),$$

all evaluated at Z^*. We conclude that all the characteristic roots of J_1 have nonpositive real parts.

Massachusetts Institute of Technology

REFERENCES

[1] FELLER, W., "On the Integral Equation of Renewal Theory," *Annals of Mathematical Statistics*, Vol. 12, 1941, pp. 243–267.
[2] ———— *Probability Theory and Its Applications*, Vol. 1, New York: John Wiley and Sons, 1950, pp. 307–363.
[3] HARRIS, T. E., "Branching Processes," *Annals of Mathematical Statistics*, Vol. 19, 1948, pp. 474–494.

[4] KOOPMANS, T., ed., *Activity Analysis of Production and Allocation*, New York: John Wiley and Sons, 1951, pp. 98–115.

[5] KREIN, M. AND S. RUTMAN, *Linear Operators Leaving Invariant a Cone in a Banach Space*, 1948, Translation No. 26 of American Mathematical Association Translation Series, 1950.

[6] LEFSCHETZ, S., *Introduction to Topology*, Princeton: Princeton University Press, 1949.

[7] LESLIE, P. H., "On the Use of Matrices in Certain Population Mathematics," *Biometrika*, Vol. 33, Nov., 1945, pp. 183–212, and Vol 35, Dec., 1948, pp. 213–245.

[8] LOTKA, A. J., *Théorie analytique des associations biologiques*, 2e Partie, Paris: Hermann, 1939, 149 pp.

[9] SAMUELSON, P., *Foundations of Economic Analysis*, Cambridge: Harvard University Press, 1947, p 438.

[10] ———— *Market Mechanisms and Maximization*, Part III, unpublished RAND Corporation Memorandum.

[11] SOLOW, R., "On the Structure of Linear Models," ECONOMETRICA, Vol. 20, No. 1, 1952, pp. 29–46.

[12] VON NEUMANN, J., "A Model of General Economic Equilibrium," *Review of Economic Studies*, Vol. 13, No. 1, 1945–1946, p. 1–9.

Econometrica, Vol. 24, No. 2 (April, 1956)

A GENERALIZATION OF THE VON NEUMANN MODEL OF AN EXPANDING ECONOMY[1]

By John G. Kemeny, Oskar Morgenstern, and Gerald L. Thompson

1. introduction

Von Neumann's model of an expanding economy was developed in 1932, published in 1937 in Vienna, and, in an English translation, again in 1945 (see [11]). While the problem of the possibility of a uniformly expanding economy had already been recognized by some economists, e.g., G. Cassel, there was no rigorous treatment in the literature until von Neumann's paper appeared. His paper has stimulated other work in this direction (see, for example, references [1, 2, 3, 4, 5, 6, 9, 13, 15, 18, 19]).

In his paper von Neumann showed that a model of an economy could be constructed for which there exists a unique rate of uniform expansion which in turn was shown to be equal to the rate of interest. In order to establish this result a number of specific economic and mathematical assumptions were required. Among the economic assumptions were the following: (1) the natural factors of production such as labor and land are available in unlimited quantities; (2) each process of production uses or produces some quantity, however small, of each good produced in the preceding period; (3) labor is held at the subsistence level, with the capitalist class investing all the proceeds obtained from the production of the preceding period.

The economist will find the first assumption quite proper because there are or have been many instances of economic development where it was true. He will more likely object to the second as being unnatural, especially if the economy studied is described in a high degree of disaggregation. The third assumption, while rare in a modern society, is nevertheless not unrealistic, for example, when policy measures are introduced that are designed to enforce rapid growth by curtailing consumption.

In this paper we accept the first assumption. By showing how outside demand can be introduced into the von Neumann model in a natural way we are able to drop the third assumption. We reject the second highly restrictive assumption and replace it by new conditions, which, we believe, have a simple, direct economic meaning. With these new conditions we obtain all of von Neumann's results (in a slightly stronger form) except for the uniqueness of the expansion rate. Instead we find a finite number of allowable expansion rates and show that prices and production can be adjusted so that any of these expansion rates

[1] The preparation of this paper was supported by the National Science Foundation by means of a grant given to the Dartmouth Mathematics Project, and in part by the Office of Naval Research by means of a contract with Princeton University.

can be obtained in the economy. In fact, for each such expansion rate there is at least one sub-economy which can expand at that rate. We give an independent characterization, similar to von Neumann's, for the maximum and minimum expansion rates. We introduce aggregation into the model and demonstrate some of its effects on expansion rates. Finally, the introduction of outside demand into the von Neumann model mentioned earlier, allows us to show that the Leontief model, if subject to expansion, is a special case of the von Neumann model of an expanding economy. This latter result has interesting connections with results of Gale, Wong, and Woodbury [4, 18, 19].

2. THE MODIFIED VON NEUMANN MODEL

We consider as a model of an economy a finite set of m processes which operate at discrete time intervals and which produce a finite number n of different goods. From an economic point of view one usually has $m > n$ because, for most goods, there are alternate ways of production so that there is a choice among production processes. From a mathematical point of view we need not, and do not, assume any relationship between m and n. The processes may be manufacturing processes but they may also represent consumption, storage, and (as we show later) outside demand. We assume constant returns to scale and the unlimited availability of the natural factors of production such as labor and land. The inputs needed for the processes at any time t are the goods produced during the preceding time period $t - 1$, plus the natural factors of production.

Each process operates at an *intensity* x where x is a real nonnegative number. Intensities are normalized so that the ith process operates at intensity x_i where $0 \leqslant x_i \leqslant 1$ and $\sum_{i=1}^{m} x_i = 1$. Thus the *intensity vector* (a row vector) $x = (x_1, \cdots, x_m)$ shall be viewed as an m-dimensional probability vector. When the ith process is operating it requires a_{ij} units of good j ($j = 1, \cdots, n$) and produces b_{ik} units of good k($k = 1, \cdots, n$) per unit of good i. Since only the ratios of these numbers are significant, the units may be chosen arbitrarily. It is assumed that a_{ij} and b_{ij} are nonnegative real numbers for all i and j. Symbolically we can represent physical production change during one time period as follows:

$$\text{(time } t - 1) \qquad xA \rightarrow xB \qquad \text{(time } t),$$

where $A = \| a_{ij} \|$ and $B = \| b_{ij} \|$. The components of the vector xA give the amounts of inputs used up in production and the components of the vector xB give the amounts produced.

Each good[2] is assigned a price y where y is a nonnegative real number. Prices are also normalized so that the jth good is assigned price y_j where $0 \leqslant y_j \leqslant 1$

[2] Labor, land, and other natural factors must be treated as free, since they are not produced. But there are simple means for entering the costs connected with these factors in the model. E.g., the cost of labor can be introduced in terms of the consumption of the worker and his family. In this approach consumer goods would be among the inputs of all processes.

and $\sum_{j=1}^{n} y_j = 1$. Thus the *price vector* (a column vector) $y = (y_1, \cdots, y_n)$ is an n-dimensional probability vector. Symbolically we can represent value changes during one time period as follows:

$$(\text{time } t - 1) \quad Ay \to By \quad (\text{time } t).$$

The components of the vector Ay give the value of the input entering into the processes and the components of the vector By give the value of goods produced by the processes.

It is assumed that there is an interest rate b (per cent) from which we derive the *interest factor* $\beta = 1 + b/100$. Interest is paid by an outside source and investment is always possible. It is also assumed that there is an expansion rate a (per cent) from which we derive the *expansion factor* $\alpha = 1 + a/100$. Because of the assumed unlimited supplies of "land and labor," i.e., the original means of production, expansion can continue indefinitely.

We are looking for vectors x and y and numbers α and β which satisfy the following five conditions. The first one is a conservation condition which says that no more goods can be used during any time period than were produced during the preceding time period. In equation form this reads

$$(1) \qquad xB \geqslant \alpha xA \quad \text{or} \quad x(B - \alpha A) \geqslant 0.$$

(Here and elsewhere we shall use the convention that, if u and v are vectors, then $u \geqslant v$ shall mean that the corresponding inequalities shall be true for the components of u and v. Also, we do not distinguish between the number zero and the zero vector since the context will always be clear.) The second condition makes the economy a profitless one, i.e., one in which a process cannot yield a return greater than that yielded by the going interest rate; in equation form this reads

$$(2) \qquad \beta Ay \geqslant By \quad \text{or} \quad (B - \beta A)y \leqslant 0.$$

The third condition requires that a zero price be charged for goods that are overproduced, in other words,

$$(3) \qquad x(B - \alpha A)y = 0.$$

The fourth condition is

$$(4) \qquad x(B - \beta A)y = 0,$$

which says that inefficient processes must be used with zero intensity.

Without further assumptions about the matrices A and B there will, in general, be no solution satisfying these conditions. Von Neumann made the following additional assumption

$$(*) \qquad a_{ij} + b_{ij} > 0, \qquad \text{for all } i \text{ and } j.$$

Intuitively, this assumption means that every process must either consume or produce a positive amount of every good. Von Neumann made this assumption to insure the uniqueness of α and to prevent the economy from breaking up into disconnected parts (cf. Sections 6 and 8). If we observe that the numbers a_{ij} and b_{ij} can be made very small this assumption does not seem unreasonable; however, it has been criticized by economists [2]. It will be seen in Section 9 that the condition is natural when the model is highly aggregated.

Observe that the following uninteresting economies satisfy all of the above conditions:

Example 1: Let A and B be matrices with $a_{ij} = 1$ and $b_{ij} = 0$ for all i and j; let $\alpha = \beta = 0$ and let x and y be arbitrary probability vectors. It is easy to see that these quantities satisfy (1)–(4) and (*). This is an economy which uses raw materials but produces nothing.

Example 2: Let A and B be matrices with $a_{ij} = 0$ and $b_{ij} = 1$ for all i and j; let $\alpha = \beta = \infty$ and let x and y be arbitrary probability vectors. It is easy to to see that these quantities satisfy (1)–(4) and (*). This is an economy which produces goods without using raw materials.

Neither of these examples corresponds to economic reality; they do, however, fit into the von Neumann model as special limiting cases. What we want to do here is to weaken the (*) assumption; when we do so we will find that examples like those mentioned above will become very annoying. We therefore impose an additional condition not contained in the original von Neumann model, namely

(5) $xBy > 0.$

Intuitively this condition means that the total value of all goods produced must be positive. Observe that Example 1 does not satisfy this condition while Example 2 does.

Although we shall occasionally use assumption (*) in this paper, our principal assumption will be another, we think economically plausible, assumption, namely

(i) every process uses some inputs, i.e., goods produced in the preceding time period, and

(ii) every good can be produced in the economy, i.e., given a good, there exists at least one process which can produce it.

These assumptions are much weaker than the von Neumann (*) assumption. They can be stated more precisely as follows:

(**)   (i) every row of A has at least one positive entry,
        (ii) every column of B has at least one positive entry.

Observe that neither of the examples above satisfies these conditions.

The analysis that follows makes use of concepts and theorems from the theory of games of strategy. It will be assumed that the reader has a certain familiarity with game theory, especially with matrix games (cf., for example, [10] and [12]). We should like to point out that game theory is here used as a mathematical tool in order to obtain mathematical results (of which only those having economic meaning are admitted). Game theory appears therefore as a mathematical technique, comparable to, say, the calculus of variations or group theory. This use of the theory does not preclude its application to a large stationary or expanding economy in a very different sense, i.e., when the participants in the economy are viewed as playing a non-zero sum n-person game. In the latter case results may be obtained that are different from those shown in the present paper, especially because of the possibility of the formation of coalitions among the players. The emergence of the theory of games as a strictly mathematical tool for the analysis of more conventional economic situations, besides its role as a model of economic reality, is a noteworthy phenomenon and gives it added significance for the economist.

We now restate conditions (**) in game theoretical terms: We consider B and $-A$ as matrix games where the maximizing player controls the rows and the minimizing player the columns. Let $v(B)$ and $v(-A)$ be the values of each of these games. Then, remembering that the entries of A and B are nonnegative, it is easy to see that the (**) conditions are equivalent to the conditions

(i) $v(-A) < 0$, and

(ii) $v(B) > 0$.

If we have numbers α and β and vectors x and y which satisfy equations (1)–(5), then these quantities will provide solutions to the economic model which hold in *every time period*. We shall then say that the economy is in *equilibrium*.

3. INTERPRETATION AS A GAME THEORY PROBLEM

We now interpret the whole problem in game-theoretic terms. It will become clear to the reader that some parts of the problem which are of game-theoretic interest are not of economic interest. We need the following lemma.

LEMMA 1: *If x, y, α, and β are solutions of (1)–(5) then $\alpha = \beta = xBy/xAy$.*

PROOF: From (5) we see that $xBy > 0$; hence from (3) and (4) $xBy = \alpha xAy = \beta xAy > 0$. From the last equation $xAy > 0$ so that $\alpha = \beta = xBy/xAy$.

Thus we need look only for solutions in which $\alpha = \beta$, i.e., the model requires that the interest rate should equal the expansion rate. Under this assumption equation (4) becomes the same as (3). Making the abbreviation $M_\alpha = B - \alpha A$, the expressions (1), (2), and (5) become

(1′) $xM_\alpha \geqslant 0$,

(2′) $M_\alpha y \leqslant 0$,

(5′) $xBy > 0$.

Observe that we have omitted expression (3) (and its equivalent (4)). This is permissible since, if we have a solution to (1′) and (2′), then such solutions must satisfy (3) as well. To see this, multiply (1′) by y, obtaining $xM_\alpha y \geqslant 0$; and multiply (2′) by x, obtaining $xM_\alpha y \leqslant 0$; these two expressions imply that $xM_\alpha y = 0$ which is (3).

If we interpret M_α as a matrix game where the maximizing player controls the rows and the minimizing player the columns we see that (1′) and (2′) imply that $v(M_\alpha) = 0$. Moreover, (1′) and (2′) show that the solutions x and y to the economic problem are optimal strategies in the game M_α. We now restate our problem in game-theoretic terms.

PROBLEM: Given nonnegative $m \times n$ matrices A and B such that $v(-A) < 0$ and $v(B) > 0$; set $M_\alpha = B + \alpha(-A)$ and find an α so that $v(M_\alpha) = 0$; then find a pair of probability vectors (x, y) such that $xBy > 0$ and such that x is optimal for the maximizing player and y is optimal for the minimizing player in the game M_α.

We shall call an α such that $v(M_\alpha) = 0$ an *allowable* α. Even if we can find an allowable α we will have to distinguish between two types of pairs of optimal strategies in the game M_α. If (x, y) is a pair of optimal strategies for M_α such that $xBy > 0$ we shall call these *economic solutions* to the game M_α; on the other hand, if (x', y') is a pair of optimal strategies for M_α such that $x'By' = 0$ we shall call them *non-economic* solutions to the game M_α. It will turn out that if the expansion rate is not unique (and perhaps even if it is unique) then there always exist non-economic solutions to the game. Since we are not interested in finding non-economic solutions we shall not mention them again, and in this sense our problem becomes more economic than game-theoretic.

4. EXISTENCE OF ECONOMIC SOLUTIONS

The purpose of this section is to discuss, under assumptions (**), the existence of economic solutions to (1′), (2′), and (5′).

Let S_m be the set of all m-dimensional probability vectors and let S_n be the set of all n-dimensional probability vectors. In what follows we shall use $x \in S_m$ to denote a strategy for the maximizing player in M_α and $y \in S_n$ to denote a strategy for the minimizing player in M_α.

LEMMA 2: *If α' and α'' $(<\alpha')$ are two distinct allowable values of α [i.e., $v(M_{\alpha'}) = v(M_{\alpha''}) = 0$] then $v(M_\alpha) = 0$ for α in the interval $\alpha' \geqslant \alpha \geqslant \alpha''$. Moreover, if x' is optimal in $M_{\alpha'}$ and y'' is optimal in $M_{\alpha''}$ then the pair (x', y'') is optimal in M_α for all α in the same interval.*

PROOF: Let x' be an optimal strategy for the maximizing player in the game $M_{\alpha'}$; then $x'M_{\alpha'} \geqslant 0$. If α is any number less than α' we have

$$x'M_\alpha = x'(B - \alpha A) = x'(B - \alpha'A) + x'(\alpha' - \alpha)A \geqslant 0,$$

hence $v(M_\alpha) \geqslant 0$.

Similarly, let y'' be optimal for the minimizing player in $M_{\alpha''}$; then $M_{\alpha''}y'' \leqslant 0$. If α is any number greater than α'' we have

$$M_\alpha y'' = (B - \alpha A)y'' = (B - \alpha''A)y'' + (\alpha'' - \alpha)Ay'' \leqslant 0,$$

hence $v(M_\alpha) \leqslant 0$.

The inequalities obtained at the conclusion of each of the two paragraphs above show that $v(M_\alpha) = 0$ and also show that (x', y'') are optimal strategies in the game M_α for $\alpha' \geqslant \alpha \geqslant \alpha''$. This concludes the proof of the lemma.

COROLLARY: *If* (*) *holds then there is at most one allowable* α.

PROOF: Suppose there were two such, α and α', with $\alpha > \alpha'$. Then let (x, y) and (x', y') be two economic solutions corresponding to these allowable α's. By the lemma the pair (x, y') is optimal at α and α' so that

$$xM_\alpha y' = xBy' - \alpha xAy' = 0$$

and

$$xM_{\alpha'}y' = xBy' - \alpha'xAy' = 0.$$

Subtracting these two equations we have

$$(\alpha' - \alpha)xAy' = 0;$$

subtracting α times the second from α' times the first we get

$$(\alpha' - \alpha)xBy' = 0;$$

hence we see that $xAy' = xBy' = 0$. Since x and y' are probability vectors we can choose indices i and j such that $x_i y'_j > 0$; then necessarily

$$x_i a_{ij} y'_j = x_i b_{ij} y'_j = 0$$

so that $a_{ij} = b_{ij} = 0$ which contradicts condition (*).

THEOREM 1: *There are at most* min (m, n) *allowable* α's *for which economic solutions to* M_α *exist.*

PROOF: For each such α there is a pair (x, y) so that $xBy > 0$; hence for each such α we can choose components (x_i, y_j) so that $x_i b_{ij} y_j > 0$; hence $xB^j > 0$ and then (1) and (3) imply that $xA^j > 0$. (A *single* superscript j on a matrix indicates the jth column of that matrix.) We next show that the indices of the components so chosen are different for different such allowable α's. Let γ and δ be two such allowable α's with $\gamma > \delta$, and let the corresponding component pairs (x_i, y_j) and (x_h, y_k) be such that

$$x_i b_{ij} y_j > 0 \qquad \text{and} \qquad x_h b_{hk} y_k > 0.$$

We must show that $i \neq h$ and $j \neq k$. We shall show $j \neq k$ and the proof of the other assertion is similar. Suppose, on the contrary, that $j = k$. By Lemma 2 there is a strategy x (corresponding to $\alpha = \gamma$) for the maximizing player which is optimal in M_α for $\delta \leqslant \alpha \leqslant \gamma$. Then, letting M_α^j be the jth column of M_α, we have

$$xM_\gamma^j \geqslant 0 \qquad \text{and} \qquad xM_\delta^j \geqslant 0.$$

However, since

$$xM_\delta^j = (xB^j - \gamma xA^j) + (\gamma - \delta)xA^j = xM_\gamma^j + (\gamma - \delta)xA^j$$

and since

$$(\gamma - \delta)xA^j > 0$$

we see that

$$xM_\delta^j = xM_\delta^k > 0.$$

By condition (3) this implies that $y_k = 0$ which, in turn, implies $x_h b_{hk} y_k = 0$, contrary to the way in which y_k was chosen.

Since to each allowable α for which there are economic solutions there corresponds an entry $b_{ij} > 0$ in the matrix B, and since the indices of two such entries are pairwise distinct we see that the maximum number of such allowable α's is equal to the longest diagonal which can be chosen in B. Because B is an $m \times n$ matrix, the longest such diagonal is min (m, n). This completes the proof of the theorem.

THEOREM 2. (*Existence theorem*):

(A) *If* (**) *holds then there is at least one and at most a finite number of allowable α's for which the game M_α has economic solutions.*

(B) (*von Neumann*). *If* (*) *holds then there is a unique allowable α.*

(C) *If* (*) *and* (**) *hold then there is a unique allowable α; moreover, for that α the game M_α has economic solutions.*

PROOF: (A) The proof of the existence of an economic solution is too lengthy to be included here, but details can be found in [8] or [16]. The proof in [8] uses the minimax theorem from the theory of games together with a perturbation argument. The proof in [16] uses the minimax theorem together with properties of full (see Section 6) optimal strategies.

By Theorem 1 there are at most a finite number of such allowable α's. The reader should observe that for each of these allowable α's there is at least one but there may be an infinite number of strategy pairs (x, y) which give economic solutions.

The reader should also observe that we can prove nothing about the magnitudes of the α's, except that they are positive and less than infinity. Obviously an α greater than one corresponds to an expanding economy (expansion *rate* and interest *rate* positive); an α equal to one corresponds to a stationary economy (expansion *rate* and interest *rate* zero); and an α less than one corresponds to a contracting economy (expansion *rate* and interest *rate* less than zero).

(B) This theorem is proved in [11] by von Neumann. It is interesting to observe that under assumption (*) alone one cannot prove the existence of solutions which satisfy (5). Example 1 in Section 2 has no solution satisfying (5).

(C) Follows from (A) and the Corollary to Lemma 1.

5. RELAXATION OF THE FREE GOODS AND INEFFICIENT PROCESSES RESTRICTIONS

Let us make the ideas of free goods and inefficient processes more precise.

DEFINITION: *Let $\alpha = \beta$ be an allowable expansion factor which has economic solutions and let (x, y) be a pair of economic solutions corresponding to this α.*

Good j is free relative to the solution (x, y) if and only if in this solution $x(B^j - \alpha A^j) > 0$ so that (to satisfy condition (3)) $y_j = 0$. (A^j and B^j indicate the jth columns of these matrices.)

Process i is inefficient relative to the solution (x, y) if and only if in this solution $(B_i - \beta A_i)y < 0$ so that (to satisfy condition (4)) $x_i = 0$. A_i and B_i indicate the ith rows of these matrices.)

Note that for a given expansion rate α and economic solution (x, y) the good j may be free while for another expansion rate α' (or perhaps even for the same expansion rate) and another solution (x', y') it could happen that good j would not be free. On the other hand there might well be goods which are free in every economic solution, cf. the definition of the set J^* in the following section. Completely analogous remarks can be made about inefficient processes.

If we are considering a deterministic model, conditions (3) and (4) are not unreasonable. If, on the other hand, we consider that the entries in the matrices A and B are technological coefficients and hence subject to possible error, it seems unreasonable that small changes in the entries of the matrices A and B should change free goods into non-free goods or inefficient processes into efficient processes and vice versa. Nevertheless this can happen as is shown by the following examples.

Example 1: Consider the following matrices:

$$A = A' = \begin{pmatrix} 1 & \epsilon \\ \epsilon & 1 \end{pmatrix}, \qquad B = \begin{pmatrix} 1 & 2\epsilon \\ \epsilon & 1 + \epsilon \end{pmatrix}, \qquad B' = \begin{pmatrix} 1 + \epsilon & \epsilon \\ 2\epsilon & 1 \end{pmatrix}$$

where $\epsilon > 0$, and consider the two models $M_\alpha = B - \alpha A$ and $M'_\alpha = B' - \alpha' A'$. The unique expansion rates for each of these models is $\alpha = \alpha' = 1$. We have

$$M_1 = \begin{pmatrix} 0 & \epsilon \\ 0 & \epsilon \end{pmatrix} \qquad \text{and} \qquad M'_1 = \begin{pmatrix} \epsilon & 0 \\ \epsilon & 0 \end{pmatrix}$$

so that good one has unit price in the first model but is free in the second, while good two is free in the first model but has unit price in the second. Observe that each entry in the matrix B' differs from the corresponding entry in the matrix B by at most ϵ so that a small change in the technological coefficients can radically change the price structure.

Example 2: Consider the following matrices:

$$A = A' = \begin{pmatrix} 1 & 2\epsilon \\ 2\epsilon & 1 \end{pmatrix}, \qquad B = \begin{pmatrix} 1 - \epsilon & \epsilon \\ 2\epsilon & 1 \end{pmatrix}, \qquad B' = \begin{pmatrix} 1 & 2\epsilon \\ \epsilon & 1 - \epsilon \end{pmatrix}$$

where $\epsilon > 0$, and consider the two models $M_\alpha = B - \alpha A$ and $M'_\alpha = B' - \alpha' A'$.

The unique expansion rates for each of these models is $\alpha = \alpha' = 1$. We have

$$M_1 = \begin{pmatrix} -\epsilon & -\epsilon \\ 0 & 0 \end{pmatrix} \quad \text{and} \quad M_1' = \begin{pmatrix} 0 & 0 \\ -\epsilon & -\epsilon \end{pmatrix}$$

so that process one is inefficient and process two is used with unit intensity in the first model while process one is used with unit intensity in the second model and process two is inefficient. Again a small change in coefficients can radically change the intensity structure.

These examples are extreme and are partly the result of using a linear model but they do illustrate the possible economic unreality of conditions (3) and (4). Suppose now that we had a solution which satisfies conditions (1), (2), and (5) but not necessarily conditions (3) and (4). In order that (2) and (5) be satisfied we must have $xAy > 0$; hence we can define the following ratios:

$f = xM_\alpha y / xAy$ = the ratio of the amount spent on overproduced goods to the amount spent on inputs;

$p = xM_\beta y / xAy$ = the ratio of the amount spent on inefficient processes to the amount spent on inputs.

Clearly condition (3) is equivalent to the condition $f = 0$ and condition (4) is equivalent to $p = 0$. If we are only looking for solutions to (1), (2), and (5), then the most we can say is that $f \geqslant 0$ and $p \leqslant 0$ which follow easily from (1) and (2).

THEOREM 3: *If (*) or (**) holds then there always exist numbers α and β and probability vectors (x, y) satisfying conditions (1), (2) and (5); moreover, for each such solution $\beta - \alpha = f - p \geqslant 0$ so that always $\beta \geqslant \alpha$.*

PROOF: Let f be any nonnegative number and p be any nonpositive number and consider the following expressions:

(1″) $xM_{\alpha+f} \geqslant 0$,

(2″) $M_{\beta+p}y \leqslant 0$,

(3″) $xM_{\alpha+f}y = 0$,

(4″) $xM_{\beta+p}y = 0$,

(5) $xBy > 0$.

These expressions are the same as expressions (1)–(5) of Section 2 if we replace α by $\alpha + f$ and β by $\beta + p$. It is easy to check that if (1″) is satisfied then so is (1), and if (2″) is satisfied then so is (2); hence, if we can find a solution to (1″)–(4″) and (5), it will furnish us automatically with a solution of (1), (2), and (5). However, if (*) or (**) is satisfied then our existence theorem (Theorem 2) immediately gives a solution to (1″)–(4″) and (5) and shows that $\alpha + f = \beta + p$, completing the proof of the theorem.

Since f can be any nonnegative number and p can be any nonpositive number, there is a continuum of such solutions. It is economically reasonable to require that f and p be made small enough in absolute value so that α and β be positive, since negative expansion or interest *factors* do not have economic meaning. The paradox raised in the two examples discussed above can now be resolved by letting f and p take on non-zero values.

A final remark can be made for the case when $p = 0$. A plausible assumption is that f, the ratio of the amount spent on overproduced goods to the total amount spent on inputs, should be very small compared to one, i.e., $f \ll 1$. From the results of the above theorem we then see that

$$0 < \beta - \alpha = f \ll 1.$$

In other words, if we replace condition (3) by the assumption that the amount of money spent on overproduced goods is very small compared to the amount spent on inputs, then solutions to the economy exist with the expansion rate lagging only slightly behind the interest rate. Analogous remarks can be made about the ratio p when $f = 0$, and when both f and p are close to zero.

6. THE EXISTENCE OF SUB-ECONOMIES

In this section of the paper we assume that condition (**) holds. The existence theorem then assures us that there are a finite number of allowable α's for which economic solutions (x, y) to M_α exist. We shall show that for any allowable α for which there are economic solutions there is a self-sufficient part of the economy, in other words a sub-economy, which can expand independently, in equilibrium, with the expansion coefficient α.

Consider one such allowable α; then $v(M_\alpha) = 0$. The minimax theorem [10, 12, 17] of the theory of games insures that there exist one or more optimal strategies for each player. The set of all optimal strategies for a player in a matrix game is convex and is spanned by a finite number of extreme points. These extreme points of the convex set of optimal strategies for a player are called *basic* optimal strategies for that player (cf. [14]). Then for each allowable α there are a finite number of basic optimal strategies for each player. Let us call a pair of basic optimal strategies (x, y) which furnish an economic solution to M_α *basic economic solutions*. We shall call the x and y which occur in basic economic solutions the x- and y-*components* of basic economic solutions.

Suppose now that there are a finite number (say $r > 1$) of allowable α's for which economic solutions exist and suppose that they are arranged in order of decreasing magnitude as follows:

$$\alpha_1 > \alpha_2 > \alpha_3 > \cdots > \alpha_r.$$

To simplify notation let us indicate the game for $\alpha = \alpha_i$ simply by M_i for $i = 1, \cdots, r$.

Let I_1 be the set of all indices of rows i of M_1 for which there is an x-component of an economic solution to M_1 with $x_i > 0$; then let I_2 be the set of indices of rows i of M_2 which are not already contained in I_1 and for which there is an

x-component of a basic economic solution to M_2 with $x_i > 0$; let I_3 be the set of indices of rows i of M_3 which are not already contained in $I_1 \cup I_2$ and for which there is an x-component of a basic economic solution to M_3 with $x_i > 0$; etc.; let I_r be the set of indices of rows of M_r which are not already contained in the set $I_1 \cup I_2 \cup I_3 \cup \cdots \cup I_{r-1}$ and for which there is an x-component of a basic economic solution to M_r with $x_i > 0$; finally, let I^* be the set of indices of all rows of M_α which are not contained in the set $I_1 \cup I_2 \cup \cdots \cup I_r$.

Let J_1 be the set of all indices of columns j of M_1 for which there is a y-component of an economic solution to M_1 with $y_j > 0$; then let J_2 be the set of indices of columns j of M_2 which are not already contained in J_1 and for which there is a y-component of a basic economic solution to M_2 with $y_j > 0$; let J_3 be the set of indices of columns j of M_3 which are not already contained in $J_1 \cup J_2$ and for which there is a y-component of a basic economic solution to M_3 with $y_j > 0$; etc.; let J_r be the set of indices of columns j of M_r which are not already contained in the set $J_1 \cup J_2 \cup \cdots \cup J_{r-1}$ and for which there is a y-component of a basic economic solution to M_r with $y_j > 0$; finally let J^* be the set of indices of all columns of M_α which are not contained in the set $J_1 \cup J_2 \cup \cdots \cup J_r$.

Now permute the rows and columns of the matrix M_α until it assumes the following form:

		J_1	J_2	J_3	$\cdots$	J_r	J^*
	I_1	M_α^{11}	0	0	$\cdots$	0	N_α^1
	I_2	M_α^{21}	M_α^{22}	0	$\cdots$	0	N_α^2
$M_\alpha =$	I_3	M_α^{31}	M_α^{32}	M_α^{33}	$\cdots$	0	N_α^3
	.	.	.	.	$\cdots$	.	.
	I_r	M_α^{r1}	M_α^{r2}	M_α^{r3}	$\cdots$	M_α^{rr}	N_α^r
	I^*	L_α^1	L_α^2	L_α^3	$\cdots$	L_α^r	Q_α

FIGURE 1

In the decomposition of Figure 1 the entries M_α^{ij} are the submatrices of M_α which have their row indices belonging to I_i and their column indices belonging to J_j. The reader will observe that we have put zeros for the matrices M_α^{ij} when $i < j$, and this, of course, needs justification which is given in Lemma 3 below. The submatrices L_α^k have their row indices in I^* and their column indices in J_k, and the submatrices N_α^k have their column indices in J^* and their row indices in I_k. The matrix Q_α has its row indices in I^* and its column indices in J^*.

The processes which have their indices in I^* are those which are never used in any economic solution, that is, they are always inefficient processes. The goods which have their indices in J^* are those which have zero price in every economic solution, hence if they are ever produced in positive quantities they are free goods. We shall be able to prove certain results about the submatrices L, M, and N but the submatrix Q can be completely arbitrary.

LEMMA 3: *If* $i < j$ *then* $M_\alpha^{ij} \equiv 0$ *for all* α, *that is,* $A^{ij} = B^{ij} = 0$. (*Here* A^{ij} *and* B^{ij} *indicate submatrices having row indices in* I_i *and column indices in* J_j.)

PROOF. Consider the game M_k, where k is any number between 1 and r. There are a finite number (say s) of basic economic optimal strategies for the first player; suppose they are x_1, x_2, $\cdots$, x_s. Let x^o be the strategy

$$x^o = \sum_{t=1}^{s} \frac{1}{s} x_t.$$

Since x^o is a convex combination of optimal strategies, it is also optimal. Moreover, it has the property that $x_i^o > 0$ if i belongs to I_k. Let us call x^o a *full* strategy corresponding to α_k. In the same way one can construct a full optimal strategy y^o for α_k.

Let x^o be a full optimal strategy for α_i and y^o be a full optimal strategy for α_j. Then Lemma 2 shows that x^o is optimal for α_j and y^o is optimal for α_i. Therefore the following equations must be satisfied

$$x^o B y^o - \alpha_i x^o A y^o = 0$$

and

$$x^o B y^o - \alpha_j x^o A y^o = 0.$$

Since $\alpha_i \neq \alpha_j$ these equations can be satisfied if and only if $x^o A y^o = x^o B y^o = 0$. Since x^o and y^o are positive on I_i and J_j respectively, this can happen only if $A^{ij} = 0$ and $B^{ij} = 0$, which in turn implies that $M_\alpha^{ij} \equiv 0$.

DEFINITION: *Let* α' *be an allowable expansion factor for* M_α *and let* (x, y) *be an economic solution corresponding to this* α'; *let* I *be the set*[3] *of indices of processes which are used, i.e., those* i *such that* $x_i > 0$; *let* J *be the set of indices of goods* j *which either have positive price or are free relative to the solution* (x, y); *finally, let* M_α^{IJ} *be the submatrix of* M_α *which has its row indices in* I *and its column indices in* J: *then we shall call* M_α^{IJ} *a sub-economy of* M_α. *Considered as an economy itself* M_α^{IJ} *can expand with the coefficient* α' *and* (x, y) *are economic solutions for the sub-economy for this* α.

Thus a sub-economy is a subset of the goods and processes of the original economy which has the same solution and same expansion coefficient as the original economy.

THEOREM 4: *Let* M_α *be an economy and let* α_1, α_2, $\cdots$, α_r *be the allowable expansion rates for which there are economic solutions; then for each* α_k *there is at least one sub-economy* M_α^{IJ} *with*

---

[3] The reader is warned not to confuse the sets I and J with the sets I_k, I^*, J_k and J^* as previously defined.

$$I \subset I_1 \cup I_2 \cup \cdots \cup I_k$$

and

$$J \subset J_1 \cup J_2 \cup \cdots \cup J_k \cup J^*$$

which can expand at the rate α_k .

PROOF: The proof is an easy consequence of the decomposition of M_α given in Figure 1 above.

COROLLARY: *The sub-economy can always be chosen so that* $I \supseteq I_k$ *and* $J \supseteq J_k$.

PROOF: Use full strategies for each player.

It is interesting to note that if new processes are added to the economy, which can be done by adding new rows to A and B and hence to M_α , the decomposition as described above may change. For example, if the new process is more efficient than an old one, then the new row of M_α will majorize an old row and the index of the old row will be relegated to the limbo of I^*. Analogously, if a new good is added to the economy, which can be done by adding new columns to A and B and hence to M_α , then again the decomposition may change. The addition of the new good might make an old good, in comparison, always a free good so that the index of the column of the old good would be shifted to J^*. Other more complicated changes can also occur.

7. CHARACTERIZATION OF THE MAXIMUM AND MINIMUM EXPANSION RATES

In this section we give a characterization of two of the allowable expansion rates. This characterization is essentially the same as that given by von Neumann [11] for the unique expansion rate which he obtains. The difference is that here we must deal with more than one expansion rate. We assume here that (**) holds.

THEOREM 5: *Let* α^0 *be the largest* α *such that there exists a vector* x *such that* xM_α $\geqslant 0$; *then* α^0 *is equal to the maximum allowable expansion factor for which economic solutions exist. In other words, the greatest (technically possible) expansion factor of the whole economy, neglecting prices, is equal to the maximum allowable* α *provided by Theorem 2.*

Similarly, let β_0 *be the smallest* β *such that there exists a vector* y *such that* $M_\beta y \leqslant 0$; *then* β_0 *is equal to the minimum allowable expansion factor for which economic solutions exist. In other words, the lowest interest factor* β *at which a profitless system of prices is possible is the minimum* $\alpha = \beta$ *provided by Theorem 2.*

PROOF: This theorem is simply a restatement of the fact that the maximum and minimum α such that $v(M_\alpha) = 0$ are also allowable α's for which economic solutions exist. For proofs of the latter fact we refer to [8] or [16].

8. DISCONNECTED SUB-ECONOMIES

Von Neumann made his (*) assumption because "it must be imposed in order to assure the uniqueness of α, β as otherwise W (the economy) might break up into disconnected parts." As we saw in the last section, if α was not unique then it could be shown that many of the entries in the matrix M_α were zeros, and there were sub-economies which could function in a self-sufficient manner. However, these sub-economies were not always completely disconnected. Intuitively, one would say that two economies are disconnected if they have different expansion rates,[4] if they use different processes with positive weight, if they put positive prices on different sets of goods, and if they can be aggregated separately. The precise definition is the following.

DEFINITION: *Let α and α' ($\neq \alpha$) be two allowable values of α for which there are economic solutions; let M_α^{IJ} and $M_\alpha^{I'J'}$ be two sub-economies which can expand at the rates α and α' respectively and such that I and I' are disjoint and $J \cap J' \subseteq J^*$ and $M_\alpha^{I'J} = M_\alpha^{IJ'} = 0$; under these assumptions we shall call M_α^{IJ} and $M_\alpha^{I'J'}$* disconnected sub-economies *of M_α*.

Economies which are not disconnected are characterized by the fact that the decomposition of Figure 1 has some non-zero entries below the M_α^{ii} entries. As we shall see in the next section, if one aggregates sub-economies which are not disconnected, then it is impossible, at least without further assumptions, to predict what effect such aggregation will have on the expansion factors. The case in which one can say something is the totally disconnected one which we proceed to define.

DEFINITION: *An economy M_α is* totally disconnected *if and only if every pair of sub-economies having different expansion rates is disconnected.*

An equivalent definition is that M_α is totally disconnected if and only if in the decomposition of Figure 1 we have $M_\alpha^{ij} = 0$ for $i > j$.

9. THE INTRODUCTION OF AGGREGATION INTO THE MODEL

By aggregation of processes or goods in the model we shall simply mean the adding together of weighted combinations of rows or columns of the matrices A and B. Such operations can most conveniently be done by pre- and post-multiplying with suitable matrices.

DEFINITION: *A process aggregating matrix P is a $p \times m$ matrix (where $1 \leqslant p \leqslant m$) having the following properties: each column of P has exactly one positive entry, each row of P has at least one positive entry and all other entries in the matrix are zeros. If $p = m$ then P is essentially a diagonal matrix and there is no aggregation, while if $p = 1$ then P is a row vector having all entries positive and we call this* total process aggregation.

A goods aggregating matrix Q is an $n \times q$ matrix (where $1 \leqslant q \leqslant n$) having the following properties: each row of Q has exactly one positive entry, each column of Q has at least one positive entry, and all other entries in Q are zeros. If $q = n$ then Q is essentially a diagonal matrix and there is no aggregation, while if $q = 1$

---

[4] This condition might also be dropped but we prefer not to do so here. Compare [4], however.

then Q is a column vector having all entries positive and we call this total goods aggregation.

It is obvious that if we start with an economy satisfying (**) and aggregate both goods and processes totally we arrive at 1×1 matrices, A and B, which satisfy the (*) condition. Even by partial aggregation we might arrive at a point where the aggregated matrices satisfy (*) and hence would obtain a unique expansion factor.

THEOREM 6: *Aggregating either processes or goods leaves unchanged or decreases the number of possible expansion factors for the economy. Moreover, if only processes are aggregated, then the magnitudes of the possible expansion factors, if anything, decrease, while if only goods are aggregated then the magnitudes of the possible expansion factors, if anything,* increase.

PROOF: The first statement is obvious since aggregation can only increase the connectedness of the economy. Let us suppose that only processes are aggregated; then the game which we must solve is PM_α. The set of strategies for the minimizing player is unchanged; hence it is clear that if α is such that $v(M_\alpha) = 0$ then $v(PM_\alpha) \leqslant 0$. From this it follows that the magnitudes of the allowable α's for which there are economic solutions must, if anything, decrease. The proof of the other statement is similar.

Theorem 6 is economically meaningful on an intuitive basis: when the number of processes is decreased the choices of methods of producing the given variety of goods become more restricted; when the number of goods is decreased, which is equivalent to obliterating distinctions among goods, the converse is the case.

The following example shows that if both goods and processes of a non-totally disconnected economy are aggregated then the expansion rate may either go up or go down by any amount.

Example. Let A and B be the following matrices:

$$A = \begin{pmatrix} 0 & 1 \\ 1 & a \end{pmatrix} \quad \text{and} \quad B = \begin{pmatrix} 0 & 2 \\ 1 & b \end{pmatrix}$$

where a and b are parameters. Before aggregation the two expansion factors are $\alpha = 1$ and $\alpha = 2$. Suppose now that we perform total aggregation of both goods and processes by letting $P = (1, 1)$ and $Q =$ column vector $(1, 1)$; then a simple computation shows that the resulting unique expansion factor α' is given by the formula $\alpha' = (3 + b)/(2 + a)$ which can be made equal to any positive number by suitable choices of a and b.

This example shows that the computation of expansion factors should not be done without an examination of the degree and kind of aggregation that has been performed on the data used. Since economic data are necessarily presented in a highly aggregated form the determination of expansion factors can, at best, be regarded as approximate. One obvious warning that should be made is that an artificial increase in expansion factors can be made by aggregating free goods with non-free goods. It is evident that this does not correspond to economic reality and therefore should be avoided.

Thus without further assumptions or restrictions on what can happen below the diagonal of the matrix it is impossible to predict what will happen when aggregation takes place. With the assumption of a completely disconnected economy one can prove a strong and economically meaningful result. Let M_α be the totally disconnected economy whose decomposition is given in Figure 2.

$$M_\alpha = $$

	J_1	J_2	J_3	$\cdots$	J_r	J^*
I_1	M_α^1	0	0	$\cdots$	0	N_α^1
I_2	0	M_α^2	0	$\cdots$	0	N_α^2
I_3	0	0	M_α^3	$\cdots$	0	N_α^3
.	.	.	.	$\cdots$	.	.
I_r	0	0	0	$\cdots$	M_α^r	N_α^r
I^*	L_α^1	L_α^2	L_α^3	$\cdots$	L_α^r	Q_α

FIGURE 2

Since the entries below the diagonal are zero it is not necessary to use double subscripts on the entries on the diagonal. Clearly M_α^1, M_α^2, $\cdots$, M_α^r are disconnected sub-economies. Let p and q be total aggregation vectors. Consider the following numbers

$$a_k = \sum_{\substack{i \in I_k \\ j \in J_k}} p_i q_j a_{ij},$$

$$b_k = \sum_{\substack{i \in I_k \\ j \in J_k}} p_i q_j b_{ij}.$$

It is easy to see that if we totally aggregate the sub-economy M_α^k then its expansion rate α_k' after aggregation is given by

$$\alpha_k' = b_k/a_k, \qquad \text{for } k = 1, 2, \cdots, r.$$

If we totally aggregate the economy M_α then its expansion rate α' after aggregation is

$$\alpha' = \frac{b_1 + b_2 + \cdots + b_r}{a_1 + a_2 + \cdots + a_r}.$$

It is a simple exercise to show that α' lies between the smallest and the largest of the α_k'. We summarize our results in the following theorem.

THEOREM 7: *Let M_α be a totally disconnected economy with sub-economies M_α^k*

for $k = 1, \cdots, r$. If α' is the unique expansion factor of M_α after total aggregation and α_k' is the unique expansion factor of M_α^k after total aggregation then

$$\min_k \alpha_k' \leqslant \alpha' \leqslant \max_k \alpha_k'.$$

10. THE INTRODUCTION OF DEMAND INTO THE VON NEUMANN MODEL

We shall now add to the von Neumann model the requirement that at each time period the economy should supply to an outside consumer a vector d of goods already being produced by the economy. Hence d is a $1 \times n$ row vector. We assume that d is always a constant fraction of the output at any given time, i.e., that the outside additional demand is expanding at the same rate as the economy.

The introduction of outside demand into the model opens up several new avenues of approach, some of which shall be studied or at least mentioned. The outside demand may be physically outside the economy, but it may also represent additional consumption by the workers within the economy. If viewed in the latter sense, we have removed the objection (noted in the introduction) to the original assumption that the model requires the restriction of the consumption by workers to the level of subsistence. As we shall see the rates of expansion and the size of the outside demand can be closely connected. The result demonstrated below that decreasing the outside demand will allow a faster growth of the economy is economically very plausible and, indeed, corroborated from observations pertaining to economic development and the role of savings.[5] The phenomenon has consequently been treated in business cycle analysis.

To simplify our equations we assume that this external demand at time t is supplied out of the production of time $t - 1$. This assumption is consistent with the interpretation of the outside demand as added consumption—i.e., as the economy expands the percentage of the total production going to the consumers remains constant. Our expressions now become

(1) $$x(B - \alpha A) \geqslant \alpha d,$$

(2) $$(B - \beta A)y \leqslant \beta e(dy),$$

(3) $$x(B - \alpha A)y = \alpha dy,$$

(4) $$x(B - \beta A)y = \beta dy,$$

(5) $$xBy > 0.$$

In expression (2) the vector e is an $n \times 1$ (column) vector each of whose entries is one. These expressions may be more briefly stated if we make greater use of the vector e. Observe that ed is an $m \times n$ matrix each of whose rows is the vector d. Then we can write the above expressions as

---

[5] The possibility of introducing cyclical components into the outside demand and hence into the behavior of the entire system easily suggests itself but we chose not to proceed in that direction at the present occasion.

(1')
$$x[B - \alpha(A + ed)] \geqslant 0,$$

(2')
$$[B - \beta(A + ed)]y \leqslant 0,$$

(3')
$$x[B - \alpha(A + ed)]y = 0,$$

(4')
$$x[B - \beta(A + ed)]y = 0,$$

(5')
$$xBy > 0.$$

Observe that these expressions correspond to (1)–(5) in Section 2 if we substitute the matrix $A' = A + ed$ for A. Hence, all of the preceding work holds and the existence theorem insures that at least one economic solution exists.

THEOREM 8: *The introduction of outside demand into the economic model has the following effect. Consider a sub-economy of the economy having a unique expansion factor.*

(*i*) *If the outside demand includes any good (produced by the sub-economy) which has a positive price, then the expansion factor of the (sub-) economy must be decreased in order to supply the outside demand.*

(*ii*) *If the outside demand for goods (produced by the sub-economy) having a positive price is decreased, then the expansion factor can correspondingly be increased.*

PROOF: (i) Let A and B be the matrices of the sub-economy. Let α, (x, y) and α', (x', y') be solutions to equations (1)–(5) of Section 2 and (1')–(5') of this section, respectively. Suppose that $\alpha' \geqslant \alpha$; then $x'[B - \alpha'(A + ed)] \geqslant 0$ implies that $x'[B - \alpha A] \geqslant 0$; and also $[B - \alpha A]y \leqslant 0$ implies that $[B - \alpha'(A + ed)]y \leqslant 0$. Hence the pair (x', y) is a game-theoretic (possibly non-economic) solution to both problems. Then we have the following two equations:

$$x'By - \alpha'x'Ay - \alpha'dy = 0,$$

$$x'By - \alpha\,x'Ay \qquad\quad = 0.$$

Subtracting the second from the first we have

$$(\alpha - \alpha')x'Ay - \alpha'dy = 0.$$

Now if $dy > 0$, i.e., if the outside demand includes non-free goods, then this equation implies that $x'Ay < 0$ which is impossible. Hence $\alpha' < \alpha$ completing the proof.

The proof of (ii) is similar to the proof of (i).

11. RELATION TO THE EXPANDING LEONTIEF MODEL

Various writers including Gale [4], Wong [18], and Woodbury [19] have discussed an expanding Leontief input-output model in which, at each time period, the goal is to produce not just enough to satisfy the internal demand plus the given external demand but at least an amount α times the total demand. The expression for this model is

$$x \geqslant \alpha(xA + d)$$

where A is the matrix which gives the internal demand and d is the external demand vector. This expression can be rewritten, using the ideas of the last section, as

$$x[I - \alpha(A + ed)] \geqslant 0.$$

This equation is identical with equation (1') of the preceding section if we replace matrix B by the identity matrix I. The principal mathematical difference between this and the von Neumann model is that there are more conditions in the von Neumann model.[6]

The question which is asked regarding the expanding Leontief model is: What is the maximum rate of expansion possible in the model? This is equivalent to the following problem:

PROBLEM: Find the largest α such that the value of the matrix game $M_\alpha = I - \alpha(A + ed)$ is zero; then find an optimal strategy x for the maximizing player, i.e., find an x such that $x[I - \alpha(A + ed)] \geqslant 0$.

We shall show that, in the sense of this problem, the expanding Leontief model is a special case of the von Neumann model.

THEOREM 9: *If the matrix $M_\alpha = [I - \alpha(A + ed)]$ is considered both as a von Neumann and a Leontief economy, then the maximum expansion factor in the Leontief model is equal to the maximum expansion factor in the von Neumann model.*

PROOF: By Theorem 5 (proved in [8] and [16]) the maximum allowable expansion factor is one for which economic solutions exist. Hence the maximum expansion factors in the von Neumann and Leontief models are the same.

Although the maximum expansion factor for the von Neumann model, when $B = I$, can be obtained from the much simpler Leontief model, it would not be correct to assume that all the information given by the von Neumann model could be obtained from the former. For example, the Leontief model does not show that when α is equal to its maximum a price structure can be put on the economy, preserving its equilibrium state, which makes the total value of all goods produced positive. Neither does it show that if α is different from one of the finite number of allowable expansion rates, there is *no* way of putting a price structure on the economy which makes the total value of all goods produced positive without upsetting the equilibrium of the model. Finally, it does not show that, at equilibrium, the interest rate is equal to the expansion rate.

Dartmouth College;
Princeton University

---

[6] From the economic point of view, there are more important differences. First of all, prices are not considered in the Leontief model. Secondly, that model considers only the flow of goods from an industry to other industries and to the outside world; it does not determine, as the von Neumann model does, the intensities of operation of the various processes.

REFERENCES

[1] Arrow, Kenneth J. and Gerard Debreu, "Existence of an Equilibrium for a Competitive Economy," *Econometrica* 22, (1954), pp. 265–290.

[2] Champernowne, D. G., "A Note on J. von Neumann's Article," *The Review of Economic Studies*, Vol. XII (1), (1945–46), pp. 10–18.

[3] Dantzig, George B., "The Programming of Interdependent Activities: Mathematical Model," Chapter II of the volume, *Activity Analysis of Production and Allocation*, edited by T. J. Koopmans, (Wiley, 1951), pp. 19–32.

[4] Gale, David, "The Closed Linear Model of Production," to be published in "Linear Inequalities and Related Systems," *Annals of Mathematics Study No. 38*, edited by H. W. Kuhn and A. W. Tucker, Princeton, 1956.

[5] Georgescu-Roegen, Nicholas, "The Aggregate Linear Production Function and Its Application to von Neumann's Economic Model," Chapter IV of the volume, *Activity Analysis of Production and Allocation*, edited by T. J. Koopmans, (Wiley, 1951), pp. 98–115.

[6] ———, "Note on the Economic Equilibrium for Nonlinear Models," *Econometrica* 22, (1954), pp. 54–57.

[7] Kakutani, Shizuo, "A Generalization of Brouwer's Fixed Point Theorem," *Duke Mathematical Journal*, vol. 8, (1951), pp. 457–9.

[8] Kemeny, John G., "Game-theoretic Solution of an Economic Problem," to be published in *Progress Report Number 2*, Dartmouth Mathematics Project, 1956.

[9] Koopmans, Tjalling C., "Introduction," Chapter 1 of the volume, *Activity Analysis of Production and Allocation*, edited by T. J. Koopmans, (Wiley, 1951), pp. 1–12.

[10] McKinsey, J., *Introduction to the Theory of Games*, New York, 1952.

[11] von Neumann, J., "Uber ein ökonomisches Gleichungssystem und eine Verallgemeinerung des Brouwerschen Fixpunktsatzes," *Ergebnisse eines mathematischen Kolloquiums*, No. 8 (1937), pp. 73–83, translated as, "A Model of General Economic Equilibrium," *Review of Economic Studies*, Vol. 13, No. 33, (1945–46) pp. 1–9.

[12] ——— and O. Morgenstern, *Theory of Games and Economic Behavior*, Princeton, (1944; third edition, 1953).

[13] Nikaido, Hukukane, "Note on the General Economic Equilibrium for Nonlinear Production Functions," *Econometrica* 22, (1954), pp. 49–53.

[14] Shapley, L. S. and R. N. Snow, "Basic Solutions of Discrete Games," *Contributions to the Theory of Games*, Annals of Mathematics Study No. 24, edited by H. W. Kuhn and A. W. Tucker, Princeton, (1950), pp. 27–35.

[15] Solow, Robert M. and Paul A. Samuelson, "Balanced Growth under Constant Returns to Scale," *Econometrica* 21, (1953), pp. 412–424.

16] Thompson, Gerald L., "Solution of a Game-theoretic Problem," to be published in "Linear Inequalities and Related Systems," *Annals of Mathematics Study No. 38*, edited by H. W. Kuhn and A. W. Tucker, Princeton, 1956.

[17] Weyl, Herrmann, "Elementary Proof of a Minimax Theorem Due to von Neumann," *Contributions to the Theory of Games*, Annals of Mathematics Study No. 24, edited by H. W. Kuhn and A. W. Tucker, Princeton (1950), pp. 19–25.

[18] Wong, Y. K., "Some Mathematical Concepts for Linear Economic Models," in *Economic Activity Analysis*, edited by Oskar Morgenstern, (Wiley, 1954), pp. 283–339.

[19] Woodbury, Max A., "Characteristic Roots of Input-output Matrices," in *Economic Activity Analysis*, edited by Oskar Morgenstern, (Wiley, 1954), pp. 365–382.

Econometrica, Vol. 25, No. 4 (October, 1957)

A MODEL EXPLAINING THE PARETO DISTRIBUTION OF WEALTH

By H. O. A. Wold and P. Whittle

The Pareto law of wealth distribution states that the density of distribution of wealth, W, is, at least for higher estate levels, proportional to a power of wealth, $W^{-\alpha-1}$. Similarly, the Pareto law has been applied to the distribution of income. For income data, the estimated values of the *Pareto parameter* α range in practice from 1.6 to 2.4 (see the table on p. 610 of [1]). Data on wealth distributions are less abundant; it would seem that the Pareto parameter is here somewhat lower, in general between 1.3 and 2.0 (see the table on p. 429 of [4], where the parameters must be adjusted upwards because rather low levels of wealth have been included). The fact that these values fall in such a narrow range, although they refer to widely separated countries and occasions, would seem to indicate a common underlying mechanism. In this paper we suggest a model which is designed primarily for the distribution of wealth. Since the formal mechanism is rather flexible, it should be possible to adapt the model so as to apply to income distributions. The model is related to earlier work by D. G. Champernowne [2] and H. Simon [3] inasmuch as it falls under the general heading of Markov stochastic processes, and with Champernowne's model there is the further resemblance that different patterns are assumed for low and high wealth groups. Our model is, however, more specific, a distinctive feature being that its parameters have definite socioeconomic interpretation and obey definite relations which can be checked with observations. In the simplest case the Pareto parameter comes out as the ratio

$$\alpha = \frac{\text{growth rate of wealth}}{\text{mortality rate}}.$$

In constructing a model of wealth distribution we assume that a person's wealth grows at compound interest during his lifetime, and upon his death is divided equally among n inheritors. Such a model will by its nature be applicable only to persons with relatively large estates.

If the number of persons in the population at time t whose estates are less than x is $N(x, t)$ then we shall suppose that the "density"

(1) $$f(x, t) = \partial N(x, t)/\partial x$$

exists and is itself differentiable with respect to x and t. These conditions could be dispensed with, but they enable us to give a simple and brief treatment.

We shall suppose that an estate of size x will during a time interval Δ grow to size $x(1+\beta\Delta) + o(\Delta)$ (so that β is the net continuous rate at which a person's net assets increase), that any person has a chance of $\gamma\Delta + o(\Delta)$ of dying in the time interval Δ, and that upon his death his estate will be distributed equally among n inheritors. We can then write down an equation for the expected change in f:

$$
\int_{x_1}^{x} f(y, t+\Delta)\, dy = (1 - \gamma\Delta) \int_{(1-\beta\Delta)x_1}^{(1-\beta\Delta)x} f(y, t)\, dy
$$

(2)

$$
+ n\gamma\Delta \int_{nx_1}^{nx} f(y, t)\, dy + o(\Delta).
$$

Differentiating equation (2) with respect to x, and letting Δ tend to zero, we obtain the linear equation

(3) $$
\frac{\partial f(x, t)}{\partial t} = -(\beta + \gamma) f(x, t) - \beta x \frac{\partial f(x, t)}{\partial x} + \gamma n^2 f(nx, t).
$$

A change of variable $y = \log x$ will transform (3) to a difference-differential equation with constant coefficients so that it is immediately apparent that the basic solution of (3) will be of the form $f = x^p e^{qt}$. This is very near the Pareto form we expect. However, an explicit solution of (3) for appropriate initial conditions by Mellin transforms shows that $f(x, t)$ will never actually tend to the Pareto form. This is not surprising, since the Pareto law cannot possibly hold for all positive x, as the integral of $x^{-\alpha-1}$ from 0 to ∞ is divergent.

To remedy matters, we shall suppose that equation (3) holds only for values of x greater than a value K. Persons with estates of K or less we shall assume to constitute a pool of lower asset holders, whose size $R(t)$ is governed by

(4) $$
\partial R(t)/\partial t = (\varkappa - \lambda) R(t) + n\gamma \int_{K}^{nK} f(y, t)\, dy.
$$

Here $\varkappa$ represents the intrinsic rate of growth of the pool, λ is the rate at which persons leave the pool to enter the "propertied" class, while the integral term represents the influx of persons who have inherited a sum insufficient to keep them in the propertied class.

Equations (3) and (4) must be supplemented by the equation

(5) $$
f(K, t) = \lambda R(t)/\beta K,
$$

which is obtained by setting the lower limits of the integrals in (2) equal to K, K, and nK respectively, adding a term $\lambda R\Delta$ to the right-hand member, and then letting $x - K$ and Δ tend to zero.

Now, equations (3)–(5) constitute a linear equation system whose solution will, as a function of time, consist of a sum of exponential terms $e^{\theta t}$. We can find the part of this solution which predominates for large t by setting

(6) $$
f(x, t) = \mu(x)e^{\theta t},
$$

(7) $$
R(t) = Qe^{\theta t}
$$

and substituting these expressions in (3)–(5) to obtain

(8) $$
(\theta + \gamma + \beta)\mu(x) + \beta x \frac{\partial}{\partial x} \mu(x) - \gamma n^2 \mu(nx) = 0,
$$

(9) $$
(\theta - \varkappa + \lambda) Q - \gamma n \int_{K}^{nK} \mu(y)\, dy = 0,
$$

(10) $$\mu(K) - \lambda Q/\beta K = 0.$$

We are now interested in determining the function $\mu(x)$ which corresponds to the greatest eigenvalue θ of the linear system (8)–(10), because this will determine the asymptotic distribution of estate size in the range $x > K$.

The general solution of equations (8)–(10), however, is no simple matter and in this paper we shall content ourselves with assuming the Pareto law

(11) $$\mu(x) = A x^{-\alpha-1}$$

to be the appropriate asymptotic solution, as indeed sampling experiments would seem to indicate. That the question system possesses solutions of type (11) is readily verified, for when $\mu(x)$ is substituted from (11) we obtain a set of three linear equations in A, Q, and θ. Eliminating these three quantities we obtain the following characteristic equation for the Pareto parameter:

(12) $$\gamma n^{1-\alpha} + \alpha\beta = \gamma + \varkappa - \lambda + \frac{\gamma\lambda n}{\alpha\beta}(1 - n^{-\alpha}).$$

This equation can be simplified considerably if we are prepared to assume that the rates of population growth in the upper and lower income brackets are equal so that

(13) $$\varkappa = \gamma(n - 1).$$

Under this condition the characteristic equation becomes

(14) $$\left(1 + \frac{\lambda}{\alpha\beta}\right)(\gamma n^{1-\alpha} - \gamma n + \alpha\beta) = 0.$$

It is the zeros of the second bracket, i.e., the solutions of

(15) $$(\beta/\gamma)\alpha = n(1 - n^{-\alpha})$$

which are appropriate, since we see from (9) and (11) that if α is a solution of (15) then θ will equal $\gamma(n - 1)$. This value of θ corresponds to the natural growth rate of the population, so that $\mu(x)$ as defined in (6) will then correspond to an equilibrium wealth distribution.

According to this simple model the parameter α depends on only two constants: n, the effective number of inheritors, and (β/γ), the ratio of the growth rate of capital to mortality rates.

The most convenient way of testing whether equation (15) is in quantitative accord with observations is to substitute likely values of n and α, and then see whether the value of (β/γ) thus obtained seems plausible. A set of (β/γ) values, calculated in this fashion, appear in Table I, below. The (β/γ) values range from 0.4 to 1.6 in the central part of the table. Now, the value of γ must be such as to give a "life expectation" of a generation, since on the average a person will hold an inherited estate for one generation. If we take a year as the unit of time, and a generation as 25 years, then we must have

$$\gamma \sim \text{\textonequarter}_{25} = 0.04.$$

Values of β/γ between 0.4 and 1.6 then correspond to values of β between 0.016 and 0.064, i.e., to asset growth rates of between 1.6 per cent and 6.4 per cent per annum. These values seem quite plausible, and encourage us to assert that the model agrees not only qualitatively but also quantitatively with observations.

TABLE I

VALUES OF (GROWTH RATE OF CAPITAL)/(MORTALITY RATE) FOR VARIOUS VALUES OF n, THE NUMBER OF INHERITORS, AND α, THE PARETO PARAMETER

α \ n	1.5	2.0	2.5	3.0	3.5
1.0	0.50	1.00	1.50	2.00	2.50
1.5	0.46	0.86	1.25	1.62	1.98
2.0	0.42	0.75	1.05	1.33	1.61
2.5	0.38	0.66	0.90	1.12	1.34
3.0	0.35	0.58	0.78	0.96	1.14

That models of the present type must inevitably lead to Pareto parameters of the right order of magnitude can be seen from the simplified case when property owners with property K come into existence at a uniform rate, while no property is inherited by individuals at all. In this case we readily verify that in the equilibrium state

$$\alpha = \gamma/\beta.$$

For $\gamma = 0.04$ and an asset growth rate of 2.5 per cent we should thus obtain

$$\alpha = 0.040/0.025 = 1.6.$$

The model can obviously be generalised in several directions, but will continue to yield a Pareto law if all changes in estates are proportional to existing estate sizes, at least if variations of γ with age are neglected. As an example of such generalisation, we could suppose that a fraction $1 - q$ of each estate is removed in death duties, and that there is a probability p_n that the residual estate will be divided equally among n inheritors. In this case equations (3) and (15) become

$$(16) \quad \partial f(x)/\partial t = -(\beta + \gamma)\, f(x) - \beta x\, \partial f(x)/\partial x + \gamma/q \sum_{1}^{\infty} p_n n^2\, f(nx/q),$$

$$(17) \qquad\qquad \alpha\beta = \gamma \sum_{1}^{\infty} p_n n[1 - (q/n)^{\alpha}].$$

Calculations show that neither of these modifications have much effect on the actual relation between α, (β/γ), and the mean n value. For example, if we set $q = 0.5$ then it is found that the central entry in Table I increases from 1.05 to 1.20.

We do not consider in this paper whether or under what conditions the Pareto distribution is the unique stable wealth distribution. It can be noted, however, that a simple graphical investigation shows that the complex roots α of (17) have all negative real parts; further, that if the gradient of the right-hand member of (17) at $\alpha = 0$ is greater than the gradient of the left-hand member then there will be a single positive real solution for α, while otherwise there will be none. That is, the condition

$$(18) \qquad \gamma \sum_{1}^{n} p_n n \log (n/q) > \beta$$

is necessary if there is to be an equilibrium solution of the Pareto form. It is conjectured that the condition is also sufficient.

We do not intend to enter here upon models for income distributions. It may be remarked, however, that our wealth distribution model leads to the same Pareto distribution if we assume that incomes are proportional to estates. Alternatively, and more realistically, it could be assumed that incomes rise exponentially with age, and that when a person dies the inheritors will have incomes which are proportional to the income of the deceased and inversely proportional to the number of heirs.

University Institute of Statistics, Uppsala, Sweden and
New Zealand Department of Scientific and Industrial Research

REFERENCES

[1] CHAMPERNOWNE, D. G. (1952): *Econometrica*, 20, 591.
[2] ——— (1953): *Economic Journal*, 63, 318.
[3] SIMON, H. (1955): *Biometrika*, 42, 425.
[4] YNTEMA, D. B. (1933): *Journal of the American Statistical Association*, 28, 423.

Econometrica 27 (1959) 30-53

COMPETITIVE VALUATION IN A DYNAMIC INPUT-OUTPUT SYSTEM[1]

By Robert M. Solow

This paper is a complement to Morishima's [9]. It generalizes the usual dynamic Leontief model by removing the restrictions that all stocks of capital goods be fully utilized, and it generalizes the usual price theory of such models by allowing prices to change and to be expected to change. The main analytical tool used is linear programming and the well-known relation between the dual variables and competitive shadow-prices. Some conclusions are reached about the ability of a system of current and futures prices to police an efficient intertemporal allocation of resources under stringent simplifying assumptions.

1. INTRODUCTION

THE PRICE-VALUATION side of the dynamic Leontief system has been pretty thoroughly neglected. So far as I know, a complete history of the literature on this subject can be given in a paragraph. There is first a bit of archaeological pre-history. In a paper in *Econometrica* [6] in 1948, David Hawkins explicitly formulated what we would now call a dynamic input-output model, in complete independence of Leontief's work which was going on at precisely that time. But Hawkins proposed what any economist would find to be an unacceptable price theory:[2] the sales revenue of each industry must just cover its current costs plus the full cost of the required new capital goods. Leontief himself passed over the valuation side of the model both in his first published discussion [7] and in the *locus classicus* [8]. However, in the spring of 1949, at the conference which gave rise to the famous Activity Analysis volume, Georgescu-Roegen discussed the dynamic Leontief model in some detail and in passing [4] proposed what I shall call the "received" doctrine in its price theory: the price of each commodity must cover its current costs plus interest on the value of the capital equipment required per unit of output. This is the system used by Zarnowitz [12]. And although he gets at it in a slightly different (and more satisfying) way, this is also the outcome of Morishima's treatment [9]. The paper by Morishima represents the fullest and most theorem-ful development of this line of thought.[3] The only contribution I have not mentioned is Goodwin's [5], and that doesn't belong here

---

[1] I am grateful to Professor Michio Morishima for many helpful ideas.

[2] It should be remembered about Hawkins' remarkable *tour de force* that he was primarily interested in the possibility of intersectoral disproportion and the generation of macroeconomic fluctuations, rather than in the programming aspects that have since stood in the foreground.

[3] Since Georgescu-Roegen discusses a "closed" system, with no non-produced input like labor, he is able to deduce a unique interest rate. Morishima, who deals with an open system, cannot.

anyway: he is interested in the disequilibrium behavior of the auction process and doesn't explicitly consider the valuation equilibrium of the dynamic system.

The received doctrine states that in the long-run competitive equilibrium of the dynamic Leontief model price equals unit cost, where unit cost includes an interest charge on the value of the unit capital requirements. If $A = (a_{ij})$ and $B = (b_{ij})$ are the $n \times n$ matrices of current input coefficients and capital coefficients respectively, a_0 is the vector of direct labor requirements, p the vector of commodity prices, p_0 the wage rate, and r the money rate of interest, the price-determining equations are:

$$p = A'p + rB'p + p_0 a_0$$

or

(1) $$(I - A)'p - rB'p = p_0 a_0.$$

For some purposes it is simpler to deal with a closed system, and in that case it is only necessary to put $a_0 = 0$ in (1).[4]

On the principle that it is nobler to give than to receive, I want to suggest an extension of the above price theory which takes explicit account of the way in which the very possibility of holding stocks knits together the behavior of prices over time. In the first place it is certainly peculiar that a price theory for a dynamic model should yield constant prices, as (1) does.[5] One might think of justifying this on the grounds that (1) represents a long-run norm about which day to day prices might fluctuate. In a sense this is true, but only leads to worse difficulties. If one starts with the presumption that prices *might* be changing, standard competitive capital theory leads to a genuine dynamic model of price change, of which (1) is indeed the stationary equilibrium. But this equilibrium is almost certainly unstable. If the initial prices and interest rate should fail to satisfy (1), there is no reason to suppose they will ever come to do so, even approximately.

It is important to realize that the proposed modification is phrased in terms of the acceleration principle and capital-output ratios only because that's the kind of model the dynamic input-output system is. The essential

---

[4] One other notational matter: Morishima distinguishes between capital goods and other goods, while Leontief does not. I will stick to Leontief's practice of assuming that any commodity might (although it need not) appear in the system as a stock. In Morishima's version this simply amounts to putting m, the number of pure flow commodities, equal to zero in his equations (4), (5), (6) and elsewhere.

[5] The von Neumann model of an expanding economy [10] also defines equilibrium to mean constant prices and interest rate. But von Neumann defined his output equilibrium to mean balanced proportional growth, and this is what takes the curse off the first definition. A constant-return-to-scale economy undergoing balanced growth is, from the valuation point of view, not changing at all, and constant prices is what one could expect.

point is not the exact form the relationships take, but the fact that the exis-tence of durable goods plus the assumption of competition has implications for intertemporal exchange. Prices at different times are not free to move independently but must satisfy certain consistency conditions.

Morishima's model and mine can be reconciled by recognizing that they represent polar assumptions about price expectation. I assume that entrepreneurs have perfect foresight and (correctly) expect prices to change, and I ask what price movements are then logically consistent. Morishima assumes that entrepreneurs always expect prices to remain constant although in fact they do change from time to time in order to clear markets, and he asks what set of constant prices (and interest rate) can actually be made to endure. It's a toss-up which assumption does more violence to reality.

In fact, as a referee has pointed out, the dynamics of price formation come from such less abstract forces as speculation, bargaining in market clearing, consumer preferences, conflicting expectations about an uncertain future, and similar kinds of behavior which find no place in the Leontief system. But it is not correct to say that there is no theory of price formation in the Leontief model any more than it would be true to say that the Ricardian theory of comparative advantage contains no theory of international exchange ratios. In both cases the theory is incomplete, but there is still point in following out the logical implications of the models as they stand. They will still have a role to play even in a more complete theory. So far it has proved hard enough to capture the dynamics of uncertainty and noncompetitive price formation even in partial models. The grand Walrasian synthesis will come by bits and pieces.

Sometime around 1952 I worked out this much and a bit more in a research paper for Professor Leontief's Harvard Economic Research Project. This was never published,[6] because at about that time Dorfman, Samuelson and I were becoming convinced that the usual (and only) formulation of the dynamic input-output model itself as a determinate causal system could be improved. Our alternative linear-programming version of the dynamic Leontief model is to be found in Chapters 11 and 12 of [3], along with our attempt to justify the introduction of optimizing choice as inescapable. If the alternative view be accepted, then it carries along with it an alternative but similar way of viewing the competitive valuation process. Some of this is sketched in [3], and I hope to be a bit more explicit below.

2. THE CASE OF CHANGING PRICES

Most models dealing in discrete time periods are subject to minor ambiguities in connection with the exact timing of events. This one is no exception.

---

[6] Although a macroeconomic version of some of the results appeared in [11], anyone used to matrix notation could easily work back from this to the full n-commodity set-up.

To keep life simple, I shall make some peculiar timing assumptions. No qualitative distortion occurs. In particular I assume that circulating capital need not be financed—that is, the current costs of a period's production (associated with the a_{ij} coefficients) are incurred simultaneously with the production and sale of output and give rise to no interest charge. Thus current costs accrue in prices of the same period in which the output is sold. In addition, I shall speak as if capital equipment were non-depreciating. This is of no consequence, since maintenance and replacement charges can be subsumed under current costs (see Morishima's Equation (5)).

Suppose a rational man were the proud owner of a sum of money equal to $\sum_1^n b_{ij} p_i(t)$. What could he do? Well, he could purchase an outfit of capital equipment with a capacity of one unit of output of commodity j per period, and set himself up in business. Or he could lend the money to someone else at the going rate of interest $r(t)$. Competitive prices, in the absence of uncertainty, must move in such a way that these two courses of action (and lots of others) are just indifferent.

If he chooses the first option, the entrepreneur will at the end of the period simultaneously incur direct costs of $\sum_0^n a_{ij} p_i(t+1)$ and sales revenue equal to $p_j(t+1)$, since he produces one unit of commodity j. In addition, he goes into the next period still owning his outfit of capital equipment (remember that depreciation is made good in current costs), which is now worth $\sum_1^n b_{ij} p_i(t+1)$.

If he lends for one period at whatever money rate of interest rules in the market, the entrepreneur will enter the next period with a sum equal to $(1+r(t))\sum_1^n b_{ij} p_i(t)$.

Since in equilibrium neither option can have an advantage over the other,

$$(2') \quad p_j(t+1) - \sum_{i=0}^n a_{ij} p_i(t+1) + \sum_{i=1}^n b_{ij} p_i(t+1) = (1+r(t)) \sum_{i=1}^n b_{ij} p_i(t).$$

An exactly similar equation can be written for each[7] commodity $j = 1, \ldots, n$. Collecting all such equations in matrix form yields

$$(2) \quad (I - A + B)' p_{t+1} = (1 + r_t)B' p_t + p_0(t + 1)a_0.$$

Note that if we put $p_t = p_{t+1} = p$, the system of difference equations (2) reduces to the linear equation (1). In other words the prices specified by the received theory are the stationary solution corresponding to the dynamic system (2). In the open system, there exists a unique meaningful stationary equilibrium satisfying (1), provided the rate of interest is less than a certain critical upper limit. (Neither (1) nor (2) provides a theory of interest, but one can easily imagine a supply-demand mechanism which would keep the

---

[7] In a more general model, one might allow for activities which are at a disadvantage compared with others, and are therefore not pursued. But if some of each commodity must be produced, the statement in the text will hold.

interest rate from rising to the critical value and rendering *all* production unprofitable.) In the closed system with $a_0 = 0$, on the other hand, there will in general be one and only one interest rate for which (1) can be solved to give meaningful prices.

There are various ways of interpreting the new price equation (2). In (2′), for instance, we can think of $n_j(t + 1) = p_j(t + 1) - \Sigma a_{ij} p_i(t + 1)$ as the net rental on a unit of capacity to produce commodity j, and the ratio of this quantity to the value of the unit of capacity, $V_j(t) = \Sigma b_{ij} p_i(t)$, is the own-rate of interest earned by such an outfit of durable capital. Then if (2′) is divided on both sides by $V_j(t)$ it becomes

$$(3) \qquad \frac{n_j(t + 1)}{V_j(t)} + \frac{V_j(t + 1) - V_j(t)}{V_j(t)} = r(t)$$

which is a well-known equilibrium condition in the theory of capital: for each asset or bundle of assets, the own-rate of interest plus the rate of appreciation equals the money-rate of interest. In slightly different language, (2) says that in each industry, profits plus capital gains are imputed as interest on the fixed capital.

Why is it that Morishima and his predecessors come up with constant prices? Where is the hidden assumption? It is in Morishima's equation (3). Ignore the q_k, which we have absorbed into the a coefficients. Then his equation states that the equilibrium price of an asset is the capitalized value of its rents. But this is true if and only if prices are known to be constant through time. The rational asset manager would hardly exchange an asset for the capitalized value of its earnings if he expected the price of the asset to rise. He would insist also on capitalizing the capital gains. This is the content of my equation (3) above. If this modification were made in Morishima's (3), his final equation (5) would correspond exactly with my (2).

Unless you simply assume that prices are forever constant, there is no reason to conclude that prices are forever constant. And if prices change and are known to be changing in known directions, the behavior of prices will be governed by (2). Justification of the assumption of fixed prices might come from the argument that transient motions will die away as the system converges to its stationary equilibrium. This question we now investigate.

3. THE DYNAMIC STABILITY OF THE PRICE AND OUTPUT MODELS

It is most convenient to study the dynamical properties of the price system

$$(2'') \qquad (B + C)' p_{t+1} = (1 + r_t) B' p_t + W$$

and the output system (see Morishima's (27))

$$(4) \qquad B x_{t+1} = (B + C) x_t - D$$

together. I have written C for the matrix $(I - A)$, W for the direct labor-cost vector $p_0 a_0$, and D for the vector of final demands.

I am going to assume that the matrix of direct capital coefficients B is nonsingular. Economically speaking this is a terrible assumption to make. It is quite possible for B to contain whole rows of zeros, since there may be many commodities which never function as stocks. Also different industries may be characterized by the same stock-structure. In general the realistic rank of B may be much less than n. No fundamental problem is introduced by this possibility, but the calculations are made more involved. Since the true dimensionality of the system is less than n, one works with a reduced set of transformed variables and converts back to the full set at the very end. To avoid this, and keep the treatment condensed, I make the stated assumption. This permits me to premultiply (2″) and (4) by $(B')^{-1}$ and B^{-1} respectively to get

$$(5) \qquad P_{t+1} = [1 + r_t] [I + (B^{-1})'C']^{-1} p_t + [B' + C']^{-1} W,$$

$$(6) \qquad x_{t+1} = (I + B^{-1}C)x_t - B^{-1}D.$$

Take (6) first. I can be brief, since the basic facts are described by Morishima in his Section III. The nature of the solution, particularly its stability properties, depends on the characteristic roots and vectors of $B^{-1}C$, assumed distinct. Let Λ be the diagonal matrix of the n characteristic roots of $B^{-1}C$. Let X be the $n \times n$ matrix whose kth column is the characteristic vector associated with λ_k. Thus $B^{-1}CX = X\Lambda$, and $(I + B^{-1}C)X = X(I + \Lambda)$. Now let x_0 be the vector of initial values for the n outputs.[8] Then it is easily verified that the unique solution of the difference-equation system (6) is

$$(7) \qquad x_t = X(I + \Lambda)^t X^{-1}(x_0 - C^{-1}D) + C^{-1}D.$$

The long-run qualitative character of the movement of outputs depends on the numbers $(1 + \lambda_k)$. Any $\lambda > 0$ contributes a geometrically-growing component (at least when measured from the stationary point $C^{-1}D$). Any $-1 < \lambda < 0$ contributes a component of geometric decay. Complex λ's lead to oscillations. There is certainly one balanced growth motion possible if A satisfies the Hawkins-Simon conditions. For then $C^{-1}B = (I - A)^{-1}B$ will be a matrix of nonnegative elements, and it will have a real positive root which is as large in absolute value as any of the other roots, and whose corresponding characteristic vector has positive components. Call this root ϱ. Then $1/\varrho$ will be a root of $B^{-1}C$, say λ_1, and the system will be capable of geometric growth like $(1 + \lambda_1)^t = (1 + 1/\varrho)^t$.

One can't say offhand whether this geometric balanced-growth path will

---

[8] The nature of Leontief's model demands that initial outputs and capital stocks be selected so that no excess capacity or undercapacity exists anywhere.

be stable or not. It is true that $|\lambda_1| \leq |\lambda_i|$ for any other characteristic root λ_i. But it does not follow from this that $|1 + \lambda_1| \leq |1 + \lambda_i|$ (for at least one i), which is what we would have to know if we were to pronounce the balanced growth path to be unstable. What we can say is that if any other characteristic root does satisfy $|1 + \lambda_i| > |1 + \lambda_1|$ then the system will eventually run into trouble. Sooner or later some one or more outputs will begin to decline—which calls the acceleration-principle technology in question—or if we permit capital to be easily decumulated, sooner or later some output will become negative. Leontief has ways of evading this difficulty [8, p. 68], and Dorfman, Samuelson and I have proposed a wholly different way of viewing the system which prevents it from ever arising.

Now let us go on to the price equations (5). Note that they are not self-contained. Counting the wage rate and the interest rate there are $n + 2$ unknown time-profiles and only n equations. As usual, we could divide each equation through by the wage rate and solve only for relative prices. That still leaves the interest rate undetermined, which is only right and proper since nothing has been said about the supply of saving or the disposition of income or the banking system or the desire for liquidity, or any of the other forces we normally incorporate in a theory of interest. I propose to let the interest rate hang, and to treat it as an arbitrary function of time. We can solve for relative prices in terms of the interest rate and the parameters of the system.

Since much the same data appear in (5) as in (6), the solutions of the two systems are closely related. The main mathematical fact is that since, as earlier shown, $X^{-1}B^{-1}CX = \Lambda$, it now follows that $X'C'[I + (B^{-1})'C']^{-1} (X'C')^{-1} = (I + \Lambda)^{-1}$. In other words the matrix $[I + (B^{-1})'C']^{-1}$ which appears in (5) has characteristic roots equal to $1/(1 + \lambda_i)$ where λ_i are the roots of the matrix $B^{-1}C$ which appears in (6), and the diagonalization is effected via the matrix $X'C' = (CX)'$.

Make the nonsingular change of variables $z_t = X'C'p_t$ in (5). There results

$$(8) \qquad z_{t+1} = (1 + r_t)(I + \Lambda)^{-1} z_t + V$$

where V is an easily calculable vector of constants. In the canonical variables z we have n separate first-order difference equations whose solution is seen to be

$$z_t = \prod_{t=0}^{t-1} (1 + r_i)(I + \Lambda)^{-t} z_0 + \text{something lengthy}.$$

By transforming back to the natural p variables, we get the solution to (5). In the blessedly simple case where the rate of interest is a constant r we find

$$z_t = (1 + r)^t (I + \Lambda)^{-t} z_0 + \text{constant}$$

or, finally,

$$(9) \qquad p_t = (1 + r)^t (X'C')^{-1}(I + \Lambda)^{-t} X'C'(p_0 - p^*) + p^*$$

where the stationary equilibrium vector p^* is none other than the solution to the "received" static price equation (1). This recalls one restriction on the "arbitrarily" chosen constant rate of interest: it must be low enough so that (1) possesses a solution none of whose components is negative. As already mentioned, there exists a range of such interest rates, with an upper bound. It is not hard to show[9] that the upper bound is λ_1, the rate of balanced growth already discussed in connection with the output model. The upper bound increases if one or more of the a_{ij} flow-coefficients or b_{ij} stock-coefficients decreases.

Now, will p_t as determined by (9) converge on the stationary price-vector p^*? This depends on the numbers $(1 + r)(1 + \lambda_i)^{-1}$. If each of them is less than 1 in modulus, the answer will be Yes. But so far as I can see at the moment, there appears to be no presumption that this will be the case. We know something about the location of the roots λ_i, but not enough to rule out the possibility or even the likelihood that the stationary price configuration p^* is an unstable equilibrium.[10]

To begin with, there are some good economic and mathematical reasons why the interest rate r should not exceed the rate of balanced growth λ_1. It was just mentioned that otherwise the stationary p^* will not even exist. In addition, see Morishima's discussion at the beginning of his Section III, recall the properties of the von Neumann model [10; and 3, Ch. 13], and our own development of the maximal properties of the balanced growth rate λ_1 in an extended Leontief model [3, pp. 297]. One can even make the case that for a closed model r will be about equal to λ_1. None of this is completely convincing, because too high an interest rate can always be compensated by a falling or less rapidly rising price level. But for the sake of the argument, let's take it that $(1 + r)(1 + \lambda_1)^{-1} < 1$.

How about the other roots? We already know, from our discussion of the stability of the balanced growth path of the output model that $|\lambda_i| \geq |\lambda_1|$. Geometrically speaking, every root λ_i lies outside the circle in the complex plane centered at the origin and passing through λ_1. Figure 1 illustrates the position. The diagram also shows the circle centered at $(-1,0)$ and passing through λ_1. Our earlier discussion showed that in the output system the balanced growth path is stable if every other root lies inside this larger circle, unstable if at least one root lies outside. The reader can see that the fact that each λ_i lies outside the smaller circle fails to provide enough information as to its location with respect to the larger circle.

[9] $(I-A'-rB')^{-1}$ must have nonnegative elements.

[10] We ought really to make some special provision to keep any prices from becoming negative even if the linear system (9) should so ordain. The resulting nonlinear equation would be harder to handle. A different tack which accomplishes the same purpose is undertaken below.

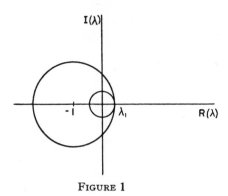

FIGURE 1

What we can say is that if *every* other root λ_i lies outside the large circle so that $|1 + \lambda_i| > |1 + \lambda_1|$ for $i = 2, \ldots, n$, and balanced growth is definitely[11] unstable, then $(1 + r)|1 + \lambda_i|^{-1} < (1 + r)(1 + \lambda_1)^{-1} < 1$ and the price model does definitely converge to p^*. On the other hand, if $|1 + \lambda_i| < |1 + \lambda_1|$ for every i, so that the balanced growth path is stable, and if r is very close to λ_1, then it seems likely that the price model will be unstable[12] and the stationary configuration p^* would be of much less intrinsic interest.

It would be useful to know some simple conditions on the matrices A and B necessary or sufficient for the stability of the dynamic price model. From the diagram it is evident that the larger is λ_1 (i.e., the more rapid the system's potential rate of balanced growth) the closer the two circles come to coinciding and the more likely it is that balanced growth is unstable and that the price model is stable. In turn, the smaller the a's and b's, the larger is λ_1.

And there I leave it.

4. SOME REMARKS ON THE CLOSED MODEL

If we put W and D equal to the null-vector in (2''), (4) and everything that follows, some very simple relationships emerge. This amounts to supposing that labor is a produced output, generated by households from consumption inputs in fixed proportions. From (7) and (9), with $D = p^* = 0$, there follows

$$(10) \qquad p_t'(I - A)x_t = (1 + r)^t p_0'(I - A)X_0,$$

which states that the present value of the net national product is a constant, never deviating from its initial value. By net national product I mean the expression $p'(I - A)x$, the aggregate value of output after intermediate prod-

---

[11] The word "definitely" is used in a peculiar sense here. Customarily we call a dynamic linear system unstable if any of its fundamental motions is unstable, for a "random" displacement will generally excite them all.

[12] Professor Morishima points out that the converse of this statement is also true.

ucts have been cancelled out; in a closed model, labor and consumption are just intermediate goods and NNP is identical with net capital formation. To repeat, (10) states that the initial NNP, if continuously reinvested at the going interest rate, will always be just sufficient to buy back the current NNP. Prices and outputs change, but in just such a way as to preserve this equality.

Again, using (2″), and (4) it can be shown that

$$p'_{t+1} Bx_{t+1} = (1 + r) p'_t Bx_t,$$

or

(11)
$$p'_t Bx_t = (1 + r)^t p'_0 Bx_0.$$

Thus a similar relation holds for the money value of the capital stock. It starts at its initial value and grows at a compound rate equal to the money rate of interest.[13]

Finally (10) and (11) imply that

$$\frac{p'_t Bx_t}{p'_t (I-A)x_t} = \frac{p'_0 Bx_0}{p'_0 (I-A)x_0},$$

that is that the ratio of the value of capital stock to the value of net output, both measured in current prices, is maintained constant throughout the motion of the system.

Somewhat similar but rather more complicated relationships hold for the open system in which final demands and the wage rate are given from the "outside."

5. A GENERALIZED LEONTIEF MODEL

Let me rewrite the basic equations (4) of the dynamic input-output model,

(12)
$$x_t = Ax_t + B(x_{t+1} - x_t) + D,$$

and look a bit more closely at its interpretation. It says that each period's gross output must exactly cover three sets of requirements: current consumption of intermediate goods (including maintenance and depreciation allowances), net capital formation to provide for the next period's gross output, and final demands.[14] To be more explicit, let us introduce a vector

[13] An identical statement holds even if the interest rate varies in time.

[14] Some may find a bit too much simultaneity in (12), because of the way that current input requirements appear to be produced simultaneously with their own use, by means of some kind of own-tail-swallowing act. This awkwardness can be avoided. Suppose the vector of commodity stocks at time zero, say S_0, covers not only the fixed capital requirements Bx_1 for the first period's production, but also covers inventories of circulating capital Ax_1 required as current inputs. Then production x_1 must provide for

of capital stocks S_t,[15] and of net investments $\Delta S_t = S_{t+1} - S_t$. Then the input-output model states

(13a) $$x_t = D_t + Ax_t + \Delta S_t,$$

(13b) $$S_t = Bx_t.$$

Here (13a) describes the allocation of gross outputs already discussed, and (13b) says that at each moment of time the capital stock must be precisely adjusted to the current flow of gross outputs. For most purposes I see no objection to the assumption that each output flow has positive value, so that no more will be produced than is necessary to cover the various demands. But (13b) is another story. If we accept the strong technological hypothesis of fixed capital coefficients, it is clear that output simply can't exceed the productive capacity of the available fixed capital. But there is nothing in technology which prevents output from failing to use up all the capacity available. All the technological hypothesis allows us to assert is

(13c) $$S_t \geq Bx_t.$$

This is more than a trivial generalization. The point is that from (13b) one can deduce $\Delta S_t = B\Delta x_t$, substitute this in (13a) and wind up with the *determinate* system (12). The principle of "no excess capacity"[16] is strong enough to define a unique output path, the only one that avoids the appearance of excess stocks.

But from (13c) one can do no such thing. In general ΔS_t and Δx_t are independent. The result is that (13a) and (13c) together do not form a determinate system. Instead they define a set of *feasible* final-demand-plus-capital-formation vectors $D + \Delta S_t$ in terms of the historically given capital stocks S_t. The choice of one among the many feasible patterns of final consumption and net investment may be made by different economic systems in different ways, but one way or another it must be made.

---

final demands, replacement of circulating capital, net investment in fixed capital, and net investment in circulating capital.

Thus $x_1 = D + Ax_1 + B(x_2 - x_1) + A(x_2 - x_1) = D + Ax_1 + (B + A)(x_2 - x_1)$

and $\qquad S_1 = S_0 - Ax_1 + Ax_1 + (B + A)(x_2 - x_1) = (B + A)x_2.$

So everything works out except that the B matrix has to be interpreted as an array of fixed *plus* circulating capital coefficients.

[15] We are tacitly assuming capital to be freely transferable from one industry to another, else we would need a whole matrix of S_{ij}'s.

[16] Of course one can (and should) argue that in a competitive system, if any component of the capital stock is in excess supply, the price or rent of its services will fall until the excess capacity is wiped out. True enough, except that when the rent has fallen to zero it can fall no further. The theory to be developed will be such that if any capital item is not fully utilized, the current rent of its services will be zero.

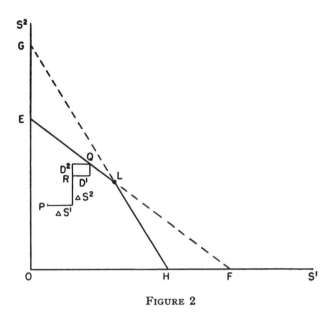

FIGURE 2

Figure 2 graphs S^1 horizontally and S^2 vertically. Point P is the endowment of capital stocks at time t. ELF represents the stocks $S^1(t + 1)$ and $S^2(t + 1)$ that could be made available if (a) there were no consumption, (b) $S^2(t)$ were freely available in unlimited amounts, and (c) the scarcity of $S^1(t)$ were the only constraint limiting production. Of course the area under ELF also represents possible outcomes if some of $S^1(t)$ were left idle.[17] GLH represents a similar locus where only S^2 is scarce. Since in fact both $S^1(t)$ and $S^2(t)$ are available in limited amounts, the polygon $OELH$ is the final feasible set of vectors S_{t+1}. Of course only points on ELH are efficient, in the sense that any other point could be unambiguously improved upon. Society can choose a point like Q, deduct amounts D_1 and D_2 for consumption, and be left with net investment shown on the diagram as ΔS^1 and ΔS^2. Then the point R represents S_{t+1} and we are ready to consider the next period.

The usual formulation of the model *requires* that society "choose" the point L, the unique point at which both stocks are fully utilized. (At Q S^1 is fully utilized, but S^2 is in excess supply.) But if the climate were getting warmer and swimming pools were S^2-intensive while snowshoes were S^1-intensive, it is hard to imagine a set of social arrangements which would insist on L as against Q.

All this is argued in great detail in [3, Ch. 11], and I repeat it here only to make this paper reasonably self-contained. If one accepts this point of

[17] An obvious modification applies if one prefers to treat capital stocks as not capable of being reduced.

view, then the dynamic input-output model loses its determinate character and the problem of choice among alternative output paths cannot be evaded. Another important conclusion follows. Each stock (including labor) must in the short run be treated as a non-reproducible fixed factor, so that there is more than one resource to be economized. Then just as in the statical case, the non-substitution theorems proved by Morishima will no longer hold. If production *can* take place with various input proportions this will now be a real advantage. If final demand *and* investment decisions call for a lot of S^1-intensive production, and S^1 is currently short, it will pay to shift to techniques light in S^1.

6. EFFICIENT PATHS

Figure 2 showed how the system can efficiently build up its stocks of capital from P to R while at the same time throwing off the required consumption vector D. Any one of an infinity of destinations other than R might have been chosen. In turn, now, R serves as an "initial" endowment of capital S_{t+1} and a new set of possibilities opens up for the next period, $t + 2$. But this new frontier of possible S_{t+2} does *not* fairly represent society's possibilities starting at P at time t. We must instead consider each alternative for S_{t+1}, like R and all the other points on ELH, and for each of them draw a locus of possible S_{t+2}. If society's vision extends over two time periods, it is the outer envelope of all the one-period frontiers beginning on ELH which constitutes the true two-period frontier.

Of course the two-period envelope can be used in exactly the same way as ELH was, to generate a three-period envelope. And so forth, for four, five, and more periods. An equivalent formulation is this: consider all feasible T-period programs which deliver specified consumption profiles and violate no constraints. Then among all such programs we look for the efficient ones, i.e., the ones which end up with terminal stocks which cannot all be simultaneously improved upon by any other program. The end points of the efficient paths will all lie along the T-period envelope just discussed.[18]

Linear programming at once suggests itself as the appropriate formalization for this model.[19] Some simplification comes from adopting equations

---

[18] The Leontief trajectory, the path which obeys (13b), is an efficient path if it is feasible. I intend to devote another paper to a closer study of the shape of the expanding envelopes. It seems likely that the Leontief equalities will play a very important role, and the more rapid the permissible rate of decumulation, the more important they become.

[19] This is by no means a full generalization of the dynamic input-output model. It allows only for those degrees of freedom which follow from the existence of durable capital goods. If in addition one recognizes the existence of alternative techniques within any period, still further necessities of choice emerge, and these have important implications for the evolution of prices. Morishima has attacked this problem [9; and an as yet unpublished paper] with remarkable results.

(13a) as they stand, solving them for x_t and substituting in (13c). The whole problem is then expressed in terms of the stock vectors. As already noted, this only involves the assumption that no commodity flow-output will be a free good in the course of the program, and so none will ever be over-produced. The model is treated this way in [3]. Here I choose to replace the $=$ by $\geq$ in (13a) and retain it explicitly, since this procedure will buy us a bit more detail in the dual price formulation. The maximum problem we are interested in is then the following:

Maximize $K'S_T$

subject to

$$(14) \begin{pmatrix} I & 0 & 0 & \ldots & 0 & 0 & -C & 0 & 0 & \ldots & 0 \\ -I & I & 0 & \ldots & 0 & 0 & 0 & -C & 0 & \ldots & 0 \\ 0 & -I & I & \ldots & 0 & 0 & 0 & 0 & -C & \ldots & 0 \\ 0 & 0 & 0 & \ldots & -I & I & 0 & 0 & 0 & \ldots & -C \\ \hdashline 0 & 0 & 0 & \ldots & 0 & 0 & B & 0 & 0 & \ldots & 0 \\ -I & 0 & 0 & \ldots & 0 & 0 & 0 & B & 0 & \ldots & 0 \\ 0 & -I & 0 & \ldots & 0 & 0 & 0 & 0 & B & \ldots & 0 \\ 0 & 0 & 0 & \ldots & -I & 0 & 0 & 0 & 0 & \ldots & B \end{pmatrix} \begin{Bmatrix} S_1 \\ S_2 \\ S_3 \\ S_T \\ \hdashline x_0 \\ x_1 \\ x_2 \\ x_{T-1} \end{Bmatrix} \leq \begin{Bmatrix} S_0 - D_0 \\ -D_1 \\ -D_2 \\ -D_{T-1} \\ \hdashline S_0 \\ 0 \\ 0 \\ 0 \end{Bmatrix}$$

where each of the submatrices appearing is $n \times n$, and K is a vector of n nonnegative weights or values assigned to the terminal stocks. As the K's vary, the solutions to these maximum problems trace out the efficient locus of terminal stocks given the technology, the initial stocks, and the required consumption profile.[20]

If there were alternative techniques for producing commodities, the technology matrix on the left of (14) would have to be enlarged to include them, and the solution of the maximum problem would specify which activities are to be used in each period.

Notice, and surprisingly enough this is sometimes important, I have not yet incorporated any constraint on the rate at which capital stocks can be decumulated. If, as Leontief and others sometimes require, we must have $S_{t+1} - S_t \geq 0$, the matrix on the left has to be enlarged. Two new blocks will appear at the bottom, namely

[20] A slightly different formulation would promote the D_t from givens to unknowns, and maximize a weighted sum of the components of $D_0, \ldots, D_{T-1}$, and S_T. In some cases it might even make sense to include $S_1, S_2, \ldots, S_{T-1}$ in the maximand–for instance if there were a possibility of war breaking out in any period and if military capability depends on the available stocks. Apart from (important) matters of technique, it seems to me that one of the great lessons to be learned from modern developments in activity analysis and linear programming is the habit of asking of any competitive system (and of some others), "What is it trying to maximize?" Naturally no naive teleology is implied.

$$\begin{pmatrix}
-I & 0 & 0 & 0 & \dots & 0 & 0 & 0 & \dots & 0 \\
I & -I & 0 & 0 & \dots & 0 & 0 & 0 & \dots & 0 \\
0 & I & -I & 0 & \dots & 0 & 0 & 0 & \dots & 0 \\
0 & 0 & I & -I & \dots & 0 & 0 & 0 & \dots & 0 \\
& & & & & & & & & \\
0 & 0 & 0 & 0 & \dots & -I & 0 & 0 & \dots & 0
\end{pmatrix}$$

and the right-hand-side vector will have a $-S_0$ and some more zeros added at the end. Obvious amendments apply if only some stocks are subject to this condition, or if a maximum rate of decumulation other than zero applies. After all, it is not so surprising that this matters for competitive pricing: if stocks can be freely run down, then consumption demands can be met by selling off stocks and the phenomenon of redundant stocks will play a much less significant role.

7. THE DUAL VALUATION PROBLEM—DECUMULATION PERMITTED

Granted perfect foresight,[21] it doesn't matter whether the Hand that chooses the target in (14) is Visible or Invisible. To get the competitive prices that make an equilibrium out of any efficient path, it is only necessary to formulate and interpret the dual problem to (14). It is:

$$\text{Minimize } (S_0 - D_0)'U_0 - \sum_{1}^{T-1} D_t' U_t + S_0' q_0$$

subject to

(15)
$$\left\{
\begin{pmatrix}
I & -I & 0 & \dots & 0 & 0 & -I & 0 & \dots & 0 \\
0 & I & -I & \dots & 0 & 0 & 0 & -I & \dots & 0 \\
0 & 0 & I & \dots & 0 & 0 & 0 & 0 & \dots & 0 \\
0 & 0 & 0 & \dots & -I & 0 & 0 & 0 & \dots & -I \\
0 & 0 & 0 & \dots & I & 0 & 0 & 0 & \dots & 0 \\
\hline
-C' & 0 & 0 & \dots & 0 & B' & 0 & 0 & \dots & 0 \\
0 & -C' & 0 & \dots & 0 & 0 & B' & 0 & \dots & 0 \\
0 & 0 & -C' & \dots & 0 & 0 & 0 & B' & \dots & 0 \\
0 & 0 & 0 & \dots & -C' & 0 & 0 & 0 & \dots & B'
\end{pmatrix}
\begin{pmatrix}
U_0 \\ U_1 \\ U_2 \\ U_{T-2} \\ U_{T-1} \\ \hline q_0 \\ q_1 \\ q_2 \\ q_{T-1}
\end{pmatrix}
\geq
\begin{pmatrix}
0 \\ 0 \\ 0 \\ 0 \\ K \\ \hline 0 \\ 0 \\ 0 \\ 0
\end{pmatrix}
\right.$$

Let us look at the constraints in detail. The first batch says

(16a) $$\qquad\qquad U_t - U_{t+1} - q_{t+1} \geq 0 \qquad (t = 0, 1, \dots, T-2),$$

(16b) $$\qquad\qquad U_{T-1} \geq K,$$

[21] It wouldn't be fair to gloss over those words and hope the reader might not notice them. Capital theory is hard enough even with this strong and sometimes paradoxical assumption. Without it, it's hard to get off the ground.

while the second batch states

(17) $-C'U_t + B'q_t \geq 0$ $(t = 0,1,\ldots,T-1)$.

Moreover, the general principles of the duality relationship tell us that if each stock and each flow is positive at every moment of time, the equality will hold in every equation of (16) and (17). It is almost certainly harmless, practically speaking, to suppose that indeed each stock is held in a positive amount throughout the T-period program. This will guarantee equality in (16). But it is more restrictive to assume all flows to be positive. If, as already mentioned, stocks can be converted freely into flows and run down as rapidly as desired, then it may turn out to be optimal when a stock is redundant to meet final demands *and* intermediate-flow demands directly out of stock, in which case some current flows may well be zero. Then the inequalities in (17) have to be respected.

Now the U's correspond to the "conservation of commodity" relations (13a) and the q's to the capital stock constraints (13c). Hence we interpret U_t as the vector of commodity-prices at time t, discounted back to the present, and q_t as the similarly discounted vector of *stock rents* at time t. In earlier notation $U_t \equiv p_t/(1+r)^t$.

We have as yet no notation for the undiscounted rents.[22] Suppose we call the undiscounted rent vector R_t. Then $q_t \equiv R_t/(1+r)^t$. With this interpretation, the dual constraints (16a) read

(18) $p_t(1+r)^{-t} - p_{t+1}(1+r)^{-t-1} - R_{t+1}(1+r)^{-t-1} \geq 0$

or, if we rearrange and assume that all stocks are always positive, so the equality holds:

(18a) $$\frac{R_j(t+1)}{p_j(t)} + \frac{p_j(t+1) - p_j(t)}{p_j(t)} = r$$

which is nothing but our old intertemporal-arbitrage equilibrium condition (3) all over again. The only additional thing we have learned is the obvious amendment that if a stock is not being held at all, there is no harm in a price configuration which would induce a holder of the stock to get rid of it.

The condition (16b) simply requires that the valuation placed on a unit of a commodity at time $T-1$ not be less than the arbitrary valuation placed on a unit stock of the commodity at time T. This is obvious, since under our assumption, a unit flow at $T-1$ can be converted to a unit stock at T costlessly, by just holding on.

---

[22] The earlier $n_j(t)$ was the rent at time t on an outfit of equipment with a capacity of one unit of commodity j. We now want the rent on a stock consisting of one unit of commodity j.

Making the already established identification in (17) we find

(19) $$C'p_t - B'R_t \leq 0$$

which states that net profits (revenue minus prime costs minus rents) can never be positive. If a commodity-flow is currently being produced, profits in its production must be zero; if the industry is producing zero output, its profit per unit may be negative.

On the assumption that all stocks are positive, so equality holds in (16a) and hence in (18) we can use (18) to eliminate R_t in (19) and there results

(20) $$(B + C)' \, p_{t+1} \geq (1 + r) \, B'p_t$$

which, apart from the inequality sign, is our old friend (2″).[23] So we have come back to the prices-changing theory with which I began, except for one important difference. You can't calculate equilibrium prices simply by solving a difference equation. If some stocks are redundant, some flows may be zero and inequalities will appear in (20). Then in order to calculate prices we have to look deeper. The significance of this is that there is no longer a divorce between the price and output systems. Visibly or invisibly caused variations in the K's will yield different efficient paths which in turn may lead to different patterns of equalities and inequalities in (20) and hence to different evolutions of the price system.

When inequalities appear and difference equations are of no avail, how can we compute the course of prices? There is nothing for it but to solve the minimum problem in (15). This has an interesting interpretation in its own right. The minimand is seen to be essentially the valuation of the initial stocks after allowance for the discounted value of final demands. Thus the competitive prices which sustain the optimal path are such as to minimize the value imputed to the initial endowment of stocks after allowing for the value placed on consumption. In addition, linear programming theory tells us that in an optimal situation, the full present value of consumption flows plus the values placed on the terminal stocks will be imputed to the initial stocks. Here too we see that the eventual price evolution will depend not only on the terminal stock values but also on the prescribed pattern of consumption flows.

The U's and q's, and hence the p's and R's, are nonnegative. Another application of duality theory tells us that if any equation of (13a) holds with an inequality, so that a particular flow in a particular period of time is ab-

[23] There are two trivial differences. Had I allowed for a variable rate of interest in interpreting U and q, a variable r_t would appear in (20). Secondly, I have been treating labor as just like any other stock and so (20) corresponds to a closed system. It would be possible to add special labor constraints in (14). This would yield new dual variables to be interpreted as discounted wage rates, and the parallel between (20) and (2″) would be complete.

solutely redundant (beyond its intermediate-good, final-demand and possibly negative net investment uses), then the corresponding component of U_t will be zero. Glancing now at (16a and b) we can go a step further. If $U_j(t) = 0$, we see from (16a) that $-U_j(t + 1) - q_j(t + 1) \geq 0$. But U_j and q_j are *never* negative. Hence $U_j(t) = 0$ implies $U_j(t + 1) = 0$ and $q_j(t + 1) = 0$. Then by induction $U_j(t + 2) = U_j(t + 3) = \ldots = U_j(T - 1) = 0$. But now from (16b) we see that $U_j(T - 1) \geq K_j$. If K_j is positive, that is if terminal stocks of commodity j are positively valued, $U_j(T - 1)$ must be positive, and working backwards we see that every $U_j(t) > 0$. Thus if it is worth having terminal stocks of a particular commodity, its flow-price must be positive at every moment of time. This in turn implies that its equation in (13a) must *always* hold with equality. If a commodity can be stored costlessly it might indeed pay to decumulate its stock, but it can never pay to decumulate more rapidly than is necessary to meet current demands, since holding until period T would always have positive payoff. Thus the only situation in which we need contemplate inequality in (13a) is for a commodity which does not enter the maximand and whose stock at some point is so large that all flow demands for the rest of the program can be met and more than met by running down the stock.

Moreover, any time a strict inequality holds in (13c), i.e., if a *stock* is at any time present in excess capital-good capacity, it follows that the corresponding component of q_t and therefore of R_t will be zero. From (18a), then, we deduce that if $R_j(t) = 0$, $p_j(t) = (1 + r)p_j(t - 1)$ and the nominal price of the commodity will increase (or decrease, if $r < 0$) simply at compound interest.

Finally, it is clear that the K's play the role of known valuations placed on terminal stocks of the various commodities. For the dual variables to imitate the results of perfect competition it is essential that all entrepreneurs take the K's (and the same K's) as given. This is the only assumption compatible with the overriding hypothesis of perfect foresight. And this is all that is essential. One might think that in addition to the terminal valuations all entrepreneurs might have to share a whole set of intermediate valuations, and that for short-run maximization to be compatible with long-run efficiency the intermediate values would have to be subject to severe and arbitrary restrictions. But the intermediate values are just the dual U's of (16) and (17). No other intermediate prices can arise—not because of some theoretical symmetry, but because of competition. Any other market prices would allow profitable intertemporal arbitrage. A gap would arise between, say, (a) maximization of discounted net worth via production over 3 periods and (b) maximization via production over 2 periods, followed by trade at current prices, followed by further production in the third period. Given certainty and competition, prices must be such as to wipe out such gaps, to make efficient activities break even and inefficient ones show a loss [**3**, pp. **318-22**]. Thus there is no arbitrariness, and the dual variables provide an image of competitive pricing.

8. THE DUAL VALUATION PROBLEM—NO DECUMULATION

Just to clinch matters, suppose we run briefly over the pricing problem under the added constraint that $S_{t+1} - S_t \geq 0$, so that no capital stock can ever be run down.[24] If we label the new vectors of dual variables $y_0, y_1, \ldots, y_{T-1}$, the constraints (17) remain unchanged, but (16a and b) become

(16c) $U_t - U_{t+1} - q_{t+1} - y_t + y_{t+1} \geq 0$ $(t = 0, 1, \ldots, T{-}2)$

(16d) $U_{T-1} - y_{T-1} \geq K.$

The new constraints (16c and 16d) will hold with equality whenever the corresponding stocks are held in positive amounts, otherwise they may stand as strict inequalities. Since capital cannot be decumulated, we can be sure that if the system starts with a positive stock of every commodity, it must continue to hold positive stocks, and so for the rest of the discussion we might as well take the equality to hold. The unchanged constraints (17) will hold with inequality whenever the corresponding output flow is positive. But now this is also a relatively harmless assumption to make. Since flow demands cannot be met by running down stocks, flows are more likely to be positive. In fact if each commodity is either part of final demand at every moment of time or directly or indirectly required as a current input to a final-demand commodity, then every flow must be positive. Thus the set of constraints (16c), (16d), (17) can be taken as a set of equations.

Does this restore the independence of the price and output system? Far from it. In the first place it will still be true that the rent on any stock will be zero if the stock is available in excess over current demands on capacity. And this is now more likely to occur, since redundant stocks cannot be converted into flows and worked off. Secondly, we have introduced a whole new set of dual variables without adding to the number of constraints. Thus there are more unknowns than equations and there is still freedom in "choosing" the prices. This means that there is still a genuine minimum problem involved, and the competitive prices will be those which minimize

$$(S_0 - D_0)'U_0 - \sum_1^{T-1} D_t'U_t + S_0'q_0 - S_0'y_0$$

subject to the constraints. Thus the particular pattern of final demands prescribed will continue to influence the optimal pattern of prices.

[24] It will be clear how to handle the more general mixed case in which stocks can be decumulated, but only at some maximum rate.

We still have to provide an interpretation of the new dual variables y_t associated with the constraints $S_{t+1} - S_t \geq 0$. The essential point is that now the possibility exists of a gap between the forward-looking market value of a capital good and its current cost of production. Suppose that at $t = 10$ it was necessary to have a large stock of marshmallow-making machinery, because D_{10} contains a large order of marshmallows. But no subsequent D_t calls for many marshmallows, and the value placed on marshmallow-machinery at the terminal date is very low. Then society is stuck with what might appropriately be called white elephants, and since future rents will be low (perhaps zero), the market will place a low valuation on them. Yet since steel, rubber, labor, and other things used to produce marshmallow-making machinery have alternative occupations, the cost of production of the machines need not fall so far. Naturally, marshmallow machines will not be produced and $S^m(t) = S^m(t + 1) = \ldots$. This sad tale could not occur in the previous formulation. If we allow capital stocks to be decomposed quite literally into their original elements and sold off as flows, then no one will ever place a lower value on a commodity stock than its flow-cost.

It is clear, on the other hand, that the market value of a stock can never exceed its cost of production, since otherwise on our assumptions, it would continue to be demanded in increasing amounts until costs were driven up to meet the market value. If a stock is actually being added to, its market value must exactly equal its unit production cost.

Any component of y_t is to be interpreted, then, as the (discounted) excess of the current flow price of the corresponding stock over the market value as built up out of future rents. If, say, $S^j(t + 1) = S^j(t)$, then $y^j(t)$ will in general be positive. If $S^j(t + 1) > S^j(t)$, then $y^j(t) = 0$.

This interpretation can be verified by assuming all the equalities to hold in (16c and d) and working backwards from $T - 1$ to earlier periods. It is easily found that

$$(21) \qquad\qquad y_t = U_t - \left(\sum_{t+1}^{T-1} q_j + K \right).$$

The expression in parentheses is the discounted sum of future rents (including terminal values), or what has already been described as the vector of market values of the various stocks; U_t is the vector of flow prices, discounted to the initial time. The flow prices will, in turn, according to (17), be equal to costs of production including rents for all produced flows, and fall short of costs of production for unproduced flows. Remember that as a concession to simplicity the model has been set up so that a commodity may have distinct stock and flow uses.

One more word on the dual constraints. Since U_t is the flow price and y_t is the excess of flow price over market value, (21) shows that $U_t - y_t = U_t^*$, say, is the vector of discounted market values. With this definition (16c and d) can be rewritten as

(22a) $$U_t^* - U_{t+1}^* - q_{t+1} \geq 0,$$

(22b) $$U_{T-1}^* \geq K.$$

Thus with cost prices replaced by market values, the new dual constraints correspond exactly to the old (16a, b). But (17) remains exactly as it was, with U's not U^*'s. Costs are computed with flow prices, not stock valuations. The reader can observe for himself how the U's and U^*'s enter the minimand, and realize once again that even if every dual constraint holds with full equality, there is still no determinate evolution of the price system independent of what happens to outputs, final demands and stocks along an efficient path to the end of the horizon

It would be fascinating to try to work out some of the comparative statical properties of the combined price and output systems, analogous to Morishima's results for the much more primitive case in which no prices change. It is easy enough to show by the methods of [1, 2] that if the final demand for a commodity should increase in a particular period, then the flow-price of that commodity in that period must increase (or at least cannot decrease). The marshmallow fable shows that what happens from then on may depend on lots of things. From (21) it can be read off that if a flow-price in period t should increase, then either the corresponding component of y_t must increase or some of the future rents to be earned on the commodity stock in question must increase. *If* the corresponding component of y_t is and remains zero, i.e., if stocks of the commodity were and still are being accumulated at time t, then some future rents must increase along with the flow-price.

A more interesting question is the effect on the evolution of prices of changes in the a_{ij} or b_{ij} coefficients, and in particular of decreases in some of them, which would correspond to technological progress. This problem can be attacked formally using the methods of Beckmann and Bailey. In the useful case one must imagine an a_{ij} or b_{ij} to change at some time t and to retain its new value through $t + 1, t + 2, \ldots, T - 1$. So far I have found nothing sufficiently edifying to justify prolonging this paper. But I recommend this as an investigation which might repay imaginative study, particularly if pursued in tandem with a closer investigation of the behavior of efficient paths in the simplest Leontief dynamic model.

9. CONCLUDING REMARKS

I keep wondering if all this is merely an arid exercise or something more. Any casual Freudian could predict how that interior dialogue would come out. It seems to me that the following conclusions emerge.

1. Capital theory is a hard subject. In particular, once we recognize the existence of durable assets, we can no longer hope to make it simple by eliminating the problem of choice and locking the system into a predetermined pattern of evolution. There are too many things to economize.

2. In particular, the whole discussion has been conducted in terms of some arbitrary K's or values placed on terminal stocks at the end of some finite horizon. This is a transparent dodge. Once we ask the obvious question, How are the K's determined?, it is obvious that they depend on what happens or is expected to happen *after* the "terminal" period. It is the essence of the future that there's always some of it left, and this poses a difficult problem for analysis. It may be that as the horizon recedes very far into the future, many of the earlier decisions become independent of the precise terminal conditions. Something like this is suggested in [3, Ch. 12].

3. The earlier price theories for the dynamic system seem to lead too easily to a determinate theory of the rate of interest. This is an optical illusion. Anything a 4 per cent rate of interest can do, a 6 per cent rate of interest can do with the nominal price level rising an additional 2 per cent per year, in a nonmonetary neoclassical system like ours. Georgescu-Roegen and Morishima get their determinacy by assuming from the beginning that price "equilibrium" means constant prices, which seems to be assuming too much. Once the movement of nominal prices becomes an endogenous part of the system, it takes one more equilibrium condition to fix the rate of interest (or the path of the rate of interest). This added condition can have to do with the supply of saving, in a system in which the disposal of income is open to choice. Or else, if the system has a money-commodity—not just a numéraire—that is, if nominal prices are always quoted in units of a particular produced commodity, then this provides an anchor for the nominal price level. We can put the nominal price of the money commodity equal to unity, and "the" rate of interest must be the own-rate of interest earned on stocks of that commodity. Equation (18a) will show how the prices of other commodities depend on their own-rates, and on "the" rate of interest.

4. The theory outlined here throws some light on what the price system (or at least a competitive price system) can and cannot be expected to do in the dynamic context of ongoing capital formation. The answer is that given all our (very strong) background assumptions about technology and *under conditions of certainty*, competitive markets (including both spot and—actually or implicitly—futures markets) will see to it that efficient activities earn zero profits and inefficient activities are penalized with losses.

This statement is subject to a variety of qualifications. In the first place, the presence of increasing returns, external economies, etc., are even more of a problem than in the static case. I say more of a problem because they are probably more prevalent in situations involving long-run accumulation of capital. Secondly, there is a wide gap between efficient activities and desirable activities, most especially in the economic development context. The Invisible Hand or, what is more to the point, the initial distribution of wealth, may implicitly choose a target in (14) but this has little claim to be called a good choice. Political intervention may take the form of announcing *convincingly* a set of terminal K weights, which are to be thought of as real values for the terminal period. After that one piece of vision at a distance, it seems as if day to day profit maximization and arbitrage will do the rest. Third, there is uncertainty. All the previous argument presupposes at least locally perfect foresight or perfect futures market. Without this unlikely gift, competitive valuations lose much of their attractiveness. One sometimes finds passages in the development literature which suggest that it is logically impossible for competitive markets to function properly in the dynamic context. This seems to be erroneous. But on closer inspection it often turns out that what is really being argued is the prevalence of uncertainty. This is far from erroneous. It is equally mistaken to believe that central planners are in some way free of uncertainty. But the great advantage of central authority is that as a great pooler of risks it can *reduce* uncertainty in a way not open to individual forecasters of the future. It would be an interesting problem to work out for this problem of efficient capital formation just how much informational and other decentralization is possible.

Massachusetts Institute of Technology

REFERENCES

[1] BAILEY, M. J.: "A Generalized Comparative Statics for Linear Programming," *Review of Economic Studies* Vol. XXIII (3), 1955-6, p. 236.

[2] BECKMANN, M.: "Comparative Statics in Linear Programming and the Giffen Paradox," *Review of Economic Studies* Vol. XXIII (3), 1955-6, p. 232.

[3] DORFMAN, R., P. SAMUELSON, AND R. SOLOW: *Linear Programming and Economic Analysis*, New York: McGraw-Hill, 1957.

[4] GEORGESCU-ROEGEN, N.: "Relaxation Phenomena in Linear Dynamic Models," Ch. V in T. Koopmans (ed.), *Activity Analysis of Production and Allocation*, New York: Wiley, 1951, p. 116.

[5] GOODWIN, R. M.: "Static and Dynamic Linear General Equilibrium Models" in *Input-Output Relations*, Leiden, 1953.

[6] HAWKINS, D.: "Some Conditions of Macroeconomic Stability," *Econometrica* Vol. 16 (4), 1948, p. 309.

[7] LEONTIEF, W. W.: "Recent Developments in the Study of Interindustrial Relations," *American Economic Review* (Papers and Proceedings), Vol. 39, May 1949, p. 211.

[8] ———: "Static and Dynamic Theory," Ch. 3 in *Studies in the Structure of the American Economy*, New York: Oxford University Press, 1953.

[9] MORISHIMA, M.: "Prices, Interest and Profits in a Dynamic Leontief System," *Econometrica*, Vol. 26 (3), 1958, p. 358.

[10] VON NEUMANN, J.: "A Model of General Equilibrium," *Review of Economic Studies*, Vol. XIII B(1), 1945, p. 1 (translation of paper first published in 1937).

[11] SOLOW, R.: "A Note on the Price Level and Interest Rate in a Growth Model," *Review of Economic Studies*, Vol. XXI (1), 1953-4, p. 74.

[12] ZARNOWITZ, V.: "Technology and the Price Structure in General Equilibrium System," *Review of Economic Studies* Vol. XXIII (2), 1955-6, p. 109.

Econometrica, Vol. 27, No. 2 (April, 1959)

SUBSTITUTION VERSUS FIXED PRODUCTION COEFFICIENTS IN THE THEORY OF ECONOMIC GROWTH: A SYNTHESIS

By Leif Johansen[1]

Most growth models are based either on the assumption of fixed production coefficients for labour and capital or on the assumption of substitutability between factors. The present paper proposes a hypothesis which is a compromise between these extremes, viz., that any *increment* in production can be obtained by different combinations of *increments* in labour and capital inputs, whereas any piece of capital which is already installed will continue to be operated by a constant amount of labour throughout its life span. First, a "general model" is presented. Next, the model is solved in different special cases. In conclusion it is suggested that the proposed hypothesis would be particularly appropriate in studying the introduction of new techniques and the relationship between population growth, the rate of saving and "structural" unemployment.

1. INTRODUCTION

The models hitherto most widely applied in the theoretical analysis of problems of economic growth can be classified in the following three groups:

(a) Models with a given capital coefficient, where the labour input does not enter the analysis explicitly, but is treated rather vaguely in supplementary comments. The models of R. F. Harrod [9], Evsey D. Domar [3][2], Hans Brems [2], Robert Eisner [5] and Ingvar Svennilson [22] exemplify this class.

(b) Models with fixed production coefficients for labour input as well as for the capital stock, or some other kind of strict complementarity. As examples one might mention the analysis of D. Hamberg [8], the work on long-range projections at the Central Planning Bureau in the Netherlands, cf. e.g., P. J. Verdoorn [25], and furthermore the more disaggregated analysis by Wassily Leontief [14], Oskar Lange [13] and other authors in the field of input-output analysis.

(c) Models with explicitly expressed possibilities of substitution between total labour input and capital stock in a traditional production function. This type of model is exemplified by the publications of Jan Tinbergen [23], Trygve Haavelmo [7], Robert Solow [19] and Stefan Valavanis-Vail [24].

Models belonging to any of these groups may, of course, contain important

---

[1] I am indebted to professor Trygve Haavelmo and Mr. Hans Jacob Kreyberg at the University of Oslo, with whom I have discussed many of the problems analysed in this paper. Mr. Kreyberg has also read through the manuscript and given useful criticism.

[2] See in particular the Foreword and Essay III: "Capital Expansion, Rate of Growth, and Employment," (*Econometrica*, April 1946 pp. 137-147).

and realistic aspects and be well suited for certain objectives. I have, however, the feeling that many theorists, whether they apply models belonging to the group (a), (b) or (c), often have been working with a "guilty conscience"[3] regarding the realism of their assumptions. The purpose of this paper is to propose a kind of synthesis between the approaches in (b) and (c) above. The synthesis will be based on the following assumptions:

(1) Any gross[4] *increment* in the rate of production can be obtained by different combinations of *increments* in capital and labour input. We may perhaps express this in another way by saying that there are ex ante substitution possibilities between capital and labour, or that there are substitution possibilities *at the margin*.

(2) Once a piece of capital is produced and has been put into operation, it will continue to operate through all its life span in cooperation with a constant amount of labour input. We may perhaps express this by saying that there are no ex post substitution possibilities, or that there are no substitution possibilities between total labour input and existing capital stock.

Even if a more flexible framework may be imagined, I have the feeling that an analysis based on the assumptions (1) and (2) above will in most cases be more realistic than an analysis based on models belonging to any of the groups, (a), (b), or (c).

The idea may of course be applied at different levels of aggregation. We shall, however, as an illustration, apply it in a pure macro-analysis of growth problems.

In Section 2 the idea is worked out more precisely and included in a rather general model. In Sections 3, 4 and 5 the solution of the model is given and some special cases are discussed. Some concluding remarks are given in Section 6.

2. THE "GENERAL" MODEL

The model to be presented in this section is, of course, not general in any absolute sense. It is only general relative to the specializations discussed in Sections 3, 4 and 5.

The model will be characterized by the following properties:

(1) There are two factors of production, labour and capital, producing an output which may be used either for consumption or for accumulation.

(2) There are substitution possibilities ex ante, but not ex post, as explained in the introduction.

[3] Cf. Evsey D. Domar [3, p. 7].

[4] That means that we have not subtracted the decline in production caused by old capital being depreciated or scrapped.

(3) From the point of time when an amount of capital is produced, it will shrink according to a given function of its age. The labour input needed to operate the capital and the production achieved shrink proportionately. Even if other interpretations are possible, this is perhaps most easily accepted if we assume that each amount of capital consists of a certain number of identical pieces or units which are operated in the same way and retain their productive efficiency during their entire life time, and that there exists a "death rate table" for these capital units. As special cases, this assumption includes the case of capital of infinite duration and the case for which all capital units have the same finite life time.

(4) New production techniques can be introduced only by means of new capital equipment. This statement is not quite clearly expressed here, but will be clarified by the formulas below.[5]

(5) We assume either that net investment is a constant fraction of net income, or as an alternative, that gross investment is a constant fraction of gross income.[6]

(6) By computing the depreciation necessary to obtain the "net" concepts introduced by (5), a unit of capital is valued in proportion to its remaining life span.

(7) The total labour force is governed by an autonomous pattern of growth.

(8) There will always be full employment of labour and capital.

It is, of course, possible to analyse the effects of points (1) through (7) with some alternative instead of point (8). That will, however, not be done in this paper. At the end of this section, we shall comment on the interpretation of assumption (8).

---

[5] This assumption probably corresponds to the idea expressed by Ingvar Svennilson [21, p. 208] in the following form: "The volume of investment, whether it constitutes a net addition to the stock of capital or not, can therefore be said to measure the rate at which capital is being modernized." Cf. also [22, p. 325]: "Technical progress will, however, mean that old capital goods are eliminated and new ones substituted." Compare further K. Maywald [15]: "It is assumed that only the best production process is used in every unit of equipment added in the course of each year to the total capacity of the industry or economy concerned. Each unit of equipment represents the technological stage of development reached in its year of origin, until the very end of its serviceable life." A similar hypothesis is also crucial, for instance, for important parts of Paul A. Baran's growth analysis [1, cf. e. g., p. 21 and pp. 78-79], and for S. G. Strumilin's analysis [20, cf. in particular p. 175].

[6] These are the savings hypotheses most widely applied in growth analysis. In his Essay VII in [3] ("Depreciation, Replacement, and Growth," *The Economic Journal*, 1953), Domar employs both hypotheses, maintaining that the gross concept is the more "applicable to a centrally directed economy, where a part of total output is set aside for investment, while the net concept is the more applicable to capitalist countries."

The unknowns that enter the model are:

$x(t)$, the rate of production at time t;

$N(t)$, the total labour force at time t;

$K(t)$, the total stock of capital at time t;

$k(t)$, the rate of gross investment at time t, i.e., $k(t)dt$ = the amount of capital produced and put into operation during the time interval $(t,\ t + dt)$;

$n(t)$, the rate of allocation of labour to newly constructed capital, i.e., $n(t)dt$ is the labour input allocated to the operation of the capital $k(t)dt$;

$y(t)$, the rate of gross increase in production at time t, i.e. the rate of increase in $x(t)$ caused by $k(t)$ and $n(t)$;

$V(t)$, the value of the capital stock at time t;

$D(t)$, the rate of depreciation at time t; and

$I(t)$, the rate of net investment at time $t = k(t) - D(t)$.

The main problem now is to provide a formal representation of a production process with the desired properties.

We first introduce the function φ describing the effects on production of the gross investment and the labour input used with this investment:

(2.1) $$y(t) = \varphi(n(t),\ k(t),\ x(t),\ t).$$

If we now assume $\partial\varphi/\partial n > 0$ and $\partial\varphi/\partial k > 0$, $n(t)$ and $k(t)$ will be substitutable factors in the process which causes a certain gross rate of increase, $y(t)$, in production.

It is perhaps reasonable to assume φ to be homogeneous of degree one in n and k. We shall, however, not introduce this specialization in the "general" model.[7]

In (2.1) we have introduced $x(t)$ as an argument besides $n(t)$ and $k(t)$. The reason for this is the following: $n(t)$ and $k(t)$ in no way indicate the "pressure" on natural resources resulting from the rate of production. This pressure may, however, have important consequences. When the pressure is already high, a greater effort in the way of increases in labour

[7] There is no immediate connection between the question of homogeneity of φ in n and k and the question of homogeneity of an ordinary production function in N and K. The arguments raised in connection with the latter question are perhaps more relevant for the role played by the argument x in φ; cf. the following discussion of this point.

Under extremely simplifying conditions we may, however, relate the function φ to traditional microeconomic production functions in the following way. Suppose that any increase in total production is generated through establishment of new firms. Suppose further that all firms which are established simultaneously have identical production functions, the form of which is denoted by $\psi(\bar{n}, \bar{k})$ where $\bar{n}$ and $\bar{k}$ stand for employment and capital per firm. In order to obtain a rate of gross increase y in

and capital may thus be required to obtain a certain increase in production. As this pressure is mainly generated through the extraction from nature of raw materials which are required in rather fixed proportion to the amount of production, $x(t)$ may perhaps be a satisfactory indicator of this so-called pressure. Arguments might, however, be raised in favour of also introducing the total stock of capital $K(t)$ and the total labour input $N(t)$ in (2.1), indicating that the *way* in which production is carried out may possibly influence the degree of pressure on natural resources.

The arguments above imply $\partial\varphi/\partial x \leq 0$.

By contrast, one might perhaps also argue that $\partial\varphi/\partial x > 0$ on the basis of "external economies."

The symbol t is introduced as a separate argument in (2.1) to take care of the possible increase in productivity through improvements in "know-how," discoveries of new natural resources, etc.

Let us now study the shrinkage in capital over time. We introduce a function $f(\tau)$ with the following interpretation : *If an amount $k(t)dt$ of capital is produced in the time interval $(t - dt,t)$, then an amount $f(\tau)k(t)dt$ of this capital will still be active at time $t + \tau$ $(\tau \geq 0)$.* It follows that $f(\tau)$ is monotonically non-increasing and that $f(0) = 1$.

As stated above (property 3) we assume that production shrinks proportionately with capital. This is equivalent to saying that if $k(\tau)d\tau$ (in cooperation with $n(\tau)d\tau$) caused an increase, $y(\tau)d\tau$, in the rate of production in the time interval $(\tau, \tau + d\tau)$, then the rate of production originating from this capital at time t equals $f(t - \tau)y(\tau)d\tau$. It is then obvious that the total rate of production at time t may be obtained by integrating the output from all layers of capital, with due account for the shrinkage:

$$(2.2) \qquad x(t) = \int_{-\infty}^{t} f(t - \tau)y(\tau)d\tau.$$

---

total production, it is then necessary to establish m new firms per unit of time, where $y = m\psi\,(\bar{n},\bar{k})$. We have further $n = m\bar{n}$ and $k = m\bar{k}$ which give $y = m\psi\,(n/m, k/m)$. This defines y as a function of n, k and m. Assume now that there exists for each expansion line in the $(\bar{n},\bar{k})$ space an optimal size of the firm (defined by the scale coefficient being equal to unity). Assume further that firms always attain this size. Then m will be a function $m(n,k)$ of n and k, and it is easily seen that $m(n,k)$ must be homogeneous of degree one in n and k. By these assumptions we get y as a function only of the variables n and k:

$$y = m(n,k)\psi\left(\frac{n}{m(n,k)}, \frac{k}{m(n,k)}\right),$$

and this function is homogeneous of degree one in n and k irrespective of the form and properties of the function ψ.

We have here for simplicity disregarded the arguments x and t in the production functions. The introduction of these arguments in ψ (for the reasons given in the text) does, however, in no way change the reasoning above.

The interpretation of $y(t)$ as the "gross" increase in $x(t)$ will now be clear. Suppose there is no shrinkage in capital, i.e., $f(\tau) \equiv 1$. Then $x(t) = \int_{-\infty}^{t} y(\tau)d\tau$ and consequently $\dot{x}(t) = y(t)$. We may therefore say that the increase $\dot{x}(t)$ consists of a gross increase $y(t)$ due to $n(t)$ and $k(t)$, while a deduction $y(t)-\dot{x}(t)$ is due to the shrinkage of the existing capital. If $f'(\tau)$ exists we have $\dot{x}(t) = y(t) + \int_{-\infty}^{t} f'(t-\tau)y(\tau)d\tau$ where $f' \leq 0$.

A reasonable condition on the function φ is that $\varphi(0,0,x,t) \equiv 0$ identically in x and t. If $n(t) = k(t) = 0$ for $t > \theta$, then we shall have $x(t) = \int_{-\infty}^{\theta} f(t-\tau)y(\tau)d\tau$ for $t \geq \theta$, and the only changes in $x(t)$ for $t > \theta$ will result from shrinkage in the existing capital. In this case, therefore, there will be no effect of increased "know‑how" after the time θ. This illustrates the condition that the increased "know‑how" in our model can be utilized only through the introduction of new capital equipment.

Let us now study the development of the labour input $n(t)$ available at any point of time to man the new capital equipment.

Our basic assumption is

(2.3) $N(t)$ is an exogenously given function of time.

This total labour force will be distributed over capital of different ages. Cooperating with the capital produced in the interval $(\tau, \tau + d\tau)$ will be the labour $n(\tau)d\tau$. At time t this will be reduced to $f(t-\tau)n(\tau)d\tau$. Accordingly, we have the following condition on the development of $n(t)$:

(2.4) $$\int_{-\infty}^{t} f(t-\tau)n(\tau)d\tau = N(t).$$

By a similar integration we obtain an expression for the total amount of capital:

(2.5) $$\int_{-\infty}^{t} f(t-\tau)k(\tau)d\tau = K(t).$$

In the traditional description of the production structure, x is related uniquely to N and K (and possibly also to t as a separate argument). In our approach it is, however, characteristic that it is in general *not* possible to derive any such unique relation which holds regardless of the development of $N(t)$ and $K(t)$. A necessary and sufficient condition for this possibility to exist is that φ be linear in n and k, and that x and t do not enter the function φ as separate arguments. (If the condition $\varphi(0,0,x,t) \equiv 0$ is abandoned, t may also enter φ. Then φ must be linear in *n*, *k* and any unique function of t).

The production model above recognizes fully the impossibility of changing at will the manning of capital equipment once constructed. There exists, however, another kind of rigidity which is not recognized above. To explain this rigidity, let us look at the capital equipment engaged in producing more capital equipment. This equipment is perhaps so constructed that it can produce only capital equipment designed to be manned in a definite way. For instance, a factory producing spinning-jennies may be equipped in such a way that it is only able to produce spinning-jennies which must be operated by a definite amount of labour. If this kind of rigidity is important, it will perhaps be difficult to realize the smooth adaption of capital equipment to the given $n(t)$-development which is implied by our model.[8] It would then perhaps be interesting to construct a model which would lie between the model presented here and one with no substitution possibilities.

Now for capital accumulation or savings. Different assumptions can be conceived of here. The possibility of *choice* open to society would make it desirable to investigate the consequences of various assumptions or to postulate some optimality criteria.[9] However, in order to conform to the most widely accepted models of growth on this point—where this paper does not attempt to make any contribution—I shall treat only the hypothesis of a fixed ratio of savings to income.

In order to define the "net" concepts, we need a rule for the valuation of capital. We then simply value a unit of capital proportionately to its remaining life span.

A newly produced unit of capital will on the average last

$$(2.6) \qquad\qquad T(0) = \int_0^\infty f(\tau)d\tau$$

periods. A unit of capital already η periods of age will on the average have

$$(2.7) \qquad\qquad T(\eta) = \frac{1}{f(\eta)} \int_\eta^\infty f(\tau)d\tau$$

periods left.[10]

We then say that a unit of capital η periods old is worth $T(\eta)/T(0)$ relative to a new one. By an integration similar to (2.5), we then get for the value of the total stock of capital

---

[8] Some rigidities of this kind must be implied by the analysis of Hans W. Singer [18], cf., e.g., p. 182: "The capital-intensive technology—which is the only now existing—. . ." and p. 183: "The absence of a technology which is at the same time modern (in the sense of incorporating the latest state of scientific knowledge) and yet in harmony with the factor endowment of under-developed countries must be classed as another major obstacle to economic development." Further, on p. 181: "In many respects, the technology of one hundred years ago would be preferable and would make their (the underdeveloped countries) economic development easier."

[9] Cf. on this point H. J. A. Kreyberg [12].

[10] Cf. Gabriel A. Preinreich [17, p. 220].

(2.8)
$$V(t) = \frac{1}{T(0)} \int_{-\infty}^{t} f(t-\tau)T(t-\tau)k(\tau)d\tau$$

which gives

(2.9)
$$V(t) = \frac{1}{T(0)} \int_{\tau=-\infty}^{t} k(\tau) \int_{\xi=t-\tau}^{\infty} f(\xi)d\xi d\tau.$$

By differentiation this gives

(2.10)
$$I(t) = \dot{V}(t) = k(t) - \frac{1}{T(0)} K(t),$$

and for depreciation the familiar formula[11]

(2.11)
$$D(t) = \frac{1}{T(0)} K(t).$$

A constant fraction a of savings applied to the net concepts then gives $I(t) = a(x(t) - 1/T(0) K(t))$, which can be written

(2.12)
$$k(t) = ax(t) + \frac{1}{T(0)} (1-a)K(t).$$

If we want to operate with a constant savings quota applied to the gross concepts, we need only neglect the last term in (2.12).

Considering our model as a whole now, we recognize that (2.1), (2.2), (2.3), (2.4), (2.5), and (2.12) where $T(0)$ is defined by (2.6) constitute 6 equations containing the six time functions $y(t)$, $n(t)$, $k(t)$, $N(t)$, $K(t)$, $x(t)$. This will be referred to in the following sections as our "general model."

One may now ask how it is that we have obtained a determinate model without any reference to the behaviour of the producers? In fact we have substitution possibilities "at the margin," and certain assumptions are therefore necessary to explain this behaviour.

The answer to this question is that a certain behaviour is tacitly implied by our assuming that $n(t)$ and $k(t)$ are always absorbed.

One explanation may be that our model applies to a centrally planned economy which at any time chooses to construct new equipment in such a way that the disposable labour is absorbed.

Another explanation may be that our model applies to an economy where production is governed by the profit motive. In that case a certain development of wages and the interest rate is implied by our model, namely, that development which makes entrepreneurs choose to absorb both the flow of savings and the flow of disposable labour at all times. These time functions for wages and the interest rate might be linked to our model. Many kinds of rigidities may, however, operate to make such smooth adaption impossible.[12]

---

[11] Cf. e.g., Essay VII in Domar [3].

[12] Cf. Robert M. Solow [19], D. Hamberg [8] and the discussion by Pilvin, Harrod, and Domar.

If the wage rate and the the rate of interest should move with rather different time shapes, a special problem would arise in connection with old capital. Capital which is constructed for instance at a time when wages are rather low and interest rates rather high may at a time of higher wages and lower interest rates be so unprofitable in use that it is scrapped prematurely or left idle for a while. Such a development may also be reflected in the valuation of the capital stock. These problems, however, are not taken care of formally in our model.[13]

In the case of a profit-motivated production process, it might be interesting to reverse the point of view described above and accepted in our model. Instead of assuming full employment of labour and capital, and implying tacitly the necessary development of wages and interest, we might assume certain developments for wages and interest, perhaps related to monetary aspects of the economy, and try to compute the time function for the possible unemployment which might occur. Such an attempt will however not be made in this paper.

The model above looks rather unmanageable in its general form. In the following sections we shall therefore work out the solutions for some special cases which are quite near to hand. The reason for working out the solution for different cases—that is, with different forms of the production function φ and the shrinkage function f—is partly that it is not obvious what functional forms are most realistic, and partly that I find it rather difficult to work out the solution if I try to combine that form of the production function (and the introduction of new techniques) which I personally find most interesting with that form of the shrinkage function which I would prefer if I had to choose.[14]

3. THE CASE WITH CAPITAL OF INFINITE DURATION

Rather important simplifications of the model are obtained if we consider the case with capital of infinite duration, i.e., the case in which

$$(3.1) \qquad\qquad f(\tau) \equiv 1 \qquad\qquad \text{for } \tau \geq 0.$$

[13] The technical changes which result from increasing "know-how," may, of course, also influence the valuation of capital. It is, however, not obvious how this ought to be introduced in the model, and I have therefore chosen to disregard it.

[14] In correspondence Robert Solow has made the following comment on an ambiguity which is not discussed above: "There is a little ambiguity involved in treating the 'physical' nature of the capital good as changing over time but at the same time assuming that the same commodity can be consumed without change. This of course is simply an aggregation difficulty; in a more complete model consumption goods will be separate from capital goods. But then in a more complete model the treatment of capital goods becomes more straightforward too. As time goes on and technical change occurs, some capital goods will be affected, others not. And one would naturally introduce different capital-labour substitution possibilities for different (including older and newer) machines, with rigidity appearing as a limiting case."

In that case (2.2) gives

(3.2)
$$x(t) = \int_{-\infty}^{t} y(\tau)d\tau.$$

Equation (2.4) gives

(3.3)
$$\int_{-\infty}^{t} n(\tau)d\tau = N(t),$$

and (2.12) gives simply

(3.4)
$$k(t) = ax(t)$$

as $T(0) = +\infty$.

In this case, there can, of course, exist costs of maintenance and repair. These costs must, however, be constant over time for every piece of capital. We can then define y and x net of these costs.

As a rather satisfactory form of φ we shall accept

(3.5)
$$\varphi(n,k,x,t) = A n^a k^b x^{-c} e^{\varepsilon t}$$

with a, b, c and ε constant. Here $a + b = 1$ is possibly a realistic hypothesis, but in general we shall not make this assumption. The coefficient c is most probably ≥ 0, but we might, as mentioned in the discussion of the "general" model, have $c < 0$ as a consequence of "external economies." ε is the relative increase in productivity per period as a result of increased "know - how," etc. In general, we shall therefore have $\varepsilon \geq 0$.

It is seen that both x and t have a neutral effect in φ in the sense that the marginal rate of substitution between n and k is not influenced by x and t.

Let us further assume an exponential growth of the labour force N, i.e.,

(3.6)
$$N(t) = N_0 e^{\nu t}$$

where ν is constant.

By differentiating (3.3) we then obtain

(3.7)
$$n(t) = \dot{N}(t) = n_0 e^{\nu t} \qquad \text{where } n_0 = \nu N_0.$$

By differentiating (3.2) we obtain $\dot{x}(t) = y(t)$. By means of (3.4), (3.5) and (3.7) we then get

(3.8)
$$\dot{x} = [A n_0^a a^b] x^{b - c} e^{(a\nu + \varepsilon)t}.$$

This is a Bernoullian differential equation[15] which can be solved to give

(3.9)
$$x(t) = \left[\frac{A n_0^a a^b (1 - b + c)}{a\nu + \varepsilon} e^{(a\nu + \varepsilon)t} + C \right]^{\frac{1}{1 - b + c}}$$

where C can be determined by means of $x(0)$. The solution is not valid for $a\nu + \varepsilon = 0$. We shall, however, disregard this special situation assuming $a\nu + \varepsilon > 0$.

---

[15] Cf. e.g., E. L. Ince [10, p. 22].

As t increases, it is here easily seen that the growth rate of $x(t)$ converges,

(3.10) $$\frac{\dot{x}(t)}{x(t)} \to \frac{a\nu + \varepsilon}{1 - b + c} \quad \text{as } t \to +\infty.$$

If we divide the solution for $x(t)$ by $N(t)$, we obtain for production per head,

(3.11) $$\frac{x(t)}{N(t)} = \frac{1}{N_0} \left[\frac{An_0^a a^b (1 - b + c)}{a\nu + \varepsilon} e^{(\varepsilon - (1-a-b+c)\nu)t} + Ce^{-(1-b+c)\nu t} \right]^{\frac{1}{1-b+c}}$$

(where $n_0 = \nu N_0$ according to (3.7)).

Here, of course, different cases may be discussed. We shall, however, consider only the case for which

(3.12) $$a > 0, b > 0, a + b \leq 1, c \geq 0, \varepsilon > 0, \nu > 0.$$

Then the last term within the bracket in (3.11) will vanish as t increases, and the solution will converge asymptotically,

(3.13) $$\frac{x(t)}{N(t)} \to \frac{1}{N_0} \left[\frac{An_0^a a^b (1 - b + c)}{a\nu + \varepsilon} \right]^{\frac{1}{1-b+c}} e^{\left[\frac{a\nu + \varepsilon}{1-b+c} - \nu \right] t}.$$

For the growth rate in (3.13) to be positive, it is necessary and sufficient that

(3.14) $$\nu < \frac{\varepsilon}{1 - (a + b) + c} \left(= \frac{\varepsilon}{c} \text{ if } a + b = 1 \right),$$

where the right hand side is always positive under our assumptions (3.12). (3.14) illustrates how an upper bound is set for the population growth by the requirement that average production shall not decline, and how this bound is influenced by technical change (the numerator of (3.14)) and by the scale properties of the production function (the denominator of (3.14)).

The most remarkable feature of the solution above is perhaps that the asymptotic growth rates given in (3.10) and (3.13) are independent of the propensity to save a.[16] Let us illustrate this by assuming two countries which are similar in all respects except for a. Asymptotically both countries will then obtain the same relative rate of growth in production per head, x/N, (and of course also in total production, x). It is, however, seen by the way in which a enters (3.13) that this asymptotic curve will lie on a higher level—and therefore the absolute rate of growth be greater—in the country with the higher propensity to save. This also implies that if both countries start from the same initial position, the country with the higher propensity to save will start out with the higher relative growth rate "before the asymptote is reached."

---

[16] This feature is not, however, dependent on our special way of introducing substitution in the model. A similar conclusion can be obtained by means of models with substitution possibilities of the traditional kind.

4. THE CASE WITH EXPONENTIAL SHRINKAGE OF CAPITAL

Let us now assume that the capital shrinkage function f defined in Section 2 has the exponential form

(4.1) $$f(\tau) = e^{-\delta\tau}.$$

This would be the case if capital units are eliminated through "accidents," and for every unit of capital existing at a point of time t there exists a probability δdt that it will be destroyed by an accident in the time interval $(t, t + dt)$, where δ is a constant independent of the age of the capital unit.

For $x(t)$ we have then

(4.2) $$x(t) = \int_{-\infty}^{t} e^{-\delta(t-\tau)}y(\tau)d\tau,$$

and similarly for $N(t)$ and $K(t)$,

(4.3) $$\int_{-\infty}^{t} e^{-\delta(t-\tau)}n(\tau)d\tau = N(t)$$

and

(4.4) $$\int_{-\infty}^{t} e^{-\delta(t-\tau)}k(\tau)d\tau = K(t).$$

Since

(4.5) $$T(0) = \int_{0}^{\infty} e^{-\delta\tau}d\tau = \frac{1}{\delta},$$

the savings equation (2.12) reduces to

(4.6) $$k(t) = ax(t) + \delta(1 - a)K(t).$$

For the growth of the labour force we shall assume, as in the preceeding section, that $N(t) = N_0 e^{\nu t}$.

In this case it turns out to be rather difficult to solve the system if we apply the function (3.5) with $c \neq 0$. Let us therefore study the special case in which

(4.7) $$\varphi(n,k,x,t) = An^a k^b e^{\varepsilon t}.$$

By differentiating (4.2) we now obtain

(4.8) $$\dot{x}(t) = y(t) - \delta x(t),$$

and similarly for $N(t)$ and $K(t)$. For $n(t)$ this now gives

(4.9) $$n(t) = n_0 e^{\nu t} \qquad \text{where } n_0 = N_0(\nu + \delta).$$

The labour force available for new capital at any time consists therefore of the growth in the total labour force plus the workers who are set free from old capital which is eliminated.

By means of the equation for $K(t)$ and (4.6) we obtain

(4.10) $$\dot{k}(t) = a\dot{x}(t) + \delta ax(t) - \delta ak(t).$$

By means of (4.7), (4.8) and (4.9) we then get the following differential equation for $k(t)$:

$$(4.11) \qquad \dot{k} = [aAn_0^a]\, e^{(a\nu+\varepsilon)t}k^b - a\delta k.$$

This is a Bernoullian equation of a slightly more complicated form than (3.8). It is solved to give

$$(4.12) \qquad k(t) = \left[\frac{An_0^a a(1-b)}{a\nu+\varepsilon+(1-b)a\delta}\, e^{(a\nu+\varepsilon)t} + Be^{-(1-b)a\delta t}\right]^{\frac{1}{1-b}},$$

where B is determined by initial conditions.

If $\delta = 0$, and accordingly $k(t) = ax(t)$, it is easily seen that (4.12) corresponds to (3.9) for $c = 0$. In the case of $\delta \neq 0$, it is not so easy to obtain the solution for $x(t)$.

We see, however, that the last term in (4.12) tends to vanish for increasing t. Let us therefore consider only the asymptotic solution

$$(4.13) \qquad \bar{k}(t) = \left[\frac{An_0^a a(1-b)}{a\nu+\varepsilon+(1-b)a\delta}\right]^{\frac{1}{1-b}} e^{\frac{a\nu+\varepsilon}{1-b}t}$$

which shows a constant relative growth rate.[17] The corresponding solution for $x(t)$, which we shall denote $\bar{x}(t)$, is then more easily obtained by means of (4.8) when we insert for y from (4.7):

$$(4.14) \qquad \bar{x}(t) = Ge^{-\delta t} + He^{\frac{a\nu+\varepsilon}{1-b}t},$$

where G is determined by initial conditions and H is given by

$$(4.15) \qquad H = \frac{(1-b)\, An_0^a \left[\dfrac{An_0^a a(1-b)}{a\nu+\varepsilon+(1-b)a\delta}\right]^{\frac{b}{1-b}}}{a\nu+\varepsilon+\delta(1-b)}.$$

Since the first term in (4.14) tends to vanish, we observe that $x(t)$ in this case will tend to increase with the same relative rate of growth as in the case studied in the perceeding section (for $c = 0$) regardless of δ (cf. (3.10)).

It is seen that under the conditions (3.12) $H > 0$. Furthermore, H is larger, the larger is a. The role played by δ is more complicated. This seems reasonable since δ not only represents the shrinkage in capital but also influences the accumulation of capital through (4.6) and, under our assumptions regarding the production process, also influences the speed with which new techniques can be introduced.[18]

---

[17] A discussion of the admissibility of this kind of approximation can be found in Hans Brems [2]. Cf. also Evsey Domar [3], Essay IX ("A Soviet Model of Growth"), pp. 231-32.

[18] Cf. the discussion of the influences of the average life time of capital in Domar [3, Essay VII].

The development of the average income x/N can be studied in a way similar to that in the preceeding section.

In the case discussed in this section, important simplification is obtained if we substitute for the net savings equation, (4.6), a gross savings equation,

$$(4.16) \qquad k(t) = \beta x(t).$$

It is then rather easy to solve the system even if we retain the production function (3.5) with c not necessarily equal to zero. The solution is

$$(4.17) \qquad x(t) = \left[C'e^{-(1-b+c)\delta t} + \frac{(1 - b + c)A n_0^a \beta^b}{av + \varepsilon + (1 - b + c)\delta} e^{(av+\varepsilon)t} \right]^{\frac{1}{1-b+c}}$$

where C' is determined by initial conditions. For $\delta = 0$, this solution clearly corresponds to (3.9). Since the first term in the bracket tends to vanish for increasing t when $\delta > 0$, a discussion of the long range development of x and x/N will follow lines similar to those of Section 3.

In this case δ also does not influence the asymptotic relative growth rate. But δ influences the *level* of the asymptotic development. It is possible for instance (remembering that $n_0 = N_0 \, (v + \delta)$ and considering N_0 as given) to demonstrate that if $a + b = 1$ and $c = 0$, we shall have the following situation: If $\varepsilon = 0$ this level will be higher the smaller is δ. But for $\varepsilon > 0$, it is possible that the level is higher the higher is δ. There will then exist a (positive) optimal δ which is larger, the larger is ε. This clearly illustrates the interrelations between δ and the speed with which new techniques are introduced within our production theory framework.

Similar cases will, of course, exist also under assumptions less restrictive than that $a + b = 1$ and $c = 0$.

What is said here is that if we have a sufficiently fast technical development, there will exist an optimal positive δ (which implies an optimal average life time for capital units) *even if we disregard the different costs of producing capital equipment with higher and lower δ.* If these cost differences are taken into account, a positive optimal value of δ will, of course, exist *a fortiori.* It would be interesting to extend our analysis in this direction in order to obtain rules for a rational selection of δ in different cases.[19]

5. THE CASE WITH A FIXED LIFE TIME FOR EACH UNIT OF CAPITAL

In this section we shall assume $f(\tau)$ to have the following form:

$$(5.1) \qquad f(\tau) = \begin{cases} 1 \text{ for } \tau \leqq \theta, \\ 0 \text{ for } \tau > \theta. \end{cases}$$

This means that every unit of capital has a finite life time θ, and that it retains its original productive capacity all through this life time.[20]

[19] Some elements for such an analysis might be found in S. G. Strumilin [20].

[20] This is the assumption adopted for instance by Domar [3, Essay VII] and by Hans Brems [2].

This further gives

(5.2) $$T(0) = \theta.$$

In this case it seems rather difficult to solve the system with production functions such as those applied in the preceeding sections. We shall therefore now have to be content with a linear and homogeneous function

(5.3) $$\varphi(n,k,x,t) = an + bk,$$

where a and b are constants.

It would perhaps be possible to add a term depending on t on the right hand side of (5.3). This would, however, not satisfy the restriction $\varphi(0,0,x,t) \equiv 0$ and would therefore not be altogether meaningful within the framework of our approach. At the end of this section we shall, however, briefly discuss the case in which a is not constant, but depends on t.

From (2.2), (2.4) and (2.5) we now get

(5.4) $$x(t) = \int_{t-\theta}^{t} y(\tau)d\tau = aN(t) + bK(t),$$

which means that there now exists a production function relating x uniquely to N and K. Formally our model in this case does not, therefore, differ from the more common growth models on this point. The concrete meaning underlying the relation is, however, still different from that of the more common production functions, as explained in Sections 1 and 2.

For the savings function we have

(5.5) $$k(t) = ax(t) + \frac{1}{\theta}(1 - a)K(t).$$

Assuming as before that $N(t) = N_0e^{\nu t}$, we obtain for $n(t)$:

(5.6) $$n(t) = n_0e^{\nu t} \quad \text{where } n_0 = \frac{\nu N_0}{1-e^{-\nu\theta}}.$$

Instead of the usual differential equations as were obtained in the preceeding sections, we now get a mixed difference-differential equation to solve:

(5.7) $$\dot{k}(t) = \gamma[k(t) - k(t-\theta)] + aa\nu N_0e^{\nu t}$$

where

(5.8) $$\gamma = \frac{1}{\theta}[1 + a(\theta b - 1)].$$

Such an equation may show many curious solutions, among them discontinuous ones. The discontinuous solutions are, however, less interesting, at any rate in growth analysis. We shall therefore restrict our discussion to continuous solutions.

The results of James and Belz [11] then imply that the solution of the homogeneous equation corresponding to (5.7) can be expressed as a sum of exponential expressions (with real and complex exponents).

Let us insert an expression $Ce^{\varrho t}$ for $k(t)$ in the equation obtained by disregarding the last term in (5.7). We then get the characteristic equation[21]

(5.9) $$\varrho = \gamma(1 - e^{-\varrho \theta}).$$

Let us first consider only the real solutions for ϱ, which are the most interesting from the point of view of growth analysis. At the end of this section we shall briefly comment on the complex solutions.

We observe first that $\varrho = 0$ is a solution of (5.9). The equation has however one more real solution if $\gamma \theta = [1 + a(\theta b - 1)] \neq 1$.[22] It is also easy to demonstrate that this solution will be a value $\varrho > 0$ if $\gamma \theta > 1$.

The latter case is, however, the more interesting from an economic point of view. The condition $\theta b > 1$, which assures $\gamma \theta > 1$, may in fact be obviously interpreted as the condition for the profitability of round-about production through the employment of capital, b representing the productivity of capital and θ its productive life time. We can therefore conclude that (5.9) has two real solutions, one equal to zero and one positive, so that we can write the solution for the homogeneous part of (5.7) as

(5.10) $$k^*(t) = C_1 + C_2 e^{\varrho t}$$

where ϱ now designates the positive root of (5.9) and C_1 and C_2 are arbitrary constants.

By adding the particular solution resulting from the last term in (5.7), we obtain the following solution for $k(t)$ (where we are still disregarding the complex solutions of (5.9)):

(5.11) $$k(t) = C_1 + C_2 e^{\varrho t} + \frac{a a \nu N_0}{\nu - \gamma(1 - e^{-\nu \theta})} e^{\nu t}.$$

For $x(t)$ we obtain by integrating $k(t)$ to give $K(t)$ and by inserting in (5.4):

(5.12) $$x(t) = C' + C'' e^{\varrho t} + a N_0 \left[1 + \frac{ab(1 - e^{-\nu \theta})}{\nu - \gamma(1 - e^{-\nu \theta})} \right] e^{\nu t}$$

where C' and C'' are constants which may be determined by means of initial conditions.[23]

For the average income we obtain

(5.13) $$\frac{x(t)}{N(t)} = \frac{1}{N_0} C' e^{-\nu t} + \frac{1}{N_0} C'' e^{(\varrho - \nu)t} + a\left[1 + \frac{ab(1 - e^{-\nu \theta})}{\nu - \gamma(1 - e^{-\nu \theta})} \right].$$

If now $\nu > \varrho$, the first two terms of (5.13) tend to vanish, and the last term remains as a constant asymptote. In this case it is easy to demonstrate that $\nu > \gamma(1 - e^{-\nu \theta})$ so that the asymptotic value for the average income is greater than a, which is obviously reasonable.

[21] Our equation (5.9) is equivalent to equation (5.3) in Domar [**3**, Essay VII].

[22] If $\gamma \theta$ should be equal to one, $\varrho = 0$ would be a double root.

[23] If we require $K(t) \to 0$ for $t \to -\infty$, then $C' = C_1 = 0$.

If $\nu < \varrho$, the second term on the right hand side of (5.13) will dominate in the long run. It is easy to prove that C'' must in this case be positive, provided that $K(t) \to 0$ for $t \to -\infty$, and x/N will therefore *increase* in the long run.

The special case $\varrho = \nu$ shall not be discussed here. (5.13) does not give the general (real, continuous) solution in this case.

The values of C' and C'' might be discussed further with reference to initial conditions. This discussion is, however, tedious and will be omitted here.

As regards the dependence of the growth rate ϱ on the parameters of the model discussed in this section, I shall only mention that ϱ now depends essentially on the propensity to save, a, and is higher the higher is a. For different values of a we have then the following possibilities: For low values of a, $\varrho < \nu$ and average income tends to a stationary value. This level is higher, the higher is a. When a is above a certain critical value, average income will, however, tend to increase in the long run, and increase faster, the higher is a.

In addition to the real solutions discussed above, the characteristic equation (5.9) contains an infinity of complex solutions. By means of the results of Frisch and Holme [6] it is easily seen[24] that in our case (with $\theta b > 1$) these complex solutions will correspond to one cycle with a period in each of the intervals (the bounds included)

$$(5.14) \qquad \left(\frac{\theta}{j + \frac{1}{2}}, \frac{\theta}{j}\right) \qquad (j = 1,2,3,\ldots),$$

i.e., in the intervals $\left(\dfrac{2}{3}\theta, \theta\right)$, $\left(\dfrac{2}{5}\theta, \dfrac{\theta}{2}\right)$, $\left(\dfrac{2\theta}{7}, \dfrac{\theta}{3}\right)$, etc.

As regards the dampening or explosion of the fluctuations, I have not reached any really general result. It is, however, rather easy to demonstrate[25]

[24] Cf. Table 2, case $C > 1$. In our case, Frisch and Holme's parameters a and c are both equal to our γ, and their C equals $\gamma\theta - \text{Log}_e \, \gamma\theta$, which is greater than 1 because we have assumed $\gamma\theta > 1$.

[25] I shall briefly give the proof by help of the results of Frisch and Holme [6]. Write $\varrho = \beta + ia$ (where a and β are of course not identical with the propensities to save used in the text). We further write $u = a\theta$ and $v = \beta\theta$. A necessary and sufficient condition for dampening is then $v < 0$. By Frisch and Holme's equation (25) we have

(i) $$v = \text{Log}_e\left(\gamma\theta \, \frac{\sin u}{u}\right)$$

where we have introduced our γ instead of Frisch and Holme's c. Now Frisch and Holme further state (p. 232) that the u's corresponding to the cyclic components in our case $[C = \gamma\theta - \text{Log}_e \gamma\theta > 1$ since $\gamma\theta > 1]$ will lie in the intervals

(ii) $$2j\pi \leqq u \leqq (2j + 1)\,\pi \qquad (j = 1,2,\ldots\ldots),$$

that means that 2π is a lower bound for any u. Since $\sin u \leqq 1$, $\gamma\theta < 2\pi$ then implies $\gamma\theta \sin u/u < 1$, which by (i) is sufficient for $v < 0$ and thus for dampening.

These results are in conformity with some results by Hans Neisser [16] and by Domar [4] in similar cases. Their analyses are however carried out in terms of pure difference equations.

that all the cycles are damped for acceptable values of γ and θ, a sufficient condition for dampening being that

(5.15) $\qquad\qquad \gamma\theta < 2\pi, \quad \text{i.e.,} \; \theta b < 1 + \dfrac{2\pi - 1}{a}.$

With the interpretation of θb given above, it is very unlikely that this condition should not be fulfilled.

The possible relevance of the results in this section for business cycle analysis and for the question of interaction between growth and cycles shall not be discussed here.

In the case discussed in this section, it seems to be rather difficult to introduce increasing technical efficiency in a satisfactory way. We might, however, introduce a changing marginal productivity of labour by leting a be a given exponential function of time:

(5.16) $\qquad\qquad \varphi(n,k,x,t) = a_0 e^{\lambda t} n + bk$

where a_0 is the marginal productivity of labour at $t = 0$ and λ is the (constant) relative rate of increase in this productivity. This satisfies $\varphi(0,0,x,t) \equiv 0$. However it obviously represents a quite special non-neutral change in productivity.

The solution for $x(t)$ with the assumption (5.16) takes the form (5.12) where $\nu + \lambda$ is substituted for ν and $a_0 (1 - e^{-(\nu+\lambda)\theta})/(1 - e^{-\nu\theta})$ is substituted for a.

The solution for $x(t)/N(t)$ then takes the form

(5.17) $\qquad\qquad \dfrac{x(t)}{N(t)} = Pe^{-\nu t} + Qe^{(\rho-\nu)t} + Re^{\lambda t}$

where P, Q and R are constants. (This solution is not valid in the special case, $\varrho = \nu + \lambda$.) When $\lambda > \varrho - \nu$, so that the last term in (5.17) will dominate in the long run, it is easily seen that R (which is independent of the initial situation except for a_0) is positive.

6. CONCLUDING REMARKS

As stated in the introductory remarks and in Section 2 of this paper, I find the hypothesis of "ex ante" substitution possibilities, but no such possibilities "ex post," more realistic than the hypotheses about the production process most widely accepted in *theoretical* growth analysis. In fact, I have the feeling that the hypothesis applied in this paper is closer to the experience of many students of economic growth who approach these questions from a "practical" point of view, and it may possibly be helpful in removing some of the "guilty conscience" of some theorists in the field who rely either on fixed coefficients or on full substitutability in a "classical" sense.

In particular, 1 find the hypothesis outlined in this paper important when technical progress is to enter the analysis as a main factor.

Sections 3, 4 and 5 show that our hypothesis does not make our models unmanageable in cases where on points other than the substitution possibilities we rely on hypotheses usually applied in theoretical growth analysis.

It seems that the conclusions are in some respects more sensitive to shifts in the *form* of the production function than they are to the shift from the assumption of substitutability in the usual sense to our assumption of substitutability only "at the margin." If the study had been directed more specially towards such subjects as, say, the importance of the rate of investment for the possibilities of adopting new techniques, the importance of obsolescence in the process of growth, the relation between population growth and "structural" unemployment, etc., then the conclusions would depend more specifically on the choice of what kind of substitutability one assumes.

Institute of Economics, University of Oslo

REFERENCES

[1] BARAN, PAUL A.: *The Political Economy of Growth*, New York: Monthly Review Press, 1957.

[2] BREMS, HANS: "Constancy of the Proportionate Equilibrium Rate of Growth: Result or Assumption?" *The Review of Economic Studies*, Vol. XXIV, February, 1957, pp. 131-138.

[3] DOMAR, EVSEY D.: *Essays in the Theory of Economic Growth*, New York: Oxford University Press, 1957.

[4] ———: "Depreciation, Replacement and Growth—and Fluctuations," *The Economic Journal*, Vol. LXVII, December, 1957, pp. 655-658.

[5] EISNER, ROBERT: "Underemployment Equilibrium Rates of Growth," *The American Economic Review*, Vol. XLII, December, 1952, pp. 820-831.

[6] FRISCH, RAGNAR AND HARALD HOLME: "The Characteristic Solutions of a Mixed Difference and Differential Equation Occurring in Economic Dynamics," *Econometrica*, Vol. III, April, 1935, pp. 225-239.

[7] HAAVELMO, TRYGVE: *A Study in the Theory of Economic Evolution*. Contributions to Economic Analysis, Amsterdam: North-Holland Publishing Company, 1954.

[8] HAMBERG, D.: "Full Capacity vs. Full Employment Growth," *The Quarterly Journal of Economics* 1952. Discussion by HAROLD PILVIN, R. F. HARROD, and EVSEY D. DOMAR, *The Quarterly Journal of Economics* 1953.

[9] HARROD, R. F.: "An Essay in Dynamic Economics," *The Economic Journal* 1953.

[10] INCE, E. L.: *Integration of Ordinary Differential Equations*, London: Oliver and Boyd, 1956.

[11] JAMES, R. W., AND M. H. BELZ: "The Significance of the Characteristic Solutions of Mixed Difference and Differential Equations," *Econometrica*, Vol. 6, October, 1938, pp. 326-343.

[12] KREYBERG, H. J. A.: "Economic Growth and Economic Welfare," *Statsøkonomisk Tidsskrift*, 1956 (Reprint No. 4 from the Oslo University Institute of Economics. In Norwegian with an English summary).

[13] LANGE, OSKAR: "Some Observations on Input-Output Analysis," *Sankhya*, 1957.

[14] LEONTIEF, WASSILY et al.: *Studies in the Structure of the American Economy*, New York: Oxford University Press, 1953.

[15] MAYWALD, K.: "The Best and the Average in Productivity Studies and in Long-Term Forecasting," *The Productivity Measurement Review*, No. 9 (Reprint Series No. 132, University of Cambridge, Department of Applied Economics.)

[16] NEISSER, HANS: "Depreciation, Replacements and Regular Growth," *The Economic Journal*, Vol. LXV, March, 1955, pp. 159-161.

[17] PREINREICH, GABRIEL A. D.: "Annual Survey of Economic Theory: The Theory of Depreciation," *Econometrica*, Vol. 6, January, 1938, pp. 219-241.

[18] SINGER, HANS W.: "Problems of Industrialization of Under-Developed Countries," in LEON H. DUPRIEZ, ed.: *Economic Progress: Papers and Proceedings of a Round Table Held by the International Economic Association*. Louvain, 1955.

[19] SOLOW, ROBERT M.: "A Contribution to the Theory of Economic Growth," *The Quarterly Journal of Economics*, Vol. XLL, February, 1956, pp. 65-94.

[20] STRUMILIN, S. G.: "The Time Factor in Capital Investment Projects," (Translated from the Russian.) in *International Economic Papers No. 1*, London and New York, 1951.

[21] SVENNILSON, INGVAR: *Growth and Stagnation in the European Economy*, Geneva, ECE, 1954.

[22] ————: "Capital Accumulation and National Wealth in an Expanding Economy," in *25 Economic Essays in Honour of Erik Lindahl*, Stockholm: *Ekonomisk Tidskrift*, 1956.

[23] TINBERGEN, JAN: "Zur Theorie der Langfristigen Wirtschaftsentwicklung," *Weltwirtschaftliches Archiv*, 1942.

[24] VALAVANIS-VAIL, STEFAN: "An Econometric Model of Growth: U.S.A., 1869-1953," *The American Economic Review*, Vol. XLV, May, 1955, pp. 208-221.

[25] VERDOORN, P. J.: "Complementarity and Long-Range Projections," *Econometrica*, Vol. 24, October, 1956, pp. 429-450.

Econometrica, Vol. 29, No. 3 (July 1961)

RATIONAL EXPECTATIONS AND THE THEORY OF PRICE MOVEMENTS[1]

BY JOHN F. MUTH

In order to explain fairly simply how expectations are formed, we advance the hypothesis that they are essentially the same as the predictions of the relevant economic theory. In particular, the hypothesis asserts that the economy generally does not waste information, and that expectations depend specifically on the structure of the entire system. Methods of analysis, which are appropriate under special conditions, are described in the context of an isolated market with a fixed production lag. The interpretative value of the hypothesis is illustrated by introducing commodity speculation into the system.

1. INTRODUCTION

THAT EXPECTATIONS of economic variables may be subject to error has, for some time, been recognized as an important part of most explanations of changes in the level of business activity. The "ex ante" analysis of the Stockholm School—although it has created its fair share of confusion—is a highly suggestive approach to short-run problems. It has undoubtedly been a major motivation for studies of business expectations and intentions data.

As a systematic theory of fluctuations in markets or in the economy, the approach is limited, however, because it does not include an explanation of the way expectations are formed. To make dynamic economic models complete, various expectations formulas have been used. There is, however, little evidence to suggest that the presumed relations bear a resemblance to the way the economy works.[2]

What kind of information is used and how it is put together to frame an estimate of future conditions is important to understand because the character of dynamic processes is typically very sensitive to the way expectations are influenced by the actual course of events. Furthermore, it is often necessary to make sensible predictions about the way expectations would change when either the amount of available information or the struc-

Errata appear following the references.

[1] Research undertaken for the project, *Planning and Control of Industrial Operations*, under contract with the Office of Naval Research. Contract N-onr-760-(01), Project NR 047011. Reproduction of this paper in whole or in part is permitted for any purpose of the United States Government.

An earlier version of this paper was presented at the Winter Meeting of the Econometric Society, Washington, D.C., December 30, 1959.

I am indebted to Z. Griliches, A. G. Hart, M. H. Miller, F. Modigliani, M. Nerlove, and H. White for their comments.

[2] This comment also applies to dynamic theories in which expectations do not explicitly appear. See, for example, Arrow, Block, and Hurwicz [3, 4].

ture of the system is changed. (This point is similar to the reason we are curious about demand functions, consumption functions, and the like, instead of only the reduced form "predictors" in a simultaneous equation system.) The area is important from a statistical standpoint as well, because parameter estimates are likely to be seriously biased towards zero if the wrong variable is used as the expectation.

The objective of this paper is to outline a theory of expectations and to show that the implications are—as a first approximation—consistent with the relevant data.

2. THE "RATIONAL EXPECTATIONS" HYPOTHESIS

Two major conclusions from studies of expectations data are the following:

1. Averages of expectations in an industry are more accurate than naive models and as accurate as elaborate equation systems, although there are considerable cross-sectional differences of opinion.

2. Reported expectations generally underestimate the extent of changes that actually take place.

In order to explain these phenomena, I should like to suggest that expectations, since they are informed predictions of future events, are essentially the same as the predictions of the relevant economic theory.[3] At the risk of confusing this purely descriptive hypothesis with a pronouncement as to what firms ought to do, we call such expectations "rational." It is sometimes argued that the assumption of rationality in economics leads to theories inconsistent with, or inadequate to explain, observed phenomena, especially changes over time (e.g., Simon [29]). Our hypothesis is based on exactly the opposite point of view: that dynamic economic models do not assume enough rationality.

The hypothesis can be rephrased a little more precisely as follows: that expectations of firms (or, more generally, the subjective probability distribution of outcomes) tend to be distributed, for the same information set, about the prediction of the theory (or the "objective" probability distributions of outcomes).

The hypothesis asserts three things: (1) Information is scarce, and the economic system generally does not waste it. (2) The way expectations are formed depends specifically on the structure of the relevant system describing the economy. (3) A "public prediction," in the sense of Grunberg and Modigliani [14], will have no substantial effect on the operation of the economic system (unless it is based on inside information). This is not quite the same thing as stating that the marginal revenue product of economics is zero,

[3] We show in Section 5 that the hypothesis is consistent with these two phenomena.

because expectations of a single firm may still be subject to greater error than the theory.

It *does not* assert that the scratch work of entrepreneurs resembles the system of equations in any way; nor does it state that predictions of entrepreneurs are perfect or that their expectations are all the same.

For purposes of analysis, we shall use a specialized form of the hypothesis. In particular, we assume:

1. The random disturbances are normally distributed.
2. Certainty equivalents exist for the variables to be predicted.
3. The equations of the system, including the expectations formulas, are linear.

These assumptions are not quite so strong as may appear at first because any one of them virtually implies the other two.[4]

3. PRICE FLUCTUATIONS IN AN ISOLATED MARKET

We can best explain what the hypothesis is all about by starting the analysis in a rather simple setting: short-period price variations in an isolated market with a fixed production lag of a commodity which cannot be stored.[5] The market equations take the form

$$C_t = -\beta p_t \qquad \text{(Demand)},$$
(3.1) $$P_t = \gamma p_t^e + u_t, \qquad \text{(Supply)},$$
$$P_t = C_t \qquad \text{(Market equilibrium)},$$

where: P_t represents the number of units produced in a period lasting as long as the production lag,

C_t is the amount consumed,

p_t is the market price in the tth period,

p_t^e is the market price expected to prevail during the tth period on the basis of information available through the $(t-1)$'st period,

u_t is an error term—representing, say, variations in yields due to weather.

All the variables used are deviations from equilibrium values.

---

[4] As long as the variates have a finite variance, a linear regression function exists if and only if the variates are normally distributed. (See Allen [2] and Ferguson [12].) The certainty-equivalence property follows from the linearity of the derivative of the appropriate quadratic profit or utility function. (See Simon [28] and Theil [32].)

[5] It is possible to allow both short- and long-run supply relations on the basis of dynamic costs. (See Holt *et al.* [17, esp. Chapters 2-4, 19]). More difficult are the supply effects of changes in the number of firms. The relevance of the cost effects has been emphasized by Buchanan [7] and Akerman [1]. To include them at this point would, however, take us away from the main objective of the paper.

The quantity variables may be eliminated from (3.1) to give

(3.2) $$p_t = -\frac{\gamma}{\beta}p_t^e - \frac{1}{\beta}u_t .$$

The error term is unknown at the time the production decisions are made, but it is known—and relevant—at the time the commodity is purchased in the market.

The prediction of the model is found by replacing the error term by its expected value, conditional on past events. If the errors have no serial correlation and $Eu_t = 0$, we obtain

(3.3) $$Ep_t = -\frac{\gamma}{\beta}p_t^e .$$

If the prediction of the theory were substantially better than the expectations of the firms, then there would be opportunities for the "insider" to profit from the knowledge—by inventory speculation if possible, by operating a firm, or by selling a price forecasting service to the firms. The profit opportunities would no longer exist if the aggregate expectation of the firms is the same as the prediction of the theory:

(3.4) $$Ep_t = p_t^e .$$

Referring to (3.3) we see that if $\gamma/\beta \neq -1$ the rationality assumption (3.4) implies that $p_t^e = 0$, or that the expected price equals the equilibrium price. As long as the disturbances occur only in the supply function, price and quantity movements from one period to the next would be entirely along the demand curve.

The problem we have been discussing so far is of little empirical interest, because the shocks were assumed to be completely unpredictable. For most markets it is desirable to allow for income effects in demand and alternative costs in supply, with the assumption that part of the shock variable may be predicted on the basis of prior information. By retracing our steps from (3.2), we see that the expected price would be

(3.5) $$p_t^e = -\frac{1}{\beta + \gamma} Eu_t .$$

If the shock is observable, then the conditional expected value or its regression estimate may be found directly. If the shock is not observable, it must be estimated from the past history of variables that can be measured.

Expectations with Serially Correlated Disturbances. We shall write the u's as a linear combination of the past history of normally and independently distributed random variables ε_t with zero mean and variance σ^2:

(3.6) $\qquad u_t = \sum_{i=0}^{\infty} w_i \varepsilon_{t-i}, \qquad E\varepsilon_j = 0, \qquad E\varepsilon_i \varepsilon_j = \begin{cases} \sigma^2 \text{ if } i = j, \\ 0 \text{ if } i \neq j. \end{cases}$

Any desired correlogram in the u's may be obtained by an appropriate choice of the weights w_i.

The price will be a linear function of the same independent disturbances; thus

(3.7) $\qquad\qquad\qquad\qquad p_t = \sum_{i=0}^{\infty} W_i \varepsilon_{t-i}.$

The expected price given only information through the $(t-1)$'st period has the same form as that in (3.7), with the exception that ε_t is replaced by its expected value (which is zero). We therefore have

(3.8) $\qquad\qquad p_t^e = W_0 E\varepsilon_t + \sum_{i=1}^{\infty} W_i \varepsilon_{t-i} = \sum_{i=1}^{\infty} W_i \varepsilon_{t-i}.$

If, in general, we let $p_{t,L}$ be the price expected in period $t+L$ on the basis of information available through the tth period, the formula becomes

(3.9) $\qquad\qquad\qquad\qquad p_{t-L,L} = \sum_{i=L}^{\infty} W_i \varepsilon_{t-i}.$

Substituting for the price and the expected price into (3.1), which reflect the market equilibrium conditions, we obtain

(3.10) $\qquad W_0 \varepsilon_t + \left(1 + \frac{\gamma}{\beta}\right) \sum_{i=1}^{\infty} W_i \varepsilon_{t-i} = -\frac{1}{\beta} \sum_{i=0}^{\infty} w_i \varepsilon_{t-i}.$

Equation (3.10) is an identity in the ε's; that is, it must hold whatever values of ε_j happen to occur. Therefore, the coefficients of the corresponding ε_j in the equation must be equal.

The weights W_i are therefore the following:

(3.11a) $\qquad\qquad\qquad\qquad W_0 = -\frac{1}{\beta} w_0,$

(3.11b) $\qquad\qquad\qquad W_i = -\frac{1}{\beta+\gamma} w_i \qquad\qquad (i = 1,2,3,\dots).$

Equations (3.11) give the parameters of the relation between prices and price expectations functions in terms of the past history of independent shocks. The problem remains of writing the results in terms of the history of observable variables. We wish to find a relation of the form

(3.12) $\qquad\qquad\qquad\qquad p_t^e = \sum_{j=1}^{\infty} V_j p_{t-j}.$

We solve for the weights V_j in terms of the weights W_j in the following manner. Substituting from (3.7) and (3.8), we obtain

(3.13) $$\sum_{i=1}^{\infty} W_i \varepsilon_{t-i} = \sum_{j=1}^{\infty} V_j \sum_{i=0}^{\infty} W_i \varepsilon_{t-i-j} = \sum_{i=1}^{\infty} \left(\sum_{j=1}^{i} V_j W_{i-j} \right) \varepsilon_{t-i} \, .$$

Since the equality must hold for all shocks, the coefficients must satisfy the equations

(3.14) $$W_i = \sum_{j=1}^{i} V_j W_{i-j} \qquad\qquad (i = 1,2,3,\dots) \, .$$

This is a system of equations with a triangular structure, so that it may be solved successively for the coefficients $V_1, V_2, V_3, \dots$.

If the disturbances are independently distributed, as we assumed before, then $w_0 = -1/\beta$ and all the others are zero. Equations (3.14) therefore imply

(3.15a) $$p_t^e = 0 \, ,$$

(3.15b) $$p_t = p_t^e + W_0 \varepsilon_t = -\frac{1}{\beta} \varepsilon_t \, .$$

These are the results obtained before.

Suppose, at the other extreme, that an exogenous shock affects all future conditions of supply, instead of only the one period. This assumption would be appropriate if it represented how far technological change differed from its trend. Because u_t is the sum of all the past ε_j, $w_i = 1$ $(i = 0,1,2,\dots)$. From (3.11),

(3.16a) $$W_0 = -1/\beta \, ,$$

(3.16b) $$W_i = -1/(\beta + \gamma) \, .$$

From (3.14) it can be seen that the expected price is a geometrically weighted moving average of past prices:

(3.17) $$p_t^e = \frac{\beta}{\gamma} \sum_{j=1}^{\infty} \left(\frac{\gamma}{\beta + \gamma} \right)^j p_{t-j} \, .$$

This prediction formula has been used by Nerlove [26] to estimate the supply elasticity of certain agricultural commodities. The only difference is that our analysis states that the "coefficient of adjustment" in the expectations formula should depend on the demand and the supply coefficients. The geometrically weighted moving average forecast is, in fact, optimal under slightly more general conditions (when the disturbance is composed of both permanent and transitory components). In that case the coefficient will depend on the relative variances of the two components as well as the supply and demand coefficients. (See [24].)

Deviations from Rationality. Certain imperfections and biases in the expectations may also be analyzed with the methods of this paper. Allowing for cross-sectional differences in expectations is a simple matter, because their aggregate effect is negligible as long as the deviation from the rational forecast for an individual firm is not strongly correlated with those of the others. Modifications are necessary only if the correlation of the errors is large and depends systematically on other explanatory variables. We shall examine the effect of over-discounting current information and of differences in the information possessed by various firms in the industry. Whether such biases in expectations are empirically important remains to be seen. I wish only to emphasize that the methods are flexible enough to handle them.

Let us consider first what happens when expectations consistently over- or under-discount the effect of current events. Equation (3.8), which gives the optimal price expectation, will then be replaced by

$$(3.18) \qquad p_t^e = f_1 W_1 \varepsilon_{t-1} + \sum_{i=2}^{\infty} W_i \varepsilon_{t-i} .$$

In other words the weight attached to the most recent exogenous disturbance is multiplied by the factor f_1, which would be greater than unity if current information is over-discounted and less than unity if it is under-discounted.

If we use (3.18) for the expected price instead of (3.8) to explain market price movements, then (3.11) is replaced by

$$(3.19a) \qquad W_0 = -\frac{1}{\beta} w_0 ,$$

$$(3.19b) \qquad W_1 = -\frac{1}{\beta + f_1 \gamma} w_1 ,$$

$$(3.19c) \qquad W_i = -\frac{1}{\beta + \gamma} w_i \qquad\qquad (i = 2,3,4,...) .$$

The effect of the biased expectations on price movements depends on the statistical properties of the exogenous disturbances.

If the disturbances are independent (that is, $w_0 = 1$ and $w_i = 0$ for $i \geqslant 1$), the biased expectations have no effect. The reason is that successive observations provide no information about future fluctuations.

On the other hand, if all the disturbances are of a permanent type (that is, $w_0 = w_1 = ... = 1$), the properties of the expectations function are significantly affected. To illustrate the magnitude of the differences, the parameters of the function

$$p_t^e = \sum_{j=1}^{\infty} V_j p_{t-j}$$

are compared in Figure 3.1 for $\beta = 2\gamma$ and various values of f_1. If current information is under-discounted ($f_1 = 1/2$), the weight V_1 attached to the latest observed price is very high. With over-discounting ($f_1 = 2$), the weight for the first period is relatively low.

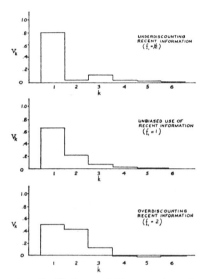

FIGURE 3.1.—Autoregression Coefficients of Expectations for Biased Use of Recent Information. ($w_0 = w_1 = \ldots = 1$).

The model above can be interpreted in another way. Suppose that some of the firms have access to later information than the others. That is, there is a lag of one period for some firms, which therefore form price expectations according to (3.8). The others, with a lag of two periods, can only use the following:

$$(3.20) \qquad p_t^{e'} = \sum_{i=2}^{\infty} W_i \varepsilon_{t-i} .$$

Then the aggregate price expectations relation is the same as (3.18), if f_1 represents the fraction of the firms having a lag of only one period in obtaining market information (that is, the fraction of "insiders").

4. EFFECTS OF INVENTORY SPECULATION

Some of the most interesting questions involve the economic effects of inventory storage and speculation. We can examine the effect by adjoining to (3.1) an inventory demand equation depending on the difference between the expected future price and the current price. As we shall show, the price expectation with independent disturbances in the supply function then turns out to have the form

$$(4.1) \qquad\qquad p_t^e = \lambda p_{t-1} ,$$

where the parameter λ would be somewhere between zero and one, its value depending on the demand, supply, and inventory demand parameters.

Speculation with moderately well-informed price expectations reduces the variance of prices by spreading the effect of a market disturbance over several time periods, thereby allowing shocks partially to cancel one another out. Speculation is profitable, although no speculative opportunities remain. These propositions might appear obvious. Nevertheless, contrary views have been expressed in the literature.[6]

Before introducing inventories into the market conditions, we shall briefly examine the nature of speculative demand for a commodity.

Optimal Speculation. We shall assume for the time being that storage, interest, and transactions costs are negligible. An individual has an opportunity to purchase at a known price in the tth period for sale in the succeeding period. The future price is, however, unknown. If we let I_t represent the speculative inventory at the end of the tth period,[7] then the profit to be realized is

$$(4.2) \qquad\qquad \pi_t = I_t(p_{t+1} - p_t) .$$

Of course, the profit is unknown at the time the commitment is to be made. There is, however, the expectation of gain.

The individual demand for speculative inventories would presumably be based on reasoning of the following sort. The size of the commitment depends on the expectation of the utility of the profit. For a sufficiently small range of variation in profits, we can approximate the utility function by the first few terms of its Taylor's series expansion about the origin:

$$(4.3) \qquad u_t = \phi(\pi_t) = \phi(0) + \phi'(0)\pi_t + \frac{1}{2}\phi''(0)\pi_t^2 + \dots .$$

The expected utility depends on the moments of the probability distribution of π:

$$(4.4) \qquad Eu_t = \phi(0) + \phi'(0)E\pi_t + \frac{1}{2}\phi''(0)E\pi_t^2 + \dots .$$

---

[6] See Baumol [5]. His conclusions depend on a nonspeculative demand such that prices would be a pure sine function, which may always be forecast perfectly.

[7] Speculative inventories may be either positive or negative.

From (4.2) the first two moments may be found to be

(4.5a) $$E\pi_t = I_t(p_{t+1}^e - p_t),$$

(4.5b) $$E\pi_t^2 = I_t^2[\sigma_{t,1}^2 + (p_{t+1}^e - p_t)^2],$$

where p_{t+1}^e is the conditional mean of the price in period $t+1$ (given all information through period t) and $\sigma_{t,1}^2$ is the conditional variance. The expected utility may therefore be written in terms of the inventory position as follows:

(4.6) $$Eu_t = \phi(0) + \phi'(0)I_t(p_{t+1}^e - p_t) + \frac{1}{2}\phi''(0)I_t^2[\sigma_{t,1}^2 + (p_{t+1}^e - p_t)^2] + \cdots.$$

The inventory therefore satisfies the condition

(4.7) $$\frac{dEu}{dI_t} = \phi'(0)(p_{t+1}^e - p_t) + \phi''(0)I_t[\sigma_{t,1}^2 + (p_{t+1}^e - p_t)^2] + \cdots = 0.$$

The inventory position would, to a first approximation, be given by

(4.8) $$I_t = -\frac{\phi'(0)(p_{t+1}^e - p_t)}{\phi''(0)[\sigma_{t,1}^2 + (p_{t+1}^e - p_t)^2]}.$$

If $\phi'(0) > 0$ and $\phi''(0) < 0$, the above expression is an increasing function of the expected change in prices (as long as it is moderate).

At this point we make two additional assumptions: (1) the conditional variance, $\sigma_{t,1}^2$, is independent of p_t^e, which is true if prices are normally distributed, and (2) the square of the expected price change is small relative to the variance. The latter assumption is reasonable because the original expansion of the utility function is valid only for small changes. Equation (4.8) may then be simplified to[8]

(4.9) $$I_t = \alpha(p_{t+1}^e - p_t),$$

where $\alpha = -\phi'(0)/\phi''(0)\sigma_{t,1}^2$.

Note that the coefficient α depends on the commodity in only one way: the variance of price forecasts. The aggregate demand would, in addition, depend on who holds the stocks as well as the size of the market. For some commodities, inventories are most easily held by the firms.[9] If an organized futures exchange exists for the commodity, a different population would

---

[8] This form of the demand for speculative inventories resembles that of Telser [31] and Kaldor [20].

[9] Meat, for example, is stored in the live animals or in any curing or ageing process.

be involved. In a few instances (in particular, durable goods), inventory accumulation on the part of households may be important.

The original assumptions may be relaxed, without affecting the results significantly, by introducing storage or interest costs. Margin requirements may, as well, limit the long or short position of an individual. Although such requirements may primarily limit cross-sectional differences in positions, they may also constrain the aggregate inventory. In this case, we might reasonably expect the aggregate demand function to be nonlinear with an upper "saturation" level for inventories. (A lower level would appear for aggregate inventories approaching zero.)

Because of its simplicity, however, we shall use (4.9) to represent inventory demand.

Market Adjustments. We are now in a position to modify the model of Section 3 to take account of inventory variations. The ingredients are the supply and demand equations used earlier, together with the inventory equation. We repeat the equations below (P_t represents production and C_t consumption during the tth period:

(4.10a) $C_t = -\beta p_t$ (Demand) ,

(4.10b) $P_t = \gamma p_t^e + u_t$ (Supply) ,

(4.10c) $I_t = \alpha(p_{t+1}^e - p_t)$ (Inventory speculation) .

The market equilibrium conditions are

(4.11) $C_t + I_t = P_t + I_{t-1}$.

Substituting (4.10) into (4.11), the equilibrium can be expressed in terms of prices, price expectations, and the disturbance, thus

(4.12) $-(\alpha + \beta)p_t + \alpha p_{t+1}^e = (\alpha + \gamma)p_t^e - \alpha p_{t-1} + u_t$.

The conditions above may be used to find the weights of the regression functions for prices and price expectations in the same way as before. Substituting from (3.6), (3.7), and (3.8) into (4.12), we obtain

(4.13)
$$-(\alpha + \beta) \sum_{i=0}^{\infty} W_i \varepsilon_{t-i} + \alpha \sum_{i=1}^{\infty} W_i \varepsilon_{t+1-i}$$
$$= (\alpha + \gamma) \sum_{i=1}^{\infty} W_i \varepsilon_{t-i} - \alpha \sum_{i=0}^{\infty} W_i \varepsilon_{t-1-i} + \sum_{i=0}^{\infty} w_i \varepsilon_{t-i} .$$

In order that the above equation hold for all possible ε's, the corresponding coefficients must, as before, be equal. Therefore, the following system of equations must be satisfied:[10]

(4.14a) $$-(\alpha +\beta)\,W_0 +\alpha W_1 = w_0 \,,$$

(4.14b) $$\alpha W_{i-1}-(2\alpha +\beta +\gamma)\,W_i +\alpha W_{i+1} = w_i \qquad (i = 1,2,3,\ldots)\,.$$

Provided it exists, the solution of the homogeneous system would be of the form

(4.15) $$W_k = c\lambda_1^{k}\,,$$

where λ_1 is the smaller root of the characteristic equation

(4.16) $$\alpha -(2\alpha +\beta +\gamma)\lambda +\alpha\lambda^2 = \alpha\,(1-\lambda)^2 -(\beta +\gamma)\lambda = 0\,.$$

λ_1 is plotted against positive values of $\alpha/(\beta +\gamma)$ in Figure 4.1.

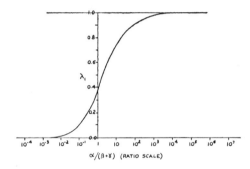

FIGURE 4.1.—Characteristic Root as a Function of $\alpha/(\beta +\gamma)$.

A unique, real, and bounded solution to (4.14) will exist if the roots of the characteristic equation are real. The roots occur in reciprocal pairs, so that if they are real and distinct exactly one will have an absolute value less than unity. For a bounded solution the coefficient of the larger root vanishes; the initial condition is then fitted to the coefficient of the smaller root.

The response of the price and quantity variables will be dynamically stable, therefore, if the roots of the characteristic equation are real. It is easy to see that they will be real if the following inequalities are satisfied:

(4.17a) $$\alpha >0\,,$$

(4.17b) $$\beta +\gamma >0\,.$$

The first condition requires that speculators act in the expectation of gain (rather than loss). The second is the condition for Walrasian stability. Hence an assumption about dynamic stability implies rather little about

[10] The same system appears in various contexts with embarrassing frequency. See Holt *et al.* [**17**] and Muth [**24**].

the demand and supply coefficients. It should be observed that (4.17) are not necessary conditions for stability. The system will also be stable if both inequalities in (4.17) are reversed (!) or if $0 > \alpha/(\beta + \gamma) > -1/4$. If $\alpha = 0$, there is no "linkage" from one period of time to another, so the system is dynamically stable for all values of $\beta + \gamma$.

Suppose, partly by way of illustration, that the exogenous disturbances affecting the market are independently distributed. Then we can let $w_0 = 1$ and $w_i = 0$ $(i \geqslant 1)$. The complementary function will therefore be the complete solution to the resulting difference equation. By substituting (4.15) into (4.14a), we evaluate the constant and find

$$(4.18) \qquad\qquad W_k = -\frac{1}{(\alpha + \beta) - \alpha \lambda_1} \lambda_1^k .$$

The weights V_k may be found either from (3.14) or by noting that the resulting stochastic process is Markovian. At any rate, the weights are

$$(4.19) \qquad\qquad V_k = \begin{cases} \lambda_1, & k = 1, \\ 0, & k > 1. \end{cases}$$

The expected price is therefore correlated with the previous price, and the rest of the price history conveys no extra information, i.e.,

$$(4.20) \qquad\qquad p_t^e = \lambda_1 p_{t-1} ,$$

where the parameter depends on the coefficients of demand, supply, and inventory speculation according to (4.16) and is between 0 and 1. If inventories are an important factor in short-run price determination, λ_1 will be very nearly unity so that the time series of prices has a high positive serial correlation.[11] If inventories are a negligible factor, λ_1 is close to zero and leads to the results of Section 3.

Effects of Inventory Speculation. Substituting the expected price, from (4.20), into (4.10), we obtain the following system to describe the operation of the market:

$$(4.21a) \qquad\qquad C_t = -\beta p_t ,$$

$$(4.21b) \qquad\qquad P_t = \gamma \lambda_1 p_{t-1} + \varepsilon_t ,$$

$$(4.21c) \qquad\qquad I_t = -\alpha(1 - \lambda_1) p_t .$$

The market conditions can be expressed in terms of supply and demand by including the inventory carryover with production and inventory carry-

---

[11] If the production and consumption flows are negligible compared with the speculative inventory level, the process approaches a random walk. This would apply to daily or weekly price movements of a commodity whose production lag is a year. Cf. Kendall [22].

TABLE 4.1
EFFECTS OF INVENTORY SPECULATION

Description	Symbol	General Formula	Approximation for Small α
1. Characteristic root	λ_1	[eq.(4.16)]	$\alpha/(\beta+\gamma)$
2. Standard deviation of prices	σ_p	$\|W_0\|(1-\lambda_1^2)^{-1/2}\sigma$	$\frac{1}{\beta}\left(1-\frac{\alpha}{\beta}\right)\sigma$
3. Standard deviation of expected price	σ_p^e	$\lambda_1\sigma_p$	$\frac{\alpha}{\beta(\beta+\gamma)}\sigma$
4. Standard deviation of output	σ_P	$(\sigma^2+\gamma^2\lambda_1^2\sigma_p^2)^{1/2}$	$\left[1+\frac{\alpha\gamma}{2\beta(\beta+\gamma)}\right]\sigma$
5. Mean producers' revenue	$EP_t\,p_t$	$\gamma\lambda_1^2\sigma_p^2+W_0\sigma^2$	$-\frac{1}{\beta}\left(1-\frac{\alpha}{\beta}\right)\sigma^2$
6. Mean speculators' revenue	$EI_t(p_{t+1}-p_t)$	$\alpha(1-\lambda_1)^2\sigma_p^2$	$\alpha\sigma^2$
7. Mean consumers' expenditure	$EC_t p_t$	$-\beta\sigma_p^2$	$-\frac{1}{\beta}\left(1-\frac{2\alpha}{\beta}\right)\sigma^2$

Notes: (1) σ is the standard deviation of the disturbance in the supply function (4.10b) with $w_0 = 1$ and $w_1 = w_2 = \ldots = 0$.
(2) $W_0 = -1/[\beta+\alpha(1-\lambda_1)]$.

forward with consumption; thus,

$$
(4.22) \qquad
\begin{aligned}
Q_t &= C_t + I_t && \text{(Demand)}, \\
Q_t &= P_t + I_{t-1} && \text{(Supply)}.
\end{aligned}
$$

Substituting from (4.21) we obtain the system:

$$(4.23a) \qquad Q_t = -[\beta +\alpha(1-\lambda_1)]p_t \qquad \text{(Demand)},$$

$$(4.23b) \qquad Q_t = [\gamma\lambda_1 - \alpha(1-\lambda_1)]p_{t-1} + \varepsilon_t \qquad \text{(Supply)}.$$

The coefficient in the supply equation is reduced while that of the demand equation is increased. The conclusions are not essentially different from those of Hooton [18]. The change is always enough to make the dynamic response stable.

If price expectations are in fact rational, we can make some statements about the economic effects of commodity speculation. (The relevant formulas are summarized in Table 4.1.) Speculation reduces the variance of prices by spreading the effect of a disturbance over several time periods. From Figure 4.2, however, we see that the effect is negligible if α is much less than the sum of β and γ. The standard deviation of expected prices first increases with α because speculation makes the time series more predictable and then decreases because of the small variability of actual prices. The variability of factor inputs and production follows roughly the same pattern (cf. Kaldor [20]).

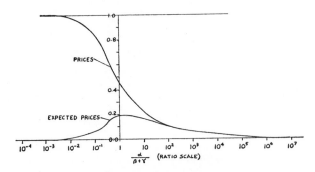

FIGURE 4.2.—Standard Deviation of Prices and Expected Prices as a Function of $\alpha/(\beta + \gamma)$ for $\beta = \gamma$.

In Figure 4.3 we see that mean income to speculators is always positive and has a maximum value slightly to the left of that for expected prices. Producers' revenue and consumers' expenditures both increase with α. Consumers' expenditures increase at first a little faster than the revenue of the producers. The effect of speculation on welfare is therefore not obvious.

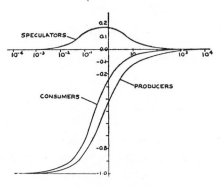

FIGURE 4.3.—Mean Income of Producers and Speculators, and Mean Expenditures of Consumers as a Function of $\alpha/(\beta + \gamma)$ for $\beta = \gamma$.

The variability of prices for various values of γ/β is plotted as a function of α/β in Figure 4.4. The general shape of the curve is not affected by values of γ/β differing by as much as a factor of 100. The larger the supply coefficient, however, the sharper is the cut-off in price variability.

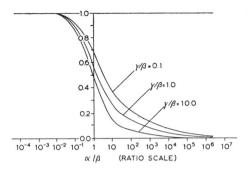

FIGURE 4.4—Standard Deviation of Prices for Various Values of γ/β as a Function of α/β.

5. RATIONALITY AND COBWEB THEOREMS

It is rather surprising that expectations have not previously been regarded as rational dynamic models, since rationality is assumed in all other aspects of entrepreneurial behavior. From a purely theoretical standpoint, there are good reasons for assuming rationality. First, it is a principle applicable to all dynamic problems (if true). Expectations in different markets and systems would not have to be treated in completely different ways. Second, if expectations were not moderately rational there would be opportunities for economists to make profits in commodity speculation, running a firm, or selling the information to present owners. Third, rationality is an assumption that can be modified. Systematic biases, incomplete or incorrect information, poor memory, etc., can be examined with analytical methods based on rationality.

The only real test, however, is whether theories involving rationality explain observed phenomena any better than alternative theories. In this section we shall therefore compare some of the empirical implications of the rational expectations hypothesis with those of the cobweb "theorem." The effects of rational expectations are particularly important because the cobweb theorem has often been regarded as one of the most successful attempts at dynamic economic theories (e.g., Goodwin [13]). Few students of agricultural problems or business cycles seem to take the cobweb theorem very seriously, however, but its implications do occasionally appear. For example, a major cause of price fluctuations in cattle and hog markets is sometimes believed to be the expectations of farmers themselves (Jesness [19]). Dean and Heady [10] have also suggested more extensive governmental forecasting and outlook services in order to offset an increasing tendency toward instability of hog prices due to a secular decrease in the elasticity of demand.

Implications of Cobweb Theorems. If the market equilibrium conditions of (3.1) are subjected to independent shocks in the supply function, the prediction of the theory would be

(5.1) $$E\left(p_t \mid p_{t-1}, p_{t-2}, \ldots\right) = -\frac{\gamma}{\beta} p_t^e .$$

As a result, the prediction of the cobweb theory would ordinarily have the sign opposite to that of the firms. This, of course, has been known for a long time. Schultz noted that the hypothesis implies farmers do not learn from experience, but added: "Such a behavior is not to be ruled out as extremely improbable" [27, p. 78].

The various theories differ primarily in what is assumed about price expectations. The early contributors (through Ezekiel [11]) have assumed that the expected price is equal to the latest known price. That is,

(5.2) $$p_t^e = p_{t-1} .$$

Goodwin [13] proposed the extrapolation formula,

(5.3) $$p_t^e = p_{t-1} - \varrho(p_{t-1} - p_{t-2}) .$$

That is, a certain fraction of the latest change is added on to the latest observed price. Depending on the sign of ϱ, which should be between -1 and $+1$, we can get a greater variety of behavior. It is still the case, however, that farmers' expectations and the prediction of the model have the opposite sign.

A third expectations formula is much more recent. The adaptive expectations model, used by Nerlove [25], satisfies the following equation:

(5.4) $$p_t^e = p_{t-1}^e + \eta(p_{t-1} - p_{t-1}^e) .$$

The forecast is changed by an amount proportional to the most recently observed forecast error. The solution of the difference equation gives the price expectation as a geometrically weighted moving average:

(5.5) $$p_t^e = \eta \sum_{j=0}^{\infty} (1 - \eta)^j p_{t-j} .$$

Certain properties of the cobweb models are compared with the rational model in Table 5.1 for shocks having no serial correlation. Such comparisons are a little treacherous because most real markets have significant income effects in demand, alternative costs in supply, and errors in both behavioral equations. To the extent that these effects introduce positive serial correlation in the residuals, the difference between the cobweb and rational models would be diminished. Subject to these qualifications, we shall compare the two kinds of models according to the properties of firms' expectations and the cyclical characteristics of commodity prices and output.

Expectations of Firms. There is some direct evidence concerning the quality of expectations of firms. Heady and Kaldor [16] have shown that, for the period studied, average expectations were considerably more

TABLE 5.1

PROPERTIES OF COBWEB MODELS

	Expectation p_t^e	Prediction $E(p_t\|p_{t-1},\dots)$	Stability Conditions
(A) Classical (Schultz-Tinbergen-Ricci)	p_{t-1}	$-\dfrac{\gamma}{\beta}p_t^e$	$\gamma < \beta$
(B) Extrapolative (Goodwin)	$(1-\varrho)p_{t-1} + \varrho p_{t-2}$ $(-1 < \varrho < 1)$	$-\dfrac{\gamma}{\beta}p_t^e$	$\dfrac{\gamma}{\beta} < \begin{cases} \dfrac{1}{1-2\varrho}, & \varrho \leqslant \dfrac{1}{3} \\[2mm] \dfrac{1}{\varrho}, & \varrho \geqslant \dfrac{1}{3} \end{cases}$
(C) Adaptive (Nerlove)	$\eta\sum\limits_{j=1}^{\infty}(1-\eta)^{j-1}p_{t-j}$ $(0 < \eta < 1)$	$-\dfrac{\gamma}{\beta}p_t^e$	$\dfrac{\gamma}{\beta} < \dfrac{2}{\eta}-1$
(D) Rational	0	0	$\beta + \gamma \neq 0$
(E) Rational (with speculation)	$\lambda_1 p_{t-1}$ $(0 < \lambda_1 < 1)$	$\lambda_1 p_{t-1}$	$\alpha > 0$ $\beta + \gamma > 0$

Note: The disturbances are normally and independently distributed with a constant variance.

accurate than simple extrapolation, although there were substantial cross-sectional differences in expectations. Similar conclusions concerning the accuracy have been reached, for quite different expectational data, by Modigliani and Weingartner [23].

If often appears that reported expectations underestimate the extent of changes that actually take place. Several studies have tried to relate the two according to the equation:

$$(5.6) \qquad\qquad p_t^e = bp_t + v_t',$$

where v_t' is a random disturbance. Estimated values of b are positive, but less than unity (see, e.g., Theil [33]). Such findings are clearly inconsistent with the cobweb theory, which ordinarily requires a negative coefficient. We shall show below that they are generally consistent with the rational expectations hypothesis.

Bossons and Modigliani [6] have pointed out that the size of the estimated coefficient, $\hat{b}$, may be explained by a regression effect. Its relevance may be seen quite clearly as follows. The rational expectations hypothesis states that, in the aggregate, the expected price is an unbiased predictor of the actual price. That is,

(5.7) $p_t = p_t^e + v_t, \qquad E p_t^e v_t = 0, \qquad E v_t = 0.$

The probability limit of the least squares estimate of b in (5.6) would then be given by

(5.8) $\text{Plim } \hat{b} = (\text{Var } p^e)/(\text{Var } p) < 1.$

Cycles. The evidence for the cobweb model lies in the quasi-periodic fluctuations in prices of a number of commodities. The hog cycle is perhaps the best known, but cattle and potatoes have sometimes been cited as others which obey the "theorem." The phase plot of quantity with current and lagged price also has the appearance which gives the cobweb cycle its name.

A dynamic system forced by random shocks typically responds, however, with cycles having a fairly stable period. This is true whether or not any characteristic roots are of the oscillatory type. Slutzky [30] and Yule [34] first showed that moving-average processes can lead to very regular cycles. A comparison of empirical cycle periods with the properties of the solution of a system of differential or difference equations can therefore be misleading whenever random shocks are present (Haavelmo [15]).

The length of the cycle under various hypotheses depends on how we measure the empirical cycle period. Two possibilities are: the interval

TABLE 5.2

CYCLICAL PROPERTIES OF COBWEB MODELS

	Serial Correlation Of Prices, r_1	Mean Interval Between Successive Upcrosses, L	Mean Interval Between Successive Peaks or Troughs, L'
(A) Classical	$r_1 = -\dfrac{\gamma}{\beta} < 0$		
(B) Extrapolative	$r_1 = \dfrac{-\gamma(1-\varrho)}{\beta + \gamma\varrho} < 0$	$2 \leqslant L \leqslant 4$	$2 \leqslant L' \leqslant 3$
(C) Adaptive	$-\dfrac{\eta\gamma}{\beta} \leqslant r_1 \leqslant 0$		
(D) Rational	$r_1 = 0$	$L = 4$	$L' = 3$
(E) Rational - with storage	$r_1 = \lambda_1 > 0$	$L > 4$	$3 \leqslant L' \leqslant 4$

Note: The disturbances are assumed to be normally and independently distributed with a constant variance. β and γ are both assumed to be positive.

between successive "upcrosses" of the time series (i.e., crossing the trend line from below), and the average interval between successive peaks or troughs. Both are given in Table 5.2, which summarizes the serial correlation of prices and mean cycle lengths for the various hypotheses.[12]

That the observed hog cycles were too long for the cobweb theorem was first observed in 1935 by Coase and Fowler [8, 9]. The graph of cattle prices presented given by Ezekiel [11] as evidence for the cobweb theorem implies an extraordinarily long period of production (five to seven years). The interval between successive peaks for other commodities tends to be longer than three production periods. Comparisons of the cycle lengths should be interpreted cautiously because they do not allow for positive serial correlation of the exogenous disturbances. Nevertheless, they should not be construed as supporting the cobweb theorem.

Carnegie Institute of Technology

REFERENCES

[1] AKERMAN, G.: "The Cobweb Theorem; A Reconsideration," *Quarterly Journal of Economics*, 71: 151–160 (February, 1957).

[2] ALLEN, H. V.: "A Theorem Concerning the Linearity of Regression," *Statistical Research Memoirs*, 2: 60–68 (1938).

[3] ARROW, K. J., AND L. HURWICZ: "On the Stability of Competitive Equilibrium I," *Econometrica*, 26: 522–552 (October, 1958).

[4] ARROW, K. J., H. D. BLOCK, AND L. HURWICZ: "On the Stability of Competitive Equilibrium II," *Econometrica*, 27: 82–109 (January, 1959).

[5] BAUMOL, W. J.: "Speculation, Profitability, and Stability," *Review of Economics and Statistics*, 39: 263–271 (August, 1957).

[6] BOSSONS, J. D., AND F. MODIGLIANI: "The Regressiveness of Short Run Business Expectations as Reported to Surveys—An Explanation and Its Implications," *Unpublished*, no date.

[7] BUCHANAN, N. S.: "A Reconsideration of the Cobweb Theorem," *Journal of Political Economy*, 47: 67–81 (February, 1939).

[8] COASE, R. H., AND R. F. FOWLER: "The Pig-Cycle in Great Britain: An Explanation," *Economica*, 4 (NS): 55–82 (1937).

[9] ————: "Bacon Production and the Pig-Cycle in Great Britain," *Economica*, 2 (NS): 143–167 (1935). Also "Reply" by R. Cohen and J. D. Barker, pp. 408–422, and "Rejoinder" by Coase and Fowler, pp. 423–428 (1935).

[10] DEAN, G. W., AND E. O. HEADY: "Changes in Supply Response and Elasticity For Hogs," *Journal of Farm Economics*, 40: 845–860 (November, 1958).

[11] EZEKIEL, M.: "The Cobweb Theorem," *Quarterly Journal of Economics*, 52: 255–280 (February, 1938). Reprinted in *Readings in Business Cycle Theory*.

[12] FERGUSON, T.: "On the Existence of Linear Regression in Linear Structural Relations," *University of California Publications in Statistics*, Vol. 2, No. 7, pp. 143–166 (University of California Press, 1955).

[12] See Kendall [21, Chapters 29 and 30, especially pp. 381 ff.] for the relevant formulas.

[13] GOODWIN, R. M.: "Dynamical Coupling With Especial Reference to Markets Having Production Lags," *Econometrica*, 15 : 181–204 (1947).

[14] GRUNBERG, E., AND F. MODIGLIANI: "The Predictability of Social Events," *Journal of Political Economy*, 62: 465–478 (December, 1954).

[15] HAAVELMO, T.: "The Inadequacy of Testing Dynamic Theory by Comparing Theoretical Solutions and Observed Cycles," *Econometrica*, 8: 312–321 (1940).

[16] HEADY, E. O., AND D. R. KALDOR: "Expectations and Errors in Forecasting Agricultural Prices," *Journal of Political Economy*, 62: 34–47 (February, 1954).

[17] HOLT, C. C., F. MODIGLIANI, J. F. MUTH, AND H. A. SIMON: *Planning Production, Inventories, and Work Force* (Prentice-Hall, 1960).

[18] HOOTON, F. G.: "Risk and the Cobweb Theorem," *Economic Journal*, 60: 69–80 (1950).

[19] JESNESS, O. B.: "Changes in the Agricultural Adjustment Program in the Past 25 Years," *Journal of Farm Economics*, 40: 255–264 (May, 1958).

[20] KALDOR, N.: "Speculation and Economic Stability," *Rev. Economic Studies*, 7: 1–27 (1939–1940).

[21] KENDALL, M. G.: *The Advanced Theory of Statistics*, Vol. II (Hafner, 1951).

[22] ————: "The Analysis of Economic Time-Series—Part I: Prices," *Journal of the Royal Statistical Society, Series A*, 116 : 11–34 (1953).

[23] MODIGLIANI, F., AND H. M. WEINGARTNER: "Forecasting Uses of Anticipatory Data on Investment and Sales," *Quarterly Journal of Economics*, 72: 23–54 (February, 1958).

[24] MUTH, J. F.: "Optimal Properties of Exponentially Weighted Forecasts," *Journal of the American Statistical Association* 55: 299–306 (June, 1960).

[25] NERLOVE, M.: "Adaptive Expectations and Cobweb Phenomena," *Quarterly Journal of Economics*, 73: 227–240 (May, 1958).

[26] ————: *The Dynamics of Supply: Estimation of Farmers' Response to Price* (John Hopkins Press, 1958).

[27] SCHULTZ, H.: *The Theory and Measurement of Demand* (University of Chicago Press, 1958).

[28] SIMON, H. A.: "Dynamic Programming Under Uncertainty with a Quadratic Criterion Function," *Econometrica*, 24: 74–81 (1956).

[29] ————: "Theories of Decision-Making in Economics," *American Economic Review*, 49: 223–283 (June, 1959).

[30] SLUTZKY, E.: "The Summation of Random Causes as the Source of Cyclic Processes," *Econometrica*, 5: 105–146 (April, 1937).

[31] TELSER, L. G.: "A Theory of Speculation Relating Profitability and Stability," *Review of Economics and Statistics*, 61: 295–301 (August, 1959).

[32] THEIL, H.: "A Note on Certainty Equivalence in Dynamic Planning," *Econometrica*, 25: 346–349 (April, 1957).

[33] ————: *Economic Forecasts and Policy* (North-Holland, 1958).

[34] YULE, G. U.: "On a Method of Investigating Periodicity in Disturbed Series," *Transactions of the Royal Society*, London, A, 226: 267–298 (1927).

(Errata, 1972) The normality assumption on page 317 is not required in the subsequent analysis. Reference to the relation between regression and normality in footnote 4 is not correct. I am indebted to Professor G. O. Bierwag for raising this question.

The linearity of the regression function associating prices and expected prices with the exogenous disturbances was not established in the paper. This can be shown and the analysis can be simplified considerably by taking expectations directly, rather than by using the assumed linear regression functions. It has the further advantage of relating the expectations problem more directly to Bayesian analysis of output decisions under conditions of uncertainty rather than that of risk alone. Observations along these lines have been made to me by Professors R. M. Cyert, M. DeGroot, M. Nerlove, and D. Orr.

Econometrica, Vol. 30, No. 2 (April, 1962)

BUFFER STOCKS, SALES EXPECTATIONS, AND STABILITY: A MULTI-SECTOR ANALYSIS OF THE INVENTORY CYCLE[1]

By Michael C. Lovell

A multi-sector buffer-stock inventory model is developed in an attempt to resolve the problem of aggregation involved in deriving implications for the stability of the economy from a consideration of inventory practices of individual firms. It is demonstrated that stability depends upon a multitude of parameters, some of which are suppressed in aggregative model construction. The economy is necessarily unstable when perfect, if myopic expectations are assumed. With naive expectations stability becomes a definite possibility, particularly if firms attempt only a delayed adjustment of inventories to the equilibrium level. Although the empirical evidence marshaled in order to illustrate the application of the theorems does not prove sufficiently accurate to permit precise conclusions, it is apparent that the conditions for stability may well be satisfied for reasonable values of the system's parameters. Tax schemes which have been suggested as means of stabilizing fluctuations in inventory investment are appraised in the concluding section.

INTRODUCTION

IMPLICATIONS for the stability of the economy of inventory practices of individual firms are appraised in this study. Eric Lundberg [28] and Lloyd Metzler [29] have both formulated macroeconomic models of the inventory cycle. My approach resembles Metzler's in that a simple servomechanism type of behavior is attributed to the individual firm. Production is conceded to be time consuming. Inventories of finished goods are held as buffer stocks in order that unanticipated demand may be satisfied. The entrepreneur attempts to adjust inventories to the appropriate level in the face of incomplete knowledge of future sales.

My approach departs from the macro approach adopted by Metzler and Lundberg in that I consider complications that arise in aggregating the behavioral patterns assumed for the individual firm in deriving conclusions concerning the dynamic properties of the economy. In contrast with the procedure of traditional macroanalysis I consider the implications of a *multitude* of interacting firms all attempting to adjust inventories to a level deemed appropriate in the face of incomplete knowledge of future market

[1] This paper was read at the December, 1960 Econometric Society Meetings. It constitutes a revision of certain materials appearing in my doctoral dissertation [26, Ch, 2], a research project supervised by Wassily Leontief. I am indebted to the Earhart Foundation, the Social Science Research Council, and the Cowles Foundation for Research in Economics for financial support. Robert Dorfman, James Henderson, Karen Hester, Lawrence Krause, and Charles Ying as well as Professor Leontief have provided helpful comments. Remaining errors are my responsibility, of course.

conditions.[2] An analysis of stability conditions for the multi-sector model reveals that dynamic properties depend upon a multitude of parameters, some of which are suppressed in aggregative model construction. Conditions for stability are found to differ fundamentally from those developed by Metzler in his macroanalysis.

In a discussion of the implications for stability of alternative inventory practices it is most appropriate to start, as in the theory of competition, with a discussion of the behavior of the individual firm. The second stage of the analysis is that of deriving the behavior of individual industries from the assumed firm behavior. Then the interrelations between the various industries must be considered in connecting the equations representing the behavior of the individual sectors in order to obtain a model of the whole economy. Finally, dynamic properties of the model for alternative values of its parameters have to be explored.

In order to make this difficult task tractable, numerous simplifying assumptions must be made. The inventory behavior pattern attributed to the individual firm is relatively simple. Capacity restraints on the level of output are ignored. Time is treated as a discrete unit. It is assumed that the production period is the same for all commodities and, in addition, that the production processes are synchronized so that output begins at the same point of time for all firms; essentially, the production process is of the "point-input point-output" type so frequently encountered in capital theory. In addition, price phenomena are neglected throughout the discussion. None of these assumptions is without precedent in either the literature of managerial economics on optimal inventory policy or in the multitude of aggregative economic models of the accelerator and related theories.

Granted that simplifying assumptions must be made in any analysis, it may still be asked whether an appropriate set has been chosen for the problem at hand. My own empirical investigation of the behavior of manufacturers' inventories in the United States suggests that the buffer-stock model does provide an appropriate framework for examining finished goods inventory

[2] The challenge raised is similar to that faced by Goodwin [16] and Chipman [10] in their disaggregation of the multiplier process. My task is more difficult in that a crucial role is explicitly assigned to errors of expectations and inventory stocks. In the development of the matrix and multi-sector multiplier theories, no explicit mention was made of the role of inventories. Chipman acknowledges in a more recent paper that "in the multiplier approach demand for outputs is regarded as preceding the production of inputs, the initial production of outputs being made possible by the temporary depletion of inventories of inputs" [11, p. 5]. The specification of stability conditions for the multi-sector multiplier has been made in abstraction from this fact. It will be found that the multiplier models of Goodwin and Chipman are only a special, restricted case of the model presented here. Under more realistic assumptions, the conditions for stability are found to differ fundamentally from those they specified.

behavior [27]. Manufacturers apparently attempt only a delayed adjustment type of inventory behavior. They tolerate a considerable departure of actual inventories from the optimum level rather than attempt an immediate adjustment of inventories on the basis of inprecise estimates of future market conditions. This complication was introduced into the theoretical analysis. Contrariwise, no empirical support was found for the hypothesis that manufacturers speculate in inventories, adjusting their holdings of stocks in response to anticipated price changes. Consequently, it seems appropriate to neglect the complications of speculation in the theoretical study. Unfortunately, I have not succeeded in introducing unfilled orders into the theoretical analysis, although the empirical evidence suggests they are a factor of considerable importance in determining the desired level of stocks of purchased materials and goods in process.

The assumption of price rigidity, motivated by convenience, serves to suppress the roles of speculative inventory holdings and substitution. A statement by J. R. Hicks suggests that a theoretical investigation of the properties of a model involving price rigidity is worth while [22, p. 145]:

> Both the manufacturer and the retailer are, for the most part, "price makers" rather than "price takers"; they fix their prices and let the quantities they sell be determined by demand. A model in which quantities bear the brunt of disequilibrium fits most of the facts distinctly better [than the model of *Value and Capital*].

In addition to facilitating the derivation of theorems concerning the stability implications of buffer-stock inventory behavior, the assumption of price rigidity makes it possible to muster within the confines of this paper relevant data for the United States economy in an attempt to determine whether the conditions for stability are satisfied. If the assumption of price rigidity were abandoned, the difficulties involved in empirical investigation would be increased by whole orders of magnitude.

Empirical and theoretical research are complementary. A theoretical investigation may assist the econometrician by providing limits on the range of models that have to be tested. Although the assumption of profit maximization may serve partially to restrict the hypotheses to be considered, major simplification is almost inevitably involved in moving from theorems derived from that assumption to the equations of a completely specified model. Examination of the dynamic implications of conceivable modes of behavior provides a second source of a priori knowledge. The theoretical investigation of stability conditions for the buffer-stock inventory model suggests appropriate a priori restrictions for empirical research by revealing which types of inventory behavior on the part of the individual firm imply reasonable dynamic properties for the economy.

The model developed in this paper belongs to a general family of multi-sector dynamic models which includes the input-output approach utilized by the United States Government to investigate on an industry by industry basis the impact of mobilization for the Korean war.[3] In dynamic input-output analysis inventories usually are either relegated to the final bill of goods or assumed to behave in accordance with an elementary version of the accelerator principle uncomplicated by lags in the adjustment process or errors made by firms in anticipating future sales volume. Although it may be appropriate to neglect such complications in the analysis of problems relating to long-run economic growth, my empirical investigations of inventory behavior in the United States indicate that errors made by firms in anticipating future sales and adjustment lags served to curtail substantially inventory accumulation during the Korean emergency [27]. The theoretical framework presented in Part I of this paper provides an appropriate vehicle for considering these two complications of actual inventory behavior in analyzing on an industry by industry basis such problems as the economic impact of mobilization for limited war.

PART I. A MULTI-SECTOR INVENTORY MODEL

A. *The Behavior of the Firm*

It seems appropriate to assume that under conditions of price rigidity entrepreneurs will carry inventories for the purpose of avoiding the unsatisfied market that would otherwise occur whenever demand exceeds anticipated sales. When demand exceeds expectations, inventories are reduced below the planned level; conversely, when sales fall short of anticipated demand, unplanned inventories are accumulated. The production level of the next period is then set so as to either exceed or fall short of anticipated sales in order to restore inventories to the desired level.[4] The excess over actual sales of goods available at the end of the production period is held as inventory and must be considered in formulating production plans for the next period. Although an essentially intuitive approach similar to that of Metzler [30] will be followed in the subsequent paragraphs where the details of this argument are spelled out, it must be mentioned that Edwin Mills has demonstrated that

[3] A discussion of two Air Force models was presented by Holley [23, 24]. Chenery and Clark have discussed the United States Emergency Models [9].

[4] Entrepreneurs in fact have the option of eliminating excess stocks by price reductions and of raising prices in periods of shortage. This type of behavior has been excluded by the assumption of price rigidity. Paul A. Samuelson has derived stability conditions for a model in which price adjustments occur when existing stocks exceed an equilibrium level as a result of a divergence between current production and consumption [34, p. 275–6].

under appropriate conditions this type of firm behavior is at least consistent with the assumption of profit maximization [**31**].

The distinction between the equilibrium and planned level of inventories proves to be crucial. It will be assumed that the firm's equilibrium level of inventory is linearly related to sales. If $I^e(t)$ represents the equilibrium inventory for the firm at time t and $\bar{X}(t)$ anticipated sales, this assumption may be expressed by the equation

$$(1.1) \qquad\qquad I^e(t) = c + b\bar{X}(t) \qquad\qquad (t = 1,2,3,\ldots)\,.$$

The parameter b, the marginal desired inventory coefficient, relates the equilibrium level of inventories to sales volume. Metzler and Lundberg assumed that firms attempt an immediate adjustment of inventories to this equilibrium level. In actual practice, costs involved in changing production levels and adjusting the size of stocks apparently lead firms to attempt only a partial adjustment of actual inventories to the desired level in any one period. If this flexible accelerator complication is introduced, the level of inventories planned for period t, $I^p(t)$, is determined by the equation

$$(1.2) \qquad I^p(t) = d[I^e(t) - I^a(t-1)] + I^a(t-1)\,, \qquad 0 < d \leqslant 1\,,$$

where $I^a(t-1)$ represents actual inventories in the preceding period.[5]
If the reaction coefficient d is precisely one, planned and equilibrium inventories are identical. But if d is less than unity, the planned adjustment in inventory is a proportion d of the discrepancy between the actual and the equilibrium level of inventories.

Entrepreneurs set the level of output at the beginning of the production period in an attempt to obtain the planned level of inventories on the basis of anticipations concerning future sales volume. Therefore, output $Q(t)$ is determined by the equation

$$(1.3) \qquad\qquad Q(t) = \bar{X}(t) + I^p(t) - I^a(t-1)\,.$$

If sales anticipations turn out to be correct, production will just suffice to meet the demand and to adjust inventories to the planned level. But when actual sales, $X(t)$, exceed anticipations, the extra demand can be met only by running inventory down below the planned level. On the other hand, surplus inventory will be accumulated when sales fall short of anticipations. Actual inventory, therefore, is given by the equation

$$(1.4)\; I^a(t) = I^p(t) + \bar{X}(t) - X(t) = cd + (1+bd)\bar{X}(t) - X(t) + (1-d)I^a(t-1)\,.$$

---

[5] This is the distributed lag type of investment function suggested by Goodwin [**17**] and utilized by Chenery [**8**] and others in empirical work.

Substituting from (1.1) and (1.2) into equation (1.3) yields

$$Q(t) = (1 + bd)\bar{X}(t) + cd - dI^a(t-1)$$

As a first step toward eliminating the inventory term note that the fact that the above equation holds for all t, including $t-1$, obviously implies

$$Q(t-1) - (1+bd)\bar{X}(t-1) - cd + dI^a(t-2) = 0$$

Combining these last two equations yields;

$$Q(t) = (1+bd)[\bar{X}(t) - \bar{X}(t-1)] - d[I^a(t-1) - I^a(t-2)] + Q(t-1).$$

Further simplification is possible for the actual change in inventory is identical to the discrepancy between output and actual sales; that is,

$$I^a(t-1) - I^a(t-2) \equiv Q(t-1) - X(t-1) .$$

Simple substitution now serves to eliminate the inventory terms from the equation explaining the level of output:

$$(1.5) \quad Q(t) = (1+bd)\bar{X}(t) - (1+bd)\bar{X}(t-1) + (1-d)Q(t-1) + dX(t-1) .$$

The output of the firm may be determined from anticipated sales and last period's output and sales volume if the magnitude of the marginal desired inventory and reaction coefficients are known.

While it will be assumed that the output of each firm in the economy is determined in this fashion, it must be observed that wide fluctuations in sales might lead to conditions in which equation (1.5) could not represent the determination of a firm's output. First, a rapid fall in sales might imply negative outputs in order that the desired fraction of excess inventories could be eliminated within a single period; in reality, inventories cannot be liquidated at a rate higher than actual sales. Secondly, inventories cannot be negative. At least for relatively small fluctuations, however, these complications may be neglected; the output of each firm in the economy may be assumed to be determined by equation (1.5).

It is interesting to note that if the product of the marginal desired inventory coefficient times the delayed adjustment term equals minus one $(bd = -1)$, the output of the firm is completely independent of whatever sales anticipations the entrepreneur happens to hold and depends only upon output and sales in the preceding period. If sales anticipations are at any fixed unchanging level, $\bar{X}_t = \bar{X}_{t-1}$, output is again found to depend only upon past output and sales. The complications created by the anticipations term may also be avoided if it is assumed that firms correctly anticipate next period's demand for their product. With perfect foresight, $\bar{X}_t = X_t$, equation (1.5) reduces to

$$(1.6) \quad Q(t) = (1+bd)X(t) + (d-1-bd)X(t-1) + (1-d)Q(t-1) .$$

Such a procedure achieves simplification at the expense of suppressing the complications of real interest. Sales anticipations and consequent errors in planning are most easily introduced if naive expectations are assumed. If $\bar{X}(t) = X(t-1)$, equation (1.5) becomes

$$(1.7) \quad Q(t) = (1 + d + bd)X(t-1) - (1 + bd)X(t-2) + (1-d)Q(t-1) .$$

B. *The Industry and the Economy*

A uniformity assumption facilitates the derivation of the economic implications of the assumption that the multitude of firms in the economy behave according to equation (1.7); it will be assumed that all firms producing a given commodity have the same marginal desired inventory and delayed adjustment coefficients. Since these are the only parameters entering into the linear equations determining the output of each firm, the total output of a commodity may be derived as a function of past industry sales and outputs by simply summing the quantities and sales figures over all the individual firms in the industry. If $X_{ij}(t)$ and $Q_{ij}(t)$ stand for the sales and output of the ith firm in the jth industry at time t, the uniformity assumption implies the following relationship between sales and outputs in each of the n industries constituting the economy

$$(1.8) \quad \sum_i Q_{ij}(t) = (1 + b_j d_j + d_j) \sum_i X_{ij}(t-1) - (1 + b_j d_j) \sum_i X_{ij}(t-2)$$
$$+ (1-d_j) \sum_i Q_{ij}(t-1) \qquad (j = 1, 2, \ldots, n) .$$

Thus the uniformity assumption permits a reduction in the complexity of the system by replacing the multitude of equations in a given industry by a single equation explaining industry output on the basis of past sales.[6] It proves convenient to rewrite equation (1.8) in more compact matrix notation as

$$(1.8') \quad Q_t = (I + BD + D)X_{t-1} - (I + BD)X_{t-2} + (I - D)Q_{t-1} .$$

Here Q_t and X_t are column vectors whose components represent industry output and sales, respectively; I is the identity matrix, and B and D are diagonal matrices of marginal desired inventory and adjustment coefficients, respectively.

---

[6] It may be observed that the output of a whole industry, but not that of any individual firm, is determined on the basis of past sales and output of that industry. The output of the individual firm is indeterminate, a problem also encountered in the theory of pure competition under the assumption of constant costs. Samuelson suggests that "under the purest conditions of competition the boundaries of the (firm) . . . become vague and ill-defined, and also unimportant." [34, p. 79]. Here too we need not be concerned with the scale of operation of the individual firm; only the output of the industry is of interest.

The assumption of uniform desired inventory and adjustment coefficients for all firms in a given industry does not suffice to provide a deterministic economic model. In addition to (1.8) other equations connecting sales volume with the outputs of the various industries are required. One possible procedure might be to assume that only one commodity is produced in the economy and that all sales are made directly to consumers. The consumption function could then be employed to relate sales to the level of output. This procedure was utilized by Metzler in the development of his theory of the inventory cycle. Although this is common practice in the construction of business cycle models it is not necessary to neglect all aggregation problems in this way. There is an alternative, less restrictive, disaggregated approach. When this more realistic procedure is followed the conditions for stability are altered in a most fundamental fashion.

A system of equations relating the sales of each sector to the level of output of all sectors is required. Let production conditions be assumed to be the same for all the firms in a given industry. Let sales be regarded as the sum of purchases by all other firms for production purposes and a final bill of goods representing government demand, consumption, and sales that are not related to current and past levels of output.[7] Since we assume that no stocks of inputs are held, purchases of commodities at time t by each sector must be related to the quantity that the sector plans to produce in the next period. The inputs required for production purposes may be considered as specified by a matrix of technological coefficients $A = (a_{ij})$, where $a_{ij} \geqslant 0$ represents the quantity of output of sector i required per unit of output of the jth sector. The n equations relating sales of each sector to the output of all other industries, because of the production lag, have the form

$$x_{it} = \sum_j a_{ij} Q_{j,t+1} + y_{it} \qquad (i = 1,\ldots, n)$$

or in matrix notation

$$(1.9) \qquad\qquad X_t = AQ_{t+1} + Y_t .$$

Sales are equal to the inputs required for output forthcoming in the next period[8] plus Y_t, the final bill of goods vector whose components represent

---

[7] Later it is explained how consumption may be included endogenously within the basic framework of the model rather than assumed to be independent of current levels of activity.

[8] The time lag in equation (1.9) is crucial. This type of formulation is essential if production is regarded as a time consuming process. The differential equation models discussed by Georgescu-Roegen [15], David Hawkins [20], and Leontief [25] assumed that production is instantaneous. The essence of the inventory problem may well lie in the fact that production does require time. Although an alternative time lag formulation may be appropriate for analyzing other problems relating to growth as

sales of each commodity that are independent of output. The equation is meaningful, of course, only if $X_t \geqslant 0$ and $Q_t \geqslant 0$. The components of the matrix A of technological coefficients might be regarded as fixed if substitution were not a technological possibility and if constant returns to scale prevailed. The technological assumption of fixed proportions need not be adopted as the assumption of price rigidity, already introduced in the development of the inventory behavior equation for individual firms, together with constant returns to scale, serves to establish the same result. Under either set of assumptions, the empirical counterpart of the A matrix is provided by the Leontief input-output matrix of flow coefficients.

Alternative interpretations of the A matrix are possible. For example, we could restrict attention to three sectors only: manufacturing, wholesale, and retail trade. Another interpretation of the A matrix is provided by the Hayekian type of technology in which higher stages of production feed their output to the lower stages. Such special cases of the general problem are all subsumed within the analysis that follows.

With the aid of equation (1.9), a simple process of substitution suffices to eliminate the expression for sales from equation (1.8') so as to have a system of equations involving past and present levels of industry outputs and the final bill of goods alone. This yields

$$(1.10) \quad Q_t = (I + BD + D)(AQ_t + Y_{t-1}) - (I + BD)(AQ_{t-1} + Y_{t-2}) + (I - D)Q_{t-1} \, .$$

A transformation of this expression for quantity reveals that current levels of output may be explained by past output levels and the magnitude of the final bill of goods

$$Q_t = [I - (I + BD + D)A]^{-1} \{ [I - D - (I + BD)A]Q_{t-1} + (I + BD + D)Y_{t-1} - (I + BD)Y_{t-2} \} \, ,$$

or more briefly

$$(1.11) \quad Q_t = TQ_{t-1} + M(I + BD + D)Y_{t-1} - M(I + BD)Y_{t-2},$$

where

$$M \equiv [I - (I + BD + D)A]^{-1}$$

and

$$T \equiv M[I - D - (I + BD)A] = I - MD(I - A).$$

opposed to cyclical phenomena, it seems clear that a model of inventory behavior has to recognize that the inputs used in the production of a commodity must have been fabricated in an earlier period.

From this last equation it is apparent that a complete, deterministic model of the economy is obtained when the technological coefficients describing production conditions, as summarized by matrix equation (1.9), are combined with the set of equations giving the level of output for each industry when firms pursue a buffer-stock inventory policy.

Utilization of a matrix of technological coefficients to achieve closure abstracts from fixed investment in plant and equipment, buildings, and so forth. Baumol has implied, in a discussion of an aggregative model, that the buffer-stock type of behavior may be attributed to *all* investment, to explain a divergence between ex ante and ex post investment [5]. Only a rephrasing of the argument to follow rather than a substantive change would be required in order to include fixed investment in this way. Alternatively, non-inventory investment may be relegated to the final bill of goods. Another procedure would be to rewrite equation (1.9) in the form $X_t = AQ_{t+1} + E(Q_t - Q_{t-1})$, where E is a matrix of capital and purchased material accelerator coefficients. When such a procedure is followed in order to explain capital accumulation the inventory model proves difficult to handle analytically, but it might be the most fruitful method to apply in empirical applications of the model.

Consumption expenditure can be relegated to the final bill of goods if it may be assumed to be independent of current income. Alternatively, consumption expenditure may be made dependent upon the current level of output by a slight reinterpretation of certain coefficients. No fundamental change in the structure of the model is required. The relation of consumption of individual commodities to labor income may be expressed by the equation

$$(1.12) \qquad\qquad C_t = C + A^c y_t \,,$$

where A^c is a column vector whose components represent marginal propensities to consume by commodity type and C is a vector of constant components of consumption expenditure. Income, the scalar y_t, may in turn be considered to depend upon the level of output, Q_{t+1}, according to the extent to which labor is utilized to produce a unit of output, and possibly the level of income itself, for labor may be consumed directly. This gives the equation

$$(1.13) \qquad\qquad y_t = A^r Q_{t+1} + a_{oo} y_t \,,$$

where $A^r = (a_{o1}, a_{o2}, \ldots, a_{on})$, a row vector, and a_{oo} are defined in a fashion similar to the coefficients of A. Substituting, one obtains

$$(1.14) \qquad\qquad C_t = C + \left(\frac{1}{1 - a_{oo}}\right) A^c A^r Q_{t+1} \,.$$

Here $A^c A^r$ is an $n \times n$ matrix, of course. Equation (1.9) can be replaced by the relation

$$(1.15) \qquad\qquad X_t = \left[A + \left(\frac{1}{1 - a_{oo}}\right) A^c A^r \right] Q_{t+1} + Y_t + C \,.$$

By substituting $A^* = A + [1/(1-a_{oo})] A^c A^r$ into equation (1.15) it is made identical in form to (1.9); the equations derived with (1.9) for the case in which all consumption was relegated to the final bill of goods may clearly be made immediately applicable to the more general case. No additional equations for the final model are obtained when this procedure is utilized to open the buffer-stock inventory model with respect to consumption; there remains but one equation of (1.11) for each industry in the economy.[9]

PART II. STATICS AND DYNAMICS

Implications for the behavior of the economy through time of alternative assumptions concerning the nature of expectations, of technological improvement, and of adjustments in marginal inventory and reaction coefficients are of fundamental interest. As a prelude to the analysis of these complex questions within the framework of the multi-sector inventory model developed in the preceding section, it is convenient to review certain basic concepts.

A. *The Static Solutions*

The first step in the analysis of the properties of the buffer-stock inventory model is to observe its behavior under static conditions. If output and the final bill of goods remain at some fixed levels, call them Q and Y, we have from equation (1.10)

$$(2.1) \qquad Q = (I + BD + D)(AQ + Y) - (I + BD)(AQ + Y) + (I - D)Q .$$

This expression simplifies to

$$(2.2) \qquad\qquad\qquad Q = AQ + Y ,$$

an equation identical to a balance relation encountered in open input-output

---

[9] An alternative procedure giving somewhat greater flexibility may be followed in order to introduce consumption complications. Let us regard the oth sector as the labor sector. Then a_{oj} must be the quantity of labor required per unit of the jth output and a_{io} the slope of the (linear) Engel curve relating consumption of commodity i to income. Various lags in consumption behavior may now be considered by appropriate specification of the parameter b_o. Labor income at time t is $x_{ot} = \sum_j a_{oj} q_{j,t+1}$ by equation (1.9). Now if $b_o = -1$ and $d_o = 1$ we have by equation (1.8) that $q_{o,t+1} = x_{ot}$; since the goods required for "production" at time $t+1$ are purchased at time t, this is equivalent to unlagged consumption behavior! If, on the other hand, $b_o = -2$, we have $q_{ot} = x_{t-2}$ and consumption is lagged *one* period, as with the Robertsonian consumption function. If b_o lies between these two limits, consumption depends on both past and current income.

analysis. The static equilibrium of the inventory model for an unchanging final bill of goods, a vector of constant outputs, is

$$(2.3) \qquad\qquad Q = [I - A]^{-1} Y \,.$$

It is clear that the equilibrium output for each sector of the economy depends only upon the matrix of flow coefficients and the final bill of goods; the magnitudes of the marginal desired inventory and reaction coefficients do not enter into the static solution. The equilibrium solution and certain complications of mathematical interest are familiar from static input-output analysis.[10]

B. *The Homogeneous Solution*

The task of analyzing the dynamic properties of the model represented by the simultaneous system of equations (1.11) is facilitated, just as with the single difference equations encountered in aggregative business cycle analysis, by working in terms of deviations from the static solution. This procedure will be most fully appreciated if a problem of prediction is considered. It may be observed that (1.11) is the "reduced form" of the system of equations (1.10); the vectors Y_t and Y_{t-1} are exogenous and the vector Q_{t-1} constitutes the predetermined variables of the system; the vector of endogenous variables Q_t is to be determined. If one desires to predict future levels of production on the assumption that equation (1.11) portrays the behavior of the economy, the prediction has to be conditional upon knowledge of the path of the unexplained exogenous variables, the final bill of goods vector Y_t. Suppose, in order to facilitate the argument, that the final bill of goods is a known constant vector Y.[11] If Q_o is the vector of current output, the level of

[10] The model is called feasible in the static sense if $Y \geqslant 0$ implies that the static solution Q is nonnegative. A theorem established by Hawkins and Simon [21] implies that the system is feasible if it is self-contained in the sense that there exists no production process which requires in order to produce a unit of output (both directly as an input and indirectly in the production of other commodities required as inputs) one or more units of its own output. This is a most reasonable assumption for an economy in which production does not require time, for otherwise some process would have to be unprofitable under any set of non-negative prices, not all zero. When production requires time, no production process need involve a loss even when the self-contained condition is violated, but only if the rate of interest is negative. While this possibility has been considered by von Neumann [35] and Irving Fisher [14, pp. 191–2], I shall exclude from consideration technologies implying a negative rate of interest and assume that the technology is that of an efficient economy so that the model is feasible in the static sense.

[11] The assumption that the final bill of goods is fixed is introduced only to simplify the discussion; it is not essential to the argument. The procedure for a fluctuating final bill of goods is analogous to that utilized in analyzing the elementary case where only a single difference equation is involved. The conditions for stability are independent of

output of each sector for the next period is given by the matrix expression $Q_1 = TQ_o + MDY$; substituting this result into equation (1.11) yields $Q_2 = T^2Q_o + (T + I)MDY$. Clearly, the assumptions permit prediction for any number of periods into the future.

This clumsy, iterative procedure may be circumvented by working in terms of deviations from equilibrium. Observe that by definition the static solution obtained by application of (2.2) must satisfy (2.1). Consequently, subtraction of the equilibrium solution Q from the vector of actual outputs Q_t as given by (1.10) yields the homogeneous equation

$$(2.4) \quad Q_t - Q = (I + BD + D)A(Q_t - Q) + [I - D - (I + BD)A](Q_{t-1} - Q)$$
$$= T(Q_{t-1} - Q),$$

the last equality following from the definition of T presented in the derivation of (1.11). By induction on this last equation one obtains the homogeneous solution,

$$(2.5) \qquad\qquad Q_t - Q = T^t(Q_o - Q).$$

All that is necessary to obtain Q_t from this homogeneous solution is to add Q to both sides

$$(2.6) \qquad\qquad Q_t = T^t(Q_o - Q) + Q,$$

where Q is provided by equation (2.2).

C. The Stability of Equilibrium

The stability of a difference equation system is most conveniently discussed with reference to the homogeneous equation (2.5). Will the system converge to the static solution Q for all initial deviations from equilibrium? Equation (2.5) reveals that this concept of stability requires

$$\lim_{t \to \infty} T^t(Q_o - Q) = 0, \qquad \text{for all vectors } (Q_o - Q).$$

Only the transition matrix T has to be considered in resolving the issue of stability. Stability requires that all of the characteristic roots of T lie within the unit circle on the complex plane. Is the multi-sector buffer-stock inventory model stable? This issue is to be explored in Part III of this paper.[12]

---

the time path of the final bill of goods. An economist's accounts of the procedure for the special, single difference equation problem is given by Allen [3, Ch. 6] and for the more general case by Leontief [25, pp. 63–5].

[12] Other dynamic properties in addition to stability are also important. Of particular interest is the question of dynamic feasibility. It is clear that if the marginal desired inventory coefficients are nonnegative, sufficiently small disturbances could not cause a stable system to degenerate into a state of negative stocks or outputs. The complication of feasibility for larger disturbances might be dealt with by embedding the model

D. *Stochastic Complications*

Stochastic disturbances are frequently introduced into dynamic models in order to represent variables omitted from the analysis. For the buffer-stock model they may be assigned a particularly important role. Stochastic disturbances can result if the assumption of static expectations is introduced only as an approximation. The assumption that actual expectations are yesterday's sales plus a disturbance with zero expected value is much more palatable than the rigid condition that $\bar{X}_t = X_{t-1}$.

Fortunately, the dynamic properties of the type of linear system under consideration is not complicated in any essential way when stochastic shocks are introduced. Suppose that the true equation describing the generation of outputs is of the form

$$(2.7) \qquad Q_t = TQ_{t-1} + MDY + \varepsilon_t,$$

where ε_t is a vector of random variables with zero expected value. More precisely, if $\mathscr{E}$ is the expected value operator, assume $\mathscr{E}(\varepsilon_t) = 0$ and $\mathscr{E}(\varepsilon_t \varepsilon_t') = \mathscr{E}(\varepsilon \varepsilon')$ for all positive integers t. Then it can be shown, although not within the space available here, that the deterministic scheme already developed describes the path of *expected* if not actual output

$$(2.8) \qquad \mathscr{E}(Q_t) = T\mathscr{E}(Q_{t-1}) + MDY.$$

Of course, how concerned one is with $\mathscr{E}(Q_t)$ and in particular the limit$_{t\to\infty}$ $\mathscr{E}(Q_t)$ depends upon the magnitude of the discrepancies between the actual level of output determined by the stochastic scheme and its expected value. Let $E_t = Q_t - \mathscr{E}(Q_t)$ represent this error. Interest centers on the variance-covariance matrix of errors $\mathscr{E}(E_t E_t')$. Although the matrix depends in an essential fashion upon the distance t into the future which we are attempting to predict, the linear nature of the system means that if the non-stochastic system is stable, if in other words $T^t \to 0$, then limit$_{t\to\infty}$ $\mathscr{E}(E_t E_t')$ exists. It follows immediately that the variance of the prediction errors is bounded. This means that the conditions of stability for the nonstochastic system are pertinent for the more realistic case in which random shocks are introduced. The theorems developed in the next section are of interest in the appraisal of a stochastic version of the buffer-stock inventory model.

---

discussed here within a larger, possibly piecewise linear system; it would then be but one of several possible regimes; the nature of the alternative regimes and the rules for switching from one regime to the next would have to be specified unambiguously. Leontief modified the Hawkins dynamic model in this way; see [25, pp. 68 – 76]. For the buffer-stock model these complications cannot be explored within the compass of this paper.

PART III. SOME DYNAMIC IMPLICATIONS OF BUFFER-STOCK INVENTORY
BEHAVIOR

In comparative statics the effects of changes in a model's parameters upon
its equilibrium solution are examined. For the multi-sector inventory model,
only the matrix A of technological coefficients together with the final bill of
goods Y are involved in the determination of the static solution. Comparative
dynamics is concerned with contrasting possible paths that an economy
might follow in adjusting through time under alternative assumptions concerning the magnitude of the system's parameters. We shall see that the
marginal desired inventory coefficients and the reaction coefficients as well
as the A matrix influence the dynamic behavior of the buffer-stock inventory
economy.

Two fundamental questions are to be considered: Does the delayed adjustment, flexible accelerator complication observed in actual buffer-stock
inventory behavior help to stabilize the economy? Do errors made by firms
in forecasting future sales volume contribute to economic instability; would
more accurate expectations serve to stabilize the economy? It proves convenient to follow a twofold line of attack in demonstrating that only the
first of these questions can be answered in the affirmative. The behavior of
the model with all reaction coefficients equal to unity will be contrasted
with the delayed reaction case in which the flexible accelerator coefficients
are less than one. In addition, the case of static expectations will be compared
with the hypothetical situation in which entrepreneurs anticipate correctly
next period's demand for their product.

In the presentation of the argument it proves essential to place certain
restrictions upon the types of technologies that will be considered. The theorems are developed under the restriction that the economy be self-contained
in the sense of Hawkins and Simon [21]. This is equivalent to the condition
that the characteristic roots of A are all within the unit circle on the complex
plane. As has already been mentioned, this guarantees the existence of a
feasible static solution for any positive final bill of goods. In addition, the
matrix A of flow coefficients will be assumed to be equivalent under a
similarity transformation to a diagonal matrix; while this is not truly
restrictive,[13] it does facilitate the proofs of certain theorems. It will also be
helpful to agree as a matter of notation that if A is any square matrix and λ_i is
a characteristic root of A, then $|\lambda_i|$ is the modulus of λ_i and $r(A) \equiv \max_i |\lambda_i|$.
In the development of the conditions for stability, frequent use is made of

---

[13] No empirical investigation could lead to the rejection of this assumption for
Bellman [6, p. 25] has shown that for any square matrix $A = (a_{ij})$ and $\varepsilon > 0$ there
exists a matrix $A^* = (a_{ij}^*)$ with the desired property and such that $|a_{ij} - a_{ij}^*| \leqslant \varepsilon$.

properties of the characteristic roots of square nonnegative (Frobenius) matrices presented by Debreu and Herstein [12].

A. *Static Expectations with Immediate Adjustment Behavior*

The contrast between the stability properties of the multi-sector buffer-stock inventory model and those of the macro-inventory cycle theory of Lloyd Metzler is most easily demonstrated by considering the restricted case of immediate adjustment behavior under the assumption of naive expectations. Metzler found that under the assumption of naive expectations his single commodity economy was stable if and only if the marginal propensity to consume is less than unity [29, pp. 117–8]. The following theorem, proved in the Appendix, establishes a necessary condition for stability of the multi-sector model.

THEOREM I: *If T is defined by* (1.11) *with D = I and B $\geqslant$ 0, then*

$$\lambda^+ < \frac{1}{3 + 2 \max(b_i)} \text{ implies } r(T) < 1 ,$$

and

$$r(T) < 1 \text{ implies } \lambda^+ < \frac{1}{3 + 2 \min(b_i)} .$$

Recognition of the multi-commodity nature of the economy reveals that even if the marginal propensity to consume is zero, stability under the assumption of immediate adjustment requires that the largest characteristic root of the matrix of technological coefficients be less than one-third.[14] This condition does not suffice if any of the marginal desired inventory coefficients is greater than zero.[15] A priori considerations suggest that Metzler's restric-

---

[14] Because Metzler neglects production conditions entirely, the special single commodity case of the disaggregated model is not identical to Metzler's. Metzler implicitly assumed that only labor enters into the production process, excluding the possibility that today's output is begot by the marriage of labor service with commodity inputs produced in the past.

[15] While negative marginal desired inventory coefficients seem unreasonable, it is interesting to note that if $B = -2I$ and $D = I$ the buffer-stock inventory model (1.10) simplifies to $Q_t = AQ_{t-1} + Y_t$, the matrix or multi-sector multiplier of Goodwin [16] and Chipman [10]. It is well known that this system is stable if the economy is feasible in the static sense that $Y \geqslant 0$ implies that the static solution Q is necessarily nonnegative. The Hawkins-Simon condition indicates that it is reasonable to assume that this condition is met. While it can be shown that the model is necessarily feasible in the dynamic sense that $Y_t \geqslant 0$ and $X_o \geqslant 0$ imply $X_t \geqslant 0$ for $t = 1,2$, the initial size of the inventory endowment places an absolute ceiling on the level of output that can be obtained without the contradiction of negative inventories. It seems appropriate to restrict our discussion to the case in which $B \geqslant 0$.

tion upon the marginal propensity to consume is satisfied. While a priori considerations also suggest that the characteristic roots of A are all less than unity in absolute value, nothing implies that they are less than one-third.

The theoretical results raise an empirical question concerning the actual values of the characteristic roots of A. Max A. Woodbury reports a figure of 0.5414 for the largest characteristic root of an 18×18 input-output matrix based on data for the year 1939 [36]. My own calculations performed on a 10×10 input-output matrix for the year 1947 yielded a dominant root of 0.55, a figure remarkably similar to that reported by Woodbury. Inspection of matrices of six, eleven, and twenty-one sectors published by the Harvard Economic Research Project [32] revealed that in every case the largest characteristic root was larger than one half.[16] This establishes that stability is not compatible with immediate adjustment behavior for reasonable values of λ^+, the dominant root of A.

A further difficulty with the assumption that firms attempt an immediate adjustment of inventories to their equilibrium level must be mentioned. Even if we chose to reject the empirical evidence and assumed that the immediate-adjustment buffer-stock model were stable, the system would still have a most undesirable property. If the reaction coefficient is unity, stability implies that the transition matrix T is nonpositive.[17] This means that if the system were stable, it would be prone to generate a cycle with most peculiar characteristics. A simple example will serve to illustrate this strange cycle. Suppose that the economy were initially in equilibrium with some given final bill of goods Y. If the final bill of goods changes to Y^*, $0 \leqslant Y^* \leqslant Y$, the output of each sector must fall in the next period below the new equilibrium level. Then in the subsequent period they must all rise above their equilibrium value, and so forth. For this type of disturbance, the length of the inventory cycle is two time periods. Such a saw-tooth cycle necessarily develops once every sector is producing below the equilibrium level, as in a depression. All this follows from the fact that a necessary condition for stability, $T \leqslant 0$, together with $(Q_t - Q) \leqslant 0$, implies $T(Q_t - Q) = Q_{t+1} - Q \geqslant 0$. The conclusion that the inventory cycle will be of two production time periods in length holds, of course, only for a particular if common type of disturbance. Nevertheless, the possibility of an inventory cycle of such curious form demonstrates that immediate adjustment behavior can give rise to cycles of an entirely different type from those that plague the American economy.

---

[16] Although the precise determination of the characteristic roots of a matrix is a difficult computational task, a lower bound for the largest characteristic root can be easily determined for A is nonnegative. Specifically, $r(A) \geqslant \min_j \Sigma_i a_{ij}$ and $r(A) \leqslant r(A^*)$ if $A \leqslant A^*$.

[17] This statement is established in the Appendix in proving Theorem I.

B. *Static Expectations with Delayed Adjustment*

A first step in demonstrating that delayed adjustment behavior may contribute to stability is provided by the following theorem, proved in the Appendix, concerning necessary conditions for stability.

THEOREM II: *If*

$$T = I - [I - (I + BD + D)A]^{-1} D(I - A) ,$$

where $D = diag(d_i) \geqslant 0$, $B = diag(b_i) \geqslant 0$, *and* $A \geqslant 0$, $r(A) < 1$, *then* $r(T) < 1$ *implies*:

(i) $$D > 0 ,$$

(ii) $$r(K) < 1 , \text{ where } K \equiv (B + I)DA(I - A)^{-1} ,$$

(iii) $$\lambda^+ < \frac{2 - min(d_i)}{2 - min(d_i) + 2\, min(b_i d_i + d_i)} .$$

Of course, even if these conditions are satisfied, the economy may still be unstable.

If empirical evidence were to reveal that any of these three conditions were not satisfied, we could conclude that the system is unstable. Estimates derived from time series data must be utilized in calculating the upper bound on λ^+ compatible with stability as appropriate cross section data on inventory holdings are not currently available. In my empirical study of manufacturing inventory investment in the United States covering the period 1948–55 [27], estimates were derived of the marginal desired inventory and reaction coefficients for finished goods inventory held by both durable and by nondurable firms. These point estimates yield an upper bound on λ^+ of 0.93, a figure safely above the estimated λ^+ of 0.54. A second set of coefficients is provided by data including purchased material and goods in process as well as finished goods inventory but broken down into five durable goods industries; examination of these estimates yielded an upper bound of 0.90 on λ^+.[18] These calculations neglect wholesale and retail trade inventories. Since the point estimates cannot be regarded as precise, we cannot be certain that the conditions of Theorem II are satisfied.[19] The evidence thus proves

---

[18] The data appear in Tables II and III of [27]. For finished goods inventory, the nondurable sector yields $min(d_i) = .0649$ and $min(b_i d_i + d_i) = .0707$. For the total inventory analysis values of .0554 and .1092 respectively are provided by primary metals and nondurables.

[19] The finished goods nondurable estimate of d is not significantly different from zero at the .05 level, suggesting that there is reason to suspect that condition (i) of Theorem II may *not* be satisfied.

inconclusive; all that can be said is that no basis is provided for concluding that the economy is unstable by considering the available data in conjuncture with Theorem II.

The next theorem specifies conditions assuring that T has no *real* roots greater than unity in absolute value.

THEOREM III: *If* $t_i = \alpha_i + \beta_i\sqrt{-1}$ *denotes a characteristic root of* T, *then*

$$\lambda^+ < \frac{2 - max(d_i)}{2 - max(d_i) + 2\,max(b_i d_i + d_i)}$$

implies

$$-1 < \alpha_i < 1\,,$$

provided

$$I \geqslant D > 0 \ and \ B \geqslant 0\,.$$

If the conditions of Theorem III are satisfied, T might still be unstable, but it would have to be an instability dominated by an explosive cycle.

An inspection of empirical estimates of the parameters of the model obtained with the finished goods inventory data yields a bound on λ^+ of 0.80; for the inventory data including purchased materials and goods in process the bound is 0.68.[20] Since both these figures are well above $\lambda^+ \doteq 0.54$, the calculations suggest that the transitions matrix of the buffer-stock inventory model cannot have a real root greater than unity in absolute value. While the system might be unstable, it would have to be dominated by an explosive cycle.

It is difficult to specify conditions assuring that explosive oscillations will not take place. One procedure, not too pleasing empirically, is to invoke a stronger uniformity assumption. Earlier in the analysis when the problem of aggregating from the firm to the industry level was encountered, it was assumed that all firms in a given industry have the same marginal desired inventory coefficient. In order to specify conditions assuring stability of the multi-sector model the strong uniformity assumption that there are no interindustry differences in the reaction and marginal desired inventory coefficients proves convenient.[21]

[20] Durables provided $max(d_i) = .1829$ and $max(b_i d_i + d_i) = .2379$ for finished goods inventory. Transportation equipment data yielded maximum coefficients of .3160 and .3987 respectively.

[21] While this is not too happy an assumption, it is a mistake to conclude that it completely circumvents the problem of aggregation. The strong uniformity assumption does not serve to collapse the multi-sector model into the single equation form derived under the traditional procedure or macroanalysis. Roy Harrod is mistaken in arguing [25, p. 282]: "...it is necessary to frame the concept of an entrepreneur, who is representative in two respects, namely: (i) demand for his output must expand at the same rate

The strong uniformity assumption means that there exist scalars b and d such that $bI = B$ and $dI = D$. Under this assumption and with static expectations, the transitions matrix reduces to

(3.1) $$T = [I - (1 + bd + d)A]^{-1}[(1 - d)I - (1 + bd)A] .$$

With strong uniformity the following function maps the characteristic roots λ_i of A into the roots t_i of the transitions matrix T:[22]

(3.2) $$t(b, d, \lambda) = \frac{1 - d - (1 + bd)\lambda}{1 - (1 + bd + d)\lambda} .$$

The strong uniformity assumption yields a necessary and sufficient condition for stability.

THEOREM IV: *If T is defined as in (1.11) with $B = bI \geqslant 0$ and $D = dI > 0$,*

then $r(T) < 1$ if and only if $\lambda^+ < \dfrac{2 - d}{2 + d + 2bd}$.

If the point estimates of $d = 0.152$ and $b = 0.276$ obtained when finished goods inventory data aggregated over all manufacturing industries are regarded as precise [27], Theorem IV implies that the inventory cycle will be stable if and only if $\lambda^+ < .84$. While this gives a considerable margin of safety over the estimated value of λ^+ of 0.54, it neglects movements in purchased material and goods in process stocks. If all inventories are assumed to behave in accordance with the buffer-stock model, the appropriate levels of d and b to utilize in testing for stability are 0.430 and 0.389 respectively; if these estimates are regarded as precise, stability is possible if and only if $\lambda^+ < .57$. This bound is uncomfortably close to 0.54, the dominant root Max A. Woodbury calculated for a matrix of technological flow coefficients,

---

that the economy as a whole is expanding; and (ii) he must be psychologically representative, in the sense that his reaction to recent experience is an average one. He must be average in his make-up of courage and prudence, of optimism and pessimism... The formula that correctly describes the behavior of this representative entrepreneur may be applied to the macro economy." While this uniformity assumption might be invoked to justify the use of aggregative data to estimate the parameters of the buffer stock inventory equation, it must be observed that under no circumstances does it suffice to justify the application of the iterative predictive procedure mentioned in Part II, Section B to aggregative empirical models of the economy.

[22] Since $PAP^{-1} = \Lambda = \mathrm{diag}(\lambda_i)$, $PTP^{-1} = [I - (1 + bd + d)A]^{-1}[1 - d)I - (1 + bd)A]$ a diagonal matrix. This also implies that the characteristic vectors of A and T are identical; if A is indecomposable, the strong uniformity assumption implies that T can have but one characteristic vector with all components of the same sign. There also exists a left characteristic vector of relative prices $p' \geq 0$ with the interesting property that $p'Q_t = t(b,d,\lambda)p'Q_{t-1} + p'Y$; evaluated in terms of this vector of relative prices, the value of output grows at a constant rate that is independent of initial conditions.

without consumption. While the point estimates suggest that the conditions for stability are satisfied, it is clear that a slightly different configuration of measurement errors or the inclusion of consumption might well have led to the opposite conclusion.[23]

Under the strong uniformity assumption equation (3.2) may be utilized in conjunction with estimates of d and b to transform the characteristic roots of A into corresponding roots of T. The calculations of Max A. Woodbury yielded the two complex roots $\lambda_2 = -.1969 \pm .0871i$ as well as the dominant root of $\lambda_1^+ = .541$ already mentioned [36, p. 381]. The corresponding roots of T obtained by substituting these roots into equation (3.2) together with the finished goods estimates of d and b are $t_1 = .803$ and $t_2 = .853 \pm .0016i$. When the estimates of d and b provided by the regressions involving data on purchased materials and goods in process as well as finished goods are utilized in the calculations, the corresponding roots of T are $t_1 = -.459$ and $t_2 = .610 \pm 0.0128i$. As expected, both sets of roots imply a stable inventory cycle. It is interesting to observe that in both cases Woodbury's second root yields a root of T implying a cycle of long period, the transformation having reduced the imaginary portion of the root considerably. Notice too that although $|\lambda_1| > |\lambda_2|$, this ranking is reversed in the process of transforming the roots of A into roots of T; in both cases $|t_1| < |t_2|$. It must be remembered that the dominating root of T is not necessarily obtained by transforming the larger roots of A. Since not all the roots of A are available, it is impossible to determine whether the roots of T reported above are the dominating ones.

These calculations have been presented only in order to illustrate the application of the theorems. Although the estimates of the characteristic roots of T may be suggestive, they can hardly be regarded as precise. More is involved than the errors of measurement inevitably encountered in estimating the parameters of a system. Although fluctuations in purchased material and goods in process as well as finished goods inventory were taken into account in deriving the estimates of the characteristic roots of T, the calculations were based on the assumption that both fixed investment and consumption spending were relegated to the final bill of goods. Another set of calculations involving a different level of closure yielded a highly explosive characteristic root of 3.15![24] While it can be claimed that for reasonable values of the param-

---

[23] Slight changes in λ^+ lead to large changes in t^+, for $\lambda^+ = .54$, $d = .43$ and $b = .389$, yield $\partial t(d,b,\lambda)/\partial \lambda = -13$.

[24] These calculations included consumption but excluded fixed investment and stocks of purchased materials and goods in process. The strong uniformity assumption was not utilized. Immediate adjustment was assumed for certain inventory holding sectors. Since performing the calculations I have been advised that the unpublished stage-of-fabrication breakdown of inventory data for individual industries utilized in estimating the b_i and d_i are extremely unreliable and inappropriate for my purposes. Details of the calculations are provided in [26, Ch. V).

eters of the system delayed adjustment buffer-stock inventory behavior *may* be stable, the possibility of instability cannot be excluded. Even this weak conclusion is encouraging, however, for with the Metzler assumption of immediate adjustment, instability was inevitable for reasonable values of λ^+.

The effects upon the stability of the economy of changes in the parameters of the system may be evaluated, at least under the strong uniformity assumption. The lower the marginal desired inventory coefficient, other things being equal, the larger the dominant root of A that is compatible with stability. The slower the speed of adjustment, provided it remains positive, the more likely the economy is to be stable. The effects of changes in technology upon the stability of the system can also be evaluated. Suppose that the economy becomes more efficient as a result of technological change that dominates in the sense that the new input-output matrix $\tilde{A}$ has the property $0 \leqslant \tilde{A} \leqslant A$, where A is the old input-output matrix; then $r(\tilde{A}) \leqslant r(A)$.[25] Clearly, an improvement in technology that dominates the old methods of production does not contribute to instability.

C. *Alternative Assumptions Concerning Expectations*

Consideration of the stability properties of the buffer-stock inventory model under the assumption that the volume of sales anticipated by entrepreneurs are simply a naive projection of current levels revealed that stability is incompatible with Metzler's assumption of immediate adjustment behavior for reasonable values of the dominant root of the input-output matrix. When the possibility of delayed adjustment was admitted, stability was implied by estimates of the system's parameters for the United States economy. Is stability a possibility even with immediate adjustment behavior under alternative assumptions about expectations? This question will now be considered.

Intuition might well suggest that instability is the consequence of errors of judgment resulting from imperfect foresight. Furthermore, my own empirical investigations of observed manufacturers' sales and inventory behavior [27] suggest that manufacturers' expectations are considerably more accurate than is implied by the assumption of naive expectations. Analytical difficulties are presented by the most interesting case in which expectations are assumed to lie between the value obtained by a naive projection and actual development. Let us content ourselves with exploring the consequences of the assumption that expectations are perfect in the myopic sense that anticipations of sales volume for the next period are precisely fulfilled.[26] An

---

[25] If $\tilde{A}$ is indecomposable and $\tilde{A} \neq A$, then $r(\tilde{A}) < r(A)$.

[26] It might be objected that the assumption of perfect foresight provides a meaningless context in which to explore the consequences of buffer-stock behavior. In a similar vein, D. H. Robertson complained that in the Keynesian analysis of the interest rate

analysis of the implications of perfect foresight demonstrates that the unstable elements of the buffer-stock model are not the simple consequence of errors of expectations.

In order to explore the implications of perfect foresight it is necessary to substitute $\bar{X}_t = X_t$ in the matrix version of equation (1.5), the expression for output in terms of current anticipations and past experience. In addition, the input-output relationship $X_t = AQ_{t+1} + Y$ may be utilized in order to reduce the system to

$$(3.3) \quad Q_t = (I + BD)(AQ_{t+1} + Y) - (I + BD)(AQ_t + Y) + (I - D)Q_{t-1} + D(AQ_t + Y).$$

The following theorem is proved in the Appendix.

THEOREM V: *The system of simultaneous difference equations* (3.3) *is unstable if either*
(i) $D = I$ *and* $B \geqslant 0$, *or*
(ii) *there exist scalars b and d such that* $I > D = dI > 0$ *and* $B = bI \geqslant 0$.

Perfect foresight implies instability with immediate adjustment behavior; even when the assumption of immediate adjustment is relaxed, the system remains unstable, at least under the strong uniformity assumption.

The case of perfect foresight is not the only alternative to the assumption of naive expectations. As a third case, suppose that the expectations of entrepreneurs are completely independent of current and past sales; for definiteness, let us assume that $\bar{X}_t = X$ for all t, including $t-1$. Then it follows from the matrix version of equation (1.5) and (1.9) that

$$(3.4) \quad Q_t = (I - D)Q_{t-1} + DX_{t-1} = (I - D)Q_{t-1} + DAQ_t + Y.$$

The dynamic behavior of this system is completely independent of the marginal desired inventory coefficients. In the appendix we establish

THEOREM VI: *Difference equation system* (3.4) *is stable provided* $I \geqslant D > 0$.

Consideration of two alternatives to the assumption of naive expectations

---

"the organ which secretes it has been amputated, and yet it somehow still exists—a grin without a cat" [33, p. 36]. By assuming perfect foresight, the very element of errors of judgment required to justify the existence of buffer stock inventories has been eliminated. A sufficient defense of the procedure is provided by observing that it is necessary to analyze the consequences of perfect foresight in order to demonstrate that instability is not simply the consequence of errors of expectations. The problem is of further interest in that the implications of stochastic disturbances may be analyzed within essentially the same framework, as was pointed out above, Part II, Section D.

suggests that instability is not simply the consequence of errors of foresight. With perfect anticipations, stability is incompatible with immediate adjustment behavior. Even with delayed adjustment, perfect foresight implies instability under the strong uniformity assumption. The second alternative considered, the case in which expectations are completely independent of actual experience, provided an example of a system that is necessarily stable; while this alternative is unrealistic, it does serve to indicate that the issue of stability hinges in part upon the particular assumptions one chooses to make about the nature of expectations.

PART IV. SUMMARY AND CONCLUSIONS

The stability conditions derived in this paper for the buffer-stock inventory model stand in marked constrast to the dynamic properties of the Walrasian model of multiple competitive markets. Lloyd Metzler has shown in a brilliant article that the stability of competition does not depend upon the speed of adjustment if all commodities are gross substitutes [30]. Theoretical investigations of the role of expectations within the framework of a purely competitive environment by Enthoven, Arrow, and Nerlove suggest that the stability of a competitive economy in which all commodities are gross substitutes may be independent of errors of expectations [4, 13]. In contrast, both errors in anticipating future sales volume and speeds of adjustment have been shown in this paper to play an important role in the determination of the dynamic properties of an inventory holding economy involving price rigidity. Both of these complications have to be considered in evaluating policy measures advanced as means of stabilizing the economy.

The magnitude of fluctuations in the inventory component of GNP is widely recognized.[27] As a consequence, tax measures designed to stabilize inventory investment have been proposed. Moses Abramovitz suggested that a tax on the average value of inventories, by inducing firms to operate with lower stocks, would contribute to economic stability [2, pp. 293-4]. Albert G. Hart argues that "a tax at a substantial rate (25 per cent, say) to be applied each quarter to the value of any increase *or* decrease in each firm's inventory, compared with the same date a year previously," might better contribute to the same objective, provided the scheme were feasible administratively [19, pp. 452–3].

The multi-sector buffer-stock inventory model provides a theoretical framework helpful in evaluating such policy issues. A tax on the size of inventory holdings designed to reduce the average value of inventories might well miss its objective of dampening cycles in economic activity engendered

---

[27] In his analysis of inventory behavior in the inter-war period, Moses Abramovitz revealed that the inventory component of GNP was subject to major fluctuations from peaks to troughs of the business cycle [1, ch. 21].

by fluctuations in inventories. A reduction in the size of inventories that entrepreneurs desire to hold at relevant levels of output does not insure increased stability, for the crucial marginal desired inventory coefficients might still be larger than before. While it might be argued that the adoption of the alternative proposal, a tax levied each quarter on the *change* in the value of inventories from the corresponding quarter of the preceding year, would necessarily lower the marginal desired inventory coefficient, this would by no means establish that such a tax would contribute to the stability of the economy. *Ceteris paribus*, the faster entrepreneurs attempt to adjust inventories to the desired level, the less likely the economy is to be stable. A tax on inventory investment might well reduce the size of the marginal desired inventory coefficients; the possibility that it would raise the reaction coefficient by inducing firms to attempt a tighter inventory policy must also be admitted.

Restraint is also called for in evaluating the implications of a possible trend on the part of manufacturers toward a policy of closer control on inventories during the post-war period in the United States. Arthur F. Burns has suggested [7, p. 14]:

> There is... strong evidence that the businessmen of our generation manage inventories better than did their predecessors... success in economizing on inventories has tended to reduce the fluctuations of inventory investment relative to the scale of business operations and this in turn has helped to moderate the cyclical swings in production.

The argument of this paper demonstrates that the adoption of inventory practices that are more efficient from the point of view of the individual firm and lead to a reduction in average inventory levels does not necessarily contribute to stability.

The multi-sector model incorporates the economy's technological coefficients, a set of additional parameters suppressed in macro-business-cycle analysis. A government policy of encouraging innovation and technological advance might be expected to contribute to stability under fairly general conditions for a change in technology that dominates serves to reduce the largest characteristic root of A. While it is conceivable that a policy of encouraging technological advance might be more effective than taxing inventory investment as a means of stabilizing the economy as well as encouraging growth, it is clear that much involved analysis will be required before it will be possible to determine precisely what policy measures will indeed contribute to a more stable economy.

APPENDIX

Before presenting proofs of the theorems stated in the text it is convenient to establish the following Lemma. $\varphi(M)$ denotes the largest of the real parts of the characteristic roots of M, any square matrix.

LEMMA: *Let* $Q \equiv -(I-A)[I-A-(B+I)DA]^{-1}D$, *so that* $(I\ A)T\ (I-A)^{-1} = I+Q$, *and let* $t_i = \alpha_i + \beta_i\sqrt{-1}$ *be any characteristic root of* T. *Then*

$$\left.\begin{array}{c} r(Q) < 2 \\ \varphi(Q) < 0 \end{array}\right\} \text{ implies } |\alpha_i| < 1.$$

Furthermore,

$$\left.\begin{array}{c} r(Q) < 2 \\ \varphi(Q) < 0 \\ Q + I \leqslant 0 \end{array}\right\} \text{ implies } r(T) < 1 .$$

Proof. The roots q_i of Q and t_i of T are related by the equation $q_i + 1 = t_i$ for $Q + I$ is equivalent under a similarity transformation to T; the first statement follows immediately from this equality. These two conditions in themselves do not suffice to assure stability as T might have a large imaginary root. The third condition, $Q + I \leqslant 0$, assures that the dominant root of T is real [12], hence less than unity in absolute value.

The proofs of Theorems II and III will be considered before that of Theorem I.

Proof of Theorem II. Suppose $r(T) < 1$. Let $Q \equiv -(I-A)[I-A-(B+I)DA]^{-1}D$, so that $(I-A)T(I-A)^{-1} = I+Q$. Now if some $d_i = 0$, $|D| = 0$. Hence $|Q| = 0$ and therefore $\varphi(Q) \geqslant 0$. But this leads to a contradiction, for $r(T) = r(I+Q) < 1$ implies $\varphi(Q) < 0$, proving (i).

To prove (ii) observe that $Q^{-1} = D^{-1}(K-I)$, where $K \geqslant 0$ as it is the product of nonnegative matrices. Since $D > 0$, all the off-diagonal elements of Q^{-1} as well as $(K-I)$ are nonnegative; therefore Q^{-1} and $K-I$ both belong to a generalization of a class of matrices considered by Metzler. $\varphi(Q) < 0$ if and only if $\varphi(Q^{-1}) < 0$ if and only if $\varphi(K-I) < 0$, the last implication following from a theorem of Metzler [30] as generalized by Enthoven and Arrow [13]; see also [4]. Now $\varphi(K-I) < 0$ is equivalent to $r(K) < 1$, which is (ii), for $K \geqslant 0$ implies that its dominant root is real and positive.

To prove (iii) observe that $r(T) = r(Q+I) < 1$ implies $r(Q) < 2$. By conditions (i) and (ii) we also have $D > 0$ and $(K-I)^{-1} \leqslant 0$; hence $Q = (K-I)^{-1}D \leqslant 0$. Now

$$Q \frac{1}{\min(d_i)} \leqslant (K-I)^{-1} \leqslant Q \frac{1}{\max(d_i)} \leqslant 0 .$$

Application of a well-known theorem concerning nonnegative matrices [12] together with $r(Q) < 2$ yields:

$$\frac{2}{\min(d_i)} > \frac{r(Q)}{\min(d_i)_i} \geqslant r[(K-I)^{-1}] = \frac{1}{1-r(K)} \geqslant \frac{r(Q)}{\max(d_i)},$$

or $\min(d_i) < 2 - 2r(K)$.

In addition, the inequality $\min(b_i d_i + d_i) A (I - A)^{-1} \leqslant (B + I) DA (I - A)^{-1} = K$ implies

$$\min(b_i d_i + d_i) r[A (I - A)^{-1}] = \min(b_i d_i + d_i) \left(\frac{\lambda^+}{1 - \lambda^+}\right) \leqslant r(K) .$$

consequently,

$$\min(d_i) < 2 - 2r(K) \leqslant 2 - 2 \min(b_i d_i + d_i) \left(\frac{\lambda^+}{1 - \lambda^+}\right) ,$$

from which condition (iii) follows immediately.

Proof of Theorem III. The restriction on λ^+ implies

$$\max(d_i) < 2 - 2 \max(b_i d_i + d_i) \left(\frac{\lambda^+}{1 - \lambda^+}\right) .$$

Now $0 \leqslant K = (B + I)DA (I - A)^{-1} \leqslant \max (b_i d_i + d_i) A (I - A)^{-1}$; therefore, the restriction on λ^+ implies

$$r(K) \leqslant \max (b_i d_i + d_i) \left(\frac{\lambda^+}{1 - \lambda^+}\right) < 1 \qquad \text{and also} \qquad 2[1 - r(K)] > \max (d_i) .$$

Since it was demonstrated in establishing condition (ii) of Theorem II that $r(K) < 1$ implies $\varphi(T - I) = \varphi(Q) < 0$, it only remains to establish that $r(T - I) < 2$. Observe that

$$r(K) < 1 \text{ implies } (K - I)^{-1} \leqslant Q \frac{1}{\max (d_i)} \leqslant 0 ,$$

yielding

$$r[(K - I)^{-1}] = \frac{1}{1 - r(K)} \geqslant \frac{r(Q)}{\max (d_i)}, \text{ or } \max (d_i) \geqslant r(Q)[1 - r(K)] .$$

This, together with the fact that $2[1 - r(K)] > \max (d_i)$, yields $r(Q) = r(T - I) < 2$, as required.

Proof of Theorem I. Since $D = I$, the first inequality of Theorem I is equivalent to that of Theorem III. Consequently, the inequality implies via the Lemma, that T has no root with real part greater than unity. In order to establish the first statement of Theorem I it is only necessary to observe that $D = I$ implies that $Q + I = (K - I)^{-1}D + I = I - D - KD - K^2 D - \dots \leqslant 0$, for $K \geqslant 0$ the convergence of the series following from the condition that $r(K) < 1$. The second statement of Theorem I follows immediately from Theorem II with $D = I$.

Proof of Theorem IV.
Let $t(b, d, \lambda) = [1 - d - \lambda - bd\lambda]/[1 - (1 + bd + d)\lambda]$ be the function mapping the roots of A into the corresponding roots of T under the strong homogeneity assumption.
Theorems II and III establish that $|t(b, d, \lambda)| < 1$ if and only if $\lambda < (2 - d)/(2 + d + 2bd)$ for *real* λ. It is only necessary to demonstrate that $|t(b, d, \lambda^+)| < 1$ implies $|t(b, d, \lambda)| < 1$

where $\lambda = \gamma + \delta\sqrt{-1}$ is any other, possibly complex root of A. From the definition of $t(b,d,\gamma)$ it follows that

$$|t(b,d\lambda)| = \frac{|1-d-\lambda-bd\lambda|}{|1-(1+bd+d)\lambda|} = +\sqrt{\frac{[1-d-(1+bd)\gamma]^2 + (1+bd)^2\delta^2}{[1-(1+bd+d)\gamma]^2 + (1+bd+d)^2\delta^2}}.$$

By Theorem III, $-1 < t(b,d,\gamma) < 1$, or $[1-d-(1+bd)\gamma]^2 < [1-(1+bd+d)\gamma]^2$. In addition, $d > 0$, so $(1+bd)^2 > (1+bd+d)^2$. This establishes that the ratio of the terms under the radical in the equation is less than unity, for both terms in the denominator of the ratio are larger than the corresponding terms of the numerator. Consequently, $t(b,d,\lambda^+) < 1$ implies $t(b,d,\lambda) < 1$.

Proof of Theorem V. $D = I$ implies that the homogeneous form of (3.3) reduces to

$$Q_t = (I + B)AQ_{t+1} - (I + B)AQ_t + AQ_t \quad \text{or} \quad (I-A)Q_t = (I + B)AQ_{t+1} - (I + B)AQ_t.$$

Premultiplying by $(I-A)^{-1}$ yields $Q_t = RQ_{t+1} - RQ_t$, where $R \equiv (I-A)^{-1}(I + B)A \geqslant 0$.

Although stability of $Q_{t+1} = R^{-1}(I + R)Q_t$ requires $r[R^{-1}(I + R)] < 1$, $R > 0$ implies that $r[R^{-1}(I + R)] = [1 + r(R)]/r(R) > 1$, establishing instability for the case of immediate adjustment.

The strong uniformity assumption facilitates the analysis of the delayed adjustment case by permitting us to write the homogeneous form of (3.3) as

$$Q_{t+1} = \{[(1 + bd)A]^{-1}(1 - dA) + I\}Q_t + [(1 + bd)A]^{-1}(d - 1)Q_{t-1}.$$

If we adopt a new definition of commodities in terms of the composite bundles of goods $Z_t = PQ_t$, this becomes

$$Z_{t+1} = \{I + [(1 + bd)A]^{-1}(1 - dA)\}Z_t + [(1 + bd)A]^{-1}(d - 1)Z_{t-1}.$$

But each of the matrices in this last equation is diagonal. Consequently, the new definition of commodities in terms of composite bundles of goods Z_t effectively separates variables so that there are now n independent second order difference equations of the form

$$z_i(t) + \gamma_{i1}z_i(t-1) + \gamma_{i2}z_i(t-2) = 0 \qquad (i = 1,2,...,n; t = 1,2,...)$$

where

$$\gamma_{i1} = -1 - \frac{(1 - d\lambda_i)}{(1 + bd)\lambda_i},$$

$$\gamma_{i2} = \frac{1 - d}{(1 + bd)\lambda_i}.$$

Clearly, all n of these difference equations must be stable if (3.3) is to be stable. It will be shown that if the matrix of technological coefficients $A \geqslant 0$ is indecomposable and $r(A) < 1$, then at least one of these n difference equations is unstable. $\lambda^+ = r(A) > 0$ is a root of A. Consequently, the corresponding difference equation of the set (2.15) has real coefficients. Samuelson has specified that a necessary condition for stability of a second order difference equation with real coefficients is that $1 + \gamma_1 + \gamma_2 > 0$. [34, p. 456]. Applying this test to the equation corresponding to the largest root of A, however, reveals that $1 + \gamma_1^+ + \gamma_2^+ = d(\lambda^+ - 1)/[(1 + bd)\lambda^+] < 0$, the numerator being negative and the denominator positive for b and d are positive and λ^+ is positive but less than unity.

Proof of Theorem VI. The homogeneous form of equation (3.4) implies

$$(I - DA)Q_t = (I - D)Q_{t-1} \text{ or } D(I - A)Q_t = -(I - D)Q_t + (I - D)Q_{t-1}.$$

Consequently, $Q_t = (I + R)^{-1}RQ_{t-1}$ where $R \equiv (I - A)^{-1}(D^{-1} - I) > 0$. Since $R > 0$, $r[(I + R)^{-1}R] = r(R)[1 + r(R)]^{-1} < 1$, as was to be shown.

Cowles Foundation for Research in Economics at Yale University

REFERENCES

[1] ABRAMOVITZ, MOSES: *Inventories and Business Cycles, with Special Reference to Manufacturers' Inventories*, New York: National Bureau of Economic Research 1950.

[2] ———: "Inventory Policy and Business Stability," *Regularization of Business Investment*, Conference of The Universities-National Bureau Committee for Economic Research, Princeton: Princeton University Press, 1954, pp. 285–96.

[3] ALLEN, R. G. D.: *Mathematical Economics*, London: Macmillan, 1956.

[4] ARROW, KENNETH J., AND M. NERLOVE: "A Note on Expectations and Stability," *Econometrica*, 26 (April, 1958), pp. 297–305.

[5] BAUMOL, W. J.: "Notes on Some Dynamic Models," *Economic Journal*, LVIII (December, 1948), pp. 506–21.

[6] BELLMAN, RICHARD: *Stability Theory of Differential Equations*, New York: McGraw-Hill, 1953.

[7] BURNS, ARTHUR F.: "Progress Towards Economic Stability," *American Economic Review*, L (March, 1960), pp. 1–19.

[8] CHENERY, HOLLIS B.: "Overcapacity and the Acceleration Principle," *Econometrica*, 20 (January, 1952).

[9] CHENERY, HOLLIS B., AND PAUL G. CLARK: *Interindustry Economics*, New York: John Wiley and Sons, Inc., 1959.

[10] CHIPMAN, JOHN S.: *The Theory of Inter-sectoral Money Flows and Income Formation*, Baltimore: Johns Hopkins Press, 1951.

[11] ———: "A Note on Stability, Workability, and Duality in Linear Economic Models," *Metroeconomica*, VI (April, 1954) pp. 1–10.

[12] DEBREU, GERARD, AND I. N. HERSTEIN: "Nonnegative Square Matrices." *Econometrica*, 21 (October, 1953) pp. 597–607.

[13] ENTHOVEN, ALAIN C., AND KENNETH J. ARROW: "A Theorem on Expectations and the Stability of Equilibrium," *Econometrica*, 24 (July, 1956), pp. 288–93.

[14] FISHER, IRVING: *The Theory of Interest*, New York: Macmillan, 1930.

[15] GEORGESCU-ROEGEN, NICHOLAS: "Relaxation Phenomena in Linear Dynamic Models," *Activity Analysis of Production and Allocation*, ed. by T. C. Koopmans, New York: John Wiley and Sons, Inc., 1951, pp. 116–131.

[16] GOODWIN, R. M.: "The Multiplier as Matrix," *Economic Journal*, LIX (December, 1949), pp. 537–555.

[17] ———: "Secular and Cyclical Aspects of the Multiplier and the Accelerator," *Income, Employment and Public Policy: Essays in Honor of Alvin H. Hansen*, New York: Norton and Co., 1948, pp. 108–32.

[18] HARROD, R. F.: *Economic Essays*, New York: Harcourt Brace, 1952.

[19] HART, ALBERT G.: "Government Measures Designed to Promote Regularization of Business Investment," *Regularization of Business Investment*, see [2] pp. 451–57.

[20] HAWKINS, DAVID: "Some Conditions of Macroeconomic Stability," *Econometrica*, 16 (October, 1948), pp. 309–22.

[21] HAWKINS, DAVID, AND HERBERT A. SIMON: "Note: Some Conditions of Macroeconomic Stability," *Econometrica*, 17 (July-October, 1949), pp. 245–48.

[22] HICKS, J. R.: "Methods of Dynamic Analysis," 25 *Economic Essays in Honour of Erik Lindahl*, Stockholm: Ekonomisk Tidskrift, 1956.

[23] HOLLEY, JULIAN L.: "A Dynamic Model: I. Principles of Model Structure," *Econometrica*, 20 (October, 1952), pp. 616–42.

[24] ———: "A Dynamic Model: II. Actual Model Structures and Numerical Results," *Econometrica*, 21 (April, 1953), pp. 298–324.

[25] LEONTIEF, WASSILY, et. al.: *Studies in the Structure of the American Economy*, New York: Oxford University Press, 1953.

[26] LOVELL, MICHAEL C.: "Inventories and Stability: An Interindustry Analysis," Unpublished Ph.D. Dissertation, Harvard University, March, 1959.

[27] ———: "Manufacturers' Inventories, Sales Expectations, and the Acceleration Principle," *Econometrica*, July, 1961.

[28] LUNDBERG, ERIK: *Studies in the Theory of Economic Expansion*, New York: Kelley and Millman, 1955.

[29] METZLER, LLOYD A.: "The Nature and Stability of Inventory Cycles," *Review of Economic Statistics*, XXIII (August, 1941), pp. 113–129.

[30] ———: "Stability of Multiple Markets: The Hicks Conditions," *Econometrica*, 13 (October, 1945), pp. 277–292.

[31] MILLS, E. S.: "Expectations, Uncertainty, and Inventory Fluctuations," *Review of Economic Studies*, XXII (1954–5), pp. 15–22.

[32] *Report on Research for* 1953, Cambridge: Harvard Economic Research Project, 1954 (hectographed).

[33] ROBERTSON, D. H.: "Mr. Keynes and the Rate of Interest," *Essays in Monetary Theory*, London: Staples Press, 1940, pp. 11–49.

[34] SAMUELSON, PAUL A.: *Foundations of Economic Analysis*, Cambridge: Harvard University Press, 1947.

[35] VON NEUMANN, JOHN: "A Model of General Economic Equilibrium," *Review of Economic Studies*, XIII (1945–6), pp. 1–9.

[36] WOODBURY, MAX A.: "Characteristic Roots of Input-Output Matrices," *Economic Activity Analysis*, ed. by Oskar Morgenstern, New York: John Wiley and Sons, Inc., 1954, pp. 365–82.

Econometrica, Vol. 30, No. 4 (October, 1962)

THE ACCUMULATION OF RISKY CAPITAL:
A SEQUENTIAL UTILITY ANALYSIS

Edmund S. Phelps[1]

This paper presents a utility analysis of personal saving in which the only storable asset, capital, exposes its holder to the risk of capital gain or loss. The consequences of this risk and the effect of other parameters upon the optimal consumption policy is analyzed by means of dynamic programming.

THIS PAPER investigates the optimal lifetime consumption strategy of an individual whose wealth holding possibilities expose him to the risk of loss. The vehicle of analysis is a stochastic, discrete-time dynamic programming model that postulates an expected lifetime utility function to be maximized. All wealth consists of a single asset, called capital.

The problem described belongs mainly to the theory of personal saving. Models of saving behavior thus far have been entirely deterministic [4, 7, 8, 11, 12, 13],[2] whereas, in fact, the saver is typically faced with the prospect of capital gain or loss. So it seems appropriate to determine whether the results of the conventional theory carry over or have to be qualified upon admitting capital risk into the theory.[3] The question also arises as to the effect of capital risk itself upon the level of consumption. This neglected factor may play a role in the explanation of certain inter-group differences in saving behavior.

These questions are easier to raise than to answer, and this paper is frankly an exploratory effort. No generality or definitiveness is claimed for the results obtained. A brief outline of the paper and sketch of some of these results follow.

In the first two sections, a utility function and a stochastic capital growth process are postulated and discussed. Subsequently, the "structure" of the optimal consumption policy, that is, the way in which consumption depends upon the individual's age and capital, is established. One's expectations, based on existing "deterministic" theory, are confirmed: Optimal consumption is an increasing function of both age and capital. Little else appears deducible without further restrictions upon the utility function.

---

[1] For helpful discussions on this subject I am grateful to T. N. Srinivasan and S. G. Winter.

[2] An exception is a Cowles Foundation Discussion Paper by Martin Beckmann [2]. That paper (which deals with wage rather than capital uncertainty) uses a technique similar to the one here.

[3] The model below resembles Ramsey's more than contemporary models [7, 11] so that it is largely his results that are modified.

Thereafter attention is confined to certain monomial utility functions. These special cases cannot yield general theorems but they do have the function of providing counter-examples to conjectures and of serving to suggest other hypotheses for empirical test.

For example, it is shown that the classical phenomenon of "hump saving" [8, 12] need not occur, quite apart from reasons of time preference, if capital is risky. Instead a low-capital "trap" region is possible in which it is optimal to maintain or decumulate capital, no matter how distant the planning horizon.

These utility functions all make consumption linear homogeneous in capital and permanent nonwealth income, and linear in each of these variables. But the straight-line classroom consumption function is not really upheld: Consumption cannot be expressed as a function of aggregate expected income because expected wage income (treated as certain) and expected capital income have different variances, whence different impacts upon the level of consumption. The marginal propensity to consume out of risky income is smaller than out of sure income. This result may help to explain why households which depend primarily upon (risky) capital income (e.g., farmers, wealthy heirs) are comparatively thrifty.

Finally, we consider the effect upon the consumption level of variations in the riskiness and in the expected rate of return of capital (given capital and nonwage income). Not surprisingly, the direction of effect of both are unpredictable without knowledge of the type of utility function; the familiar conflict between substitution and income effects applies as much to risk as to the rate of return. Two closely related utility functions give opposite results. But it is interesting that risk always "opposes" return. Where increase of the rate of return raises (reduces) the propensity to consume, an increase in risk reduces (raises) it; and where return has no effect, neither does risk.

1. THE BEHAVIOR OF CAPITAL

Capital is treated as homogeneous in the sense that each unit of the asset experiences the same rate of return.[4]

The individual's consumption opportunities occur at discrete, equally spaced points in time. These points divide the lifetime of the consumer into N periods. The state of the system at the beginning of each period, $n = 1$, $2, \ldots, N$, is described by the variable x_n, the amount of capital then on hand. At this time the individual chooses to consume some amount c_n of this capital.

---

[4] Alternatively, capital might have been envisioned more like identical female rabbits. In any short time period, some units of the asset would multiply while others not. This might be termed subjective or *ex ante* homogeneity.

The unconsumed capital is left to grow at a rate which is not then known. In addition to the capital growth, the individual receives an amount, y, of nonwealth income at the end of the period. This income is the same each period. Consequently the amount of capital available for consumption in the next period is given by the difference equation

$$(1.1) \qquad x_{n+1} = \beta_n(x_n - c_n) + y, \qquad\qquad x_1 = k,$$

where $\beta_n - 1$ is the rate of return earned on capital in the nth period.

We shall assume that the random variables β_n are independent and drawn from the same probability distribution. There are m possible rates of return, $0 \leqslant \beta_i$, $i = 1, 2, \ldots, m$. The probability of the ith rate of return will be denoted by p_i (the same from period to period). In addition we shall assume that $\bar{\beta} = \Sigma_1^m \, p_i \beta_i > 1$ so that the consumer expects capital to be productive. However, $\Sigma_1^m \, p_i(\beta_i - \bar{\beta})^2 > 0$, and so the realized return may differ from the expected one.

2. THE UTILITY FUCTION

This model postulates a consumer who obeys the axioms of the von Neumann-Morgenstern utility theory. His consumption strategy (or policy) can therefore be viewed as maximizing the expected value of utility, which is determined up to an increasing linear transformation.

Second, we suppose that the lifetime utility associated with any consumption history is a continuously differentiable function of the amount consumed at the beginning of each period.

The lifetime utility function is assumed to be of the independent and additive form

$$(2.1) \qquad U = \sum_{i=1}^{N} \alpha^{n-1} u(c_n), \qquad\qquad 0 < \alpha \leqslant 1.$$

The implications of this functional form are several. Preferences for the consumption "chances" or distributions of any period are invariant to the consumption levels befalling the individual in other periods (separability). Preferences among consumption subhistories in the future are independent of the age of the individual (stationarity). Preference for a consumption strategy is independent of or unaffected by any serial correlation in the random consumption sequence associated with that strategy (independence).[5]

---

[5] However the necessary and sufficient conditions for independence of utilities when choice takes place under uncertainty have yet to be investigated. The independence of utilities when choice takes place in an environment of certainty has been axiomatized by Debreu [6]. The meaning of additivity with a variable utility discount factor and an infinite number of periods has also been investigated by Koopmans [9].

The same axioms which yield the von Neumann-Morgenstern utility indicators also imply that $U(c_1, \ldots, c_N)$ is bounded from above and below.[6]
Consequently $u(c_n)$ is also a bounded function. Let $\bar{u}$ and $\underline{u}$ denote the upper
and lower bounds of $u(c_n)$, respectively.

Finally, we postulate that the individual strictly prefers more consumption
to less (monotonicity) and that he is strictly averse to risk (concavity). The
latter means that for every pair of consumption histories $(c_1, \ldots, c_N)$ and
$(c_1^o, \ldots, c_N^o)$ to which he is not indifferent, he will strictly prefer the certainty
of the compromise history $\theta c + (1 - \theta)c^o$ to the mixed prospect offering him
the history c with probability θ and the history c^o with probability $1 - \theta$,
$0 < \theta < 1$. It follows trivially that $u(c_n)$ is a strictly increasing and strictly
concave function.

3. DERIVATION OF THE FUNCTIONAL EQUATIONS

We seek the consumption strategy (or, equivalently, policy)—denoted
by the sequence of functions $\{c_n(x)\}$ for $x \geqslant 0$, $n = 1, 2, \ldots, N$—which
maximizes expected lifetime utility:

$$(3.1) \qquad\qquad J_N(c) = \exp_\beta U$$

subject to the relation (1.1). Notice that the optimal c_n, $n = 1, \ldots, N$, will
be a stochastic rather than a predetermined function of n.

To treat this variational problem we turn to the technique of dynamic
programming [3]. Observing that the maximum expected value of lifetime
utility depends only upon the number of stages in the process and the initial
capital, k, we define the function

$$(3.2) \qquad\qquad w_N(k) = \max J_N(c)$$

where the maximum is taken over all admissible policies. The function defined
may be interpreted as the utility-of-wealth function of the optimizing consumer having N periods of life remaining.

Next one reduces the problem with N decision variables to a sequence of
N problems, each involving only one policy variable, the decision which
must be taken at the current moment. This approach leads to the following
functional equations:[7]

---

[6] A proof of boundedness may be found in [1] and [5]. The proof uses the "continuity axiom" and a generalization of the St. Petersburg game, the idea for which
Arrow [1] credits to K. Menger.

[7] The argument starts with the observation that with the elapse of each period the
individual is confronted with another multistage decision problem which differs only
in having one less stage and, in general, a different initial capital. By the "principle of

$$(3.3) \quad w_N(x) = \max_{0 \le c \le x} [u(c) + \alpha \sum_{i=1}^{m} p_i w_{N-1}(\beta_i(x - c) + y)], \qquad N \ge 2,$$

and

$$(3.4) \qquad\qquad w_1(x) = \max_{0 \le c \le x} u(c)$$

which defines the utility of wealth in the single stage process. Without a subscript, the symbol c shall always denote the value of consumption in the first period of the (not necessarily original) multistage process. Similarly x shall denote capital at the start of whatever process is being considered.

4. PROPERTIES OF THE OPTIMAL CONSUMPTION POLICY

A number of standard results follow from this model: First, the optimal consumption strategy is unique; the optimum value of c_n is a unique function of x_n for every n.

The proof consists of showing that the utility of wealth function is strictly concave if the utility of consumption function is strictly concave; therefore the maximand in each period is a strictly concave function of current consumption, whence the maximizing consumption level is unique.[8]

Second, consumption is an increasing function of capital and age. The latter result depends upon the further assumption made now that $\alpha\bar{\beta} > 1$. It will become clear in the next section that this inequality is also a necessary condition for positive accumulation of capital.

The proof is rather involved and is omitted here. It can be shown that if $\alpha\bar{\beta} > u'(0)/u'(y)$ then, with $N \ge 2$ periods remaining, consumption is the following function of capital:

$$(4.1) \qquad\qquad c = \begin{cases} 0, & 0 \le x \le \bar{x}_N, \\ c_N(x), & x \ge \bar{x}_N, \end{cases}$$

where $c_N(x) = 0$ at $x = \bar{x}_N$, $c_N'(x) > 0$, and $c_N(x) < x$. The function $c_N(x)$

---

optimality" [3], if the individual's consumption strategy is optimal for the original N-stage process then that part of the strategy relating to the last N-1 stages must also constitute a complete optimal strategy with respect to the new N-1 stage process. This principle, equation (1.1), the additive utility function (3.1) and the definition (3.2) combine to yield the sequence of equations in the unknown utility of wealth functions in (3.3) and (3.4).

[8] Readers who are unfamiliar with this type of proof may wish to consult [3]. Proofs of the result above and of the other results stated but not proved in this section can be found in an earlier version of this paper (same title) by the author, published as Cowles Foundation Discussion Paper No. 109, which is available on request to the Cowles Foundation.

represents the interior portion of the solution where consumption is not constrained by the nonnegativity requirement.

It can be further shown that the marginal utility of wealth declines with age and capital and that the "consumption function" in (4.1) shifts leftward and upward as age increases:

$$w_1'(x) < w_2'(x) < \ldots < w_N'(x) < \ldots,$$

(4.2)
$$c_2(x) > \ldots > c_N(x) > \ldots,$$

$$0 < \bar{x}_2 < \ldots < \bar{x}_N < \ldots.$$

Of course, when $N = 1$, $c = x$.

In the other case, where $\alpha\bar{\beta} \leqslant u'(0)/u'(y)$, the constraint that consumption cannot exceed capital becomes binding for $N = 2$ and possibly for larger N—when capital is sufficiently small. If there is a value of $x \geqslant 0$ for which $c_N(x) = x$ then, denoting this value by $\hat{x}_N$, we obtain

$$c = \begin{cases} x, & 0 \leqslant x \leqslant \hat{x}_N, \\ c_N(x), & x \geqslant \hat{x}_N. \end{cases}$$

Again, as age increases, N decreases, the marginal utility of wealth function decreases and the consumption function shifts upward. Consequently the intersection where $c = x$ shifts rightward:

$$\hat{x}_2 > \ldots > \hat{x}_N \geqslant 0.$$

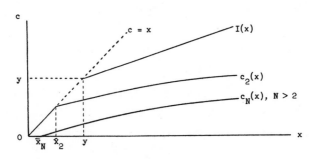

FIGURE 1

A typical possibility is graphed in Figure 1. This consumption function is of the second type. As N becomes small, the consumption schedule shifts upward. When $N = 2$, the function intersects the $c = x$ line. When $N = 1$, $c = x$ at all x.

The $I(x)$ function is defined in the next section.

5. CONDITIONS FOR EXPECTED ACCUMULATION

The preceding theorems confirm our expectations about the qualitative behavior of optimal consumption. They do not go far enough to permit inferences about the behavior of capital as a function of age and initial capital. One might ask if the model generates "hump saving" [**8, 12**], so important in the theory of aggregate capital formation. The "hump saver" saves when he is young and dissaves as he grows older. Therefore we ask: Can one find a value of N sufficiently large to induce the individual to save —more precisely, to cause the expected value of his subsequent capital to exceed the value of his present capital?[9]

Let us define "expected income," $I(x)$, to be the amount of consumption such that the expected value of capital in the next period equals present capital. Now $\exp x_{n+1} = y + \bar{\beta}(x_n - c_n)$. Expected stationarity, $\exp x_{n+1} = x_n$, implies $c_n = (y/\bar{\beta}) + [(\bar{\beta} - 1)/\bar{\beta}] x_n = I(x)$. Expected income is displayed as a function of capital in Figure 1. Our question is then whether, in the limit, as N approaches infinity, $c_N(x) < I(x)$ for all $x \geqslant y$.

The answer is clear cut when capital is riskless. Then $\beta_i = \beta$ for all i and we obtain the following recurrence relation in the limiting utility of wealth function:

$$(5.1) \qquad w(x) = \max_c \{u(c) + \alpha w(\beta(x - c) + y)\} .$$

The maximum is an interior one for $x \geqslant y$ so that $c(x)$ defined by

$$(5.2) \qquad u'(c) - \alpha \beta w'(\beta(x - c) + y) = 0$$

determines c as a function of x.

Differentiating totally with respect to x gives

$$(5.3) \quad w'(x) = \alpha \beta w' (\beta(x - c) + y) + c'(x) [u'(c) - \alpha \beta w'(\beta(x - c) + y)]$$
$$= \alpha \beta w'(\beta(x - c) + y) \qquad \text{[by (5.2)]}.$$

Since $w'(x)$ is monotone decreasing, (5.3) implies that $x_{n+1} > x_n$ if and only if $\alpha \beta > 1$. Therefore, denoting the limiting consumption function by $c(x)$, $c(x) < I(x)$ for all $x \geqslant y$.

This simple result fails to extend to risky capital. When $\beta_i \neq \bar{\beta}$ for some i, (5.3) becomes

$$(5.4) \qquad w'(x) = \alpha \Sigma p_i \beta_i w'(\beta_i(x - c) + y) .$$

From (5.4) no general conclusions concerning the conditions for expected capital growth can be drawn. Of course capital cannot be expected to grow

---

[9] Of course, an affirmative answer would not be very interesting if the necessary value of N exceeds human life expectancy!

very long unless $\bar{\beta} > 1$. But $\alpha\bar{\beta} > 1$ is insufficient to guarantee "expected" capital growth.[10]

It is clear that the critical value which $\alpha\bar{\beta}$ must exceed if capital growth is to be expected will depend upon the distribution of β_i and the shape of the marginal utility function $w'(x)$. The only practical procedure here is to investigate the implications for capital growth of particular classes of utility functions.

6. IMPLICATIONS OF SELECTED MONOMIAL UTILITY FUNCTIONS

In this section we investigate the implications of certain types of monomial utility functions for the consumption function and for the expected path of capital.

We consider first the utility function[11]

$$(6.1) \qquad\qquad u(c_n) = \bar{u} - \lambda c_n^{-\gamma}, \qquad\qquad \bar{u}, \gamma > 0, \lambda > 1.$$

Solving successively for the sequence of unknown functions $\{w_n(x)\}$, $N = 1, 2, \ldots$, yields

$$w_N(x) = \bar{u}(1 + \alpha + \ldots + \alpha^{N-1}) - \lambda(\alpha b^{-\gamma})^{N-1}[1 + (\alpha b^{-\gamma})^{\frac{-1}{\gamma+1}} +$$
$$(6.2)$$
$$\ldots + (\alpha b^{-\gamma})^{\frac{-(N-1)}{\gamma+1}}]^{\gamma+1}[x + (b^{-1} + \ldots + b^{-(N-1)})y]^{-\gamma}$$

and

$$(6.3) \quad c_N(x) = \cfrac{(\alpha b^{-\gamma})^{\frac{-(N-1)}{\gamma+1}}}{1 + (\alpha b^{-\gamma})^{\frac{-1}{\gamma+1}} + \ldots + (\alpha b^{-\gamma})^{\frac{-(N-1)}{\gamma+1}}}[x + (1 + b + \ldots + b^{N-2})y]$$

where

$$b = (\Sigma p_i \beta_i^{-\gamma})^{\frac{-1}{\gamma}}.$$

[10] Several plausible cases are the following. First, there may be no capital level at which the expected returns to saving repays the risks. Or it may be that the individual can "afford" the risks of net expected saving only when capital exceeds a critical value at which $c(x)$ intersects $I(x)$ from above. In the opposite case, additional wealth is worth the risks only as long as capital falls short of the level where $c(x)$ intersects $I(x)$ from below.

[11] The function (6.1) fails to have the boundedness property assumed up to this point and thus it contradicts the "continuity axiom" mentioned in Section 2. Whatever the merits of that axiom, the function has received sufficient study in the context of deterministic models [4, 12, 13] to deserve our attention here.

If the reader applies (6.3) to $c_{N+1}(x)$ and uses (6.2) he will obtain an expression for $w_{N+1}(x)$ having the same form as (6.2). Note also that if $\alpha = \beta_i = 1$ for all i, formula (6.3) calls for consuming a fraction $1/N$ of the individual's net worth, $x + (N-1)y$.

Provided that $\alpha b^{-\gamma} < 1$ (for which $\alpha < 1$, $\beta > 1$, $\gamma > 0$ is sufficient in the certainty case), the expressions in (6.2) and (6.3) converge as N approaches infinity, giving the solutions to the "infinite stage" process:

$$(6.4) \qquad w(x) = \frac{\bar{u}}{1-\alpha} - \lambda \left[\frac{(\alpha b^{-\gamma})^{\frac{-1}{\gamma+1}}}{(\alpha b^{-\gamma})^{\frac{-1}{\gamma+1}} - 1} \right]^{\gamma+1} \left(x + \frac{y}{b-1} \right)^{-\gamma}$$

and

$$(6.5) \qquad c(x) = \left(1 - (\alpha b^{-\gamma})^{\frac{1}{\gamma+1}} \right) \left(x + \frac{y}{b-1} \right).$$

This limiting consumption function is useful as an approximation to $c_N(x)$ for large N.

(i) *Properties of the consumption function.*

A number of properties of the consumption functions (6.3) and (6.5) can be observed immediately. First, the consumption function is linear homogeneous in capital and nonwealth income. Of two households, both having identical utility functions like (6.1), if one household enjoys twice the capital and nonwealth income of the other, it will also consume twice as much.

Second, consumption is linear in capital and nonwealth income. The coefficient of wealth, $\partial c/\partial x$, may be called the marginal propensity to consume (MPC) out of wealth.

The convergence condition $\alpha b^{-\gamma} < 1$ insures that $\partial c/\partial x > 0$. And $\partial c/\partial x < 1$ for all finite α, $b > 0$.

The coefficient $\partial c/\partial y$ may be called the MPC out of "permanent," sure, (nonwealth) income. Clearly $\partial c/\partial y > 0$ if and only $b > 1$ (given the convergence condition). What can be said concerning this condition?

When capital is risky (that is, when $\beta_i \neq \bar{\beta}$ for some i), then $b < \bar{\beta}$.[12] Therefore the postulate $\bar{\beta} > 1$ does not imply $b > 1$. We see thus that Keynes' "psychological law" stating that MPC > 0 applies only if capital has a positive net expected productivity and only if capital is sufficiently productive at that. However, we do observe positive MPC and if we were to

---

[12] To see this, draw a diagram showing $\beta_i^{-\gamma}$ as a function of β_i. Since $\beta^{-\gamma}$ is a convex function of β, $\Sigma\, p_i \beta_i^{-\gamma} > \bar{\beta}^{-\gamma}$ whence $b = (\Sigma\, p_i \beta_i^{-\gamma})^{-1/\gamma} < \bar{\beta}$.

fit this model to data we should presumably find that $b > 1$. At any rate, we shall assume $b > 1$ unless we indicate the contrary.

Is the MPC also less than one, as Keynes had it? Of course, with $b > 1$, the MPC out of an income stream beginning sufficiently far in the future is bound to be less than one. Usually one considers the effect on (immediate) consumption of immediate income. To do that in the present model—where the paycheck is received at the end of the period—suppose capital increases by the same amount as y, as if last period's paycheck were increased too. Is this MPC out of "immediate," nonwealth income smaller than one?

This MPC is

$$\left[1 - (\alpha b^{-\gamma})^{\frac{1}{\gamma+1}}\right]\frac{b}{b-1}$$

and is smaller than one if and only if $\alpha b > 1$.

This is an interesting condition. This same condition, we show now, is necessary and sufficient for positive capital accumulation at all possible values of income and capital.

Note first that $c(x) < I(x)$ for all $x \geqslant y$—causing the expected growth of capital—if and only if $c(y) < y$ and $c'(x) \leqslant I'(x)$. Now $c(y)/y$ equals the MPC just analyzed so that $\alpha b > 1$ means $c(y) < y$. The condition that $c'(x) < I'(x)$ is

$$1 - (\alpha b^{-\gamma})^{\frac{1}{\gamma+1}} < \frac{\bar{\beta} - 1}{\bar{\beta}}$$

for which $\alpha b > 1$ is sufficient (although unnecessary).[13]

The significance of this exercise lies in the possibility that $1 < b \leqslant 1/\alpha$, in which case capital will be expected to grow only if it exceeds a certain threshold. Suppose $\alpha b = 1$. Then all nonwealth income is consumed and there is "net expected saving"—that is, $c(x) < I(x)$—only if $x > y$, i.e., only if the individual starts the period with some capital over and above his just-received wage of the previous period. Otherwise there will be no "hump saving" (in this case), even though $\bar{\beta} > 1/\alpha$.

A comparison of the MPC's leads to an interesting finding: The greater nonwealth income, y, as a proportion of total expected income, $I(x)$, the larger is the ratio of consumption to expected income. This is because the MPC out of (sure, immediate) nonwealth income, $c'(x)b/(b-1)$, is greater than the consumption effect of that increase in current capital which is required to raise expected income by one dollar. Writing

$$x = \frac{\bar{\beta}}{\bar{\beta} - 1}\left[I(x) - \frac{y}{\bar{\beta}}\right],$$

---

[13] Note that all these conditions reduce to $b > 1$ if $\alpha = 1$.

we see that the latter consumption effect is $c'(x)\,\bar{\beta}/(\bar{\beta}-1)$. Recalling that $b < \bar{\beta}$, we find that "sure" income has the stronger effect. This implies that, among households who have like utility functions and who face the same capital growth process, those whose expected income depends relatively heavily on risky capital will be observed to be relatively thrifty. This may help to explain why wealthy heirs, farmers, and certain other groups save a comparatively large proportion of their incomes. Further, the result suggests that capital income and labor income ought not to be aggregated in econometric analyses of consumption.

(ii) Variations of risk and return.

The last question taken up here relates to the effect upon consumption of variations in the riskiness and expected return from capital. Since the consumption function is linear homogeneous we can write

$$c = \frac{\partial c}{\partial x}\, x + \frac{\partial c}{\partial y}\, y ,$$

whence these variations influence consumption through the marginal propensities, which are a function of b (and independent of x and y).

Let us consider first the effect of variations in risk and return on the value of b.

An increase in the expected return on capital is defined here as a uniform shift in the probability distribution of β_t which leaves all its moments the same except the mean, $\bar{\beta}$. Such a shift increases $\bar{\beta}$ and b.

What effect has risk on the value of b? When capital is risky, $b < \bar{\beta}$. Thus the presence of risk (as distinct from marginal increases therein) decreases b.

Hence, capital's (net) productivity and its riskiness affect consumption in the opposite direction.

A second kind of risk effect results from a change in the degree of risk, somehow measured.

A probability distribution which offers a simple measure of risk is the uniform or rectangular distribution. This is a two-parameter distribution with mean $\bar{\beta}$ and range $2h$. The variance is $h^2/3$ so that h is the measure of risk.

We show now that increases in h reduce b so that the "structural" and "marginal" effect of risk on b are in the same direction. Noting that $db/dh < 0$ means $db^{-\gamma}/dh > 0$, we examine $b^{-\gamma}$.

By definition of b,

$$b^{-\gamma} = \int_{\bar{\beta}-h}^{\bar{\beta}+h} \beta^{-\gamma} \left(\frac{1}{2h}\right) d\beta .$$

Evaluating the integral we find

$$b^{-\gamma} = \frac{1}{(1-\gamma)2h}\left[(\bar{\beta}+h)^{1-\gamma} - (\bar{\beta}-h)^{1-\gamma}\right].$$

Differentiating with respect to h yields

$$\frac{db^{-\gamma}}{dh} = \frac{1}{2(1-\gamma)h^2}\left[(\bar{\beta}-h)^{-\gamma}(\bar{\beta}-\gamma h) - (\bar{\beta}+h)^{-\gamma}(\bar{\beta}+\gamma h)\right].$$

Assuming $\gamma > 1$, $db^{-\gamma}/dh > 0$ if and only if

$$\frac{\bar{\beta}-\gamma h}{\bar{\beta}+\gamma h} < \left(\frac{\bar{\beta}-h}{\bar{\beta}+h}\right)^{\gamma}.$$

β equal to zero is excluded, for otherwise b is not defined. Consequently $h < \bar{\beta}$ and the right hand side of the inequality must be positive. But so may be the left hand side (if $\gamma < \bar{\beta}/h$). The following shows the inequality is satisfied for all $\gamma > 1$.

Dividing both sides of the inequality by $\bar{\beta}$, and defining $z = h/\bar{\beta}$, we obtain

$$\frac{1-\gamma z}{1+\gamma z} < \left(\frac{1-z}{1+z}\right)^{\gamma}$$

which, taking the logarithm of both sides, we find to be satisfied if and only if

$$\log(1-\gamma z) - \log(1+\gamma z) < y\left[\log(1-z) - \log(1+z)\right].$$

Expansion of the logarithmic functions into Taylor's series yields

$$\left(-\gamma z - \frac{(\gamma z)^2}{2} - \frac{(\gamma z)^3}{3} - \cdots\right) - \left(\gamma z - \frac{(\gamma z)^2}{2} + \frac{(\gamma z)^3}{3} - \cdots\right)$$

$$< \gamma\left[\left(-z - \frac{z^2}{2} - \frac{z^3}{3} - \cdots\right) - \left(z - \frac{z^2}{2} + \frac{z^3}{3} - \cdots\right)\right]$$

whence

$$\left(\gamma z + \frac{(\gamma z)^3}{3} + \frac{(\gamma z)^5}{5} + \cdots\right) > \left(\gamma z + \frac{\gamma z^3}{3} + \frac{\gamma z^5}{5} + \cdots\right).$$

This inequality can be seen to hold for all $\gamma > 1$. Therefore a marginal increase in risk reduces the value of b. Recalling that an increase in the expected return increases b, we note that changes in risk and return have opposite effects on consumption.

We consider now the effect of a change in b upon consumption. Does the substitution effect dominate here—so that a rise in b encourages

saving and reduces consumption? Or does the income effect dominate?
Turning first to $\partial c/\partial x$, we see from (6.5) that an increase in b raises $\partial c/\partial x$.
Turning next to $\partial c/\partial y$, we note from (6.5) that $\partial c/\partial y = 1/(b-1) \cdot \partial c/\partial x$.
It would appear that a rise in b might reduce $\partial c/\partial y$, because of the downward
recapitalization (using $1/(b-1)$) of the y stream, if b were sufficiently small
$(b > 1)$. It can be shown that $d(\partial c/\partial y)/db \geqslant 0$ if and only if $(\alpha b^{-\gamma})^{-1/(\gamma+1)} \leqslant$
$(1 + b\gamma)/(1 + \gamma)$. If $\alpha = 1$ this is satisfied for all $b > 1$; otherwise it is
satisfied only for values of b above some value $\hat{b} > 1$.

Thus, if there is no utility discount, the income effect dominates here;
then a rise in the expected return on capital weakens the incentive to save and
an increase in risk compels more saving in order to reduce the insecurity of
the future. But if the future is discounted, the individual feels "poorer";
then a rise in the expected return may encourage saving up to a point, after
which the income effect dominates; this point comes sooner the smaller is y.
In either case, risk and return variations have opposing qualitative effects
upon consumption.

(iii) *Other utility functions.*

To see that the implications of the utility function (6.1) for the effects of
variations in risk and return are not general, one has only to modify the
utility function thus:

$$(6.6) \qquad u(c_N) = \lambda c^\gamma, \qquad \lambda > 0, \ 0 < \gamma < 1 \ .$$

All the equations (6.2)–(6.5) continue to hold with the difference that λ and γ
are then replaced by $-\lambda$ and $-\gamma$, respectively. Hence the limiting consumption function is

$$(6.7) \qquad c(x) = \left[1 - (\alpha b^\gamma)^{\frac{1}{1-\gamma}} \right]\left(x + \frac{y}{b-1} \right)$$

where $b^\gamma = \Sigma p_i \beta_i^\gamma$.

An increase in $\bar{\beta}$, other moments of the distribution unchanged, will increase b.

Once again the effect of risk is easy to ascertain. Since β^γ is a concave
function of β, $\Sigma p_i \beta_i^\gamma < \bar{\beta}^\gamma$ whence $b = (\Sigma p_i \beta_i^\gamma) < \bar{\beta}$.

Turning finally to the effect of a marginal increase in risk upon b, we find
that the "natural" result $db^\gamma/dh < 0$ (meaning that global and marginal risk
effects have like signs) depends upon the condition $(\bar{\beta} - \gamma h)/(\bar{\beta} + \gamma h) >$
$[(\bar{\beta} - h)/(\bar{\beta} + h)]^\gamma$, which is satisfied for all $\gamma < 1$.

Once again, risk and return work in opposite directions.

Consider now the effect of an increase in b upon consumption. Unlike the previous example, $\partial c/\partial x$ decreases with increasing b, as can be seen from (6.7); the substitution effect dominates the income effect. And, as (6.7) clearly shows, $\partial c/\partial y$ is also a decreasing function of b for all values of $b > 1$; the downward recapitalization of future income merely reinforces the substitution effect against the weaker income effect.

Thus an increase in expected return encourages saving while an increase of the riskiness of capital discourages saving. The implications of the utility function (6.6) are essentially opposite to those of the utility function (6.1).

To what can this contrast of results be attributed? The utility function is determined only up to a linear transformation, meaning that we can set $\bar{u} = 0$ in (6.1) without effect. Doing this reveals that both (6.1) and (6.6) are constant-elasticity utility functions with elasticity parameter γ. The income effect dominates (unless b is small and y large) in the elastic case and the substitution effect dominates in the inelastic case.

Finally we examine a utility function that can produce some odd results, the logarithmic function in (6.8):

$$(6.8) \qquad\qquad u(c_N) = \log c_N .$$

It appears to be impossible to solve for $c_N(x)$ explicitly in terms of x and y except in the case $y = 0$. Then we easily find

$$(6.9) \qquad w_N(x) = (1 + \alpha + \ldots + \alpha^{N-1}) \log x + v(\theta, \alpha, N)$$

where $v(\theta, \alpha, N)$ depends only upon the parameters, denoted by θ, of the probability distribution of β_t, α and N, and not upon x.

Also

$$(6.10) \qquad c_N(x) = \frac{x}{1 + \alpha + \ldots + \alpha^{N-1}} .$$

When the utility function is logarithmic, the optimum consumption rate is independent both of the expected return and riskiness of capital. Consumption is linear homogeneous in capital. As N is increased, the consumption function flattens asymptotically until, in the limit,

$$(6.11) \qquad\qquad c(x) = (1 - \alpha)x .$$

A limiting function exists only if $\alpha < 1$.[14]

Cowles Foundation for Research in Economics

---

[14] For certain utility functions the existence of a limiting solution does not require $\alpha < 1$. Ramsey [12] argued that boundedness was sufficient but a condition on the elasticity or rate of approach to the upper bound is also necessary, at least in models not containing risk. Samuelson and Solow [14] assume that the upper utility bound is attained at a finite consumption rate, which is not a necessary condition.

REFERENCES

[1] ARROW, K. J.: *Bernoulli Utility Indicators for Distributions Over Arbitrary Spaces*, Technical Report No. 57 of the Department of Economics, Stanford University, July, 1958.

[2] BECKMANN, M. J.: "A Dynamic Programming Model of the Consumption Function," Cowles Foundation Discussion Paper No. 69, March 1959.

[3] BELLMAN, R.: *Dynamic Programming*, Princeton: Princeton University Press, 1957.

[4] CHAMPERNOWNE, D. G.: Review of "A Theory of the Consumption Function" by Milton Friedman, *Journal of the Royal Statistical Society*, Series A, Vol. 121, Part I, 1958.

[5] CHERNOFF, H., AND L. MOSES: *Elementary Decision Theory*, New York: John Wiley and Sons, 1959.

[6] DEBREU, G.: "Topological Methods in Cardinal Utility Theory," *Mathematical Methods in the Social Sciences*, Stanford: Stanford University Press, 1960.

[7] FRIEDMAN, M.: *A Theory of the Consumption Function*, Princeton: Princeton University Press, 1957.

[8] GRAAFF, J. DE V.: "Mr. Harrod on Hump Saving," *Economica*, February, 1950, pp. 81–90.

[9] KOOPMANS, T. C.: "Stationary Ordinal Utility and Impatience," *Econometrica*, April, 1960, pp. 287–309.

[10] MARKOWITZ, H. M.: *Portfolio Selection*, New York: John Wiley and Sons, 1959.

[11] MODIGLIANI. F., AND R. BRUMBERG: "Utility Analysis and the Consumption Function: An Interpretation of Cross-Section Data," in K. Kurihara, ed., *Post-Keynesian Economics*, New Brunswick, New Jersey: Rutgers University Press, 1954.

[12] RAMSEY, F. P.: "A Mathematical Theory of Saving," *Economic Journal*, December, 1928, pp. 543–559.

[13] ROBERTSON, D. H.: *Lectures on Economic Principles*, Vol. II, Ch. 5, pp. 69–87.

[14] SAMUELSON, P. A., AND R. M. SOLOW: "A Complete Capital Model Involving Heterogeneous Capital Goods," *Quarterly Journal of Economics*, November, 1956, pp. 537–562.

Econometrica, Vol. 31, No. 1–2 (January–April, 1963)

TURNPIKE THEOREMS FOR A GENERALIZED LEONTIEF MODEL[1]

By Lionel W. McKenzie

Theorems are proved on the convergence of efficient paths in certain closed linear models of production to the Neumann ray (of maximal proportional expansion). Radner's theorem is generalized, in the first theorem, to convergence to a facet of the production cone which contains the Neumann ray. Then the weak convergence is extended in the second theorem from convergence to the facet to convergence to the ray itself.

1. INTRODUCTION

A TURNPIKE THEOREM is concerned with efficient paths of accumulation in von Neumann models of economic expansion. The von Neumann model is a closed linear model of production [2] in which the outputs of one period furnish the inputs of the next period. The only goods which appear explicitly are those which exist as stocks at the ends of periods. These stocks are available in their entirety for use in the production processes of the following period, that is, they are not drawn upon for "unproductive" consumption by households.

In this context, efficiency is defined with reference to the terminal stocks [13]. That is, a path of accumulation lasting N periods is efficient if no other path, starting from the same initial stocks and complying with the technical restraints, reaches larger terminal stocks after N periods.

Von Neumann considered paths of proportional expansion of stocks which achieve the largest possible rate of expansion. We may call these paths Neumann rays. Associated with such a path is a set of prices at which processes in use earn zero profits and no processes can earn positive profits. We may call these the Neumann prices for the path. If the technology is such that all goods are ultimately needed to sustain any production, the Neumann ray will involve the production of all goods, and, under appropriate additional assumptions, it will be a unique and efficient path. If these assumptions are relaxed, however, there may be different Neumann rays for different subsets of stocks, where each ray realizes a largest rate of increase for a particular subset [5]. Also, the Neumann ray may not be unique, but lie in a convex set of Neumann rays, each realizing the same maximal growth rate. Finally, the Neumann ray need not be an efficient path in terms of all goods involved [9].

In any case, a turnpike theorem [1] is a theorem that establishes, for some

[1] This paper was presented in its original version to the Stillwater meetings of the Econometric Society, August, 1961. The research was supported by a grant of the National Science Foundation.

type of efficient path, that the path stays near a Neumann ray (or a set of Neumann rays) for most of the time as the period of accumulation becomes long.

The most basic turnpike theorem that has so far been reached is that of Roy Radner [13]. However, in order to obtain definite convergence to the Neumann ray, he finds it necessary to assume that only one process is profitable when the Neumann prices prevail. In the terminology which I shall use this means that the Neumann facet of the production cone is one-dimensional. It has been pointed out by David Gale [2, p. 295] that there always exists a Neumann ray which can be generated by as few as n basic processes. This clearly implies that if the Neumann ray is unique it must not be in the relative interior of a facet of dimension greater than or equal to n.[2] However, it seems unusually restrictive to insist upon dimensionality equal to one. Indeed, in the presence of distinct industries without external economies, the one dimensional case cannot occur.

In this paper I state the Radner theorem explicitly in terms of the Neumann facet. We prove convergence of this facet by an analogue of the argument used by Radner. In order to proceed further than this and obtain a convergence to the Neumann ray, which lies in the Neumann facet, we must specialize the technology. We shall assume the Leontief model in its most general form. The production coefficients are variable, and durable capital goods are present. The essential restriction which remains is that joint production in the sense of current output does not occur. Of course, a process may have joint outputs in the form of a stock of durable capital remaining at the end of the period. It is the presence of durable capital which distinguishes this model from the simpler Leontief models appearing in Hicks [3], Morishima [11], and McKenzie [8]. For the simpler model slightly stronger theorems have been obtained. The production model here is a generalization of the fixed coefficient model described by Morishima [10] and Solow [14]. It is also closely related to the model with variable coefficients used by Morishima [12]. In comparison with the original Dorfman, Samuelson, and Solow discussion [1], the production processes are disaggregated into industries, and the theorem is global rather than local.

It should be said that the model is stated in Leontief terms for the sake of the familiar reference, and because the Leontief restrictions will imply the more general conditions which underlie the theorems in a formal sense. A restatement, free of the Leontief terms, and more general sufficient conditions for the validity of the theorems will be given briefly.

---

[2] Otherwise the removal of some basic processes can easily eliminate all expressions for the ray involving less than $n + 1$ basic processes without eliminating the ray from the production cone. Then Gale's result is contradicted.

Having secured convergence to the Neumann facet by Radner's method, we then show that, under certain assumptions on the processes which span this facet, convergence to the Neumann ray can be obtained as well. In this part of the paper considerable use is made of methods developed for the fixed coefficients model by Tsukui [15] and Uzawa [16].

From all of these explorations it seems to the writer that the original Dorfman, Samuelson, and Solow conjecture that efficient paths in the Neumann model tend to converge to Neumann paths is, as a general presumption, doubtful. The central characteristic which these paths do have is convergence to Neumann facets, when appropriate facets exist. It appears that appropriate facets need *not* always exist.[3] Convergence to Neumann rays is a more special phenomenon.

It should be added that the sense in which convergence occurs in Theorems 1 and 2 of this paper is not the usual one. What is meant, for example, is that the path is near the Neumann facet except for a small part of the total time. This has been dubbed by Inada "The Weak Turnpike Theorem" [4, p. 24].

2. THE MODEL

The model may be thought of simply as a Leontief model with period structure, capital goods, and variable coefficients. The most convenient representation is the Neumann one where stocks of goods existing at the end of a period are converted by production into other stocks during the next period. Let the number of goods, and thus the number of industries, be n. Then an n by n matrix B may represent the inputs into the processes, each column being the input vector of a particular industry. If the consumption of goods in production during the period is similarly represented by another n by n matrix A, the outputs of the processes will be given by $I - A + B$. Thus the input-output matrix representing the processes in use is $\begin{bmatrix} I - A + B \\ - B \end{bmatrix}$. The processes in use will, of course, depend on the prices, both at the end of the first period and at the end of the second. As a consequence of competition, these processes must realize zero profits, while all others realize zero or negative profits. Of course, the set of processes meeting these conditions need not be unique, and not every set of prices for the two periods will permit the conditions to be satisfied at all. We know from activity analysis, however, that an appropriate set of prices will exist if the productive processes can be efficiently used.

---

[3] Sidney Winter has explored some aspects of this problem [17]. My colleague, Hugh Rose, has suggested that an assumption of structural stability for the efficient paths under small perturbations of the parameters that differ from zero would exclude the non-turnpike cases.

Let a_j be the jth column of A and b_j, the jth column of B. Let D_j be a set of (a_j, b_j) which can appear together in the jth process, that is, $\begin{pmatrix} 1 - a_j + b_j \\ - b_j \end{pmatrix}$ is an input-output combination which is possible for the industry which produces the jth good. The technology is specified initially by the following two assumptions:

ASSUMPTION I: D_j is compact, convex, and not empty.

ASSUMPTION II: $b_j \geqslant a_j > 0$, for $(a_j, b_j) \varepsilon D_j$.[4]

We define a transformation set T in E_{2n} as all $(-y^t, y^{t+1})$ such that

(1)
$$\begin{bmatrix} I - A + B \\ - B \end{bmatrix} x^{t+1} \geqslant \begin{pmatrix} y^{t+1} \\ -y^t \end{pmatrix},$$

for some $x^{t+1} \geqslant 0$ and some $(a_j, b_j) \varepsilon D_j$. T is a closed convex cone, and $T \cap (0, \Omega) = (0, 0)$.

The inequality in (1) may be interpreted as meaning that goods may be disposed of without cost. Equation (1) is a linear activities model of the type described by Koopmans [6]. His postulates A, B, C, D (pp. 48–57) are immediate in this case. However, T is not necessarily polyhedral, since D_j need not be so.

In this model the using up of durable capital is represented as a destruction of a part of the stock.[5] This may not always give an adequate picture, although it may be less objectionable when all stocks are growing than when some are being depleted. Also, service industries do not appear directly, in particular, the households which produce labor services. These industries are integrated with the commodity producing industries. That is, their stocks of goods are merged with the stocks of the industries that consume their services according to the quantity of services consumed during the period.

We call a square matrix M reducible if it can be put, by the same transpositions of rows and columns, in the form $\bar{M} = \begin{bmatrix} E & F \\ O & G \end{bmatrix}$, where E and G are square submatrices. Let us suppose that B is written so that b_{ij} refers to an input of the ith good into a process of the industry which produces the jth good.

We shall say that a square matrix M with nonpositive off-diagonal elements

---

[4] I shall use the convention that for two vectors x and y, $x \geqslant y$ means $x_i \geqslant y_i$, all i, while $x > y$ means $x_i \geqslant y_i$, all i, and $x_i > y_i$, some i, and $x >> y$ means $x_i > y_i$, all i. The analogous convention is used for $\leqslant$, $<$, and $<<$.

[5] This is perhaps a small step in the direction of partially relaxing the "no joint supply" assumption. See [3, p. 87].

has a dominant diagonal, which is positive. Moreover, $(I - A)x > 0$ for some $x > 0$ implies that B is irreducible.

ASSUMPTION III: There are $(a_j, b_j)\ \varepsilon\ D_j$, $j = 1, \ldots, n$, such that $(I - A)$ has a dominant diagonal, which is positive. Moreover, $(I - A)x > 0$ for some $x > 0$ implies that B is irreducible.

3. SOME PROPERTIES OF THE MODEL

In this section we make Assumptions I, II, and III. We shall use the literature freely to derive some implications of our assumptions. First, we show

LEMMA 1: For given A, B with $(a_j, b_j)\ \varepsilon\ D_j$, $j = 1, \ldots, n$, all stocks may expand together if and only if $(I - A)$ has a dominant diagonal.

Proof. By (1), for x^1, y^0, y^1,

$$(I - A)\, x^1 + Bx^1 \geqslant y^1, \qquad - Bx^1 \geqslant - y^0 .$$

Then, $(I - A)\, x^1 \geqslant y^1 - y^0$. We use [7, p. 50]. If $y^1 - y^0 \gg 0$, $(I - A)'$ has a dominant diagonal, and this implies that $(I - A)$ has one also. On the other hand, if $(I - A)$ has a dominant diagonal, $(I - A)^{-1}$ exists and $(I - A)^{-1} \geqslant 0$. Thus $x^1 \geqslant 0$ exists for any $y^1 - y^0 \geqslant 0$.

This allows us to prove

LEMMA 2: There exist $y \gg 0$, $p \gg 0$, and $\alpha > 1$ such that $(-y, \alpha y)\ \varepsilon\ T$, and $-p \cdot w + \alpha^{-1} p \cdot z \leqslant 0$ for $(-w, z)\ \varepsilon\ T$.

Proof. We depend on Gale [2]. His Assumptions 1, 2, and 3 are immediate. Then his Theorem 1 gives appropriate $y > 0$, $p > 0$, $\alpha > 0$, for an α which is maximal. By Assumption III and Lemma 1, the maximal expansion rate exceeds 1 in the model. However, $\alpha > 1$ implies by Assumption III that in the choice of the (a_j, b_j), which realize α, B is irreducible. Then by Theorem 4 of Gale, $y \gg 0$, and, by Lemma 1, $I - A$ has a dominant diagonal.

Define $\bar{A} = B(I - A)^{-1}$. Since $(I - A)^{-1} \geqslant 0$ and has a positive diagonal, $\bar{A}$ is also irreducible. Then if no stock is being depleted, the model (1) can be written

$$(2) \qquad \begin{bmatrix} I + \bar{A} \\ - \bar{A} \end{bmatrix} \bar{x}^{t+1} \geqslant \begin{pmatrix} y^{t+1} \\ - y^t \end{pmatrix},$$

for $\bar{x}^{t+1} \geqslant 0$. In particular, the form (2) is possible for $(-y, \alpha y)\ \varepsilon\ T$. Now suppose $p_i = 0$ for some i. Let δ_i have $\delta_{ii} = 1$, $\delta_{ij} = 0$, $j \neq i$, where $\delta_i\ \varepsilon\ E_n$.

Let J be the set of all i such that $p_i = 0$. Then $\Sigma_{i \epsilon j} \left[-p \cdot \bar{a}_i + \alpha^{-1} p \cdot (\delta_i + \bar{a}_i) \right]$ < 0, where $\bar{a}_i$ is the ith column of $\bar{A}$, since $\bar{A}$ is irreducible and $\alpha > 1$. However, $y_i > 0$ implies $\bar{x}_i > 0$. Moreover, $-p \cdot w + \alpha^{-1} p \cdot z \leqslant 0$ for $(-w, z) \, \varepsilon \, T$ implies $-p \cdot \bar{a}_j + \alpha^{-1} p \cdot (\delta_j + \bar{a}_j) \leqslant 0$, for $j = 1, \ldots, n$. Multiplying (2) on both sides with $(p, \alpha^{-1} p)$, we see that the strict inequality for $j = i$ is not consistent with $-p \cdot y + \alpha^{-1} p \cdot \alpha y = 0$, so $p_i = 0$ cannot occur, and $p \gg 0$.

I will refer to the ray generated by y satisfying the conditions of Lemma 2 as a Neumann ray. An associated p will be termed a Neumann price vector, and α is the Neumann expansion rate. We now need some results on efficient paths. Let $(-y^t, y^{t+1}) \, \varepsilon \, T$ for $t = 0, \ldots, N - 1$. We shall say that the path is efficient if $w^N \geqslant y^N, - w^0 \geqslant -y^0$, and $(-w^t, w^{t+1}) \, \varepsilon \, T$, for $t = 0, \ldots, N - 1$ implies $w^N = y^N$. It may be proved:

LEMMA 3: If $(-y^t, y^{t+1})$, $t = 0, \ldots, N - 1$, is an efficient path, there exist price vectors (p^t), with $p^t > 0$ such that

(3)
$$-p^t \cdot y^t + p^{t+1} \cdot y^{t+1} = 0, \quad \text{and}$$
$$-p^t \cdot w^t + p^{t+1} \cdot w^{t+1} \leqslant 0,$$

for all $(-w^t, w^{t+1}) \, \varepsilon \, T$. If $p^N \gg 0$, the converse is also true.

Proof. This theorem for the case where T is polyhedral was proved by Koopmans [6, Theorems 5.4.1, pp. 82–83, and 5.9, p. 89]. In the polyhedral case $p^N \gg 0$ can be obtained. Otherwise, the situation is not very different. In Koopmans' terminology, y^0 is the vector of primary goods; y^t for $t = 1, \ldots, N - 1$ is a vector of intermediate goods; and y^N is the vector of final goods. Negative prices for intermediate goods cannot appear because of free disposal [6, p. 91]. Also $p^t = 0$ would imply $p^{t+1} = 0$ by the second relation of (3) and Assumptions I and II. Since $p^N > 0$, $p^t > 0$ holds for all t.

If (3) were satisfied and $p^N \gg 0$, but the path were not efficient, there would be another path having $z^N > y^N$, and $-z^0 \geqslant -y^0$. Adding up the second relations of (3), we obtain $-p^0 \cdot z^0 + p^N \cdot z^N \leqslant 0$. But adding up the first relations we obtain $-p^0 \cdot y^0 + p^N \cdot y^N = 0$, which implies $-p^0 \cdot z^0 + p^N \cdot z^N > 0$. Since this is a contradiction, no such path is possible. The results of Malinvaud [9] also approximate this lemma, except that he treats the goods of every period as final goods.

We see from the converse statement of Lemma 3 that the path $(-y, \alpha y)$ found in Lemma 2 is efficient for arbitrary $N > 0$.

4. CONVERGENCE TO THE NEUMANN FACET

I now wish to consider certain relations which exist in this model between efficient paths and Neumann rays. In particular, we shall consider the tendency of efficient paths to the Neumann facet. A facet $F(p,q)$ of T is defined whenever $-p \cdot w + q \cdot z \leqslant 0$ for all $(-w,z) \varepsilon T$. Then $F(p,q)$ is the set of all $(-w,z) \varepsilon T$ for which the equality is satisfied. Obviously, every facet contains 0, and is a closed, convex cone with vertex 0.

Let P be the set of Neumann price vectors, p, which satisfy the conditions of Lemma 2 and have $\Sigma p_i = 1$.[6] P is a closed, convex set in E_n. If p^* is in the relative interior of P, for any $p \varepsilon P$ there is a $p' \varepsilon P$ such that $p^* = \beta p + (1 - \beta)p', 0 < \beta < 1$. We define the Neumann facet as $F(p^*, \alpha^{-1}p^*) = F^*$, where p^* is any p in the relative interior of P. From the expression for p^* above, we see that $F^* = \cap_{p \varepsilon P} F(p, \alpha^{-1}p)$. Thus F^* is well defined in terms of P. Also from the expression of F^* in terms of p^*, we see that it is closed.

I now present, with appropriate modifications, the argument of Radner [13]. Let the norm of a vector $|z| = \Sigma |z_i|$, the sum of the absolute values of the components. Let the angle between two vectors z and w be $d(z,w) = \Sigma |z_i/|z| - w_i/|w||$, that is, the norm of the vector joining the normalized vectors. However, if $|z| = 0$, or $|w| = 0$, $d(z,w)$ is undefined. If C is a nonempty set of vectors, let $d(z,C) = \inf d(z,w)$ for $w \varepsilon C$.

LEMMA 4: For any $\varepsilon > 0$, there is $\delta > 0$ such that for any $(-w,z) \varepsilon T$ with $d((-w,z), F^*) > \varepsilon$, $-(\alpha - \delta)p^* \cdot w + p^* \cdot z \leqslant 0$.

Proof. The set $T_1 = \{z | (-w,z) \varepsilon T \text{ and } \Sigma w_i = 1\}$ is bounded. For assume there is a sequence (w^s, z^s) such that $\Sigma w_i^s = 1$ and $\Sigma z_i^s \to \infty$. Consider the derived sequence $(-w^{s'}, z^{s'})$ where $w^{s'} = w^s/\Sigma z_i^s$ and $z^{s'} = z^s/\Sigma z_i^s$. This sequence is bounded, and there is a point of accumulation $(-\bar{w}, \bar{z})$. Since T is closed, $(-\bar{w}, \bar{z}) \varepsilon T$. But $\bar{w} = 0$, which implies by Assumption II and (1) that $\bar{z} = 0$, contradicting the hypothesis.

Now suppose there is $\varepsilon > 0$ and a sequence $(-w^s, z^s)$ in T such that $d((-w^s, z^s), F^*) \geqslant \varepsilon$, while $p^* \cdot z^s/p^* \cdot w^s \to \alpha$. Define $w^{s'} = w^s/\Sigma w_i^s$, $z^{s'} = z^s/\Sigma w_i^s$. Then the sequence $(-w^{s'}, z^{s'})$ is bounded, since $z^{s'}$ lies in T_1. There is a point of accumulation $(-\bar{w}, \bar{z}) \varepsilon T$. Then $-\alpha p^* \cdot \bar{w} + p^* \cdot \bar{z} = 0$ and $(-\bar{w}, \bar{z}) \varepsilon F^*$, contradicting the hypothesis. Since $p^* \cdot z^s/p \cdot w^s \leqslant \alpha$ always holds in T, the δ of the lemma must exist.

We are now able to prove:

THEOREM 1: *Under Assumptions I, II, and III, let* $(-y^t, y^{t+1})$, $t = 0, \ldots,$

---

[6] Notice that any $(p, \alpha^{-1}p)$ satisfying the inequality of the lemma satisfy (3) for any $(-y, \alpha y) \varepsilon T$. Thus all such $(-y, \alpha y)$ are efficient and form a convex set on the boundary of T, which, indeed, lies in a single closed facet.

$N — 1$, *be an efficient path where* $y_i^0/|y^0| \geqslant \eta > 0$. *Then for any* $\varepsilon > 0$ *there is a number* N_1 *such that the number of periods in which* $d((-y^t, y^{t+1}), F^*) \geqslant \varepsilon$ *cannot exceed* N_1.

Proof. Choose the maximal y^* on a Neumann ray with $y^* \leqslant y^0$ and consider the path $(-\alpha^t y^*, \alpha^{t+1} y^*)$, $t = 0, \ldots, N — 1$. This is a feasible path from y^0 lasting N periods. Let $\varepsilon > 0$. For all t for which $d((-y^t, y^{t+1}), F^*) \geqslant \varepsilon$, it follows from the lemma that

$$p^* \cdot y^{t+1} \leqslant (\alpha — \delta)\, p^* \cdot y^t$$

for some $\delta > 0$. At the same time we know that for each $t = 0, \ldots, N — 1$,

$$p^* \cdot y^{t+1} \leqslant \alpha p^* \cdot y^t ,$$

since $(-y^t, y^{t+1}) \, \varepsilon \, T$ by assumption. Therefore, if $d((-y^t, y^{t+1}), F^*) \geqslant \varepsilon$ for N' periods, we have for $N \geqslant N'$

$$p^* \cdot y^N \leqslant (\alpha — \delta)^{N'} \alpha^{N-N'} p^* \cdot y^0 .$$

By Lemma 3 there is a price sequence (p^t), $p^t > 0$, associated with any efficient path $(-y^t, y^{t+1})$, $t = 0, \ldots, N — 1$, satisfying (3). Also $p^N \cdot y^N \geqslant p^N \cdot w^N$ for any feasible path $(-w^t, w^{t+1})$ with $w^0 \leqslant y^0$. Let $k = \max p_i^N / p_i^*$, $i = 1, \ldots, n$. Then

$$p^N \cdot y^N \leqslant k p^* \cdot y^N$$

and

$$p^N \cdot y^N \leqslant k(\alpha — \delta)^{N'} \alpha^{N-N'} p^* \cdot y^0 .$$

Thus $p^N \cdot y^N \geqslant p^N \cdot \alpha^N y^*$ implies

$$k(\alpha — \delta)^{N'} \alpha^{N-N'} (p^* \cdot y^0) \geqslant \alpha^N (p^N \cdot y^*),$$

or

$$1 > \left(\frac{\alpha — \delta}{\alpha}\right)^{N'} \geqslant k^{-1} \frac{p^N \cdot y^*}{p^* \cdot y^0} = h > 0 .$$

Thus $N' \leqslant \log h / [\log(\alpha — \delta) — \log \alpha] > 0$, both numerator and denominator being negative. Since $\log h \to — \infty$ as $h \to 0$, we must bound h from below to finish the proof.

We note, first, that h does not change when p^N or p^* is multiplied by an arbitrary positive number. Hence we are free to choose $|p^N| = |p^*| = 1$. We also choose $\eta \leqslant y_i^*/|y^*|$, $i = 1, \ldots, n$. Let $p_{i_1}^* \leqslant p_i^*$ for $i = 1, \ldots, n$. Then k^{-1} cannot be less than $p_{i_1}^*$. Moreover, $p^N \cdot y^* \geqslant \eta |y^*| \geqslant \eta^2 |y^0|$. The last inequality follows from the choice of y^* so that $y_i^* = y_j^0 \geqslant \eta |y^0|$, for some i and j. Then $h \geqslant p_{i_1}^* (\eta^2 |y^0|/|y^0|) = \eta^2 p_{i_1}^* > 0$. Then we may choose

$$N_1 = \log (\eta^2 p_{i_1}^*)/(\log(\alpha — \delta) — \log \alpha) > 0.$$

We have explicitly used the Leontief model stated in (1) and Assumptions I, II, and III to obtain the convergence to the Neumann facet. However, this is a very special model for that result. What we have in fact appealed to, beyond the general von Neumann model, is that there exist a positive Neumann ray and positive associated price vector. Thus Theorem I may be restated in these terms.

5. UNIQUENESS OF THE NEUMANN RAY

It has now been shown that any efficient path departing from positive stocks, each of which exceeds a given (arbitrary) quantity, cannot stay away from a neighborhood of the Neumann facet for more than a fixed number of periods. However, the Neumann facet may include stock vectors y for a wide range of stock compositions. Radner assumed the facet to be one dimensional to eliminate this possibility. But the facet certainly may be as much as n-dimensional in E_{2n}, and its projection into the space of the first or last n components of $(-y^t, y^{t+1})$ can also be n-dimensional. In our model, however, it is possible to proceed further after strengthening the assumptions. The chief purpose of this strengthening is to make the Neumann ray unique. However, the Neumann facet will be n-dimensional even with the stronger assumptions.

We will say that a set D contained in E_{2n} is relatively strictly convex if it is strictly convex in the smallest subspace containing it. We now assume in place of I,

ASSUMPTION I': D_j is compact, *relatively strictly* convex, and not empty.

And we assume in place of III,

ASSUMPTION III': There are $(a_j, b_j) \varepsilon D_j, j = 1, \ldots, n$, such that $(I - A)$ has a dominant diagonal. Moreover, $(I - A) x > 0$ for some $x > 0$ implies that B is irreducible *and nonsingular*.

The assumptions are the same as before except for the words in italics which are added.

The effect of strict convexity of D_j is to make the (a_j, b_j), which appear in an efficient path, unique if stocks are growing and prices are positive. That is, each industry has a unique process available. However, if all stocks are expanding, all n industries must be active. We prove

LEMMA 5: With Assumptions I', II, III', $y^{t+1} \gg y^t$ along an efficient path implies that the related A and B are unique if (p^t, p^{t+1}) may be chosen positive.

Proof. From (1) $y^{t+1} \gg y^t$ implies $x^{t+1} \gg 0$. But by the second relation of (3), $p^{t+1}(I - A + B) - p^t B \leqslant 0$. Then, since $x^{t+1} \gg 0$, the first relation of (3) implies $p^{t+1}(I - A + B) - p^t B = 0$. Suppose there is A', B', and $p^{t+1}(I - A' + B') - p^t B' = 0$, where $(A', B') \neq (A, B)$. Let $A'' = uA + vA'$, $B'' = uB + vB'$, where $u, v > 0$, $u + v = 1$. Now A'' and B'' also satisfy this equation, and a column (a_j, b_j) of (A'', B'') may, by Assumption I', be multiplied by $1 - \varepsilon$ for small $\varepsilon > 0$ without leaving D_j. Also positive prices imply $p^{t+1}(- A'' + B'') - p^t B'' \ll 0$. Thus we may choose A''' and B''' equal to $(1 - \varepsilon) A''$ and $(1 - \varepsilon) B''$, respectively, so that $p^{t+1}(I - A''' + B''') - p^t B''' \gg 0$, contradicting the second relation of (3). Therefore, A and B are unique.

It is an immediate consequence of Lemma 5 that the A and B matrices which generate a Neumann path $(y, \alpha y)$ of Lemma 2 are unique. This follows from $p^* \gg 0$ and $\alpha > 1$. We may, indeed, go further to prove

LEMMA 6: With Assumptions I', II, III', the Neumann ray and the Neumann price vector are unique.

Proof. Since all goods are produced, it must be that $\alpha^{-1} p^*(I - A + B) - p^* B = 0$. Then from the positivity of p^*, we deduce that (1) must hold with equality for $(y, \alpha y)$. Write $(I - A + B) x = \alpha y$ and $-Bx = -y$. Since $(I - A)$ is nonsingular by Lemma 1, we may rewrite this in the form of (2), $(I + \bar{A})\bar{x} = \alpha y$ and $\bar{A}\bar{x} = y$, with $\bar{x} \gg 0$. Then $\bar{x} = \bar{A}^{-1}y$, or

$$(I + \bar{A}^{-1})y = \alpha y,$$

where $\bar{A} = B(I - A)^{-1} \geqslant 0$. $\bar{A}^{-1}$ exists by the nonsingularity of B assumed in III'.

We see that y is a characteristic vector of $(I + \bar{A}^{-1})$. But from the proof of Lemma 2, $\bar{A}$ is irreducible. Then, from the Frobenius theory, it has a unique positive characteristic ray, to which there corresponds a simple positive root. Since $\bar{A}$ and $(I + \bar{A}^{-1})$ have the same characteristic vectors, y lies in this ray, and it is unique up to multiplication by a positive number. Similar considerations apply to p^*, which is a positive characteristic vector for $(I + \bar{A})^{-1}$ on the left. This proves the lemma.

The Neumann facet F^* is now the set of $(-w, z)$ which satisfy (1) with equality with the A and B proper to the Neumann ray. If a path lasting N periods lies on the Neumann facet, it may be expressed by the difference equation

(4) $$y^{t+1} = (I + \bar{A}^{-1})y^t,$$

$t = 0, \ldots, N - 1$. We will first investigate certain sequences which satisfy

(4). Later these results will be extended to paths which lie near the Neumann facet. We may also define $C = (1/\alpha)(I + \bar{A}^{-1})$. C has the same characteristic vectors as $(I + \bar{A}^{-1})$, and if λ is a characteristic root of $(I + \bar{A}^{-1})$, λ/α is a characteristic root of C. In particular, 1 is a simple characteristic root of C and the only characteristic root with a positive characteristic vector. Following Uzawa, I shall call $(I - \bar{A}^{-1})$, or C, a Frobenius matrix; and α, or 1, respectively, the Frobenius root. A Frobenius matrix is defined by Uzawa [16, pp. 2–3] as a square matrix with a unique simple positive root with a positive characteristic vector, on the left and also on the right.

6. CONVERGENCE TO THE NEUMANN RAY

In order to insure that solutions of (4) with $y^t > 0$ will converge to the Neumann ray, our assumptions must be slightly strengthened again. Let $\bar{A}$ generate a Neumann path according to (2). Then we assume

ASSUMPTION IV: $(I + \bar{A}^{-1})$ is nonsingular.[7] Furthermore, if λ is a characteristic root of $(I + \bar{A}^{-1})$ and $|\lambda| = \alpha$, $\lambda = \alpha$.

I now use arguments which are related to those of Uzawa [16] and Tsukui [15]. Let U_n be an n-dimensional vector space over the complex numbers. For $z \, \varepsilon \, U_n$ we may write $z = u + iv$, where u and v are real vectors in E_n.[8] The angle d is well defined over U_n, except at the origin. Suppose that the sequence (y^t), $t = 0, \ldots, N - 1$, $y^t \, \varepsilon \, U_n$, satisfies (4). Let $y^* \gg 0$ lie on the Neumann ray, and $S = \{z | u \geqslant 0, v = 0, \text{ and } |z| = 1\}$.

LEMMA 7: There are $N_0 > 0$, $\eta > 0$, such that $y^0 \geqslant 0$, $d(y^N, S) < \eta$, and $N > N_0$ imply $d(y^*, y^t) \leqslant \varepsilon$ for $0 \leqslant N' \leqslant t \leqslant N'' \leqslant N$, where $(N'' - N')/N \geqslant 1 - \delta$, for arbitrary $\varepsilon > 0$, $\delta > 0$.

Proof. Let p^* be a Neumann price vector. $p^* \gg 0$ is a characteristic vector of C on the left for the root 1. It will be sufficient to consider $z^t = \alpha^{-t} y^t$, for $t = 0, \ldots, N - 1$, which satisfies

(4') $z^{t+1} = Cz^t$,

since $d(y^t, y^*) = d(z^t, y^*)$. Moreover, since (4') is linear, we may assume

[7] Since B has already been assumed nonsingular in Assumption III', this amounts to assuming $I - A + B$ to be nonsingular.

[8] Let $z = u + iv$, $w = x + iy$, where u, v, x, and y are real vectors in E_n. The inner product $z \cdot w$ in U_n is defined as $(u - iv) \cdot (x + iy)$. Also if $D = A + iB$, A and B real, $Dz = (A + iB)(u + iv)$, and $zD = (u + iv)(A - iB)$. With these conventions we may use the same notations for operations in U_n and in E_n.

$|z^0| = 1$. Let S_2 (S_3) be the invariant subspace of U_n associated with roots λ_i with $|\lambda_i| < (>) 1$. S_2 is spanned by vectors $w_1, \ldots, w_{n_1}$ such that $(C - \lambda_{i_r})^{s_r} w_r = 0$ for some λ_i with $|\lambda_i| < 1$, and s_r an integer no greater than n_1, and correspondingly for S_3. Since the root 1 is simple, the complex space U_n may be represented as the sum of S_2, S_3, and the one-dimensional subspace spanned by y^*, which we shall call S_1. Consider $p^* \cdot [(C - \lambda_{i_r})^{s_r} w_r] = 0$. But $p^*(C - \lambda_{i_r})^{s_r} w_r = (1 - \lambda_{i_r})^{s_r} (p^* \cdot w_r)$. Since $(1 - \lambda_{i_r}) \neq 0$, $p^* \cdot w_r = 0$. With a similar argument for S_3, we see that $p^* \cdot w = 0$ for $w \, \varepsilon \, S_2 + S_3$.

Let $|z| = 1$ for $z > 0$, and let $|z|$ otherwise be arbitrary. We may write $z = z_1 + z_2 + z_3$, where $z_1 \, \varepsilon \, S_1$, $z_2 \, \varepsilon \, S_2$, and $z_3 \, \varepsilon \, S_3$. Let C_2 represent the linear transformation which is the restriction to S_2 of the linear transformation represented by C. Then $C_2^t \to 0$ as $t \to \infty$, since all the characteristic roots λ_i of C_2 have $|\lambda_i| < 1$. Moreover, for all z such that $|z| = 1$, the term z_2 in the direct product representation has $|z_2| < h$ for some $h > 0$. Otherwise, there is a sequence z^s with $|z_2^s| \to \infty$ and $|z^s| = 1$. Then $z^s/|z_2^s| \to 0$, and $z_2^s/|z_2^s|$ has a point of accumulation $\bar{z}_2$ with $|\bar{z}_2| = 1$, which belongs both to S_2 and to $S_1 + S_3$. However, this contradicts the linear independence of the components of the sum, so $|z_2| < h$ must hold for some h. Finally, for any given z_2, $C_2^t z_2 \to 0$, as $t \to \infty$. Also $|C_2^t z_2|$ is a continuous function of z_2. Therefore, N_1 may be chosen for any given $\varepsilon_1 > 0$, so that $|C_2^t z_2^0| = |z_2^t| < \varepsilon_1$ for $t \geqslant N_1$, uniformly for $|z_2| \leqslant h$, that is, for $|z^0| = 1$.

We have assumed that $|z^0| = 1$. This implies that $|z_1^0| < h'$ for some $h' > 0$, where z_1^0 is the Neumann ray component of z^0. The argument for this bound corresponds to that used to bound the S_2 component of z for $|z| = 1$. Let $\eta < \min d(x, w)$ for $x, w \neq 0$, $x \, \varepsilon \, S$, $w \, \varepsilon \, S_2 + S_3$. Since $p^* \cdot x \neq 0$ for $x \, \varepsilon \, S$, S and $S_2 + S_3$ are disjoint. Then a positive minimum of $d(x, w)$ is provided by the fact that S and the set of normalized elements of $S_1 + S_2$ are compact.

Consider $z = z_1 + w$, where $z_1 \, \varepsilon \, S_1$ and $w \, \varepsilon \, S_2 + S_3$. Suppose we have both that $d(z, S) \leqslant \eta$ and $|z_1| < h'$. I claim that $|w| < k$ for some $k > 0$. If not, there are sequences z^i, w^i with $z^i = z_1^i + w^i$ and $w^i \, \varepsilon \, S_2 + S_3$, where $d(z^i, S) \leqslant \eta$, $|z_1^i| < h'$, and $|w^i| \to \infty$ for $i = 1, 2, \ldots$. Let $z^{i'}$, $z_1^{i'}$, $w^{i'}$ equal $z^i/|w^i|$, $z_1^i/|w^i|$, $w^i/|w^i|$, respectively; since these sequences are bounded they have points of accumulation, $\bar{z}$, $\bar{z}_1$, $\bar{w}$. Moreover, $d(\bar{z}, S) \leqslant \eta$. However, $\bar{z}_1 = 0$, so $\bar{z} \, \varepsilon \, S_2 + S_3$. Since this contradicts the definition of η, the number k must exist. However, if z^t satisfies (4'), $z_1^t = z_1^0$, so $|z_1^t| < h'$ whenever $|z_1^0| < h'$. Then, if $d(z^t, S) < \eta$, the foregoing argument implies that $|z_2^t + z_3^t| < k$. Thus $|z_3^t| - |z_2^t| < k$ or $|z_3^t| < k + \varepsilon_1$ for $t \geqslant N_1$.

Consider $z^{N-t} = C^{-1} z^{N-t+1}$. The roots of C^{-1} are λ_i^{-1} and the associated subspaces are the same as for C. Thus the restriction C_3^{-t} of C^{-t} to S_3 goes to 0 as $t \to \infty$. Then, as before, there is an $N_2 > 0$ such that $t > N_2$ implies $|z_3^{N-t}| < \varepsilon_2$, for any given $\varepsilon_2 > 0$ and any $|z_3^N| < k + \varepsilon_1$.

Finally, $d(z^t, z_1^t)$ is a continuous function of z^t for fixed $z_1^t = z_1^0 \neq 0$. Therefore, for any $\varepsilon > 0$ there is an $\varepsilon_3 > 0$ such that $|z^t - z_1^t| < \varepsilon_3$ implies $d(z^t, z_1^t) < \varepsilon$. Choose $\varepsilon_1 + \varepsilon_2 < \varepsilon_3$. Let $N' = N_1$ and $N'' = N - N_2$. Choose N so that $(N'' - N')/N = 1 - (N_1 + N_2)/N \geqslant 1 - \delta$. Then for $N' \leqslant t \leqslant N''$, we have $|z^t - z_1^t| = |z_2^t + z_3^t| < \varepsilon_3$. Thus $d(y^t, y^*) = d(z^t, z_1^t) < \varepsilon$ for $N' \leqslant t \leqslant N''$. It is clear that the argument holds for $N > N_0$ if it holds for N_0. This completes the proof of the lemma.

If Lemma 7 is to be useful to us we must extend it to paths $(-y^t, y^{t+1}) \ \varepsilon \ T$ where $d((-y^t, y^{t+1}), F^*)$ is sufficiently small, but where $(-y^t, y^{t+1})$ does not necessarily satisfy (4). This will be done by showing that such a path (y^t) stays near a sequence $(y^{t'})$ which satisfies (4) and consequently converges to y^* in terms of the angle d. This result is expressed in

LEMMA 8: Let $(-y^t, y^{t+1}) \ \varepsilon \ T$. For any $N, \delta > 0$, there is an $\varepsilon > 0$ such that $d((-y^t, y^{t+1}), F^*) < \varepsilon$ for $t = 0, \ldots, N - 1$, implies there is a sequence $(y^{t'})$ in E_n where $(-y^{t'}, y^{t+1'})$ satisfies (4) for $t = 0, \ldots, N - 1$, and $d(y^t, y^{t'}) < \delta$, for $t = 0, \ldots, N$. ε depends on N and δ.

Proof. The proof will be by induction. All ε's and δ's in the argument are positive. Suppose the theorem is valid for $t = \tau, 0 \leqslant \tau \leqslant N - 1$. Then ε may be chosen so that $d(y^t, y^{t'}) < \delta_1$ for $t \leqslant \tau$, where $(-y^{t'}, y^{t+1'})$ satisfies (4) for $t \leqslant \tau - 1$. Then choose $y^{\tau+1'} = (I + \bar{A}^{-1}) y^{\tau'}$. Since $d((-y^\tau, y^{\tau+1}), F^*) < \varepsilon$, there is a $(-z, w) \ \varepsilon \ T$ such that $w = (I + \bar{A}^{-1})z$ and $d((-y^\tau, y^{\tau+1}), (-z, w)) < \varepsilon$.

We may choose $(-z, w)$ equal in norm to $(-y^\tau, y^{\tau+1})$. Then $|(-y^\tau, y^{\tau+1}) - (-z, w)| < \varepsilon |(-y^\tau, y^{\tau+1})|$. By the proof of Lemma 4, there is a $\varrho > 0$ such that $(-y^\tau, y^{\tau+1}) \ \varepsilon \ T$ implies $|(-y^\tau, y^{\tau+1})| < \varrho |y^\tau|$. Therefore, $|y^\tau - z| + |y^{\tau+1} - w| < \varepsilon \varrho |y^\tau|$. Also, from the definition of F^*, we may choose ε so that $|p^* \cdot (y^{\tau+1} - \alpha y^\tau)| < \delta_2 |y^\tau|$ for an arbitrary δ_2. Then, using the fact that $p^* \gg 0$, we have, for small δ_2, $|y^{\tau+1}|/|y^\tau| > \delta_3$ for some δ_3. As $\varepsilon \to 0$, $|y^\tau - z|/|y^\tau| \to 0$ and $|y^{\tau+1} - w|/|y^\tau| \to 0$. Moreover, each of these vectors is eventually bounded away from zero, that is, $y^\tau/|y^\tau|$, $z/|y^\tau|$, etc. Since d is continuous for nonzero arguments, this implies that ε may be chosen small enough so that $d(y^\tau, z) + d(y^{\tau+1}, w) < \delta_4$ for arbitrary δ_4. Then $d(y^{\tau'}, z) < \delta_1 + \delta_4$. By the linearity of the right side of (4), for $\delta_1 + \delta_4$ small enough, $d(y^{\tau+1'}, w) < \delta_5$, where δ_5 may be as small as we like. Thus $d(y^{\tau+1}, y^{\tau+1'}) < \delta_6 = \delta_4 + \delta_5$. Finally, both δ_1 and δ_6 may be made smaller than δ by choice of ε.

This completes the induction except for the first step. To begin, choose $(-y^{0'}, y^{1'}) = (-z, w)$, where $d((-y^0, y^1), (-z, w)) < \varepsilon$, and $|-z, w| = |-y^0, y^1|$. Then by the argument above, $d(y^0, z) + d(y^1, w) < \delta$ for ε small enough. Note that a single ε suffices for all paths $(-y^t, y^{t+1})$ which satisfy the conditions of the Lemma.

Theorem 1 may now be combined with Lemmas 7 and 8 to give

THEOREM 2: *Under Assumptions I', II, III', and IV, let* $(-y^t, y^{t+1})$, $t = 0,\ldots, N - 1$, *be any efficient path where* $y_i^0/|y^0| \geqslant \eta > 0$. *Then for any* η, ε, $\delta > 0$ *there is a number* N', *such that* $N > N'$ *implies that* $d(y^*, y^t) < \varepsilon$ *for* v *periods where* $v/N \geqslant 1 - \delta$.

Proof. We shall first use Lemmas 7 and 8 to turn convergence to the Neumann facet into convergence to the Neumann ray. Then Theorem 1 provides the necessary convergence to the facet. By Lemma 8, we may choose, for arbitrary N_1 and $\eta_1 > 0$, an $\varepsilon_1 > 0$ such that if $d((-y^t, y^{t+1})$, $F^*) < \varepsilon_1, t = 0, \ldots, N_1 - 1$; then, for some sequence $(y^{t'})$ satisfying (4), $d(y^t, y^{t'}) < \eta_1$. Notice that this means $d(y^{t'}, S) < \eta_1$, since $y^t > 0$ for all t.

On the other hand, by Lemma 7, we may choose N_1 and η_1 for an arbitrary $\delta_1 > 0$ such that, for any sequence $(y^{t'})$, $t = 0,\ldots, N_1$, with $y^{0'} > 0$ and $d(y^{N_1'}, S) < \eta_1$, which satisfies (4), $d(y^{t'}, y^*) < \varepsilon/2$ for v_1 periods where $v_1/N_1 \geqslant 1 - \delta_1$. We take $\eta_1 < \varepsilon/2$. Then for the appropriate ε_1 and N_1, $d(y^t, y^*) < \varepsilon/2 + \eta_1 < \varepsilon$ for at least v_1 periods.

Now, by Theorem 1, for a path (y^t) which satisfies the hypothesis, and an arbitrary N', $d((-y^t, y^{t+1})$, $F^*) < \varepsilon_1$, for at least $(1 - [N_2/N'])$ N' periods where N_2 is a fixed positive number. We choose N' so that $N_1 (N_2 + 2)/N' < \delta_1$. Then the whole interval N' contains at least $(N' - N_1 (N_2 + 2))/N_1$ disjoint intervals of length at least N_1 during each of which $d((-y^t, y^{t+1})$, $F^*) < \varepsilon_1$. Then, in each such interval, $d(y^t, y^*) < \varepsilon$ for at least v_1 periods where $v_1 \geqslant (1 - \delta_1)N_1$. Thus for the whole path $d(y^t, y^*) < \varepsilon$ holds for at least v periods where $v \geqslant (N' - N_1 (N_2 + 2))(1 - \delta_1)$ periods. Finally, we may choose δ_1 so that $(1 - [N_1(N_2 + 2)/N'])(1 - \delta_1) > (1 - \delta_1)^2 > 1 - \delta$. The theorem is proved with this N' and $v = (1 - \delta)N'$, if we note that our choice of δ_1 also suffices for any $N > N'$, since N_1, N_2, and δ_1 are not affected by increasing N'.

7. A MORE GENERAL STATEMENT

It may have occurred to the reader already that the Leontief statement of the model is a little artificial. Suppose the Neumann ray is unique.* If we let F be an n by n output matrix and E an n by n input matrix, possibly with some zero columns, we may write the processes which span the Neumann facet as $\begin{pmatrix} F \\ -E \end{pmatrix}$. This facet has dimension less than or equal to n. Then our $I - A = F - E$. Thus, conditions laid on $I - A$ may in this formulation be put on $F - E$, in particular, that the off-diagonal elements be nonpositive and that there be a dominant diagonal. Also, E may be assumed irreducible and nonsingular, and a column e_j of E may have $e_j > 0$.

* And lies in the relative interior of the Neumann facet.

In place of $(I + \bar{A}^{-1})$, we now have FE^{-1}, and the provisions of Assumption IV may be applied to it. In fact, once we have arrived at the Neumann facet, a sufficient assumption for the convergence proof is simply that FE^{-1} be a nonsingular Frobenius matrix, with no special assumptions on $F - E$. Also, irreducibility of E is not necessary.

Of course, our assumptions have, except for Assumption IV, been applied in a wider context than the Neumann facet. They have been used to insure that $y^* \gg 0$, $p^* \gg 0$, and $\alpha > 1$, the substance of Lemma 2. However, this is more than is needed to obtain convergence to a facet. Let us define a Neumann ray by conditions like those of Lemma 2. That is, for $y > 0$, the statement that (y) is a Neumann ray means that $(-y, \alpha y)\ \varepsilon\ T$ for $\alpha > 0$, and there is a $p > 0$ such that $-p \cdot w + \alpha^{-1} p \cdot z \leqslant 0$ for $(-w, z)\ \varepsilon\ T$. We also add the condition introduced by Kemeny, Morgenstern, and Thompson [5], $p \cdot y > 0$. Then the Neumann facet containing this ray may be defined just as before. Consider an efficient path which begins at y^0 and terminates at y^N, where the associated price vector is p^N. It is sufficient that $y^0 \geqslant y^*$ for some y^* on a Neumann ray, where $y_i^* > 0$ for $p_i^N > 0$, and $p_i^N > 0$ implies $p_i^* > 0$. This is easily confirmed from the proof of Theorem 1. In other words, there must exist an appropriate p^*, y^* for the efficient path in question. Different efficient paths may well use different p^*, y^*. Indeed, if there are alternative Neumann paths with different α and $p^* \cdot y^* > 0$, different Neumann facets will be used. An efficient path will seek the Neumann facet which satisfies the proper conditions for it. Our assumptions were calculated to cause all efficient paths to seek the same facet, but this is a special case.

The analysis of Kemeny, Morgenstern, and Thompson has illuminated the question of the non-uniqueness of the Neumann balanced growth paths which satisfy $p^* \cdot y^* > 0$. We now see the relevance of the condition $p^* \cdot y^* > 0$ to economics. It if is not met, the balanced growth path will not satisfy the turnpike conditions for *any* efficient path, so *there is no Neumann facet, corresponding to this p^*, y^*, to serve a turnpike function.*

In a general statement, it may be desirable, where such existence assumptions are necessary, to make them directly. For example, if we assume directly that $y^* \gg 0$ on some Neumann facet, then this facet is the only one which T possesses which allows the turnpike conditions to be met. If, also, $p^* \gg 0$, it will serve for every efficient path.

In order to achieve something stronger than convergence to a Neumann facet, assumptions must be made about the processes which lie in that facet. If these are n in number and both input and output matrices have rank n, our analysis may be carried out as above. These assumptions are, however, too strong. Suppose the processes have sets of input and output vectors which are linearly independent although fewer than n. Let the number of these processes be $r < n$. If submatrices E_r and F_r can be selected, involving positively priced goods, where $F_r E_r{}^{-1}$ is a nonsingular, Frobenius matrix, the same arguments may be applied as before. They will insure convergence of the activity levels x^t to x^*, which gives convergence of y^t to y^* at the same time. There is, of course, more to be said about this.

University of Rochester
Rochester, New York

REFERENCES

[1] DORFMAN, ROBERT, PAUL SAMUELSON, AND ROBERT SOLOW: *Linear Programming and Economic Analysis*, New York, 1958, chapter 12.

[2] GALE, DAVID: "The Closed Linear Model of Production," *Linear Inequalities and Related Systems*, edited by Kuhn and Tucker, Princeton, 1956.

[3] HICKS, J. R.: "Prices and the Turnpike, I., The Story of a Mare's Nest," *Review of Economic Studies*, February, 1961.

[4] INADA, KEN-ICHI: "Balanced Growth and Intertemporal Efficiency in Capital Accumulation," unpublished manuscript, 1961.

[5] KEMENY, J. G., OSKAR MORGENSTERN, AND G. L. THOMPSON: "A Generalization of the von Neumann Model of an Expanding Economy," *Econometrica*, April, 1956.

[6] KOOPMANS, TJALLING: "Analysis of Production as an Efficient Combination of Activities," *Activity Analysis of Production and Allocation*, edited by Koopmans, New York, 1951.

[7] MCKENZIE, LIONEL: "Matrices with Dominant Diagonals and Economic Theory," *Mathematical Methods in the Social Sciences*, edited by Arrow, Karlin, and Suppes, Stanford, 1960.

[8] ———: "Price-Quantity Duality and the Turnpike Theorem," paper presented to the Econometric Society, December, 1960.

[9] MALINVAUD, EDMOND: "Capital Accumulation and Efficient Allocation of Resources," *Econometrica*, April, 1953.

[10] MORISHIMA, MICHIO: "Prices, Interest, and Profits in a Dynamic Leontief System," *Econometrics*, July, 1958.

[11] ———: "Proof of a Turnpike Theorem: The No Joint Production Case," *Review of Economic Studies*, February, 1961.

[12] ———: "Some Properties of a Dynamic Leontief System with a Spectrum of Techniques," *Econometrica*, October, 1959.

[13] RADNER, ROY: "Paths of Economic Growth That Are Optimal with Regard Only to Final States," *Review of Economic Studies*, February, 1961.

[14] SOLOW, ROBERT: "Competitive Valuation in a Dynamic Input-Output System," *Econometrica*, January, 1959.

[15] TSUKUI, JINKICHI: "On a Theorem of Relative Stability," *International Economic Review*, May, 1961.

[16] UZAWA, HIROFUMI: "Causal Indeterminacy of the Leontief Dynamic Input-Output System," unpublished manuscript, 1961.

[17] WINTER, SYDNEY: "A Boundedness Property of the Closed Linear Model of Production," RAND P-2384, July, 1961.

Econometrica, Vol. 32, No. 1–2 (January–April, 1964)

PERSISTENCE OF CONTINUAL GROWTH NEAR THE VON NEUMANN RAY: A STRONG VERSION OF THE RADNER TURNPIKE THEOREM[1]

BY HUKUKANE NIKAIDÔ

This paper strengthens the Radner turnpike theorem by examining, under a few reasonable additional assumptions, the mode of the convergence of efficient paths to the von Neumann ray. Continual proximity to the turnpike is established for long-term efficient paths of economic growth except in a common number of initial and final consecutive periods. This result consolidates the Radner theorem and thereby confirms what the originators of the turnpike proposition undoubtedly had in mind.

IT SEEMS THAT nothing has been more challenging to mathematical economists during the last two or three years than the "turnpike" problem. It is concerned with a question of whether or not optimal paths of economic growth trace out catenary motions near the balanced growth path, the so-called turnpike, as the span of programming periods gets longer.[2] It will continue to bewitch many people, since only some very special cases of turnpike phenomena have definitely been brought to light by a few authors[3] such as Hicks [2], Morishima [4], and Radner [5], whose results jointly embellish the February, 1961 issue of *The Review of Economic Studies*. Among these results, Radner's seems to be the most suggestive for further studies in the formulation of the problem as well as in the method of proof. Radner proved, in an elegant way, that, for any thin neighbouring cone of the balanced growth ray, any optimal paths starting at a common initial position stay within the cone except for a finite common number of periods. In spite of this splendid result, however, Radner's theorem has been criticized because of one dubious point left untouched. The criticism points out that there is no assurance that the system will not run off the neighbouring cone around the half-way point of the entire programming period. An optimal path may several times enter and leave the neighbouring cone at intermediate periods which are far from both the intitial and the terminal periods. In other words, no evidence has yet been given for the belief that these running-off periods are concentrated around the initial and terminal periods. On this ground, Radner's results are often referred to as a "weak"

[1] This research was based on a grant from the Ministry of Education, Japan. An earlier version of this paper was circulated as ISER Discussion Paper No. 27, June, 1962, The Institute of Social and Economic Research, Osaka University. The writer should like to acknowledge the stimulus he received upon reading the draft of a paper [6] by Dr. J. Tsukui on a turnpike theorem for a Leontief type model. It was because of this paper that the writer was led to conjecture and prove the present results. He also benefited from valuable comments by D. Gale, N. Georgescu-Roegen, S. Ichimura, M. Morishima, and a referee of this paper.

[2] For general expositions of the turnpike problem see [1, 2].

[3] [3, 6] are more recent contributions to the problem. They prove turnpike theorems for some Leontief-type models in the explicit presence of a capital coefficient matrix, but on some stringent assumptions.

turnpike theorem,[4] or, more jokingly, as a "hop-skip-jumping" turnpike theorem.

The purpose of this paper is to show that this phenomenon of half-way turning off does not really occur in the Radner case, provided some additional, but plausible, assumptions are explicitly imposed upon technological possibilities and the society's preferences about the terminal states of paths of economic growth. In non-mathematical terms, the additional assumption about technology implies that goods can be combined as inputs *in any proportion* to produce some outputs which may, or may not, be zero. This suggests, but need not imply, the presence of some costless disposal processes. On the other hand, another assumption requires that society prefers one state to another if the former provides a larger amount of each good than the latter.

It is also assumed that the von Neumann ray is generated by a positive vector.

These assumptions are sufficiently general to be satisfied by almost all economically meaningful cases. The discussion in the following sections is intended to justify the writer's belief that the Radner theorem should be classified as a "strong," rather than a "weak," turnpike theorem, as one assuring true catenary movements near the turnpike. To be more precise, it will be shown in this paper that under these additional assumptions, the Radner turnpike theorem can be put in the following form:

For any thin neighbouring cone of the balanced growth ray there is a number k such that any optimal path $x(t)$ starting at a common initial state continually stays within the cone except for the k initial periods and the k terminal periods, that is, during most periods t of the program given by $k \leq t \leq N - k$, regardless of the whole span N of programming periods.

The writer believes that this result suggests the powerfulness of the Radner theorem.

For simplicity's sake, the proof will proceed in two steps. The first step will give a proof for the case where free disposability prevails, a case which may deserve independent attention. Then, in the second step, the general case will be reduced to the free disposal case. The method of proof is similar to that of Radner, but consists of a more prudent application of the latter.

1. THE RADNER TURNPIKE THEOREM RECONSIDERED

1.1. To begin with, for the sake of the reader's convenience, the Radner turnpike theorem, in somewhat modified notation, will be outlined as briefly as possible. The theorem is concerned with optimal paths of growth of an economy whose state is described by an n-dimensional vector x, the components of x standing,

---

[4] Professor Inada was the first to point out this peculiar feature of the Radner turnpike theorem. Cf. [3]. However, he also freed it from this peculiarity later in [7], independently of the present writer.

e.g., for the amounts of capital stocks. Whenever one finds it convenient to speak of x in explicit reference to a period t, we write $x(t)$.

The economy has a set of possible technologies, which transform $x(t)$ to $x(t+1)$. These possible pairs of input-output configurations form a technology set T in the nonnegative orthant of a $2n$-dimensional Euclidean space R^{2n}. Radner assumes the following conditions on T.

ASSUMPTION A.1:[5] *T is a closed convex cone in the nonnegative orthant of a 2n-dimensional Euclidean space.*

ASSUMPTION A.2: *If $(0,y)$ is in T, then $y=0$.*
A sequence $\{x(t)\}_{t=0}^{N}$ is said to be feasible, given $x(0)=x^{o}$, if $(x(t), x(t+1))\in T$ *for $t=0,1,2,\ldots, N-1$.* Such a sequence describes a mode of economic growth which extends over N periods.

1.2. Moreover, the economy has preferences among feasible sequences. These preferences depend only upon the terminal states $x(N)$ of such sequences. The preference is represented by a numerical function $u(x)$ defined on the nonnegative orthant of an n-dimensional Euclidean space R^{n}. Radner's assumptions on $u(x)$ are as follow:

ASSUMPTION A.3: *$u(x)$ is nonnegative and continuous, and there is an a such that $u(a)>0$.*

ASSUMPTION A.4: *$u(x)$ is quasi-homogeneous.*[6]

Given N, the span of programming periods, and $x(0)=x^{o}$, the initial state, a u-optimal sequence is a feasible sequence that maximizes $u(x(N))$ among all feasible sequences $\{x(t)\}_{t=0}^{N}$ of span N.

1.3. For any vectors x and y in R^{n}, $x'y$ stands for the inner product given by $\sum_{i=1}^{n}x_iy_i$. The norm $\|x\|$ of a vector x in R^{n} is $(x'x)^{\frac{1}{2}}$. Frequent use will be made of these concepts in the sequel. Radner assumes furthermore:
(i) There are an $\hat{x}\geq 0$, a price vector $p\geq 0$, and an interest factor (growth factor, at the same time) $\rho>0$ such that
(i.1) $(\hat{x}, \rho\hat{x})\in T$;
(i.2) $p'(y-\rho x)\leq 0$ for any $(x,y)\in T$;
(ii)[7] $p'(y-\rho x)<0$ for all $(x,y)\in T$ that are not proportional to $(\hat{x}, \rho\hat{x})$;

---

[5] Radner did not assume convexity in proving his weak turnpike theorem. Our A.1 is just his assumption A1′ in [5, p. 101].

[6] See [5]. The concept of quasi-homogeneity is irrelevant to our discussion, and so its definition may be omitted.

[7] We follow Radner in assuming (ii), though, as he noted, it implicitly postulates some sort of strict convexity and therefore is not met by the Leontief type models, nor the original von Neumann model. See the introduction and Remark 1 of [5].

(iii) there is a number $K>0$ such that $u(x)\leq Kp'x$ for all $x\geq 0$;

(iv)[8] an initial vector x^o is given such that for some $L>0$, and N_o, there is a feasible sequence from x^o to $L\hat{x}$ in N_o periods;

(v) for some numbers $\hat{u}>0$ and N_1, and some vector y for which $u(y)=\hat{u}$, there is a feasible sequence from $\hat{x}$ to y in N_1 periods.

1.4. It has been proved by Radner in a very elegant way that under Assumptions A.1-A.4 and (i)-(v) the following theorem holds.

RADNER'S TURNPIKE THEOREM: *For any $\varepsilon>0$ there is a number k such that, for any programming span N and any u-optimal sequence $\{x(t)\}_{t=0}^N$ with $x(0)=x^o$, the number of periods in which*

(1) $$\left\|\frac{x(t)}{\|x(t)\|} - \hat{x}\right\| \geq \varepsilon$$

holds can not exceed k, provided $\|\hat{x}\|=1$.

The implication of the theorem is obvious.[9] It states the important result that any u-optimal sequence lies in the $\mathscr{E}$-neighbouring cone $\{x|\quad \|x/\|x\| - \hat{x}\| < \varepsilon\}$ of the balanced growth path $\{\rho^t\hat{x}\}$ except possibly for k periods.

1.5. As was pointed out in the introductory discussion, however, these exceptional periods are not assured to be concentrated about initial periods and terminal periods. Some of them may possibly be intermediate periods which are far from both the starting period 0 and the last period N. Thus it is of some interest to detect further economically meaningful conditions that exclude this pathological phenomenon of half-way running off. We shall give here some of these conditions, under which Radner's theorem can be restated in the following form:

A STRONG TURNPIKE THEOREM: *For any $\varepsilon>0$ there is a number k such that, for any programming span N and any u-optimal sequence $\{x(t)\}_{t=0}^N$ with $x(0)=x^o$ we have, upon the normalization $\|\hat{x}\|=1$,*

(2) $$\left\|\frac{x(t)}{\|x(t)\|} - \hat{x}\right\| < \varepsilon \quad \text{for} \quad k\leq t\leq N-k.$$

This theorem means that any optimal sequence lies entirely in the $\mathscr{E}$-neighbouring cone of the balanced growth path in all periods extending from k to $N-k$.

1.6. Our *additional assumptions* are as follow:

(α) *For any $x\geq 0$ there is some y such that $(x,y)\in T$.*

---

[8] Regarding (iv) and (v), see Radner's Remarks 3 and 4 in [5].
[9] Cf. [1, 2].

(β) $\hat{x} > 0$.

(γ) *The preference indicator $u(x)$ satisfies*:

$$x > y \geq 0 \quad \text{implies} \quad u(x) > u(y).$$

(α) implies that any combination of goods at any proportion can be transformed into some output. Note that in (α) it does not matter whether or not $y = 0$. (β) is self-explanatory. (γ) slightly strengthens A.3, but not too much from the economic point of view.

In the following two sections we shall prove that, if (α), (β), and (γ) are assumed in addition to Radner's basic assumptions A.1-A.4. and (i)-(v), the strong turnpike theorem also holds.

2. PROOF FOR THE CASE OF FREE DISPOSABILITY

2.1. Assumption (α) is closely related to, but weaker than, the following assumption of free disposability, as given by Radner himself:

ASSUMPTION A.5: *If $x^* \geq x$, $y \geq y^* \geq 0$ and $(x,y) \in T$, then $(x^*, y^*) \in T$.*

In order to make the crucial points of our proof as clear as possible and to bring into relief the role played by free disposability in the proof, the discussion will be done in two steps. In this section, the proof will be given first for the case of free disposability. Then, in the following section, the general case will be reduced to the free disposal case. Thus, A.5 is assumed in this section. It is noted, however, that one needs A.5 only when proving Lemma 4.

2.2. The proof begins by noting some simple results on the norm $\|\cdot\|$.

Take $\hat{x}$ and p in (i), (ii), and (β). We may assume, without loss of generality, that

$$(3) \qquad \|\hat{x}\| = 1, \quad p'\hat{x} = 1.$$

As is well known, any vector x in R^n can be uniquely decomposed to a sum of its orthogonal projection $\theta(x)\hat{x}$ on the straight line spanned by $\hat{x}$ and its orthogonal complement $e(x)$. Explicitly, we have

$$(4) \qquad x = \theta(x)\hat{x} + e(x),$$

where

$$(5) \qquad \theta(x) = \hat{x}'x.$$

Then, we have

LEMMA 1: $x \neq 0$, $\|(x/\|x\|) - \hat{x}\| < \delta$, $\delta > 0$ *imply* $\|e(x)\| < \delta\|x\|$.

PROOF: By decomposing $x/\|x\|$ to the sum $\theta(x/\|x\|)\hat{x}+e(x/\|x\|)$ and noting that $e(x/\|x\|)$ is orthogonal to $\theta(x/\|x\|)\hat{x}-\hat{x}$, we see

$$\delta^2>\left\|\frac{x}{\|x\|}-\hat{x}\right\|^2=\left\|\theta\left(\frac{x}{\|x\|}\right)\hat{x}-\hat{x}\right\|^2+\left\|e\left(\frac{x}{\|x\|}\right)\right\|^2\geqq\left\|e\left(\frac{x}{\|x\|}\right)\right\|^2=\|e(x)\|^2/\|x\|^2.$$

This proves the lemma.

2.3. Consider any feasible sequences $\{x(t)\}_{t=0}^{N}$, with $x(0)=x^o$.

LEMMA 2:

(I)   *For each of these sequences,*

$$p'x(t+1)/\rho^{t+1}\leqq p'x(t)/\rho^t \qquad (t=0,1,\ldots,N-1).$$

(II) $p>0$.

(III)   *There is a number $\Delta>0$ such that*

$$\|x(t)/\rho^t\|\leqq\Delta \qquad (t=0,1,\ldots,N)$$

holds uniformly for all of these sequences of any span N.

(IV)   *There is a number $\Gamma>0$ such that*

$$p'x(N)/\rho^N\geqq\Gamma$$

holds uniformly for all u-optimal sequences starting at x^o with $N\geqq N_o+N_1$.

PROOF: (I) Since $(x(t),x(t+1))\in T$, we have, by (i.2), $p'x(t+1)\leqq\rho p'x(t)$, which, if divided by ρ^{t+1}, yields (I).

(II) If some components of p vanish, there is some $x\geq0$ such that $p'x=0$. By (α), there exists some $y\geq0$ such that $(x,y)\in T$ for this x. Then, by (i.2), $p'(y-\rho x)\leqq0$. But, since $p'y\geqq0$ and $p'x=0$, we have $p'(y-\rho x)=0$. This implies, in view of (ii), (x,y) is proportional to $(\hat{x},\rho\hat{x})$, so that $p'\hat{x}$ must also vanish, contradicting assumption (β).

(III) By (I), $p'x(t)/\rho^t\leqq p'x(0)$. Since $p'>0$ by (II) and $x(t)/\rho^t$ is nonnegative, this implies the desired uniform boundedness.

(IV) As was shown by Radner,[10] there is, in view of (iv) and (v), a feasible sequence $\{\bar{x}(t)\}_{t=0}^{N}$ with $\bar{x}(0)=x^o$ such that $u(\bar{x}(N))=L\rho^{N-N_o-N_1}\hat{u}>0$. Because of the u-optimality of $\{x(t)\}_{t=0}^{N}$ and in view of (iii), it follows that $Kp'x(N)\geqq u(x(N))$ $\geqq u(\bar{x}(N))=L\rho^{N-N_o-N_1}\hat{u}>0$. Hence $p'x(N)/\rho^N\geqq L\hat{u}/K\rho^{N_o+N_1}=\Gamma>0$, which holds uniformly for all u-optimal sequences at issue.

---

[10] See Remarks 3 and 4 in [5].

An immediate consequence of these two lemmas is

LEMMA 3: *Let* $\{x(t)\}_{t=0}^{N}$ *be any feasible sequence with* $x(0)=x^{o}$. *If* $x(t)\neq0$ *and* $\|(x(t)/\|x(t)\|)-\hat{x}\|<\delta$ *for some* t, *then* $\|e(x(t)/\rho^{t})\|<\delta\Delta$ *for the same* t.

The proof is immediate, so that it may be omitted.

2.4. The following lemma is very important to our proof.

LEMMA 4: *Let* $\{x(t)\}_{t=0}^{N}$ *be any u-optimal sequence with* $x(0)=x^{o}$. *If* $\|e(x(r)/\rho^{r})\|$ $<\eta$ *and* $\|e(x(s)/\rho^{s})\|<\eta$ *for some* r, s *and* $\eta>0$, *then*

$$\left|\theta\left(\frac{x(r)}{\rho^{r}}\right)-\theta\left(\frac{x(s)}{\rho^{s}}\right)\right|<2\eta\max_{i}[\|p\|, 1/\min \hat{x}_{i}]$$

for the same r *and* s.

PROOF: Without loss of generality, we may assume that $r<s$. Using (I) of Lemma 2, $p'x(s)/\rho^{s}\leq p'x(r)/\rho^{r}$, so that

$$p'\left(\theta\left(\frac{x(s)}{\rho^{s}}\right)\hat{x}+e\left(\frac{x(s)}{\rho^{s}}\right)\right)\leq p'\left(\theta\left(\frac{x(r)}{\rho^{r}}\right)\hat{x}+e\left(\frac{x(r)}{\rho^{r}}\right)\right).$$

Hence, by rearrangement, and in view of $p'\hat{x}=1$,

$$\theta\left(\frac{x(s)}{\rho^{s}}\right)-\theta\left(\frac{x(r)}{\rho^{r}}\right)=\left(\theta\left(\frac{x(s)}{\rho^{s}}\right)-\theta\left(\frac{x(r)}{\rho^{r}}\right)\right)p'\hat{x}\leq p'e\left(\frac{x(r)}{\rho^{r}}\right)-p'e\left(\frac{x(s)}{\rho^{s}}\right)$$

$$\leq\|p\|\left(\left\|e\left(\frac{x(r)}{\rho^{r}}\right)\right\|+\left\|e\left(\frac{x(s)}{\rho^{s}}\right)\right\|\right)<2\eta\|p\|.$$

On the other hand, we wish to show that

$$\theta\left(\frac{x(r)}{\rho^{r}}\right)-\theta\left(\frac{x(s)}{\rho^{s}}\right)=\omega<\max_{i}\frac{2\eta}{\hat{x}_{i}}.$$

Suppose that $\omega\geq\max_{i}2\eta/\hat{x}_{i}$. Let

$$\hat{w}=\tfrac{1}{2}\left(\theta\left(\frac{x(r)}{\rho^{r}}\right)+\theta\left(\frac{x(s)}{\rho^{s}}\right)\right)\hat{x}.$$

Since $\frac{\omega}{2}\hat{x}_{i}\geq\eta>\left\|e\left(\frac{x(r)}{\rho^{r}}\right)\right\|\geq-e_{i}\left(\frac{x(r)}{\rho^{r}}\right)$ and $\frac{\omega}{2}\hat{x}_{i}\geq\eta>\left\|e\left(\frac{x(s)}{\rho^{s}}\right)\right\|\geq e_{i}\left(\frac{x(s)}{\rho^{s}}\right)$

for all the components $i=1,2,\ldots,n$, we have

$$\frac{x(r)}{\rho^r} = \theta\Big(\frac{x(r)}{\rho^r}\Big)\hat{x} + e\Big(\frac{x(r)}{\rho^r}\Big) > \Big(\theta\Big(\frac{x(r)}{\rho^r}\Big) - \frac{\omega}{2}\Big)\hat{x} = \hat{w},$$

$$\frac{x(s)}{\rho^s} = \theta\Big(\frac{x(s)}{\rho^s}\Big)\hat{x} + e\Big(\frac{x(s)}{\rho^s}\Big) < \Big(\theta\Big(\frac{x(s)}{\rho^s}\Big) + \frac{\omega}{2}\Big)\hat{x} = \hat{w}.$$

Note that $(\hat{w}, \rho\hat{w})\in T$. Therefore, $\hat{w} < x(r)/\rho^r$ implies, by free disposability A.5, that $(x(r)/\rho^r, \rho\hat{w})\in T$. Hence, $(x(r), \rho^{r+1}\hat{w})\in T$. On the other hand, because $x(s)/\rho^s < \hat{w}$, we can choose a positive vector $\hat{v}$ such that $x(s) + \rho^s\hat{v} < \rho^s\hat{w}$ and $\hat{v}$ is proportional to $\hat{x}$. But, as $(\rho^{s-1}\hat{w}, \rho^s\hat{w})\in T$, free disposability A.5 implies that $(\rho^{s-1}\hat{w}, x(s) + \rho^s\hat{v})\in T$. These results mean that the sequence of span N

$$x(0), \ldots, x(r), \rho^{r+1}\hat{w}, \rho^{r+2}\hat{w}, \ldots, \rho^{s-1}\hat{w}, x(s) + \rho^s\hat{v}, \ldots, x(N) + \rho^N\hat{v}$$

is feasible. Then applying (γ) to $x(N) + \rho^N\hat{v}$ and $x(N)$ entails $u(x(N) + \rho^N\hat{v}) > u(x(N))$, which contradicts the u-optimality of $\{x(t)\}_{t=0}^N$. The desired inequality will readily be obtained by combining these results together.

LEMMA 5: *Under the same assumptions as in Lemma 4, we have*

$$0 \leqq p'\frac{x(t)}{\rho^t} - p'\frac{x(t+1)}{\rho^{t+1}} < 4\eta \max_i [\|p\|, 1/\min \hat{x}_i]$$

for any t such that $r \leqq t \leqq s-1$.

PROOF: A simple evaluation of upper bounds, based on Lemma 4, gives, for r and s, with $r < s$,

$$0 \leqq p'\frac{x(r)}{\rho^r} - p'\frac{x(s)}{\rho^s} = \theta\Big(\frac{x(r)}{\rho^r}\Big) - \theta\Big(\frac{x(s)}{\rho^s}\Big) + p'\Big(e\Big(\frac{x(r)}{\rho^r}\Big) - e\Big(\frac{x(s)}{\rho^s}\Big)\Big)$$

$$\leqq \Big|\theta\Big(\frac{x(r)}{\rho^r}\Big) - \theta\Big(\frac{x(s)}{\rho^s}\Big)\Big| + \|p\|\Big(\Big\|e\Big(\frac{x(r)}{\rho^r}\Big)\Big\| + \Big\|e\Big(\frac{x(s)}{\rho^s}\Big)\Big\|\Big)$$

$$< 2\eta \max_i [\|p\|, 1/\min \hat{x}_i] + 2\eta\|p\| \leqq 4\eta \max_i [\|p\|, 1/\min \hat{x}_i].$$

Therefore, in view of (I) in Lemma 2, we finally have

$$0 \leqq p'\frac{x(t)}{\rho^t} - p'\frac{x(t+1)}{\rho^{t+1}} \leqq p'\frac{x(r)}{\rho^r} - p'\frac{x(s)}{\rho^s} < 4\eta \max_i [\|p\|, 1/\min \hat{x}_i]$$

for any t between r and $s-1$.

2.5. We are now ready to prove the strong turnpike theorem.

PROOF OF THE THEOREM. As was proved by Radner,[11] for any $\varepsilon > 0$ we can choose a positive τ with $\rho > \tau$ such that $x \neq 0$, $(x, y) \in T$ and $\|x/\|x\| - \hat{x}\| \geqq \varepsilon$ imply $p'y \leqq \tau p'x$

Now choose $\eta > 0$ and $\delta > 0$ in such a fashion that

$$(6) \qquad 4\eta \max \left[\|p\|, \; 1/\min_i \hat{x}_i \right] < \left(1 - \frac{\tau}{\rho} \right) \Gamma \,,$$

$$(7) \qquad \delta \Delta < \eta \,,$$

$$(8) \qquad \delta \leqq \varepsilon \,.$$

Since A.1.-A.4. and (i)-(v) are assumed, the original Radner Turnpike Theorem holds, so that for this δ there is a number $k = k(\delta)$ such that

$$(9) \qquad \left\| \frac{x(t)}{\|x(t)\|} - \hat{x} \right\| < \delta$$

for any u-optimal sequences with $x(0) = x^o$ except for k periods. In view of (IV) in Lemma 2, it is noted that $\|x(t)\| > 0$ in (9). Now, suppose that $N > k$, and for each of these sequences let r and s be the first and last periods in which (9) is valid. Then,

$$\left\| \frac{x(r)}{\|x(r)\|} - \hat{x} \right\| < \delta \quad \text{and} \quad \left\| \frac{x(s)}{\|x(s)\|} - \hat{x} \right\| < \delta \,.$$

Accordingly, in view of (6), (7) and Lemmas 3 and 5, we have, for $r \leqq t \leqq s-1$,

$$(10) \qquad 0 \leqq p' \frac{x(t)}{\rho^t} - p' \frac{x(t+1)}{\rho^{t+1}} < (1 - \tau/\rho)\Gamma \,.$$

Suppose that for some t between r and $s-1$ we would have $\|(x(t)/\|x(t)\|) - \hat{x}\| \geqq \varepsilon$. Then, $p'x(t+1) \leqq \tau p'x(t)$, so that

$$p' \frac{x(t)}{\rho^t} - p' \frac{x(t+1)}{\rho^{t+1}} \geqq \left(1 - \frac{\tau}{\rho} \right) p' \frac{x(t)}{\rho^t} \geqq \left(1 - \frac{\tau}{\rho} \right) \Gamma \,,$$

in the light of (I) and (IV) in Lemma 2. But this contradicts (10). Taking (8) into account, we have thereby shown that

$$\left\| \frac{x(t)}{\|x(t)\|} - \hat{x} \right\| < \varepsilon \qquad (r \leqq t \leqq s) \,.$$

Note that r and s may vary with the u-optimal sequence in question. But it is sure that $r + (N-s) \leqq k$ by the very result due to Radner. Therefore, we have, *a fortiori*,

$$\left\| \frac{x(t)}{\|x(t)\|} - \hat{x} \right\| < \varepsilon \qquad (k \leqq t \leqq N-k)$$

for any u-optimal sequences with $x(0) = x^o$ whenever $N \geqq 2k$, as was to be shown.

---

[11] See Lemma in [5, p. 102].

3. PROOF OF THE GENERAL CASE

3.1. The general case in which A.5 holds no longer, but (α) is valid will be dealt with by imbedding the given system in an extended system where free disposability A.5 prevails. This will begin with enlarging the technology set T by means of the addition of all the conceivable disposal processes. Then it will be easy to show that the strong turnpike theorem holds in the enlarged system. The final necessary step of the argument will be to see that u-optimal sequences in the original system still remain u-optimal in the enlarged system.

3.2. The enlarged technology set, which will be called the *disposal hull* of T and designated by $\tilde{T}$, is defined by

$$\tilde{T} = \{(\tilde{x}, \tilde{y}) | \tilde{x} \geq x, \ y \geq \tilde{y} \geq 0 \quad \text{for some} \quad (x, y) \in T \} \ .$$

An important, but immediate fact is that $\tilde{T}$ admits free disposability A.5.

3.3. We consider, for the time being, an economy having $\tilde{T}$ as a technology set but having the same preference indicator $u(x)$ as in the original system.

LEMMA 6: *If A.1-A.4 and* (i)-(v) *together with* (α), (β), *and* (γ) *are assumed on T, the strong turnpike theorem holds for any u-optimal sequences in $\tilde{T}$, starting at x^0.*

PROOF: If A.1-A.5 and (i)-(v) together with (β) and (γ) are shown to be satisfied in $\tilde{T}$, the lemma will be true by virtue of the result for the free disposal case proved in Section 2. To begin with, let us check on A.1 and A.2. The convexity, nonnegativity, and cone property of $\tilde{T}$ in A.1 as well as the impossibility of the land of Cockaigne, A.2, under the technology set $\tilde{T}$ are immediately seen, so that the proof may be omitted. We shall prove, however, the rather non-evident fact that $\tilde{T}$ is closed. In fact, let $(\tilde{x}^v, \tilde{y}^v) \in \tilde{T} (v = 1, 2, \ldots)$ and $\lim \tilde{x}^v = \tilde{x}$, $\lim \tilde{y}^v = \tilde{y}$. There exist, by definition, $(x^v, y^v) \in T (v = 1, 2, \ldots)$ such that $\tilde{x}^v \geq x^v \geq 0$, $y^v \geq \tilde{y}^v \geq 0$ $(v = 1, 2, \ldots)$. Since $\{\tilde{x}^v\}$ is convergent, $\{x^v\}$ is bounded. Then, the corresponding $\{y^v\}$ must be bounded,[12] by A.1 and A.2. Hence, we may assume, without loss of generality, that $\{x^v\}$ and $\{y^v\}$ converge to some x and y, respectively. Since T is closed, we have, in the limit, $\tilde{x} \geq x \geq 0$, $y \geq \tilde{y} \geq 0$ and $(x, y) \in T$, which proves that $(\tilde{x}, \tilde{y}) \in \tilde{T}$. Therefore $\tilde{T}$ is closed. Thus, A.1 and A.2 are also true for $\tilde{T}$. On the other hand, A.3 and A.4 are trivial, because they have no bearing on the technology set, whereas the prevalence of A.5 in $\tilde{T}$ was already noted. To see the prevalence of the remaining conditions (i)-(v), (β), and (γ), however, it suffices to note that the same $\hat{x}$, p, and ρ which served as von Neumann configurations for T can play the corresponding role for $\tilde{T}$. Indeed, take the same $\hat{x}$, p, and ρ. Then, (iii), (iv), (v), (β), and (γ), which are assumed to

---

[12] If $\|x^v\| \leq \alpha$, $(x^v, y^v) \in T$ and $\lim \|y^v\| = \infty$, then we may assume that $(x^v/\|y^v\|, y^v/\|y^v\|)$ converges to some $(0, y) \in T$ with $y \neq 0$. This contradicts A.2.

hold for T, automatically hold *a fortiori* in $\tilde{T}$, a super set of T. Let us show the validity of (i) and (ii) in $\tilde{T}$. First, (i.1) is trivially true. Next, for any $(\tilde{x},\tilde{y}) \in \tilde{T}$, there is, by definition, some $(x,y) \in T$ such that $\tilde{x} \geq x, y \geq \tilde{y}$. In consequence, we have $p'(\tilde{y} - \rho\tilde{x}) \leq p'(y - \rho x) \leq 0$, proving (i.2). If, furthermore, $p'(\tilde{y} - \rho\tilde{x}) = 0$, then $\tilde{x} = x$, $\tilde{y} = y$, and $p'(y - \rho x) = 0$, because p is positive by Lemma 2. Therefore, by virtue of (ii) for $T, (\tilde{x}, \tilde{y})$ must be proportional to $(\hat{x}, \rho\hat{x})$, which proves (ii) for $\tilde{T}$. We have thereby shown that A.1–A.5, (i)-(v), together with (β) and (γ), are valid in $\tilde{T}$.

3.4. We now proceed to the next step of our argument. From a general point of view, an optimal sequence in the original technology set may cease to be optimal in a larger technology set. However, if (α) is assumed, and if the technology set is enlarged by the addition of disposal processes, it can be shown that no such possibility arises. To prove this plausible, yet non-evident fact, let us introduce the concept of additivity A.0, a structural property of the technology set which is weaker than A.1.

ASSUMPTION A.0. *If* (x^1, y^1) *and* (x^2, y^2) *are in* T, *then* $(x^1 + x^2, y^1 + y^2)$ *is in* T.

We shall prove

LEMMA 7: *If* T *satisfies* A.0, (α) *and if* $u(x)$ *is nondecreasing, then any u-optimal sequence in* T, *starting at an* x^o, *remains to be u-optimal even in* $\tilde{T}$.

PROOF: Suppose that a u-optimal sequence $\{x(t)\}_{t=0}^{N}$ with $x(0) = x^o$ were not u-optimal in $\tilde{T}$. Then there would exist a feasible sequence $\{\tilde{x}(t)\}_{t=0}^{N}$ in $\tilde{T}$, with $\tilde{x}(0) = x^o$, such that

$$(11) \qquad u(\tilde{x}(N)) > u(x(N)) .$$

By definition, there are N pairs of input-output configurations (z^t, y^{t+1}) such that

$$(12) \qquad (z^t, y^{t+1}) \in T \qquad (t = 0, 1, \ldots, N-1),$$

$$(13) \qquad x^o = \tilde{x}(0) \geq z^o, \quad y^N \geq \tilde{x}(N), \quad y^t \geq \tilde{x}(t) \geq z^t \qquad (t = 1, 2, \ldots, N-1) .$$

Since $x^o - z^o \geq 0$, there is, by (α), some v^1 such that $(x^o - z^o, v^1) \in T$. Then, in view of (13), $y^1 + v^1 - z^1 \geq 0$, so that, again by (α), there is some v^2 satisfying $(y^1 + v^1 - z^1, v^2) \in T$. Repeating this procedure we can obtain N pairs of input-output configurations in T, that is, $(x^o - z^o, v^1)$, $(y^t + v^t - z^t, v^{t+1})$ $(t = 1, 2, \ldots, N-1)$. Thus, adding them to the corresponding configurations in (12), respectively, based on A.0, we finally get a feasible sequence in T of span N, starting at x^o,

$$x^o, \, y^1 + v^1, \, y^2 + v^2, \ldots, \, y^{N-1} + v^{N-1}, \, y^N + v^N .$$

But, in view of the nondecreasingness of $u(x)$, (11) and (13) imply $u(y^N + v^N) \geq$

$u(y^N) \geqq u(\tilde{x}(N)) > u(x(N))$, which contradicts the u-optimality of $\{x(t)\}_{t=0}^{N}$. This completes the proof.

3.5. We are now in a position to prove the Strong Turnpike Theorem under additional assumptions (α), (β), and (γ). In fact, by Lemma 7, any u-optimal sequence in T, starting at x^o, does not lose its u-optimality in $\tilde{T}$. And, by Lemma 6, the Strong Turnpike Theorem holds for u-optimal sequences in $\tilde{T}$. Therefore, it holds in particular for such sequences in T.

The Institute of Social and Economic Research, Osaka University

REFERENCES

[1] DORFMAN, R., P. A. SAMUELSON, AND R. M. SOLOW: *Linear Programming and Economic Analysis* (McGraw-Hill, 1958).
[2] HICKS, J. R.: "Prices and the Turnpike I: The Story of a Mare's Nest," *Review of Economic Studies*, Vol. XXVIII (2), 1961.
[3] MCKENZIE, L. W.: "Turnpike Theorems for a Generalized Leontief Model," *Econometrica*, Vol. 31 (1, 2), 1963.
[4] MORISHIMA, M.: "Proof of a Turnpike Theorem: The No Joint Production Case," *Review of Economic Studies*, Vol. XXVIII (2), 1961.
[5] RADNER, R.: "Paths of Economic Growth That Are Optimal with Regard Only to Final States: A Turnpike Theorem," *Review of Economic Studies*, Vol. XXVIII (2), 1961.
[6] TSUKUI, J.: "Efficient and Balanced Growth Paths in Dynamic Input-Output Systems— A Turnpike Theorem," *Rironkeizaigaku*, Vol. XIII (1), 1962.

Added in proof:

[7] INADA, K.: "Some Structural Characteristics of Turnpike Theorems," forthcoming in *Review of Economic Studies*.

Econometrica, Vol. 33, No. 4 (October, 1965)

MONEY AND ECONOMIC GROWTH[1]

BY JAMES TOBIN

In non-monetary neo-classical growth models, the equilibrium degree of capital intensity and correspondingly the equilibrium marginal productivity of capital and rate of interest are determined by "productivity and thrift," i.e., by technology and saving behavior. Keynesian difficulties, associated with divergence between warranted and natural rates of growth, arise when capital intensity is limited by the unwillingness of investors to acquire capital at unattractively low rates of return. But why should the community wish to save when rates of return are too unattractive to invest? This can be rationalized only if there are stores of value other than capital, with whose rates of return the marginal productivity of capital must compete. The paper considers monetary debt of the government as one alternative store of value and shows how enough saving may be channeled into this form to bring the warranted rate of growth of capital down to the natural rate. Equilibrium capital intensity and interest rates are then determined by portfolio behavior and monetary factors as well as by saving behavior and technology. In such an equilibrium, the real monetary debt grows at the natural rate also, either by deficit spending or by deflation.

1. THE PURPOSE of this paper is to discuss the rôle of monetary factors in determining the degree of capital intensity of an economy. The models I shall use in discussing this question are both aggregative and primitive. But I believe they serve to illuminate the basic points I wish to make. At any rate, I have taken the designation of this talk as a "lecture" as a license to emphasize exposition rather than novelty and sophistication. And my subject falls naturally and appropriately in the tradition of Irving Fisher of my own university.

Fisher and Keynes, among others, have drawn the useful and fruitful analytical distinction between choices affecting the disposition of income and choices affecting the disposition of wealth. The first set of choices determines how much is saved rather than consumed and how much wealth is accumulated. The second set determines in what forms savers hold their savings, old as well as new. Considerable economic discussion and controversy have concerned the respective rôles of these two kinds of behavior, and their interactions, in determining the rate of interest.

[1] This is the Fisher Lecture that was presented at the Joint European Conference of the Econometric Society and The Institute of Management Sciences in Zürich, September 11, 1964.

2. Most models of economic growth are nonmonetary. They offer no place for significant choices of the second kind—portfolio choices. They admit only one type of asset that can serve wealth owners as a store of value, namely reproducible capital. It is true that some of these models, particularly disaggregated variants, may allow savers and owners of wealth to choose between different kinds or vintages of capital. But this is the only scope for portfolio choice they are permitted. Different questions arise when monetary assets are available to compete with ownership of real goods. I shall proceed by reviewing how the intensity and yield of capital are determined in a typical aggregative nonmonetary model of economic growth, and then indicating how their determination is modified by introducing monetary assets into the model.

3. In a nonmonetary model of growth and capital accumulation, so long as saving continues it necessarily takes the form of real investment. And so long as saving and investment augment the capital stock faster than the effective supplies of other factors are growing, nothing prevents the yields on capital investment from being driven to zero or below. Of course, low or negative yields may cause people to reduce or discontinue their saving or even to consume capital. This classical reaction of saving to the interest rate may help to set an upper limit to capital deepening and a lower bound to the rate of return on capital. But clearly this kind of brake on investment causes no problems of underemployment and insufficiency of aggregate demand. Increased consumption automatically replaces investment.

4. I can illustrate in Figure 1 the manner in which saving behavior determines capital intensity and the rate of interest in a nonmonetary growth model. (For the basic construction of the diagram I am indebted to my Yale colleague, John Fei, but he is not responsible for my present use of it.)

In Figure 1 the horizontal axis measures capital intensity k, the quantity of capital (measured in physical units of output) per effective manhour of labor. The significance of the term "effective" is to allow for improvements in the quality of labor inputs due to "labor-augmenting" technological progress. Thus, if a 1964 manhour is equivalent as input in the production function to two manhours in the base period, say 1930, then k measures the amount of capital per man half-hour 1964 or per manhour 1930.

The vertical axis measures various annual rates. Curve AA' represents y, the average annual product of capital. Since output and capital are measured in the same physical units, this variable has the dimension, pure number per year. It is the reciprocal of the famous capital-output ratio. In accordance with usual assumptions about the production function, y is shown to decline as capital intensity k becomes deeper. Curve MM' represents the corresponding marginal product of capital.

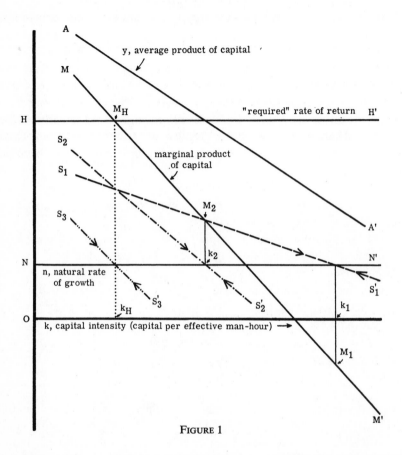

FIGURE 1

For present purposes it will be convenient to regard the average product y, shown by AA', and the corresponding marginal product of capital MM', as referring to output net of depreciation. If depreciation is a constant proportion δ of the capital stock, the average gross product of capital would simply be $y + \delta$, and the marginal gross product would likewise be uniformly higher than MM' by the constant δ. In Figure 1 MM' becomes zero or negative for sufficiently intense use of capital. There are, of course, some technologies—Cobb-Douglas, for example—in which the marginal gross product is always positive. But depreciation can nevertheless make the marginal net product negative.

Even after this allowance for depreciation, the yield on durable capital relevant to an investment-saving decision is not always identical with the marginal product of capital at the time of the decision. The two will be identical if the marginal product is expected to remain constant over the lifetime of the new capital. But if it is expected to change because of future innovations or because of future capital deepening or capital "shallowing" in the economy, the relevant marginal efficiency of current new investment is a weighted average of future marginal products. I shall, however, ignore this distinction in what follows and use the marginal product in Figure 1 as at least an indicator of the true rate of return on capital. For the most part I shall be concerned with equilibrium situations where the two are stationary and therefore identical.

A curve like $S_1 S_1'$ reflects saving behavior. It tells the amount of net saving and investment per year, per unit of the existing capital stock. Therefore it tells how fast the capital stock is growing. In Harrod's terminology, this is the "warranted rate of growth" of the capital stock. The particular curve $S_1 S_1'$ is drawn so that its height is always the same proportion of the height of $A_1 A_1'$. This represents the common assumption that net saving is proportional to net output.

The effective labor force, in manhours, is assumed to grow at a constant rate n, independent of the degree of capital intensity. The "natural rate of growth" n depends on the natural increase in the labor force and on the advance of labor-augmenting technology. This conventional growth-model assumption is indicated in Figure 1 by the horizontal line NN'.

5. So much for the mechanics of Figure 1. Now what determines the development and ultimate equilibrium value, if any, of capital intensity? A rate of growth of capital equal to n will just keep capital intensity constant. If the "warranted" rate of growth of capital exceeds the "natural" rate of growth of labor n, then capital deepening will occur. If capital grows more slowly than labor, k will decline. These facts are indicated in the diagram by the arrows in curve $S_1 S_1'$. With the saving behavior assumed in $S_1 S_1'$, the equilibrium capital intensity is k_1. The corresponding stationary marginal product is M_1. To emphasize the point suggested above, M_1 in the diagram is negative.

A different kind of saving behavior is depicted by $S_2 S_2'$. Here the ratio of net investment to output declines with k. The reason would be that capital deepening lowers the yield on saving and therefore increases the propensity to consume. With saving behavior $S_2 S_2'$, the ultimate equilibrium has a capital intensity k_2 and a marginal product M_2.

6. The theory of interest sketched in Section 5 is classical. The rate of return on capital, in long-run equilibrium, is the result of the interaction of "productivity" and "thrift," or of technology and time preference. To dramatize the conflict of this theory and monetary theories of interest, I shall begin with an extreme case—so extreme that the crucial monetary factor is not even specified explicitly. Some growth models assume a lower limit on the marginal product of capital

of quite a different kind from the limit that thrift imposed in Section 5. Harrod, for example, argues that investors will simply not undertake new investment unless they expect to receive a certain minimum rate of return. Savers, on the other hand, are not discouraged from trying to save when yields fall to or below this minimum. The result is an impasse which leads to Keynesian difficulties of deficient demand and unemployment. In Harrod's model these difficulties arise when the warranted rate of growth at the minimum required rate of profit exceeds the natural rate. The rate of saving from full employment output would cause capital to accumulate faster than the labor force is growing. Consequently, the marginal product of capital would fall and push the rate of return on investment below the required minimum.

In Figure 1, suppose HH to be the required minimum. Then, correspondingly, k_H is the maximum capital intensity investors will tolerate. Yet the saving behavior depicted in the diagram would, if it were actually realized, push marginal product toward M_1 and capital intensity toward k_1, given saving behavior $S_1 S_1'$ (or M_2 and k_2, given saving behavior $S_2 S_2'$). It is this excess of *ex ante* S over I which gives rise to the Keynesian difficulties.

The opposite problem would arise if there were a *maximum* return on investment *below* the equilibrium return (M_1 or M_2) to which saving behavior by itself would lead. At this maximum, the warranted rate of growth would fall short of the natural rate. So long as actual yields on investment exceeded the critical maximum, investment demand would be indefinitely large. In any event it would exceed saving.

The consequences of this impasse in Harrod's model are less clear than the events that follow the deflationary or Keynesian impasse. At this stage the two cases lose their symmetry. Though it is possible for output to fall short of the technologically feasible, when *ex ante* investment is less than *ex ante* saving, it is not possible for output to surpass its technological limits in the opposite case. Presumably an excess of *ex ante* investment is an "inflationary gap," and its main consequence is a price inflation which somehow—for example, through forced saving—eliminates the discrepancy. But this only makes the point that monetary assets had better be introduced explicitly. For it is scarcely possible to talk about inflation in a nonmonetary model where there is no price level to inflate.

7. I have spoken of Harrod's model, but I have the impression that the concept of a required rate of profit plays a key rôle in other theories of growth, notably those of Mrs. Robinson and Mr. Kaldor. Indeed I understand one of the key characteristics of their models—one of the reasons their authors consider them "Keynesian" growth models in distinction to classical models of the type sketched in Section 5 above—is that they separate the investment decision from saving behavior.

A minimal rate of return on capital (a required rate of profit) cannot exist in a vacuum, however. It must reflect the competition of other channels for the placement of saving. For a small open economy, a controlling competitive rate might be set by the yield available on investment abroad. This would, however, leave unexplained the existence of such a limit for a closed economy, whether a national economy or the world as a whole. In any case the growth models under discussion are closed economy models.

In a closed economy clearly the important alternative stores of value are monetary assets. It is their yields which set limits on the acceptable rates of return on real capital and on the acceptable degree of capital intensity. To understand these limits, both how they are determined and how they may be altered, it is necessary to introduce monetary assets into the model explicitly. It is necessary to examine the choices of savers and wealth owners between these assets and real capital. I continue, I remind you, to make the useful distinction between saving-consumption choices, on the one hand, and portfolio choices on the other. The choices I am about to discuss are portfolio choices; that is, they concern the forms of saving and wealth rather than their total amounts.

8. The simplest way to introduce monetary factors is to imagine that there is a single monetary asset with the following properties:

(a) It is supplied only by the central government. This means that it represents neither a commodity produced by the economy nor the debts of private individuals or institutions.

(b) It is the means of payment, the medium of exchange, of the economy. And it is a store of value by reason of its general acceptability in the discharge of public and private transactions.

(c) Its own-yield (i.e., the amount of the asset that is earned by holding a unit of the asset a given period of time) is arbitrarily fixed by the government. This may, of course, be zero but is not necessarily so.

Furthermore, it will be convenient for expository reasons to introduce money in two stages, avoiding in the first stage the complications of a variable value of money, a variable price level. Suppose, to begin with, that the value of money in terms of goods is fixed. The community's wealth now has two components: the real goods accumulated through past real investment and fiduciary or paper "goods" manufactured by the government from thin air. Of course the non-human wealth of such a nation "really" consists only of its tangible capital. But, as viewed by the inhabitants of the nation individually, wealth exceeds the tangible capital stock by the size of what we might term the fiduciary issue. This is an illusion, but only one of the many fallacies of composition which are basic to any economy or any society. The illusion can be maintained unimpaired so long as the society does not actually try to convert all of its paper wealth into goods.

9. The simplest kind of two-asset portfolio behavior is the following: If the yields of the two assets differ, wealth owners will wish to place all of their wealth

in the asset with the higher yield. If they are the same, wealth owners do not care in what proportions they divide their wealth between the two assets. Evidently, if there are positive supplies of both assets, they can be willingly held in portfolios only if the two yields are equal. On this assumption about portfolio behavior, it is easy to see how the institutionally determined rate of interest on money controls the yield of capital. In particular, it is this rate of interest which is the minimal rate of profit that leads to the deflationary impasse discussed in Section 6 above.

At the same time, we can see two ways in which government policy can avoid this impasse. Returning to Figure 1, suppose that HH is the yield on money and therefore the minimal yield acceptable to owners of capital. The corresponding capital intensity is k_H. One measure the government could take is to reduce the yield on money, say to M_1. Such a reduction might—and in Figure 1 it does—entail a negative rate of interest on money, reminiscent of the "stamped money" proposals of Silvio Gesell. Manipulation of interest rates on monetary assets within more normal limits is, in more realistically complex models, accomplished by the usual instruments of central banking.

Alternatively, the government could channel part of the community's excessive thrift into increased holdings of money. Thus, let us now interpret $S_1 S_1'$ to measure the amount by which the public wishes to increase its total wealth relative to its existing holdings of capital. This leads to the Harrod impasse if all the saving must take the form of capital. But if only part of it goes into capital accumulation, if in particular the rate of increase of the capital stock can be lowered to $S_3 S_3'$, then all will be well. Equilibrium capital intensity will be k_H, consistent with maintaining the marginal product of capital at the required level HH. This can be done if the government provides new money to absorb the saving represented by the difference between $S_1 S_1'$ and $S_3 S_3'$.

The only way for the government to achieve this is continuously to run a deficit financed by issue of new money. The deficit must be of the proper size, as can be

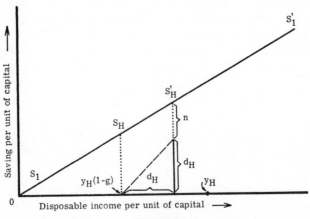

FIGURE 2

illustrated by Figure 2. Here saving is measured vertically, and output and income horizontally. Both are measured in proportion to the capital stock, as in Figure 1. y_H is the output per unit of capital corresponding to the required equilibrium capital intensity k_H. Government purchases of goods and services are assumed to be a fraction g of output. Consequently, $y_H(1-g)$ is output available for private use, and if the budget is balanced it is also the disposable income of the population. Taking $S_1 S_1'$ as the function relating saving to disposable income, S_H is the amount of private saving, (relative to the capital stock) when the budget is balanced. By assumption, however, this is too much investment—it causes the warranted rate to exceed the natural rate. Now n is the natural rate of growth; it is therefore the "right" amount of investment relative to the capital stock. A deficit of d_H (per unit of capital) will do the trick. It increases disposable income to $y_H(1-g)+d_H$, and this raises total saving to S_H'. But of this, d_H is acquisition of government debt, leaving only n for new tangible investment.

The arithmetic is simple enough: Since

(1) $\qquad S = s[y(1-g)+d]=d+n$,

(2) $\qquad \dfrac{d}{y} = \dfrac{s(1-g)-n/y}{1-s}$ gives the required deficit as a fraction of income.

On these assumptions about portfolio choice, the size of the government debt, here identical to the stock of money, does not matter. The deficit must absorb a certain proportion of income, as given in (2). But since wealth owners will hold money and capital in any proportions, provided their yields are in line, the size of the cumulated deficit is immaterial.

The opposite case would correspond to Harrod's inflationary impasse. Just as there is a deficit policy that will resolve the deflationary impasse, so there is a surplus policy that will remedy the opposite difficulty. In this case a balanced budget policy would leave the yield on capital so high that no one wants to hold money. To get the public to hold money it is necessary to increase capital intensity and lower the marginal product of capital. But a higher capital intensity takes more investment relative to output. To achieve a higher investment ratio, the resources that savers make available for capital formation must be supplemented by a government budget surplus. The mechanics of this can be seen by operating Figure 2 in reverse.

10. The portfolio behavior assumed in Section 9 is too simple. A more realistic assumption is that the community will hold the two assets in proportions that depend on their respective yields. There is a whole range of rate differentials at which positive supplies of both assets will be willingly held. But the greater the supply of money relative to that of capital, the higher the yield of money must be relative to that on capital. I shall not review the explanations that have been offered

for this kind of rate-sensitive portfolio diversification. One explanation runs in terms of risk-avoiding strategy where one or both yields are imperfectly predictable. Other explanations are associated with the specific functions of money as means of payment. Yield differentials must compensate for the costs of going back and forth between money and other assets. They must also offset the value of hedging against possible losses in case of unforeseen and exigent needs for cash.

The demand for money, presumably, depends also on income. Other things equal (i.e., asset yields and total wealth), more money will be required and less capital demanded the higher the level of output.

11. One implication of the assumption about portfolio behavior made in Section 10 can be stated very simply. Capital deepening in production requires monetary deepening in portfolios. If saving is so great that capital intensity is increasing, the yield on capital will fall. Given the yield on money, the stock of money per unit of capital must rise. Provided the government can engineer such an increase, capital deepening can proceed. There is a limit to this process, however. As in the previous cases discussed, there is an equilibrium capital intensity. Monetary deepening cannot push capital intensity beyond this equilibrium because the deficit spending required would leave too little saving available for capital formation.

In such an equilibrium, the shares of money and capital in total wealth must be constant so that their yields can remain constant. To maintain the fixed relation between the stocks, money and capital must grow at the same rate. That is, new saving must be divided between them in the same ratio as old saving.

Let $m(k, r)$ be the required amount of money per unit of capital when the capital intensity is k and the yield of money is r. We know that m is an increasing function of r: more money is demanded when its yield is higher. At the moment, we are taking r as fixed. I take m to be also an increasing function of k because an increase in k lowers the yield of capital. It is true that an increase in k also lowers y and therefore reduces the strict transactions demand for means of payment. But I assume the yield effects of variations in capital intensity to be the more powerful.

Let w (for "warranted") be the rate of growth of the capital stock, and let d represent, as before, the deficit per unit of existing capital. Then, constancy of amount of money per unit of capital at $m(k, r)$ requires that $d=m(k, r)w$. Assuming as before that saving is a constant proportion of disposable income, the basic identity is essentially the same as (1) above:

$$S=s(y(1-g)+d)=d+w .$$

Using the fact that $d=m(k, r)w$, we have

(3) $$w(k, r) = \frac{sy(k)(1-g)}{1+(1-s)m(k, r)}.$$

In equilibrium $w=n$: the warranted and natural rates must be equal. The equilibrium degree of capital intensity is the value of k that equates $w(k, r)$ in (3) to n.

I have written w and y in (3) as functions of k as a reminder that these variables, as well as m, depend directly or indirectly on capital intensity. Since y is a decreasing and m an increasing function of k, it is clear that w declines with k. Moreover, the amount by which w in (3) falls short of the hypothetical w for $m=0$ $(sy(1-g))$ increases with k.

This analysis may be presented diagrammatically, following the format of Figure 1. In Figure 3, $S_1 S_1'$ reflects, as before, the balanced budget $(d=0)$ saving function, with saving a constant fraction of disposable income. This would be the warranted rate of growth of capital if m were zero. $W_1 W_1'$ represents for every capital intensity the warranted rate of growth of capital, assuming that the stock of money is adjusted to that capital intensity and maintained in that adjustment by deficit spending. The intersection of $W_1 W_1'$ with NN', the natural rate of growth, gives the equilibrium capital intensity k_1. As before, the equilibrium yield on capital is M', its marginal product at k_1. This yield, however, is not necessarily equal to the yield on money r.

The curve $W_1 W_1'$ is drawn for a particular yield on money $\bar{r}_1$. Lowering the yield on money, say to $\bar{r}_2$, would shift the curve to the right, to $W_2 W_2'$ —increasing equilibrium capital intensity and lowering the equilibrium rate of return on capital.

12. I turn now to the more interesting and realistic case where the value of money in terms of goods is variable. Its variability has two important consequences. The real value of the monetary component of wealth is not under the direct control of the government but also depends on the price level. And the real return on a unit of money—a favorite concept of Fisher—consists not only of its own-yield but also of the change in its real value.

Once again, we may ask whether there is an equilibrium capital intensity and, if so, how it is determined. The analysis of Section 11 tells us that there is an equilibrium capital intensity associated with a stable price level. But this requires a particular fiscal policy that maintains through deficit spending of the right magnitude just the right balance between stocks of money and capital. Now what happens when fiscal policy is determined independently so that a stable price level cannot necessarily be maintained?

In particular, suppose that a balanced budget policy is followed and the nominal stock of money remains constant. Real capital gains due to deflation play the same rôle as deficits did in Section 11. That is, they augment real disposable income and they absorb part of the propensity to save. Therefore, we can use the same apparatus as before, illustrated in Figure 3, to find the equilibrium capital intensity.

There is, however, one important difference. In the equilibrium the real stock of money must be increasing as fast as the capital stock, namely at the natural rate n. In the present instance this can happen only if the price level falls at rate n. If so, the real return on money r is not simply the nominal yield $\bar{r}$ but $\bar{r}+n$. Consequently the demand for money will be larger than if prices were expected to remain stable.

Equilibrium will require a greater stock of money per unit of capital and a lower capital intensity if deflation is substituted for money creation. This is indicated in Figure 3 where $W_3 W_3'$ is the curve corresponding to a yield on money n points higher than the yield behind $W_1 W_1'$

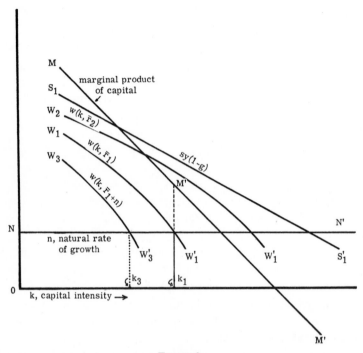

FIGURE 3

13. It is natural to ask whether there are symmetrical *equilibrium* situations in which a budget surplus or inflation is called for. The most obvious symmetrical case occurs when the natural rate of growth of the effective labor force is negative. But this is not a very interesting case of "growth."

The Harrod inflationary impasse, discussed above, would mean that at the hypothetical equilibrium capital intensity and rate of profit achievable when 100 per cent of saving goes into capital formation there is zero demand for money. Any money in existence, therefore, would have to be wiped out by surpluses or price increases; but these would be temporary rather than permanent.

One might, I suppose, imagine the public to desire a negative monetary position, i.e., to be net debtors to the government. Then there would be an equilibrium in which the public's net debt to the government grows in real value at the natural rate, thanks either to budget surpluses (with which the government acquires IOU's from its citizens) or to price inflation. In either case capital formation exceeds normal saving because the public saves extra either through taxes and the government budget or through the necessity to provide for the increased real burden of its debt to the government.

A negative monetary position is not as far-fetched as it sounds, if "money" is interpreted in a broad sense to connote the whole range of actual fixed-money-value assets, not just means of payment. It is quite possible, then, for the government to be a net creditor over this entire category of assets, while still providing a circulating medium of exchange.

14. So far only the existence of an equilibrium path of the kind described in Section 12 has been discussed. Its stability is something else again. I can only sketch the considerations involved.

What happens when the community is thrown out of portfolio balance either by some irregularity in technological progress, labor force growth, saving behavior, change in yield expectations, or portfolio preferences? If the result of the shock is that the public has too much capital and too little money for its tastes, goods prices will fall faster or rise more slowly than before. In the opposite case, the public will try to buy capital with money and will push prices up faster or retard their decline.

Evidently there are two effects, at war with each other. One we might call the Pigou effect, the other the Wicksell effect. The Pigou effect is stabilizing. Consider the case of a deflationary shock. The accelerated decline in prices, by augmenting the real value of existing money balances, helps to restore portfolio balance. Moreover, by increasing total real wealth it retards the flow of saving into capital formation. The Wicksell effect is destabilizing. An accelerated decline in prices means a more attractive yield on money and encourages a further shift in portfolio demand in the same direction as the original shock. The issue depends on the speed with which price movements are translated into expectations. If this process is sluggish—expectations are inelastic—then the stabilizing Pigou effect will win out. But if current experience has a heavy weight in formation of expectations, the system can be unstable.*

15. In classical theory, the interest rate and the capital intensity of the economy are determined by "productivity and thrift," that is, by the interaction of technology and saving propensities. This is true both in the short run, when capital is being accumulated at a rate different from the growth of the labor force, and in the long-run stationary or "moving stationary" equilibrium, when capital intensity is constant. Keynes gave reasons why in the short run monetary factors and portfolio decisions modify, and in some circumstances dominate, the determination of the interest rate and the process of capital accumulation. I have tried to show here that a similar proposition is true for the long run. The equilibrium interest rate and degree of capital intensity are in general affected by monetary supplies and portfolio behavior, as well as by technology and thrift.

Cowles Foundation for Research in Economics, Yale University

* The last three sentences have been added to the original version, and the remainder of the stability discussion of section 14 has been deleted.

Econometrica, Vol. 34, No. 4 (October, 1966)

OPTIMUM GROWTH IN AN AGGREGATIVE MODEL OF CAPITAL ACCUMULATION: A TURNPIKE THEOREM[1]

By David Cass

This paper presents an analysis of the behavior of growth paths which are optimum with respect to the social welfare generated by consumption over a finite planning period. The principal result is the establishment of a (modified) golden rule turnpike property for such paths.

1. INTRODUCTION AND SUMMARY

RECENT CONTRIBUTIONS to the theory of optimum economic growth, for example, in [1, 3, 9 or 11], like Ramsey's seminal work [6], have been primarily concerned with the implications of maximizing the social welfare generated by the entire stream of future consumption. As an alternative formulation, in this paper it is postulated that only the social welfare associated with future consumption over some finite period is of direct concern; generations beyond the horizon are accounted for only insofar as a lower bound on the terminal capital stock is prescribed. Then, within a closed, aggregative framework, the behavior of growth paths which are optimum with respect to this social welfare is investigated.

Our central result is to exhibit a general property of such optimum growth paths. Stated loosely, this property is that any economy pursuing optimum growth over a sufficiently long period would spend all except at most an initial and final phase of the period performing nearly golden rule balanced growth (appropriately defined for a possibly nonzero social discount rate). *Hence, we have generalized the turnpike property of essentially pure production models, originally elaborated by Dorfman, Samuelson, and Solow [2], and later explored by many others, in an important direction: A similar result is shown to hold when the intrinsic value of consumption— over and above its indirect contribution to the continuation of production—is explicitly accounted for.*

The plan of the paper is as follows: In the next section we introduce the now standard aggregative model of capital accumulation and a precise definition of the social welfare enjoyed within the economy described by this model. In Section 3 we characterize and then discuss the general behavior of optimum growth paths.

[1] Work on this paper was begun while I was the recipient of a Haynes Foundation dissertation fellowhip at Stanford University; it was also supported in part by the National Science Foundation under grants GS-420 to the University of Chicago and GS-88 to the Cowles Foundation for Research in Economics at Yale University. The paper itself has benefited greatly from lively discussions at Stanford (in the Quantitative Analysis Workshop) and later at the University of Chicago (in an informal summer seminar on growth theory conducted by Professor H. Uzawa). A similar analysis by Samuelson [7] came to my attention after the paper was completed.

Finally, in Section 4, we formulate and then demonstrate the optimum growth turnpike property.

2. THE MODEL AND DEFINITION OF SOCIAL WELFARE

We assume the closed, aggregative model of capital accumulation first closely analyzed by Solow [8]. Briefly, the behavior of this simple economy over time is described by three relations:

(1) $\quad y = f(k)$,

an aggregate production function, relating the output per capita of a single, homogeneous good to the capital-labor ratio;

(2) $\quad c(t) + z(t) = y(t)$, $\quad c(t) \geqslant 0$, $\quad z(t) \geqslant 0$,

the allocation of current output per capita between instantaneous consumption and gross investment per capita;[2] and

(3) $\quad \dot{k}(t) = z(t) - \lambda k(t)$, with $k(0) = k^0$, given $\lambda = n + \mu > 0$, $k^0 > 0$,

the growth of capital per head from the historically given initial capital-labor ratio k^0, when the labor force (and population) is expanding exogenously at the positive rate n, and the capital stock is depreciating, independently of use, at the positive rate μ.

The production function is assumed to exhibit, in addition to constant returns to scale, positive marginal productivity of either factor, as well as a diminishing marginal rate of substitution between factors, expressed by the conditions

(4) $\quad f(k) > 0$, $\quad f'(k) > 0$, $\quad f''(k) < 0$ for $k > 0$.

Moreover, both the importance and limitation of roundaboutness in production are assumed to be further represented by the limit conditions

(5) $\quad \lim_{k \to 0} f'(k) = \infty$, $\quad \lim_{k \to \infty} f'(k) = 0$.

Finally, as should be clear from (1), there is no technical change in this economy.

It is worthwhile mentioning that the aggregative "neoclassical" technology outlined in the preceding paragraphs is a special case of the two-sector "neoclassical" technology of Uzawa [10]; most of the results to be presented carry over directly into that more general formulation, in which the available techniques for producing capital goods differ from those for producing consumption goods. Because it

---

[2] It is necessary in what follows that the allocation process be mildly well behaved. Therefore, it is convenient at this point simply to assume the stronger condition that $c(t)$ and $z(t)$ are piecewise continuous. This can be interpreted as an approximation of the fact that the planning and execution of abrupt changes in any given allocation scheme require time.

simplifies the exposition, and also because no further insight is gained otherwise, we choose to carry out the analysis for the special case.

Social welfare over any finite period $[0, T]$ is presumed to be adequately represented by the functional

(6) $$W = \int_0^T U[c(t)]e^{-\delta t}\,dt, \qquad \text{given } -\infty < \delta < \infty,$$

that is, by the discounted sum over the period of some index, $U(\cdot)$, of the rate of per capita consumption. For short, we refer to this index as the instantaneous utility function. The latter is assumed to increase at a decreasing rate,

(7) $$U'(c) > 0, \quad U''(c) < 0 \text{ for } c > 0,$$

and to increase very rapidly for small but very slowly for large rates of per capita consumption,

(8) $$\lim_{c \to 0} U'(c) = \infty, \quad \lim_{c \to \infty} U'(c) = 0.$$

The conditions in (7) can be interpreted, by reference to the discrete analogue of (6), to represent a diminishing marginal rate of substitution between rates of per capita consumption at any two points of time. And the limit conditions (8) are essentially, first, one possible continuous generalization of the imposition of a minimum subsistence level, and second, the condition of nonsatiation.

Finally, as mentioned in the introduction, we assume that the growth paths which this economy is free to follow are constrained by the additional nontechnological requirement

(9) $$k(T) \geqslant k^T, \qquad \text{given } k^T \geqslant 0,$$

that the terminal capital-labor ratio be at least as large as some prescribed minimum.

3. OPTIMUM GROWTH PATHS WITHIN A FINITE HORIZON

The problem confronting, say, the technical staff of the central planning board is to determine the growth path $\{(c(t), z(t), k(t)): 0 \leqslant t \leqslant T\}$ maximizing the welfare criterion (6), subject to the feasibility constraints (1)-(3) and the terminal condition (9). For easy reference, this problem can be stated concisely as:

(10)
$$
\begin{cases}
\text{Specify the growth path} \qquad (c, z, k) \\[6pt]
\text{which maximizes social welfare } \int_0^T U(c)e^{-\delta t}\,dt \\[6pt]
\text{subject to } c + z = f(k), \qquad c \geqslant 0,\ z \geqslant 0, \\[6pt]
\qquad \dot{k} = z - \lambda k, \qquad \text{with } k(0) = k^0, \text{ and } k(T) \geqslant k^T \\[6pt]
\text{and given } 0 < T < \infty, \quad -\infty < \delta < \infty, \quad \lambda > 0,\ k^0 > 0, \text{ and } k^T \geqslant 0.
\end{cases}
$$

In (10) and hereafter, variables such as c, z, and k are understood to be functions of t when not explicitly so denoted.

In order that (10) be a meaningful problem, it is necessary that k^T and T be chosen so that the minimum terminal capital-labor ratio is attainable within the existing technology and feasible within the prescribed period. Formally, these restrictions can be expressed by the constraint

$$(k^T, T) \in A$$

where A, the set of attainable and feasible terminal parameters, is defined by

$$A = \{(k^T, T): 0 \leqslant k^T < \bar{k}, \ g(k^T, T) \geqslant 0\},$$

with

(11) $\bar{k} = \hat{k}, \quad \text{for } k^0 \leqslant \hat{k}$

       $= k^0, \text{for } \hat{k} < k^0,$

where $f(\hat{k}) = \lambda \hat{k}$, and

(12) $g(k^T, T) = T - \displaystyle\int_{k^0}^{k^T} \frac{dk}{f(k) - \lambda k}, \quad \text{for } k^0 \leqslant k^T$

       $= \displaystyle\int_{k^0}^{\max(k^T, \hat{k})} \frac{dk}{f(k) - \lambda k} - T, \quad \text{for } k^0 > k^T.$

Equations (11) and (12) follow directly from the structure of the technology postulated in the last section: The former defines the maximum attainable capital-labor ratio starting from any $k^0 > 0$, while the latter merely displays the difference between the prescribed period and the minimum time required to go from k^0 to k^T, when $k^0 \leqslant k^T$ (or between the maximum time permitted in going from k^0 to k^T and the prescribed time, when $k^0 > k^T$, the less interesting case).

As a further comment before presenting the solution to (10), let us emphasize that the (effective) social discount rate δ need not be positive. Indeed, for any finite social discount rate and any feasible growth path generating consumption per capita c, from (2), (4), (7), and (11) it follows that

$$\int_0^T U(c) e^{-\delta t}\, dt \leqslant \frac{U[f(\bar{k})]}{\delta}(1 - e^{-\delta T}) < \infty,$$

social welfare is bounded from above.[3] Thus, one obvious and permissible interpretation of the welfare functional (6) is purely classical: It represents total individual welfare over the period under consideration. On our other assumptions —in particular that the current labor force $L(t)$ and the current total population

---

[3] Of course, if δ is positive, or if δ is zero and a suitable level of saturation is admitted, then our formulation of the problem (10) is also meaningful for the limiting case $T \to \infty$. However, as Koopmans (Proposition K in [3]) has shown, even if a modification of Ramsey's bliss device is used, if δ is negative, then the limiting case $T \to \infty$ of the corresponding problem has no solution. This result is relevant to our later interpretation of the optimum growth turnpike.

$P(t)$ grow at the same positive rate n, so that the former is a fixed proportion γ of the latter—such an interpretation can be expressed explicitly by

$$W = \int_0^T P(t)u[c(t)]dt = \int_0^T U[c(t)]e^{-\delta t}dt,$$

where

$$U[c(t)] = \frac{L(0)}{\gamma}u[c(t)] \text{ and } \delta = -n < 0.$$

Now the index $U(\cdot)$ is simply a constant multiple of the instantaneous utility function of the representative individual in our egalitarian economy $u(\cdot)$, providing a motivation for the reference introduced in the previous section.

To characterize the optimum growth paths, we appeal to Pontryagin's Maximum Principle (Sections 1.6, 1.8 in [4]), which applies to the problem (10) if the variables are redefined in such a way that the gross investment ratio s,

$$0 \leqslant s = \frac{z}{f(k)} \leqslant 1,$$

can be treated as an explicit control parameter. By introducing the imputed price of a unit of gross investment per head,

(13) $q = q(t)$,

and the imputed value of gross national product per capita,

(14) $\psi = U(c) + qz$,

and then applying the theorem to the Hamiltonian expression representing the present imputed value of net national product per capita,

$$(\psi - q\lambda k)e^{-\delta t},$$

the following theorem is obtained:

The necessary conditions for an optimum growth path are that there exists a continuous imputed price (13) such that

(15) $\dot{q} = (\delta + \lambda)q - U'(c)f'(k) = \dfrac{d\left(\int_t^T \dfrac{\partial[\psi - q\lambda k]}{\partial k}e^{-\delta(\tau - t)}d\tau\right)}{dt}$

and

(I) $q(T) \geqslant 0$, with equality for $k(T) > k^T$,

the imputed price changes as if, say, the central planning board exercises perfect foresight with respect to the net marginal value product of capital, while the terminal imputed price is zero if $k(T) > k^T$ or nonnegative if $k(T) = k^T$;

(16) $c + z = f(k)$, $c \geqslant 0$, $z \geqslant 0$,

and

(17) $\quad \left(\dfrac{\partial\psi}{\partial z}\right)_{c=f(k)-z} = -U'(c)+q \leqslant 0$, *with equality for* $z>0$,

the allocation between current consumption and current gross investment per capita is feasible and maximizes the imputed value of gross (and net) national product at each point of time;

(18) $\quad \dot{k} = z - \lambda k$, *with* $k(0)=k^0$,

and

(II) $\quad k(T) \geqslant k^T$,

the growth of the capital-labor ratio is feasible, while the terminal capital-labor ratio is at least as large as the prescribed minimum.

It should be clear that all the above valuations are in terms of the instantaneous utility of the rate of per capita consumption.

Conditions (15)–(18), (I), and (II) are also sufficient. In demonstrating this fact, it is further easily shown that if an optimum growth path exists, then it is unique. Hence, we can state as a second theorem:

Suppose we have found a feasible path (c^1, z^1, k^1) *and an imputed price* q^1 *which satisfy* (15)–(18), (*I*), *and* (*II*). *Then consider any other distinct feasible path* (c^2, z^2, k^2) *satisfying* (16), (18), *and* (*II*). *By "distinct" is meant*

$$k^1(\tau) \neq k^2(\tau) \text{ for some } 0 < \tau < T,$$

which, because of the continuity of k on any feasible path, implies

(19) $\quad k^1(t) \neq k^2(t)$ *for* $t \in I(\tau)$,

where $I(\tau)$ *is some open interval around* τ. *It follows that*

(20) $\quad \displaystyle\int_0^T \{U(c^1) - U(c^2)\} e^{-\delta t}\, dt > 0$,

the first path is strictly better than the second.

To prove this result, we perform various manipulations on the integral in (20). Thus,

$$\int_0^T \{U(c^1) - U(c^2)\} e^{-\delta t}\, dt = ,$$

adding and subtracting $U'(c^1)(c^1 - c^2)$ and the zero expressions $q^1(z^j - \lambda k^j - \dot{k}^j)$, $j=1, 2$, derived from (18), within the braces under the integral,

$$\int_0^T \{U(c^1) - U(c^2) - U'(c^1)(c^1 - c^2) + U'(c^1)(c^1 - c^2)$$

$$+ q^1(z^1 - \lambda k^1 - \dot{k}^1) - q^1(z^2 - \lambda k^2 - \dot{k}^2)\} e^{-\delta t}\, dt = ,$$

adding and subtracting $U'(c^1)f'(k^1)(k^1-k^2)$, substituting for $c^j, j=1, 2$, from (16), and rearranging terms, all again within the braces under the integral,

$$\int_0^T \{U(c^1)-U(c^2)-U'(c^1)(c^1-c^2)+(q^1-U'(c^1))(z^1-z^2)$$

$$+(U'(c^1)f'(k^1)-\lambda q^1)(k^1-k^2)$$

$$+U'(c^1)(f(k^1)-f(k^2)-f'(k^1)(k^1-k^2))-q^1(k^1-k^2)\}e^{-\delta t}\,dt> ,$$

utilizing the strict concavity of $f(\cdot)$ in conjunction with (19), and the concavity of $U(\cdot)$, and integrating by parts the expression

$$\int_0^T q^1(k^1-k^2)e^{-\delta t}\,dt ,$$

$$\int_0^T \{(q^1-U'(c^1))(z^1-z^2)+(\dot{q}^1+U'(c^1)f'(k^1)-(\delta+\lambda)q^1)(k^1-k^2)\}e^{-\delta t}\,dt$$

$$-[q^1(k^1-k^2)e^{-\delta t}]\Big|_0^T \geqslant,$$

applying the optimality conditions (15) and (17),

$$-[q^1(k^1-k^2)e^{-\delta t}]\Big|_0^T \geqslant 0 ,$$

substituting from the initial condition in (18) and the terminal conditions (I) and (II).

An analysis of the solutions to the pair of autonomous differential equations (15) and (18), given the relations (16) and (17), is presented in detail in [1], and these results are exhibited here in Figure 1. The general behavior of the unique optimum growth path for any given initial capital-labor ratio, $k^0>0$, and any prescribed minimum terminal capital-labor ratio and time horizon which are attainable and feasible, $(k^T, T) \in A$—referred to hereafter as the unique optimum growth path specified by (k^0, k^T, T)—can thus be derived from a close examination of this phase diagram. Therefore, before we present the central results of this paper, we detour and mention the several features depicted in Figure 1.

$\dot{k}=0, \dot{q}=0$—The singular curves for each differential equation considered separately. They divide the half-plane $k \geqslant 0$ into four regions of behavior for the system of differential equations, as labeled and illustrated.

S—The curve for which $z=0$ and (17) is satisfied with equality. Thus it can best be represented as the boundary of specialization in consumption: for all points on or below (above) S, gross investment is zero (strictly positive). Notice that our assumption (8), that marginal utility approaches infinity as consumption per capita approaches zero, in conjunction with the optimality conditions specifying imputa-

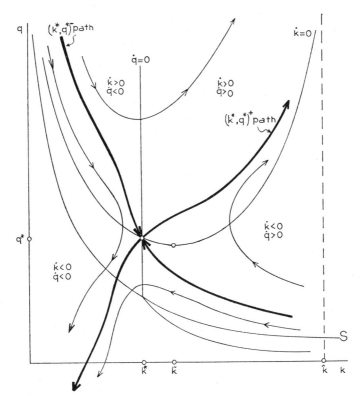

FIGURE 1.—The nature of the solutions to the optimality conditions.

tion and allocation, imply that the contrary specialization in investment is never optimum over a finite interval of time.

$\hat{k}$—Previously defined by (11), $\hat{k}$ can be further interpreted as the maximum long-run attainable capital-labor ratio: For any $k^0 > 0$, specialization in investment would result in an asymptotic approach to $\hat{k}$. Although the cases for which $k^0 \geqslant \hat{k}$ are probably not particularly interesting—a point which would be debatable in an open model allowing foreign aid or virtually unlimited borrowing in the international capital market—as they present no essential complication, we will only implicitly restrict our attention to the cases for which $k^0 < \hat{k}$.

$\tilde{k}$—This is the golden rule capital-labor ratio, defined by $f'(\tilde{k}) = \lambda$. Thus, balanced growth at $\tilde{k}$ yields the golden rule growth path, denoted by $(\tilde{c}, \tilde{z}, \tilde{k})$, $\tilde{c} = f(\tilde{k}) - \lambda\tilde{k}$, and $\tilde{z} = \lambda\tilde{k}$. It can be interpreted as the one balanced growth path which would be forever voluntarily maintained as optimum, given the ethical judgment that there is to be no discrimination among generations, i.e., a zero social discount rate, either because of size or timing.

(k^*, q^*)—The point representing the unique balanced growth path and imputed price defined by the singular solution of the system (15)–(18), $f'(k^*) = \delta + \lambda$,

$z^* = \lambda k^*$, $c^* = f(k^*) - z^*$, and $q^* = U'(c^*)$. For $\delta \neq 0$, (c^*, z^*, k^*) differs from the golden rule growth path. However, it is proved in [1] that if there is social impatience, i.e., a positive social discount rate, then it is again the one balanced growth path which would be forever voluntarily maintained as optimum. Though (c^*, z^*, k^*) is not such a "best" balanced growth path when the social discount rate is negative, we take the liberty of referring to any balanced growth path at a capital-labor ratio k^* as a (modified) golden rule growth path.

It should be mentioned explicitly that the (modified) golden rule growth path is attainable if and only if $k^* < \hat{k}$, which condition provides a lower bound on δ. That is, if $k^* < \hat{k}$, then $\delta + \lambda = f'(k^*) > f'(\hat{k})$, or $\delta > f'(\hat{k}) - \lambda = \rho$, where ρ is some finite negative number, as $\lambda = f'(\tilde{k}) > f'(\hat{k})$ by the strict concavity of $f(\cdot)$. The implication for our analysis is that, in any society in which the material well-being of the average individual of tomorrow's generation is vastly more important than that of today's—perhaps because of rapid population growth—although the optimum growth path specified by (k^0, k^T, T) always exists, for large T the turnpike becomes the maximum attainable balanced growth path $(0, \hat{z}, \hat{k})$, $\hat{z} = f(\hat{k})$, and not the (modified) golden rule growth path (c^*, z^*, k^*). We neglect this possibility and hereafter simply assume $\delta > \rho$.

$(k^*, q^*)^-$ and $(k^*, q^*)^+$ paths—The singular point (k^*, q^*) is a saddle point, with its stable branches the $(k^*, q^*)^-$ path, and its unstable branches the $(k^*, q^*)^+$ path. It is also shown in [1] that for $\delta > 0$, some portion of the $(k^*, q^*)^-$ path is the unique optimum growth path specified by $(k^0, 0, \infty)$.

Before continuing the analysis, two comments about emphasis and notation will be helpful. First, although the system (15)–(18) along with the terminal conditions (I) and (II) characterize any unique optimum growth path in terms of the real variables c, z, and k and the imputed price q, most of the discussion in the remainder of this and the following section will emphasize only the real stock variable k and the imputed price q. This is possible because we can reformulate (16) and (17) as

(17') $c = \min\{h(q), f(k)\} = c(k, q)$,   and

(16') $z = f(k) - c(k, q) = z(k, q)$,   where

(21) $h(q) = U'^{-1}(q) > 0$,   for $q \geqslant 0$
              $= +\infty$,   for $q < 0$,   with

(22) $h'(q) = \dfrac{1}{U''[h(q)]} < 0$,   and

(23) $\lim_{q \to 0} h(q) = \infty$, $\lim_{q \to \infty} h(q) = 0$,

utilizing the postulated properties of the instantaneous utility function (7) and (8). Hence, the system (15)–(18) can be reduced to a pair of autonomous differential equations in the variables k and q,

(18') $\dot{k} = z(k, q) - \lambda k$,   with $k(0) = k^0$,   and

(15') $\dot{q} = (\delta + \lambda)q - U'[c(k, q)]f'(k)$.

Such simplification is primarily a matter of convenience; the same relations (16') and (17') which enable us to ignore the real flow variables c and z also readily allow us to convert results in terms of k and q, where relevant, into terms of c or z.

Second, in accordance with this emphasis, we adopt the procedure of referring to a particular solution to the system (15)–(18) as the (k^j, q^j) path, where the point (k^j, q^j) is some easily distinguished feature of the particular solution. Also, the backward and forward (in time) segments of the (k^j, q^j) path from the point (k^j, q^j) are expressly referred to as the $(k^j, q^j)^-$ and $(k^j, q^j)^+$ paths, respectively. And, when the need arises, any segment of a (k^j, q^j) path is explicitly denoted by $\{(k^j(t), q^j(t)): 0 \leqslant t \leqslant T\}$, with initial or terminal values $(k^j(0), q^j(0))$ or $(k^j(T), q^j(T))$—though occasionally for the last we drop superscripts if the possibility of resulting confusion is small.

For example, a distinguishing feature of the solution discussed in the fourth preceding paragraph is its asymptotic properties with respect to the point (k^*, q^*). Hence, it is referred to as the (k^*, q^*) path, and its branches as the $(k^*, q^*)^-$ and $(k^*, q^*)^+$ paths, while later on, some segment of the solution will be denoted by $\{(k^*(t), q^*(t)): 0 \leqslant t \leqslant T_1^q\}$.

Now, in order both to prepare the way for the next section, as well as to gain further insight into the present formulation and solution of the optimum growth problem, it is worthwhile utilizing the information implicit in Figure 1 to scrutinize more closely some particular optimum growth paths. Specifically, for this discussion we assume that k^0 and k^T are given such that $0 < k^0 < k^T < k^*$, but allow T to take on all values permitted within A. One possible interpretation is that we are restricting attention to a relatively underdeveloped economy with moderate growth ambitions (provided, for example, T is sufficiently large and δ is close to zero). Similar observations can be made concerning the analogous set of optimum growth paths given any configuration of initial and minimum terminal capital-labor ratios.

Within the set of particular optimum growth paths specified by (k^0, k^T, T), given $0 < k^0 < k^T < k^*$ with $(k^T, T) \in A$, we can distinguish two types. On the first type of path, k increases steadily from $k(0) = k^0$ to $k(T) = k^T$, while q decreases steadily to $q(T) = q^T \geqslant q^\alpha$, where q^α is defined by

(24) $\dot{k} = 0 \Big|_{k = k^T}$.

Let us denote these as (k^T, q^T) paths. On the second type of path, k first increases from $k(0) = k^0$ to $k^{T^*} \in (k^T, k^*)$, and then decreases to $k(T) \geqslant k^T$, while again q

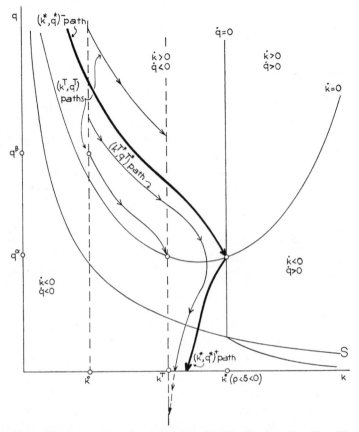

FIGURE 2.—The optimum growth paths specified by (k^0, k^T, T), given $0 < k^0 < k^T < k^*$ with $(k^T, T) \in A$.

decreases steadily to $0 \leqslant q(T) = q^T < q^\alpha$. Let us denote these as (k^{T^*}, q^{T^*}) paths, where q^{T^*} is defined by

$$(25) \qquad \left. \dot{k} = 0 \right|_{k = k^{T^*}}.$$

Observe that each type of path, exemplified in Figure 2, is labeled according to the point at which k approaches closest to k^*.

By the foregoing definitions, $\dot{k} > 0$ on any (k^T, q^T) or $(k^{T^*}, q^{T^*})^-$ path, while $\dot{k} < 0$ on any $(k^{T^*}, q^{T^*})^+$ path. On the other hand, with respect to the behavior over time of per capita consumption, as $\dot{q} < 0$ on either type of path, from (17') and (22),

$$(26) \qquad \dot{c} = h'(q)\dot{q} > 0$$

when the economy is not specializing in consumption, but

$$(27) \qquad \dot{c} = f'(k)\dot{k} = -\lambda f'(k)k < 0$$

when the economy is specializing in consumption. Thus, as a glance at Figure 2 will verify, $\dot{c}>0$ on any (k^T, q^T) or $(k^{T*}, q^{T*})^-$ path, while $\dot{c}>0$ initially but possibly $\dot{c}<0$ finally on any $(k^{T*}, q^{T*})^+$ path.

Such behavior can, of course, be related to the length of the period of direct concern $[0, T]$, for short, the planning period. More precisely, a falling capital-labor ratio would be observed if and only if our relatively underdeveloped economy pursues optimum growth for a planning period of length $T>\tau_1$, and decreasing per capita consumption for a planning period of length $T>\tau_2>\tau_1$.

The general method by which τ_1 and τ_2 are determined also underlies our later results. Hence, it is useful to detail it here.

Given the set of optimum growth paths from $k(0)=k^0$ to $k(T)\geqslant k^T$, suppose we want to compare the lengths of the planning periods associated with portions (including the whole) of any two. Then, if one path traverses the interval $[k^i, k^j]$ (or $[q^i, q^j]$), while the other traverses at least the same interval, both monotonically, by comparing the rates of change of k (or q), the relative lengths of the planning periods associated with the common interval can be easily ascertained. Note that such an unequivocal comparison is only possible here by virtue of the facts (a) that the solution to the pair (15′) and (18′) through any point (k, q) for which $k\geqslant 0$ is unique,[4] and (b) that from (15′)–(18′) and (22),

(28) $\qquad \dfrac{\partial k}{\partial q} = -h'(q)>0 \,, \quad$ for (k, q) above S

$\qquad\qquad = 0 \,, \qquad\qquad$ for (k, q) below S, and

(29) $\qquad \dfrac{\partial \dot{q}}{\partial k} = -f''(k)q>0 \,, \qquad\qquad\qquad$ for (k, q) above S

$\qquad\qquad = -\{U''[f(k)]f'(k)^2 + U'[f(k)]f''(k)\}>0, \quad$ for (k, q) below S.

Thus, for example, by comparing $\dot{k}$ over $[k^0, k^T]$ on each (k^T, q^T) path and $\dot{q}$ over $[q^\alpha, q^\beta]$ on each (k^{T*}, q^{T*}) path with the same quantities on the particular (k^T, q^T) path for which $q(T)=q^\alpha$ (see Figure 2), we demonstrate that τ_1 is defined by the planning period associated with this particular (k^T, q^T) path. Similarly, a comparison of each (k^{T*}, q^{T*}) path with the particular (k^{T*}, q^{T*}) path for which $q(T)=U'[f(k^T)]$ (or $z(T)$ just becomes zero) yields the planning period associated with the latter to define $\tau_2>\tau_1$.

Such comparisons[5] also enable us to assert the uniform approach of first, the

[4] It is straightforward to show that the RHS of (15′) and (18′) satisfies the Lipschitz condition on any closed, bounded, and convex region of the half-plane $k\geqslant 0$. Hence, this pair satisfies the conditions of the basic existence and uniqueness theorem for systems of differential equations. See, for example, pp. 20–22 and 159–67 in [5], which contain an especially clear statement and proof of this theorem, assuming that the RHS of the system has continuous partial derivatives (though actually requiring only that the RHS satisfies the Lipschitz condition).

[5] In conjunction with the theorem concerning the uniform continuity with respect to initial conditions of the solutions to systems of differential equations whose RHS satisfy the Lipschitz condition. Again see [5], pp. 192–99.

(k^T, q^T) path to the minimum time feasible path—which would appear in our diagram as the horizontal line at $q = \infty$ from k^0 to k^T—as T decreases from τ_1, and second, the (k^{T*}, q^{T*}) path to the portions of the (k^*, q^*) path sketched in Figure 2 as T increases from τ_1. As a preface to the next section, we stress that the last implies that the optimum growth path spends a relatively and absolutely longer middle length of the planning period close to the (modified) golden rule growth path.

As a final comment, consider the fact that for any (k^{T*}, q^{T*}) path which terminates beyond the minimum terminal target, that is, with $q^{T*}(T) = 0$ and $k^{T*}(T) > k^T$, its continuation which returns to $q(\tau) < 0$ and $k(\tau) = k^T$ (see Figure 2) also nominally satisfies all the optimality conditions except (I) for some $\tau > T$. Indeed, (I) is intended to rule out this continued (k^{T*}, q^{T*}) path as a possible optimum growth path—the reason being that it is easily shown that the (k^{T*}, q^{T*}) path with a comparable planning period $[0, \tau]$, but with termination beyond the minimum terminal target, is strictly better. The interpretation of this result is straightforward and, in addition, helps to clarify the relation between prescribing an arbitrary terminal target, while simultaneously attempting to maximize an interim welfare criterion. Suppose that, instead of the terminal condition $k(T) \geqslant k^T$, we had postulated the exact terminal target $k(T) = k^T$. Then, any continued (k^{T*}, q^{T*}) path would be optimum for some T. However, the resultant negative imputed prices on the final portion of such a path would mean that to use the existing capital stock to provide positive gross investment would be definitely detrimental, in particular, in reaching the desired target. That is, if negative gross investment were permitted within the technology available, say, in the extreme case, by some finite maximum rate of deliberate destruction, then it would be optimum over the final stage of that growth path. On the other hand, noting that $U'(c)$, the marginal value of per capita consumption, is always positive, it would also be true that over that same final stage the use of the existing capital stock to provide positive consumption is always definitely beneficial. Hence, there would be some inconsistency between both reaching the arbitrary terminal target and maximizing welfare while doing so. The upshot of this discussion is therefore that by introducing the relaxed terminal condition, we preclude this particular sort of inconsistency, and thereby end up with possibly both more welfare and more capital—though it should be mentioned that there remains in our formulation a more fundamental inconsistency arising from the somewhat arbitrary imposition of any terminal constraints, that is, the implicit discrimination against generations beyond the horizon.

4. THE OPTIMUM GROWTH TURNPIKE PROPERTY

We are now in a position to present our central result, stated precisely in the following theorem:

Given any positive number $\varepsilon > 0$, define the closed, rectangular ε-neighborhood

N(ε) of the (modified) golden rule growth path by

(30) $N(ε) = \{(k, q): \mid k - k^* \mid \; \leqslant ε, \mid q - q^* \mid \; \leqslant ε\}$.

Then, for the unique optimum growth path $\{(k,(t), q(t)): 0 \leqslant t \leqslant T\}$ specified by the initial and terminal parameters (k^0, k^T, T), there exist two finite times $0 \leqslant T_1 < \infty$ and $0 \leqslant T_2 < \infty$,

(31) $T_1 = T_1(ε, k^0), \quad T_2 = T_2(ε, k^T)$,

such that $(k(t), q(t)) \in N(ε)$ whenever $T_1 \leqslant t \leqslant T - T_2$.

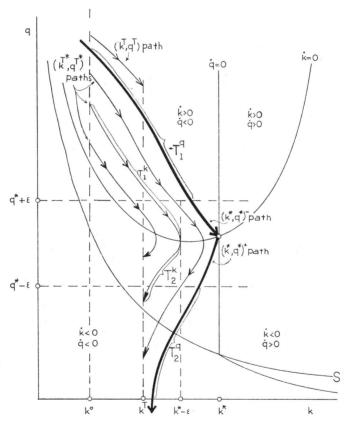

FIGURE 3.—The optimum growth turnpike property: $k^0 < k^T < k^*$.

Thus, defining the "sufficiently long period" mentioned in the introduction by

(32) $T > T_1 + T_2$,

the theorem asserts a strong turnpike property for optimum growth over any planning period $[0, T]$, in the sense that it states that such growth occurs within an arbitrarily small neighborhood of the "best" balanced growth path, except possibly over some initial or terminal phase. We also emphasize that this theorem is stated in terms of both the real stock variable k and the imputed price variable q—the reason being that the concept of optimum growth advanced in this paper is intimately related to the flow variable c, and the turnpike property thereby encompasses it, along with the remaining flow variable of the model, z, by virtue of the relations (16') and (17').

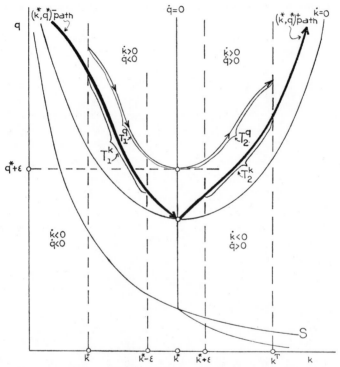

FIGURE 4.—The optimum growth turnpike property: $k^0 < k^* < k^T$.

That the theorem is true has already been suggested by the delineation of the limiting (k^T, q^T) and (k^{T*}, q^{T*}) paths; further heuristic proof is developed by reference to the constructions presented in Figures 3 and 4. Without loss of generality, we can assume that $|\, k^0 - k^* \,| > \varepsilon$ and $|\, k^T - k^* \,| > \varepsilon$. We also only consider the case for which $k^0 < k^*$, as the alternative case is essentially similar, and, for the first part of the discussion, the subcase analyzed in the last section for which $0 < k^0 < k^T < k^*$.

Thus, for given k^0 and k^T, $0 < k^0 < k^T < k^*$, we initially examine a set of (k^T, q^T) and (k^{T*}, q^{T*}) paths. In order to make relevant comparisons in this set, we distinguish the lengths of planning period associated with first, the particular

$(k^{T*}, q^{T*})^-$ and $(k^{T*}, q^{T*})^+$ paths on which $k^{T*} = k^* - \varepsilon$,[6] and second, the portions of the $(k^*, q^*)^-$ and $(k^*, q^*)^+$ paths which just intersect the lines $k = k^0$ and $q = q^* + \varepsilon$, or the lines $q = q^* - \varepsilon$ and the prior of $k = k^T$ or $q = 0$, respectively. Denote the former by T_1^k and T_2^k and the latter by T_1^q and T_2^q, as in Figure 3.

Employing the method outlined earlier, it is easily established through direct comparison that $T_1^k + T_2^k$ is longer than the planning period associated with any (k^{T*}, q^{T*}) path which does not enter $N(\varepsilon)$, and therefore is also longer than the planning period associated with any (k^T, q^T) path. Of equal consequence, it is likewise easily demonstrated that either T_1^k or T_1^q (either T_2^k or T_2^q) is longer than the length of planning period associated with the entrance of any (k^{T*}, q^{T*}) path into $N(\varepsilon)$ (the departure of any (k^{T*}, q^{T*}) path out of $N(\varepsilon)$).

Hence, we have justified the use of the lengths of planning period T_1^k or T_1^q and T_2^k or T_2^q to define the times whose existence is asserted by

(33) $T_1 = \max(T_1^k, T_1^q)$ and $T_2 = \max(T_2^k, T_2^q)$,

in the case of any (k^T, q^T) path or any (k^{T*}, q^{T*}) path which does not enter $N(\varepsilon)$, because the segment of planning period $[T_1, T - T_2]$ is empty, while in the case of any (k^{T*}, q^{T*}) path which does enter $N(\varepsilon)$, because the path enters or departs $N(\varepsilon)$ in at most a length of time T_1 or T_2, respectively.

The arguments establishing the times T_1 and T_2 for the other subcases are also quite straightforward:

For $k^T < k^0 < k^*$, we can distinguish (k^0, q^0) paths, on which both k and q decrease steadily from $k(0) = k^0$ and $q(0) = q^0 \leqslant q^\alpha$, where q^α is defined by

(24') $k = 0 \Big|_{k=k^0}$,

from (k^{0*}, q^{0*}) paths, on which k first increases from $k(0) = k^0$ to $k^{0*} \in (k^0, k^*)$, and then decreases to $k(T) \geqslant k^T$, while q decreases steadily, where q^{0*} is defined by

(25') $k = 0 \Big|_{k=k^{0*}}$.

Therefore, this subcase is essentially the same as that discussed in the preceding paragraphs, but with the superscript T replaced by the superscript 0.

For $k^0 < k^* < k^T$, on all optimum growth paths k increases steadily from $k(0) = k^0$ to $k(T) = k^T$, while q first decreases to $q^{\infty*} \in (q^*, \infty)$, and then increases. Denote these paths, in analogy with our other notation, as $(k^{\infty*}, q^{\infty*})$ paths, where $k^{\infty*}$ is

---

[6] It is implicitly assumed in the ensuing argument that the curve $\dot{k} = 0$ going away from the point (k^*, q^*) intersects the line $k = k^* - \varepsilon$ before it intersects either of the lines $q = q^* \pm \varepsilon$ (see Figure 3). Then, this particular (k^{T*}, q^{T*}) path is the optimum path which just enters $N(\varepsilon)$; for $k^{T*} > k^* - \varepsilon$ ($k^{T*} < k^* - \varepsilon$), the (k^{T*}, q^{T*}) path enters (does not enter) $N(\varepsilon)$. An argument analogous to that in the text can be presented to cover each of the other possibilities, but for our purpose it would entail needless added complication.

defined by

$$(34) \qquad \dot{q} = 0 \Big|_{q=q\infty^*} \quad \text{or } k^{\infty^*} = k^*.$$

Then, the lengths of the planning period associated with first, the particular $(k^{\infty^*}, q^{\infty^*})^-$ and $(k^{\infty^*}, q^{\infty^*})^+$ paths on which $q^{\infty^*} = q^* + \varepsilon$, and second, the portions of the $(k^*, q^*)^-$ and $(k^*, q^*)^+$ paths which just intersect the lines $k = k^0$ and $k = k^* - \varepsilon$ or the lines $k = k^* + \varepsilon$ and $k = k^T$, respectively, can be utilized to define T_1 and T_2 as in (33). This subcase is illustrated in Figure 4.

It only remains to show that T_1 depends primarily on the parameters k^0 and ε, and T_2 primarily on k^T and ε. (Of course, these times also depend on the parameters and functions defining the underlying model.) This is most directly accomplished thusly: For notational convenience, we again concentrate on the subcase for which $0 < k^0 < k^T < k^*$. Then, on either the particular $(k^{T^*}, q^{T^*})^-$ and $(k^{T^*}, q^{T^*})^+$ paths on which $k^{T^*} = k^* - \varepsilon$ (note that the choice of these particular paths depends on ε), or the $(k^*, q^*)^-$ and $(k^*, q^*)^+$ paths, both k and q are monotonic functions of time. It follows that on any of these paths k is a unique function of q, and conversely. Hence, by separating variables and integrating, (15′) and (18′) yield

$$T_1^k = -\int_{k^*-\varepsilon}^{k_0} \frac{dk^{T^*}}{z[k^{T^*}, q^{T^*}(k^{T^*})] - \lambda k^{T^*}} = T_1^k(k^0, \varepsilon),$$

$$\vdots$$

$$T_2^q = \int_{q^*-\varepsilon}^{\max(0, q^*(k^T))} \frac{dq^*}{(\delta + \lambda)q^* - U'(c[k^*(q^*), q^*])f'(k^*(q^*))} = T_2^q(k^T, \varepsilon),$$

which, along with (28), entail the asserted result.

Cowles Foundation for Research in Economics and Yale University

REFERENCES

[1] CASS, D.: "Optimum Growth in an Aggregative Model of Capital Accumulation," *Review of Economic Studies*, Vol. 32 (1965).

[2] DORFMAN, R., P. A. SAMUELSON, AND R. M. SOLOW: *Linear Programming and Economic Analysis*, Chapter 12, New York: McGraw-Hill Book Company, 1958.

[3] KOOPMANS, T. C.: "On the Concept of Optimal Economic Growth," *Semaine D'Etude sur le Rôle de L'Analyse Econométrique dans la Formulation de Plans de Développement*, Rome: Pontificia Academia Scientiarum, 1965.

[4] PONTRYAGIN, L. S., V. G. BOLTYANSKII, R. V. GAMKRILEDZE, AND E. F. MISCHENKO, *The Mathematical Theory of Optimal Processes*, New York and London: Interscience Publishers, 1962.

[5] ————: *Ordinary Differential Equations*, Reading, Mass.: Addison-Wesley Publishing Co., 1962.

[6] RAMSEY, F. P.: "A Mathematical Theory of Saving," *Economic Journal*, Vol. 38 (1928).

[7] SAMUELSON, P. A.: "A Catenary Turnpike Theorem Involving Consumption and the Golden Rule," *American Economic Review*, Vol. 55 (1965).

[8] SOLOW, R. M.: "A Contribution to the Theory of Economic Growth," *Quarterly Journal of Economics*, Vol. 32 (1956).

[9] SRINIVASAN, T. N.: "Optimal Savings in a Two-Sector Model of Growth," *Econometrica*, Vol. 32 (1964).

[10] UZAWA, H.: "On a Two-Sector Model of Economic Growth," *Review of Economic Studies*, Vol. 29 (1962).

[11] ———: "Optimal Growth in a Two-Sector Model of Capital Accumulation," *Review of Economic Studies*, Vol. 31 (1964).

INDEX